W9-CDO-758

591
W659
2013

world development report 20 13

Jobs

About the cover

In almost every language there is a range of words related to jobs, each emphasizing a different angle. Some words hint at the nature of the activity being performed, evoking the skill or expertise that is required. Others refer to the volume of human inputs used in production, bringing images of effort and conveying a sense of physical exertion. There are also words associated with the sheer numbers of people engaged in economic activity, which are more easily associated with aggregate statistics. In other cases, what seems to be at stake is a contractual relationship, involving mutual obligations and a degree of stability. In some languages, there are even words to designate the place where the person works, or at least a slot in a production process. This multiplicity of words clearly shows that jobs are multi-dimensional and cannot be characterized by a single term or measured by a single indicator.

Words related to jobs do not always translate well from one language to another, as the range of options available in each case can be different. If languages shape thinking, there are times when the ways in which people refer to jobs seem to be at odds. Gaps probably arise from the different characteristics of jobs being emphasized in different societies. They also suggest that jobs' agendas can differ across countries.

In many languages, words related to jobs serve not only as common nouns but also as proper nouns. Throughout history family names have been associated with specific skills or trades: Vankar in Hindi, Hattori in Japanese, Herrero in Spanish, or Mfundisi in Zulu, just to mention a few. The use of job-related words as household identifiers shows that people associated themselves with what they did. Nowadays, people aspire to choose their jobs based on what motivates them and on what could make their lives more meaningful. In almost every language there are also several words to express the lack of a job. Almost invariably these words have a negative connotation, close in spirit to deprivation; at times they even carry an element of stigma. In all these ways, language conveys the idea that jobs are more than what people earn, or what they do at work: they are also part of who they are.

world development report **2013**

DISCARD
DISCARD
CHAMPLAIN COLLEGE

Jobs

THE WORLD BANK
Washington, DC

© 2012 International Bank for Reconstruction and Development / The World Bank
1818 H Street NW, Washington DC 20433
Telephone: 202-473-1000; Internet: www.worldbank.org

Some rights reserved

1 2 3 4 15 14 13 12

This work is a product of the staff of The World Bank with external contributions. Note that The World Bank does not necessarily own each component of the content included in the work. The World Bank therefore does not warrant that the use of the content contained in the work will not infringe on the rights of third parties. The risk of claims resulting from such infringement rests solely with you.

The findings, interpretations, and conclusions expressed in this work do not necessarily reflect the views of The World Bank, its Board of Executive Directors, or the governments they represent. The World Bank does not guarantee the accuracy of the data included in this work. The boundaries, colors, denominations, and other information shown on any map in this work do not imply any judgment on the part of The World Bank concerning the legal status of any territory or the endorsement or acceptance of such boundaries.

Nothing herein shall constitute or be considered to be a limitation upon or waiver of the privileges and immunities of The World Bank, all of which are specifically reserved.

Rights and Permissions

This work is available under the Creative Commons Attribution 3.0 Unported license (CC BY 3.0) **http://creativecommons.org/licenses/by/3.0.** Under the Creative Commons Attribution license, you are free to copy, distribute, transmit, and adapt this work, including for commercial purposes, under the following conditions:

Attribution—Please cite the work as follows: **World Bank. 2012.** *World Development Report 2013: Jobs.* **Washington, DC: World Bank. DOI: 10.1596/978-0-8213-9575-2.** License: Creative Commons Attribution CC BY 3.0.

Translations—If you create a translation of this work, please add the following disclaimer along with the attribution: *This translation was not created by The World Bank and should not be considered an official World Bank translation. The World Bank shall not be liable for any content or error in this translation.*

All queries on rights and licenses should be addressed to the Office of the Publisher, The World Bank, 1818 H Street NW, Washington, DC 20433, USA; fax: 202-522-2625; e-mail: pubrights@worldbank.org.

Softcover
ISSN: 0163-5085
ISBN: 978-0-8213-9575-2
e-ISBN: 978-0-8213-9576-9
DOI: 10.1596/978-0-8213-9575-2

Hardcover
ISSN: 0163-5085
ISBN: 978-0-8213-9620-9
DOI: 10.1596/978-0-8213-9620-9

Photo credits:
page 67: Garimpeiros (independent prospectors) at the Serra Pelada gold mine, in Brazil © Sebastião Salgado/Amazonas—Press Images. Used with permission of Sebastião Salgado/Amazonas—Press Images. Further permission required for reuse.

page 91: Day laborer in a pineapple plantation in Pontian, Malaysia © Justin Guariglia/Redux. Used with permission of Justin Guariglia/Redux. Further permission required for reuse.

page 145: Shopkeeper and a friend at a foodstuff shop in Mpape, Nigeria © Ayemoba Godswill/World Bank; Rural migrants working in construction in China © Curt Carnemark/World Bank.

page 222: Farmers in a pomegranate field in Tajikistan © Gennadiy Ratushenko/World Bank; Wage worker at a garment factory in Vietnam © Lino Vuth/World Bank; Street vendor in Kabul, Afghanistan © Steve McCurry/Magnum Photos; Drying peppers in the street in Mexico © Curt Carnemark/World Bank.

page 248: Employees at a call center in Poland © Piotr Malecki/Panos Pictures.

page 318: Worker at a construction site in Jakarta, Indonesia © Sebastião Salgado/Amazonas—Press Images. Used with permission of Sebastião Salgado/Amazonas. Further permission required for reuse.

Cover design: Will Kemp, World Bank
Interior design: Debra Naylor

Contents

Boxes

Figures

Maps

Tables

Foreword

Today, jobs are a critical concern across the globe—for policy makers, the business community, and the billions of men and women striving to provide for their families.

As the world struggles to emerge from the global crisis, some 200 million people—including 75 million under the age of 25—are unemployed. Many millions more, most of them women, find themselves shut out of the labor force altogether. Looking forward, over the next 15 years an additional 600 million new jobs will be needed to absorb burgeoning working-age populations, mainly in Asia and Sub-Saharan Africa.

Meanwhile, almost half of all workers in developing countries are engaged in small-scale farming or self-employment, jobs that typically do not come with a steady paycheck and benefits. The problem for most poor people in these countries is not the lack of a job or too few hours of work; many hold more than one job and work long hours. Yet, too often, they are not earning enough to secure a better future for themselves and their children, and at times they are working in unsafe conditions and without the protection of their basic rights.

Jobs are instrumental to achieving economic and social development. Beyond their critical importance for individual well-being, they lie at the heart of many broader societal objectives, such as poverty reduction, economy-wide productivity growth, and social cohesion. The development payoffs from jobs include acquiring skills, empowering women, and stabilizing post-conflict societies. Jobs that contribute to these broader goals are valuable not only for those who hold them but for society as a whole: they are good jobs for development.

The *World Development Report 2013* takes the centrality of jobs in the development process as its starting point and challenges and reframes how we think about work. Adopting a cross-sectoral and multidisciplinary approach, the Report looks at why some jobs do more for development than others. The Report finds that the jobs with the greatest development payoffs are those that make cities function better, connect the economy to global markets, protect the environment, foster trust and civic engagement, or reduce poverty. Critically, these jobs are not only found in the formal sector; depending on the country context, informal jobs can also be transformational.

Building on this framework, the Report tackles some of the most pressing questions policy makers are asking right now: Should countries design their development strategies around growth or focus on jobs? Are there situations where the focus should be on protecting jobs as opposed to protecting workers? Which needs to come first in the development process—creating jobs or building skills?

The private sector is the key engine of job creation, accounting for 90 percent of all jobs in the developing world. But governments play a vital role by ensuring that the conditions are in place for strong private sector–led growth and by alleviating the constraints that hinder the private sector from creating good jobs for development.

The Report advances a three-stage approach to help governments meet these objectives. First, policy fundamentals—including macroeconomic stability, an enabling business environment, investments in human capital, and the rule of law—are essential for both growth and job creation. Second, well-designed labor policies can help ensure that growth translates into employment opportunities, but they need to be complemented by a broader approach to job creation that looks beyond the labor market. Third, governments should strategically identify which jobs would do the most for development given their specific country context, and remove or offset the obstacles that prevent the private sector from creating more of those jobs.

In today's global economy, the world of work is rapidly evolving. Demographic shifts, technological progress, and the lasting effects of the international financial crisis are reshaping the employment landscape in countries around the world. Countries that successfully adapt to these changes and meet their jobs challenges can achieve dramatic gains in living standards, productivity growth, and more cohesive societies. Those that do not will miss out on the transformational effects of economic and social development.

The *World Development Report 2013* is an important contribution to our collective understanding of the role of jobs in development. Its insights will provide valuable guidance for the World Bank Group as we collaborate with partners and clients to advance their jobs agendas. Working together, we can foster job creation and maximize the development impact of jobs.

Jim Yong Kim
President
The World Bank Group

Acknowledgments

This Report was prepared by a team led by Martín Rama, together with Kathleen Beegle and Jesko Hentschel. The other members of the core team were Gordon Betcherman, Samuel Freije-Rodriquez, Yue Li, Claudio E. Montenegro, Keijiro Otsuka, and Dena Ringold. Research analysts Thomas Bowen, Virgilio Galdo, Jimena Luna, Cathrine Machingauta, Daniel Palazov, Anca Bogdana Rusu, Junko Sekine, and Alexander Skinner completed the team. Additional research support was provided by Mehtabul Azam, Nadia Selim, and Faiyaz Talukdar. The team benefited from continuous engagement with Mary Hallward-Driemeier, Roland Michelitsch, and Patti Petesch.

The Report was cosponsored by the Development Economics Vice Presidency (DEC) and the Human Development Network (HDN). Overall guidance for the preparation of the Report was provided by Justin Lin, former Senior Vice President and Chief Economist, Development Economics; Martin Ravallion, acting Senior Vice President and Chief Economist, Development Economics; and Tamar Manuelyan-Atinc, Vice President and Head of the Human Development Network. Asli Demirgüç-Kunt, Director for Development Policy, oversaw the preparation process, together with Arup Banerji, Director for Social Protection and Labor.

Former World Bank President Robert B. Zoellick, President Jim Yong Kim, and Managing Directors Caroline Anstey and Mahmoud Mohieldin provided invaluable insights during the preparation process. Executive Directors and their offices also engaged constructively through various meetings and workshops.

An advisory panel, comprising George Akerlof, Ernest Aryeetey, Ragui Assaad, Ela Bhatt, Cai Fang, John Haltiwanger, Ravi Kanbur, Gordana Matković, and Ricardo Paes de Barros, contributed rich analytical inputs and feedback throughout the process.

Seven country case studies informed the preparation of the Report. The case study for Bangladesh was led by Binayak Sen and Mahabub Hossain, with Yasuyuki Sawada. Nelly Aguilera, Angel Calderón Madrid, Mercedes González de la Rocha, Gabriel Martínez, Eduardo Rodriguez-Oreggia, and Héctor Villarreal participated in Mexico's case study. The study for Mozambique was led by Finn Tarp, with Channing Arndt, Antonio Cruz, Sam Jones, and Fausto Mafambisse. For Papua New Guinea, Colin Filer and Marjorie Andrew coordinated the research. The South Sudan study was led by Lual Deng, together with Nada Eissa. AbdelRahmen El Lahga coordinated the Tunisian work, with the participation of Ines Bouassida, Mohamed Ali Marouani, Ben Ayed Mouelhi Rim, Abdelwahab Ben Hafaiedh, and Fathi Elachhab. Finally, Olga Kupets, Svitlana Babenko, and Volodymyr Vakhitov conducted the study for Ukraine.

The team would like to acknowledge the generous support for the preparation of the Report by the Government of Norway through its Ministry of Foreign Affairs, the multidonor Knowledge for Change Program (KCP II), the Nordic Trust Fund, the Government of Denmark through its Royal Ministry of Foreign Affairs, the Swiss State Secretariat for Economic Affairs (SECO), the Canadian International Development Agency (CIDA), the Government of Sweden through its Ministry for Foreign Affairs, and the Government of Japan through its Policy and Human Resource Development program. The German Ministry for Economic Cooperation and Development Cooperation (BMZ) through the German Agency for International Cooperation (GIZ) organized a development forum that brought together leading researchers from around the world in Berlin.

Generous support was also received for the country case studies by the Australian Agency for International Development (AusAID), Canada's International Development Research Centre (IDRC), the Government of Denmark through its Royal Ministry of Foreign Affairs, the Japan International Cooperation Agency (JICA) through the JICA Institute, and the United Nations University World Institute for Development Economics Research (UNU-WIDER). The United Kingdom's Overseas Development Institute (ODI) assisted the team through the organization of seminars and workshops.

A special recognition goes to the International Labour Organization (ILO) for its continued engagement with the team. José Manuel Salazar-Xiriñachs and Duncan Campbell coordinated this process, with the participation of numerous colleagues from the ILO. Interagency consultations were held with the International Monetary Fund (IMF), the Organisation for Economic Co-operation and Development (OECD), and the United Nations Economic and Social Council (ECOSOC). The team also benefited from an ongoing dialogue with the International Trade Union Confederation (ITUC).

Country consultations were conducted in Bangladesh, Canada, China, Denmark, Finland, France, Germany, India, Japan, the Republic of Korea, Mexico, Mozambique, Norway, Papua New Guinea, Singapore, Sweden, Switzerland, Tunisia, Turkey, Ukraine, and the United Kingdom. All consultations involved senior government officials. Most included academics, business representatives, trade union leaders, and members of civil society. In addition, bilateral meetings were held with senior government officials from Australia, the Netherlands, South Africa, and Spain.

Consultations with researchers and academics were arranged with the help of the African Economic Research Consortium (AERC) in Kenya, the Economic Research Forum (ERF) in the Arab Republic of Egypt, and the Latin American and Caribbean Economic Association (LACEA) in Chile. The Institute for the Study of Labor (IZA) organized special workshops with its research network in Germany and Turkey, coordinated by Klaus Zimmerman. Forskningsstiftelsen Fafo in Norway undertook a household survey in four countries, which this Report draws on.

The production of the Report and the logistics supporting it were assured by Brónagh Murphy, Mihaela Stangu, Jason Victor, and Cécile Wodon, with a contribution by Quyên Thúy Đinh. Ivar Cederholm coordinated resource mobilization. Irina Sergeeva and Sonia Joseph were in charge of resource management. Martha Gottron, Bruce Ross-Larson, Gerry Quinn, and Robert Zimmermann participated in the editing of the Report. The Development Data Group, coordinated by Johan Mistiaen, contributed to the preparation of its statistical annex.

The Office of the Publisher coordinated the design, typesetting, printing, and dissemination of both the hard and soft versions of the Report. Special thanks go to Mary Fisk, Stephen McGroarty, Santiago Pombo-Bejarano, Nancy Lammers, Stephen Pazdan, Denise Bergeron, Andres Meneses, Theresa Cooke, Shana Wagger, Jose De Buerba, and Mario Trubiano, as well as to the Translations and Interpretation Unit's Cecile Jannotin and Bouchra Belfqih.

The team also thanks Vivian Hon, as well as Claudia Sepúlveda, for their coordinating role; Merrell Tuck-Primdahl for her guidance on communication; Vamsee Krishna Kanchi and Swati P. Mishra for their support with the website; Gerry Herman for his help with the preparation of the movie series associated with the Report; and Gytis Kanchas, Nacer Mohamed Megherbi, and Jean-Pierre S. Djomalieu for information technology support.

Many others inside and outside the World Bank contributed with comments and inputs. Their names are listed in the Bibliographical Note.

Abbreviations and data notes

ABBREVIATIONS

ADB	Asian Development Bank
ALMP	active labor market program
ARB	Asociación de Recicladores de Bogotá (Bogotá Association of Recyclers)
BPO	business process outsourcing
CAFTA	Central America Free Trade Agreement
CASEN	Chile National Socioeconomic Characterization
CIRAD	Centre de coopération internationale en recherche agronomique pour le développement (Center for International Cooperation in Agronomic Research for Development)
CFA	Committee on Freedom of Association
COSATU	Confederation of South African Trade Unions
CSR	corporate social responsibility
ECLAC	Economic Commission for Latin America
ECOSOC	United Nations Economic and Social Council
EMBRAPA	Brazilian Agricultural Research Corporation
EPL	employment protection legislation
EPZ	export processing zone
EU	European Union
FAO	Food and Agriculture Organization of the United Nations
FAFO	Forskningsstiftelsen Fafo (Fafo Research Foundation)
FDI	foreign direct investment
FACB	freedom of association and collective bargaining
GATT	General Agreement on Tariffs and Trade
GATS	General Agreement on Trade in Services
GDP	gross domestic product
GNP	gross national product
HOI	Human Opportunity Index
I2D2	International Income Distribution Database
IC	Industrial Council
ICLS	International Conference of Labour Statisticians
ICTWSS	Database on Institutional Characteristics of Trade Unions, Wage Setting, State Intervention and Social Pacts
IDA	Industrial Disputes Act (India)
IDRC	International Development Research Center
IEA	International Energy Agency
IFC	International Finance Corporation
IFPRI	International Food Policy Research Institute
ILO	International Labour Organization

IMF	International Monetary Fund
IPCC	International Panel on Climate Change
ISSP	International Social Survey Programme
IT	information technology
IZA	Forschungsinstitut zur Zukunft der Arbeit (Institute for the Study of Labor)
KILM	Key Indicators of the Labor Market
KUT	Korea University of Technology and Education
MDG	Millennium Development Goal
MERCOSUR	Mercado Común del Sur (Southern Cone Common Market)
MFA	Multi-Fiber Arrangement
MGNREGA	Mahatma Gandhi National Rural Employment Guarantee Act
MIS	Management Information System
NASSCOM	National Association of Software and Service Companies
NEET	not in education, employment, or training
NGO	nongovernmental organization
ODI	Overseas Development Institute
OECD	Organisation for Economic Co-operation and Development
PISA	Programme of International Student Assessment
PPP	purchasing power parity
R&D	research and development
RMB	renminbi
SEWA	Self Employed Women's Association
SEZ	special economic zone
SME	small and medium enterprise
SNA	System of National Accounts
SOE	state-owned enterprise
TEWA	Termination of Employment of Workmen Act
TFP	total factor productivity
TVE	technical and vocational education
UISA	Unemployment Insurance Savings Accounts
UN	United Nations
UNDP	United Nations Development Programme
UNECE	United Nations Economic Commission of Europe
UNEP	United Nations Environment Programme
UNESCO	United Nations Educational, Scientific and Cultural Organization
WDR	World Development Report
WTO	World Trade Organization
WIEGO	Women in Informal Employment: Globalizing and Organizing

DATA NOTES

The use of the word *countries* to refer to economies implies no judgment by the World Bank about the legal or other status of territory. The term *developing countries* includes low- and middle-income economies and thus may include economies in transition from central planning, as a matter of convenience. Dollar figures are current U.S. dollars, unless otherwise specified. *Billion* means 1,000 million; *trillion* means 1,000 billion.

Moving jobs center stage

Jobs are the cornerstone of economic and social development. Indeed, development happens through jobs. People work their way out of poverty and hardship through better livelihoods. Economies grow as people get better at what they do, as they move from farms to firms, and as more productive jobs are created and less productive ones disappear. Societies flourish as jobs bring together people from different ethnic and social backgrounds and nurture a sense of opportunity. Jobs are thus transformational—they can transform what we earn, what we do, and even who we are.

No surprise, then, that jobs are atop the development agenda everywhere—for everyone from policy makers to the populace, from business leaders to union representatives, from activists to academics. Looking to seize opportunities for job creation presented by massive demographic shifts, technological innovations, global migrations of people and tasks, and deep changes in the nature of work, policy makers ask difficult questions:

- Should countries build their development strategies around growth or should they rather focus on jobs?

- Can entrepreneurship be fostered, especially among the many microenterprises in developing countries, or are entrepreneurs born?

- While jobs can contribute to social cohesion, is there anything governments can do about it, apart from trying to support job creation?

- Are greater investments in education and training a prerequisite for employability, or can skills be built through jobs?

- Should efforts to improve the investment climate target the areas, activities, or firms with greater potential for job creation?

- What is the risk that policies to foster job creation in one country will come at the expense of jobs in other countries?

- When confronted with large shocks and major restructuring, is it advisable to protect jobs and not just people?

- How can the reallocation of workers be accelerated from areas and activities with low productivity to those with greater potential?

Individuals value jobs for the earnings and benefits they provide, as well as for their contributions to self-esteem and happiness. But some jobs have broader impacts on society. Jobs for women can change the way households spend money and invest in the education and health of children. Jobs in cities support greater specialization and the exchange of ideas, making other jobs more productive. Jobs connected to global markets bring home new technological and managerial knowledge. And in turbulent environments, jobs for young men can provide alternatives to violence and help restore peace.

Through their broader influence on living standards, productivity, and social cohesion, these jobs have an even greater value to society than they do for the individual. But some jobs can have negative spillovers. Jobs supported through transfers or privilege represent a burden to others or undermine their opportunities to find remunerative employment. Jobs damaging the environment take a toll on everybody. Thus it is that some jobs do more for development, while others may do little, even if they are appealing to individuals.

Which jobs have the greatest development payoffs depends on the circumstances. Countries differ in their level of development, demography, endowments, and institutions. Agrarian societies face the challenge of making agricultural jobs more productive and creating job opportunities outside farms. Resource-rich countries need to diversify their exports, so that jobs are connected to global markets rather than supported through government transfers. Formalizing countries need to design their social protection systems in ways that extend their coverage without penalizing employment.

A vast majority of jobs are created by the private sector. Governments, though, can support—or hinder—the private sector in creating jobs. The idea that development happens through jobs sheds new light on the strategies, policies, and programs governments can pursue. Strategies should identify which types of jobs would have the highest development payoffs, given a country's circumstances. Policies should remove the obstacles that prevent the private sector from creating jobs. Programs for generating employment may also be warranted, for instance, in conflict-affected countries. But the costs and benefits of these policies and programs have to be assessed, taking into account the potential spillovers from jobs, both positive and negative.

At a more practical level, this jobs lens on development leads to a three-layered policy approach:

- *Fundamentals.* Because jobs provide higher earnings and broader social benefits as coun-

tries grow richer, the policy environment must be conducive to growth. That requires attending to macroeconomic stability, an enabling business environment, human capital accumulation, and the rule of law.

- *Labor policies.* Because growth alone may not be enough, labor policies need to facilitate job creation and enhance the development payoffs from jobs. Policies can address labor market distortions while not being a drag on efficiency. But they should avoid distortionary interventions that constrain employment in cities and global value chains—and provide voice and protection for the most vulnerable.

- *Priorities.* Because some jobs do more for development than others, it is necessary to identify the types of jobs with the greatest development payoffs given a country's context, and to remove—or at least offset—the market imperfections and institutional failures that result in too few of those jobs being created.

The centrality of jobs for development should not be interpreted as the centrality of labor policies and institutions. Nearly half the people at work in developing countries are farmers or self-employed and so are outside the labor market. And even in the case of wage employment, labor policies and institutions may or may not be the main obstacle to job creation. Often, the most relevant obstacles lie outside of the labor market. The catalysts for job creation may be policies that make cities work better, help farmers access and apply appropriate agricultural techniques, or allow firms to develop new exports. Jobs are the cornerstone of development, and development policies are needed for jobs.

Jobs wanted

To many, a "job" brings to mind a worker with an employer and a regular paycheck. Yet, the majority of workers in the poorest countries are outside the scope of an employer-employee relationship. Worldwide, more than 3 billion people are working, but their jobs vary greatly. Some 1.65 billion are employed and receive reg-

1.6 billion people working for a wage or a salary

1.5 billion people working in farming and self-employment

77% labor force participation by women in Vietnam

28% labor force participation by women in Pakistan

39% of the **manufacturing jobs** are in **microenterprises** in Chile

97% of the **manufacturing jobs** are in **microenterprises** in Ethiopia

2x employment growth in a firm **in Mexico** over 35 years

10x employment growth in a firm **in the United States** over 35 years

115 million children working in **hazardous conditions**

21 million victims of **forced labor**

600 million jobs needed over **15 years** to keep current employment rates

90 million people working abroad

621 million youth neither working nor studying

22x the **productivity gap** between manufacturing firms in the 90th and 10th percentiles **in India**

9x the **productivity gap** between manufacturing firms in the 90th and 10th percentiles **in the United States**

10 million entrants to the labor force per year in Sub-Saharan Africa

30 million postsecondary students in China

3% international migrants as a share of the world population

60% foreign-born population in Kuwait, Qatar, and the United Arab Emirates

ular wages or salaries. Another 1.5 billion work in farming and small household enterprises, or in casual or seasonal day labor. Meanwhile, 200 million people, a disproportionate share of them youth, are unemployed and actively looking for work. Almost 2 billion working-age adults, the majority of them women, are neither working nor looking for work, but an unknown number of them are eager to have a job. Clarifying what is meant by a job is thus a useful starting point.

The meaning of the words used to describe what people do to earn a living varies across countries and cultures. Some words refer to workers in offices or factories. Others are broader, encompassing farmers, self-employed vendors in cities, and caregivers of children and the elderly. The distinction is not merely semantic. The varied meanings hint at the different aspects of jobs that people value. And views on what a job is almost inevitably influence views on what policies for jobs should look like.

For statisticians, a job is "a set of tasks and duties performed, or meant to be performed, by one person, including for an employer or in self-employment."[1] Jobs are performed by the employed. These are defined as people who produce goods and services for the market or for their own use. But the statistical definition is mute about what should not be considered a job. International norms view basic human rights as the boundaries of what is unacceptable. Among them are the United Nations Universal Declaration of Human Rights (1948) and the International Labour Organization Declaration on Fundamental Principles and Rights at Work (1998), which further specifies core labor standards. Combining these different perspectives, jobs are activities that generate income, monetary or in kind, without violating human rights.

Different places, different jobs

The world of work is particularly diverse in developing countries. This variety refers not only to the number of hours worked and the number of jobs available, the usual yardsticks in industrial countries, but also to the characteristics of jobs. Two main aspects stand out. One is the prevalence of self-employment and farming.[2] The other is the coexistence of traditional and modern modes of production, from subsistence agriculture and low-skilled work to technology-driven manufacturing and services and highly skilled knowledge work.

While nearly half of the jobs in the developing world are outside the labor market, the shares of wage work, farming, and self-employment differ greatly across countries.[3] Nonwage work represents more than 80 percent of women's employment in Sub-Saharan Africa—but less than

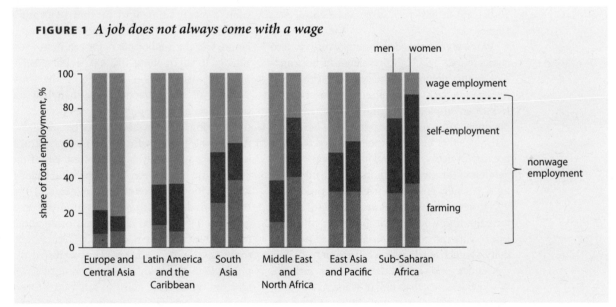

FIGURE 1 *A job does not always come with a wage*

Source: World Development Report 2013 team.
Note: Data are for the most recent year available.

FIGURE 2 *Among youth, unemployment is not always the issue*

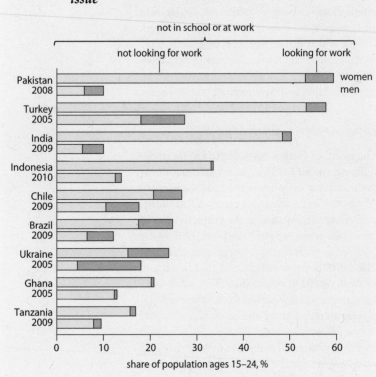

Source: World Development Report 2013 team.

20 percent in Eastern Europe and Central Asia (figure 1).

Work across the developing world is also characterized by a high prevalence of informality, whether defined on the basis of lack of firm registration, lack of social security coverage, or lack of an employment contract. Informal employment is not under the purview of labor regulations, either because of their limited scope or because of deliberate avoidance or evasion. Regardless of the specific definition used, informality is generally associated with lower productivity. However, this does not necessarily mean that formalization would result in greater efficiency. Informality can be a symptom of lower productivity as much as it can be a cause of it.[4]

Gender and age differences are striking. Worldwide, fewer than half of women have jobs, compared with almost four-fifths of men. In Pakistan, 28 percent of women but more than 82 percent of men participate in the labor force, whereas participation rates are above 75 percent

for both men and women in Tanzania and Vietnam. Beyond these stark contrasts in participation, women continue to earn significantly less than men, and the differences are not fully explained by education, experience, or sector of work. While a growing share of youth between ages 15 and 24 allocate most of their time to schooling and training, youth unemployment is still alarming in some countries (above 40 percent in South Africa since early 2008 and above 50 percent in Spain in early 2012).[5] Even in countries where it is low, youth unemployment is twice the national average or more. In addition, 621 million young people are "idle"—not in school or training, not employed, and not looking for work. Rates of idleness vary across countries, ranging between 10 and 50 percent among 15- to 24-year-olds (figure 2).[6] Many youth work in unpaid jobs; if paid, they are less likely to have social insurance.[7]

The changing world of work

This complex picture is compounded by massive demographic shifts. To keep employment as a share of the working-age population constant, in 2020 there should be around 600 million more jobs than in 2005, a majority of them in Asia and Sub-Saharan Africa. While some countries have experienced very large increases in their labor force—nearly 8 million new entrants a year in China since the mid-1990s and 7 million in India—others face a shrinking population. Ukraine's labor force, for example, is estimated to fall by about 160,000 people a year.[8]

Rapid urbanization is changing the composition of employment. More than half the population in developing countries is expected to be living in cities and towns before 2020.[9] As a result, the growth of the nonagricultural labor force will vastly exceed the growth of the agricultural labor force. This structural change, which in industrial countries took decades, now transforms lives in developing countries in a generation. Structural change can bring about remarkable improvements in efficiency, and some developing countries have narrowed the productivity gap with industrial countries rapidly. But others have failed to catch up.[10] Overall, the gap between developing and developed regions remains wide.

Globalization is also changing the nature of jobs. Industrial countries are shifting from primary and traditional manufacturing industries toward services and knowledge-intensive activities.[11] At the same time, technological improvements and outsourcing to developing countries are leading to a decline in medium-skilled jobs.[12] Production tasks have been splintered so that they can be performed in different locations.[13] Transnational companies have built integrated value chains to tap into national skill pools around the world.[14] Outsourcing is occurring in services as well as in manufacturing. The share of developing countries in exports of world services nearly doubled to 21 percent between 1990 and 2008.[15]

Technology is changing the way workers and firms connect, through their access to much larger, even global, employment marketplaces. Some of the new marketplaces operate through the internet; others use mobile phone technology.[16] Part-time and temporary wage employment are now major features of industrial and developing countries. In South Africa, temporary agency workers make up about 7 percent of the labor force; the temporary staffing industry provides employment to an average of 410,000 workers a day. In India, the number of temporary workers that employment agencies recruit grew more than 10 percent in 2009 and 18 percent in 2010.[17]

This changing landscape of global production has also brought about shifts in skill endowments and in the world distribution of top talent. China and India rank high in perceived attractiveness as outsourcing hubs because of their exceptionally high ratings in the availability of skills.[18] India has close to 20 million students in higher education, nearly as many as the United States; both countries are outpaced by China, with 30 million postsecondary students.[19] The United States still accounts for a large share of top scores in international student assessments, but the Republic of Korea has the same share as Germany, and both are closely followed by the Russian Federation. The number of high-performing students in Shanghai alone is one-fifth that of Germany and about twice that of Argentina.[20]

The role of the private sector

In such rapidly changing times, the private sector is the main engine of job creation and the source of almost 9 of every 10 jobs in the world.

Between 1995 and 2005, the private sector accounted for 90 percent of jobs created in Brazil, and for 95 percent in the Philippines and Turkey.[21] The most remarkable example of the expansion of employment through private sector growth is China. In 1981, private sector employment accounted for 2.3 million workers, while state-owned enterprises (SOEs) had 80 million workers.[22] Twenty years later, the private sector accounted for 74.7 million workers, surpassing, for the first time, the 74.6 million workers in SOEs (figure 3).

In contrast to the global average, in some countries in the Middle East and North Africa, the state is a leading employer, a pattern that can be linked to the political economy of the post-independence period, and in some cases to the abundance of oil revenues.[23] For a long period, public sector jobs were offered to young college graduates. But as the fiscal space for continued expansion in public sector employment shrank, "queuing" for public sector jobs became more prevalent, leading to informality, a devaluation of educational credentials, and forms of social exclusion.[24] A fairly well-educated and young labor force remains unemployed, or underemployed, and labor productivity stagnates.[25]

Overall, countries have been successful at creating jobs. More people have jobs now than ever before, and those jobs provide generally higher earnings. Indeed, amid rapid social and economic change, poverty has declined in developing countries. The share of the population of the developing world living on less than US$1.25 a day (in purchasing power parity) fell from 52 percent in 1981 to 22 percent in 2008, or from 1.94 billion people to 1.29 billion.[26] This reduction is the result of multiple factors, but the creation of millions of new, more productive jobs, mostly in Asia but also in other parts of the developing world, has been the main driving force.[27]

Jobs are vulnerable to economic downturns, though, much more so in the private sector than the public sector. Short-term crises may wipe out years of progress. They may start in a single country but now, through globalization, spread over entire regions or to the world. The recent financial crisis created 22 million new unemployed in a single year. Growth in total employment, hovering around 1.8 percent a year before 2008, fell to less than 0.5 percent in 2009, and by 2011 had not yet reached its pre-crisis level.[28]

FIGURE 3 *In China, employment growth is led by the private sector*

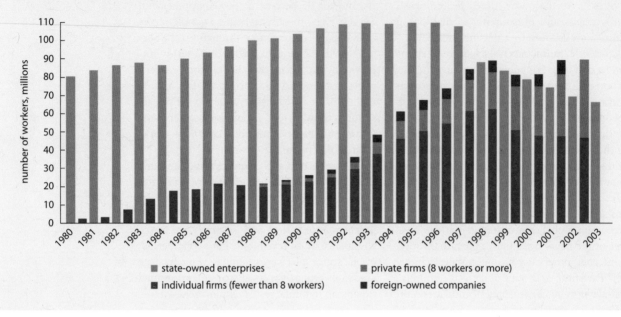

Source: Kanamori and Zhao 2004.
Note: Data for foreign-owned companies in 2002 and for non-state-owned enterprises in 2003 are not available.

Policy responses to prevent and mitigate the impact of crises involve different combinations of instruments, with potentially diverse implications for jobs.[29]

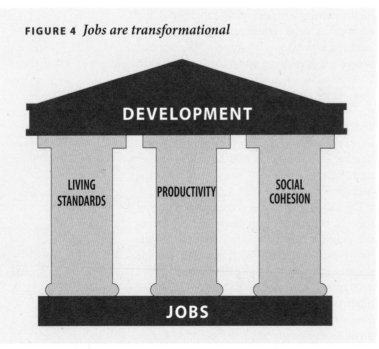

FIGURE 4 *Jobs are transformational*

Source: World Development Report 2013 team.

Demography, urbanization, globalization, technology, and macroeconomic crises bring about formidable jobs challenges. Countries that fail to address them may fall into vicious circles of slow growth in labor earnings and job-related dissatisfaction affecting a sizable portion of the labor force.[30] Youth unemployment and idleness may be high, and women may have fewer job opportunities, leaving potential economic and social gains untapped.[31] A repeating pattern of small gains in living standards, slow productivity growth, and eroding social cohesion can set in. In contrast, countries that address these jobs challenges can develop virtuous circles. The results—prosperous populations, a growing middle class, increased productivity, and improved opportunities for women and youth—may then be self-reinforcing.

Development happens through jobs

Jobs are more than just the earnings and benefits they provide. They are also the output they generate, and part of who we are and how we interact with others in society. Through these outcomes, jobs can boost living standards, raise productivity, and foster social cohesion (figure 4).

Jobs are what we earn

Jobs are the most important determinant of living standards. For most people, work is the main source of income, especially in the poorest countries. Many families escape or fall into poverty because family members get or lose a job. Opportunities for gainful work, including in farming and self-employment, offer households the means to increase consumption and reduce its variability. Higher yields in agriculture, access to small off-farm activities, the migration of family members to cities, and transitions to wage employment are milestones on the path to prosperity.[32] And as earnings increase, individual choices expand—household members can choose to stay out of the labor force or to work fewer hours and dedicate more time to education, to retirement, or to family.

Earnings from work increase with economic development, and the benefits associated with jobs improve as well. The relationship is not mechanical, but growth is clearly good for jobs (figure 5). Admittedly, as economies become more developed, the average skills of jobholders increase, implying that observations across countries are not strictly comparable, as they do not refer to identical workers. But growth also improves the living standards of workers whose skills have not changed.

More than two decades of research on poverty dynamics, spanning countries as different as Canada, Ecuador, Germany, and South Africa, show that labor-related events trigger exits from poverty.[33] These events range from the head of a household changing jobs to family members starting to work and to working family members earning more. Conversely, a lack of job opportunities reduces the ability of households to improve their well-being.[34] In a large set of qualitative studies in low-income countries, getting jobs and starting businesses were two of the main reasons for people to rise out of poverty.[35]

Quantitative analysis confirms that changes in labor earnings are the largest contributor to poverty reduction (figure 6). In 10 of 18 Latin American countries, changes in labor income explain more than half the reduction in poverty, and in another 5 countries, more than a third. In Bangladesh, Peru, and Thailand, changes in education, work experience, and region of residence mattered, but the returns to these characteristics (including labor earnings) mattered most. Just having work was not enough, given that most people work in less developed economies. What made a difference for escaping poverty was increasing the earnings from work.[36]

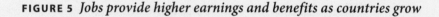

FIGURE 5 *Jobs provide higher earnings and benefits as countries grow*

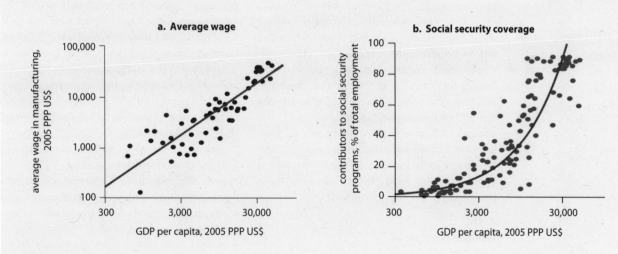

a. Average wage

b. Social security coverage

Source: World Development Report 2013 team.
Note: GDP = gross domestic product; PPP = purchasing power parity. Each dot represents a country.

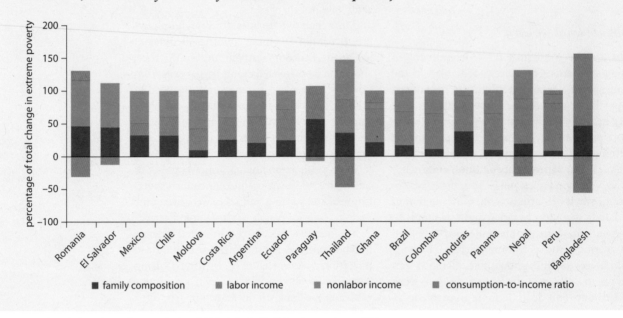

FIGURE 6 *Jobs account for much of the decline in extreme poverty*

Sources: Azevedo and others 2012; Inchauste and others 2012; both for the World Development Report 2013.

Note: Family composition indicates the change in the share of adults (ages 18 and older) within the household. *Labor income* refers to the change in employment and earnings for each adult. *Nonlabor income* refers to changes in other sources of income such as transfers, pensions, and imputed housing rents. If a bar is located below the horizontal axis, it means that that source would have increased, instead of decreased, poverty. The changes are computed for Argentina (2000–10); Bangladesh (2000–10); Brazil (2001–09); Chile (2000–09); Colombia (2002–10); Costa Rica (2000–08); Ecuador (2003–10); El Salvador (2000–09); Ghana (1998–2005); Honduras (1999–2009); Mexico (2000–10); Moldova (2001–10); Panama (2001–09); Paraguay (1999–2010); Peru (2002–10); Nepal (1996–2003); Romania (2001–09); and Thailand (2000–09). The changes for Bangladesh, Ghana, Moldova, Nepal, Peru, Romania, and Thailand are computed using consumption-based measures of poverty, while the changes for the other countries are based on income measures.

Beyond their fundamental and immediate contribution to earnings, jobs also affect other dimensions of well-being, including mental and physical health. Not having a job undermines life satisfaction, especially in countries where wage employment is the norm and where the lack of opportunities translates into open unemployment rather than underemployment. Among those employed, the material, nonmaterial, and even subjective characteristics of jobs can all have an impact on well-being.[37] Other features such as workplace safety, job security, learning and advancement opportunities, and health and social protection benefits are valued by workers. But relatively few jobs offer these advantages in developing countries.

Jobs are what we do

Economic growth happens as jobs become more productive, but also as more productive jobs are created and less productive jobs disappear. These gains may ultimately be driven by new goods, new methods of production and transportation, and new markets, but they materialize through a constant restructuring and reallocation of resources, including labor.[38] Net job creation figures hide much larger processes of gross job creation and gross job destruction. On average across developing countries, between 7 and 20 percent of jobs in manufacturing are created within a year, but a similar proportion disappear (figure 7).[39]

Because economies grow as high-productivity jobs are created and low-productivity jobs disappear, the relationship between productivity gains and job creation is not mechanical. In the medium term, employment trends align closely with trends in the size of the labor force, so growth is truly jobless in very few cases. In the short term, however, innovations can be associated with either increases or decreases in employment.[40] The popular perception is that productivity grows through downsizing, but some firms are able to achieve both productivity and employment gains.[41] In Chile, Ethiopia, and Romania, successful "upsizers" contributed to output and employment growth substantively; sometimes they are more numerous than the successful "downsizers."[42] And the combination of private sector vibrancy and state sector restructuring led to rapid output and employment growth in transition economies and in China in the late 1990s and the early 2000s.[43]

Successful upsizers tend to be younger, leaner, and more innovative.[44] But overall, large firms are both more innovative and more productive. They invest more in machinery. They are much more likely than small firms to develop new product lines, to introduce new technology, to open and close plants, to outsource, and to engage in joint ventures with foreign partners.[45] These firms produce more with a given amount of labor, and export more as well. They also pay substantively higher wages than micro- and small enterprises (figure 8). In developing countries, however, many people work in very small and not necessarily very dynamic economic units.

Family farms dominate in agriculture. At 1.8 and 1.2 hectares, respectively, average farm size is small in Sub-Saharan Africa, and especially in Asia.[46] The Green Revolution has led to both higher cereal yields and more job creation because the new technologies are labor intensive. But progress has been uneven across regions and has not taken place on a large scale in Sub-Saharan Africa. More mechanized farms have higher productivity, but constraints in land markets usually slow mechanization; without it, yields per hectare tend to be higher on smaller farms.

Outside agriculture there are massive numbers of microenterprises and household businesses (figure 9). These small units play significant roles in job creation, even in high-middle-income countries. They account for 97 percent of employment in the manufacturing sector in Ethiopia, but still for a sizable 39 percent in Chile. In the services sector, their role is often more important. Even in Eastern European countries, where the private sector is only two decades old, microenterprises are the source of 10 to 20 percent of employment in manufactur-

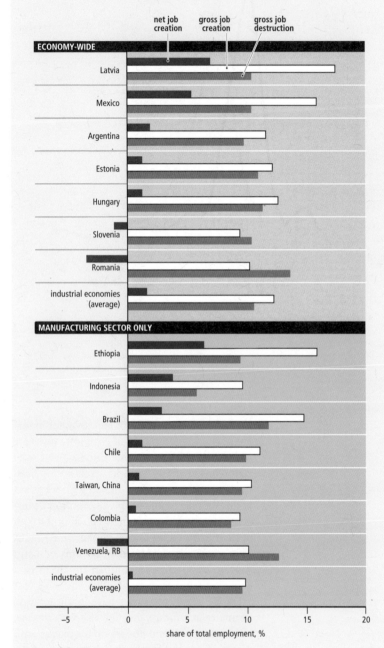

FIGURE 7 *Simultaneous job creation and destruction characterize all economies*

Sources: World Development Report 2013 team estimates based on Bartelsman, Haltiwanger, and Scarpetta 2009b and Shiferaw and Bedi 2010.
Note: The figure shows annual job flows. Data are from Argentina (1996–2001); Brazil (1997–2000); Canada (1984–97); Chile (1980–98); Colombia (1983–97); Estonia (1996–2000); Ethiopia (1997–2007); Finland (1989–97); France (1989–97); Germany (1977–99); Hungary (1993–2000); Indonesia (1991–94); Italy (1987–94); Latvia (1983–98); Mexico (1986–2000); the Netherlands (1993–95); Portugal (1983–98); Romania (1993–2000); Slovenia (1991–2000); Taiwan, China (1986–91); the United Kingdom (1982–98); the United States (1986–91, 1994–96); and República Bolivariana de Venezuela (1996–98).

FIGURE 8 *Larger firms pay higher wages*

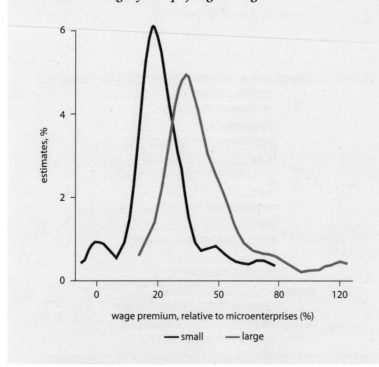

Source: Montenegro and Patrinos 2012 for the World Development Report 2013.
Note: The figure uses 138 household and labor force surveys spanning 33 countries over 1991–2010. The horizontal axis reports the estimated wage premium of small firms (10 to 50 workers) and large firms (more than 50 workers) relative to microenterprises, controlling for worker characteristics.

ing and 30 to 50 percent of employment in services. The large numbers of economic units are associated with a very wide dispersion of total factor productivity. In India, even within narrowly defined sectors, a manufacturing plant at the 10th percentile of the distribution generates 22 times less output than a plant in the 90th percentile would produce with the same inputs. This pattern is similar in a number of Latin American countries. By comparison, the ratio is 1 to 9 in the United States.[47]

While microenterprises have lackluster performance as a group, they are also very diverse. Microenterprises and household businesses are a means of survival for the poor and a way of diversifying out of farming activities. On average, their owners do not earn much.[48] But in middle-income countries, many among the owners of micro- and small enterprises are as entrepreneurial as their peers in industrial countries. Their weak performance may be due to an adverse investment environment—for example, limited access to credit.[49] Yet a small number of micro-

enterprises, the gazelles, invest and earn higher returns.[50]

While large firms are more productive, they were not all born large. In industrial countries, some of the more resounding successes, from Honda to Microsoft, started in garages. Many successful companies in developing countries also grew out of small household businesses. Thailand's Charoen Pokphand Group, founded in 1921 as a small seed shop in Bangkok by two brothers, has grown into one of the largest multinational conglomerates in agribusiness, operating in 15 countries and encompassing close to 100 companies. India's Tata Group transformed from a Mumbai-based family-owned trading firm in the late 19th century to a multinational conglomerate, comprising 114 companies and subsidiaries across eight business sectors on several continents. Many of China's successful clusters, such as the footwear industry in Wenzhou, also started from small family businesses working close to each other.[51]

Unfortunately, in many developing countries, larger and older firms tend to be stagnant while smaller and younger enterprises are prone to churning. A vibrant dynamic process is usually absent. In Ghana, many firms were born large and showed little growth over 15 years; in Portugal, by contrast, many firms born as microenterprises grew substantially.[52] The majority of firms in India is also born small, but they tend to stay small, without displaying much variation in employment over their life cycle. A revealing comparison involves the size of 35-year old firms relative to their size at birth. In India, the size declines by a fourth; in Mexico, it doubles. In the United States, it becomes 10 times bigger.[53] The potential gains from greater entrepreneurial vibrancy, and from a more substantial reallocation of labor from low- to high-productivity units, are sizable.[54] But helping those gains materialize is a daunting task.

Jobs are who we are

Having, or not having, a job can shape how people view themselves and relate to others. While some jobs can be empowering, in extreme cases a lack of job opportunities can contribute to violence or social unrest. Youth may turn to gangs to compensate for the absence of identity and belonging that a job might provide. In Ecua-

FIGURE 9 *The employment share of microenterprises is greater in developing countries*

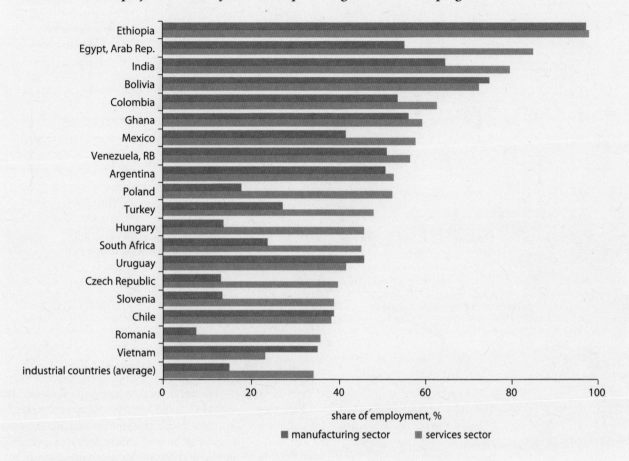

Sources: World Development Report 2013 team estimates and EUROSTAT.

Note: Microenterprises are firms, formal or informal, with fewer than 10 workers. Data for developing countries are from Argentina (2006–10), Bolivia (2005, 2007), Chile (2006, 2009), Colombia (2009), the Czech Republic (2005–07), the Arab Republic of Egypt (2006), Ethiopia (1999), Ghana (1991), Hungary (2007–08), India (2004, 2009), Mexico (2004–10), Poland (2005–07), Romania (2005–07), Slovenia (2005–07), South Africa (2005–07), Turkey (2006–10), Uruguay (2009), República Bolivariana de Venezuela (2004–06), and Vietnam (2009). Data for industrial countries are from Austria, Belgium, Denmark, Finland, France, Germany, Greece, Italy, Luxembourg, the Netherlands, Norway, Portugal, Spain, Sweden, and the United Kingdom over 2005–07.

dor, for instance, they did so "because they were searching for the support, trust, and cohesion—social capital—that they maintained their families did not provide, as well as because of the lack of opportunities in the local context."[55]

The workplace can be a place to encounter new ideas and interact with people of different genders or ethnicities. Bosnians interviewed in the late 1990s commented that "the area in which there is the greatest support for ethnic co-operation is in the workplace."[56] Business people in Trinidad and Tobago reported that they interacted with people of a wider range of ethnicities at work than they did in their social lives.[57] Networks can also exclude. In Morocco, people

whose fathers did not have formal sector jobs were significantly less likely to have such jobs themselves.[58]

The distribution of jobs within society—and perceptions about who has access to opportunities and why—can shape expectations for the future and perceptions of fairness. Children's aspirations may be influenced by whether their parents have jobs and the types of jobs they have. The Arab Spring was not merely about employment. But disappointment, especially among youth, about the lack of job opportunities and frustration with the allocation of jobs based on connections rather than merit echoed across countries.

FIGURE 10 *People who are unemployed, or do not have motivating jobs, participate less in society*

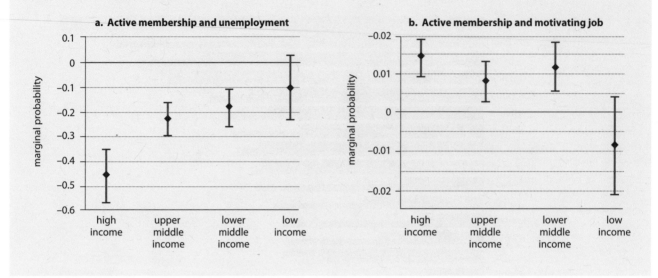

Source: Wietzke and McLeod 2012 for the World Development Report 2013.
Note: The vertical axis shows the probability of the respondent being an active member of one or more of nine types of associations, controlling for the income, education, and demographic characteristics of respondents. In panel a, the probability is linked to being unemployed, and panel b to having a job characterized as cognitive, creative, or independent. The vertical lines indicate the 95 percent confidence interval of the estimated probability.

Jobs influence how people view themselves, how they interact with others, and how they perceive their stake in society.[59] Jobs also can have collective consequences. They can shape how societies handle collective decision making, manage tensions between diverse groups, and avoid and resolve conflicts. The relationship is not immediate or direct, however. Jobs are only one factor contributing to the capacity of societies to manage collective decision making peacefully. And social cohesion can in turn influence jobs by shaping the context in which entrepreneurs make business decisions.

Trust beyond one's own group and civic engagement are two indicators of social cohesion. Unemployment and job loss are associated with lower levels of both trust and civic engagement (figure 10). While causality is difficult to establish, there is more than just a correlation at stake. Indonesian men and women who were working in 2000 but not in 2007 were less likely to be participating in community activities than those still at work. And those who were working in 2007 but not in 2000 were significantly more likely to be involved in the community than those who were still out of work.[60]

The nature of jobs matters as well. Jobs that empower, build agency, and respect rights are associated with greater trust and willingness to participate in civil society. Jobs that create economic and social ties may build incentives to work across boundaries and resolve conflict. And if people believe that job opportunities are available to them either now or in the future, their trust in others and their confidence in institutions may increase. Ultimately, jobs can influence social cohesion through their effects on social identity, networks, and fairness.

Valuing jobs

Not all forms of work are acceptable. Activities that exploit workers, expose them to dangerous environments, or threaten their physical and mental well-being are bad for individuals and societies alike. Child prostitution and forced labor contravene principles of human dignity and undermine individual and collective well-being. Today, an estimated 21 million people globally are victims of bonded labor, slavery, forced prostitution, and other forms of involuntary work.[61]

In 2008, 115 million children between the ages of 5 and 17 were involved in hazardous work.[62] International norms of human rights and labor standards reject forced labor, harmful forms of child labor, discrimination, and the suppression of voice among workers.

Beyond rights, the most obvious outcome of a job is the earnings it provides to its holder. These earnings can be in cash or in kind and may include a range of associated benefits. Other characteristics, such as stability, voice, and fulfillment at work, also affect subjective well-being. Several of these dimensions of jobs have been combined into the concept of Decent Work, introduced by the International Labour Organization (ILO) in 1999.[63] Defined as "opportunities for women and men to obtain decent and productive work in conditions of freedom, equity, security and human dignity," this concept has been used by many governments to articulate their policy agendas on jobs. The concept of Decent Work has also been embraced by the United Nations and several international organizations and endorsed by numerous global forums.

As jobs provide earnings, generate output, and influence identity, they shape the well-being of those who hold them—and they also affect the well-being of others. To understand how much jobs contribute to development, it is necessary to assess these effects—the spillovers from jobs. Jobs that generate positive spillovers have a greater value to society than they have to the individual who holds the job, while the opposite is true when spillovers are negative. Intuitively, many people have notions about such broader payoffs. When asked about their most preferred jobs, respondents in China, Colombia, Egypt, and Sierra Leone give different answers from those they offer when asked to identify the most important jobs to society (figure 11). Working as a civil servant or as a shop owner is generally preferred by individuals, while teachers and doctors are quite often mentioned as the most important jobs for society.

Who gets a job makes a difference too, and not just for individuals. In a society that values poverty reduction, jobs that take households out of hardship generate a positive spillover, because they improve the well-being of those who care. Female employment also matters beyond the individual. An increase in the share of household income contributed by women often results in improvements in children's educational attainment and health. In Bangladesh, where the garment industry employs women in large numbers, the opening of a garment factory within commuting distance of a village is seen as a signal of opportunity and leads to increased schooling for girls.[64] Among disadvantaged castes in Southern Indian villages, an increase of US$90 in a woman's annual income is estimated to increase schooling among her children by 1.6 years.[65]

Similarly, a job created or sustained through foreign direct investment (FDI) matters for other jobs, and thus for other people. With the investment come knowledge and know-how. These raise productivity not only in the foreign subsidiary but also among local firms interacting with the subsidiary or operating in its vicinity. Such knowledge spillovers are sizable in low- and middle-income countries.[66] Conversely, a job in a protected industry that needs to be supported through transfers (either by taxpayers or by consumers) generates a negative spillover, even more so when the need for protection is associated with the use of outdated technology that results in high environmental costs.

Jobs can also affect other people by shaping social values and norms, influencing how groups coexist and manage tensions. In Bosnia and Herzegovina and the former Yugoslav Republic of Macedonia, surveys found that the number of people willing to work together or do business with someone of a different ethnicity was greater than the number of people in favor of interethnic cooperation in schools or neighborhoods.[67] And in the Dominican Republic, a program targeted to youth at risk shows that jobs can change behaviors with positive implications for society. Participation in the Programa Juventud y Empleo (Youth and Employment Program), which provides a combination of vocational and life skills training, reduced involvement in gangs, violence, and other risky behaviors.[68]

For the same level of earnings and benefits, the larger the positive spillovers from a job, the more transformational the job can be, and the greater its value to society. In everyday parlance, good jobs are those that provide greater well-being to the people who hold them. But good jobs for development are those with the highest value for society. Understanding these wider

FIGURE 11 *Views on preferred jobs and most important jobs differ*

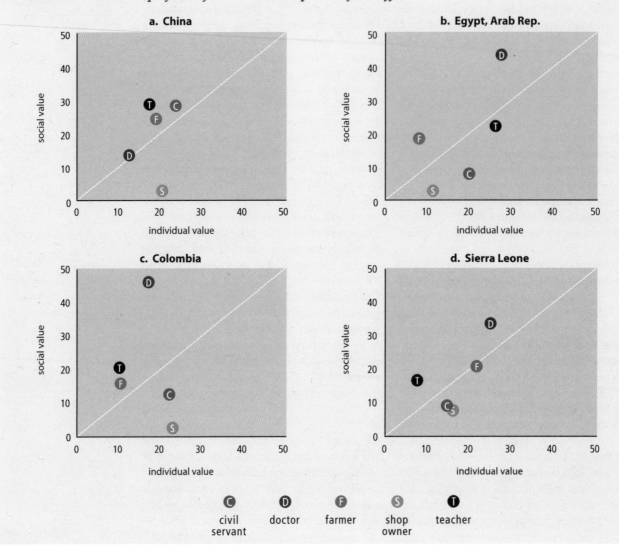

Sources: Bjørkhaug and others 2012; Hatløy and others 2012; Kebede and others 2012; and Zhang and others 2012; all for the World Development Report 2013.
Note: The figure shows the share of respondents who would want the job for themselves (individual value) and those who think the job is good for society (social value).

payoffs to jobs has shaped recent development thinking.[69]

Spillovers from jobs can be identified across all three transformations (figure 12). Some directly affect the earnings of others, as when a job is supported through government transfers, or restrictive regulations that reduce employment opportunities for others. Other spillovers take place through interactions: in households in the case of gender equality, at the workplace when knowledge and ideas are shared, or in society more broadly in the case of networks. Spillovers also occur when jobs and their allocation con-

tribute to common goals, such as poverty reduction, environmental protection, or fairness.

Because a job can affect the well-being of others as well as that of the jobholder, two jobs that may appear identical from an individual perspective could be different from a social perspective (figure 13). The individual perspective provides a useful starting point, because it often coincides with the social perspective. A high-paying job in Bangalore's information technology sector is probably good for the worker; it is also good for India because it contributes to the country's long-term growth. In other cases, the two perspectives may conflict. For instance, Vietnam's poverty rate declined with unprecedented speed in the 1990s when land was redistributed to farmers and agricultural commercialization was liberalized.[70] From the individual perspective, farming jobs involve difficult working conditions, substantial variability in earnings, and no formal social protection. But they can make a major contribution to development, as a ticket out of poverty for many. Conversely, bloated public utilities often offer a range of privileges to their employees even if the utilities themselves provide only limited coverage and unreliable services and are obstacles to economic growth and poverty reduction. Such jobs may look appealing from an individual perspective, but are less so to society.

Jobs agendas are diverse . . . but connected

Jobs challenges are not the same everywhere. Creating more jobs may be a universal goal, but the types of jobs that can contribute the most to development depend on the country context. Jobs that connect the economy to the world may matter the most in some situations; in others,

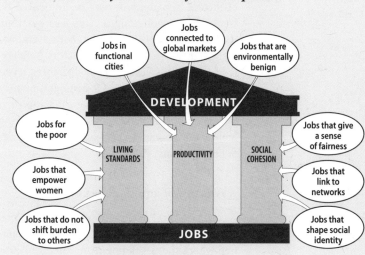

FIGURE 12 *Some jobs do more for development*

Source: World Development Report 2013 team.

the biggest payoff may be for jobs that reduce poverty or defuse conflict. Certainly, the level of development matters. The jobs agenda is not the same in an agrarian economy as in one that is rapidly urbanizing. It is bound to be different still in countries already grappling with how far the formal economy can be extended.

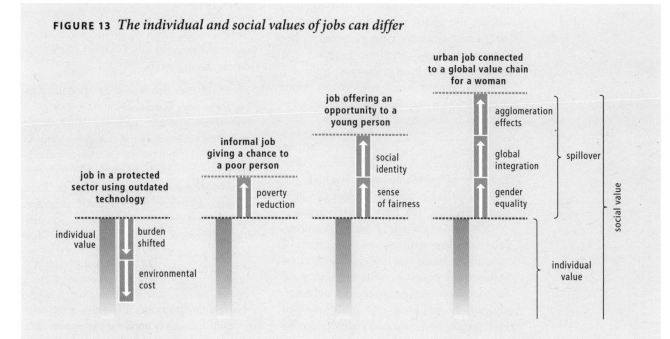

FIGURE 13 *The individual and social values of jobs can differ*

Source: World Development Report 2013 team.

But the nature of good jobs for development in a particular context is not simply a function of income per capita. It may be influenced by conflict that is ongoing or still reverberating. A country's geography or its natural endowments can also be determining factors. Small island nations have unique jobs challenges, as do resource-rich economies. Or demography may be the key characteristic—witness the imposing but very different challenges in countries facing high youth unemployment and those with aging populations.

A typology of jobs challenges

A country's level of development, institutional strength, endowments, and demography define where the development payoff from jobs is greatest. The jobs agenda in one country will thus be different from that in another country, depending on their dominant features. The challenges facing countries as they move along the development path are illustrated by the agrarian, urbanizing, and formalizing cases:

- *Agrarian countries.* Most people are still engaged in agriculture and live in rural areas. Jobs that improve living standards have a substantial development payoff because of high poverty rates. Cities need to be more functional to reap the benefits from agglomeration and global integration, so jobs that set the foundation for cities to eventually become economically dynamic are good jobs for development. Even in the most optimistic scenario, however, it may take decades before urbanization is complete, so increasing productivity in agriculture is a priority.

- *Urbanizing countries.* Productivity growth in agriculture has risen enough to free up large numbers of people to work in cities. Job opportunities for women, typically in light manufacturing, can have positive impacts on the household allocation of resources. Jobs that deepen the global integration of urbanizing countries, especially in higher-value-added export sectors, are also good for development. As countries urbanize, congestion, pollution, and other costs of high density become increasingly serious, so

jobs that do no environmental damage have particularly positive development impacts.

- *Formalizing countries.* Large and growing urban populations generally lead to more developed economies, where a fairly substantial proportion of firms and workers are covered by formal institutions and social programs. But further increasing formality to levels typical of industrial countries involves tradeoffs between living standards, productivity, and social cohesion. There is a premium on jobs that can be formalized without making labor too costly and on jobs that reduce the divide between those who benefit from formal institutions and those who do not.

In some countries, the jobs challenge is shaped by demography and special circumstances affecting particular groups.

- In *countries with high youth unemployment* young people do not see opportunities for the future. Many of these countries have large youth bulges, which can put downward pressure on employment and earnings. Many also have education and training systems that are not developing the kinds of skills needed by the private sector. On closer inspection, the problem is often more on the demand side than the supply side, with limited competition reducing employment opportunities, especially in more skill-intensive sectors. In these settings, removing privilege in business entry and access to jobs is likely to have large development payoffs.

- *Aging societies* also face generational issues, but these stem from a shrinking working-age population and the high cost of providing and caring for a growing number of elderly people. The impact of the declining working-age population can be mitigated through policies for active aging, ensuring that the most productive members of society, including the highly skilled elderly, can work. Containing the increase in pension, health care, and long-term care costs can be achieved through reforms in program design, but these reforms can be a source of social strain.

Natural endowments, including geography, and institutions can create unique jobs challenges.

- *Resource-rich countries* may have substantial foreign exchange earnings, but this wealth may not translate into employment creation beyond the exploitation of natural resources. Indeed, the abundance of foreign exchange can hamper the competitiveness of other export activities. Some resource-rich countries distribute part of their wealth through transfers or subsidized public sector jobs, while relying on migrants to do menial work. This approach can maintain living standards but at the expense of productivity growth and social cohesion. In those countries, jobs that support the diversification of exports can have large development payoffs.

- *Small island nations,* because of their size and remoteness, cannot reap the benefits from agglomeration and global integration except through tourism. So the productivity spillovers from jobs are limited, as are employment opportunities outside basic services and government. Outmigration offers an alternative for improving living standards, while return migration and diaspora communities can stimulate the diffusion of new business ideas among locals.

- In *conflict-affected countries,* the most immediate challenge is to support social cohesion. Employment for ex-combatants or young men vulnerable to participation in violence takes on particular importance. With fragile institutions and volatile politics, attracting private investment and connecting to global value chains may be out of reach for quite some time. Yet construction can boom even in poor business environments, and it is labor intensive. Investments in infrastructure can not only support social cohesion through their direct employment impact, they can also be a step in preparing for future private sector job creation.

These criteria are not mutually exclusive. Chad and the Democratic Republic of Congo are both resource rich and conflict affected; Jordan and Armenia are formalizing and also have high youth unemployment. Still, looking through the jobs lens and focusing on the key features of the different country types can help identify more clearly the kinds of jobs that would make the greatest contribution to development in each case. This focus allows for a richer analysis of the potential tradeoffs between living standards, productivity, and social cohesion in a specific context. It provides clues about the obstacles to job creation and, ultimately, the priorities for policy makers (figure 14).

Migration of people—and of jobs

The movement of people and jobs implies that jobs challenges, while being country specific, also have a global scope. These processes have implications for living standards and productivity at both the sending and the receiving ends, and they can transform families and entire communities, for better or for worse. Tradeoffs are inevitable, and coping with them only through the policies of receiving countries alone may prove unsatisfactory.

At the turn of the 21st century, there were more than 200 million international migrants worldwide, nearly 90 million of them workers. Many migrants are temporary or seasonal workers who eventually return home. Some countries are mainly recipients, while others are sources, and yet others neither host nor send significant numbers of migrants (map 1). Some are large recipients either in absolute numbers (for instance, the United States) or in relative terms (Jordan and Singapore). Migrants from Bangladesh, Mexico, and India represent a large share of total migrants worldwide; Fiji, Jamaica, and Tonga have a large share of their population overseas. Figures for some of the smaller countries are striking. For instance, about a fifth of all Salvadorians live abroad, while more than 60 percent of the populations of Kuwait, Qatar, and the United Arab Emirates are foreign-born.[71]

International migration increases the incomes of migrants and their families through earnings and remittances. The majority of the studies find either no effect or a very small negative effect on the labor earnings of locals in receiving countries. Migrants also contribute to global output if their productivity abroad is higher than it would be at home, which is usually the case. They may even contribute to output in the sending country, as networks of migrants and returnees channel investments, innovation,

FIGURE 14 *Good jobs for development are not the same everywhere*

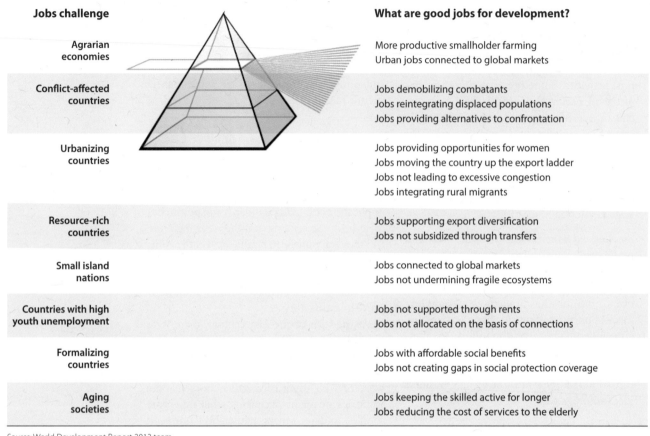

Jobs challenge	What are good jobs for development?
Agrarian economies	More productive smallholder farming Urban jobs connected to global markets
Conflict-affected countries	Jobs demobilizing combatants Jobs reintegrating displaced populations Jobs providing alternatives to confrontation
Urbanizing countries	Jobs providing opportunities for women Jobs moving the country up the export ladder Jobs not leading to excessive congestion Jobs integrating rural migrants
Resource-rich countries	Jobs supporting export diversification Jobs not subsidized through transfers
Small island nations	Jobs connected to global markets Jobs not undermining fragile ecosystems
Countries with high youth unemployment	Jobs not supported through rents Jobs not allocated on the basis of connections
Formalizing countries	Jobs with affordable social benefits Jobs not creating gaps in social protection coverage
Aging societies	Jobs keeping the skilled active for longer Jobs reducing the cost of services to the elderly

Source: World Development Report 2013 team.

and expertise. Social effects are more mixed. On the positive side, migration connects people from different cultures in ways bound to widen their horizons. On the negative side, the separation from family and friends can be a source of distress and isolation. Migration may also bring racial prejudice and heighten social tensions in host countries, especially when migrants are secluded in segregated occupations or neighborhoods, preventing their integration in society.

Jobs are on the move as well. The past four decades have been marked by the outsourcing of manufacturing tasks from industrial countries to the developing world, especially to East Asia (figure 15). More recently, the same pattern is observable for service tasks. In fact, services are the fastest-growing component of global trade. Developing countries are now exporting not only traditional services, such as transportation and tourism, but also modern and skill-intensive services, such as financial intermediation, computer and information services, legal and technical support, and other business services. India was the pioneer, but other countries— Brazil, Chile, China, and Malaysia, to name a few—have also seized the opportunity.[72]

The obvious winners of job migration are the workers and entrepreneurs in countries to which industries and splintered service jobs have migrated. This migration, along with the transfer of new technologies and advanced management methods, contributes to productivity growth and higher living standards. The hidden winners of job migration are consumers worldwide. The improved international division of labor increases the availability of goods and services and enhances the possibility of gaining from trade. The clear losers are those who have seen their jobs disappear because of the declining competitiveness of their industries and services. Among the losers, many skilled workers find comparable jobs without a substantial loss in salary, but oth-

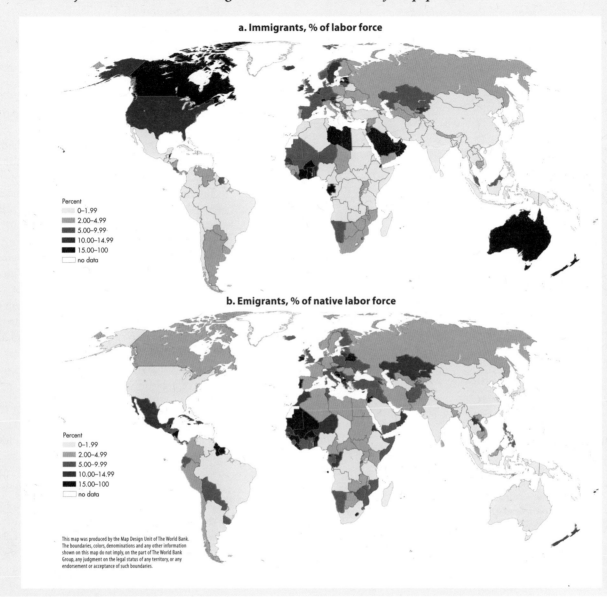

MAP 1 *Only in some countries are migrants a substantial share of the population*

a. Immigrants, % of labor force

Percent
- 0–1.99
- 2.00–4.99
- 5.00–9.99
- 10.00–14.99
- 15.00–100
- no data

b. Emigrants, % of native labor force

Percent
- 0–1.99
- 2.00–4.99
- 5.00–9.99
- 10.00–14.99
- 15.00–100
- no data

This map was produced by the Map Design Unit of The World Bank. The boundaries, colors, denominations and any other information shown on this map do not imply, on the part of The World Bank Group, any judgment on the legal status of any territory, or any endorsement or acceptance of such boundaries.

Sources: World Development Report 2013 team based on Özden and others 2011, and Artuc and others 2012, using census data around 2000.

ers do not. Low-skilled workers or those with industry- or occupation-specific skills that are no longer in demand are those who suffer most.

Policies through the jobs lens

While it is not the role of governments to create jobs, government functions are fundamental for sustained job creation. The quality of the civil service is critically important for development, whether it is teachers building skills, agricultural extension agents improving agricultural productivity, or urban planners designing functional cities. Temporary employment programs for the demobilization of combatants are also justified in some circumstances. But as a general rule it is the private sector that creates jobs. The role of government is to ensure that the conditions are in place for strong private-sector-led

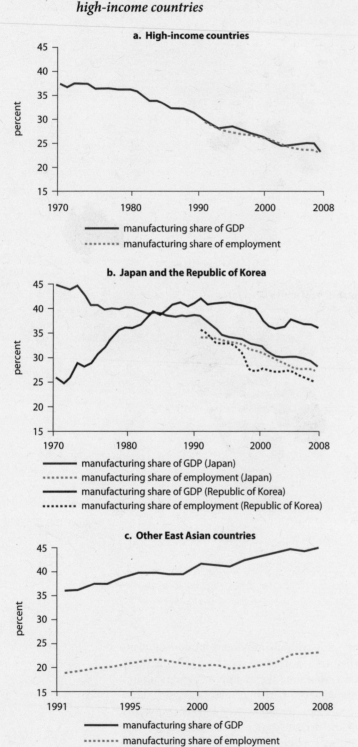

FIGURE 15 *Manufacturing jobs have migrated away from high-income countries*

a. High-income countries

- manufacturing share of GDP
- ⋯⋯ manufacturing share of employment

b. Japan and the Republic of Korea

- manufacturing share of GDP (Japan)
- ⋯⋯ manufacturing share of employment (Japan)
- manufacturing share of GDP (Republic of Korea)
- ▪▪▪ manufacturing share of employment (Republic of Korea)

c. Other East Asian countries

- manufacturing share of GDP
- ⋯⋯ manufacturing share of employment

Sources: World Development Report 2013 team estimates based on data from the United Nations Industrial Development Organization (UNIDO) and the United Nations Statistics Division.
Note: Japan is not included in panel a. GDP = gross domestic product.

growth, to understand why there are not enough good jobs for development, and to remove or mitigate the constraints that prevent the creation of more of those jobs.

Government can fulfill this role through a three-layered policy approach (figure 16):

- *Fundamentals.* Because jobs improve with development, providing higher earnings and benefits as countries grow rich, a prerequisite is to create a policy environment that is conducive to growth. Macroeconomic stability, an enabling business environment, human capital accumulation, and the rule of law are among the fundamentals. Ensuring macroeconomic stability involves containing volatility and avoiding major misalignments of relative prices. Adequate infrastructure, access to finance, and sound regulation are key ingredients of the business environment. Good nutrition, health, and education outcomes not only improve people's lives but also equip them for productive employment. The rule of law includes protection of property rights and also the progressive realization of rights at work, to avoid a situation where growth coexists with unacceptable forms of employment.

- *Labor policies.* Because growth does not mechanically deliver employment, a second layer is to ensure that labor policies do not undermine job creation and instead enhance the development payoffs from jobs. But labor market imperfections should not be addressed through institutional failures. Instead, they should remain on a range—a plateau—where negative efficiency effects are modest. Labor policy should avoid two cliffs: the distortionary interventions that clog the creation of jobs in cities and in global value chains, and the lack of mechanisms for voice and protection for the most vulnerable workers, regardless of whether they are wage earners. The first cliff undermines the development payoffs from agglomeration and global integration; the second leads to low living standards and a social cohesion deficit.

- *Priorities.* Because some jobs do more for development than others, it is necessary to understand where good jobs for development lie, given the country context. More selective policy interventions are justified when incentives are distorted, resulting in too few of those jobs. If this is the case, policies should remove the market imperfections and institutional failures that prevent the private sector from creating more good jobs for development. If the failures and imperfections cannot be clearly identified, or cannot be easily removed, offsetting them may be an option, but the costs and benefits of doing so need to be carefully assessed.

Fundamentals: Ensuring the basics

Macroeconomic stability. Volatility hurts employment and earnings, often immediately. According to a recent estimate, a 1.0 percent decline in gross domestic product (GDP) is associated with an increase in the unemployment rate of 0.19 percentage point in Japan, 0.45 percentage point in the United States, and 0.85 percentage point in Spain.[73] In developing countries, where farming and self-employment are more prevalent and income support mechanisms are more limited, the short-term impact of macroeconomic instability is less on open unemployment and more on earnings from work.[74]

Volatility can originate internally or be caused by external shocks. Internally, it is often the outcome of unsustainable budget deficits and lax monetary policy. But tight budgets and rigid monetary policy rules may not be a magic wand. Budget deficits are more or less worrisome depending on how quickly an economy is growing, whereas the independence of central banks needs to be weighed against the overall coherence of the country's development strategy. Assessing the soundness of macroeconomic management requires taking account of the impact of fiscal and monetary policies on economic growth.[75]

Volatility may also result from external shocks, including natural disasters and crises originating abroad. Precautionary policies can cushion those shocks, if and when they occur. Most often, short-term stimulus or adjustment packages are needed—but these tend to be less effective in the developing world than in developed countries because of lower multiplier effects.[76]

Avoiding exchange rate misalignment is necessary to sustain a vibrant export sector—and thus to create jobs connected to international markets and global value chains. Surges in a country's foreign exchange earnings generally

FIGURE 16 *Three distinct layers of policies are needed*

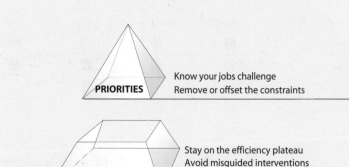

PRIORITIES
Know your jobs challenge
Remove or offset the constraints

LABOR POLICIES
Stay on the efficiency plateau
Avoid misguided interventions
Provide voice and extend protection

FUNDAMENTALS
Macroeconomic stability
An enabling business environment
Human capital
Rule of law and respect for rights

Source: World Development Report 2013 team.

lead to an overvaluation of its currency, making imports more affordable and exports less competitive. Resource-rich countries face similar pressures for their currencies to appreciate, and the commodity booms of the last few years have only made these pressures stronger. Currency overvaluation can also happen in countries where large volumes of foreign assistance are needed to jump-start development, cope with natural disasters, or facilitate recovery after a conflict. An analysis of 83 developing countries between 1970 and 2004 confirms that aid fosters growth (albeit with decreasing returns) but induces overvaluation and has a negative impact on export diversification.[77]

An enabling business environment. Finance, infrastructure, and business regulations set the quality of the investment climate and thus influence job creation by private firms. Access to finance, a chief constraint to business expansion in countries in every development phase, is the top constraint in low- and upper-middle-income countries (figure 17). Financial markets have the potential to allocate resources toward more productive uses, thwart the channeling of resources to those with political connections or economic power, and expand financial in-

FIGURE 17 *Finance and electricity are among the top constraints faced by formal private enterprises*

Constraint	Firm size			Income level				All
	Small	Medium	Large	Low	Lower middle	Upper middle	High	
Access to finance	●	●	○	◐	●	●	○	●
Power shortage	◐	◐	●	●	○			◐
Lack of skills			○				●	
Informal competition	○	○			◐	○		○
Tax rates				○		◐	◐	

● most severe   ◐ second-most severe   ○ third-most severe

Source: IFC, forthcoming.
Note: The analysis is based on World Bank enterprise surveys covering 46,556 firms in 106 countries. Small firms have fewer than 20 employees, medium firms have 21–99, and large firms 100 and more.

clusion. But regulatory oversight is needed to ensure transparency and competition in how funds are allocated.[78] The financial crisis of 2008 reopened heated debates on the appropriate regulation of the financial sector and the need to balance prudence and stability with innovation and inclusion.

Access to affordable and quality infrastructure is a prerequisite for firms to operate. Power shortages are the number-two constraint to firm growth and job creation mentioned by entrepreneurs the world over—and number one in low-income countries. Telecommunications allow for a better flow of information with suppliers and customers, and the internet and mobile technology facilitate the spread of new ideas. Roads provide greater access to markets, as do ports and airports.[79] The way infrastructure is regulated is important as well. Inadequate pricing policies and regulations amplify the gap in needed infrastructure services. In many countries, monopolies based on political connections have led to reduced quantities of infrastructure services at higher prices and lower quality.[80]

Business regulation also affects the opportunities for businesses to grow and create jobs. Regulations can increase the cost of doing business, in money or in time needed to comply. Steps taken to meet requirements or to pay fees are a burden for businesses, as are delays or discretionary decisions, such as those for permits or licenses. There is great variation across firms in the same location with regard to the time it takes to comply with regulations or to receive permits.[81] Business regulations also affect competition and thus the pressure to innovate and increase productivity. Across countries, regulations on business entry are inversely correlated with productivity and firm creation, with stronger effects in sectors that have higher rates of entry.[82] In Mexico, easing entry requirements increased business registration and employment and drove down consumer prices, largely through creating new firms rather than formalizing informal firms.[83]

Human capital. Good outcomes in nutrition, health, and education are development goals in themselves, because they directly improve people's lives. But they also equip people for productive employment and job opportunities—and through this channel, human capital drives economic and social advances. There is robust evidence from throughout the world that an additional year of schooling raises earnings substantially, and that this earnings premium reflects the higher productivity of more educated workers.[84] Together, nutrition, health, and education combine to form human skills and abilities that have been powerfully linked to productivity growth and poverty reduction in the medium to longer run.[85] Also, better health brings, directly, higher labor productivity. As such, human capital is a fundamental ingredient for desirable job outcomes.

Human capital formation is cumulative. Of crucial importance are adequate health and nutrition during "the first 1,000 days," from conception to two years of age. Brain development in this time period affects physical health, learning abilities, and social behavior throughout life.[86] Ensuring adequate nutrition, health, and cognitive stimulation through a nurturing environment from the womb through the first years raises returns to later child investments significantly.[87] While foundations are laid early on, human capital and skills continue to be formed throughout childhood and young adulthood. Schooling is fundamental for the further development of cognitive and social skills until the end of the teenage life. Social skills remain malleable through adolescence and the early adult years.[88] Young adults can continue into more specialized skill-building, including at tertiary levels, but success depends on whether the generic skills needed to learn and adapt to different tasks and problem-solving environments have been acquired. These general skills are especially important in more dynamic economic environments.

Unfortunately, the evidence shows that many countries are falling short in building up the human capital of their children and youth. The quality of delivery systems has often failed to keep pace with the expansion of access to basic social services. In a large majority of developing countries that took part in the Programme for International Student Assessment (PISA) in 2009, at least one-fifth of 15-year-old students were functionally illiterate (not reaching at least level 2 in the PISA reading assessment).[89]

The rule of law. Across countries, the presence of institutions that protect property rights, uphold the rule of law, and rein in corruption is associated with higher levels of development.[90] Property rights foster private sector growth by allowing firms to invest without the fear that their assets will be stolen or confiscated.[91] The ability to enforce contracts widens the circle of potential suppliers and customers, as personal connections become less important in establishing trust.[92] The rule of law has direct implications for the growth of firms and jobs. Entrepreneurs who believe their property rights are secure reinvest more of their profits than those who do not.[93] Conversely, rampant crime and violence are likely to drive firms away and discourage domestic and foreign investment.[94] Across countries, investment climate surveys consistently find crime and corruption to be obstacles to conducting business.[95]

An effective judicial system is a key institution for enforcing property rights and reducing crime and corruption. An independent, accountable, and fair judiciary can contribute to private sector growth and job creation by enforcing the rules that govern transactions and by helping ensure that the costs and benefits of growth are fairly distributed. The justice system can enforce contracts, reduce transaction costs for firms, and create a safe and more predictable business environment.[96] And effective courts increase the willingness of firms to invest.[97]

An institutional environment that respects rights is an important ingredient of the rule of law and a foundation for good jobs for development. The ILO's core labor standards provide a floor in the areas of child labor, forced labor, discrimination, and freedom of association and collective bargaining.[98] Health and safety at work also call for attention by governments and employers. Ensuring that standards are applied in practice requires providing access to information to workers and employers. It also implies expanding legal coverage to workers in jobs that fall outside formal laws and regulations. Associations of informal workers can inform them about their rights, help them use legal mechanisms, and offer them collective voice.[99]

Labor policies: Avoiding the two cliffs

A malfunctioning labor market may prevent economic growth from translating into more and better jobs. Traditional analyses focus on labor supply, labor demand, and their matching to explain why there may not be enough employment, or not enough wage employment in the case of developing countries. By not addressing labor market imperfections, or by creating them, labor policies can indeed constrain job creation, even seriously. In many cases, however, the constraints to creating transformational jobs are not connected to the labor code. The low productivity of smallholder farming in agrarian economies is probably more closely related to failures in agricultural research and extension. And the lack of competition in technologically advanced activities that could boost the demand for skilled work in countries with high youth employment is more likely to stem from cronyism and political favoritism.

There is no consensus on what the content of labor policies should be. Views are polarized, reflecting differences in fundamental beliefs. To some, labor market regulations and collective bargaining are sources of inefficiency that reduce output and employment, while protecting insiders at the expense of everyone else. In this view, unemployment insurance and active labor market programs create work disincentives and are a waste of money. To others, these policies provide necessary protection to workers against the power of employers and the vagaries of the market. They can even contribute to economic efficiency by improving information, insuring against risks, and creating conditions for long-term investments by both workers and firms.

Advocates of both views can find examples to support their positions. Those who see labor policies and institutions as part of the problem point to the impressive long-term job creation record of the United States, a country with limited interventions in the labor market. They also point to the protective job security rules that have impeded young people from finding work in many North African and Southern European countries. By contrast, those who see labor policies as part of the solution point to job-sharing as decisive in Germany's relative success in weathering the financial crisis.

A careful review of the actual effects of labor policies in developing countries yields a mixed picture. Most studies find that impacts are modest—certainly more modest than the intensity of the debate would suggest.[100] Across firm sizes and country levels of development, labor policies and regulations are generally not among the top three constraints that formal private enterprises face. Excessive or insufficient regulation of labor markets reduces productivity. But in between these extremes is a plateau where effects enhancing and undermining efficiency can be found side by side and most of the impact is redistributive, generally to the advantage of middle-aged male workers (as opposed to owners of capital, women, and younger workers).

In most countries that have been studied, job security rules and minimum wages have a small effect on aggregate employment. These rules offer benefits for those who are covered, while negative effects tend to be concentrated on youth, women, and the less skilled. In Colombia and Indonesia, minimum wage increases had only a modest overall effect but the employment impact was stronger for young workers.[101] Regulations more clearly affect job flows, creating "stickiness" in the labor market and slowing the pace of labor reallocation.[102] While this hinders economic efficiency, the evidence on productivity is fairly inconclusive, though admittedly scarce.[103]

In developing countries, collective bargaining does not have a major impact outside the public sector and activities characterized by limited competition, where there are rents to share.[104] Unions consistently raise wages for workers. Studies place this premium in the 5 to 15 percent range in Mexico; around 5 percent in Korea; and at 10 to 20 percent in South Africa.[105] The costs in terms of reduced jobs are not so clear, however. In some countries, though not all, the tradeoff seems to be lower employment, but even then the magnitudes are relatively small. The limited evidence on union effects on productivity is also mixed.[106] The main challenges are extending voice to those who are not wage earners, so that the constraints facing their farms and microenterprises can be addressed, and organizing collective bargaining in a way that enhances productivity.

Active labor market programs, such as training, employment services, wage subsidies, and public works, have a mixed record.[107] When they are not well grounded in the needs and realities of the labor market or when administration is poor and not transparent, they are of little use or even worse. When they are well designed and implemented, they can help facilitate job matching, mitigate the negative impacts of economic downturns, and fill the gap when employers or workers underinvest in training (figure 18). Even when this is the case, though, effects tend to be modest, so expectations about what active labor market policies can achieve need to be held in check.

Social insurance coverage is limited even in the most formalized developing countries. Unemployment insurance can help workers manage the risks of job loss, but it can also weaken job search efforts. When unemployment insurance, pensions, health care, and other benefits are financed through the payroll, high contribution rates can create hiring disincentives. In developing countries where formal sectors are small, funding these programs through general taxation is increasingly discussed,[108] but any taxes create distortions. In the end, there is no substitute for affordable social protection benefits that are valued by workers. The main issue is coherently integrating social protection and social assistance to minimize gaps and overlaps.

In sum, labor policies and institutions can improve labor market information, manage risk, and provide voice. But these advantages can come at the expense of labor market dynamism, reduced incentives for job creation and job search, and a gap in benefits between the covered and uncovered. The challenge is to set labor policies on a plateau—a range where regulations and institutions can at least partially address labor market imperfections without reducing efficiency. Labor market rules that are too weak or programs that are too modest or nonexistent can leave problems of poor information, unequal power, and inadequate risk management untreated. In contrast, rules that are too stringent and programs that are too ambitious can compound market imperfections with institutional failures.

The focus on good jobs for development offers some insights to assess where the edges of the plateau, the cliffs, may lie. At one end of the plateau are labor policies that slow job creation in cities, or in global value chains, and make countries miss out on jobs supporting agglomeration effects and knowledge spillovers. Forgoing the development payoffs from urbanization and global integration would be a consequence of falling off the cliff. This is not necessarily an argument for minimum regulation. There is also scope for arrangements strengthening spatial coordination, and thus increasing efficiency, as suggested by China's recent experience with collective bargaining.

At the other end of the plateau, the absence of mechanisms for voice and protection for those who do not work for an employer, or do so in the informal sector, is also a concern. Extending voice for workers who are often among the poorest may result in higher living standards. Limiting abuses by employment intermediaries should enhance efficiency, and building inclusive social protection systems can contribute to greater social cohesion. The experience of India's Self Employed Women's Association and

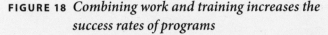

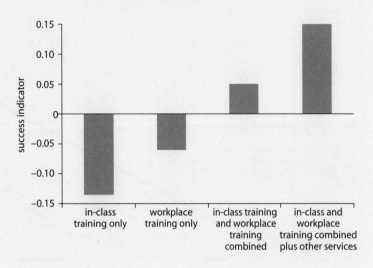

FIGURE 18 *Combining work and training increases the success rates of programs*

Source: Fares and Puerto 2009.
Note: The figure shows the correlation coefficient between type of training and reported success of a program, with success defined as improving employment or earnings and being cost-effective.

the health insurance program for the poor in Vietnam are encouraging in this respect.[109] This cliff may be less visible than excessive labor market rigidity, but it is no less real.

Priorities: Realizing the development payoffs from jobs

In addition to ensuring that the fundamentals support growth and that labor policies are adequate, decision makers can help realize the development payoffs that come from jobs. Some jobs do more than others for living standards, productivity, and social cohesion. What those jobs are depends on the country context—its level of development, demography, endowments, and institutions. In some circumstances, there will be no constraints to the emergence of good jobs for development, and no specific policy will be needed. In others, governments can support the private sector in creating more of these jobs. Sometimes this can be achieved by removing constraints that impede the creation of jobs with high development payoffs. When this is not possible, policies can be more proactive and bypass the constraints, provided that the gains to society from doing so outweigh the cost.

FIGURE 19 *A decision tree can help set policy priorities*

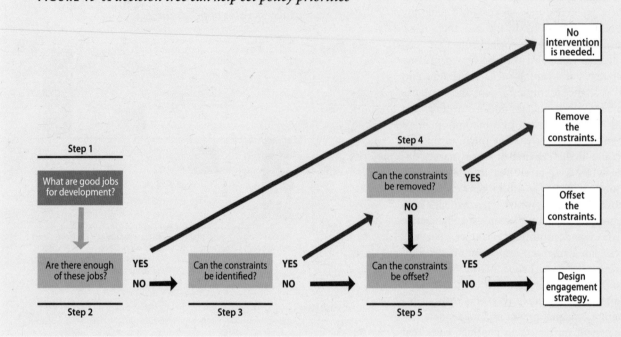

Source: World Development Report 2013 team.

A simple approach to setting policy priorities follows five steps (figure 19):

- *Step one: What are good jobs for development?* Assessing the development payoffs from jobs in a particular country context is the first step in identifying priorities. The nature of those jobs varies with the characteristics of the country, including its phase of development, demography, endowments, and institutions. Jobs challenges are not the same in agrarian economies, resource-rich countries, conflict-affected countries, or in countries with high youth unemployment. And the jobs with the greatest development impact differ as well, resulting in diverse jobs agendas.

- *Step two: Are there enough of these jobs?* A country may or may not face constraints in creating good jobs for development. For example, light manufacturing can offer employment opportunities for women, with significant impacts on poverty. If a boom is under way, the development value of new manufacturing jobs might materialize. But it might not if, for example, inadequate urbanization policies limit the establishment of new firms.

In the absence of gaps of this sort, it is difficult to justify government interventions beyond establishing the fundamentals and adopting adequate labor policies.

Data and analysis can be used to identify misaligned incentives, indicated by a gap between the individual and the social value of jobs. Several research areas deal with these gaps. For instance, the tools of public finance can measure the tax burden that applies to capital and labor and assess the cross-subsidization between individuals or firms. The methods of labor economics can uncover gaps between the actual earnings of specific groups of workers and their potential earnings, or between the social and individual returns to schooling. Poverty analyses help in identifying the kind of jobs that are more likely to provide opportunities to the poor, or the locations where job creation would have a greater impact on reducing poverty. Productivity studies allow for quantifying the spillovers from employment in foreign-owned investment companies, or in cities. Environmental studies shed light on the carbon footprint and pollution created by various types of jobs. And values surveys can discover which types of jobs provide social networks and social identity.

- *Step three: Can the constraints be identified?* The gaps between the individual and social values of specific types of jobs indicate unexploited spillovers from jobs. The gaps typically arise from market imperfections and institutional failures that cause people to work in jobs that are suboptimal from a social point of view, lead firms to create jobs that are not as good for development as they should be, or connect people less through jobs than would be socially desirable. But identifying those constraints is not always easy. For instance, a broad set of cultural, social, and economic forces may result in insufficient employment opportunities for women. Similarly, the obstacles to more jobs in cities could be in the land market, or in the institutional arrangements to coordinate urban development, or in the ability to raise revenue to finance infrastructure.

- *Step four: Can the constraints be removed?* If the institutional failures and market imperfections leading to misaligned incentives can be identified, reforms should be considered. It is a good economic principle to target reforms on the failures and imperfections at the root of the problem. Where reforms are technically and politically feasible, policy makers can directly tackle the major constraints hindering the creation of more good jobs for development by the private sector.

- *Step five: Can the constraints be offset?* Reforms might not be feasible, technically or politically. Or perhaps the constraints for jobs are not identifiable. An alternative then is to adopt offsetting policies that can restore the incentives for job creation. For instance, if a diffuse but entrenched set of norms and beliefs makes it difficult for women to work, efforts could aim at increasing their employability through targeted investments in social and physical infrastructure (box 1). Similarly, if politically charged regulations slow down the reallocation of labor toward more productive activities, urban infrastructure and logistics could enhance the attractiveness of jobs in cities and jobs connected to world markets.

But there are cases when constraints can neither be removed nor offset. An engagement strategy involving a deeper analysis of the options and buy-in by key stakeholders is needed then.

Policy making to remove or offset constraints needs to be selective and supported by good public finance principles. The costs and benefits of policy options need to be assessed, but calculations are different when the overall development impact is the guiding objective. An employment program to demobilize ex-combatants in a conflict-affected country could be assessed in terms of whether the earnings gains of participants justify the program costs, but a full accounting should also incorporate the potentially positive effects from reintegration and peace building. In the Democratic Republic of Congo, the cost of an integration program for ex-combatants was about US$800 per beneficiary.[110] Such a program would likely be judged as cost inefficient by traditional standards. Whether or not it is still worth implementing depends on the value policy makers attach to social cohesion benefits. These benefits should be stated for the policy decision to be transparent.

Diverse jobs agendas, diverse policy priorities

Some countries have successfully set policy to bring out the development payoffs from jobs, in ways that provide a model to others.

As an *agrarian country*, in the 1990s Vietnam concentrated on increasing productivity in agriculture, freeing labor to work in rural off-farm employment and eventually supporting migration to cities. In 1993, more than 70 percent of employment was in agriculture, 58 percent of the population lived in poverty, and famine was still a real concern.[111] Two decades later, Vietnam is the second-largest exporter of rice and coffee; the largest exporter of black pepper and cashew nuts; and a top exporter of tea, rubber, and seafood products. Poverty has declined dramatically. Combined with a strong emphasis on agricultural extension, land reform and deregulation led to rapidly growing agricultural productivity on very small farm plots. These policies were part of a broader package of reforms, or *Doi Moi*, that took Vietnam from central planning to a market economy with a socialist orientation.[112] Policies also aimed at

BOX 1 *How does women's labor force participation increase?*

Some developing countries have experienced important increases in women's labor participation over a relatively short period of time. Nowhere has the change been faster than in Latin America. Since the 1980s, more than 70 million women have entered the labor force, raising the female labor participation rate from 36 percent to 43 percent. In Colombia, the rate increased from 47 percent in 1984 to 65 percent in 2006. By contrast, in the Middle East and North Africa, women's labor force participation has only grown by 0.17 percentage points per year over the last three decades.

Recent research attributes this rapid transformation to increases in labor force participation among married or cohabiting women with children, rather than to demographics, education, or business cycles. Changes in social attitudes contributed to the transformation, but this is a complex area with limited scope—and justification—for direct policy intervention. For instance, women's participation rates are very low in the West Bank and Gaza, particularly among married women. But this cannot be mechanically attributed to religion, as countries like Indonesia have high participation rates. Other social norms and regulations prevent women from participating, despite their willingness and capacity to do so.

While the scope to influence social attitudes is limited, evidence suggests that public policies and programs in other areas have an important role to play. It also suggests that a combination of targeted investments and interventions in social and physical infrastructure can modify women's labor force participation and the returns to their earnings. These investments can be categorized into three groups. They can address shortages in the availability of services (such as lack of electricity or daycare facilities) that force women to allocate large amounts of time to home production. They can make it easier for women to accumulate productive assets, such as education, capital, and land, facilitating their entry into high-productivity market activities. And they can remove norms or regulations that imply biased or even discriminatory practices, preventing women from having equal employment opportunities.

There are successful experiences with targeted investments and interventions of each of these three sorts. Public provision or subsidization of child care can reduce the costs women incur at home when they engage in market work. Examples include publicly provided or subsidized day care such as Estancias Infantiles in Mexico, Hogares Comunitarios in Colombia, and similar programs in Argentina and Brazil. Improvements in infrastructure services—especially in water and electricity—can free up women's time spent on domestic and care work. Electrification in rural South Africa, for instance, has increased women's labor force participation by about 9 percent. Correcting biases in service delivery institutions, such as the workings of government land distribution and registration schemes, allows women to own and inherit assets. Finally, the use of active labor market policies, the promotion of networks, and the removal of discriminatory regulations are important to make work more rewarding for women.

Sources: World Development Report 2013 team based on Amador and others 2011, Chioda 2012, and World Bank 2011d.

creating employment opportunities outside agriculture. The country opened to foreign investors, first in natural resource exploitation and light manufacturing, and then more broadly in the context of its accession to the World Trade Organization in 2007. Registered FDI increased fourfold in just two years, from 1992 to 1994; over the past five years, FDI inflows exceeded 8 percent of GDP.[113]

Rwanda, a conflict-affected country, has rebounded after the ethnic conflict and destruction of the mid-1990s. By 2000, Rwanda's economy had returned to precrisis levels as a result of the cessation of conflict as well as an aggressive package of reforms.[114] Growth has continued, reaching an estimated 8.8 percent in 2011, and the poverty rate fell by 12 percentage points between 2005 and 2010. In the wake of the conflict, the government supported the reintegration and demobilization of more than 54,000 former combatants. In 2012, 73 percent of ex-combatants expressed satisfaction with their social integration, and 85 percent of community members felt there was trust between the two groups.[115] While ex-combatants were only a small share of Rwanda's population of 10 million, their reintegration had payoffs for social cohesion. Rwanda has built on this start by rejuvenating the private sector through reforms of institutions and business regulations.[116] The coffee industry has created thousands of new jobs.[117]

Chile, a resource-rich country, has managed its copper riches in a way compatible with job creation in nonresource sectors. Home to more than a quarter of the world's copper reserves, Chile diversified its exports and its economy while effectively managing resource-related risks such as currency appreciation and inflation. Unemployment fell to single digits from around 20 percent in the early 1980s.[118] A resource stabilization fund (since 1987) together with a transparent fiscal rule (since 1999) allowed the country to save for difficult times and avoid a loss of competitiveness. Governance reforms in all areas of public sector management promoted accountability and transparency. An active export-oriented growth policy, including the welcoming of foreign investment, supported productivity spillovers from jobs connected to global markets. Competitive innovation funds for nonmineral export sectors, especially in agribusiness, have broadened the export base.[119] The public budget boosted education spending, which almost doubled between 1990 and 2009, leading to an unprecedented expansion of secondary and tertiary education.[120]

Slovenia has successfully tackled its very *high youth unemployment* rate, reducing the ratio of youth to adult unemployment from three in the 1990s to around two today.[121] The success in reducing youth unemployment cannot be attributed to spending on active labor market programs (about average for transition countries), liberalizing the labor market (rules remain more restrictive than the average in developed countries), or low minimum wages (still on the high side).[122] Potential distortions from these policies seem to be somewhat offset, however, by a model of consensus-based decision making whereby trade unions and employer organizations, with broad coverage, set wages that respond well to macroeconomic trends and sectoral productivity.[123] Sustained growth before the global crisis is ultimately responsible for much of Slovenia's decline in youth unemployment. Taking advantage of European integration, the economy successfully restructured its export sector. Very good infrastructure and a fairly well-skilled workforce helped as well.

Examples of successful policies can actually be found across the entire typology of jobs challenges (figure 20). As an *urbanizing country*, *Korea* carefully designed and phased policies to accompany the transition of jobs from agriculture to light manufacturing and then to industries with higher value added.[124] Land development programs were established first, followed by a land-use regulation system, and then by comprehensive urban planning. Housing and transportation policies held the diseconomies of urbanization in check. *Tonga*, a *small island nation*, is actively using the Recognized Seasonal Employer program launched by

New Zealand in 2007 to provide employment opportunities through migration, leading to higher remittances, improved knowledge of agricultural techniques, computer literacy, and English-language skills.[125] *Brazil* provides an example of a rapidly *formalizing country*. Over the past decade, job creation in the formal sector has been three times as rapid as in the informal sector. Just in the five years leading up to the crisis, the formal share of total employment increased by about 5 percentage points.[126] Non-contributory social protection programs such as Bolsa Familia, a simplification of tax rules for small business, increased incentives for firms to formalize their workers, and improved enforcement of tax and labor regulations contributed to this success. *Poland*, an *aging society*, has seen its employment ratio increase from 60 percent in 2006 to 65 percent in 2009. This was due to changes in the application of eligibility rules of disability pensions, and pension reforms adjusting the level of benefits down as life expectancy increases. In 2012, a new wave of pension reforms raised the retirement age to 67 for men and women from the current 65 for men and 60 for women.[127]

Connected jobs agendas: Global partnerships for jobs

Policies for jobs in one country can have spillovers to other countries, both positive and negative. An important issue is whether international coordination mechanisms could influence government decisions to enhance the positive spillovers and mitigate the negative. Several areas lend themselves to more and better coordination.

Rights and standards. Cross-border mechanisms exist to set standards and provide channels for improving compliance with rights. ILO conventions can influence domestic legislation and be a channel for voice and coordination internationally, as demonstrated by the process of adopting the conventions for home-based and domestic workers. The support for core labor standards in the 1998 Declaration on Fundamental Principles and Rights at Work suggests that countries respond to pressure from the international community.[128] Yet the pressure only goes so far. The persistence of forced labor, children working in hazardous conditions, discrimi-

FIGURE 20 *Which countries succeeded at addressing their jobs challenges and how?*

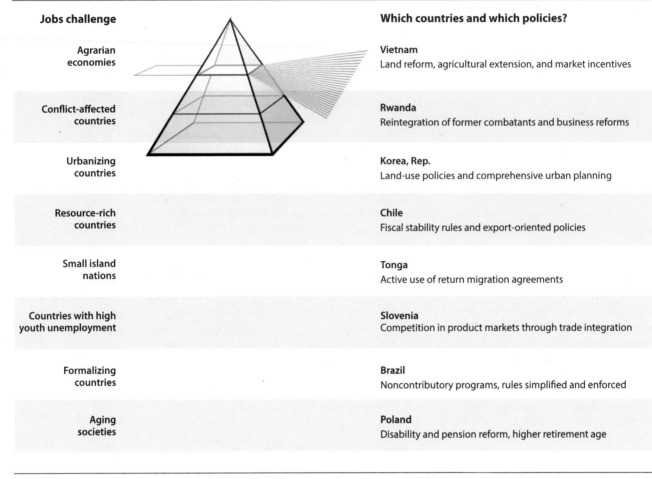

Jobs challenge	Which countries and which policies?
Agrarian economies	**Vietnam** Land reform, agricultural extension, and market incentives
Conflict-affected countries	**Rwanda** Reintegration of former combatants and business reforms
Urbanizing countries	**Korea, Rep.** Land-use policies and comprehensive urban planning
Resource-rich countries	**Chile** Fiscal stability rules and export-oriented policies
Small island nations	**Tonga** Active use of return migration agreements
Countries with high youth unemployment	**Slovenia** Competition in product markets through trade integration
Formalizing countries	**Brazil** Noncontributory programs, rules simplified and enforced
Aging societies	**Poland** Disability and pension reform, higher retirement age

Source: World Development Report 2013 team.

nation, and lack of voice suggest that ratification on its own is not sufficient.

Trade agreements are a potential instrument for international coordination on rights. They can incorporate incentives for attention to voice and working conditions by linking trade access to the adoption and enforcement of labor laws and standards. Whether linking rights to trade actually leads to better outcomes for workers on either side of a trade agreement is less clear. Labor clauses can be used as a protectionist tool, undermining trade and employment opportunities in developing countries. Moreover, in the absence of capacity and institutions to monitor and enforce compliance, trade agreements on their own can be weak instruments. For instance, Cambodia's successful bilateral trade agreement with the United States was accompa-

nied by two projects, one to build capacity for monitoring working conditions in garment factories and one to support an arbitration council to resolve collective labor disputes.[129]

Beyond the initiatives of governments through conventions and trade agreements, a growing emphasis is being placed on private sector accountability and the broader corporate social responsibility (CSR) agenda, whereby companies voluntarily bring social and environmental concerns into their operations.[130] Codes of conduct are most likely to be adopted by companies based in the European Union and North America, which then make engagement with labor standards a condition of business with suppliers. But there is limited evidence on the extent to which codes of conduct translate into improved enforcement of standards. Because of the complexity of global supply chains, seasonal and temporary workers are outside the reach of CSR frameworks. Workers outside of global supply chains are not covered.[131] To be effective, CSR efforts should focus more on building the capacity of local firms to comply and the capacity of labor inspectorates to do their work.

Trade and investment. International trade in goods has been gradually liberalized over time, and the notion that freer trade is mutually beneficial for the transacting parties is now widely shared. However, many developing countries still lack the competitiveness to harness the benefits from global integration. Direct assistance to reduce logistic costs and improve the competitiveness of firms and farms is thus a priority. Aid for trade has increased substantially and now accounts for about a third of total aid to developing countries. But there is scope for making the assistance more effective, by focusing on the export activities most suited to address the specific jobs challenges that recipient countries face. Increasing the involvement by the private sector would also enhance the effectiveness of the assistance.[132]

In contrast to trade in goods, progress in services liberalization has been slow, at both the multilateral and the regional levels. Offers to the Doha Round currently being negotiated promise greater security in access to markets but no additional liberalization compared to the policies in force.[133] Services are characterized by well-known market imperfections—from network externalities in infrastructure to asymmetric information and moral hazard in finance—and are thus subject to more pervasive regulations. Liberalizing trade in services requires adequate domestic regulation. Setting up markets for electricity, or cushioning the social impacts of large distributors on retail trade, is challenging.[134] Not surprisingly, liberalization of services is much less advanced in developing countries than in industrial countries.[135]

The productivity gains from liberalizing services would be substantial. Many services are inputs into the production process. Electricity, finance, telecommunications, and trade have a direct impact on business costs, affecting the competitiveness of downstream sectors. By boosting job creation and raising labor earnings, these productivity gains should also lead to improved living standards. Social impacts

can be more mixed. They are clearly positive when cell phones connect people (and especially the poor) to product markets, to employment opportunities, or to government services. They can be negative when the disappearance of retail trade leads to the decline of urban centers and affects the livelihoods of older shopkeepers who may not find alternative employment easily. An adequate sequencing of services liberalization and domestic regulatory reform is needed to manage these tradeoffs, and, in doing so, address the concerns of developing countries.[136] International collaboration can fill the knowledge gaps and facilitate implementation.[137]

International agreements can also promote global public goods. One case in point is gender equality. Trade is not gender neutral, implying that liberalization changes women's access to jobs. Traditionally men were more likely to have "brawn jobs," involving stronger physical requirements, while "brain jobs" involving dexterity, attention, or communication—from stitching garments to processing data—present more opportunities for women. Call centers in Delhi and Mumbai employ more than 1 million people, most of them women. Preferential access for imports from sectors with more "brain jobs" can thus create employment opportunities for women in countries where gender equality is far from attained.[138] But as countries move up the ladder of global value chains, gender opportunities can change. This was the case in Malaysia, where the share of women working in manufacturing declined in the mid-1980s.[139]

Migration. In contrast to the movement of goods and services across borders, few international agreements pertain to migration in general and the migration of workers in particular. Those in existence have limited coverage. ILO conventions 97 and 143, in force since 1952 and 1978, refer to the prevention of discrimination or abusive conditions against migrants and call for penalties and sanctions against those who promote clandestine or illegal migration. But they have been ratified by only 49 and 23 countries, respectively. Liberalizing the provision of services by natural persons, in line with Mode 4 of the General Agreement on Trade in Services (GATS), is not on the agenda of many countries, industrial or developing. And the United Nations international convention on the rights of migrant workers and their families, which entered into force in 2003, has been ratified by only 22 countries—mostly sending countries.

While migration occurs across borders, legislation is mostly driven by country-specific laws. This is an area where a global perspective is warranted, but views on what needs to be done are diverse. One view focuses on the large earnings differentials between countries, suggesting that global productivity and poverty reduction would accelerate enormously with the free movement of labor.[140] Another perspective focuses instead on national security and the protection of communities and their cultures, implying the need for barriers to contain migration. Yet another highlights the moral imperative of protecting the human rights of migrants, no matter their legal status, and giving shelter to those who suffer any form of persecution.[141] None of these views suffices, however, because any one of them alone cannot address the complex tradeoffs that migration poses for policy design.

In many instances, both sending and receiving countries can benefit from migration through a collaborative approach. Most abuses perpetrated by traffickers, firms, or workers are associated with illegal migrant flows, so the formalization of these flows is a basic tool for protecting the rights of migrant workers. This formalization cannot be enforced without the cooperation of institutions in both sending and receiving countries. That is why bilateral agreements are also needed, with provisions for quotas by occupation, industry, region, and duration of stay.[142] The agreements can distinguish between temporary movements of workers and steps to permanent migration, with conditions and protocols to go from one to another. They can include considerations about taxation, social security, and even financing higher education—a special concern in the case of "talent" migration. These agreements can design incentives so that stakeholders in both sending and receiving countries have an interest in enforcing the provisions.[143]

Jobs are center stage, but where are the numbers?

A significant research and data agenda lies ahead. Further analysis is needed on the relationship between jobs and movements in and out of poverty; the dynamics of micro- and small enterprises in the informal sector; and the links between jobs and human behaviors and norms. Research on the magnitude of spillovers from jobs could identify good jobs for development tailored to country contexts. Another important research area concerns the impact of jobs on the acquisition of cognitive and noncognitive skills, and how this impact varies depending on the characteristics of the job and the person who holds it. Similarly, more evidence on productivity spillovers from jobs across cities with different characteristics would have a high value for development policy. Estimates of the environmental impacts of different types of jobs are, today, scarce at best. In the area of labor policies, more empirical work is needed on the boundaries of the plateau, depending on the characteristics of the country. More research is also needed on how international trade, investment across borders, and migration affect the composition of employment across countries. More solid knowledge on the sequencing of international commitments and domestic policies related to services could address the reluctance of developing countries to make further progress in the direction of liberalization and reap the gains from global integration.

Setting policy priorities for jobs needs to be based on reliable data. Given that a large share of the people at work in developing countries are not wage employees, and that even fewer have a formal sector job, the measurement of employment is challenging. Determining which jobs have the greatest payoffs for poverty reduction requires linking information on a household's income or consumption with information on the employment of its members. Understanding which economic units create more jobs, or whether labor reallocation leads to substantial growth rather than just churning, requires information on the inputs and outputs of very diverse production units. Assessing how the composition of employment affects trust and willingness to participate in society requires information on individual values and behaviors.

The paucity of empirical analyses on the employment impact of the global crisis in developing countries and the difficulty of comparing measures of informal employment across countries suggest that data quality and availability remain a constraint for policy making. Much effort goes into measuring unemployment rates, and measuring them often.[144] But open unemployment is not a very telling indicator in countries where a large fraction of the labor force is not salaried. The Millennium Development Goal on eradicating poverty lists four indicators to monitor progress toward the employment target, defined as "achieving full and productive employment and decent work for all, including women and young people." But these indicators only partially capture advances in the quantity and quality of jobs in the developing world.[145]

Today's challenges for labor statistics can be regrouped into three key areas: data gaps; data quality issues; and planning, coordination, and communication issues. Data gaps concern countries where labor statistics do not exist at all or are collected only sporadically. Whenever such statistics exist, data quality is a concern throughout the statistical production chain, from the use of appropriate definitions to questionnaire design, from sampling frame to interviewer processes, and from data entry and coding to verification and estimation procedures. Planning, coordination, and communication issues arise when different institutions are responsible for collecting and disseminating the data.[146]

A quarter of a century ago, a renewed emphasis on poverty reduction as the key objective of development policy launched a long-term data effort. Across the world, information on household living standards was collected through standardized surveys. The sampling methods and the variable definitions used were duly documented. And the data and documentation were made available to researchers and practitioners whenever possible. For jobs, employment modules attached to household surveys used for poverty analyses would need to be standardized and include informal firms and microenterprises in establishment surveys. Such an approach would move jobs center stage.

* * *

Countries have a choice in responding to the jobs challenges of demographics, structural shifts, technological progress, and periodic macroeconomic crises. They can simply pursue growth, ensure that the labor market functions well, and hope that jobs will follow. Or they can recognize that growth does not mechanically deliver the jobs that do most for development. Jobs for women, jobs in cities and in global value chains, and jobs providing voice and protection for the most vulnerable in society may come high on the list. The precise nature of the jobs challenge depends on a country's geography, endowments, institutions, and level of development. What is common to all is the need to remedy the institutional failures and market imperfections that prevent the private sector from creating more of those good jobs for development. Countries can then return to the difficult questions posed at the outset. For each of them, there is a conventional wisdom that practitioners do not consider to be totally satisfactory. The jobs lens in development does not lead to a flat rejection of the conventional wisdom, but to a qualification of when it holds and when it does not.

In short, countries can leave themselves open to small gains in living standards, slow productivity growth, and fractious societies. Or, by addressing their jobs challenges, they can enjoy a self-reinforcing pattern of more prosperous livelihoods, rising productivity, and the stronger social cohesion that comes from improving employment opportunities and fairness in access to jobs.

Growth strategies or jobs strategies? The conventional wisdom is to focus on growth as a precondition for continued increases in living standards and strengthened social cohesion. But lags and gaps among the three transformations of living standards, productivity, and social cohesion are not uncommon. The impact of growth on poverty reduction varies considerably across countries. And in some cases, growth is not accompanied by increased social cohesion—even though poverty may fall and living standards improve for some, the expectations of others remain unfulfilled. The employment intensity of different sectors and fairness in access to employment opportunities matter as well. It is thus jobs that bring together the three transformations.

Tradeoffs among improving living standards, accelerating productivity growth, and fostering social cohesion arguably reflect a measurement problem, more than a real choice. If growth indicators captured the intangible social benefits from jobs, from lower poverty to greater social cohesion, a growth strategy and a jobs strategy would be equivalent. But a growth strategy may not pay enough attention to female employment, or to employment in secondary cities, or to idleness among youth. When potentially important spillovers from jobs are not realized, a jobs strategy may provide more useful insights.

Can entrepreneurship be fostered? The conventional wisdom is that most micro- and small enterprises in developing countries are just forms of survivorship, with limited chances to grow. But self-employed workers account for a large share of employment in developing countries. Even if only a fraction of them succeeded in building a viable business, the aggregate impact on living standards and productivity would be substantial. Moreover, in developing countries many large enterprises are born large, often the result of government support or privileged access to finance and information. Breaking privilege is one more reason why the success of micro- and small enterprises is so important.

Management practices are important in explaining firm productivity, even in small and medium-size firms. The capacity to acquire skills and to apply them to business is one of the most important characteristics of successful entrepreneurs. Yet markets fail to nurture entrepreneurship, because knowledge spillovers imply that some of the returns to acquiring or developing new managerial ideas and knowledge are appropriated by others. And the potential to absorb management practices differs greatly among beneficiaries. Observable characteristics of small business owners can predict entrepreneurial potential, and programs to upgrade their managerial capacity have been shown to make a difference. Programs targeted to small business owners with entre-preneurial potential can thus make a substantial difference in living standards and productivity.

Can policies contribute to social cohesion? The conventional wisdom is that a lack of jobs is detrimental to social cohesion, but other than ensuring full employment there is little that governments can or should do. Yet open unemployment is not the main challenge in many countries, as the characteristics of jobs also matter. While not all jobs can positively affect social cohesion, those that shape social identity, build networks—particularly for excluded groups—and increase fairness can help defuse tensions and support peaceful collective decision making.

Measures that support inclusion, extend access to voice and rights, and improve transparency and accountability in the labor market can increase the extent to which people perceive that they have a stake in society. This perception can be especially critical when risks of social unrest from youth unemployment and conflict are high. Employment programs can undermine social cohesion if they have weak governance or divisive targeting, but can have positive effects when they are well-designed. Jobs policies for youth at risk can incorporate counseling and training in conflict resolution. Public works programs can facilitate community participation and engagement between citizens and local authorities. Policies can thus focus not only on the number of jobs, but on expanding job opportunities for excluded groups.

Skills or jobs—what comes first? The conventional wisdom is that investing in skills will lead to job creation and to higher productivity and labor income. High unemployment and skills mismatches are often attributed to shortcomings in education and training systems. But in reality they can also result from market distortions, which send the wrong signals to the education system or lead to a lack of dynamism in private firms. In such situations, massive investments in training systems, as seen in many parts of the world, might show disappointing results as hoped-for job outcomes do not materialize.

A core set of basic skills, both cognitive and social, is necessary for productive employment, and they cannot just be acquired on the job. Without such generic skills, the prospects of improving employment opportunities and earnings are thin. Skills are also critical for countries to move up the value-added ladder, as they can ignite innovation, produce the benefits of mutual learning, and hence lead to job creation themselves. But in between, much learning can happen through work: job opportunities can shape social skills and create demand for education and training. Learning on the job leads to significantly higher earnings in many settings, with the return to one year of work experience being around a third to half of the return to an additional year of schooling.

A targeted investment climate? The conventional wisdom is that a level playing field is preferable because governments do not have enough information to pick winners and targeting can be captured by interest groups. But given the often limited fiscal space and administrative capacity of developing countries, creating an enabling business environment across the board can be challenging, and the relevant question is how policy priorities should be set. The conventional wisdom views targeting with a skepticism that stems from failed experiences with industrial policy. However, targeting may not necessarily be aimed at industrial sectors. Supporting job creation in sectors with high rates of female employment, or productivity gains in smallholder farming, or more jobs connected to global value chains may have high development payoffs depending on country contexts.

When there is clarity about where the good jobs for development are, and there is sufficient information to understand what can be done to support the creation of those jobs, a targeted investment climate may be warranted. But this is provided that targeted interventions can be designed in a way that makes them resilient to capture by interest groups. The risk of capture is easier to contain when the number of beneficiaries is very large, such as the case of farmers, urban businesses, and female micro-entrepreneurs. It is much higher in the case of industrial policy.

Competing for jobs? The conventional wisdom is that the number of jobs is not finite, so that policies for jobs in one country cannot be harmful to other countries. Indeed, in the medium to long term, total employment is roughly determined by the size of the labor force. But policies may alter global trade, investment, and migration flows, affecting the composition of employment. The concern is that the share of good jobs for development may decline in one country as it increases in another. Policies aimed at capturing a larger global share of the jobs with the largest productive spillovers can reduce well-being abroad, even if global well-being increases.

However, not all efforts to support job creation amount to beggar-thy-neighbor policies. Whether they do so depends on the type of instruments used and the nature of the spillovers from jobs. A key question is what purpose policies serve. Policies that aim to improve compliance with rights, prosecuting forced labor and harmful forms of child labor, amount to providing a global public good. On the other hand, policies that aim at reaping the benefits from productive externalities may adversely affect other countries, especially when they undermine an open trading system and are not aligned with a country's dynamic comparative advantage.

Protecting workers or protecting jobs? The conventional wisdom is that policies that protect people are preferable, because they mitigate welfare losses while at the same time allowing the reallocation of labor, hence supporting creative destruction. Protecting jobs that are no longer economically viable through government transfers and employment protection legislation freezes an inefficient allocation of resources. Protecting jobs also entails a high risk of capture. It may lead to enduringly unproductive jobs, stifle technological advance, prevent structural change, and eventually undermine growth.

However, there are times when many jobs are lost or threatened at once and few are being created. There are also jobs generating substantial productivity spillovers, whose disappearance in large numbers can lead to ghost towns and depressed regions. Protecting people should have primacy if shocks are idiosyncratic—if the employment dislocation is local and limited and if turnover continues to be the norm. Protecting jobs may be warranted in times of systemic crises or major economic restructuring. But job protection policies can create permanent inefficiency, especially in countries with weak institutions, making it indispensable to establish and enforce trigger rules and sunset clauses that define the extent and size of the protection.

How to accelerate the reallocation of workers? The conventional wisdom is to focus policy on removing the labor market rigidities that keep workers in firms or areas with low productivity. But reforms may not always be politically feasible. In India, complex and cumbersome labor market institutions have unambiguously negative effects on economic efficiency but these institutions have remained largely untouched for 60 years.

Tolerance for the avoidance or evasion of distortive regulation can help contain their cost but not ensure dynamism. In India, widespread noncompliance has been the dominant response to cumbersome labor regulations. However, labor-intensive manufacturing sectors remain sluggish despite buoyant performance of the overall economy. Other countries with similarly stringent regulatory obstacles have accomplished more efficiency-enhancing labor reallocation by actively taking advantage of productivity spillovers from jobs in industrial clusters, dynamic cities, or global value chains to make the regulations less binding. In Sri Lanka, the development of export processing zones (EPZs) drove the takeoff of the garment industry. In Brazil, the surge of internal migration is closely associated with the country's continuing integration into the global economy and a development policy that favors clusters and agglomeration. In China, labor reallocation is rooted in the development of competitive cities, supported by regional competition and experimentation. A strategic focus on enhancing productivity spillovers from jobs, through urbanization and global integration, can overcome the labor rigidity.

Jobs drive development
They should not be an afterthought of growth

Some have greater development payoffs
It is not just the number of jobs

Jobs are created by the private sector
Public action sets the stage

Many jobs in developing countries are in farms and very small firms
Informal is normal

Some work is unacceptable
Rights should not be overlooked

One size does not fit all
Jobs challenges vary across countries

Get the policy fundamentals right
They have a bearing regardless of the jobs challenge

The main constraints to job creation may lie elsewhere
Labor policies matter less than assumed

Set priorities for public action
Focus on the jobs with greater development payoffs

Data and cooperation on cross-border investments and migration lag
A global agenda for jobs is needed

Notes

1. Article 2, ILO 2007. Also see UN 2009.
2. Ghose, Majid, and Ernst 2008.
3. Gindling and Newhouse 2012 for the World Development Report 2013.
4. Kanbur 2009.
5. International Labour Organization, Department of Statistics, http://laborsta.ilo.org/sti/sti_E.html.
6. Lyon, Rosati, and Guarcello 2012 for the World Development Report 2013.
7. World Bank 2006b.
8. World Development Report 2013 team estimates based on data from the International Labour Organization, http://laborsta.ilo.org/applv8/data/EAPEP/eapep_E.html, and World Development Indicators, http:/data-worldbank.org/data/catalog/world-development-indicators.
9. United Nations 2011.
10. Lin 2012; Pagés 2010; World Bank 1992.
11. European Centre for the Development of Vocational Training 2008.
12. Autor and Dorn 2011; Gratton 2011; Holzer and Lerman 2009.
13. Feenstra 2010.
14. Brown, Ashton, and Lauder 2010. See Selim 2012 for the World Development Report 2013.
15. Goswami, Mattoo, and Sáez 2011.
16. Examples include oDesk, https://www.odesk.com/; Babajob, http://www.babajob.com/; Google Trader (for example, http://www.google.co.ug/africa/trader/search?cat=jobs); and SoukTel, http://www.souktel.org/.
17. TeamLease 2010.
18. A.T. Kearney 2011.
19. UNESCO Institute of Statistics, http://stats.uis.unesco.org/unesco/TableViewer/tableView.aspx?ReportId=175.
20. WDR team estimates of the top 20 percent of ratings among countries in the 2009 Programme for International Student Assessment of 15 year-olds. See http://www.pisa.oecd.org.
21. International Labour Office database on labor statistics, Laborsta, http://laborsta.ilo.org/e.
22. Private sector employment refers here to "private firms" and to "individuals" according to the official Chinese classsification. The former are defined as for-profit units invested in and established by natural persons or controlled by persons using more than seven workers. The latter includes units that hire fewer than eight workers. Foreign-invested firms and collectives are not part of the private sector in official statistics. For more details, see Kanamori and Zhao (2004).
23. Nabli, Silva-Jáuregui, and Faruk Aysan 2008.
24. Assaad 2012; Assaad and Barsoum 2007.
25. Mryyan 2012; Gatti and others 2012; Stampini and Verdier-Choucane 2011; ILO 2011.
26. Based on an update by the WDR team of Chen and Ravallion (2010).
27. World Bank 2011b.
28. ILO 2012a.
29. ILO and World Bank 2012.
30. Bell and Blanchflower 2011; Farber 2011.
31. World Bank 2011c.
32. Ravallion 2009.
33. Inchauste 2012 for the World Development Report 2013.
34. Baulch 2011; Fields and others 2003.
35. Narayan, Pritchett, and Kapoor 2009.
36. Azevedo and others 2012 for the World Development Report 2013. This report uses methods developed by authors, including Paes de Barros and others (2006) and Bourguignon and Ferreira (2005).
37. Blanchflower and Oswald 2011.
38. Haltiwanger 2011; Nelson 1981; Schumpeter 1934.
39. Bartelsman, Haltiwanger, and Scarpetta 2009; Davis, Haltiwanger, and Schuh 1996.
40. Bartelsman, Haltiwanger, and Scarpetta 2009.
41. Baily, Bartelsman, and Haltiwanger 1996.
42. World Development Report 2013 team estimates.
43. Bartelsman, Haltiwanger, and Scarpetta 2004; Brandt, Van Biesebroeck, and Zhang 2012; Lin 2012; Rutkowski and others 2005.
44. World Development Report 2013 team estimates, and Dutz and others 2011.
45. Ayyagari, Demirgüç-Kunt, and Maksimovic 2011; IFC, forthcoming.
46. South Africa is excluded from this estimate because it is an outlier, with average farm size of 288 hectares.
47. Hsieh and Klenow 2009; Pagés 2010.
48. Banerjee and Duflo 2011; Fox and Sohnesen 2012; Schoar 2010; Sutton and Kellow 2010.
49. de Soto 1989; Perry and others 2007.
50. Grimm, Kruger, and Lay 2011; McKenzie and Woodruff 2008.
51. Mertens 2011; Witze 2010.
52. Sandefur 2010.
53. Hsieh and Klenow 2011.
54. Bartelsman, Haltiwanger, and Scarpetta 2009; Haltiwanger 2011; Hsieh and Klenow 2009; Syverson 2011.
55. Moser 2009, 240.
56. Dani and others 1999, 3.
57. Kilroy 2011.
58. Gatti and others 2012.

59. Akerlof and Kranton 2010.
60. Giles, Mavridis, and Witoelar 2012 for the World Development Report 2013.
61. ILO 2012b.
62. ILO 2010.
63. ILO 2002.
64. Heath and Mobarak 2011.
65. Luke and Munshi 2011.
66. Alfaro and Chen 2011; Romer 1993.
67. UNDP 2003a; UNDP 2003b.
68. Ibarraran and others 2012.
69. As an example, recent World Development Reports on youth (World Bank 2006b), geography (World Bank 2009b), conflict (World Bank 2011a), and gender (World Bank 2011c) look at spillovers from jobs in different contexts.
70. Glewwe 2004.
71. IOM 2010.
72. Goswami, Mattoo, and Sáez 2011.
73. Ball, Leigh, and Loungani 2012.
74. World Bank 2012, various issues.
75. Commission on Growth and Development 2008.
76. Kraay 2012.
77. Elbadawi, Kaltani, and Soto 2009.
78. King and Levine 1993; Levine 2005.
79. IFC, forthcoming.
80. Foster and Briceño-Garmendia 2010.
81. Djankov, Freund, and Pham 2010; Hallward-Driemeier, Khun-Jush, and Pritchett 2010.
82. Klapper, Laeven, and Rajan 2006.
83. Bruhn, 2008.
84. See, for example, Psacharopoulos and Patrinos (2004); Montenegro and Patrinos 2012 for the World Development Report 2013.
85. See, for example, Hanushek and Woessmann (2008) and Commander and Svejnar (2011) on the productivity link. Structural change and poverty links are explored in Lee and Newhouse (2012) for the World Development Report 2013.
86. Engle and others 2007; Grantham-McGregor and others 2007; Heckman 2008; Walker and others 2007; Young and Richardson 2007.
87. Engle and others 2007.
88. Heineck and Anger 2010; Cunha, Heckman and Schennach 2010.
89. OECD PISA 2009, http://www.pisa.oecd.org.
90. IMF 2003; Rodrik 2000.
91. Keefer 2009; North 1981, 1990.
92. Acemoglu, Johnson, and Robinson 2001; North 1990; Rodrik, Subramanian, and Trebbi 2004.
93. World Bank 2004.
94. World Bank 2010.
95. World Bank 2004.
96. World Bank 2004.
97. Laeven and Woodruff 2007.
98. ILO 1998.
99. Chen and others 2012 for the World Development Report 2013.
100. Betcherman 2012.
101. Alatas and Cameron 2003; Arango and Pachón 2004; Rama 2001; SMERU Research Institute 2001.
102. Haltiwanger, Scarpetta, and Schweiger 2008.
103. Betcherman 2012 for the World Development Report 2013; Freeman 2009; OECD 2006.
104. Aidt and Tzannatos 2002.
105. Freeman 2009.
106. Aidt and Tzannatos 2002.
107. Card, Kluve, and Weber 2010; OECD 2006; Almeida and others 2012 for the World Development Report 2013.
108. Bird and Smart 2012; Levy 2008.
109. Bhatt 2006; Chen and others 2012 for the World Development Report 2013.
110. World Bank 2010. Note that this unit cost is the aggregate cost of the Multi-Country Demobilization and Reintegration Program, including all forms of reintegration support, not only employment.
111. Glewwe 2004.
112. Rama 2009.
113. World Development Indicators 2012. World Development Indicators, World Bank, Washington, DC. http://data-worldbank.org/data-catalog/world-developmentindicators.
114. World Bank 2007.
115. Rwanda Demobilization and Reintegration Commission 2012.
116. Rwanda was named a top reformer by *Doing Business* in 2010.
117. Dudwick and Srinivasan, forthcoming; World Bank 2011a.
118. World Development Indicators 2012. World Development Indicators, World Bank, Washington, DC. http://data-worldbank.org/data-catalog/world-developmentindicators.
119. Consejo Nacional de Innovación 2008; World Bank 2008.
120. World Bank 2006a; World Development Indicators 2011. World Development Indicators, World Bank, Washington, DC. http://data-world bank.org/data-catalog/world-development indicators.
121. OECD 2010.
122. OECD 2009.
123. OECD 2009.
124. Yusuf and Nabeshima 2006; Park and others 2011.
125. See World Bank 2010; Gibson, McKenzie, and Rohorua 2008.
126. Fajnzylber, Maloney, and Montes-Rohas 2011; OECD and ILO 2011.
127. World Bank 2011d.

128. Chau and Kanbur (2002) find evidence of a peer effect whereby ratification depends on the number of similar countries that have already ratified the convention.

129. Adler and Hwang 2012 for the World Development Report 2013.

130. Levi and others 2012 for the World Development Report 2013; Newitt 2012 for the World Development Report 2013.

131. Locke, forthcoming; Locke, Quin, and Brause 2007.

132. Hoekman 2011.

133. Borchert, Gootiiz and Mattoo 2011.

134. François and Hoekman 2010.

135. Hoekman and Mattoo 2011.

136. Fink, Mattoo, and Rathindran 2003; François and Hoekman 2010.

137. Hoekman and Mattoo 2011.

138. World Bank 2011c.

139. Randriamaro 2007.

140. See, for instance, Winters and others (2002); World Bank (2005).

141. See, for instance, EFRA (2011) and Angenendt (2012).

142. Regional agreements, such as the European Union's Schengen area, can also cover specific areas such as visas or social security of migrant workers. Several Latin American countries, Spain, and Portugal have been developing common principles about social security rights and regulations for migrants.

143. For a discussion on these issues, see Pritchett (2006).

144. Sixty-five countries produce monthly or quarterly labor force surveys, whereas 116 produce annual surveys.

145. The four indicators are GDP per employed person (a measure of productivity), the employment-to-population rate, the proportion of the employed population living on less than US$1.25 a day (the so-called working poor), and the proportion of own-account and unremunerated workers in employed population (also called vulnerable workers). See United Nations Development Group 2010.

146. ILO 2012c. See Kanbur and Svejnar (2009) on the importance of data for labor analysis and policy

References

The word *processed* describes informally reproduced works that may not be commonly available through libraries.

A.T. Kearney. 2011. *Offshoring Opportunities amid Economic Turbulence: A.T. Kearney Global Services Location Index, 2011.* Chicago: A.T. Kearney Global Services Location Index.

Acemoglu, Daron, Simon Johnson, and James A. Robinson. 2001. "The Colonial Origins of Comparative Development: An Empirical Investigation." *American Economic Review* 91 (5): 1369–401.

Adler, Daniel, and Hans Hwang. 2012. "From Law on the Books to Law in Action: A Note on the Role of Regulation in the Production of Good Jobs in Cambodia's Garment Sector." Background paper for the WDR 2013.

Aidt, Toke, and Zafiris Tzannatos. 2002. *Unions and Collective Bargaining: Economic Effects in a Global Environment.* Washington, DC: World Bank.

Akerlof, George A., and Rachel E. Kranton. 2010. *Identity Economics: How Our Identities Shape Our Work, Wages, and Well-Being.* Princeton, NJ: Princeton University Press.

Alatas, Vivi, and Lisa Ann Cameron. 2003. "The Impact of Minimum Wages on Employment in a Low Income Country: An Evaluation Using the Difference-in-Differences Approach." Policy Research Working Paper Series 2985, World Bank, Washington, DC.

Alfaro, Laura, and Maggie Xiaoyang Chen. 2011. "Selection, Reallocation, and Knowledge Spillovers: Identifying the Impact of Multinational Activity on Aggregate Productivity." Paper presented at the World Bank Conference on Structural Transformation and Economic Growth, Washington, DC, October 6.

Almeida, Rita, David Margolis, David Robalino, and Michael Weber. 2012. "Facilitating Labor Market Transitions and Managing Risks." Background paper for the WDR 2013.

Amador, Diego, Raquel Bernal and Ximena Peña 2011. "The Rise in Female Participation in Colombia: Fertility, Marital Status or Education?" Background paper for the World Development Report 2012.

Angenendt, Steffen. 2012. "Migration and Social Inclusion—Looking through the Good Jobs Lens." In *Moving Jobs to the Center Stage,* BMZ (Bundesministerium fuer Wirtschaftliche Zussamenarbeit), Berlin Workshop Series. Berlin.

Arango, Carlos, and Angelica Pachón. 2004. "Minimum Wages in Colombia: Holding the Middle with a Bite on the Poor." Borradores de Economía Serie 280, Banco de la República de Colombia, Bogotá.

Artuc, Erhan, Frederic Docquier, Caglar Özden, and Chris Parsons. 2012. "Education Structure of Global Migration Patterns: Estimates Based on Census Data." World Bank, Washington DC. Processed.

Assaad, Ragui. 2012. "The MENA Paradox: Higher Education but Lower Job Quality." In *Moving Jobs to the Center Stage.* BMZ (Bundesministerium fuer Wirtschaftliche Zussamenarbeit), Berlin Workshop Series. Berlin.

———. 1997. "The Effects of Public Sector Hiring and Compensation Policies on the Egyptian Labor Market." *World Bank Economic Review* 11 (1): 85–118.

Assaad, Ragui, and Ghada Barsoum. 2007. "Youth Exclusion in Egypt: In Search of 'Second Chances.'" Middle East Youth Initiative Working Paper Series 2, Wolfensohn Center for Development, Dubai School of Government, Dubai.

Autor, David H., and David Dorn. 2011. "The Growth of Low-Skill Service Jobs and the Polarization of the U.S. Labor Market." Massachusetts Institute of Technology, Cambridge, MA. Processed.

Ayyagari, Meghana, Asli Demirgüç-Kunt, and Vojislav Maksimovic. 2011. "Firm Innovation in Emerging Markets: The Roles of Governance and Finance." *Journal of Financial and Quantitative Analysis* 46 (6): 1545–80.

Azevedo, João Pedro, Gabriela Inchauste, Sergio Olivieri, Jaime Saavedra Chanduvi, and Hernan Winkler. 2012. "Is Labor Income Responsible for Poverty Reduction? A Decomposition Approach." Background paper for the WDR 2013.

Baily, Martin Neil, Eric J. Bartelsman, and John Haltiwanger. 1996. "Downsizing and Productivity Growth: Myth or Reality?" *Small Business Economics* 8 (4): 259–78.

Ball, Laurence, Daniel Leigh, and Prakash Loungani. Forthcoming. "Okun's Law: Fit at 50?" Working Paper, International Monetary Fund, Washington, DC.

Banerjee, Abhijit V., and Esther Duflo. 2011. *Poor Economics: A Radical Rethinking of the Way to Fight Global Poverty.* New York: Public Affairs.

Bartelsman, Eric, John Haltiwanger, and Stefano Scarpetta. 2004. "Microeconomic Evidence of Creative Destruction in Industrial and Developing Countries." Discussion Paper Series 1374, Institute for the Study of Labor, Bonn.

———. 2009. "Measuring and Analyzing Cross-Country Differences in Firm Dynamics." In *Producer Dynamics: New Evidence from Micro Data*, ed. Timothy Dunne, J. Bradford Jensen, and Mark J. Roberts, 17–76. Cambridge, MA: National Bureau of Economic Research.

Baulch, Bob, ed. 2011. *Why Poverty Persists: Poverty Dynamics in Asia and Africa.* Cheltenham, U.K.: Edward Elgar.

Bell, David N. F., and David G. Blanchflower. 2011. "The Crisis, Policy Reactions and Attitudes to Globalization and Jobs." Discussion Paper Series 5680, Institute for the Study of Labor, Bonn.

Betcherman, Gordon. 2012. "Labor Market Institutions: A Review of the Literature." Background paper for the WDR 2013.

Bhatt, Ela. 2006. *We Are Poor But So Many: The Story of Self-Employed Women in India.* New York: Oxford University Press.

Bird, Richard M., and Michael Smart. 2012. "Financing Social Expenditures in Developing Countries: Payroll or Value Added Taxes?" International Center for Public Policy Working Paper Series 1206, Andrew Young School of Policy Studies, Georgia State University, Atlanta.

Bjørkhaug, Ingunn, Anne Hatløy, Tewodros Kebede, and Huafeng Zhang. 2012. "Perception of Good Jobs: Colombia." Background paper for the WDR 2013.

Blanchflower, David G., and Andrew J. Oswald. 2011. "International Happiness." Working Paper Series 16668. National Bureau of Economic Research, Cambridge, MA.

Borchert, Ingo, Batshur Gootiiz, and Aaditya Mattoo. 2011. "Services in Doha: What's on the Table?" In *Unfinished Business: The WTO's Doha Agenda*, ed. Will Martin and Aaditya Mattoo, 115–44. London: London Publishing Partnership.

Bourguignon, François, and Francisco H. G. Ferreira. 2005. "Decomposing Changes in the Distribution of Household Incomes: Methodological Aspects." In *The Microeconomics of Income Distribution Dynamics in East Asia and Latin America*, ed. François Bourguignon, Francisco H. G. Ferreira, and Nora Lustig, 17–46. Washington, DC: World Bank.

Brandt, Loren, Johannes Van Biesebroeck, and Yifan Zhang. 2012. "Creative Accounting or Creative Destruction? Firm-Level Productivity Growth in Chinese Manufacturing." *Journal of Development Economics* 97 (2): 339–51.

Brown, Philip, David Ashton, and Hugh Lauder. 2010. *Skills Are Not Enough: The Globalization of Knowledge and the Future of the UK Economy.* Wath upon Dearne, U.K.: U.K. Commission for Employment and Skills.

Bruhn, Miriam. 2008. "License to Sell: The Effect of Business Registration Reform on Entrepreneurial Activity in Mexico." Policy Research Working Paper Series 4538, World Bank, Washington, DC.

Card, David, Jochen Kluve, and Andrea Weber. 2010. "Active Labour Market Policy Evaluations: A Meta-Analysis." *Economic Journal* 120 (11): 452–77.

Chau, Nancy H., and Ravi Kanbur. 2001. "The Adoption of International Labor Standards Conventions: Who, When and Why?" In *Brookings Trade Forum: 2001*, ed. Nancy H. Chau, Ravi Kanbur, Ann E. Harrison, and Peter Morici, 113–56. Washington, DC: Brookings Institution.

Chen, Martha, Chris Bonner, Mahendra Chetty, Lucia Fernandez, Karin Pape, Federico Parra, Arbind Singh, and Caroline Skinner. 2012. "Urban Informal Workers: Representative Voice and Economic Rights." Background paper for the WDR 2013.

Chen, Shaohua, and Martin Ravallion. 2010. "The Developing World Is Poorer Than We Thought, but No Less Successful in the Fight against Poverty." *Quarterly Journal of Economics* 125 (4): 1577–625.

Chioda, Laura. 2012. *Work and Family: Latin America and Caribbean Women in Search of a New Balance.* Washington, DC: World Bank.

Commander, Simon, and Jan Svejnar. 2011. "Business Environment, Exports Ownership, and Firm Performance." *Review of Economics and Statistics* 93 (1): 309–37.

Commission on Growth and Development. 2008. *The Growth Commission Report: Strategies for Sustained Growth and Inclusive Development.* Washington, DC: Commission on Growth and Development.

Consejo Nacional de Innovación. 2008. *Hacia una Estrategia Nacional de Innovación para la Competitividad.* Santiago: Consejo Nacional de Innovación.

Cunha, Flavio, James J. Heckman, and Susanne Schennach. 2010. "Estimating the Technology of Cognitive and Noncognitive Skill Formation." *Econometrica* 78 (3): 883–931.

Dani, Anis, Sarah Forster, Mirsada Muzur, Dino Djipa, Paula Lytle, and Patrizia Poggi. 1999. *A Social Assessment of Bosnia and Herzegovina.* Washington, DC: World Bank.

Davis, Steven J., John C. Haltiwanger, and Scott Schuh. 1996. *Job Creation and Destruction.* Cambridge, MA: MIT Press.

de Soto, Hernando. 1989. *The Other Path: The Invisible Revolution in the Third World.* New York: Harper & Row.

Djankov, Simeon, Caroline Freund, and Cong S. Pham. 2010. "Trading on Time." *Review of Economics and Statistics* 92 (1): 166–73.

Dudwick, Nora, and Radhika Srinivasan, with Jose Cueva and Dorsati Madani. Forthcoming. *Creating Value Chains in Africa's Fragile States: Are Value Chains an Answer?* Directions in Development Series. Washington, DC: World Bank.

Dutz, Mark A., Ioannis Kessides, Stephen O'Connell, and Robert D. Willig. 2011. "Competition and Innovation-Driven Inclusive Growth." Policy Research Working Paper Series 5852, World Bank, Washington, DC.

EFRA (European Union Agency for Fundamental Rights). 2011. *Fundamental Rights of Migrants in an Irregular Situation in the European Union.* Luxembourg: Publications Office of the European Union.

Elbadawi, Ibrahim, Linda Kaltani, and Raimundo Soto. 2009. *Aid, Real Exchange Rate Misalignment and Economic Performance in Sub-Saharan Africa.* Santiago: Universidad Católica de Chile.

Engle, Patrice L, Maureen M. Black, Jere R. Behrman, Meena Cabral de Mello, Paul J. Gertler, Lydia Kapiriri, Reynaldo Martorell, and Mary Eming Young. 2007. "Strategies to Avoid the Loss of Developmental Potential in More than 200 Million Children in the Developing World." *Lancet* 369 (9557): 229–42

European Centre for the Development of Vocational Training. 2008. *Future Skill Needs in Europe, Medium-Term Forecast, Synthesis Report.* Brussels: European Centre for the Development of Vocational Training.

Fajnzylber, Pablo, William F. Maloney, and Gabriel V. Montes-Rojas. 2011. "Does Formality Improve Micro-Firm Performance? Quasi-Experimental Evidence from the Brazilian SIMPLES Program." Discussion Paper Series 4531, Institute for the Study of Labor, Bonn.

Farber, Henry S. 2011. "Job Loss in the Great Recession: Historical Perspective from the Displaced Workers Survey, 1984–2010." Discussion Paper Series 5696, Institute for the Study of Labor, Bonn.

Fares, Jean, and Olga Susana Puerto. 2009. "Towards Comprehensive Training." Social Protection Discussion Paper Series 0924, World Bank, Washington, DC.

Feenstra, Robert C. 2010. *Offshoring in the Global Economy: Microeconomic Structure and Macroeconomic Implications.* Cambridge, MA: MIT Press.

Fields, Gary, Paul Cichello, Samuel Freije-Rodriguez, Marta Menendez, and David Newhouse. 2003. "Household Income Dynamics: A Four-Country Story." *Journal of Development Studies* 40 (2): 30–54.

Fink, Carsten, Aaditya Mattoo, and Randeep Rathindran. 2003. "An Assessment of Telecommunications Reform in Developing Countries." *Information Economics and Policy* 15 (4): 443–66.

Foster, Vivien, and Cecilia Briceño-Garmendia, eds. 2010. *Africa's Infrastructure: A Time for Transformation.* Washington, DC: World Bank.

Fox, Louise, and Thomas Sohnesen. 2012. "Household Enterprise in Sub-Saharan Africa: Why They Matter for Growth, Jobs, and Poverty Reduction." Policy Research Working Paper Series 6184, World Bank, Washington, DC.

François, Joseph F., and Bernard Hoekman. 2010. "Services Trade and Policy." *Journal of Economic Literature* 48 (3): 642–92.

Freeman, Richard. 2009. "Labor Regulations, Unions, and Social Protection in Developing Countries: Market Distortions or Efficient Institutions?" In *Handbook of Development Economics,* Volume 5, ed. Dani Rodrik and Mark Rosenzweig, 4657–702. Amsterdam: Elsevier.

Gatti, Roberta, Diego Angel-Urdinola, Joana Silva, and Andras Bodor. 2012. *Striving for Better Jobs: The Challenge of Informality in the Middle East and North Africa.* Washington, DC: World Bank.

Ghose, Ajit K., Nomaan Majid, and Christoph Ernst. 2008. *The Global Employment Challenge.* Geneva: International Labour Organization.

Gibson, John, David McKenzie, and Halahingano Rohorua. 2008. "How Pro-Poor is the Selection of Seasonal Migrant Workers from Tonga Under

New Zealand's Recognized Seasonal Employer Program." Working Paper Series 4698, World Bank, Washington, DC.

Giles, John, Dimitris Mavridis, and Firman Witoelar. 2012. "Subjective Well-Being, Social Cohesion, and Labor Market Outcomes in Indonesia." Background paper for the WDR 2013.

Gindling, T. H., and David Newhouse. 2012. "Self-Employment in the Developing World." Background paper for the WDR 2013.

Glewwe, Paul W. 2004. "An Overview of Economic Growth and Household Welfare in Vietnam in the 1990s." In *Economic Growth, Poverty and Household Welfare in Vietnam*, ed. Paul Glewwe, Bina Agarwal, and David Dollar, 1–26. Washington, DC: World Bank.

Goswami, Arti Grover, Aaditya Mattoo, and Sebastián Sáez, eds. 2011. *Exporting Services: A Developing Country Perspective*. Washington, DC: World Bank.

Grantham-McGregor, Sally, Yin Bun Cheung, Santiago Cueto, Paul Glewwe, Linda Richter, Barbara Strupp, and the International Child Development Steering Group. 2007. "Development Potential in the First 5 Years for Children in Developing Countries." *Lancet* 369 (January): 60–70.

Gratton, Lynda. 2011. *The Shift: The Future of Work Is Already Here*. London: HarperCollins.

Grimm, Michael, Jens Kruger, and Jann Lay. 2011. "Barriers to Entry and Returns to Capital in Informal Activities: Evidence from Sub-Saharan Africa." *Review of Income and Wealth* 57 (S1): S27–S53.

Hallward-Driemeier, Mary, Gita Khun-Jush, and Lant Pritchett. 2010. "Deals Versus Rules: Policy Implementation Uncertainty and Why Firms Hate It." Working Paper Series 16001, National Bureau of Economic Research, Cambridge, MA.

Haltiwanger, John. 2011. "Globalization and Economic Volatility." In *Making Globalization Socially Sustainable*, ed. Marc Bacchetta and Marion Jansen, 119–46. Geneva: International Labour Organization and World Trade Organization.

Haltiwanger, John, Stefano Scarpetta, and Helena Schweiger. 2008. "Assessing Job Flows across Countries: The Role of Industry, Firm Size, and Regulations." Working Paper 13920. National Bureau of Economic Research, Cambridge, MA.

Hanushek, Eric A., and Ludger Woessmann. 2008. "The Role of Cognitive Skills in Economic Development." *Journal of Economic Literature* 46 (3): 607–88.

Hatløy, Anne, Tewodros Kebede, Huafeng Zhang, and Ingunn Bjørkhaug. 2012. "Perception of Good Jobs: Sierra Leone." Background paper for the WDR 2013.

Heath, Rachel, and Mushfiq Mobarak. 2011. "Supply and Demand Side Constraints on Educational Investment: Evidence from Garment Sector Jobs and a Girls' Schooling Subsidy Program in Bangladesh." Yale University, New Haven, CT. Processed.

Heckman, James J. 2008. "The Case for Investing in Disadvantaged Young Children." *In Big Ideas for Children: Investing in Our Nation's Future*, 49–58. Washington, DC: First Focus.

Heineck, Guido, and Silke Anger. 2010. "The Returns to Cognitive Abilities and Personality Traits in Germany." *Labour Economics* 17 (3): 535–46.

Hoekman, Bernard. 2011. "Aid for Trade: Why, What, and Where Are We?" In *Unfinished Business? The WTO's Doha Agenda*, ed. Will Martin and Aaditya Mattoo, 233–54. London: London Publishing Partnership.

Hoekman, Bernard, and Aaditya Mattoo. 2011. "Services Trade Liberalization and Regulatory Reform: Re-invigorating International Cooperation." Policy Research Working Paper Series 5517, World Bank, Washington, DC.

Holzer, Harry, and Robert Lerman. 2009. *The Future of Middle-Skill Jobs*. Washington, DC: Center on Children and Families, Brookings Institution.

Hsieh, Chang-Tai, and Peter J. Klenow. 2009. "Misallocation and Manufacturing TFP in China and India." *Quarterly Journal of Economics* 124 (4): 1403–48.

———. 2011. "The Life Cycle of Plants in India and Mexico." Chicago Booth Research Paper 11-33, Booth School of Business, University of Chicago.

Ibarrarán, Pablo, Laura Ripani, Bibiana Taboada, Juan Miguel Villa, Brigida Garcia. 2012. "Life Skills, Employability and Training for Disadvantaged Youth: Evidence from a Randomized Evaluation Design." IZA Conference Paper, May 12, 2012. Processed.

IFC (International Finance Corporation). Forthcoming. *IFC Job Study: Assessing Private Sector Contributions to Job Creation*. Washington, DC: IFC.

ILO (International Labour Organization). 1998. Declaration on Fundamental Principles and Rights at Work. Adopted by the International Labour Conference at its 86th session, ILO, Geneva, June 18.

———. 2002. *Decent Work and the Informal Economy*. Geneva: ILO.

———. 2007. Resolution Concerning Updating the International Standard Classification of Occupations. Adopted by the Tripartite Meeting of Experts on Labour Statistics on Updating the International Standard Classification of Occupations, ILO, Geneva, December 6.

———. 2010. *Accelerating Action against Child Labour*. Geneva: ILO.

———. 2011. *Global Employment Trends for Youth*. Geneva: ILO.

———. 2012a. *Global Employment Trends 2012: Preventing a Deeper Jobs Crisis.* Geneva: ILO.

———. 2012b. *ILO Global Estimate of Forced Labour: Results and Methodology.* Geneva: ILO.

———. 2012c. "What Are the Key Challenges Facing Labour Statistics Today?" ILO, Geneva. Processed.

ILO and World Bank. 2012. *Inventory of Policy Responses to the Financial and Economic Crisis: Joint Synthesis Report.* Washington, DC: ILO and World Bank.

IMF (International Monetary Fund). 2003. "Growth and Institutions." In *World Economic Outlook: April 2003; Growth and Institutions,* 95–128. Washington, DC: IMF.

Inchauste, Gabriela. 2012. "Jobs and Transitions out of Poverty: A Literature Review." Background paper for the WDR 2013.

Inchauste, Gabriela, Sergio Olivieri, Jaime Saavedra Chanduvi, and Hernan Winkler. 2012. "Decomposing Recent Declines in Poverty: Evidence from Bangladesh, Peru, and Thailand." Background paper for the WDR 2013.

IOM (International Organization for Migration). 2008. *World Migration Report 2008: Managing Labor Mobility in the Evolving Global Economy.* Geneva: IOM.

———. 2010. *World Migration Report 2010. The Future of Migration: Building Capacities for Change.* Geneva: IOM.

Kanamori, Tokishi, and Zhijun Zhao. 2004. *Private Sector Development in the People's Republic of China.* Manila: Asian Development Bank Institute.

Kanbur, Ravi. 2009. "Conceptualizing Informality: Regulation and Enforcement." *Indian Journal of Labour Economics* 52 (1): 33–42.

Kanbur, Ravi, and Jan Svejnar, eds. 2009. *Labor Markets and Economic Development.* Routledge.

Kebede, Tewodros, Anne Hatløy, Huafeng Zhang, and Ingunn Bjørkhaug. 2012. "Perception of Good Jobs: Egypt." Background paper for the WDR 2013.

Keefer, Philip. 2009. "Governance." In *The SAGE Handbook of Comparative Politics,* ed. Todd Landman and Neil Robinson, 439–62. London: SAGE Publications.

Kilroy, Austin. 2011. "Business Bridging Ethnicity." Ph.D. thesis, Massachusetts Institute of Technology, Cambridge, MA.

King, Robert, and Ross Levine. 1993. "Finance and Growth: Schumpeter Might Be Right." *Quarterly Journal of Economics* 108 (3): 717–37.

Klapper, Leora, Luc Laeven, and Raghuram Rajan. 2006. "Entry Regulation as a Barrier to Entrepreneurship." *Journal of Financial Economics* 82 (3): 591–629.

Kraay, Aart. 2012. "How Large Is the Government Spending Multiplier? Evidence from World Bank Lending." *Quarterly Journal of Economics* 127 (2): 1–59.

Laeven, Luc, and Christopher Woodruff. 2007. "The Quality of the Legal System, Firm Ownership, and Firm Size." *Review of Economics and Statistics* 89 (4): 601–14.

Lee, Jean, and David Newhouse. 2012. "Cognitive Skills and Labor Market Outcomes." Background paper for the WDR 2013.

Levi, Margaret, Christopher Adolph, Aaron Erlich, Anne Greenleaf, Milli Lake, and Jennifer Noveck. 2012. "Aligning Rights and Interests: Why, When, and How to Uphold Labor Standards." Background paper for the WDR 2013.

Levine, Ross. 2005. "Finance and Growth: Theory and Evidence." In *Handbook of Economic Growth,* ed. Philippe Aghion and Steven Durlauf, 865–934. Amsterdam: Elsevier.

Levy, Santiago. 2008. *Good Intentions, Bad Outcomes, Social Policy, Informality, and Economic Growth in Mexico.* Washington, DC: Brookings Institution Press.

Lin, Justin Yifu. 2012. *Demystifying the Chinese Economy.* Cambridge, U.K.: Cambridge University Press.

Locke, Richard. Forthcoming. *Beyond Compliance: Promoting Labor Justice in a Global Economy.* New York: Cambridge University Press.

Locke, Richard, Fei Quin, and Alberto Brause. 2007. "Does Monitoring Improve Labor Standards? Lessons from Nike." *Industrial and Labor Relations Review* 61 (1): 3–31.

Luke, Nancy, and Kaivan Munshi. 2011. "Women as Agents of Change: Female Income and Mobility in India." *Journal of Development Economics* 94 (1): 1–17.

Lyon, Scott, Furio C. Rosati, and Lorenzo Guarcello. 2012. "At the Margins: Young People neither in Education nor in Employment." Background paper for the WDR 2013.

Maloney, William F., and Jairo Núñez Méndez. 2003. "Measuring the Impact of Minimum Wages: Evidence from Latin America." Working Paper Series 9800, National Bureau of Economic Research, Cambridge, MA.

McKenzie, David, and Christopher Woodruff. 2008. "Experimental Evidence on Returns to Capital and Access to Finance in Mexico." *World Bank Economic Review* 22 (3): 457–482.

Mertens, Brian. 2011. "Forbes Asia's Businessman of the Year." *Forbes Asia Magazine,* December 5.

Montenegro, Claudio E., and Harry Anthony Patrinos. 2012. "Returns to Schooling around the World." Background paper for the WDR 2013.

Moser, Caroline O. N. 2009. *Ordinary Families, Extraordinary Lives: Assets and Poverty Reduction in*

Guayaquil, 1978–2004. Washington, DC: Brookings Institution.

Mryyan, Nader. 2012. "Demographics, Labor Force Participation, and Unemployment in Jordan." Working Paper Series 670, Economic Research Forum, Giza, Egypt.

Nabli, Mustapha K., Carlos Silva-Jáuregui, and Ahmet Faruk Aysan. 2008. "Authoritarianism, Credibility of Reforms, and Private Sector Development in the Middle East and North Africa." Working Paper Series 443, Economic Research Forum, Cairo.

Narayan, Deepa, Lant Pritchett, and Soumya Kapoor. 2009. *Moving Out of Poverty: Success from the Bottom Up.* New York: Palgrave Macmillan; Washington, DC: World Bank.

Nelson, Richard R. 1981. "Research on Productivity Growth and Productivity Differences: Dead Ends and New Departures." *Journal of Economic Literature* 19 (3): 1029–64.

Newitt, Kirsten. 2012. "Private Sector Voluntary Initiatives on Labour Standards." Background paper for the WDR 2013.

North, Douglass C. 1981. *Structure and Change in Economic History.* New York: W. W. Norton.

———. 1990. *Institutions, Institutional Change and Economic Performance.* New York: Cambridge University Press.

OECD (Organisation for Economic Co-operation and Development). 2006. *OECD Employment Outlook: 2006.* Paris: OECD.

———. 2009. *OECD Reviews of Labour Market and Social Policies: Slovenia.* Paris: OECD.

———. 2010. *Off to a Good Start? Jobs for Youth.* Paris: OECD.

OECD and ILO. 2011. G20 Country Policy Briefs: Brazil—Share of Formal Employment Continues to Grow. Paris: OECD and ILO.

Özden, Çaglar, Christopher Parsons, Maurice Schiff, and Terrie L. Walmsley. 2011. "Where on Earth Is Everybody? The Evolution of Global Bilateral Migration 1960–2000." *World Bank Economic Review* 25 (1): 12–56.

Paes de Barros, Ricardo, Mirela de Carvalho, Samuel Franco, Rosane Mendoça. 2006. "Uma Análise das Principais Causas da Queda Recente na Desigualdade de Renda Brasileira." *Revista Econômica* 8(1): 117–147.

Pagés, Carmen, ed. 2010. *The Age of Productivity: Transforming Economies from the Bottom Up.* New York: Palgrave Macmillan.

Park, Jaegil, Daejong Kim, Yongseok Ko, Funnan Kim, Keunhyun Park, and Keuntae Kim. 2011. "Urbanization and Urban Policies in Korea." Korea Research Institute for Human Settlements.

Perry, Guillermo E., William F. Maloney, Omar S. Arias, Pablo Fajnzylber, Andrew D. Mason, and Jaime Saavedra-Chanduvi. 2007. *Informality: Exit and Exclusion.* Washington, DC: World Bank.

Pritchett, Lant. 2006. *Let Their People Come: Breaking the Gridlock on Global Labor Mobility.* Washington, DC: Center for Global Development.

Psacharopoulos, George, and Harry Anthony Patrinos. 2004. "Returns to Investment in Education: A Further Update." *Education Economics* 12 (2): 111–34.

Rama, Martín. 2001. "The Consequences of Doubling the Minimum Wage: The Case of Indonesia." *Industrial and Labor Relations Review* 54 (4): 864–81.

———. 2009. "Making Difficult Choices: Vietnam in Transition." Working Paper Series 40, Growth and Development Commission, World Bank, Washington, DC.

Randriamaro, Zo. 2007. *Gender and Trade: Overview Report (2006).* Brighton, U.K.: BRIDGE.

Ravallion, Martin. 2009. "Are there lessons for Africa from China's Success against Poverty?" *World Development* 37 (2): 303–13.

Rodrik, Dani. 2000. "Institutions for High-Quality Growth: What They Are and How to Acquire Them." *Studies in Comparative International Development* 35 (3): 3–31.

Rodrik, Dani, Arvind Subramanian, and Francesco Trebbi. 2004. "Institutions Rule: The Primacy of Institutions over Geography and Integration in Economic Development." *Journal of Economic Growth* 9 (2): 131–65.

Romer, Paul Michael. 1993. "Idea Gaps and Object Gaps in Economic Development." *Journal of Monetary Economics* 32 (3): 543–73.

Rutkowski, Jan, Stefano Scarpetta, Arup Banerji, Philip O'Keefe, Gaëlle Pierre, and Milan Vodopivec. 2005. *Enhancing Job Opportunities: Eastern Europe and the Soviet Union.* Washington, DC: World Bank.

Rwanda Demobilization and Reintegration Commission. 2012. *Tracer: Community Dynamics and Payment Verification Study.* Kigali: Rwanda Demobilization and Reintegration Commission.

Sandefur, Justin. 2010. "On the Evolution of the Firm Size Distribution in an African Economy." Working Paper Series 2010-5, Centre for the Study of African Economies, Oxford.

Schoar, Antoinette. 2010. "The Divide between Subsistence and Transformational Entrepreneurship." In *Innovation Policy and the Economy,* vol. 10, ed. Josh Lerner and Scott Stern, 57–81. Cambridge, MA: National Bureau of Economic Research.

Schumpeter, Joseph Alois. 1934. *The Theory of Economic Development: An Inquiry into Profits, Capital, Credit, Interest, and the Business Cycle.* Cambridge, MA: Harvard University Press.

Selim, Nadia. 2012. "Innovation for Job Creation." Background paper for the WDR 2013.

Shiferaw, Admasu, and Arjun S. Bedi. 2010. "The Dynamics of Job Creation and Job Destruction: Is Sub-Saharan Africa Different?" Poverty, Equity and Growth Discussion Papers 22, Courant Research Centre, Göttingen, Germany.

SMERU Research Institute. 2001. *Wage and Employment Effects of Minimum Wage Policy in the Indonesian Urban Labor Market.* Jakarta: SMERU Research Institute.

Stampini, Marco, and Audrey Verdier-Choucane. 2011. "Labor Market Dynamics in Tunisia: The Issue of Youth Unemployment." Discussion Paper Series 5611, Institute for the Study of Labor, Bonn.

Sutton, John, and Nebil Kellow. 2010. *An Enterprise Map of Ethiopia.* London: International Growth Centre.

Syverson, Chad. 2011. "What Determines Productivity?" *Journal of Economic Literature* (49) 2: 326–65.

TeamLease. 2010. *Temp Salary Primer 2010.* Ahmedabad, India: TeamLease Services Pvt. Ltd.

United Nations. (UN). 2009. *System of National Accounts.* New York: UN.

————. 2011. *World Urbanization Prospects: The 2011 Revision.* New York: United Nations, Department of Economic and Social Affairs.

UNDP (United Nations Development Programme). 2003a. *Early Warning Report: FYR Macedonia.* New York: UNDP.

————. 2003b. *Early Warning System: Bosnia and Herzegovina.* New York: UNDP.

United Nations Development Group. 2010. *Thematic Paper on MDG1: Eradicate Extreme Poverty and Hunger, Review of Progress.* New York: United Nations.

Walker, Susan P., Theodore D. Wachs, Julie Meeks Gardner, Betsy Lozoff, Gail A. Wasserman, Ernersto Pollitt, and Julie A. Carter. 2007. "Child Development: Risk Factors for Adverse Outcomes in Developing Countries." *Lancet* 369 (9556): 145–57.

Wietzke, Frank-Borge, and Catriona McLeod. 2012. "Jobs, Well-Being, and Social Cohesion: Evidence from Value and Perception Surveys." Background paper for the WDR 2013.

Winters, Alan, Terrie Walmsley, Zhen Kun Wang, and Roman Grynberg. 2002. "Negotiating the Liberalization of the Temporary Movement of Natural Persons." University of Sussex Discussion Paper 87, Sussex, U.K.

Witze, Morgen. 2010. "Case Study: Tata." *Financial Times,* December 29.

World Bank. 1992. *World Development Report 1992: Development and the Environment.* New York: Oxford University Press.

————. 2004. *World Development Report 2005: A Better Investment Climate for Everyone.* New York: Oxford University Press.

————. 2005. *Global Economic Prospects: Economic Implications of Remittances and Migration.* Washington, DC: World Bank.

————. 2006a. *Chile Development Policy Review.* Washington, DC: World Bank.

————. 2006b. *World Development Report 2007: Development and the Next Generation.* Washington, DC: World Bank.

————. 2007. *Rwanda: Toward Sustained Growth and Competitiveness, Volume I, Synthesis and Priority Measures.* Washington, DC: World Bank.

————. 2008. *Chile: Toward a Cohesive and Well Governed National Innovation System.* Washington DC: World Bank.

————. 2009a. *Doing Business 2010.* Washington, DC: World Bank.

————. 2009b. *World Development Report 2009: Reshaping Economic Geography.* Washington, DC: World Bank.

————. 2010. MDRP (Multi-Country Demobilization and Reingration Program) Report. Washington, DC: World Bank.

————. 2011a. *World Development Report 2011: Conflict, Security, and Development.* Washington, DC: World Bank.

————. 2011b. *More and Better Jobs in South Asia.* Washington, DC: World Bank.

————. 2011c. *World Development Report 2012: Gender Equality and Development.* Washington, DC: World Bank.

————. 2011d. *Capabilities, Opportunities and Participation. Gender Equality and Development in the Middle East and North Africa Region.* A Companion Report to the *World Development Report 2012.* Washington, DC: World Bank.

————. 2011e. "Fueling Growth and Competitiveness in Poland through Employment, Skills, and Innovation." Technical report, World Bank, Washington, DC.

————. 2012. *Job Trends.* Washington, DC: World Bank.

Young, Mary Eming, and L. M. Richardson, eds. 2007. *Early Child Development From Measurement to Action: A Priority for Growth and Equity.* Washington, DC: The World Bank.

Yusuf, Shahid, and Kaoru Nabeshima. 2006. *Post-Industrial East Asian Cities: Innovation for Growth.* Palo Alto: Stanford University Press.

Zhang, Huafeng, Ingunn Bjørkhaug, Anne Hatløy, and Tewodros Kebede. 2012. "Perception of Good Jobs: China." Background paper for the WDR 2013.

The jobs challenge

Demographic transitions, structural change, technological progress, and global volatility are changing the world of work. Yet, traditional farming and self-employment remain dominant in many countries.

Worldwide, more than 3 billion people have jobs, but the nature of their jobs varies greatly. Some 1.65 billion have regular wages or salaries. Another 1.4 billion work in farming and small household enterprises, or in casual or seasonal day labor. The majority of workers in the poorest countries are engaged in these types of work, outside the scope of an employer-employee relationship. Another 200 million people, a disproportionate share of them youth, are unemployed and actively looking for work. Almost 2 billion working-age adults are neither working nor looking for work; the majority of these are women, and an unknown number are eager to have a job.[1]

The jobs challenge facing the world is multi-faceted, ranging from improving aspects of the work people do, to supporting the reallocation of people to better jobs, to creating jobs for those who want to work. Youth bulges in some countries are bringing in millions of new job seekers. Sub-Saharan Africa's labor force grows by about 8 million people every year. South Asia's grows by 1 million people every month. Elsewhere, the working population is rapidly aging, and more and more workers are putting off retirement. By 2020, more than 40 million additional jobs will be needed for people 65 years and older.[2]

Structural and technological changes are moving more people from rural areas to cities.

In the next 15 years, half of the population in developing countries will reside in urban areas, the result of a migration that is rapidly shifting work from the farm to the factory or the street. The rural-urban shift generally improves individual well-being, especially for those who find wage employment. Still, workers' share of global income may be declining, a pattern attributed in part to globalization and technological change. Wages for the same occupation are converging across countries, but a higher premium is paid for more skilled occupations. Women's earnings still lag behind those of men, and the fraction of them who work varies enormously across countries. While women's labor force participation exceeds 75 percent in Vietnam, it is only 28 percent in Pakistan.

As the world changes, so do jobs. Despite improvements in workers' education levels, many firms report that they have difficulty finding the skilled workers they seek. Part-time and temporary work appear to be increasing. In India and South Africa, for example, there has been a sharp rise in the number of temporary employment services and labor brokers. Outsourcing was once concentrated in manufacturing, but new technology is now enabling the splintering of tasks in services. Meanwhile, new platforms on the internet and mobile phones offer innovations for matching workers and employers, and not only for highly skilled jobs.

A job, but not always a salary

To many, the word *job* brings to mind a worker with an employer and a regular paycheck. Yet, this narrow definition excludes nearly 1.4 billion people who work for a living. The concept of a job is actually much broader than wage employment. Jobs are activities that generate actual or imputed income, monetary or in kind, formal or informal. But not all forms of work can be deemed jobs. Activities performed against the will of the worker or involving violations of fundamental human rights should not be considered jobs. Some other activities that entail work effort, such as cooking and cleaning at home, are not considered jobs unless they are performed by people hired and paid for the work.

Multiple forms of work

Defining and measuring jobs is challenging because the ways people spend their time and work are diverse (question 1). Economists usually distinguish between work and leisure, but the reality is more complex. Time can be allocated to nonproduction and production activities. The first category includes time spent eating, sleeping, schooling, and at recreation. Production includes both market and nonmarket work. Whether an activity is considered production can be assessed based on a third-person test: "if an activity is of such character that it might be delegated to a paid worker, then that activity shall be deemed productive."[3]

Patterns in time allocated to production differ across countries and over time. Jobs that span eight hours a day, five days a week, with paid vacation, are not the norm in developing countries. Some jobs involve a few hours of work during certain days of the week or certain weeks of the year; others entail long hours most days of the week almost every week of the year. Some people have had only one job in the previous week, while others have engaged in two or more jobs. In 2011, temporary employment represented more than one-fifth of total wage employment in the Republic of Korea and Spain, but around 5 percent in Australia and the Slovak Republic.[4]

The measurement of unemployment or underemployment is equally challenging. Some people would like to work more hours, whereas others would rather not. More than 15 percent of those employed in Armenia, Colombia, Guatemala, and Peru, but less than 3 percent in Hungary, Pakistan, Portugal, and the United States worked fewer hours than desired.[5] Some people who would like to work have no job. Unemployment rates vary over the business cycle; around 2009 and 2010, when the worst of the international crisis hit most countries in the world, they ranged from more than 20 percent in South Africa and Spain to less than 5 percent in Austria, Korea, Malaysia, Singapore, Sri Lanka, and Thailand.[6]

The world of work is more diverse in developing countries than in developed countries. This diversity refers not only to the number of hours worked and number of jobs available, usual yardsticks in developed countries, but also to characteristics of jobs. Two main aspects stand out. First, there is prevalence of self-employment, which often makes measures of unemployment and underemployment inadequate.[7] Second, the coexistence of traditional and modern modes of production leads to large variations in the nature of work, from subsistence agriculture and menial work to technology-driven manufacturing and services.

Work across the developing world is characterized by a high prevalence of informality, whether defined on the basis of firm registration, social security coverage, or a written employment contract. Informal employment is not under the purview of labor regulations, either because of their limited scope or because they are deliberately avoided or evaded. Regardless of the specific definition used, informal employment is generally associated with lower productivity. However, this does not necessarily mean that firm registration, social security coverage, or a written contract would result in greater efficiency. Informality can be a symptom of lower productivity as much as it can be a cause of it.

Different places, different jobs

Self-employment and farming represent almost half the jobs in the developing world. The vast majority of those in self-employment work in small enterprises with no paid employees.[8]

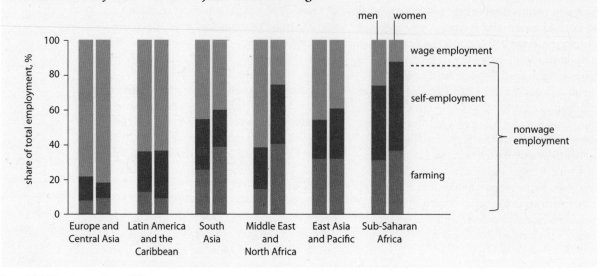

FIGURE 1.1 *A job does not always come with a wage*

Source: World Development Report 2013 team.
Note: Data are for the most recent year available.

But shares of wage work, farming, and self-employment differ greatly by gender and across countries. Nonwage work represents more than 80 percent of women's employment in Sub-Saharan Africa, but less than 20 percent in countries of Eastern Europe and Central Asia (figure 1.1).

Gender differences are also striking.[9] Worldwide, less than 50 percent of women have jobs, whereas almost 80 percent of men do. Roughly 50 percent of both working men and working women are wage earners, but this statistic hides substantial variation across countries and regions. Women are significantly underrepresented in wage employment in low- and lower-middle-income countries, but are more likely than men to work for wages in middle-income countries. In countries such as Pakistan, where 28 percent of women but more than 82 percent of men participate in the labor force, wage employment is a much lower share of total employment among women than among men. Even in countries such as Tanzania and Vietnam, where participation rates are above 75 percent for both men and women, wage employment still lags behind for women. Beyond these stark contrasts, women continue to earn significantly less than men. And these differences are not fully explained by education, experience, or sector of work.

A growing share of youth, typically defined as people ages 15 to 24, is in schooling or in training. Still, youth unemployment reaches alarming levels in some countries (above 40 percent in South Africa since early 2008 and above 50 percent in Spain in early 2012).[10] Even in countries where it is relatively low, the youth unemployment rate is twice or more the national average. In addition, a large share of young people are considered "idle"—not in education, not employed, and not in training or looking for work (figure 1.2).[11] In some countries, more than one-third of 15- to 24-year-olds are idle; in most countries, unemployment rates are small compared to idleness rates.[12] In many cases, when youth work they do so in unpaid jobs. If paid, they are less likely to have access to social security.[13]

Although child labor is in decline, it still affects 1 in 8 children (1 in 14 in the case of hazardous work). The International Labour Organization (ILO) defines child labor as any work by a child under age 12 or, for a child above age 12, any work that impedes education or is damaging to health and personal development. Worldwide, 306 million children were at work in

2008. Of these, 215 million were engaged in activities that constituted child labor, and 115 million were involved in hazardous work.[14] Most of these children are unpaid family workers or participate in farming. More than half live in Asia and the Pacific; but the share is highest is in Sub-Saharan Africa, where child labor affects 1 in 4 children (or 65 million of them).

Youth bulges, aging societies, and migrant nations

Demographic shifts can be massive, but they do not always go in the same direction. The most populous countries in the world have experienced very large increases in their labor force: nearly 8 million new entrants a year in China and 7 million a year in India since the early 1990s. (These rates are now decelerating rapidly, particularly in China.) Many smaller countries face large relative increases, even if the absolute numbers are less astounding. In other countries, the overall population and the labor force are shrinking. For example, Ukraine's labor force is estimated to decrease by 0.75 percent annually, the equivalent of approximately 160,000 fewer people every year.[15]

A simple conceptual exercise illustrates the challenges raised by these dramatic demographic transitions. To keep the ratio of employment to working-age population constant, in 2020, there should be around 600 million more jobs than in 2005. More than 175 million of them, or nearly 1 million a month, would be needed in East Asia and the Pacific as well as in South Asia (figure 1.3). The number of jobs in Sub-Saharan Africa would have to increase by about 50 percent, which translates into employment growth of 2.7 percent a year. But in Eastern Europe and Central Asia, where populations are aging, only 2.4 million new jobs would be needed during the same period.

The age structure of the labor force, not simply its size, matters as well. Youth are staying in school longer and entering the labor market later, whereas adults are living longer and healthier lives. The labor force participation rate of people 65 years of age and older has remained relatively stable over the past two decades. Even with a stable participation rate, however, close to

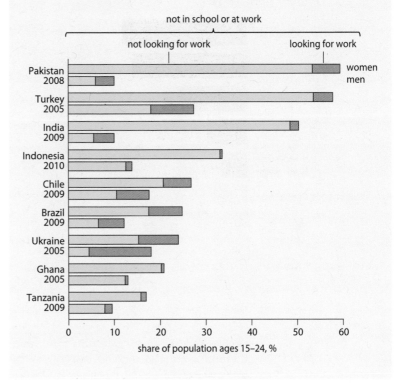

FIGURE 1.2 *Among youth, unemployment is not always the issue*

Source: World Development Report 2013 team.

42 million jobs will have to be generated by 2020 to cope with the growth in the number of older people. One-quarter of these jobs will need to be in China, even though the size of the Chinese labor force will have started to decline in absolute terms.[16]

International migration is also changing the size and composition of the labor force in many countries. At the turn of the century, there were more than 200 million international migrants worldwide, and nearly 90 million of them were workers. If international migrants constituted a nation, theirs would be the fifth-largest in the world, ahead of Brazil. Precise estimates diverge but there is agreement that migrants represent nearly 3 percent of the world population.[17]

These aggregate figures hide important differences across countries. Some are large migration recipients either in absolute numbers (for instance, the United States) or in relative terms

FIGURE 1.3 *Employment growth is needed to cope with population growth*

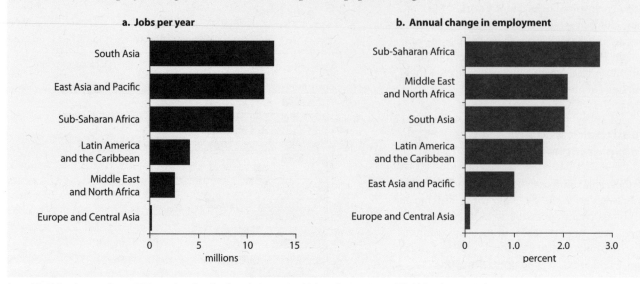

Source: World Development Report 2013 team based on data from the International Labour Organization and World Development Indicators.
Note: Estimations are for the period 2005–20, based on projected population growth assuming constant employment rates.

(Jordan and Singapore). Migrants from countries such as Bangladesh, India, and Mexico represent a large share of total migrants worldwide; countries such as Fiji, Jamaica, and Tonga have a large share of their population overseas. Figures for some of the smaller countries are striking. For instance, nearly one-fifth of all Salvadorians live abroad, while more than three-fifths of the population in Kuwait, Qatar, and the United Arab Emirates is foreign-born.[18]

Cities, wages, and women

Economic development brings significant changes in the composition of the labor force, a process known as structural transformation.[19] Before 2020, more than half of the total population in developing countries is expected to be living in cities and towns.[20] That means that the growth of the nonagricultural labor force will vastly exceed the growth of the agricultural labor force.[21] Urbanization derives from growth in agricultural productivity that sustains higher standards of living. It can also be associated with rapid economic growth at the aggregate level, because urban jobs tend to be more productive than rural jobs. But that has not always

been the case.[22] Population movements away from agriculture were indeed associated with rapid economic growth in East Asia; much less so in Sub-Saharan Africa (figure 1.4).

Technological change induces families to increase market production in place of home production.[23] Structural change has increased the time devoted to consumption or investment activities but it has also meant more work. In some cases, structural change has even led to reduced leisure,[24] particularly for workers who shift to market jobs with low productivity.[25] In the past, this process of structural change often took decades, but in many developing countries, it is transforming lives within a generation (box 1.1).

The shift from home to market production is not gender neutral, because women have tended to specialize in home production whereas men traditionally have focused more on market production. As women move into jobs, they often continue to work at home. When both jobs and home activities are considered, women are generally busier than men. This is so in rich and poor countries. Evidence from Sub-Saharan Africa, Europe, and India shows that women spend more time on production activities than men do.[26] But when they take on jobs—especially

FIGURE 1.4 *Moving from farms to cities does not always bring economic growth*

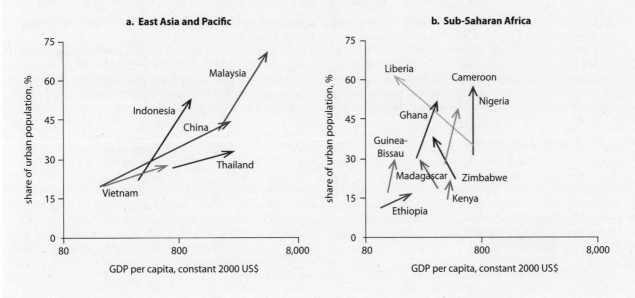

Source: World Development Indicators.
Note: Data correspond to changes between 1985 and 2010. GDP = gross domestic product.

BOX 1.1 *The nature of work and leisure change as cities develop*

The process of structural transformation can be seen today in small and medium-size cities throughout the developing world. The process has been so fast that most people, even young ones, remember the old rural setting. As they have embraced the traits of modern urban life, their jobs and their leisure have changed so much that they do not contemplate returning to the old mores.

A neighborhood of 5,000 outside the city of Tangerang, Indonesia, started coming to life 25 years ago, when iron, rubber, garment, and thread factories sprang up in the surrounding areas. Some in the neighborhood still work as farmhands. But most women and men earn their living in the factories, as well as in a variety of jobs that rose up alongside them. Many men drive *ojeks* (motorcycle taxis); women sell sweets and other items by the gates of the factories. Residents also make a living through home-based garment piecework, handicrafts such as broom-making, and construction work; some are civil servants and teachers. Poorer women collect and resell scraps of fabric. The flow of newcomers has also offered an income-generating opportunity to local families from renting rooms for lodging. Seemingly everyone in the neighborhood has a cell phone and gets around on their own motorcycle.

A 28-year-old steelworker and father of one said that getting factory work used to be a lot easier when the community was newer. Junior high school graduates were still accepted for work then. Now, he said, production workers must have at least a senior high school degree, and vocational school graduates under age 30

are preferred. Practices surrounding recruitment have also become tighter. "It is public knowledge," he added, "that to be accepted in the company, candidates must have an inside connection because more and more people need work, while the number of job opportunities is limited." Many factory workers in the neighborhood work on a six-month contract and hope for its renewal. The best local job available is often reported to be running one's own business. Even when faced with possible unemployment, a 41-year-old noted he had "never thought of returning to the village. That is desperate. Don't be desperate. Find another job and don't get picky."

Comparing the situation now to the early days, a local official described the neighborhood's busy market as "cleaner and more strategic now, and there are more sellers or merchants, so there are more options. Public transportation to the market is more accessible now. It used to be hard to find, and the streets used to be muddy." He estimated that poverty in the neighborhood had fallen by half, from 20 percent at the turn of the century to around 10 percent now. He indicated that the neighborhood had weathered the global financial crisis well and that factory workers had been able to keep their jobs. These changes to work come with changes in leisure. Young men now spend time on computer chats and playing video games. "We used to send letters through the post office," recalls a 22-year-old. "Now, nobody wants to go to the post office. . . . It's beneath them. Now everyone has cell phones."

Source: World Bank 2011a.

BOX 1.2 *Jobs bring earnings opportunities to women, but also new difficulties*

Jobs can transform women's roles in households and in society more broadly. In a community of 3,000 inhabitants outside Durban, South Africa, 80 percent of the women were estimated to be working outside their home, mainly as teachers and nurses but also in offices and retail outlets or with the police. Women did not have such opportunities 10 years ago. "Women are no longer regarded as housewives," a young woman remarked in a Durban focus group.

In a bustling neighborhood in East Jakarta, in Indonesia, women work as street sellers, peddling food, glasses, plates, and carpets. Young women explained that selling carpets is hard work that women do "because they have to help support their families. Their husbands' jobs don't generate enough income." With more education than their elders, young women in this area of Jakarta are more likely to be working in the nearby ceramic factory or in one of the shops or beauty salons in the neighborhood's markets or at the new shopping malls in the city.

In a poor neighborhood of Santiago de los Caballeros, the second-largest city in the Dominican Republic, only a few women sold clothes and sweets in the streets a decade ago. Many are now earning incomes from activities such as selling lottery tickets or running small clothing stores and beauty salons. The incomes of these women are vitally important to their families because men are struggling. Factory opportunities and other jobs associated with the city's free trade zone have been shrinking in recent years. Participants in a Santiago focus group said that women found work more easily than men because employers have "more confidence in them [the women]."

Increased labor force participation is not without challenges. The women in Santiago worry about their safety because of assaults, theft, and gang violence; many think it is too dangerous to work at night. Despite the expansion of work opportunities, mobility continues to be a constraint not only because of poor transportation and safety risks but also because of the roles women play as income-earners and as caregivers in the household. In rural areas, women face difficulties in traveling for farm work and other jobs outside their villages because of traditional cultural and gender norms.

In a semi-urban area outside Cuzco, in Peru, large numbers of women are now engaged in home-based handicrafts, sewing, and diverse agricultural activities. Outside the home, they take up farm jobs, run their own small shops or restaurants, or work for hire in these places. The women explained, however, that they consider home-based activities (such as raising livestock) to be better jobs than jobs outside the home, because "it's peaceful work, and we can look after the kids."

Women encounter many difficulties in commuting across cities for work. In Lautoka, an urban area in Fiji, the local economy is stagnant, and women are working in much larger numbers to help their households cope. Focus group participants explained that only men "can take up jobs in a different town . . . but not the wife because she has responsibilities at home to look after the kids and in-laws."

Source: World Bank 2011a.

those that are outside the household setting—their economic role changes (box 1.2).

Jobs are changing in surprising ways

New technologies, globalization, and structural transformation have brought about remarkable improvements in efficiency. Some developing countries have managed to narrow the productivity gap with industrial countries in only a few decades.[27] But others have failed to catch up and the gap remains considerable for all developing regions (figure 1.5).

The nature of work is changing as well. Industrial countries are experiencing a sustained shift away from primary and traditional manufacturing industries toward services and knowledge-intensive jobs. At the same time, technology improvements and greater reliance on outsourcing to developing countries is leading to a decline in middle-skilled jobs.[28] Technology has allowed production tasks to be splintered and therefore performed in different locations.[29]

Transnational companies have built integrated value chains and can tap into national skill pools around the world.[30] Outsourcing is occurring in services as well as manufacturing. The share of developing countries in exports of world services rose from 11 percent in 1990 to 21 percent in 2008.[31] India has led the way in the information technology (IT) sector, but other countries, such as the Arab Republic of Egypt, have begun to focus attention on exporting services.[32]

This changing landscape of global production has also brought about shifts in skills endowments and in the distribution of top talent across countries. India and China rank high in perceived attractiveness as hubs of outsourcing because of their exceptionally high ratings in people skills and availability.[33] India has close to 20 million students in higher education, nearly as many as the United States; both countries are outpaced by China, with 30 million postsecondary students.[34] The United States still accounts for a large share of international top scorers in student assessments, but Korea has the same share as Germany, and both are closely followed

FIGURE 1.5 *Labor productivity remains low in developing countries*

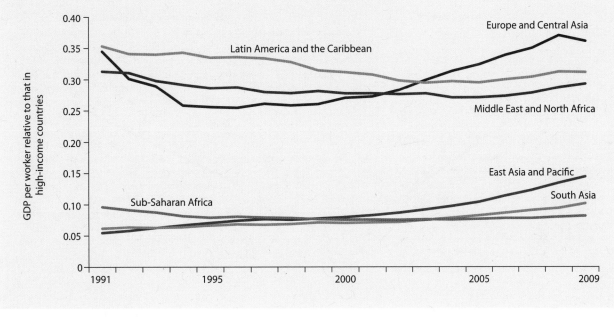

Source: World Development Indicators.
Note: GDP = gross domestic product. Ratio is measured in 2005 purchasing power parity US$.

by the Russian Federation. The number of high-performing students in the city of Shanghai alone is one-fifth of that of Germany and about double that of Argentina.[35]

Skills are not one-dimensional, however. Different jobs require different combinations of manual skills (needed for physical tasks), cognitive skills (needed for mental tasks), and social skills (needed to interact with others). The distribution of employment by occupation can be used to estimate the skill intensity of production. As incomes rise, countries tend to use fewer manual skills in production, and more nonroutine cognitive skills.[36] However, even for a given level of gross domestic product (GDP) per capita, countries can use nonroutine skills to varying degrees (figure 1.6).[37]

Technological progress expands the possibilities for emerging and even low-income countries to create jobs in higher-skilled production activities as well as to link to international value chains in services and manufacturing. In other words, technological progress enables countries to diverge from a linear evolutionary path from manual skill intensity to the use of higher-order cognitive and social skills.[38] India and China top the list of countries in an index measuring their

attractiveness as hubs for the outsourcing of services. Ghana and Senegal, ranked 26th and 28th, come in significantly ahead of emerging market powerhouses like South Africa or Turkey.[39] High-skilled niches are developing the world over. They tend to be located in close proximity to centers of higher education in metropolitan areas with good infrastructure, from Cairo's Smart Village Business Park to Ghana's IT Enabled Service Industry cluster. [40] Bangalore and Chennai in India and Suzhou in China have emerged as global research and development hotspots.

Technology itself is changing the way workers and firms connect, through their access to much larger, even global, marketplaces for employment. Some of these marketplaces operate through the Internet; others use mobile phone technology.[41] These changes are affecting workers in developing countries and not just those in high-skilled occupations. *Babajobs*, for example, was launched in 2009 and is now the largest digital marketplace for blue-collar jobs in India, with more than 320,000 job listings and more than 80,000 job seekers.

With changes in technology and the organization of work, permanent jobs are becoming

FIGURE 1.6 *The skills mix changes with economic development*

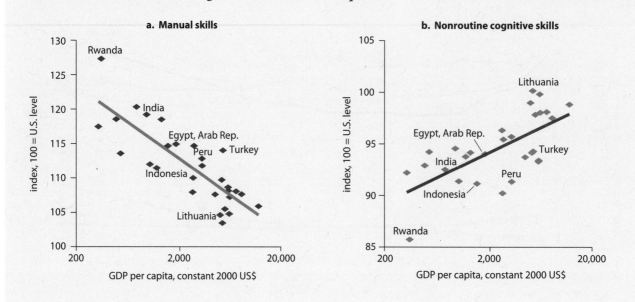

Source: Aedo and others 2012 for the World Development Report 2013.
Note: GDP = gross domestic product. All skill intensities are measured relative to the U.S. level. Each data point shows the skill intensity of national production, derived from transcribing the occupational structure to individual skills, following Autor, Levy, and Murnane 2003.

less common. Part-time and temporary wage employment (also called nonstandard employment) is now a major feature of industrial countries. More than half the firms in the United States expect to raise the share of their part-time and temporary employees over the next five years.[42] The trend is also evident in developing countries (box 1.3).

People's jobs may not match their aspirations. Surveys in high-income countries show that as many as half of all workers—among both self-employed and wage employees—would prefer to be their own bosses.[43] Percentages are lower in low- and middle-income countries, where a larger fraction of the labor force works in household enterprises or on farms. On average, about one-fourth of adults from 35 countries in Eastern Europe and Central Asia prefer self-employment, but the rate varies from 10 percent in Azerbaijan and Hungary to 43 percent in Belarus and Turkey.[44] In poorer countries, self-employment is often a choice of last resort, in part because of the inability to find salaried employment.[45] Owning a small business is a goal to which the poor do not always aspire.[46]

Prosperity, but a changing distribution of earnings

Earnings from work increase with economic development, and the benefits associated with jobs improve as well (figure 1.7). The relationship is not mechanical, but growth is unambiguously good for jobs. Part of the change in earnings and benefits stems from the higher average skills that economies gain as they become more developed; part comes from workers with the same skills enjoying better opportunities.

Poverty has declined in the developing world, to a large extent through jobs. The share of the population of the developing world living on less than US$1.25 a day (in purchasing power parity, or PPP) fell from 52 percent in 1981 to 22 percent in 2008, or from 1.94 billion to 1.29 billion people.[47] This reduction is the result of multiple factors, but the creation of millions of new, more productive jobs, mostly in Asia but also in other parts of the developing world, has been the main driving force.[48] More people have jobs now than ever before, and those jobs provide generally higher earnings.

BOX 1.3 *The temporary staffing industry is growing in developing countries*

A decade ago, the temporary staffing industry was seen as irrelevant outside of high-income countries. But it is now growing rapidly in some developing countries, even beyond large cities.[a] This growth is often viewed as a response to the complex regulatory framework facing employers. Temporary staffing also allows more flexibility in the management of peak workloads and in adjusting staffing levels up or down in line with business demands.

Depending on the context, the temporary staffing industry employs different types of workers, from mainly entry-level, previously unemployed workers seeking to gain experience to highly educated, mid-level career employees looking to fast-track their careers.

In South Africa, temporary workers make up about 7 percent of the labor force; the temporary staffing industry provides employment to an average of 410,000 workers a day.[b] Finance—the sector in the statistics that includes temporary staffing—was a close second to retail in employment growth from 1994 to 2009. Unskilled jobs and service-related occupations dominate the employment distribution within the labor brokering subsector. A worker employed in temporary staffing services is less likely to contribute to pension funds or health insurance and is generally seen as more vulnerable.

Temporary forms of employment have existed in India for decades, partly as a way to circumvent rigid labor laws.[c] However, the modern industry of temporary staffing is only 15 years old, and is developing rapidly. The number of temporary workers recruited by labor brokers grew more than 10 percent in 2009 and 18 percent in 2010. According to some media reports, workers are quitting permanent jobs to move into more attractive temporary roles. Some firms claim that as many as 15 percent of new recruits are permanent employees switching to temporary jobs.[d] Competition in the Indian temporary staffing industry is strong. Agencies have introduced lower recruitment fees to gain more market share and to drive growth. Large temporary staffing firms are entering niche activities such as business consulting (Manpower) and training (TeamLease).[e]

As temporary staffing grows, so do calls to examine the regulatory framework of the industry.[f] Some of those calls focus on addressing vulnerability. Workers in these jobs typically face lower earnings (because a portion of the pay is diverted to temporary staffing agencies). They also face a lack of benefits, coverage by labor laws, and job security. Other efforts focus on professionalizing the industry. For instance, in 2011 TeamLease and seven other staffing firms formed the Indian Staffing Federation to advocate for changes in labor laws and more acceptance for the industry in a country where a vast majority of the labor force is unorganized.

Source: World Development Report 2013 team.
a. Dourgarian (2011) remarks that it is not the Group of 8 countries that led the pack in the growth in the staffing industry in 2011, but the BRICs (Brazil, India, the Russian Federation, and China), along with Indonesia, Mexico, and Pakistan.
b. The discussion on South Africa is drawn from Bhorat (2012) for the World Development Report 2013.
c. World Bank 2011b.
d. TeamLease 2010.
e. Bajaj 2011.
f. ILO 2011; Musgrave 2009.

FIGURE 1.7 *Jobs provide higher earnings and benefits as countries grow*

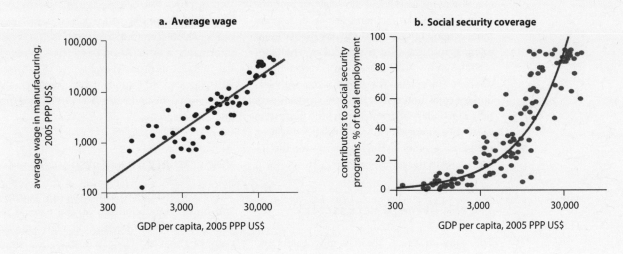

Source: World Development Report 2013 team.
Note: GDP = gross domestic product; PPP = purchasing power parity. Each dot represents a country.

Yet in a majority of countries, both industrial and developing, the share of labor in total income is declining.[49] This trend, which has been observed since the mid-1980s and early 1990s, has been attributed to various forces, from technological progress biased toward skilled workers to global competition undermining workers' bargaining power. The entrance of China and India in world trade has doubled the size of the globalized labor force, hence reducing the price of labor relative to that of other factors of production.[50]

Changes in the distribution of income in recent years have actually taken place not only between factors of production but between workers. Two distinctions are relevant in this respect: between high- and low-skill workers, and between those who work in tradable sectors and those who do not. Tradable sectors produce goods and services that can be exported or imported, such as shirts or computers. A turning point came in the mid-1990s, when labor earnings in developing countries started to grow faster than those in industrial countries, regardless of level of skill. But the trend is more pronounced in tradable sectors, whereas low-skill workers in nontradable sectors continue to be the most disadvantaged (figure 1.8).

The relatively lower wages among low-skill workers compared with high-skill workers, particularly in nontradable sectors in developing countries, are consistent with an increase in returns to education. Returns to education measure the wage premium on higher educational attainment for workers of the same sex with the same age and work experience. In all regions, more schooling is associated with higher labor earnings, but the gain is not linear. The labor earnings of workers with tertiary education are double or more than those of workers with secondary education only. However, workers with only a secondary education earn little more than those with elementary education. The education premium is generally higher the lower the income level of the country (figure 1.9).

The role of the private sector

The solution to all these demographic and technological challenges rests with the private sector. That does not mean that the government does not have a role to play. The quality of the civil service is critically important for development, whether it is teachers building skills, agricultural extension agents improving agricultural productivity, or urban planners designing functional cities. Public works programs or employment programs for the demobilization of combatants are also justified in some circumstances. But the private sector is the main engine of job creation and the source of roughly nine of 10 jobs in the world. Between 1995 and 2005, the private sector accounted for almost 90 percent of jobs created in Brazil. In the Philippines and Turkey, the fraction reached 95 percent.[51]

But the most remarkable example of the expansion of employment through private sector growth is the case of China. In 1981, private sector employment accounted for 2.3 million workers while state-owned enterprises (SOEs) had 80 million workers. Two decades later, employment in private sector firms accounted for 74.7 million workers surpassing, for the first time, the 74.6 million workers in SOEs (figure 1.10).[52]

In contrast to the global average, in some countries in the Middle East and North Africa, the state keeps a leading role as an employer—a pattern that can be linked to the political economy of the post-independence period and, in some cases, to the abundance of oil revenues.[53] For a long period, public sector jobs were offered to young college graduates. In recent years, however, the fiscal space for continued expansion in public sector employment shrank, and "queuing" for public sector jobs became more prevalent, leading to increasing transitions into informality, a devaluation of education credentials, and forms of social exclusion.[54] A relatively well-educated and young labor force remains unemployed, or underemployed, and labor productivity stagnates.[55]

Vulnerability on a global scale

Jobs are vulnerable to economic downturns—and much more so in the private than in the public sector. Short-term crises may wipe out years of progress. They may start in a single country and through globalization spread over entire regions or, as in the recent one, to the

FIGURE 1.8 *Wages in developing countries are catching up*

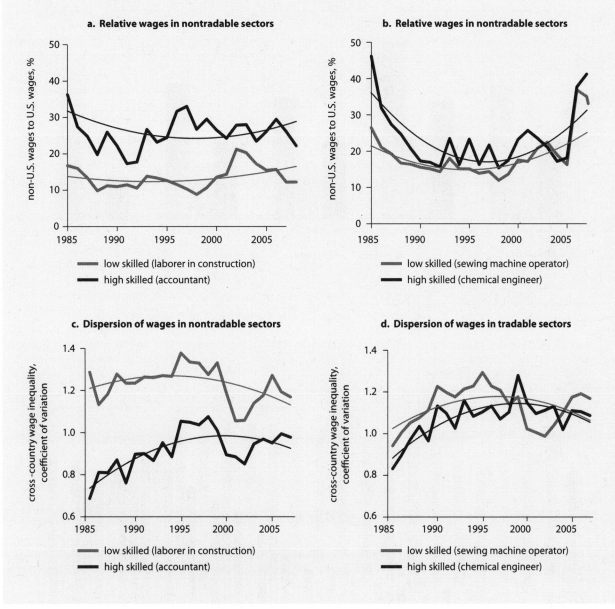

a. Relative wages in nontradable sectors

low skilled (laborer in construction)
high skilled (accountant)

b. Relative wages in nontradable sectors

low skilled (sewing machine operator)
high skilled (chemical engineer)

c. Dispersion of wages in nontradable sectors

low skilled (laborer in construction)
high skilled (accountant)

d. Dispersion of wages in tradable sectors

low skilled (sewing machine operator)
high skilled (chemical engineer)

Source: Based on Oostendorp 2012 for the World Development Report 2013.
Note: The database used to construct this figure contains wage data by occupations for an unbalanced panel of more than 150 countries from 1983 to 2008. The data are derived from the International Labour Organization (ILO) October Inquiry database by calibrating the data into a normalized wage rate for each occupation. For a description of the data, see Freeman, Oostendorp, and Chor 2011. The vertical axis in panels a and b represents the ratio between U.S. wages and non-U.S. wages. The vertical axis in panels c and d represents the coefficient of variation of wages—a measure of wage inequality—across all countries in the sample.

whole world. In 1995, a financial crisis in Mexico engulfed most of Latin America as well as other emerging countries. In 1997, a speculative attack on Thailand's currency severely affected the economies of Indonesia, Malaysia, and Korea. In 2007, an alarming rise in food prices begot problems with food supply and inflation, increasing poverty and reducing real wages in parts of the developing world.[56]

FIGURE 1.9 *Returns to education are higher in poorer countries*

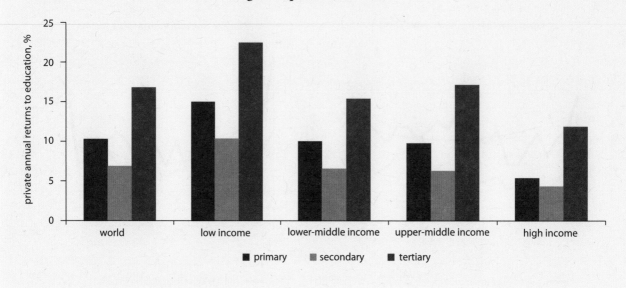

Source: Montenegro and Patrinos 2012 for the World Development Report 2013.
Note: Reported figures are unweighted averages of country-level private returns, for the most recent year within the period 2000–10 in a sample of 69 countries.

FIGURE 1.10 *In China, employment growth is led by the private sector*

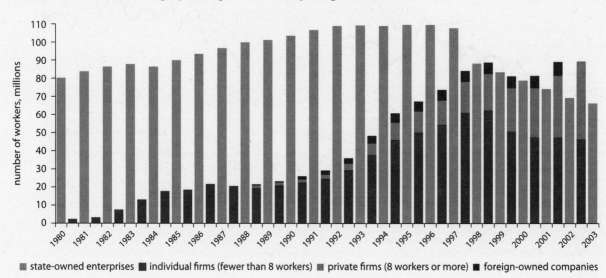

Source: Kanamori and Zhao 2004.
Note: Data for foreign-owned companies in 2002 and for non-state-owned enterprises in 2003 are not available.

In 2008, the bursting of asset price bubbles and the resulting collapse of financial institutions in the United States and some European countries initiated a crisis of worldwide span, creating 22 million new unemployed in a single year. Growth in total employment, which had been hovering around 1.8 percent a year before 2008, fell to less than 0.5 percent in 2009, and by

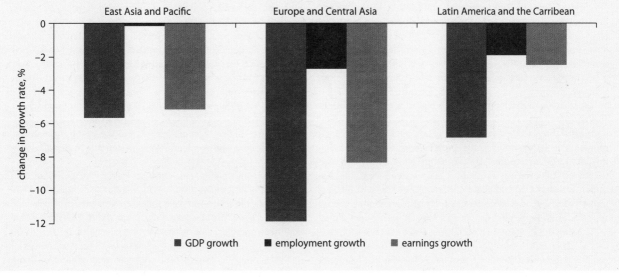

FIGURE 1.11 *In developing countries, the crisis affected earnings more than employment*

East Asia and Pacific   Europe and Central Asia   Latin America and the Carribean

change in growth rate, %

■ GDP growth   ■ employment growth   ■ earnings growth

Source: Khanna, Newhouse, and Paci 2010.
Note: GDP = gross domestic product. The vertical axis measures the difference in growth rates before and after the beginning of the crisis.

2011 had not yet returned to its pre-crisis level.[57] As Europe struggles with high levels of public debt, vulnerabilities in its banking sector, and uncertainties about the euro, and as growth decelerates in China and India, it is by no means clear that the global crisis is over.

The impact of the 2008–09 crisis varied across developing countries. Some, such as the Baltic countries, the Kyrgyz Republic, Mexico, Romania, Russia, South Africa, and Turkey, had absolute declines in employment; other countries such as Brazil, China, and Indonesia experienced only a brief deceleration. Country-specific studies shed further light on employment impacts across different population groups. For example, it is estimated that the crisis cost China between 20 million and 36 million jobs, particularly among migrant workers in export-oriented sectors.[58] In Mexico, it caused a decline of half a million jobs between 2008 and the second quarter of 2009, particularly among women, youth, and older workers, as well as a 10 percent drop in real wages.[59] In Indonesia, although the effects of the crisis were mild, young, casual, and informal workers were affected.[60] Across countries, the young bore the largest brunt.[61]

Adjustment patterns, in terms of jobs lost or earnings declines, also varied in developing countries. The less formalized the labor market, the more earnings shrank and the less employment numbers gave away. In Central and Eastern Europe, where the labor market is largely formalized, the growth rate of GDP dropped on average by 12 percentage points, employment contracted by 3 percent, and earnings fell by more than 8 percent (figure 1.11).[62] In East Asia, where formal employment rates are very low, the average decline in GDP growth was 5.5 percentage points and total employment numbers barely changed.[63]

The policy response to the crisis was unprecedented in its scale, but it also involved different combinations of instruments, with potentially different implications for jobs. Fiscal stimulus across the world amounted to US$5.5 trillion in purchasing power parity, with China, Japan, and the United States accounting for more than 70 percent of it.[64] Of 77 countries for which data are available, 80 percent used fiscal expansion. Higher-income countries favored tax cuts, higher unemployment benefits, and direct support for enterprises. Low- and middle-income countries boosted expenditures, including spending on training and income-support measures.[65] Across countries, responses mainly aimed at preventing or mitigating employment

BOX 1.4 *Responses to the crisis went beyond income support for the unemployed*

Countries worldwide used an array of policy responses to confront the jobs crisis. Macroeconomic stimulus and targeted sector policies were supplemented by policies to strengthen income support for those affected; measures to boost labor demand through wage subsidies, credit policies, and public works programs; and investments in skills and tailor-made employment services for those most affected.

Globally, unemployment insurance played a minor role. Only 15.4 percent of the unemployed received benefits during the crisis, because of the low effective coverage of unemployment insurance programs. In 23 countries in the Organisation for Economic Co-operation and Development, Central Europe, and Latin America, the duration of benefits was extended. Countries with large informal sectors or without unemployment schemes relied on a mix of cash transfers and public works schemes to provide additional income support for those in need. Colombia's Familias en Acción—a program focusing on strengthening nutrition and education for children—increased its coverage from 1.8 million to 2.7 million families. Argentina expanded the coverage of family benefits to all informal sector workers.

Countries across all income levels took measures to boost labor demand. Of the resources devoted to creating and protecting jobs, high-income countries spent more than half (56 percent) on credit policies for firms. They also implemented work-sharing arrangements to cushion the impact of the crisis. Take-up rates for these initiatives reached 3.3 percent of the employed in Italy, 3.2 percent in Germany, and 2.7 percent in Japan.

Low- and middle-income countries spent 67 percent of their resources on direct job creation measures and public works programs. Mexico, for example, extended its temporary works program to around 250,000 workers, or 0.5 percent of the labor force. Wage subsides were popular in Europe. They were most often implemented through a reduction in social security contributions and were targeted to small and medium enterprises or to disadvantaged groups such as long-term job seekers and the young. To reach an effective scale in a timely manner, though, countries needed to have had such programs in place before the crisis.

In comparison, efforts to ramp up training, employment services, or specific support programs for vulnerable groups were relatively modest in scope and scale. Building or maintaining skills took the lion's share of the budget in this category, with Chile, Italy, Mexico, Turkey, and the United States spending the most.

Overall, countries with more mature social protection systems as well as established employment programs were able to respond quickly and reduce the impact of the crisis on jobs. With few exceptions, though, little is known about possible unintended effects of their programs such as whether preserving some jobs came at the expense of destroying others. Careful impact analysis is only in its initial stages.

Sources: ILO and World Bank 2012.

losses, rather than trying to offset earnings shortfalls (box 1.4).

* * *

Demography, urbanization, globalization, technological progress, and macroeconomic crises bring about formidable jobs challenges. Countries that fail to address them may fall into vicious circles of slow growth in labor earnings and job-related dissatisfaction affecting a sizable portion of the labor force.[66] Youth unemployment and idleness may be high, and women may face limited job opportunities, leaving potential economic and social gains untapped.[67] A repeating pattern of small gains in living standards, slow productivity growth, and eroding social cohesion may emerge. In contrast, countries that successfully address these job challenges can develop virtuous circles. The results—prosperous populations, a growing middle class, increased productivity, and improved opportunities for women and youth—may then be self-reinforcing.

What is a job?

The world of work is diverse, especially in developing countries, and it is changing rapidly. Against this backdrop, the diversity of the words used to describe what people do to earn a living across countries and cultures should not be surprising. Even people who speak the same language can have vastly different interpretations of the meaning of a *job*. For some, the word conjures up an image of a worker in an office or a factory, with an employer and a regular paycheck. Others may think of farmers, self-employed vendors in cities, and caregivers of children or elderly relatives.

Work matters and words matter

The varied interpretations capture the different aspects of jobs that people value. A woman in Hanoi, Vietnam, explained, "an old woman who just sells vegetables can gain respect from others and people listen to her."[68] A man who had worked his way out of poverty in Satgailijhara, Bangladesh, linked the value of his job as a rice farmer to being able to invest in his children, "I have been able to get my children educated. That's the best achievement in life."[69]

Ela Bhatt, a lawyer and the founder of Self Employed Women's Association (SEWA) in India, described her struggle with the language of work, given the multiplicity of tasks that people do every day and over time: "A small farmer works on her own farm. In tough times, she also works on other farms as a laborer. When the agriculture season is over, she goes to the forest to collect gum and other forest produce. Year round, she produces embroidered items either at a piece rate for a contractor or for sale to a trader who comes to her village to buy goods. Now, how should her trade be categorized? Does she belong to the agricultural sector, the factory sector, or the home-based work sector? Should she be categorized as a farmer or a farm worker? Is she self-employed or is she a piece-rate worker?"[70]

These questions are not merely semantic. The words and categories that are used to describe work have tangible implications. Views on what a job is and what it means almost inevitably influence views on what policies for jobs should look like. Those for whom the word *job* is associated with the image of a worker in an office or a factory, with an employer and a paycheck, may focus on a supportive investment climate for firms. Those for whom the word also encompasses farming, street vending, waste picking, and domestic employment may think of jobs policies as including land reform, agricultural extension, urban policies, or the provision of voice to the most vulnerable workers.

According to the International Conference of Labour Statisticians (ICLS), which sets standard definitions for official use across countries, a job is "a set of tasks and duties performed, or meant to be performed, by one person, including for an employer or in self-employment."[71] Under this definition, a *job* is not the same as *employment*. The existence of job vacancies and people with more than one job means that the number of jobs is greater than the number of people employed. The existence of unemployment means that people do not find the jobs they want. Jobs refer to tasks, while the wage employed, farmers, and the self-employed refer to the people who do them.

Some gray areas

The ICLS definition excludes some forms of work from official employment statistics. The employed are part of the economically active population, defined as people who contribute to "the production of goods and services as defined by the United Nations systems of national accounts and balances."[72] The system of national accounts (SNA) includes "all production actually destined for the market, whether for sale or barter," as well as the production of goods for one's own use, but "excludes all production of services for own final consumption within households."[73] This definition thus leaves out of official statistics activities such as child-rearing, care of the elderly, or home cooking, as well as traveling to work.

Some countries are starting to develop estimates of these other types of activities. The SNA offers guidelines to countries for producing satellite accounts reflecting forms of household work that are not considered jobs. According to these guidelines, "a job can refer to unpaid household service and volunteer work performed by one person for a household outside the SNA production boundary but within the general production boundary."[74] Mexico, for instance, has used this guidance to estimate the value of unremunerated activities in households, such as housekeeping and child care. These activities represented nearly a quarter of Mexican GDP between 2003 and 2009 and were equivalent to about two-thirds of worker wages and benefits.[75]

Informality is another important gray area. After nearly four decades of debates about the concept of informality, there is still no consensus on what is meant by informal jobs. Some schools of thought link informality to characteristics of firms—whether the business is registered or pays taxes. Others focus on characteristics of workers—whether they are covered by social protection or have an employment contract. And yet others stress modes of production and levels of productivity to define informality. A consensus is starting to emerge on how to measure informality, but the definitions used still leave out types of work that some consider informal. Meanwhile, relatively few countries produce regular statistics on informality (box 1.5).

BOX 1.5 *Few countries produce statistics on informality*

The concept of dual economies has an old lineage.[a] Based on the recognition of dual economies and the Harris and Todaro two-sector model, the term *informality* was first coined by a U.K. anthropologist in a paper about Ghana. The concept gained popularity with a widely cited report from a mission of the International Labour Organization (ILO) to Kenya.[b] Since then, studies on informality have proliferated, and the concept has become standard in development studies, labor economics, and other disciplines. Today the causes and implications of informality are the subject of an intense academic debate and an extended research agenda aimed at understanding how labor markets function in developing countries.[c]

A variety of approaches can be used to measure informality, informal employment, and the informal sector. Measurement becomes even more complex when informality is combined with other concepts like illegal and underground activities or nonstandard work. The lack of systematic country-level data on informality has led researchers to construct their own estimates using similar but not identical criteria, which sometimes lead to diverging conclusions.

Recommendations on the measurement of informality were first drafted in 1993 by the 15th International Conference of Labour Statisticians (ICLS). Four years later, the United Nations created the Delhi Group to document and recommend methods for defining and collecting data on the informal sector. In 2003, the 17th ICLS, through the document "Guidelines Concerning a Statistical Definition of Informal Employment," introduced a definition of informal employment and a series of rules for its measurement. Since 2006,

the Delhi Group has been working with the ILO on a forthcoming "Manual of Surveys of Informal Employment and Informal Sector." In 2008, the newest version of the United Nation's system of national accounts adopted most of the previous resolutions and recommendations on the measurement of informality. That resulted in a broad definition that includes both the informal sector and informal employment. However, gray areas remain in relation to activities such as farming, independent professionals, and activities among rural workers in general.

Few countries produce regular official statistics on informality. The dearth of data is apparent in global repositories such as the ILO's Key Indicators of the Labor Market database, which, in its most recent version, includes data on informality for only 60 countries.[d] A report on informality across the world by the ILO and Women in Informal Employment: Globalizing and Organizing (WIEGO) makes systematic use of the most thorough definition of informality, covering informal employment and employment in informal firms, to present data on 47 countries.[e] The ILO-WIEGO report shows informality rates ranging from 40 percent in Uruguay and 42 percent in Thailand to 75 percent in Bolivia and 80 percent in India.

The extent of informality varies with differences in productivity across firms and workers, as well as with differences in the nature of regulations and the degree to which they are enforced. Whether informality is the result of exit, exclusion, uneven enforcement, or low firm productivity is still a matter of debate. Better measurement can provide information on the magnitude of informality and provide more data for the advancement of studies in this area.

Source: World Development Report 2013 team.
a. Boeke 1942; Lewis 1954.
b. Harris and Todaro 1970; Hart 1973; ILO 1972.
c. A few among the most recent are Guha-Khasnobis and Kanbur 2006; Perry and others 2007; Kanbur 2009; Blades, Ferreira, and Lugo 2011; and Vanek and others 2012.
d. ILO Key Indicators of the Labour Market (database).
e. Vanek and others 2012.

What is not a job?

While views about what a job means vary, a broad consensus exists on the types of activities that should never be considered a job. International norms define basic human rights as the boundaries of what is unacceptable. The United Nations Universal Declaration of Human Rights, which the UN General Assembly embraced unanimously in 1948, provides for the right to work and protection from discrimination.[76] The Declaration on Fundamental Rights and Principles at Work adopted at the ILO conference in 1998 further specifies core labor standards that call for an end to forced and compulsory labor, child labor, and labor discrimination, and that provide for freedom of association and collective bargaining.[77] Most countries have ratified the conventions on forced labor, child labor, and discrimination; fewer have ratified the conventions on freedom of association and collective bargaining (figure 1.12).[78]

While international agreements help define what forms of work are unacceptable, in practice many people work in activities that violate their rights. Some 21 million people are estimated to be subject to forced labor, and around 1 million to trafficking.[79] In many cases, forced labor is inflicted upon minorities or groups that are discriminated against, such as migrants, women, and indigenous people. Migrant workers in sweatshops in Latin America, child soldiers in conflict-afflicted areas of Africa, people trafficked for sexual exploitation in Europe and Asia, and temporary migrant workers under sponsorship contracts in the Middle East are the subjects of the most conspicuous forms of forced labor and trafficking in the world.

Child labor provides another striking example (box 1.6). Although it is covered by the core labor standards and many countries have ratified the relevant ILO conventions and the UN Convention on the Rights of the Child, the ILO estimates that 115 million children worldwide were involved in hazardous work in 2008. Measurement is complicated by legal and moral concerns, as well as by the flawed design of surveys that may induce parents to misreport children's work.[80] These statistics may actually represent only a lower boundary on the size of the problem.

Recent research shows that children work for diverse and complex reasons.[81] They range from household poverty to the relative accessibility and affordability of schooling and from the preferences of families and even children regarding work and play to the influence of technological change, international trade, and ur-

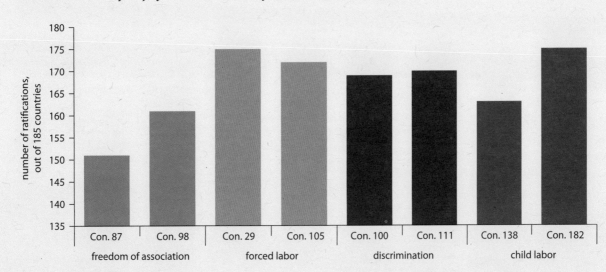

FIGURE 1.12 *A majority of countries have ratified the core labor standards*

BOX 1.6 *Not all child work is child labor*

According to the International Labour Organization (ILO), children engaged in child labor include "all persons aged between 5 and 17 years who during a specified time period were engaged in one or more of the following activities: (a) hazardous work; (b) worst forms of child labor other than hazardous work; and (c) other forms of child labor (depending on age of the child and weekly hours worked)."[a] The "worst forms of child labor" include any work that jeopardizes the health, safety, or morals of a child. Such work is determined to be hazardous depending on its specific nature, the demands on children in particular industries, and the general working conditions. Apart from hazardous work, the worst forms of child labor include all forms of slavery, bondage, military conscription, trafficking, and using, procuring, or offering children for prostitution, pornography, or other illicit activities.

This definition of child labor is governed by two ILO Conventions (132 and 182), two ILO recommendations (146 and 190), and the UN Convention on the Rights of the Child. However, international standards also provide countries with some latitude in setting allowed boundaries for the involvement of children in productive activities (regarding ages or the definition of hazardous work, for example). The standards also permit limited work in the performance of household chores or in light productive activities that are not considered harmful.

Source: World Development Report 2013 team.
a. ILO 2008a.

banization. Children in wealthier households may, in some settings, be engaged in child labor if household assets and access to finance, land, or other resources generate more demand for work from household members.[82] Child labor

may affect schooling, health, fertility, and behavior, although establishing these links has been challenging. Rarely is there a one-to-one tradeoff between school and work. In many places, the majority of children who work are also attending school. Moreover, a child may have dropped out of school for reasons unrelated to child labor. The participation of children 12 years and older in family farming and small household enterprises can in some cases contribute to the acquisition of skills.[83]

In sum, *jobs* are activities that generate actual income, monetary or in kind, and do not violate fundamental rights and principles at work. This definition includes the categories of work covered by ICLS guidelines: wage or salary employment, employers, members of cooperatives, family workers (including unpaid family members), and the self-employed. In many instances, however, these categories may fail to uniquely or clearly classify certain individuals. For instance, small farmers are sometimes wage employed or self-employed, but they may also be employers if they hire unpaid family workers. Jobs include labor activities that generate income for the household, even if no income measure can be attributed to a person's specific labor, as in the case of household enterprises and farming.

By this definition, jobs are much broader than just working in an office or a factory, with an employer and a regular paycheck.

Garimpeiros (independent prospectors) at the Serra Pelada gold mine, in Brazil

© Sebastião Salgado/Amazonas—Press Images

Notes

1. World Development Report 2013 team estimates.
2. World Development Report 2013 team estimates based on data from the International Labour Organization, http://laborsta.ilo.org/applv8/data/EAPEP/eapep_E.html, and World Development Indicators, http:/data-worldbank.org/data/catalog/world-development-indicators.
3. Reid 1934, 11.
4. Organisation for Economic Co-operation and Development Employment database, http://www.oecd.org/employment/database. Temporary work refers to a mixture of seasonal jobs, fixed-term contracts, on-call workers, and temporary help agency workers that varies by country, depending on national definitions and available statistics.
5. Lee, McCann, and Messenger 2007.
6. ILO Department of Statistics, "Short term indicators of the labour market," http://laborsta.ilo.org/sti/sti_E.html.
7. Ghose, Majid, and Ernst 2008.
8. Gindling and Newhouse 2012 for the World Development Report 2013.
9. World Bank (2011c) offers a more in-depth review of these issues.
10. ILO Department of Statistics, "Short term indicators of the labour market," http://laborsta.ilo.org/sti/sti_E.html.
11. Youth not in employment, education, or training are also sometimes referred to as "NEETs." See the statistical annex for more information. Kovrova, Lyon, and Rosati 2012 for the World Development Report 2013; Ranzani and Rosati 2012 for the World Development Report 2013.
12. Lyon, Rosati, and Guarcello 2012 for the World Development Report 2013.
13. World Bank 2006.
14. ILO 2010.
15. United Nations Population Division, World Population Prospects 2011; ILO, Labor Force Participation Estimates and Projections.
16. Rozelle and Huang 2012 and estimates from International Labour Office database on labor statistics, Laborsta, http://laborsta.ilo.org/, October 2011.
17. IOM 2008; Lucas 2005; Özden and others 2011.
18. IOM 2010.
19. Chenery and Syrquin 1975; Clark 1940; Kuznets 1966; Rostow 1960.
20. UN 2011b.
21. Herrmann and Khan 2008.
22. This is the main observation that sparked the research on the informal sector: Harris and Todaro 1970; Hart 1973; ILO 1972. For a recent study of the process of structural change in Africa, see Losch, Freguin-Gresh, and White (2012).
23. Freeman and Schettkat 2005; Ngai and Pissarides 2008.
24. Bardasi and Wodon 2006; Lee, McCann, and Messenger 2007; Maddison 2001; Ramey and Francis 2009.
25. Bardasi and Wodon 2010; Gammage 2010.
26. Charmes 2006; Gálvez-Muñoz, Rodríguez-Modroño, and Domínguez-Serrano 2011; Hirway and Jose 2012. Burda, Hamermesh, and Weil (2011) argue that differences in total work by gender change over the business cycle but converge over the long term.
27. ILO 2009a; Pagés 2010.
28. Autor and Dorn 2011; Gratton 2011; Holzer and Lerman 2009.
29. Feenstra 2010.
30. Brown, Ashton, and Lauder 2010. For U.S. parent companies, according to the National Science Foundation, the share of research performed by Asia-located affiliates outside of Japan rose from 5 to 14 percent from 1997 to 2008, mainly in China, Korea, Singapore, and India (http://nsf.gov/statistics/seind12/c4/c4s4.htm).
31. Goswami, Mattoo, and Sáez 2011.
32. Goswami, Mattoo, and Sáez 2011.
33. A.T. Kearney 2011.
34. United Nations Educational, Scientific and Cultural Organization Institute of Statistics, http://stats.uis.unesco.org/unesco/TableViewer/tableView.aspx?ReportId=175.
35. WDR team estimates of the top 20 percent of PISA ratings among 12 countries in the 2009 Programme for International Student Assessment (PISA) of 15-year-olds.
36. This skill definition broadly follows Autor, Levy, and Murnane (2003) and Acemoglu and Autor (2011). Other approaches distinguish, for example, between cognitive, noncognitive, and technical skills (World Bank 2010) or cognitive/problem solving, learning, personal/behavioral/ethical, and social and communication skills (ILO 2008b).
37. Aedo and others 2012 for the World Development Report 2013.
38. Brown, Ashton, and Lauder 2010.
39. A.T. Kearney 2011.
40. Yoshino 2011.
41. Examples include oDesk (https://www.odesk.com/), babajob (http://www.babajob.com/), Google trader (for example, http://www.google.co.ug/africa/trader/search?cat=jobs), and SoukTel (http://www.souktel.org/).
42. McKinsey Global Institute 2011.

43. Blanchflower, Oswald, and Stutzer 2001. More recent (2005) data of the International Social Survey Programme show similar patterns.

44. WDR team estimates from the 2010 Life in Transitions Survey.

45. Banerjee and Duflo 2011; Perry and others 2007.

46. Banerjee and Duflo 2011. Although, it is not always the case that the self-employed always report lower well-being. In their study from Ghana, Falco and others 2012 for the WDR 2013 find that informal firm owners who employ others are on average substantially happier than formal workers.

47. Based on an update by the authors Chen and Ravallion 2010.

48. World Bank 2011b.

49. Guscina 2006; Lübker 2007; Rodriguez and Jayadev 2010.

50. Bentolila and Saint-Paul 2003; Freeman 2008.

51. International Labour Office database on labor statistics, Laborsta, http://laborsta.ilo.org/.

52. The definition of "private sector" in China is broad and sometimes not clearly defined in official statistics. There is differentiation between what are labeled "private firms" (a profit-making unit invested in and established by natural persons or controlled by persons hiring more than seven workers) and "individual firms" (those with fewer than eight employees). Foreign-invested firms and collectives are not part of the private sector in official statistics. For more details, see Kanamori and Zhao (2004).

53. Nabli, Silva-Jaurengui, and Faruk Aysan 2008.

54. Assaad 2012; Assaad and Barsoum 2007.

55. Mryyan 2012.

56. For a study of previous crises, see Fallon and Lucas (2002). For the food price crisis, see Ivanic and Martin (2008).

57. ILO 2012a.

58. Giles and others 2012 for the World Development Report 2013. These losses were temporary and currently worker shortages are experienced instead.

59. Freije-Rodriguez, Lopez-Acevedo, and Rodriguez-Oreggia 2011.

60. McCulloch, Grover, and Suryahadi 2011.

61. Cho and Newhouse 2010.

62. Khanna, Newhouse, and Paci 2010.

63. Khanna, Newhouse, and Paci 2010; World Bank 2012.

64. ILO and World Bank 2012.

65. ILO and World Bank 2012; Robalino, Newhouse, and Rother forthcoming.

66. Bell and Blanchflower 2011; Farber 2011.

67. World Bank 2011c.

68. World Bank 2011a.

69. Narayan, Pritchett, and Kapoor 2009, 19.

70. Bhatt 2006, 17.

71. Article 2, ILO 2007. Also see UN (2009).

72. Article 9, ILO 1982, http://www.ilo.org/wcmsp5/groups/public/---dgreports/---stat/documents/normativeinstrument/wcms_087481.pdf.

73. UN 2009, 6–7.

74. ILO 2009b, 42.

75. INEGI 2011.

76. UN 1948, http://www.un.org/en/documents/udhr/, article 23 (1).

77. ILO 1998.

78. The core international labor standards are the subject of eight conventions covering the four areas: Convention 87 (1948), the Freedom of Association and Protection of the Right to Organize Convention; Convention 98 (1949), the Right to Organize and Collective Bargaining Convention; Convention 29 (1930), the Forced Labour Convention; Convention 105 (1957), the Abolition of Forced Labour Convention; Convention 100 (1951), the Equal Remuneration Convention; Convention 111 (1958), the Discrimination (Employment and Occupation) Convention; Convention 138 (1973), the Minimum Age Convention; and Convention 182 (1999), the Worst Forms of Child Labour Convention. See "Conventions," NORMLEX Database: Information on International Labour Standards, International Labour Organization, Geneva. ILO (2012). http://www.ilo.org/dyn/normlex/en/.

79. Andrees and Belser 2009; ILO 2009c; ILO 2012b.

80. Dillon and others 2012.

81. Basu 1999; Basu and Tzannatos 2003; Cigno and Rosati 2005; Edmonds 2008.

82. Del Carpio and Loayza 2012; Hazarika and Sarangi 2008.

83. Edmonds (2008) offers a review of the theoretical and empirical evidence on child labor.

References

The word *processed* describes informally reproduced works that may not be commonly available through libraries.

A.T. Kearney. 2011. *Offshoring Opportunities amid Economic Turbulence: A.T. Kearney Global Services Location Index, 2011.* Chicago: A.T. Kearney Global Services Location Index.

Acemoglu, Daron, and David Autor. 2011. "Skills, Tasks and Technologies: Implications for Employment and Earnings." In *Handbook of Labor Economics* Volume 4, ed. Orley Ashenfelter and David E. Card. Amsterdam: Elsevier.

Aedo, Cristian, Jesko Hentschel, Javier Luque, and Martin Moreno. 2012. "Skills Around the World: Structure and Recent Dynamics." Background paper for the WDR 2013.

Andrees, Beate, and Patrick Belser. 2009. *Forced Labour: Coercion and Exploitation in the Private Economy*. Geneva: International Labour Organization.

Assaad, Ragui. 2012. "The MENA Paradox: Higher Education but Lower Job Quality." In *Moving Jobs to the Center Stage*. Berlin: BMZ (Bundesministerium für Wirstchaftliche Zussamenarbeit), Berlin Workshop Series.

Assaad, Ragui, and Ghada Barsoum. 2007. "Youth Exclusion in Egypt: In Search of 'Second Chances.'" Middle East Youth Initiative Working Paper Series 2, Wolfensohn Center for Development, Dubai School of Government, Dubai.

Autor, David H., and David Dorn. 2011. "The Growth of Low-Skill Service Jobs and the Polarization of the U.S. Labor Market." Massachusetts Institute of Technology, Cambridge, MA. Processed.

Autor, David H., Frank Levy, and Richard J. Murnane. 2003. "The Skill Content of Recent Technological Change: An Empirical Exploration." *Quarterly Journal of Economics* 118 (4): 1279–333.

Bajaj, Vikas. 2011. "Outsourcing Giant Finds It Must Be Client, Too." *New York Times*, November 30.

Banerjee, Abhijit V., and Esther Duflo. 2011. *Poor Economics: A Radical Rethinking of the Way to Fight Global Poverty*. New York: Public Affairs.

Bardasi, Elena, and Quentin Wodon. 2006. "Poverty Reduction from Full Employment: A Time Use Approach." Munich Personal RePEc Archive Paper 11084, Munich.

———. 2010. "Working Long Hours and Having No Choice: Time Poverty in Guinea." *Feminist Economics* 16 (3): 45–78.

Basu, Kaushik. 1999. "Child Labor: Cause, Consequence, and Cure, with Remarks on International Labor Standards." *Journal of Economic Literature* 37 (3): 1083–119.

Basu, Kaushik, and Zafiris Tzannatos. 2003. "Child Labor and Development: An Introduction." *World Bank Economic Review* 17 (2): 145–6.

Bell, David N. F., and David G. Blanchflower. 2011. "The Crisis, Policy Reactions and Attitudes to Globalization and Jobs." Discussion Paper Series 5680, Institute for the Study of Labor, Bonn.

Bentolila, Samuel, and Gilles Saint-Paul. 2003. "Explaining Movement in the Labor Share." *Contributions to Macroeconomics* 3 (1).

Bhatt, Ela. 2006. *We Are Poor but So Many: The Story of Self-Employed Women in India*. New York: Oxford University Press.

Bhorat, Haroon. 2012. "Temporary Employment Services in South Africa." Background paper for the WDR 2013.

Blades, Derek, Francisco H. G. Ferreira, and Maria Ana Lugo. 2011. "The Informal Economy in Developing Countries: An Introduction." *Review of Income and Wealth* 57 (Special Issue): S1–S7.

Blanchflower, David G., Andrew J. Oswald, and Alois Stutzer. 2001. "Latent Entrepreneurship across Nations." *European Economic Review* 45 (4–6): 680–91.

Boeke, Julius H. 1942. *Economies and Economic Policy in Dual Societies*. Haarlem: Tjeenk Willnik.

Brown, Philip, David Ashton, and Hugh Lauder. 2010. *Skills Are Not Enough: The Globalization of Knowledge and the Future of the UK Economy*. Wath upon Dearne, U.K.: United Kingdom Commission for Employment and Skills.

Burda, Michael C., Daniel S. Hamermesh, and Philippe Weil. 2011. "Total Work, Gender and Social Norms." Working Paper Series 13000, National Bureau of Economic Research, Cambridge, MA.

Charmes, Jacques. 2006. "A Review of Empirical Evidence on Time Use in Africa from UN-Sponsored Surveys." In *Gender, Time Use, and Poverty in Sub-Saharan Africa*, ed. C. Mark Blackden and Quentin Wodon, 39–72. Washington, DC: World Bank.

Chen, Shaohua, and Martin Ravallion. 2010. "The Developing World Is Poorer Than We Thought, but No Less Successful in the Fight against Poverty." *Quarterly Journal of Economics* 125 (4): 1577–625.

Chenery, Hollis Burnley, and Moises Syrquin. 1975. *Patterns of Development, 1957–1970*. London: Oxford University Press.

Cho, Yoonyoung, and David Newhouse. 2010. "How Did the Great Recession Affect Different Types of Workers? Evidence from 17 Middle-Income Countries." Discussion Paper Series 5681, Institute for the Study of Labor, Bonn.

Cigno, Alessandro, and Furio C. Rosati. 2005. *The Economics of Child Labour*. Oxford: Oxford University Press.

Clark, Colin. 1940. *The Conditions of Economic Progress*. London: Macmillan & Company.

Del Carpio, Ximena, and Norman Loayza. 2012. "The Impact of Wealth on the Amount and Quality of Child Labor." Policy Research Working Paper Series 5959, World Bank, Washington, DC.

Dillon, Andrew, Elena Bardasi, Kathleen Beegle, and Pieter Serneels. 2012. "What Explains Variation in Child Labor Statistics? Evidence from a Survey Experiment in Tanzania." *Journal of Development Economics* 98 (1): 136–47.

Dourgarian, Gregg. 2011. "Five Staffing Industry Trends for 2011." *Staffing Talk*, January 3.

Edmonds, Eric. 2008. "Child Labor." In *Handbook of Development Economics*, Vol. 4, ed. T. Paul Shultz and John Strauss, 3607–709. Oxford: North Holland Elsevier.

Falco, Paolo, William Maloney, Bob Rijkers, and Mauricio Sarrias. 2012. "Subjective Well-Being, Informality, and Preference Heterogeneity in Africa." Background paper for the WDR 2013.

Fallon, Peter, and Robert Lucas. 2002. "The Impact of Financial Crises on Labor Markets, Household Incomes and Poverty: A Review of Evidence." *World Bank Research Observer* 17 (1): 21–45.

Farber, Henry S. 2011. "Job Loss in the Great Recession: Historical Perspective from the Displaced Workers Survey, 1984–2010." Discussion Paper Series 5696, Institute for the Study of Labor, Bonn.

Feenstra, Robert C. 2010. *Offshoring in the Global Economy: Microeconomic Structure and Macroeconomic Implications.* Cambridge, MA: MIT Press.

Freeman, Richard B. 2008. "The New Global Labor Market." *Focus* 26 (1): 1–6.

Freeman, Richard, Remco H. Oostendorp, and Davin Chor. 2011. "The Standardized ILO October Inquiry 1953–2008." National Bureau of Economic Research, Cambridge, MA.

Freeman, Richard, and Ronald Schettkat. 2005. "Marketization of Household Production and the EU-US Gap in Work." *Economic Policy* 20 (41): 5–50.

Freije-Rodriguez, Samuel, Gladys Lopez-Acevedo, and Eduardo Rodriguez-Oreggia. 2011. "Effects of the 2008–09 Economic Crisis on Labor Markets in Mexico." Policy Research Working Paper Series 5840, World Bank, Washington, DC.

Gálvez-Muñoz, Lina, Paula Rodríguez-Modroño, and Mónica Domínguez-Serrano. 2011. "Work and Time Use By Gender: A New Clustering of European Welfare Systems." *Feminist Economics* 17 (4): 125–57.

Gammage, Sarah. 2010. "Time Pressed and Time Poor: Unpaid Household Work in Guatemala." *Feminist Economics* 16 (3): 79–112.

Ghose, Ajit K., Nomaan Majid, and Christoph Ernst. 2008. *The Global Employment Challenge.* Geneva: International Labour Organization.

Giles, John, Albert Park, Fang Cai, and Yang Du. 2012. "Weathering a Storm: Survey-Based Perspectives on Employment in China in the Aftermath of the Global Financial Crisis." Policy Research Working Paper Series 5984, World Bank, Washington, DC.

Gindling, T. H., and David Newhouse. 2012. "Self-Employment in the Developing World." Background paper for the WDR 2013.

Goswami, Arti Grover, Aaditya Mattoo, and Sebastián Sáez, eds. 2011. *Exporting Services: A Developing Country Perspective.* Washington, DC: World Bank.

Gratton, Lynda. 2011. *The Shift: The Future of Work Is Already Here.* London: HarperCollins.

Guha-Khasnobis, Basudeb, and Ravi Kanbur, eds. 2006. *Informal Labour Markets and Development.* New York: Palgrave Macmillan.

Guscina, Anastasia. 2006. *Effects of Globalization on Labor's Share in National Income.* Washington, DC: International Monetary Fund.

Harris, John R., and Michael P. Todaro. 1970. "Migration, Unemployment and Development: A Two-Sector Analysis." *American Economic Review* 60 (1): 126–42.

Hart, Keith. 1973. "Informal Income Opportunities and Urban Employment in Ghana." *Journal of Modern African Studies* 11 (1): 61–89.

Hazarika, Gautam, and Sudipta Sarangi. 2008. "Household Access to Microcredit and Child Work in Rural Malawi." *World Development* 36 (5): 843–59.

Herrmann, Michael, and Haider Khan. 2008. "Rapid Urbanization, Employment Crisis and Poverty in African LDCs: A New Development Strategy and Aid Policy." Munich Personal RePEc Archive Paper 9499, Munich.

Hirway, Indira, and Sunny Jose. 2012. "Understanding Women's Work Using Time-Use Statistics: The Case of India." *Feminist Economics* 17 (4): 67–92.

Holzer, Harry, and Robert Lerman. 2009. *The Future of Middle-Skill Jobs.* Washington, DC: Center on Children and Families, Brookings Institute.

ILO (International Labour Organization). 1972. *Employment, Incomes and Equality: A Strategy for Increasing Productive Employment in Kenya.* Geneva: ILO.

———. 1982. Resolution Concerning Statistics of the Economically Active Population, Employment, Unemployment and Underemployment. Adopted by the Thirteenth International Conference of Labour Statisticians, ILO, Geneva, October 29.

———. 1998. Declaration on Fundamental Principles and Rights at Work. Adopted by the International Labour Conference at its Eighty-sixth Session, ILO, Geneva, June 18.

———. 2007. Resolution Concerning Updating the International Standard Classification of Occupations. Adopted by the Tripartite Meeting of Experts on Labour Statistics on Updating the International Standard Classification of Occupations, ILO, Geneva, December 6.

———. 2008a. Resolution Concerning Statistics of Child Labour. Adopted by the Eighteenth International Conference of Labour Statisticians, ILO, December 5.

———. 2008b. *Skills for Improved Productivity, Employment Growth and Development.* Geneva: ILO.

———. 2009a. *Protecting People, Promoting Jobs: A Survey of Country Employment and Social Protection Policy Responses to the Global Economic Crisis.* Geneva: ILO.

———. 2009b. *Report of the Conference, 18th International Conference of Labour Statisticians.* Geneva: ILO.

———. 2009c. *The Cost of Coercion.* Geneva: ILO.

———. 2010. *Accelerating Action against Child Labour.* Geneva: ILO.

———. 2011. *Private Employment Agencies, Promotion of Decent Work and Improving the Functioning of Labour Markets in Private Services Sectors.* Geneva: ILO.

———. 2012a. *Global Employment Trends 2012: Preventing a Deeper Jobs Crisis.* Geneva: ILO.

———. 2012b. *ILO Global Estimate of Forced Labour 2012: Results and Methodology.* Geneva: ILO.

———. 2012c. NORMLEX Database: Information System on International Labour Standards. ILO, Geneva. http://www.ilo.org/dyn/normlex/en/f?p=NORMLEXPUB:1:0.

ILO and World Bank. 2012. *Inventory of Policy Responses to the Financial and Economic Crisis: Joint Synthesis Report.* Washington, DC: ILO and World Bank.

INEGI (Instituto Nacional de Estadística y Geografía de México). 2011. *Sistema de Cuentas Nacionales de México. Cuenta Satélite del Trabajo no Remunerado de los Hogares de México, 2003–2009.* Mexico, DF: INEGI.

IOM (International Organization for Migration). 2008. *World Migration Report 2008: Managing Labor Mobility in the Evolving Global Economy.* Geneva: IOM.

———. 2010. *World Migration Report 2010—The Future of Migration: Building Capacities for Change.* Geneva: IOM.

Ivanic, Maros, and Will Martin. 2008. "Implications of Higher Global Food Prices for Poverty in Low-Income Countries." *Agricultural Economics* 39 (1): 405–16.

Kanamori, Tokishi, and Zhijun Zhao. 2004. *Private Sector Development in the People's Republic of China.* Manila: Asian Development Bank Institute.

Kanbur, Ravi. 2009. "Conceptualizing Informality: Regulation and Enforcement." *Indian Journal of Labour Economics* 52 (1): 33–42.

Khanna, Gaurav, David Newhouse, and Pierella Paci. 2010. "Fewer Jobs or Smaller Paychecks? Labor Market Impacts of the Recent Crisis in Middle-Income Countries." Economic Premise April 2010, Number 11, Poverty Reduction and Equity Group and the Human Development Network Social Protection Division, World Bank, Washington, DC.

Kovrova, Irina, Scott Lyon, and Furio Camillo Rosati. 2012. "NEET Youth Dynamics in Indonesia and Brazil: A Cohort Analysis." Background paper for the WDR 2013.

Kuznets, Simon. 1966. *Modern Economic Growth.* New Haven, CT: Yale University Press.

Lee, Sangheon, Deidre McCann, and Jon C. Messenger. 2007. *Working Time around the World.* New York: Routledge; Geneva: International Labour Organization.

Lewis, W. Arthur. 1954. "Economic Development with Unlimited Supplies of Labor." *The Manchester School* 22 (2): 139–91.

Losch, Bruno, Sandrine Freguin-Gresh, and Eric Thomas White. 2012. *Structural Transformation and Rural Change Revisited: Challenges for Late Developing Countries in a Globalizing World.* Washington, DC: World Bank.

Lübker, Malte. 2007. "Labour Shares." Technical Brief 1, International Labour Organization, Geneva.

Lucas, Robert E. B. 2005. *International Migration and Economic Development: Lessons from Low-Income Countries.* Cheltenham, U.K.: Edward Elgar Publishing.

Lyon, Scott, Furio C. Rosati, and Lorenzo Guarcello. 2012. "At the Margins: Young People neither in Education nor in Employment." Background paper for the WDR 2013.

Maddison, Angus. 2001. *The World Economy: A Millennial Perspective.* Paris: Organisation for Economic Co-operation and Development.

McCulloch, Neil, Amit Grover, and Asep Suryahadi. 2011. *The Labor Market Impact of the 2009 Financial Crisis in Indonesia.* Sussex, U.K.: Institute of Development Studies.

McKinsey Global Institute. 2011. *An Economy That Works: Job Creation and America's Future.* Washington, DC: McKinsey Global Institute.

Montenegro, Claudio E., and Harry Anthony Patrinos. 2012. "Returns to Schooling around the World." Background paper for the WDR 2013.

Mryyan, Nader. 2012. "Demographics, Labor Force Participation, and Unemployment in Jordan." Working Paper Series 670, Economic Research Forum, Giza, Egypt.

Musgrave, Amy. 2009. "Labor Broking Industry Likely to Face Regulation." *Business Day,* August 25.

Nabli, Mustapha K., Carlos Silva-Jáuregui, and Ahmet Faruk Aysan. 2008. "Authoritarianism, Credibility of Reforms, and Private Sector Development in the Middle East and North Africa." Working Paper Series 443, Economic Research Forum, Cairo.

Narayan, Deepa, Lant Pritchett, and Soumya Kapoor. 2009. *Success from the Bottom Up.* Vol. 2 of *Moving Out of Poverty.* New York: Palgrave Macmillan; Washington, DC: World Bank.

Ngai, Rachel L., and Christopher A. Pissarides. 2008. "Trends in Hours and Economic Growth." *Review of Economic Dynamics* 11 (2): 239–56.

Oostendorp, Remco. 2012. "The Occupational Wages around the World (OWW) Database: Update for

1983–2008." Background paper for the WDR 2013.

Özden, Çaglar, Christopher Parsons, Maurice Schiff, and Terrie L. Walmsley. 2011. "Where on Earth Is Everybody? The Evolution of Global Bilateral Migration 1960–2000." *World Bank Economic Review* 25 (1): 12–56.

Pagés, Carmen, ed. 2010. *The Age of Productivity: Transforming Economies from the Bottom Up.* New York: Palgrave Macmillan.

Perry, Guillermo E., William F. Maloney, Omar S. Arias, Pablo Fajnzylber, Andrew D. Mason, and Jaime Saavedra-Chanduvi. 2007. *Informality: Exit and Exclusion.* Washington, DC: World Bank.

Ranzani, Marco, and Furio Camillo Rosati. 2012. "The NEET Trap: A Dynamic Analysis for Mexico." Background paper for the WDR 2013.

Ramey, Valerie A., and Neville Francis. 2009. "A Century of Work and Leisure." *American Economic Journal: Macroeconomics* 1 (2): 189–224.

Reid, Margaret. 1934. *Economics of Household Production.* New York: John Wiley and Sons.

Robalino, David, David Newhouse, and Friederike Rother. Forthcoming. "Labor and Social Protection Policies during the Crisis and Recovery." In *Labor Markets in Developing Countries during the Great Recession: Impacts and Policy Responses*, ed. Arup Banerji, David Newhouse, David Robalino, and Pierella Paci. Washington, DC: World Bank.

Rodriguez, Francisco, and Arjun Jayadev. 2010. "The Declining Labor Share of Income." Human Development Research Paper 2010/36, United Nations Development Programme, New York.

Rostow, Walt Whitman. 1960. *The Stages of Economic Growth: A Non-Communist Manifesto.* Cambridge, U.K.: Cambridge University Press.

Rozelle, Scott, and Jikun Huang. 2012. "China's Labor Transition and the Future of China's Rural Wages and Employment." Background paper for the WDR 2013.

TeamLease. 2010. *Temp Salary Primer 2010.* Ahmedabad, India: TeamLease Services Pvt. Ltd.

UN (United Nations). 1948. Universal Declaration of Human Rights. Adopted by the UN General Assembly, New York, December 10.

———. 2009. *System of National Accounts.* New York: UN.

———. 2011b. *World Urbanization Prospects: The 2011 Revision.* New York: UN, Department of Economic and Social Affairs.

Vanek, Joann, Martha Chen, Ralf Hussmanns, James Heintz, and Françoise Carré. 2012. *Women and Men in the Informal Economy: A Statistical Picture.* Geneva: Women in Informal Employment: Globalizing and Organizing and International Labour Organization.

World Bank. 2006. *World Development Report 2007: Development and the Next Generation.* Washington, DC: World Bank.

———. 2010. *Stepping Up Skills for More Jobs and Higher Productivity.* Washington, DC: World Bank.

———. 2011a. *Defining Gender in the 21st Century: Talking with Women and Men around the World, A Multi-Country Qualitative Study of Gender and Economic Choice.* Washington, DC: World Bank.

———. 2011b. *More and Better Jobs in South Asia.* Washington, DC: World Bank.

———. 2011c. *World Development Report 2012: Gender Equality and Development.* Washington, DC: World Bank.

———. 2012. *Job Trends.* Washington, DC: World Bank.

Yoshino, Yutaka, ed. 2011. *Industrial Clusters and Micro and Small Enterprises in Africa: From Survival to Growth.* World Bank Directions in Development Series. Washington, DC: World Bank.

Jobs are transformational

Introduction to Part 1

Economic development is about improvements in living standards supported by productivity growth. It also involves social change associated with urbanization, integration in the world economy, and the drive toward gender equality. All of these transformations are related to jobs. The development process is about some jobs becoming better and others disappearing, about people taking jobs and changing jobs, and about jobs migrating to other places within and across countries. Development often entails the movement of labor from rural, agricultural, and mostly subsistence activities to urban, nonagricultural, and mostly market-oriented activities. This movement transforms the lives of families and communities, the organization of firms, and the norms and values of societies. It can boost productivity and improve living standards and also affect the cohesiveness of society. Jobs are thus a key driver of development.

- *Living standards:* Jobs provide earnings opportunities to lift people out of poverty, raise their consumption, and contribute to individual well-being more broadly.

- *Productivity:* Through job creation and destruction within sectors and reallocations across sectors and countries, jobs are also at the root of economic growth.

- *Social cohesion:* Jobs define who people are in many ways; by shaping values and be-

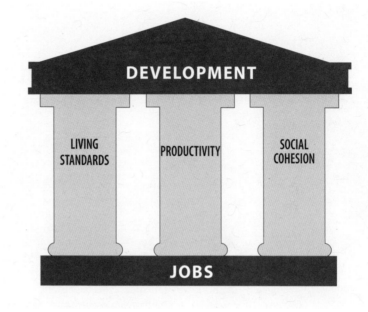

haviors, they can influence trust and civic engagement.

Distinguishing these three transformations provides an understanding of how jobs contribute to development. People's well-being is the ultimate goal, and the transformation of living standards captures this link directly. But sustained improvements in living standards are impossible without productivity growth or when resources are wasted through confrontation. That is why it is necessary to look at the three transformations jointly.

CHAPTER 2

Jobs and living standards

Jobs are the main source of income for the majority of households and a key driver of poverty reduction. But their contribution to well-being goes beyond the earnings they provide.

Jobs are the most important determinant of living standards around the world. For the vast majority of people, their work is the main source of income, especially in the poorest countries. And jobs-related events are the most frequent reasons for families to escape or fall into poverty. Furthermore, as earnings increase, individual choices expand—household members can opt to stay out of the labor force or to work fewer hours and dedicate more time to education, retirement, or family. Opportunities for gainful work, including in farming and self-employment, offer households the means to increase consumption and reduce its variability. Higher crop yields, access to small off-farm enterprise activities, the migration of family members to cities, and transitions to wage employment are milestones on the path to prosperity.

In addition to their fundamental and immediate contribution to earnings, jobs affect other dimensions of well-being, positively and negatively. Not having a job undermines mental health, especially in countries where wage employment is the norm and the lack of employment opportunities translates into open unemployment rather than underemployment. But a job prone to occupational accidents or work-related diseases can damage physical health or worse. More generally, monetary, nonmonetary, and even subjective characteristics of jobs can all have an impact on well-being (box 2.1).

Jobs also influence how workers see themselves and relate to others. Most people feel that jobs should be meaningful and contribute to society. Together with other objective job characteristics, the self-esteem a job provides is an important determination of satisfaction with life.

Jobs improve material well-being

Over the course of a country's development, higher productivity and labor earnings allow households to allocate more time to investment and consumption activities and less to production. Thus, schooling and retirement gain importance relative to work. For the past century or so, the number of hours worked by youth in industrial countries has declined steadily as access to education has increased. Similarly, the number of years in retirement has increased in parallel with longer life expectancy.[1] Higher earnings also facilitate longer periods of job seeking, especially among younger household members, often leading to higher unemployment rates. Among men and women of prime age (25 to 54), total working hours (market and nonmarket) have remained relatively stable, with the main change being the growing share of market activities among women (figure 2.1). These general trends are not ironclad, however.

BOX 2.1 *There are many dimensions of living standards and many ways to measure them*

Debates on how to define and measure living standards go far back in social sciences. The work by Rowntree and Booth in late 19th century England is usually mentioned as seminal, especially in relation to the measurement of poverty. In the 1930s, the creation of the System of National Accounts concentrated on measuring the total market value of the goods and services produced in an economy and made gross domestic product (GDP) per capita the main indicator of living standards in general. By the 1970s and 1980s, there was a growing agreement that important aspects of well-being, such as health status, or exposure to crime, pollution, and urban congestion, were not fully accounted for in GDP. Research also showed that the distribution of material amenities affected individual well-being. There is now consensus that living standards depend not only on average incomes and consumption but also on access to benefits as diverse as health and education, sanitation and housing, and security and freedom.[a]

There are ongoing systematic efforts to collect individual, household, and community data to better understand and compare living standards in developing and developed countries. Complete poverty profiles for different groups of the population within a country, based on the comparison of income or consumption aggregates to international or national poverty lines, have proliferated. Microdata collection efforts have allowed a close monitoring

of standards of living and poverty reduction worldwide. Advances toward the first Millennium Development Goal (Eradicate extreme poverty) have been documented using global monetary poverty measures. The availability of richer datasets, in turn, has supported the emergence of newer measures of living standards, many of them multidimensional in nature. These measures combine both monetary and nonmonetary indicators of well-being, as well as information on their distribution across different population groups.[b]

Despite this progress, important controversies remain, particularly on which indicators are more appropriate for gauging each dimension of well-being and on the weights that should be attributed to each. Some recent proposals even suggest a revamping of statistical systems to formulate better measures of production that take into consideration changes in the quality of goods, government services, and time allocated to home activities and leisure. There are also proposals to include among measures of living standards subjective indicators of well-being and indicators on the level and sustainability of human, physical, and environmental assets.[c] Other proposals emphasize subjective indicators building on a philosophical point of view.[d] Aggregating indicators and comparing them over time and across space becomes more intricate in this case, because of differences in values and beliefs.

Source: World Development Report 2013 team.

a. Adelman and Morris 1973; Chenery and Syrquin 1975; Nordhaus and Tobin 1973; Sen and Hawthorn 1987; Steckel 1995; Streeten 1979.

b. Among these indicators are the Human Development Index (UNDP 1990), the Human Opportunity Index (Paes de Barros and others 2009), and a large variety of multidimensional poverty indexes (Alkire and Foster 2011; Bourguignon and Chakravarty 2003; Kakwani and Silber 2008). See also OECD 2011.

c. Fitoussi, Sen, and Stiglitz 2010.

d. This is the case, for instance, of the measures of Gross National Happiness in Bhutan by the Center for Bhutan Studies.

The nature of production, consumption, and investment activities varies across countries as well. In some, low hours of work among youth are associated more with idleness than with schooling; in others, schooling has proceeded at an accelerated pace. Similarly, job characteristics change with development. In rural economies where agricultural activities predominate, the purpose of household production is often direct consumption. Less developed economies tend to be characterized by more working time dedicated to jobs without wage payments, including farming and other types of self-employment. Development changes the organization of work from home to market production.[2] As economies develop, more work is remunerated through wages and salaries. This reallocation is usually accompa-

nied by higher market participation among women.[3] Developed and developing economies allocate a similar share of the day to work. But women allocate a larger share than men to activities not directly generating income (figure 2.2).

Jobs do not automatically guarantee sustained improvements in earnings and well-being. Working people often remain mired in poverty. In many countries, adults in poor households are more likely to be working than those in nonpoor households. The poor are not usually characterized by lack of jobs or hours of work; they often have more than one job and work long hours, but their jobs are poorly remunerated (box 2.2).

In more affluent societies, a larger share of income is derived from capital, transfers (social

FIGURE 2.1 *Working hours vary across ages*

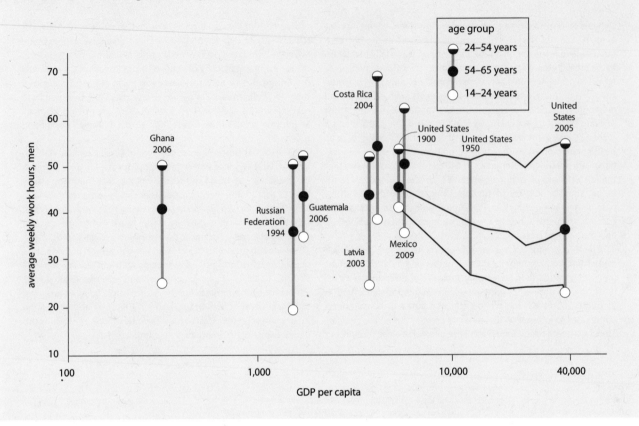

Sources: Berniell and Sanchez-Paramo 2011; Ramey and Francis 2009.
Note: GDP = gross domest product. The vertical axis measures weekly hours spent on production activities (market and nonmarket work), including some outside the boundaries of the system of national accounts, such as child care. The measure does not include time allocated to schooling or leisure. The horizontal axis measures real GDP per capita in 2000 US$.

assistance), or savings (social insurance and pensions). Still, the majority of households worldwide make their living through their work, and labor earnings represent the largest share of total household income (figure 2.3). The main change that comes with development is the composition of labor income.[4]

Job-related events are the main escape route from poverty in developing and developed countries alike. More than two decades of research on poverty dynamics, spanning countries as different as Canada, Ecuador, Germany, and South Africa, show that labor-related events trigger household exits from poverty (figure 2.4). These events range from the head of a household taking a new job, to family members starting to work, to working family members earning more from their labor. In a large set of

qualitative studies in low-income countries, getting jobs and starting businesses were two of the main reasons people gave to explain their rise out of poverty.[5] Conversely, a lack of job opportunities reduces the ability of households to improve their well-being.[6]

Jobs are not the only force that determines whether a household escapes from poverty. Demographic changes, such as the arrival of a newborn, relatives moving in, or a family split because of death or separation, affect expenditures per capita, hence the household's poverty status. The same is true of changes in nonlabor income from assets or transfers, be they private remittances, public social assistance, or pensions. These developments may all interact and often occur simultaneously. For example, the migration of family members to a city for a job may

FIGURE 2.2 *Women spend more time in activities not directly generating income*

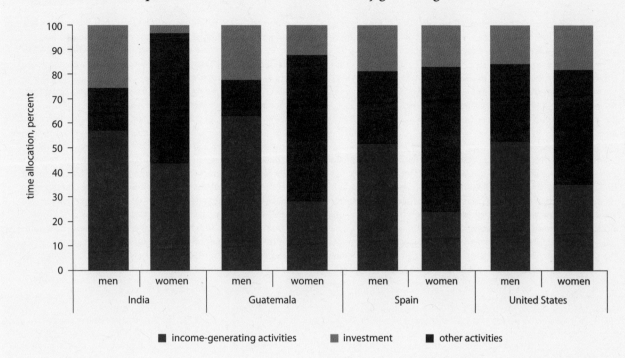

Source: World Development Report 2013 team based on ISSP 2005 for Spain and the United States, 1999 Time Use Survey of India, and 2006 Guatemala Household Survey.
Note: The figure refers to people aged 15 years and more. *Income-generating activities* is the time devoted to wage or salaried employment; farming, own-account work, self-employment with hired labor, and unpaid family labor in household enterprises; *investment* refers to time allocated to education, health care, and job search; *other activities* includes work outside the system of national accounts, for example child care, housework. Leisure and other activities associated with consumption (for example, shopping and social interactions), as well as sleep, are not included.

improve the well-being not only of the migrants but also of those who stay in the rural village. In addition to receiving remittances, those who stay behind may have access to the migrants' land to cultivate and work more as a result.[7]

With all these changes occurring at the same time, gauging the contribution of labor earnings to poverty reduction is difficult. However, recent methods allowing to decompose changes in poverty by sources of income confirm the fundamental contribution of change in labor earnings (figure 2.5). In 10 of 18 countries considered for the analysis, labor income explains more than half of the change in poverty, as measured by the US$2.50-a-day poverty line. In another 5 countries, it accounts for more than a third of the reduction in poverty.[8] A further decomposition of the contribution of labor income to poverty reduction in Bangladesh, Peru, and Thailand found that changes in individual characteristics

(education, work experience, or region of residence) were important, but that the returns to these characteristics mattered more. Among those returns is the relative price of labor.[9]

The connection between jobs and poverty reduction is not mechanistic, and not all transitions out of poverty require a change in the type of work undertaken. Changes in the productivity of the same job may also be at play. In Bangladesh and Vietnam, for example, poverty transitions have been dominated not by changes in income sources from farm to nonfarm income, but by higher income within the same sector.[10]

Richer insights on the connection between labor-related events and transitions out of poverty can be obtained from studies that follow the same households over extended periods of time. Studies in several countries in Asia and in Sub-Saharan Africa show that farming and off-farm activities are intricately related and not

BOX 2.2 *Most poor people work*

It is not lack of work that defines the poor. This realization has brought to the fore the concept of the working poor, and questions about who they are, and why they remain poor even when they have jobs. First studied by researchers in some countries such as the United States, this concept of the working poor is now recognized globally. The International Labour Organization (ILO) has included the working poor in its statistics since the mid-1990s, and measurements of this group have been added as a Millennium Development indicator.

The working poor are defined as employed persons in households whose members are living below one of the two international poverty lines—either US$1.25 or US$2 a day.[a] Household expenditure surveys allow for a classification of the population as poor and nonpoor, based on the level of consumption per person. These surveys also provide information on household members who work. According to the ILO's most recent estimate, 910 million workers—nearly 30 percent of total global employment—were living on less than US$2 a day.[b] The incidence is much higher among low-income countries. It reaches 63.7 percent in Africa and 54.2 percent in Asia.[c]

Caution is needed in interpreting this concept, however. Outside the group of the working poor, there may be individuals who have very low labor earnings but whose expenditures are above the poverty line because they have other sources of income such as private transfers or earnings from social insurance or social assistance programs. In other words, being excluded from the category of working poor does not mean one has high labor earnings.

Another concept that indicates whether job earnings are sufficient to ensure an adequate standard of living for a person or a household is the living wage. This is the level of earnings that would provide a satisfactory standard of living to workers and their families. But moving from this definition to measurement is difficult. With more than half of all working people engaged in nonwage work, accurate measures of labor earnings may not be available. Moreover, there are diverse interpretations of what constitutes a standard family and a lack of consensus on computation methods.[d] An alternative is measuring the percentage of the population that cannot reach the poverty line with labor incomes only, as the Poverty Labor Trend Index in Mexico does.[e]

Source: World Development Report 2013 team.
Notes: For a review of the working poor in developed countries, see Blank, Danziger, and Schoeni (2006) and Brady, Fullerton, and Cross (2010); for developing countries, see Fields (2011). The content and scope of the Millennium Development Goals can be found in United Nations, "We Can End Poverty, 2015: Millennium Development Goals," United Nations, New York.
a. Indicator 18, "Poverty, income distribution and the working poor," KILM (Key Indicators of the Labour Market) (database), 7th ed. 2011, International Labour Organization, Geneva.
b. ILO 2011, 41–42.
c. Estimates are for 2009 for a selection of low-income countries from the ILO KILM.
d. Anker 2011.
e. Poverty Labor Trend Index, National Council for the Evaluation of Social Development Policy (CONEVAL), Mexico City.

FIGURE 2.3 *Jobs are the most important source of household income*

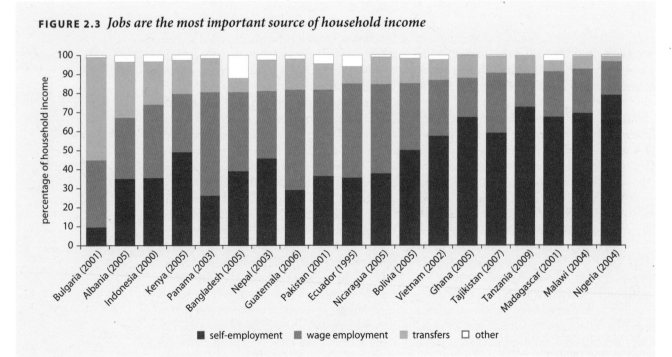

Source: Covarrubias and others 2012 for the World Development Report 2013.

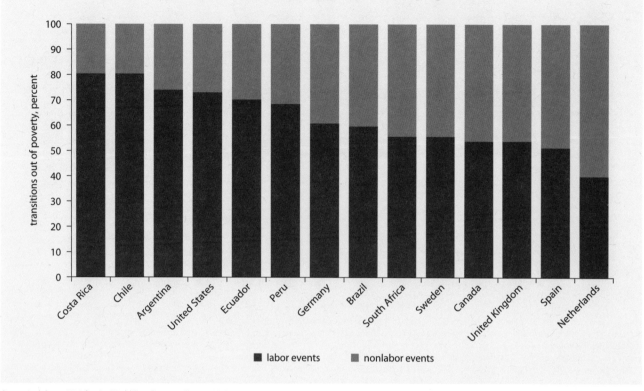

FIGURE 2.4 *Jobs take households out of poverty, especially in developing countries*

labor events   nonlabor events

Source: Inchauste 2012 for the World Development Report 2013.
Note: Nonlabor events include changes in nonlabor earnings (such as rents or pensions) and demographic changes. A trigger event is defined as the most important event occurring during a poverty reduction spell among a set of mutually exclusive categories of events such as changes in family structure, in sources of income, and in needs of the household.

necessarily substitutes for each other. Access to land, increases in farm yields, and access to markets are fundamental for the growth of off-farm jobs and hence for diversification in family incomes.[11] Simply having work is not what matters most, according to these studies, since most people work in rural economies. What is important for escaping poverty is deriving greater earnings from work.

Other factors of production are critical for explaining poverty reduction through jobs, particularly in rural areas. Studies from Uganda and Pakistan, using rural data spanning 4 and 10 years respectively, show that higher agricultural productivity, the growing commercialization of agriculture, and an increase in cash crop production contributed substantially to poverty reduction. The increase in the price of cash crops over this period also helped.[12] Improvements in land rights and better access to input and output markets, due to infrastructure in-

vestments, also raised the odds of escaping poverty, particularly in Uganda. All of these factors affect the labor productivity of farmers but originate in land markets or food markets rather than labor markets.

The largest poverty reductions documented are associated with jobs in agriculture. The cases of China and Vietnam, in the 1980s and 1990s respectively, testify to the importance of agricultural productivity and the forces unleashed by land reform, investments in rural infrastructure, and off-farm job opportunities.[13] In rural China, poverty reduction was associated with off-farm activities, but the workers engaged in these activities tended to be those who had benefited from increased farm incomes and by obtaining more education.[14] Furthermore, easier access to off-farm employment and opportunities for migration reduced the exposure of households to income shocks. A similar pattern of events has been documented in other Asian and Sub-

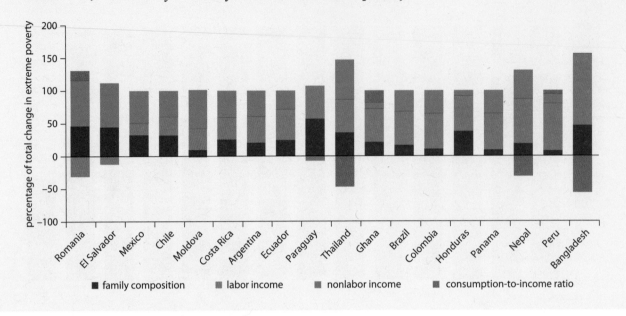

FIGURE 2.5 *Jobs account for much of the decline in extreme poverty*

■ family composition   ■ labor income   ■ nonlabor income   ■ consumption-to-income ratio

Sources: Azevedo and others 2012; Inchauste and others 2012; both for the World Development Report 2013.

Note: Family composition indicates the change in the share of adults (ages 18 and older) within the household. *Labor income* refers to the change in employment and earnings for each adult. *Nonlabor income* refers to changes in other sources of income such as transfers, pensions, and imputed housing rents. If a bar is located below the horizontal axis, it means that that source would have increased, instead of decreased, poverty. The changes are computed for Argentina (2000–10); Bangladesh (2000–10); Brazil (2001–09); Chile (2000–09); Colombia (2002–10); Costa Rica (2000–08); Ecuador (2003–10); El Salvador (2000–09); Ghana (1998–2005); Honduras (1999–2009); Mexico (2000–10); Moldova (2001–10); Panama (2001–09); Paraguay (1999–2010); Peru (2002–10); Nepal (1996–2003); Romania (2001–09); and Thailand (2000–09). The changes for Bangladesh, Ghana, Moldova, Nepal, Peru, Romania, and Thailand are computed using consumption-based measures of poverty, while the changes for the other countries are based on income measures.

Saharan African countries. Whereas poverty reduction in rural areas in Asia is associated with diversification into nonfarm activities, in Sub-Saharan Africa, it may be more closely associated with increases in farm productivity.[15]

Jobs and relapses into poverty are also connected. Widespread shocks such as droughts, floods, and conflicts can drive households into poverty or even chronic poverty. Events specific to individuals, such as illness or poor health of the head of household, can have the same effect. In these cases it is not joblessness per se that pushes families into poverty but rather the destruction of personal and household assets.[16] And even taking these shocks into account, job loss of the head of household remains a critical determinant of a fall into poverty.[17]

The poor clearly rely on their labor to make a living. The death or disability of an income earner significantly increases the odds of falling into poverty or remaining poor, particularly among households with few assets. Studies from Uganda and Pakistan show that the share of household members who work also has a considerable impact. Households with rising dependency ratios were more likely to remain poor or fall into poverty, while households whose share of working-age adults increased were less likely to fall into poverty or remain in a state of poverty.[18]

Jobs are more than just earnings

Jobs have consequences beyond wages and earnings. Other aspects such as workplace safety, stability, commuting time, learning and advancement opportunities, entitlements to pension benefits, and other amenities are highly valued by some workers. However, quantifying the monetary value of these other aspects of a job is not easy. Comparable surveys in Jianyang,

BOX 2.3 *The value of job attributes can be quantified through hedonic pricing*

Workers place a value on jobs that goes beyond income. At the individual level, people assess the impact a job might have on their physical and mental well-being, as well as on their families. In addition to the earnings the job provides, they can value the stability of a job, its earnings, the possibilities of advancement, or the flexibility of working hours. Workers might also value how well a job connects them to society, the prestige associated with it, or its contribution to social goals.

Hedonic pricing assesses how people value specific job characteristics through their job satisfaction or happiness more broadly. Indicators of subjective well-being are linked through statistical analysis to various job characteristics, including earnings. Statistical methods can be used to assess the contribution of each of these job characteristics to happiness or job satisfaction.

The weights associated with different job characteristics in the estimated hedonic price function allow an assessment of the value workers attach to each job characteristic. The monetary value of a job characteristic can be assessed by comparing the corresponding weight in the hedonic price function with the weight of earnings. Thus, for instance, a hedonic function reveals the share of earnings respondents would be willing to forgo in exchange for stability, or for creativity at work, or for a job providing voice in the workplace.[b]

Using surveys commissioned for this Report, hedonic valuation of health insurance benefits range from 1.5 percent of hourly wages in Colombia and China to 4.2 percent in Egypt and 5.1 percent in Sierra Leone.[a] This is significantly lower than the explicit valuations answered by those surveyed: 4.9 percent in China, 10 percent in Colombia and Sierra Leone, and, at the highest, 25 percent in Egypt. This indicates that the revealed preference of individuals for health insurance benefits in the job are lower than the price they express they would be willing to pay. Hedonic pricing can also identify the revealed preference to pay for other less tangible job characteristics. Salaried workers in Colombia, China, and Egypt would forgo up to 1.5 percent of hourly wages for jobs that are "meaningful." In Egypt, salaried workers reveal a price tag equivalent of up to 2.1 percent of hourly wages for jobs that are non-manual or nonroutine.

This approach is especially relevant in the assessment of job benefits. These benefits involve a deduction from earnings in exchange for access to a pension in old age, for instance. Jobholders typically value these benefits, but they may value them less than the associated deductions in earnings through social security contributions. If the expected value of the pension is low or uncertain, they may prefer to remain in the informal sector. In contrast, a well-designed program that allows longevity risks to be pooled with other jobholders may be valued by the jobholder more than the deductions associated with participation.

Source: World Development Report 2013 team.
a. Calculations by the World Development Report 2013 team of the FAFO (Forskningsstiftelsen Fafo [Fafo Research Foundation]) 2012 Survey on Good Jobs.
b. Recent examples are Hintermann, Alberini, and Markandya 2010 and Falco and others 2012.

China; Risaralda, Colombia; Cairo and Fayoum, the Arab Republic of Egypt; and Port Loko and Free Town, Sierra Leone, showed the limited ability of respondents to attach a monetary value to job benefits, despite expressing willingness to pay.[19] Among those who do give an explicit valuation, the willingness to pay for pension benefits goes from 5 percent of monthly wages in China to 7 percent in Colombia and 13 percent in Egypt. Lower values are given for transportation allowances (2, 1, and 7 percent, respectively), but having a permanent contract is valued more, especially in Egypt (3, 8, and 22 percent, respectively) (box 2.3).

Characteristics of jobs have other less tangible, but no less real, effects on well-being. In particular, jobs can have a direct impact on workers' health, a key component of human development and personal well-being (box 2.4). Exposure to hazardous substances causes an estimated 651,000 deaths annually, mainly in developing countries. Work-related acci-

dents and diseases kill an average of 6,000 people a day, or 2.2 million a year. Most of these deaths (1.7 million) result from work-related diseases; the remainder is linked to fatal accidents in the workplace and during commutes to or from work.[20] Every year, more than 400 million people (nearly 15 percent of the global labor force) suffer from occupational accidents or illnesses involving work-related diseases. In some cases, the incidence is intolerably high: half of slate pencil workers in India and 37 percent of the miners in Latin America suffer from some stage of silicosis (an occupational lung disease caused by inhalation of silica dust).[21] Mental health can be threatened by abusive relations between managers and workers and sexual harassment. Health risks are not confined to wage employment. Collecting and carrying water or cooking over open stoves, as many self-employed workers do, poses risks, and these risks are more likely to affect women than men.[22]

BOX 2.4 *Work can pose risks to health and safety*

Surveys of workers in garment factories in three countries underscore the health and safety hazards they face in their jobs. Garment workers in Indonesia, Jordan, and Haiti have reported physical stresses linked to work, including hunger, thirst, and severe fatigue.

In Indonesia, more than half the workers surveyed reported that they had experienced severe thirst often or every day. Heat is a likely contributor. Asked whether the factory is too hot or too cold, only about half (52 percent) reported that temperature was not a concern. Occupational safety is an issue for many: 59 percent of workers reported concerns about dangerous equipment; 73 percent were concerned about accidents; 64 percent, about dusty or polluted air; and 69 percent, about chemical odors.

In factories in Jordan, 37 percent of workers reported concerns about dangerous equipment, and 45 percent reported concerns about accidents and injuries.

In Haiti, 40 percent of workers reported that they had experienced severe fatigue or exhaustion occasionally, often, or every day; 41 percent reported frequent headaches, dizziness, backaches, or neck aches. A stunning 63 percent of workers reported that they had experienced severe thirst often or every day.

Source: IFC and ILO 2011.

Occupational accidents and work-related diseases have economic costs. These costs are difficult to compute because the estimates ought to include spending on health care and sickness benefits, as well as the forgone earnings from workdays lost. Estimating these costs is particularly difficult in the case of the self-employed. The few studies that have tried to do so suggest that the burden on society could be high. In Spain, in the industrial sector alone, these costs were estimated to amount to 1.72 percent of gross domestic product (GDP) in 2004. In Mauritius, the cost of work-related injuries represented around 2.8 percent of GDP in 2003.[23] Global estimates put the cost associated with work-related sickness at around 4 percent of GDP.[24]

Opportunities to participate in labor markets for people with disabilities vary across countries. The employment ratio of people with disabilities ranges from 70 percent, in Poland, to 20 percent, in Switzerland and Zambia, lower than the ratio for the overall population.[25] Disabilities may be preexisting conditions or the result of job-related injuries or conditions. Different labor outcomes among persons with disabilities stem from productivity differentials, from disincentives created by the system of social benefits, and from discrimination. In any case, a lower employment rate is one of the main channels through which disability may lead to poverty.

In countries where wage employment is the norm, joblessness may severely affect well-being. Together with income, social status has been recognized as an important factor in the development and maintenance of mental health.[26] Studies document the detrimental effects of unemployment and the positive effects when finding a job.[27] Medical research has associated unemployment with stress, depression, heart disease, and alcoholism.[28] Psychological hardship, marital dissolutions, and suicide have also been associated with job loss.[29] Depression and stress-related illnesses are becoming more common with the expansion of outsourcing, labor informality, and mobility in the modern workplace.[30]

The impact of unemployment on mental health appears to occur independently of the availability of social insurance or other mechanisms of protection.[31] This is because the psychological hardship of unemployment is also associated with social stigma. Studies show that a worker who is unemployed or who has a vulnerable job faces less duress if the phenomenon is more pervasive or if there is less inequality in the incidence of unemployment or the distribution of vulnerable jobs. This finding demonstrates the close interaction between a person's job and their place in society.[32]

Jobs and life satisfaction

Happiness, both a personal goal and a social aspiration, is related to employment status. A large body of literature shows that unemployed people report lower happiness and life satisfaction than their employed counterparts.[33] For instance, in Indonesia subjective well-being increases when gaining a job and decreases when losing it.[34] Some researchers argue that this discontent is transitory, but others point out that, as long as concerns about job stability persist, so does unhappiness. This "unhappiness effect" is more typically reported in men than in women, but evidence indicates that women are affected by the unemployment of their spouse.

The lack of employment can lower the self-esteem and undermine the social status of other family members.[35]

When jobs are in short supply and unemployment becomes a problem, people change their expectations and attitudes. Data from the World Value Surveys for a large set of countries (both developed and developing) show that higher unemployment rates are associated with lower ambitions to do meaningful work, perhaps indicating that a lack of available jobs impels individuals to accept any job.

It is not only one's joblessness that may be important to life satisfaction. In the United Kingdom, the unemployed are less unhappy in districts in which the unemployment rate is higher, suggesting that joblessness always hurts but that it hurts less if there are many unemployed people in the local area.[36] The effect on happiness of not having a job seems to be partially offset by the lower social stigma when the lack of jobs is widespread. Joblessness also leads to a loss of contact with people through the workplace and to a contraction in related social networks, which can erode social capital and undermine the sense of engagement with others.[37]

Simply having a job does not guarantee higher life satisfaction. Feeling insecure at work because of earnings variability, job instability, or health and safety concerns also affects a person's sense of well-being (figure 2.6).[38] For wage workers, the type of contract and its duration are important; part-timers and seasonal workers express less job satisfaction. Even workers with long-term contracts may feel insecure.[39] In factories in Haiti, Jordan, and Vietnam, earnings from work did not influence the reported level of life satisfaction, but working conditions did.[40] In more developed countries, jobs that provide more autonomy are linked to higher life satisfaction.[41]

Most research on the links between jobs and life satisfaction has been conducted in settings where wage employment is the norm. A growing literature on life satisfaction in developing regions, where a smaller share of those who work are wage earners, shows that farmers have the lowest levels of life satisfaction relative to other workers and the unemployed (figure 2.7). Meanwhile, wage workers and the self-

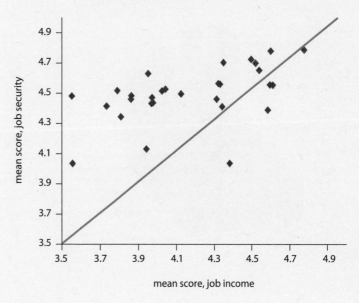

FIGURE 2.6 *Workers often care more about job security than about income*

Source: ISSP 2005.

Note: The analysis covers 29 countries, each represented in the figure by a dot. Respondents scored the importance of job security and job income on a scale from 1 to 5, with 5 = very important, 4 = important, 3 = neither important nor unimportant, 2 = unimportant, 1 = not important at all.

employed have higher levels of satisfaction than the unemployed.

Whether the self-employed express greater satisfaction than wage workers depends on the context. In industrial countries and in Eastern Europe and Central Asia, life satisfaction is, on average, similar among both groups, but in Latin America, it is substantially lower among the self-employed.[42]

Jobs contribute to how people view themselves and relate to others. Most people feel strongly that their jobs should be meaningful and contribute to society. A 2005 survey of 29 countries asked people about the characteristics that they valued in their jobs.[43] Over three-quarters reported that it is important to have a job that is useful to society, and a similar share agreed that it is important that their jobs help other people. In nine countries, the share who reported that it is important for jobs to be socially useful was higher than the share reporting that high income is important. While most of these are high-income countries, preferences for

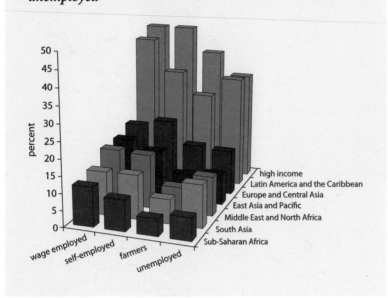

FIGURE 2.7 *Life satisfaction is lower among farmers and the unemployed*

Sources: Gallup 2009, 2010.

socially useful and high-income jobs did not differ greatly in the Dominican Republic, Mexico, or South Africa.

Job satisfaction and other measures of nonmaterial well-being such as happiness or identity may be affected by cultural differences and social norms. Notwithstanding this, other health variables used as proxies of job satisfaction such as absence of fear or sadness also show an association with working conditions. Research for Haiti, Jordan, and Vietnam finds working conditions such as basic hygiene and health, workplace facilities, or presence of unions to be associated with fewer feelings of fear or sadness.[44]

* * *

Jobs have an impact on the well-being of the person who holds them, but they can also have an impact on the well-being of others. Some jobs bring more poverty reduction and, as such, benefit those who consider eradicating poverty to be a fundamental societal goal. Some jobs promote higher employment rates among women, giving more say on the way household resources are allocated, typically leading to greater spending on raising children. Gender equality, much the same as poverty reduction, is a broadly shared societal goal. Jobs that have these additional impacts do more for development. Given such spillover effects, jobs play a fundamental role in the well being of individuals and entire societies. Jobs may thus be the center piece of a development strategy (Question 2).

Rapid and sustained growth is generally viewed as the main priority for developing countries, and as a precondition for continued increases in living standards and strengthened social cohesion. Economic growth, living standards, and social cohesion can indeed move together, and they often do—as shown, for example, by the remarkable experience of East Asian economies, including the Republic of Korea and Singapore.[45] Building on the East Asian experience, the conventional wisdom is to focus on growth and assume that increased living standards and greater social cohesion will follow. This is the main tenet behind "growth strategies," "growth diagnostics," and "binding constraints analyses," all of which aim to identify and remove obstacles to economic growth and to sustain it over prolonged periods of time.

But transformations in living standards, productivity, and social cohesion do not necessarily happen at the same pace. Lags and gaps in rising living standards can be illustrated by the different impacts growth has on poverty reduction across countries. A 2 percent annual growth rate can reduce poverty rates by 1 percent in some countries and by 7 percent in others.[46] Ethiopia, Tanzania, and Zambia experienced periods of economic growth with very little change in poverty incidence.[47] On the other hand, important advances in poverty reduction have also happened during periods of slow growth, as occurred in Brazil and Mexico during the 1990s and the first half of the 2000s.[48] And in some cases, growth is not accompanied by increased social cohesion—even though poverty may fall and living standards improve for some, the expectations of others remain unfulfilled. Tunisia is a clear example in this regard: its growth rate is well above the average of the region, but it has nonetheless experienced serious social and political tensions.[49]

The recognition of these lags and gaps has led to more nuanced approaches to economic growth in which the growth being sought is "pro-poor," "shared," or "inclusive."[50] In these versions, it is not just the rate of growth that matters but also the initial distribution of income and the possibility of redistributing resources through the growth process itself and through government transfers.[51]

Behind these sensible qualifiers, it is possible to point to the role of jobs. Growth is "inclusive" when higher earnings are driven by employment opportunities for the majority of the labor force, particularly the poor. Recent studies show that the impact of economic growth on poverty reduction depends critically on the employment intensity of different sectors.[52] Employment opportunities also matter for social cohesion. It is thus jobs that bring together the three transformations.

Realizing the role jobs play implies going beyond the sequential view in which growth issues are addressed first and employment follows from increased demand. Instead, jobs are seen as a medium that can make the development transformations a reality. From a statistical point of view, the relationship between growth and employment (or unemployment) shows substantial variation over time, across countries, and across sectors. In light of this diversity, a given rate of growth does not guarantee a given level of job creation or a given composition of employment (box 2.5).

When a growth strategy may not be sufficient

Focusing on the aggregate relationship between growth and employment downplays some of the most important channels through which jobs connect to development. The very notion of employment as derived labor demand does not reflect the situation of the many working people in developing countries who are farmers and self-employed. The focus on the labor market as the transmission chain between growth and employment also does not capture the interaction of working people with others in households, at the workplace, and in society more broadly. Focusing solely on the relationship between growth and employment may fail to measure how jobs can foster gender equality, support urbanization, or contribute

BOX 2.5 *The relationship between growth and employment is not mechanical*

The statistical connection between economic growth and employment is sometimes termed Okun's Law. In 1962 Arthur Okun found that in the years immediately following World War II, a 1 percent increase in gross domestic product (GDP) in the United States brought about a 0.3 percent decline in unemployment. Since then, this empirical regularity has found support in a wide variety of countries. Recent research, however, suggests that Okun's Law is not as stable as its name implies.[a]

The debate on the stability of Okun's Law sheds light on the characteristics of economic recessions and expansions. A recent study indicates that, in industrial countries, unemployment has become more responsive to output declines over the past 20 years. This has been attributed to institutional reforms that have made labor markets more flexible. Interestingly, economies that suffer financial crises and large housing price busts (such as the United States and Spain in recent years) have deeper and longer increases in unemployment than Okun's Law would have predicted; whereas economies with large short-time work schemes (like Germany, Italy, Japan, and the Netherlands) show less unemployment than predicted.[b]

While Okun's Law relates to unemployment, other studies focus on the growth elasticity of employment. In its simplest form, this elasticity is the ratio between the percentage change in employment and the percentage change in GDP. These elasticities show great variability over time and space, too, making it difficult to forecast net job creation over the course of development. For instance, in Tanzania growth elasticities of employment declined from 1.04 in the period 1992–96 to 0.27 in the period 2004–08. Similar trends have been reported for Ethiopia, Ghana, and Mozambique.[c] In Latin America, recent estimates show that growth elasticities of employment were much lower during the global financial crisis than in previous crises. In other words, the Great Recession produced comparatively less net employment destruction in that region.[d]

While employment and unemployment are aggregates, growth may also affect the composition of unemployment. Important controversies, such as why manufacturing employment in India has stagnated despite rapid growth in the sector can be interpreted in this light.[e] Other studies show that, given their different labor intensities, economic growth in some sectors like agriculture, construction, or services generates more employment than does economic growth in manufacturing.[f] Investment projects in agribusiness in Ukraine, in construction in India, and in tourism in Rwanda have had large employment impacts, not only because of the direct jobs created but also because of indirect job creation in their large network of distribution channels.[g]

Source: World Development Report 2013 team.
a. Cazes, Verick, and Al Hussami 2011; Moosa 2012.
b. Balakrishnan, Das, and Kannan 2009.
c. Martins 2012 for the World Development Report 2013.
d. World Bank 2010.
e. Bhalotra 1998; Roy 2004.
f. Arias-Vasquez and others 2012 for the World Development Report 2013.
g. IFC, forthcoming.

to peaceful collective decision making. Understanding how to enhance these positive spillovers from jobs might be difficult when only aggregates are considered.

The case of urbanizing economies such as Bangladesh may support the idea that the three major transformations happen simultaneously. Taking advantage of their abundance of relatively low-skilled labor, such economies can engage in world markets through light manufacturing. Wage employment is created in large numbers, providing opportunities for rural migrants, and cushioning social tensions at a time of rapid social change. In Bangladesh, the expansion of the light manufacturing sector has allowed for the integration of young women into the labor market, at a time of falling fertility rates. Employment opportunities for women have in turn led to growing female schooling, better human development outcomes, and faster poverty reduction.

In practice, however, tradeoffs between the three transformations can amount to more than just lags and gaps. Depending on the nature of the jobs challenges facing a country, tensions may emerge between growth that generates jobs for living standards and growth that generates jobs for productivity growth or for social cohesion. Examples abound:

- In agrarian economies, increasing productivity in smallholder farming is fundamental for poverty reduction, given the share of the population living in rural areas. But urban jobs in activities that connect the economy to world markets and global value chains are necessary for growth. With limited resources to support both, a tradeoff between living standards and productivity may arise.

- In resource-rich countries, massive investments in extractive industries support accelerated rates of growth and connections with international markets but generate little direct (or even indirect) employment and often little poverty reduction. Moreover, the abundance of foreign exchange undermines the competitiveness of other activities, making it difficult to create productive jobs in other sectors.

- In countries with high youth unemployment, job opportunities are not commensurate with the expectations created by the expansion of education systems. And the active labor market programs needed to defuse social tensions in the short term may not do much for poverty reduction because many of the jobless come from middle-class families, and devoting public resources to finance them may reduce economic dynamism.

- In formalizing economies, there is an effort to support social cohesion by extending the coverage of social protection to as many workers as possible. Broad coverage regardless of the type of job is often seen as part of a social compact. But extending coverage without distorting incentives to work, save, and participate in formal systems is difficult and may have adverse impacts on productivity and long-term growth.

When a jobs strategy may be appropriate

Tradeoffs between improving living standards, accelerating productivity growth, and fostering social cohesion arguably reflect a measurement problem. While the contribution jobs make to output can be quantified, some of the spillovers from jobs cannot. Measured output does not increase when jobs defuse social tensions, even though these outcomes are valued by society and may increase productivity in the future. Conversely, measured output does not decline when jobs in export sectors are replaced by jobs producing for the domestic market, even though the opportunities to acquire technical and managerial knowledge through work tend to be higher in the export sectors.

If the spillovers from jobs could be appropriately quantified, the tradeoffs would be fully understood and an adequate evaluation of the output and employment potential of a given growth strategy would be possible. For example, fully accounting for the negative impact of current pollution on workers' future health would make a more complete evaluation of the output potential of a growth strategy based on a given technology. Opting for defused tensions or greater integration in world trade would lay the ground for accelerating growth in the future in a sustainable way, which a short-term evaluation based on output growth alone would fail to consider. If measures of growth captured the intangible social benefits from jobs, a growth strategy and a jobs strategy would be equivalent. However, when focusing on measured growth only, spillovers from jobs can easily be overlooked, and this is why a jobs strategy may be needed. By focusing on the spillovers from jobs, a jobs strategy highlights the different outcomes of interest in a development process.

Considering a jobs strategy is a way to call attention to the social value of jobs. A jobs strategy assesses the types of jobs that do more for development in a particular country context. It relies on qualitative and quantitative analyses to identify how jobs contribute to living standards, productivity, and social cohesion. And it seeks to identify where the constraints to the creation of the jobs with the highest development payoff lie in practice. In some cases, a jobs strategy will focus on increasing female labor participation, in others on creating employment opportunities for youth, yet in others on creating a supportive environment for the creation of jobs in cities, or jobs connected to global value chains. This may not be too different from preparing a more comprehensive growth strategy, except that jobs would be center stage.

Jobs strategies are not needed under all circumstances. A jobs strategy is warranted only when potentially important spillovers from jobs are not realized, leading to tensions between living standards, productivity, and social cohesion. When improvements in living standards, productivity, and social cohesion happen together, as was the case in several East Asian countries, and may now be the case in urbanizing economies such as Bangladesh, a growth strategy may be more appropriate. Yet even remarkably successful East Asian economies such as Korea and Singapore, which undoubtedly delivered inclusive growth over many decades, also had jobs strategies at specific points in their development histories (box 2.6).

BOX 2.6 *Korea went from a growth to a jobs strategy, and Singapore the other way around*

The Republic of Korea and Singapore are success stories combining long-term economic growth with rapid poverty reduction and strong social cohesion. But at different points in time, both countries relied on jobs strategies.

Singapore was confronted with a tense social situation at independence, with both high unemployment and inter-ethnic tension. Its first development strategy focused on jobs, housing, and wage moderation. As unemployment subsided, the next strategy was geared toward raising labor costs to encourage higher-value-added activities. This cost drive resulted in a recession, however, and since then Singapore has focused on growth, rather than jobs.

Conversely, Korea abandoned development planning in 1996, but in 2010, it adopted a jobs strategy for the next decade as its highest-level policy document. In October 2010, the Korean government launched the "National Employment Strategy 2020 for the Balance of Growth, Employment and Welfare." In the tradition of long-range plans, this national strategy has a clear target for 2020: an increase in the employment rate of the working-age population (15–64 years) to a minimum of 70 percent—the average among industrial economies. The strategy was rooted in the mismatch between macroeconomic indicators that pointed to a recovering economy and the inability of individuals—especially youth—to find adequate employment.

The strategy identifies four pillars to achieve the 70 percent target. The first recognizes the importance of collaboration between the public and private sectors for employment creation and consists of implementing economic and industrial policies in a job-friendly manner. The second aims at improving flexibility and fairness in the workplace and consists of a series of reforms to increase regulation in certain areas of the labor law, while decreasing regulation in others. Thus the 40-hour workweek became enforceable for all companies, regardless of size,[a] with the obligatory introduction of the *work time savings system*.[b] Simultaneously, regulations on duration of contracts for temporary workers and fixed-term contracts were relaxed to allow for more hiring flexibility. The third pillar focuses on increasing labor force participation and skill development of women, youth, and older workers. This involves developing the option of permanent part-time jobs, thus allowing parents to both work and care for their children, especially in sectors suffering from labor shortages and unable to fill full-time jobs. Older workers would be retained longer in the active labor force by having the option to work shorter hours under the wage peak system.[c] Last but not least, the intention is to facilitate welfare-to-work transitions, by encouraging able-bodied welfare recipients to enroll in employment assistance programs and by reinforcing their obligation to pursue employment.

Sources: World Development Report 2013 team based on Huff 1994, 1995; Republic of Korea 2010.
a. The 40-hour workweek was introduced in 2004 and applied only to companies with over 1,000 employees.
b. This system allows employees to take leave to compensate for overtime, work during holidays, or night work.
c. The wage peak system allows companies to rehire workers after they retire.

Day laborer in a pineapple plantation in Pontian, Malaysia

© Justin Guariglia / Redux

Notes

1. Gershuny 2000; Krueger and others 2009; Ramey and Francis 2009.
2. Ngai and Pissarides 2008.
3. See Hongqin, MacPhail, and Dong (2011) for the case of growing female participation in China. On the other hand, see Gammage and Mehra (1999) for the case of stagnant female participation in the Middle East.
4. Davis and others 2010.
5. Narayan, Pritchett, and Kapoor 2009.
6. See the studies cited in Baulch 2011; Fields and others 2003; and Fields and others 2007.
7. de Brauw and Giles 2008; Giles and Murtazashvili 2010.
8. Azevedo and others 2012 for the World Development Report 2013. In El Salvador and Romania, nonlabor incomes compensated for lower labor incomes as a result of the financial crisis. For Mexico, although earnings increased for the employed, this effect was compensated for by a decline in occupied adults, resulting in a relatively lower contribution of labor income to poverty reduction when compared to transfers.
9. Inchauste and others 2012 for the World Development Report 2013.
10. Dang and Lanjouw 2012.
11. Estudillo, Sawada, and Otsuka 2008; Himanshu, Bakshi, and Dufour 2011; Lanjouw and Lanjouw 2001; Lanjouw and Murgai 2009; Otsuka, Estudillo, and Sawada 2009; Takahashi and Otsuka 2009.
12. Mansuri and others 2012a for the World Development Report 2013.
13. Glewwe, Gragnolatti, and Zaman 2002; Ravallion and Chen 2007; Ravallion, Chen, and Sangraula 2009.
14. Christiaensen and others 2009; de Brauw and others 2002; Giles 2006; Giles and Yoo 2007.
15. Christiaensen and Todo 2009; Estudillo and others 2012; Himanshu and others 2011.
16. Dercon and Porter 2011; Fields and others 2003; Lawson, McKay, and Okidi 2006; Lohano 2011; Quisumbing 2011; Woolard and Klasen 2005.
17. Fields and others 2003; Fields and others 2007.
18. Mansuri and others 2012b for the World Development Report 2013.
19. Bjørkhaug and others 2012 for the World Development Report 2013; Hatløy and others 2012 for the World Development Report 2013; Kebede and others 2012 for the World Development Report 2013; Zhang and others 2012 for the World Development Report 2013.
20. ILO 2010.
21. ILO 2005.
22. Al-Tuwaijri and others 2008; Brenner 1979.
23. Estimates for both Spain and Mauritius are from Ramessur (2009).
24. ILO 2005.
25. WHO and World Bank 2011.
26. Wilkinson and Marmot 1998.
27. Baingana and others 2004; Murphy and Athanasou 1999.
28. Brenner 1971; Brenner 1975; Dooley, Catalano, and Wilson 1994; Dooley, Prause, and Ham-Rowbottom 2000.
29. Lundin and Hemmingsson 2009; Stuckler and others 2009a, 2009b.
30. ILO 2010.
31. Ouweneel 2002.
32. Helliwell and Putnam 2004; Stutzer and Lalive 2004.
33. Blanchflower and Oswald 2011; Winkelmann and Winkelmann 1998. There are valid concerns about how to compare self-reported subjective outcomes across countries and cultures. See King and others 2004.
34. Gales, Mavridis, and Witoelar 2012 for the World Development Report 2013.
35. Björklund 1985.
36. Clark and Oswald 1994.
37. Helliwell and Putnam 2004.
38. Dooley, Prause, and Ham-Rowbottom 2000; Winefield 2002.
39. Bardasi and Francesconi 2004; Origo and Pagani 2009.
40. Dehejia, Brown, and Robertson 2012 for the World Development Report 2013.
41. Wietzke and McLeod 2012 for the World Development Report 2013.
42. Graham 2008.
43. ISSP 2005.
44. Dehejia, Brown, and Robertson 2012 for the World Development Report 2013.
45. Gill and Kharas 2007; Stiglitz 1996; World Bank 1993.
46. Ravallion 2001; Ravallion 2011.
47. Bigsten and others 2003; Demombynes and Hoogeeven 2007.
48. Ferreira, Leite, and Ravallion 2010; Hanson 2010.
49. The GDP per capita (in real 2000 US$) grew in Tunisia at an annual average rate of 3.4 percent between 1990 and 2008, whereas the average for the Middle East and North Africa region was 2.0 percent in the same period (World Development Indicators).
50. There are several measures that gauge "pro-poor" growth. See Ravallion 2004.
51. Ianchovichina and Lundstrom 2009; Ravallion 2001.

52. Christiaensen, Demery, and Kuhl 2011; Loayza and Raddatz 2010.

References

The word *processed* describes informally reproduced works that may not be commonly available through libraries.

Adelman, Irma, and Cynthia Taft Morris. 1973. *Economic Growth and Social Equity in Developing Countries*. Stanford, CA: Stanford University Press.

Al-Tuwaijri, Sameera, Igor Fedotov, Ilise Feitshans, Malcolm Gifford, David Gold, Seiji Machida, Michele Nahmias, Shengli Niu, and Gabor Sandi. 2008. *Beyond Death and Injuries: The ILO's Role in Promoting Safe and Healthy Jobs*. Geneva: International Labour Organization.

Alkire, Sabina, and James Foster. 2011. "Understandings and Misunderstandings of Multidimensional Poverty Measurement." *Journal of Economic Inequality* 9 (2): 289–314.

Anker, Richard. 2011. *Estimating a Living Wage: A Methodological Review*. Geneva: International Labour Organization.

Arias-Vasquez, Javier, Jean N. Lee, and David Newhouse. 2012. "The Role of Sectoral Growth Patterns in Labor Market Development." Background paper for the WDR 2013.

Azevedo, João Pedro, Gabriela Inchauste, Sergio Olivieri, Jaime Saavedra Chanduvi, and Hernan Winkler. 2012. "Is Labor Income Responsible for Poverty Reduction? A Decomposition Approach." Background paper for the WDR 2013.

Baingana, Florence, Andrew Dabalen, Essimi Menye, Menahem Prywes, and Michael Rosholm. 2004. "Mental Health and Socio-Economic Outcomes in Burundi." Health, Nutrition and Population Discussion Paper, World Bank, Washington, DC.

Balakrishnan, Ravi, Mitali Das, and Prakash Kannan. 2009. "Unemployment Dynamics during Recessions and Recoveries: Okun's Law and Beyond." In *IMF World Economic Outlook: Rebalancing Growth*, 69–108. Washington, DC: International Monetary Fund.

Bardasi, Elena, and Marco Francesconi. 2004. "The Impact of Atypical Employment on Individual Wellbeing: Evidence from a Panel of British Workers." *Social Science & Medicine* 58 (9): 1671–88.

Baulch, Bob, ed. 2011. *Why Poverty Persists: Poverty Dynamics in Asia and Africa*. Cheltenham, U.K.: Edward Elgar Publishing.

Berniell, M. Inés, and Carolina Sanchez-Paramo. 2011. "Time Use Database." World Bank, Washington, DC. Processed.

Bhalotra, Sonia R. 1998. "The Puzzle Of Jobless Growth in Indian Manufacturing." *Oxford Bulletin of Economics and Statistics* 60 (1): 5–32.

Bigsten, Arne, Kebede Bereket, Abebe Shimeless, and Mekonnen Taddesse. 2003. "Growth and Poverty Reduction in Ethiopia: Evidence from Household Panel Surveys." *World Development* 31 (1): 87–106.

Bjørkhaug, Ingunn, Anne Hatløy, Tewodros Kebede, and Huafeng Zhang. 2012. "Perception of Good Jobs: Colombia." Background paper for the WDR 2013.

Björklund, Anders. 1985. "Unemployment and Mental Health: Some Evidence from Panel Data." *Journal of Human Resources* 20 (4): 469–83.

Blanchflower, David G., and Andrew J. Oswald. 2011. "International Happiness." Working Paper Series 16668, National Bureau of Economic Research, Cambridge, MA.

Blank, Rebecca M., Sandra K. Danziger, and Robert F. Schoeni. 2006. *Working and Poor*. New York: Russell Sage Foundation.

Bourguignon, François, and Satya Chakravarty. 2003. "The Measurement of Multidimensional Poverty." *Journal of Economic Inequality* 1 (1): 25–49.

Brady, David, Andrew Fullerton, and Jennifer Moren Cross. 2010. "More Than Just Nickels and Dimes: A Cross-National Analysis of Working Poverty in Affluent Democracies." *Social Problems* 57 (4): 559–85.

Brenner, Harvey. 1971. "Economic Changes and Heart Disease Mortality." *American Journal of Public Health* 65 (12): 606–11.

———. 1975. "Trends in Alcohol Consumption and Associated Illnesses: Some Effects of Economic Changes." *American Journal of Public Health* 65: 1279–92.

———. 1979. "Mortality and the National Economy." *The Lancet* 26: 568–73.

Cazes, Sandrine, Sher Verick, and Fares Al Hussami. 2011. "Diverging Trends in Unemployment in the United States and Europe: Evidence from Okun's Law and the Global Financial Crisis." Employment Working Paper Series 106, International Labour Organization, Geneva.

Chenery, Hollis Burnley, and Moises Syrquin. 1975. "Patterns of Development: 1950–1970." In *Redistribution with Growth: Policies to Improve Income Distribution in Developing Countries in the Context of Economic Growth*, ed. Hollis Burnley Chenery, Richard Jolly, Montek S. Ahluwalia, C. L. Bell, and John H. Duloy. Oxford: Oxford University Press.

Christiaensen, Luc, Ruchira Bhattamishra, Lei Pan, and Sangui Wang. 2009. "Pathways Out of Poverty in Lagging Regions: Evidence from Rural Western China." World Bank, Washington, DC. Processed.

Christiaensen, Luc, Lionel Demery, and Jesper Kuhl. 2011. "The (Evolving) Role of Agriculture in Poverty Reduction—An Empirical Perspective." *Journal of Development Economics* 96 (2): 239–54.

Christiaensen, Luc, and Yasuyuki Todo. 2009. "Poverty Reduction during the Rural-Urban Transformation: The Role of the Missing Middle." Paper presented at the International Association of Agricultural Economists 2009 Conference, Beijing, August 16.

Clark, Andrew, and Andrew J. Oswald. 1994. "Unhappiness and Unemployment." *Economic Journal* 104: 648–59.

Covarrubias, Katia, Benjamin Davis, Aminata Bakouan, and Stefania Di Giuseppe. 2012. "Household Income Generation Strategies." Background paper for the WDR 2013.

Dang, Hai-Anh, and Peter Lanjouw. 2012. "Measuring Poverty Dynamics and Labor Transitions with Synthetic Panels Based on Cross-Sections." Processed.

Davis, Benjamin, Katia Covarrubias, Kostas Stamoulis, Paul C. Winters, Carlogero Carletto, Esteban Quiñones, Alberto Zezza, and Stefania DiGiuseppe. 2010. "A Cross-Country Comparison of Rural Income Generating Activities." *World Development* 38 (1): 48–63.

de Brauw, Alan, and John Giles. 2008. "Migrant Labor Markets and the Welfare of Rural Households in the Developing World: Evidence from China." Policy Research Working Paper Series 4585, World Bank, Washington, DC.

de Brauw, Alan, Jikun Huang, Scott Rozelle, Linxiu Zhang, and Yigang Zhang. 2002. "The Evolution of China's Rural Labor Markets during the Reforms." *Journal of Comparative Economics* 30 (2): 329–53.

Dehejia, Rajeev, Drusilla Brown, and Raymond Robertson. 2012. "Life Satisfaction, Mental Well-Being, and Workplace Characteristics Evidence from Vietnam, Jordan, and Haiti." Background paper for the WDR 2013.

Demombynes, Gabriel, and Johannes G. Hoogeeven. 2007. "Growth, Inequality, and Simulated Poverty Paths for Tanzania, 1992–2002." *Journal of African Economies* 16 (4): 596–628.

Dercon, Stefan, and Catherine Porter. 2011. "A Poor Life? Chronic Poverty and Downward Mobility in Rural Ethiopia, 1994 to 2004." In *Why Poverty Persists: Poverty Dynamics in Asia and Africa*, ed. Bob Baulch, 65–95. Cheltenham, U.K.: Edward Elgar Publishing.

Dooley, David, Ralph Catalano, and Georjeanna Wilson. 1994. "Depression and Unemployment: Panel Findings from the Epidemiologic Catchment Area Study." *American Journal of Community Psychology* 61 (3): 745–65.

Dooley, David, JoAnn Prause, and Kathleen Ham-Rowbottom. 2000. "Inadequate Employment and High Depressive Symptoms: Panel Analyses." *International Journal of Psychology* 35: 294.

Estudillo, Jonna P., Tomoya Matsumoto, Ziauddin Hayat Chowdhury, Nandika Kumanayake, and Keijiro Otsuka. 2012. "Labor Markets, Occupational Choice, and Rural Poverty in Selected Countries in Asia and Sub-Saharan Africa." Background paper for the WDR 2013.

Estudillo, Jonna P., Yasuyuki Sawada, and Keijiro Otsuka. 2008. "Poverty and Income Dynamics in Philippine Villages, 1985–2004." *Review of Development Economics* 12 (4): 877–90.

Falco, Paolo, William Maloney, Bob Rijkers, and Mauricio Sarrias. 2012. "Subjective Well-Being, Informality, and Preference Heterogeneity in Africa." Background paper for the WDR 2013.

Ferreira, Francisco H. G., Phillippe G. Leite, and Martin Ravallion. 2010. "Poverty Reduction and Economic Growth? Explaining Brazil's Poverty Dynamics 1985–2004." *Journal of Development Economics* 93 (1): 20–36.

Fields, Gary. 2011. *Working Hard, Working Poor*. New York: Oxford University Press.

Fields, Gary, Paul Cichello, Samuel Freije-Rodriguez, Marta Menendez, and David Newhouse. 2003. "Household Income Dynamics: A Four-Country Story." *Journal of Development Studies* 40 (2): 30–54.

Fields, Gary, Robert Duval Hernández, Samuel Freije, and María Laura Sánchez Puerta. 2007. "Intragenerational Income Mobility in Latin America." *Economía* 7 (2): 101–54.

Fitoussi, Jean-Paul, Amartya Sen, and Joseph E. Stiglitz. 2010. *Mismeasuring Our Lives: Why GDP Doesn't Add Up*. New York: The New Press.

Gammage, Sarah, and Rekha Mehra. 1999. "Trends, Countertrends, and Gaps in Women's Employment." *World Development* 27 (3): 533–50.

Gershuny, Jonathan. 2000. *Changing Times: Work and Leisure in Post Industrial Society*. Oxford: Oxford University Press.

Giles, John. 2006. "Is Life More Risky in the Open? Household Risk-Coping and the Opening of China's Labor Markets." *Journal of Development Economics* 81 (1): 25–60.

Giles, John, Dimitris Mavridis, and Firman Witoelar. 2012. "Subjective Well-Being, Social Cohesion, and Labor Market Outcomes in Indonesia." Background paper for the WDR 2013.

Giles, John, and Irina Murtazashvili. 2010. "A Control Function Approach to Estimating Dynamic Probit Models with Endogenous Regressors, with an Application to the Study of Poverty Persistence in China." Policy Research Working Paper Series 5400, World Bank, Washington, DC.

Giles, John, and Kyeongwon Yoo. 2007. "Precautionary Behavior, Migrant Networks and Household Consumption Decisions: An Empirical Analysis Using Household Panel Data from Rural China." *Review of Economics and Statistics* 89 (3): 534–51.

Gill, Indermit, and Homi Kharas. 2007. *An East Asian Renaissance: Ideas for Economic Growth.* Washington, DC: World Bank.

Glewwe, Paul W., Michele Gragnolatti, and Hassan Zaman. 2002. "Who Gained from Vietnam's Boom in the 1990s?" *Economic Development and Cultural Change* 50 (4): 773–92.

Graham, Carol. 2008. "Measuring Quality of Life in Latin America: What Happiness Research Can (and Cannot) Contribute." IDB Working Paper 549, Inter-American Development Bank, Washington, DC.

Hanson, Gordon H. 2010. "Why Isn't Mexico Rich?" *Journal of Economic Literature* 48 (4): 987–1004.

Hatløy, Anne, Tewodros Kebede, Huafeng Zhang, and Ingunn Bjørkhaug. 2012. "Perception of Good Jobs: Sierra Leone." Background paper for the WDR 2013.

Helliwell, John, and Robert Putnam. 2004. "The Social Context of Well-Being." *Philosophical Transactions of the Royal Society B* 359: 1435–46.

Himanshu, Ishan Bakshi, and Camille Dufour. 2011. "Poverty, Inequality and Mobility in Palanpur: Some Preliminary Results." Asia Research Centre Working Paper 45, Asia Research Centre, London School of Economics and Political Science, London.

Himanshu, Peter Lanjouw, Abhiroop Mukhopadhyay, and Rinku Murgai. 2011. "Non-Farm Diversification and Rural Poverty Decline: A Perspective from Indian Sample Survey and Village Study Data." Asia Research Centre Working Paper 44, Asia Research Centre, London School of Economics and Political Science, London.

Hintermann, Beat, Anna Alberini and Anil Markandya. 2010. "Estimating the Value of Safety with Labour Market Data: Are the Results Trustworthy?" *Applied Economics* 42 (9): 1085–100.

Hongqin, Chang, Fiona MacPhail, and Xiao-yuan Dong. 2011. "The Feminization of Labor and the Time-Use Gender Gap in Rural China." *Feminist Economics* 17 (4): 93–124.

Huff, W. G. 1994. *The Economic Growth of Singapore: Trade and Development in the Twentieth Century.* New York: Cambridge University Press.

———. 1995. "What Is the Singapore Model of Economic Development?" *Cambridge Journal of Economics* 19 (6): 735–59.

Ianchovichina, Elena, and Susanna Lundstrom. 2009. "What Is Inclusive Growth?" World Bank, Washington, DC. Processed.

IFC (International Finance Corporation). Forthcoming. *Job Study.* Washington, DC: IFC.

IFC (International Finance Corporation) and ILO (International Labour Organization). 2011. "Baseline Data Collection: Better Work." IFC and ILO, Washington, DC. Processed.

ILO (International Labour Organization). 2005. *Facts on Safety at Work.* Geneva: ILO.

———. 2010. *Emerging Risks and New Patterns of Prevention in a Changing World of Work.* Geneva: ILO.

———. 2011. *Growth, Employment and Decent Work in the Least Developed Countries.* Geneva: ILO.

Inchauste, Gabriela. 2012. "Jobs and Transitions Out of Poverty: A Literature Review." Background paper for the WDR 2013.

Inchauste, Gabriela, Sergio Olivieri, Jaime Saavedra-Chanduvi, and Hernan Winkler. 2012. "Decomposing Recent Declines in Poverty: Evidence from Bangladesh, Peru, and Thailand." Background paper for the WDR 2013.

ISSP (International Social Survey Programme). 2005. "Module on Work Orientation." ISSP, Cologne.

Kakwani, Nanak, and Jacques Silber. 2008. *Quantitative Approaches to Multidimensional Poverty Measurement.* Basingstoke, U.K.: Palgrave Macmillan.

Kebede, Tewodros, Anne Hatløy, Huafeng Zhang, and Ingunn Bjørkhaug. 2012. "Perception of Good Jobs: Egypt." Background paper for the WDR 2013.

King, Gary, Christopher J. L. Murray, Joshua A. Salomon, and Ajay Tandon. 2004. "Enhancing the Validity and Cross-Cultural Comparability of Measurement in Survey Research." *American Political Science Review* 98 (1): 191–207.

Krueger, Alan B., Daniel Kahneman, Claude Fischler, David Schkade, Norbert Schwarz, and Arthur A. Stone. 2009. "Time Use and Subjective Well-Being in France and the U.S." *Social Indicators Research* 93 (1): 7–18.

Lanjouw, Jean O., and Peter Lanjouw. 2001. "The Rural Non-Farm Sector: Issues and Evidence from Developing Countries." *Agricultural Economics* 26 (1): 1–23.

Lanjouw, Peter, and Rinku Murgai. 2009. "Poverty Decline, Agricultural Wages, and Nonfarm Employment in Rural India: 1983–2004." *Agricultural Economics* 40 (2): 243–63.

Lawson, David, Andy McKay, and John Okidi. 2006. "Poverty Persistence and Transitions in Uganda: A Combined Qualitative and Quantitative Analysis." *Journal of Development Studies* 42 (7): 1225–51.

Loayza, Norman, and Claudio Raddatz. 2010. "The Composition of Growth Matters for Poverty Alleviation." *Journal of Development Economics* 93 (1): 137–51.

Lohano, Hari Ram. 2011. "Poverty Dynamics in Rural Sindh, Pakistan, 1987–88 to 2004–05." In *Why Poverty Persists: Poverty Dynamics in Asia and Africa*, ed. Bob Baulch, 145–86. Cheltenham, U.K.: Edward Elgar Publishing.

Lundin, Andreas, and Tomas Hemmingsson. 2009. "Unemployment and Suicide." *The Lancet* 374 (9686): 270–1.

Mansuri, Ghazala, Slesh Shrestha, Hernan Winkler, and Monica Yanez-Pagans. 2012a. "A Plot of My Own: Land Titling and Economic Mobility in Rural Uganda." Background paper for the WDR 2013.

———. 2012b. "Health or Wealth? Income Earner Death and Economic Mobility in Rural Pakistan." Background paper for the WDR 2013.

Martins, Pedro. 2012. "Growth, Employment, and Poverty in Africa: Tales of Lions and Cheetahs." Background paper for the WDR 2013.

Moosa, Imad A. 2012. "A Cross-Country Comparison of Okun's Coefficient." *Journal of Comparative Economics* 24 (3): 335–56.

Murphy, Gregory C., and James A. Athanasou. 1999. "The Effect of Unemployment on Mental Health." *Journal of Occupational and Organizational Psychology* 72 (1): 83–99.

Narayan, Deepa, Lant Pritchett, and Soumya Kapoor. 2009. *Success from the Bottom Up.* Vol. 2 of *Moving Out of Poverty.* New York: Palgrave Macmillan; Washington, DC: World Bank.

Ngai, Rachel L., and Christopher A. Pissarides. 2008. "Trends in Hours and Economic Growth." *Review of Economic Dynamics* 11 (2): 239–56.

Nordhaus, William D., and James Tobin. 1973. "Is Growth Obsolete?" In *The Measurement of Economic and Social Performance*, ed. Milton Moss, 509–64. Cambridge, MA: National Bureau of Economic Research.

OECD (Organisation for Economic Co-operation and Development). 2011. *How's Life? Measuring Well-Being.* Paris: OECD.

Origo, Federica, and Laura Pagani. 2009. "Flexicurity and Job Satisfaction in Europe: The Importance of Perceived and Actual Job Stability for Well-Being at Work." *Labour Economics* 16 (5): 547–55.

Otsuka, Keijiro, Jonna P. Estudillo, and Yasuyuki Sawada, eds. 2009. *Rural Poverty and Income Dynamics in Asia and Africa.* New York: Routledge.

Ouweneel, Piet. 2002. "Social Security and Well-Being of the Unemployed in 42 Nations." *Journal of Happiness Studies* 3 (2): 167–92.

Paes de Barros, Ricardo, Francisco H. G. Ferreira, José R. Molinas Vega, and Jaime Saavedra Chanduvi. 2009. *Measuring Inequality of Opportunities in Latin America and the Caribbean.* Washington, DC: World Bank.

Quisumbing, Agnes R. 2011. "Poverty Transitions, Shocks and Consumption in Rural Bangladesh, 1996–97 to 2006–07." In *Why Poverty Persists: Poverty Dynamics in Asia and Africa*, ed. Bob Baulch, 29–64. Cheltenham, U.K.: Edward Elgar Publishing.

Ramessur, Taruna Shalini. 2009. "Economic Cost of Occupational Accidents: Evidence from a Small Island Economy." *Safety Science* 47 (7): 973–9.

Ramey, Valerie A., and Neville Francis. 2009. "A Century of Work and Leisure." *American Economic Journal: Macroeconomics* 1 (2): 189–224.

Ravallion, Martin. 2001. "Growth, Inequality and Poverty: Looking Beyond Averages." *World Development* 29 (11): 1803–15.

———. 2004. "Pro-Poor Growth: A Primer." Policy Research Working Paper Series 3242, World Bank, Washington, DC.

———. 2011. "A Comparative Perspective on Poverty Reduction in Brazil, China and India." *World Bank Research Observer* 26 (1): 71–104.

Ravallion, Martin, and Shaohua Chen. 2007. "China's (Uneven) Progress against Poverty." *Journal of Development Economics* 82 (1): 1–42.

Ravallion, Martin, Shaohua Chen, and Prem Sangraula. 2009. "Dollar a Day Revisited." *World Bank Economic Review* 23 (2): 163–84.

Republic of Korea. 2010. *National Employment Strategy 2020 for the Balance of Growth, Employment and Welfare.* Seoul: Republic of Korea.

Roy, Dutta Sudipta. 2004. "Employment Dynamics in Indian Industry: Adjustment Lags and the Impact of Job Security Regulations." *Journal of Development Economics* 73 (1): 233–53.

Sen, Amartya, and Geoffrey Hawthorn. 1987. *The Standard of Living.* Cambridge, U.K.: Cambridge University Press.

Steckel, Richard H. 1995. "Stature and the Standard of Living." *Journal of Economic Literature* 33: 1903–40.

Stiglitz, Joseph E. 1996. "Some Lessons from the East Asian Miracle." *World Bank Research Observer* 11 (2): 151–77.

Streeten, Paul. 1979. "Basic Needs: Premises and Promises." *Journal of Policy Modeling* 1: 136–46.

Stuckler, David, Sanjay Basu, Marc Suhrcke, and Adam Coutts. 2009a. "The Public Health Effect of Economic Crises and Alternative Policy Responses in Europe: An Empirical Analysis." *The Lancet* 374 (9686): 315–23.

Stuckler, David, Sanjay Basu, Marc Suhrcke, and Martin McKee. 2009b. "The Health Implications of Financial Crisis: A Review of the Evidence." *Ulster Medical Journal* 78 (3): 142–5.

Stutzer, Alois, and Rafael Lalive. 2004. "The Role of Social Work Norms in Job Searching and Subjective Well-Being." *Journal of the European Economic Association* 2 (4): 696–719.

Takahashi, Kazushi, and Keijiro Otsuka. 2009. "The Increasing Importance of Nonfarm Income and the Changing Use of Labor and Capital in Rice Farming: The Case of Central Luzon, 1979–2003." *Agricultural Economics* 40 (2): 231–42.

UNDP (United Nations Development Programme). 1990. *Human Development Report 1990.* New York: UNDP.

WHO (World Health Organization) and World Bank. 2011. *World Report on Disability.* Washington, DC: WHO and World Bank.

Wietzke, Frank-Borge, and Catriona McLeod. 2012. "Jobs, Well-Being, and Social Cohesion: Evidence from Value and Perception Surveys." Background paper for the WDR 2013.

Wilkinson, Richard, and Michael Marmot. 1998. *Social Determinants of Health: The Solid Facts.* Geneva: World Health Organization.

Winefield, Anthony H. 2002. "The Psychology of Unemployment." In *Social, Developmental, and Clinical Perspectives*, ed. Claes von Hofsten and Lars Bäckman. Vol. 2 of *Psychology at the Turn of the Millennium.* New York: Psychology Press.

Winkelmann, Rainer, and Liliana Winkelmann. 1998. "Why Are the Unemployed So Unhappy? Evidence from Panel Data." *Economica* 65: 1–15.

Woolard, Ingrid, and Stephan Klasen. 2005. "Determinants of Income Mobility and Household Poverty Dynamics in South Africa." *Journal of Development Studies* 41 (5): 865–97.

World Bank. 1993. *The East Asian Miracle.* Washington, DC: World Bank.

———. 2010. *From Global Collapse to Recovery: Economic Adjustment and Growth Prospects in Latin America and the Caribbean.* Washington, DC: World Bank.

Zhang, Huafeng, Ingunn Bjørkhaug, Anne Hatløy, and Tewodros Kebede. 2012. "Perception of Good Jobs: China." Background paper for the WDR 2013.

CHAPTER 3

Jobs and productivity

Reallocation from low- to high-productivity jobs matters more for growth in developing countries, where differences in productivity across sectors and within sectors are wide. But reallocation often amounts to little more than churning.

Productivity growth happens as jobs become more productive, as new high-productivity jobs are created, and as low-productivity jobs disappear. In the medium term, trends in employment align closely with trends in the labor force, so there is no such a thing as jobless growth. But the short-term relationship between employment and growth is more complex. Large numbers of jobs are being created and destroyed simultaneously, leading to structural change and spatial labor reallocation. Underneath these sectoral and spatial changes are firm dynamics that result in a constant restructuring and reallocation of resources, including labor.

In developing countries, many people work in very small and not so dynamic economic units. Family farms, which often predominate in agriculture, average only 1.2 hectares in Asia, and 1.8 hectares in Sub-Saharan Africa. Outside of agriculture, microenterprises and household businesses account for a large share of employment in a majority of developing countries. These businesses make a significant contribution to gross job creation and destruction, although not necessarily to net job creation and productivity growth.

In agriculture, the Green Revolution has led to higher cereal yields and to employment growth because the new technologies are labor intensive. The progress has been uneven across regions, however. In Sub-Saharan Africa, the Green Revolution has not taken place on a large scale.

Outside of agriculture, productivity varies substantially across enterprises, implying potentially large productivity gains from job reallocation. The speed at which productivity grows also varies. Large firms are more innovative, provided that they are exposed to competition. At the other end, microenterprises are a diverse group. A vast majority of them, more prone to churning than to growth, are a means of survival for the poor. Yet some are entrepreneurial, and their success could boost wage employment.

Employment turbulence, not jobless growth

Jobless growth is a popular notion, often believed to be grounded on data. However, unemployment rates neither explode nor vanish over time, so employment trends align closely with trends in the size of the labor force. The growth of gross domestic product (GDP) certainly matters for employment growth, but in the medium term it matters less than demographics and participation rates. Data from 97 countries over the past decade confirm that a positive relationship exists between the growth of GDP per capita and the growth of employment per capita (figure

BOX 3.1 *What drives economic growth?*

At the risk of simplifying, four main forces lie behind increases in an economy's per capita output. The first is the use of more capital per unit of labor. The second is an increase in the number of people working, relative to the total population. This happens when fertility declines and the share of adults in the total population increases; it is also happens when women shift their work from household chores to income-generating activities. The third mechanism through which output can grow is by making people themselves more productive. The acquisition of skills, also known as human capital accumulation, allows a person to do more using the same amount of capital. The fourth mechanism is technological progress,

measured as changes in total factor productivity. Technological progress amounts to combining capital, labor, and skills more efficiently, while applying new knowledge.

Growth decomposition quantifies the contribution of each of these four forces to economic growth. It can be done for any particular country given sufficient data on gross domestic product, capital, employment, and human capital. Some of these variables may need to be constructed or approximated; for instance, the stock of capital in an economy is estimated based on accumulated investments, while human capital is approximated by the educational attainment of its population, corrected for the quality of education.

Source: World Development Report 2013 team.

3.1a).[1] The relationship is not very strong, but only in very few cases was growth truly jobless.

On the other hand, the short-term relationship between growth and employment is not so straightforward. Growth happens partly through the disappearance of low-productivity jobs as well as through the creation of more productive jobs.[2] So for the same sample of countries over the same decade, surges in total factor productivity (TFP) in one year were in-

deed associated with a decline in employment in the same year (figure 3.1b). Only in subsequent years did this negative employment effect wane.

Productivity growth is a turbulent process. Analyses covering economies as different as Ethiopia and the United States in different periods over the past three decades reveal the magnitude of gross job creation and gross job destruction (figure 3.2). In the manufacturing sector of developing countries, between 7 and

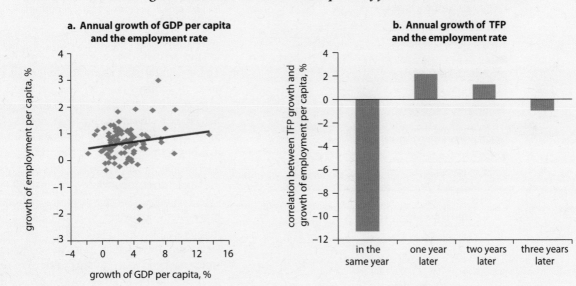

FIGURE 3.1 *Economic growth does not occur at the expense of jobs in the medium term*

a. Annual growth of GDP per capita and the employment rate

b. Annual growth of TFP and the employment rate

Source: World Development Report 2013 team estimates based on average growth decomposition accounting for years 1999–2009.
Note: GDP = gross domestic product; TFP = total factor productivity. Data are from 97 countries. Panel a presents the relationship between annual growth of GDP per capita and the growth of the employment-to-population ratio. Each dot represents a country. Panel b depicts the correlation between annual growth in total factor productivity (TFP) and employment rate growth in the same year, and in subsequent years.

FIGURE 3.2 *Simultaneous job creation and destruction characterize all economies*

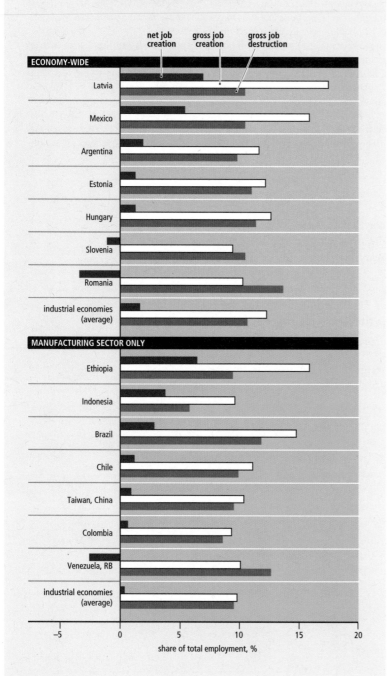

Sources: World Development Report 2013 team estimates based on Bartelsman, Haltiwanger, and Scarpetta 2009b and Shiferaw and Bedi 2010.

Note: The figure shows annual job flows. Data are from Argentina (1996–2001); Brazil (1997–2000); Canada (1984–97); Chile (1980–98); Colombia (1983–97); Estonia (1996–2000); Ethiopia (1997–2007); Finland (1989–97); France (1989–97); Germany (1977–99); Hungary (1993–2000); Indonesia (1991–94); Italy (1987–94); Latvia (1983–98); Mexico (1986–2000); the Netherlands (1993–95); Portugal (1983–98); Romania (1993–2000); Slovenia (1991–2000); Taiwan, China (1986–91); the United Kingdom (1982–98); the United States (1986–91, 1994–96); and República Bolivariana de Venezuela (1996–98).

20 percent of jobs are created every year, while a similar proportion disappear.[3] Even when aggregate employment was declining, as in the 1990s in Romania and Slovenia and in the manufacturing sector of República Bolivariana de Venezuela, many new jobs were being created. Conversely, when aggregate employment was growing by 6 percent in Mexico, jobs were disappearing at almost twice that rate.

Job flows may be associated with profound transformations in the sectoral structure of the economy. Technological change often occurs for specific products and processes, causing productivity to grow at different paces in different sectors. However, the relative weight of different sectors in the economy is determined not only by technological progress, but also by market demand and nonmarket forces. When there is an expansion of the most productive sectors, aggregate productivity increases. This composition effect, called productivity-enhancing structural change, is well documented in the case of labor shifts from agriculture to industry and services. Analysis based on more disaggregated data suggests that reallocation of labor across sectors has also been an important driver of productivity growth in several fast-growing East Asian countries. In China, it contributed 4.1 percentage points of the 7.3 percent annual growth in aggregate labor productivity over the past decade; in Vietnam, it accounted for 2.6 points out of 4.2 (figure 3.3).[4]

Job flows are also associated with changes in the spatial distribution of employment. The structural shift from agriculture in rural areas to industry and services in towns and cities may be the most visible example of spatial labor reallocation, but it is not the only one.[5] Even within sectors, job flows often have a strong spatial dimension. New plants associated with more innovative activities tend to start in large, diversified cities—incubators—with a higher density of suppliers and labor, and more fluent exchanges of information. As they mature and become more self-sufficient in information, these plants move to smaller cities, where land and wage costs are lower. As a result, many medium and small cities tend to be more specialized.[6]

The extent of spatial relocation varies across sectors and countries. For instance, in the Republic of Korea, manufacturing dominance in

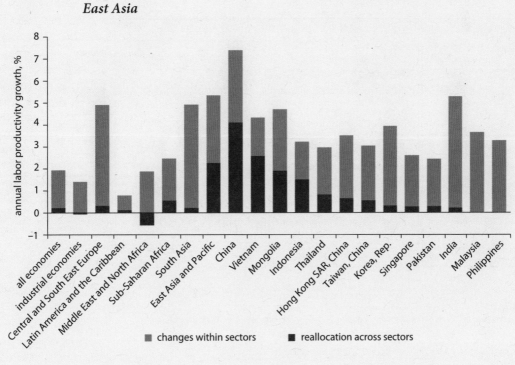

FIGURE 3.3 *Labor reallocation across sectors was a driver of productivity growth in East Asia*

■ changes within sectors   ■ reallocation across sectors

Source: World Development Report 2013 team estimates based on Kucera and Roncolato 2012.
Note: The figure shows the decomposition of labor productivity growth in 81 economies over 1999–2008 into productivity changes due to changes within sectors and reallocation across sectors. Seven sectors are considered: agriculture, hunting, forestry, and fishing; mining and utilities; manufacturing; construction; trade, restaurants, and hotels; transport, storage, and communication; and other services. The regional growth rates are weighted averages, with weights based on an economy's share in regional GDP.

urban centers has continued for a long period of time. Enterprises have been sprawling into the suburbs of urban centers rather than leapfrogging to different locations as in some industrial countries (map 3.1). Similar shifts are happening in Brazil, China, and Vietnam.[7] In India, large manufacturing enterprises are moving away from urban centers into rural locations.[8] Regardless of the nature of the shift, almost inevitably jobs are created in some places and destroyed in others.

Underneath these sectoral and spatial changes in the structure of employment are the firm dynamics connecting job flows and productivity growth. Aggregate productivity grows when existing firms become better at what they do, when more productive firms enter the market, and when less productive ones exit. It also grows when more productive firms become bigger and less productive ones become smaller. Decomposition analyses show that in most countries the main driver of aggregate productivity growth is firms becoming better at what they do (figure 3.4).[9] Entry and exit also contribute, which indicates that new firms are more productive than those exiting. In general, exiting firms see their productivity decline before they close, whereas new firms tend to attain the average levels of productivity of their industry within five years. These complex dynamics imply that at any point in time, firms with very different productivity levels coexist, even within narrowly defined industries.[10]

The popular perception that productivity grows through downsizing at the firm level is partially supported by these analyses. Indeed, in many cases, employment tends to shrink in firms experiencing rapid productivity growth.[11] But downsizing is only part of the story. There are also many successful upsizing firms, achieving both productivity growth and employment growth.[12] For instance, one-fourth of manufac-

MAP 3.1 *Manufacturing activities are sprawling out of the main urban centers in the Republic of Korea*

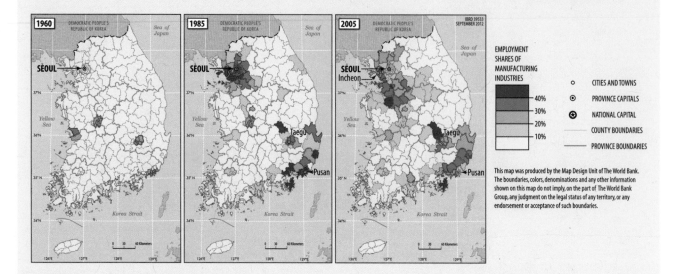

Source: Park et al. 2011.
Note: The maps show employment shares of manufacturing industries at the city or county level for 1960, 1985, and 2005.

FIGURE 3.4 *Efficiency gains at the firm level are the main driver of productivity growth*

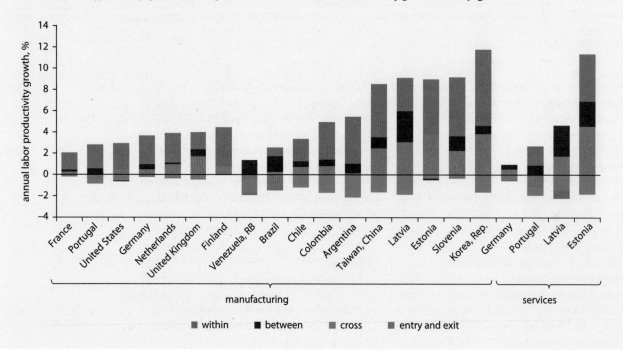

Source: Based on Bartelsman, Haltiwanger, and Scarpetta 2009b.
Note: The figure decomposes annual labor productivity growth. Data for industrial countries are from France (1990–95), the Netherlands (1992–2001), the United States (1992,1997), Portugal (1991–1994), the United Kingdom (2000, 2001), and Germany (2000–02). Data for developing economies are from Argentina (1995–2001); Brazil (2001); Chile (1985–99); Colombia (1987–98); Estonia (2000, 2001); the Republic of Korea (1988, 1993); Slovenia (1997–2001); Taiwan, China (1986, 1991, 1996); and República Bolivariana de Venezuela (1999). *Within* captures the changes at the firm level, *between* the changes in employment shares across firms, *cross* the interaction between the former two, and *entry and exit* the opening and closure of firms.

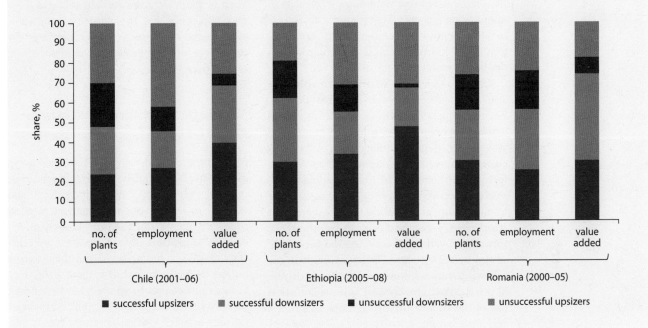

FIGURE 3.5 *Efficiency gains and employment growth can go together*

■ successful upsizers   ■ successful downsizers   ■ unsuccessful downsizers   ■ unsuccessful upsizers

Source: World Development Report 2013 team based on Amadeus Database, Bureau van Dijk, Amsterdam, and Ethiopia Large and Medium Scale Manufacturing and Electricity Industries Survey, Central Statistical Agency, Addis Ababa.

Note: no. = number. The figure shows the contribution of each of the four groups to the annual growth rate of the variable of interest. The plants considered employ at least 10 workers and exist throughout the entire period. Successful upsizers are plants that increased both labor productivity and employment, successful downsizers are plants that increased productivity but reduced employment, unsuccessful downsizers are plants that reduced employment and productivity, and unsuccessful upsizers are plants that increased employment but reduced productivity.

turing plants operating in Chile over 2001–06 were successful downsizers, consistent with the popular perception. But another one-fourth were successful upsizers, achieving both productivity and employment growth (figure 3.5). More important, the successful upsizers contributed more to production, employment, and aggregate productivity growth than the successful downsizers. Results were similar in Romania between 2000 and 2005, and in Ethiopia between 2005 and 2009. While country experiences vary, having a critical mass of successful upsizers is not uncommon.

Across countries, successful upsizers in manufacturing industries tend to be younger, leaner, and more innovative. Among survivors in the same industry and region, younger firms were more likely to be upsizers in Chile over 2001–06, and successful upsizers in Romania over 2000–05. In all three countries, survivors employing fewer than 20 employees tended to upsize fewer rather than downsize. In Romania, survivors investing more in capital per worker also tended to

be successful upsizers.[13] Recent evidence based on 26,000 manufacturers from 71 countries further shows that firms that innovated in products or processes were more likely to be successful upsizers; they not only attained higher total factor productivity than noninnovative firms; they also exhibited higher employment growth.[14]

Transition economies in Europe illustrate the links between job reallocation and productivity growth. Before reforms were implemented, these economies suffered from large distortions caused by a rigid planning system, which prevented resources from flowing to more efficient uses. Liberalization led to massive downsizing and job losses. Eventually, it also strengthened incentives, mobility, and markets, opening up space for more productive private companies. The entry of these dynamic players contributed between 20 and 50 percent of total labor productivity growth in the late 1990s. The exit of obsolete firms released resources that could be used more effectively by new or existing firms. Although lack of experience and small size often made the new firms less productive than the average firms of more advanced countries, these new firms were more efficient than domestic incumbents. They played a strong role in boosting productivity in medium- and high-technology industries and in exerting competitive pressure on existing firms.[15]

China's rapid productivity growth was also underpinned by large-scale reallocation. Beginning in 1978, economic reform efforts gradually expanded the influence of markets and deepened global integration. All of this created unprecedented opportunities for the formation of private entities, including township and village enterprises, and the entry of foreign companies. During the first decade of reform (1978–88), reallocation from agriculture to nonagriculture activities was the source of almost half of all productivity growth. In the following decades, however, the main drivers of productivity growth were labor reallocation out of the state sector, private sector vibrancy, and state sector restructuring. The scale of business entry was startling: the number of industrial firms rose from 377,000 in 1980 to nearly 8 million in 1996. The 2004 economic census reported 1.33 million manufacturing firms with annual sales above RMB 5 million.[16] Most of them were private. The entry of these new businesses and the closure of nonviable state-owned enterprises (SOEs) accounted for two-thirds of TFP growth in manufacturing sectors over 1998–2006.[17]

Most jobs are in very small farms and firms

Many people in developing countries work in very small and not very dynamic economic units—family farms, microenterprises, and household businesses. Although microenterprises are often defined as firms employing ten or fewer workers, many among them are actually one-person businesses. Given their contribution to total employment, these small economic units cannot be ignored. Understanding their dynamics is crucial to deciphering the relationship between jobs and productivity.

In family farms, hired labor is usually employed in simple tasks such as weeding and harvesting, whereas family labor usually carries out care-intensive activities such as water management, land preparation, and fertilizer application. Limited reliance on hired labor is due to the difficulty to monitor effort, and without machinery, farms cannot be expanded beyond the size manageable by the family's labor, which is typically 1 to 2 hectares.[18] Family farms dominate even in high-income countries, and owner cultivation is the most common form of land tenure, especially in Asia (figure 3.6).

At 1.2 and 1.8 hectares, respectively, average farm size is small in both Asia and Sub-Saharan Africa.[19] In Asia, farmers typically own land plots, which they supplement through tenancy contracts that facilitate transfers from relatively land-abundant to relatively labor-abundant households. Farms in Sub-Saharan Africa are slightly larger than in Asia, but size and the importance of owner farming are becoming similar in both regions.[20] There are some exceptions to this pattern. Colonial governments created large farms in some developing countries, such as estates in southern Africa, haciendas in Latin America and the Philippines, and plantations in the Caribbean. In Sub-Saharan Africa, large areas are also held as customary land—owned collectively by extended families, clans, or lineage.[21]

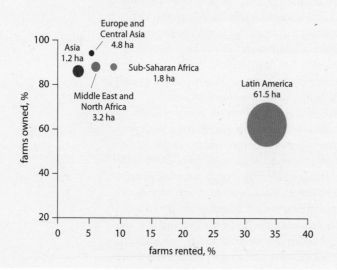

FIGURE 3.6 *Smallholder farming is dominant outside Latin America*

Source: FAO 2010.

Note: ha = hectare. Countries in Asia include: Bangladesh, India, Indonesia, the Lao People's Democratic Republic, Nepal, Pakistan, and Thailand; in Europe and Central Asia: Azerbaijan, Croatia, the Czech Republic, Georgia, the Kyrgyz Republic, Latvia, Serbia, Slovenia, and Turkey; in Latin America and the Caribbean: Brazil, Guatemala, Nicaragua, St. Lucia, St. Vincent and the Grenadines, Uruguay, República Bolivariana de Venezuela, and Virgin Islands (United States); in the Middle East and North Africa: the Arab Republic of Egypt, Jordan, Morocco, Qatar, Saudi Arabia, and Tunisia; and in Sub-Saharan Africa: Côte d'Ivoire, Ethiopia, and Madagascar.

FIGURE 3.7 *The employment share of microenterprises is greater in developing countries*

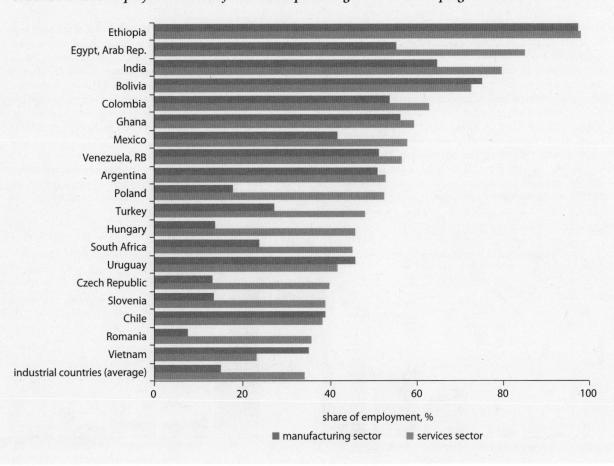

share of employment, %

■ manufacturing sector ■ services sector

Sources: World Development Report 2013 team estimates based on International Income Distribution Database (I2D2) and EUROSTAT.
Note: Microenterprises are firms, formal or informal, with fewer than 10 workers. Data for developing countries are from Argentina (2006–10); Bolivia (2005, 2007); Chile (2006, 2009); Colombia (2009); the Czech Republic (2005–07); the Arab Republic of Egypt (2006); Ethiopia (1999); Ghana (1991); Hungary (2007–08); India (2004, 2009); Mexico (2004–10); Poland (2005–07); Romania (2005–07); Slovenia (2005–07); South Africa (2005–07); Turkey (2006–10); Uruguay (2009); República Bolivariana de Venezuela (2004–06); and Vietnam (2009). Data for industrial countries are from Austria, Belgium, Denmark, Finland, France, Germany, Greece, Italy, Luxembourg, the Netherlands, Norway, Portugal, Spain, Sweden, and the United Kingdom over 2005–07.

Outside of agriculture, microenterprises and household businesses are dominant. More than 80 percent of registered manufacturing establishments in Argentina, Bolivia, El Salvador, and Mexico have fewer than 10 workers.[22] About 90 percent of manufacturing establishments employ 5 to 49 workers in China; India; Indonesia; Korea; the Philippines; and Taiwan, China.[23] The share of microenterprises is even higher outside manufacturing, reaching 94 percent in the services sector of Mexico and 98 percent in all modern sectors in Tunisia.[24] In several African and Latin American countries, the majority of informal enterprises consist of 1- to 3-person businesses.[25]

It is often claimed that most employment, and most job creation, is associated with small and medium enterprises, but that is generally not true in developing countries. In reality, micro- and small enterprises account for the bulk of employment, even in middle-income countries (figure 3.7). Their share is often underestimated, because economic censuses and plant-level surveys rarely cover the informal segment of the economy, where businesses are especially small. But data from household and labor force surveys that are representative of the entire population provide a different picture. These small enterprises play significant role in employment in manufacturing. They account for 97 percent of employment

BOX 3.2 *Microenterprises account for most job creation and destruction*

In some household and labor force surveys, employees are asked to report the size of the firm they work for, or the size of their own business if they are self-employed. This information can be used to estimate the distribution of employment by plant size. This distribution can in turn be used to correct for the omission of informal enterprises in an economic census or plant-level survey.

This approach was applied to Chile's manufacturing survey, the Annual National Industrial Survey (Encuesta Nacional Industrial Anual), which covers more than 90 percent of employment among establishments with 50 workers or more, but less than half the employment in establishments with 10 to 49 workers. Nearly 300,000 workers in microenterprises are omitted from the survey; 250,000 of them work in firms with fewer than 5 employees.

The distribution of job flows by firm size that emerges from the manufacturing survey can be adjusted based on the distribution of employment by plant size from Chile's household survey, the National Socioeconomic Characterization Survey (Encuesta de Caracterización Socioeconómica Nacional, or CASEN). Before this adjustment, larger firms seem to account for most job creation and destruction. But the adjustment shows that microenterprises contribute about 80 percent of gross job flows. This estimate should not be taken literally, because the microenterprises for which information on job creation and destruction is available are not necessarily representative—the Chilean census started to include microenterprises only in the late 1990s. But even with a margin of error, the estimate is so large that it changes the picture of job creation and job destruction.

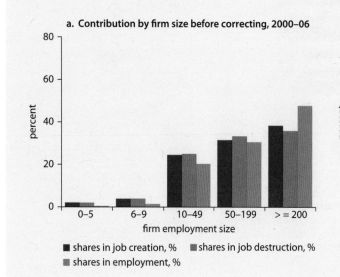

a. Contribution by firm size before correcting, 2000–06

b. Contribution by firm size after correcting, 2000–06

- shares in job creation, %
- shares in job destruction, %
- shares in employment, %

Source: World Development Report 2013 team.

in the manufacturing sector in Ethiopia and 39 percent in Chile. In services sectors, their role is often more important. Even in Eastern European countries, where private sector entry is only two decades old, microenterprises account for 10 to 20 percent of employment in manufacturing and for 30 to 50 percent of employment in services. Micro- and small enterprises also play a critical role in job creation and destruction (box 3.2).[26]

In farms, uneven technological progress

It is generally assumed that large farms are more productive. In low-income countries, however, yields per hectare tend to be higher in smaller farms, because family farms apply more labor per unit of land, even though they apply fewer purchased inputs. This inverse relationship between farm size and productivity was first observed in South Asia.[27] But it has also emerged in Sub-Saharan Africa as population pressure on the land has led to agricultural intensification. In Kenya, Malawi, Tanzania, and Uganda, a 1 percent increase in farm size is associated with a 0.1 to 0.2 percent reduction in yield.[28] The use of family labor per hectare is also inversely correlated with farm size.[29]

The relationship between crop yields and farm size emerges, because the larger, more mechanized farms have higher productivity. But

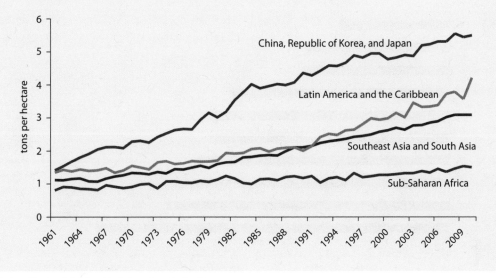

FIGURE 3.8 *Crop yields have diverged vastly across regions*

Source: FAOSTAT-Agriculture (database), Food and Agriculture Organization, Rome.
Note: Figures are weighted averages of yields for wheat, rice, and coarse crops.

constraints in land markets usually slow expansion and mechanization.[30]

The new technologies of the Green Revolution contributed to job creation because they were labor intensive. Short-statured, fertilizer-responsive, high-yielding varieties of rice and wheat were developed by international agricultural research centers in the late 1960s. The varietal improvement of other cereals such as maize followed. These varieties, as well as improved production practices, were quickly diffused, particularly in tropical Asia. The amount of inorganic fertilizer applied has steadily increased over extended periods.[31] Thanks to continual technological improvements and sustained adoption, cereal yields have increased dramatically for the past several decades.[32]

Progress has been uneven across regions, however (figure 3.8). In Sub-Saharan Africa, there is no evidence to suggest that small farmers were slower than larger farmers in adopting the new technologies. But the Green Revolution has not taken place on a large scale, even though farmland has been growing scarce because of population pressure on limited cultivable areas.[33] Feeding growing populations from a shrinking amount of farm land requires Sub-Saharan African countries to increase cereal yields.[34] Yet improved agricultural technology is location specific: improved varieties in Asia

may not be productive in Sub-Saharan Africa, and high-yielding varieties in irrigated areas may be low-yielding in rain-fed areas.[35]

The agricultural growth associated with the Green Revolution not only creates jobs in farming but also facilitates the development of the nonfarm sectors.[36] The adoption of modern technology stimulates the production and marketing of fertilizer and other purchased inputs. Increased supply of cereals stimulates the development of food markets and keeps the cost of living low for those who migrate to the cities. In addition to these backward and forward links, the increase in farmers' incomes heightens the demand for goods and services.[37] Cross-country analyses show that agricultural growth has resulted in the expansion of nonfarm sectors, particularly where the agricultural sector is large.[38]

Among firms, much churning and few gazelles

Outside of agriculture, productivity varies substantially across enterprises, implying that job reallocation could lead to large gains in aggregate productivity. In India, within a narrowly defined manufacturing industry, a plant at the 90th percentile of the TFP distribution gener-

FIGURE 3.9 *The dispersion of productivity in manufacturing is greater in developing countries*

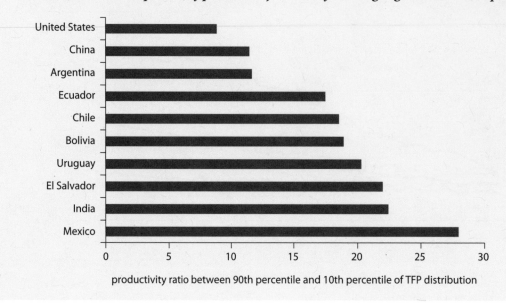

productivity ratio between 90th percentile and 10th percentile of TFP distribution

Source: Pagés 2010.

Note: TFP = total factor productivity. The figure shows the ratio of TFP among plants between the 90th and the 10th percentiles of the TFP distribution within narrowly defined industries. TFP is measured as physical productivity, as defined by Foster, Haltiwanger, and Syverson (2008). The data cover only the manufacturing sector. Data are from Argentina (2002), Bolivia (2001), Chile (2006), China (2005), Ecuador (2005), El Salvador (2005), India (1994), Mexico (2004), United States (1997), and Uruguay (2005).

ates 22 times as much output as a plant at the 10th percentile. In comparison, the estimated ratio is only 9 to 1 in the United States.[39] The dispersion of TFP is also high in a number of Latin American countries (figure 3.9). Detailed data on nonmanufacturing firms are scarcer. But the dispersion of TFP in retail businesses in Mexico, and in communication and transportation businesses in Uruguay, is also sizable.[40]

The speed at which productivity grows also varies across firms. Large firms are typically more innovative than small firms. They tend to invest more in machinery and hire more educated workers. They are also more likely than small firms to engage in activities such as developing new product lines, introducing new technology, opening and closing plants, outsourcing, and engaging in joint ventures with foreign partners (figure 3.10a). Large firms produce more with a given amount of labor, are more likely to export, and tend to export more. They also pay substantively higher wages than micro- and small enterprises (figure 3.10b). They pay a wage premium even controlling for age, education, and other worker characteristics. Not all large firms are innovative, however. When size is supported through nonmarket mechanisms,

efficiency tends to suffer. Large SOEs without foreign competitors are less innovative and productive than other large firms.[41]

For a given size, young firms are also more likely than old firms to engage in innovative activities. They also have better growth prospects, a finding consistent with evidence from industrial countries (figure 3.11).[42] For example, in the 1990s, when China was in the early stages of reform, human and financial resources were concentrated in SOEs. However, the incentive structure in these enterprises hindered innovation. In contrast, the new township and village enterprises lacked the resources to adopt new technology and import new equipment, but they were more flexible in their decision making. As a result, these younger firms were more dynamic than large SOEs, although they were less productive than large and medium private companies.[43]

In developing countries, the dispersion of productivity and growth prospects across firms is further widened by the large number of microenterprises, many of which are barely more than a means of subsistence for the poor. A majority of these microenterprises have limited capital and often even lack a fixed address.

FIGURE 3.10 *Large firms tend to perform better and to pay better than small ones*

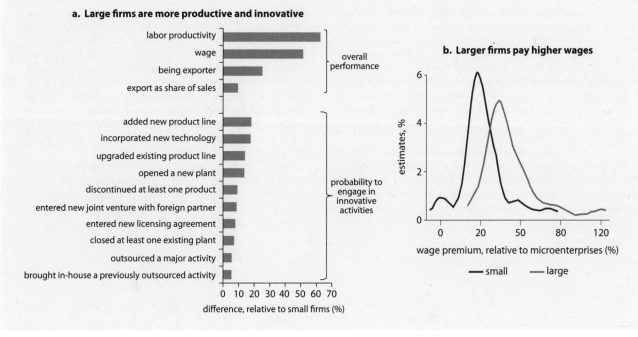

a. **Large firms are more productive and innovative**

b. **Larger firms pay higher wages**

Source: World Development Report 2013 team based on Ayyagari, Demirgüç-Kunt, and Maksimovic 2011a; and Montenegro and Patrinos 2012 for the World Development Report 2013.
Note: Panel a uses World Bank enterprise surveys covering more than 54,000 firms across 102 developing countries over 2006–10 for overall performance, and 19,000 firms across 47 developing countries over 2002–05 for innovative activities. The analysis controls for firm characteristics, industry, and country. In this panel, large firms employ 100 or more workers and small firms fewer than 20 workers. Panel b uses 138 household and labor force surveys spanning 33 countries over 1991–2010 and controls for worker characteristics. In this panel, large firms are those employing more than 50 workers and small firms 10 to 50 workers.

FIGURE 3.11 *Young firms are more likely than old ones to engage in innovative activities*

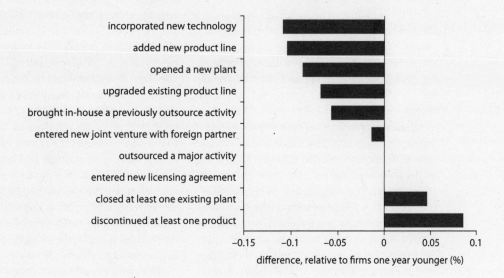

Source: World Development Report 2013 team based on Ayyagari, Demirgüç-Kunt, and Maksimovic 2011a.
Note: The figure uses World Bank enterprise surveys covering 19,000 firms across 47 developing countries over 2002–05, controlling for firm characteristics, industry, and country. Statistically insignificant estimates are reported as zeroes.

BOX 3.3 *Most microenterprises are in rural areas and engage in commerce*

Microenterprises in urban areas, and particularly those in the informal sector, tend to attract the attention of academics and policy makers. But microenterprises are prominent in rural areas as well. The surveys of micro- and small enterprises in Africa and in Latin America and the Caribbean show that fewer than half are in cities and towns with 20,000 inhabitants or more. The urban share reaches 46 percent in the Dominican Republic but is below 30 percent in all other countries surveyed. Even if rural towns are counted (generally, localities with 2,000 to 20,000 inhabitants), well over half of the enterprises are in strictly rural areas in most countries.

The vast majority of microenterprises are engaged in commerce, supporting the conventional view that associates microenterprises with street vendors and petty traders. But a significant number are involved in light manufacturing activities. According to the 1-2-3 surveys of West African countries, the most important sector in capital cities is petty trading (27.1 percent of all enterprises), followed by

other manufacturing and food (16 percent) and other services (11.8 percent). Similarly, the surveys of countries in Africa and in Latin America and the Caribbean suggest that 56 to 74 percent of micro- and small firms in urban areas, and 60 to 70 percent in rural areas, are engaged in commerce. The surveys of household enterprises in Sub-Saharan African countries show similar patterns. These surveys identify three manufacturing activities as the most important across all countries: textiles and apparel, food and beverages, and wood and forest products. These three categories account for about 75 percent of manufacturing enterprises in urban areas and nearly 90 percent of manufacturing enterprises in rural areas.

Most of the microenterprises operate from home or on the street. According to the surveys of household enterprises in Sub-Saharan Africa, 25 to 45 percent of these microfirms use home as primary point of operation, and 10 to 40 percent of them simply work on the street.

Sources: Fox and Sohnesen 2012; Grimm, Kruger, and Lay 2011; Liedholm 2002.

Many are located in rural areas, absorbing some labor slack during the low agricultural season (box 3.3). Across 18 developing countries, 44 percent of the people living on less than US$1 a day in urban areas, and 24 percent of those in rural areas, work in a nonagricultural business. On average, they do not earn much.[44]

Nonetheless, these nonfarm activities provide an important channel to diversify income for the poor. In nine Sub-Saharan African countries, most nonfarm jobs were generated by households starting businesses, rather than entering the rapidly expanding private wage sector. Despite being modest, earnings from household enterprises contribute to consumption much the same as earnings from wage employment do. And these small businesses offer an avenue for poor households to engage in gradually more productive activities.[45]

While microenterprises have a lackluster performance as a group, they are also very diverse. In middle-income countries, a significant share of the owners of micro- and small enterprises are as entrepreneurial as their peers in industrial countries. Their weak performance may be driven more by contextual factors such as limited access to credit and policy-induced barriers to access technologies and markets, than by limited capacity. In several Latin American countries, for example, entrants into self-employment tend to be workers who have ac-

cumulated human and physical capital while working for a wage or a salary. Operating microenterprises is a choice for them. Those who achieve higher productivity levels are more likely to stay in business, grow, and create job opportunities for others.[46]

A very small group of microenterprises actually displays a strong performance. This group bears similarities with the so-called "gazelles" of industrial countries—high-growth companies whose revenues increase by at least 20 percent annually for four years or more. In industrial countries, the term "gazelle" is used for companies starting from a revenue base of at least US$1 million, which makes them very big by developing-country standards. Nonetheless, the same dynamism can be found at a much smaller scale. Data from seven Sub-Saharan African countries show that the median capital stock held by urban informal enterprises is less than US$80, whereas the capital stock for those in the top quintile averages US$5,000. The average monthly profit of those in the top quintile is seven times the median monthly profit. The rate of returns to capital is also relatively high in these firms.[47] This heterogeneity among microenterprises suggests they can be an incubator for large and productive firms.

The dynamism of microenterprises matters not only for livelihoods but also for productivity growth. Large firms innovate more, but they are

FIGURE 3.12 *Surviving firms were born larger and grew less in Ghana than in Portugal*

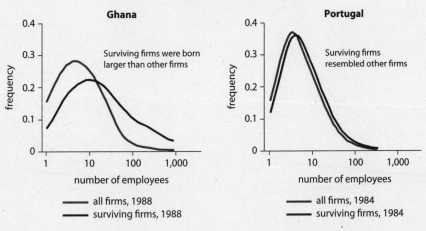

a. Initial year: All firms versus surviving firms

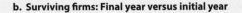

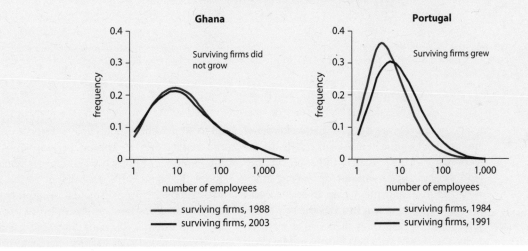

b. Surviving firms: Final year versus initial year

Sources: Cabral and Mata 2003; Sandefur 2010.

not all born large. In industrial countries, some of the more resounding successes, from Honda to Microsoft, started in garages. And many successful companies in developing countries also grew out of small household businesses. Thailand's Charoen Pokphand Group, founded in 1921 as a small seed shop in Bangkok by two brothers, has grown into one of the world's largest multinational conglomerates in agribusiness, operating in 15 countries and encompassing close to 100 companies.[48] India's Tata Group transformed from a Mumbai-based, family-owned trading firm in the late 19th century to a multinational conglomerate comprising 114 companies and subsidiaries across 8 business sectors on several continents.[49] Many of China's successful clusters, such as the footwear and electric appliance industry in Wenzhou, also started from small family businesses working close to each other.[50]

A vibrant firm life cycle is often missing, however. Larger and older firms tend to be stagnant, while smaller enterprises are prone to churning. In Ghana, for example, many firms are born large and show little growth over 15 years (figure 3.12). In Portugal, by contrast,

FIGURE 3.13 *The majority of firms grew little in India and Mexico*

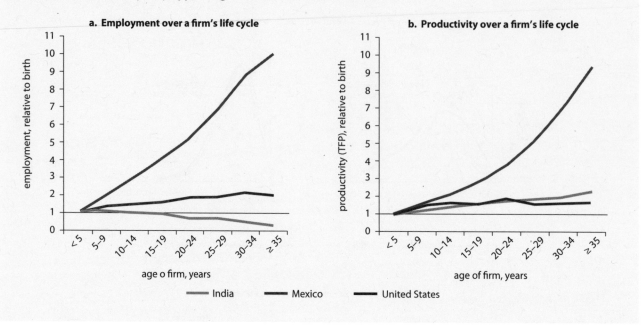

Source: Hsieh and Klenow 2011.
Note: TFP = total factor productivity. Figures show the average employment (or productivity) of firms in different age groups relative to the average employment (or productivity) of those same firms had at birth. Figures are computed using 1989–90 and 1994–95 data for India, 1998 and 2003 data for Mexico, and 1992 and 1997 data for the United States.

many more firms are born as microenterprises and grow substantially in 7 years.[51] The majority of firms are born small in India too, but they tend to stay small, without displaying much variation in employment over their life cycle. A revealing comparison involves the size of 35-year old firms relative to their size at birth. In India, the size declines by a fourth. In Mexico, it doubles. In the United States, it is 10 times larger (figure 3.13a). Productivity growth over a firm's life cycle follows similar patterns in these countries (figure 3.13b).[52]

Churning—entering and exiting at a relatively high rate—is much more common than growth among the micro- and small enterprises of developing countries. In several Sub-Saharan African and Latin American countries, about 20 percent of micro- and small enterprises enter and leave the market in the same year. A majority of closures occur within three years of starting up. Among the survivors, less than 3 percent expand by four employees or more.[53] In Vietnam,

20 to 30 percent of household enterprises leave the market over a two-year period, while the total number of household enterprises remains about the same.[54] In Sub-Saharan Africa, few household enterprises expand into employment beyond the household, as shown by the experiences of Ethiopia, Tanzania, and Madagascar.[55] In Mexico, individuals starting microenterprises are more likely to remain the sole worker than to increase the firm size (table 3.1).[56]

The wide dispersion of productivity among businesses, the large number of unsustainable microenterprises, and the stagnation of larger firms all suggest that the process of market selection and creative destruction that has underpinned the rapid growth of transition economies and East Asian countries in the past decades is weak in most developing countries. This weakness impedes labor and other resources from moving toward their most productive uses and undermines both job creation and productivity growth. Gains from tackling the difficulties faced

TABLE 3.1 *Few small firms grew in Mexico*

		Same firms by size in 2011, %			
		Own account	1–4 workers	5–9 workers	10 or more workers
Firms by size in 1987, %	Own account	51.9	12.4	0.5	0.2
	1–4 workers	22.1	49.2	3.9	1.5
	5–9 workers	7.8	35.1	22.6	13.1
	10 or more workers	4.1	15.2	14.4	44.6

Source: Fajnzylber, Maloney, and Rojas 2006.
Note: Rows do not add up to 100 percent because the owners of some of these firms may become salary workers or unemployed.

by the start-ups and removing constraints to the growth of incumbents could be sizable, but the task is daunting (question 3).[57]

* * *

Jobs can have an impact on the productivity of others, beyond the jobholder and the economic unit where they belong. Jobs that have these additional impacts do more (or less) for development. These additional impacts arise because jobs differ in the way they connect with each other, and some of the connections do not occur through markets. In functional cities, ideas are exchanged among people more effectively, making everybody more productive. In clusters, similar firms that locate next to each other tend to benefit from a broader pool of qualified workers and common support services. Firms also connect with foreign businesses through trade and investment, and, in integrating with global value chains, they can acquire more advanced knowledge, technology, and management know-how. In all these ways, specific jobs can contribute to productivity gains of others and elsewhere in the economy. But effects can be negative as well if jobs overuse natural resources or damage the environment, thus reducing aggregate productivity.

Self-employment is prevalent in developing countries, and micro- and small enterprises are a major source of livelihood for low-skilled workers. Even if only a small fraction of these tiny economic units succeeded in building a viable business, with the potential to hire others, the aggregate effect on living standards would be substantial. Their success would also matter for productivity reasons. Quite a few currently large enterprises in industrial countries started out as micro- and small family businesses. By contrast, in developing countries many large enterprises are born large, often the result of government support or privileged access to finance and information. Breaking privileges is one more reason why the success of microenterprises is so important.

Views differ on whether there is scope to help the self-employed succeed. At one time almost every self-employed person or owner of a microenterprise was seen as a potential entrepreneur, held back only by regulatory zeal and corruption. Substantial rates of return on capital for micro- and small enterprises were viewed as evidence of a potential to thrive.[58] But the pendulum has swung, and the conventional wisdom is now rather pessimistic. The large numbers of unregistered self-employed in developing countries are viewed as subsistence entrepreneurs who are trying to make ends meet, not thriving.[59] Evidence on the growth of micro- and small enterprises in several countries in Latin America and West Africa shows that most microenterprises with at least two years of operations remain at their start-up employment levels.[60] Embedded in the pessimism of the conventional wisdom is the idea that entrepreneurial ability and skills cannot be easily transferred, especially not to adults with limited formal education. In this view, entrepreneurs are born, not made. If this view is correct, attempts to convert survivorship into entrepreneurship are bound to fail. The wide dispersion of productivity across firms, including across microenterprises, suggests, however, that reality is somewhere in between the optimistic and the pessimistic view: survivorship may be dominant, but entrepreneurship is unlikely to be missing altogether.

Who is an entrepreneur?

Entrepreneurship combines innovative capacity to put new ideas into effect with managerial capacity to increase a firm's efficiency within the limits of known technology. Specific psychological traits are associated with entrepreneurship, such as a personal need for achievement, a belief in the effect of personal effort on outcomes, self-confidence, and a positive attitude toward risk. These traits are difficult to observe or measure. But surveys comparing entrepreneurs with other workers in places as diverse as China and the Russian Federation show that observable individual characteristics such as education, experience, gender, location, and age are good predictors of entrepreneurship.[61] Among microenterprises, rates of return on capital tend to be higher when their owners are more educated and experienced.

Observable characteristics of the self-employed can thus be used to identify individuals who have potential to become successful entrepreneurs.[62] To illustrate the point, a successful entrepreneur is defined as someone who employs others and is not living in poverty. The share of this group in total employment is small and relatively stable across countries at different levels of development.[63] The share of self-employed workers without paid employees, on the other hand, initially increases and then declines with GDP per capita (figure 3.14a). At its peak, which corresponds to low-income countries, the share of self-employed workers without paid employees reaches almost three-fifths of total employment. Among this group, a majority are individuals with relatively low potential to succeed. Their characteristics are closer to those of wage workers than of employers.[64]

However, if each of the self-employed workers with high potential were to create a single additional job, total employment would increase substantially, somewhat more so in low-income countries (figure 3.14b). As a share of the work-

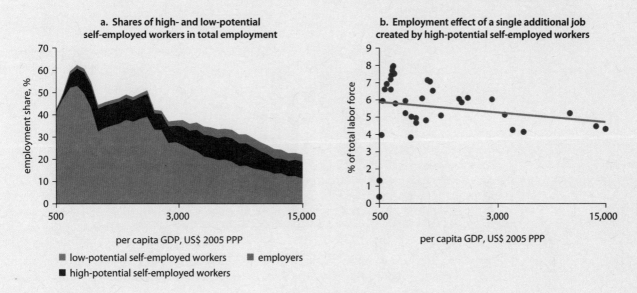

FIGURE 3.14 *Some among the self-employed have the potential to become successful entrepreneurs*

a. Shares of high- and low-potential self-employed workers in total employment

employment share, %

per capita GDP, US$ 2005 PPP

- ◼ low-potential self-employed workers   ◼ employers
- ◼ high-potential self-employed workers

b. Employment effect of a single additional job created by high-potential self-employed workers

% of total labor force

per capita GDP, US$ 2005 PPP

Sources: Gindling and Newhouse 2012 for the World Development Report 2013; World Development Report 2013 team estimates based on data from 36 countries.
Note: GDP = gross domestic product. PPP = purchasing power parity. In panel b, each dot represents a country.

ing age population, such additional job creation would amount to 8 percent in Kenya, 5 percent in the Arab Republic of Egypt and 4 percent in Costa Rica.

While this calculation is hypothetical, several studies report that observable characteristics of micro- and small informal enterprise owners, such as education and gender, are important determinants of innovation and employment growth.[65] In Mexico, after a business registration reform, informal enterprise owners with observable traits similar to those found among formal enterprise owners were more likely to register their business than those similar to wage workers.[66]

What constrains entrepreneurship?

Even potentially skilled entrepreneurs would have difficulty succeeding without access to basic infrastructure and financial resources. In their absence, managerial capacity alone may not be enough to realize productivity gains and employment expansion. The investment climate matters for business performance as well.

Removing obstacles to firm growth is thus a prerequisite to foster entrepreneurship.

Obstacles notwithstanding, entrepreneurial capacity varies substantially across microenterprises and small firms. A distinction is often made between innovative or transformative entrepreneurs and replicative or subsistence entrepreneurs.[67] The former correspond to Schumpeterian type of entrepreneurs, while the latter, who generally manage micro- and small enterprises, are followers. Such a distinction, however, does not capture the broader gradation of managerial performance that lies between the transformative and subsistence extremes. A study of the number of management practices adopted by the owners of micro- and small enterprises in Sub-Saharan Africa reveals a large variation of management scores (figure 3.15). These scores are closely associated with business performance.[68] A broad dispersion of management scores is also found among relatively larger firms in India.[69]

An emerging literature confirms the importance of management practices in explaining firm productivity. Although much of the focus is on large firms, recent studies have turned their

FIGURE 3.15 *Management scores vary widely across small enterprises in Sub-Saharan Africa*

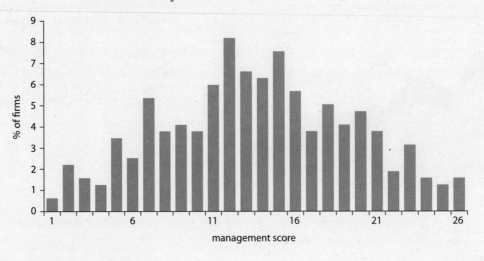

Source: Fafchamps and Woodruff 2012.
Note: The management score measures the degree to which firm owners use and master core management and business techniques. Scores are based on an evaluation of 26 techniques (26 is the highest possible score).

attention to how innovation in small and medium firms takes place. The most telling studies involve management training provided for free to randomly selected firms whose performance is then compared to that of a control group of firms. Evaluations of these programs find that the training improves the financial literacy and basic management skills of business owners. The estimated impact is also positive, but less robust, when it comes to improved business outcomes and job creation. Better outcomes are associated with business owners who already had an initial understanding of the concepts and relatively better access to financial resources.

On the other hand, similarly designed interventions to provide financial resources to microenterprises, or to process their registration with authorities, or to pay the salary of an additional employee, show mixed impacts on business performance.[70] In Mexico and Sri Lanka, grants given to microenterprises increase the income of their owners—and then only if they are male—but do not result in employment creation. In Ghana, similar grants given to female business owners do not result in significant growth of their microenterprises. In Sri Lanka, only 22 percent of eligible microenterprises took

up an offer of a wage subsidy covering 50 percent of the cost of hiring a worker for six months and 25 percent of the cost for another two months. Overall, these results suggest that lack of access to finance is not the only constraint.

Entrepreneurial skills, measured by the education of business owners and their participation in training, explain a large share of the differences in productivity across firms and regions in developing countries.[71] Yet markets fail to nurture entrepreneurship, because knowledge spillovers imply that some of the returns to acquiring or developing new managerial ideas are appropriated by others. More important perhaps, entrepreneurs themselves do not recognize the relevance of management expertise.[72] Only 3 percent of Brazil's owners of micro- and small enterprises, for instance, see management as a binding business constraint.[73] This may be an area where information and knowledge failures matter, leading to a vicious circle of low productivity, low living standards, and insufficient job creation.

The capacity to acquire skills and to apply them to business seems to be one of the most important characteristics of successful entrepreneurs. Success also depends on having core skills such as numeracy and literacy, as well as social skills. A vast literature highlights the importance of entrepreneurs' schooling as a determinant of firm growth, employment, and efficiency.[74] Russian and Chinese business owners have more entrepreneurs in their families and among childhood friends than otherwise similar individuals, suggesting that social environment also matters.[75]

Learning can also happen through jobs. Nearly half of entrepreneurs managing the 50 largest manufacturing firms in Ethiopia began their careers in trading companies, thereby learning about the market and what it takes to meet demand.[76] A large number of founders and leading entrepreneurs in the light manufacturing industries in Asia and Sub-Saharan Africa were initially traders or employees in the marketing division of large enterprises.[77]

Integration in supply chains with larger, often foreign, firms is receiving much attention as a potential source of knowledge transfers.[78] Indian entrepreneurs returning from Silicon Valley made Bangalore a hub of the information technology industry. Perhaps the most dramatic evidence attesting to the importance of learning from abroad can be found in the case of the garment industry in Bangladesh (box 3.4).

The case for targeted management training

Managerial practices are linked to differences in productivity, profitability, firm growth, and survival.[79] The development experience of the garment industry in Bangladesh suggests that entrepreneurship can be fostered by exposure to advanced management practices and technologies. But whether managerial capacity can be improved through management training is more debatable. Creativity, foresight, and risk taking are key elements of any innovative process, but the question is whether they can be diffused and nurtured.

A substantial number of experiments have been conducted in recent years, providing evidence of both successes and failures of management training interventions. Some patterns emerge from a systematic review of the available evidence. To be successful, management training must be kept simple, appropriate teaching materials must be available, and the training must

---

BOX 3.4 *What explains the boom in the garment industry in Bangladesh?*

The garment industry in Bangladesh illustrates how important it is to learn advanced management practices, marketing, and technologies from abroad. When Daewoo Corporation of Korea teamed up with Bangladesh's Desh Ltd. to produce garments for export in Bangladesh in 1979, the South Asian country had no modern industry. Little more than 20 years later, the industry was generating more than US$12.5 billion in export revenue. Women accounted for 80 percent of its 3.6 million workers

Arguably, a wide set of factors, from financial innovation to policy support, contributed to this development success. But it began in 1979, when Desh sent 130 newly recruited, educated employees to Daewoo's garment factory in Korea, where they participated in an eight-month intensive training course covering topics from sewing skills to factory management, quality control, and international procurement and marketing—skills that they then applied in the Desh factories in Bangladesh. Within a few years, almost all the trainees had left Desh to start their own garment businesses. Some of the ex-Desh workers joined new garment factories established by affluent businessmen, while others founded trading houses, which then contributed to the proliferation of garment manufacturers by providing a variety of valuable services including international procurement and marketing, sample making, and design reengineering.

Observing Desh's good start in exporting, and subsequently the success of ex-Desh workers, highly educated people started their own garment businesses, and wealthy families actively invested in the industry. As a result, the size of garment firms has been quite large since the beginning; their average size was 300 workers in 1983–84 and 700 in 2010–11. As of 2005, owners of garment firms had 15 years of schooling on average, and about 60 percent of them had completed college or university education.

Learning from abroad continued. Some entrepreneurs participated in training programs in Singapore, Japan, and Europe. Beyond garment enterprises in Korea, other newly industrial countries in East Asia followed Daewoo into operation in Bangladesh and invested in training Bangladeshi workers and managers. Thus, many Bangladeshi traders and manufacturers had work experience in garment trading and production, including the experience of working at joint ventures, before starting their current businesses.

Sources: Bangladesh Knitwear Manufacturers and Exporters Association 2012 ; Easterly 2002; Mottaleb and Sonobe 2011; Rhee 1990.

last for a certain minimum length of time. Complementing classroom teaching with instructors' visits to trainees on the job can yield significant positive effects.[80] In Mexico, for example, such on-site visits improved sales, profits, and productivity.[81] But in Ghana, on-site visits and support for microenterprises were not successful.[82] It is also possible that key entrepreneurial skills are gained more effectively through work experience in large productive firms than through training programs.[83]

Entrepreneurship training for women has had mixed results. Nurturing female entrepreneurship has the potential to create wider social benefits associated with female employment, such as changes in the household allocation of resources that improve family well-being, especially of children. Female entrepreneurship often provides employment opportunities to women that allow them to balance work and family roles. Yet providing classroom training to female microentrepreneurs in Peru had no effect on key business outcomes such as sales and profits, even when some business practices improved.[84] Classroom training complemented with on-site visits, though, yielded positive results.[85] In Pakistan and Tanzania, management training improved management practices and business outcomes for male but not female entrepreneurs.[86] These mixed results can also reflect wider constraints facing women in societies, including access to effective learning in schools.

A common finding of training evaluations is that the potential to absorb management practices differs greatly among beneficiaries. Readily observable individual characteristics can help identify those business owners with the highest potential to benefit from management training. Expert panels may be used to identify and rank micro- and small enterprises on their potential to grow, but such methods are expensive and difficult to apply on a large scale. An effective alternative is a survey questionnaire designed to capture abilities, attitudes, and management scores of potential trainees.[87] Management training itself can be used as a screening device. Trainees with high potential often undertake new investments and expand employment as a result of their training. Financial institutions could view such activity as an indication of potentially high investment returns. Programs that combine management training with financial support yield better firm performance in developing countries.[88]

Training programs can be implemented by private providers and financed by private investors with a significant interest in the success of the entrepreneurs in whom they have invested. But as long as there are knowledge spillovers and the importance of management expertise is undervalued, governments have a role to play. Given the differing capabilities among business owners, proper targeting is crucial to ensure positive returns to publicly funded programs. Randomized experiments in Ghana, Tanzania, and Vietnam indicate that the benefit of such programs generally outweighs the cost, even though the costs of implementing training programs vary greatly.[89] If the overall investment climate is not conducive to private sector growth, however, targeted training programs for better business skills will most likely return meager results.

Notes

1. Labor force is used instead of employment in figure 3.1. Over a long term (10-year period), changes in unemployment rates are small, in general, and employment in an economy is driven by the size of its labor force.
2. Haltiwanger 2011; Schumpeter 1934.
3. Gross job creation is the sum of all additions to total employment. It occurs when expanding economic units hire workers and when new economic units are created. In principle, economic units can be as small as a one-person microenterprise, but most quantitative analyses refer to establishments employing several workers. Gross job destruction is the sum of all employment losses. It occurs when economic units close or contract in size. Net job creation is the difference between these two gross flows. Job creation and destruction rates measure how many employment positions emerge or disappear in a specific period (typically one year) relative to the number of existing positions. See Bartelsman, Haltiwanger, and Scarpetta 2009b; Davis, Haltiwanger, and Schuh 1996.
4. Kucera and Roncolato 2012; McMillan and Rodrik 2011; Pieper 2000; Timmer and de Vries 2009.
5. World Bank 2009.
6. Duranton 2007, Duranton 2012 for the World Development Report 2013; Duranton and Puga 2001; Henderson 2002.
7. Park et al. 2011; World Bank 2011b.
8. Ghani, Goswami, and Kerr 2012.
9. For a discussion on how to decompose productivity growth by firm dynamics, see Foster, Haltiwanger, and Krizan (2001) and Griliches and Regev (1992).
10. Bartelsman and Doms 2000; Bartelsman, Haltiwanger, and Scarpetta 2004; Foster, Haltiwanger, and Krizan 2001; Roberts 1996; Syverson 2011; Tybout 1996, 2000. The dispersion of productivity across firms is not, by itself, sufficient to gauge the efficiency of the job creation and reallocation process. Poor market structure and institutions can distort the process. See Haltiwanger 2011; Nelson 1981.
11. Bartelsman, Haltiwanger, and Scarpetta 2004; Tybout 1996.
12. Baily, Bartelsman, and Haltiwanger 1996.
13. WDR 2013 team estimation based on Amadeus Database, the Annual National Industrial Survey of Chile, and Ethiopia Large and Medium Scale Manufacturing and Electricity Industries Survey.
14. Dutz and others 2011.
15. Bartelsman, Haltiwanger, and Scarpetta 2004; Rutkowski and others 2005.
16. Brandt and Rawski 2008; World Bank and the People's Republic of China Development Research Center of the State Council 2012.
17. Brandt, Hsieh, and Zhu 2008; Brandt and Rawski 2008; Brandt, van Biesebroeck, and Zhang 2012.
18. Hayami and Otsuka 1993.
19. South Africa is excluded from this figure because it is an outlier, with an average farm size of 288 hectares.
20. In fact, tenancy markets are emerging in Sub-Saharan Africa. See Holden, Otsuka, and Place 2009.
21. Otsuka and Place 2001.
22. Pagés 2010.
23. ADB 2009. The analysis is based on data from India (2004–05); Indonesia (2006); the Republic of Korea (2004); the Philippines (2005); and Taiwan, China (2006).
24. Rijkers and others 2012 for the World Development Report 2013; Pagés 2010.
25. Grimm, Kruger, and Lay 2011; Liedholm 2002.
26. See also Ayyagari, Demirgüç-Kunt, and Maksimovic (2011b) for analysis based on World Bank enterprise surveys; the analysis suggests that small firms contribute significantly to employment and job creation.
27. The body of literature on this subject is enormous. See Barrett, Bellemare, and Hou 2010; Carletto, Savastano, and Zezza 2011; and Larson and others 2012 for the World Development Report 2013.
28. Holden, Otsuka, and Place 2009; Larson and others 2012 for the World Development Report 2013.
29. For example, in Kenya in 2007, the family labor input per hectare in maize production was 418 hours for the top quartile of farms (measured by size), but that input reached 1,032 hours for the bottom quartile.
30. The positive relationship is found not only in such high-wage economies as Japan but also in India recently. See Foster and Rosenzweig 2011; Hayami and Kawagoe 1989.
31. Evenson and Gollin 2003.
32. World Bank 2007. Improvement in agriculture technology can lead to fast growth in productivity in the sector and convergence in aggregate productivity. On the basis of data from 50 countries over 1967–92, Martin and Mitra (2001) found that productivity growth in agriculture was faster than in manufacturing in these countries over the period.
33. However, TFP has been increasing since the early 1980s, suggesting that the Green Revolution has taken place in some areas of Sub-Saharan Africa. See Block 2012.
34. Hayami and Ruttan 1985.

35. David and Otsuka 1994.

36. Ravallion 2005; Ravallion and Chen 2007.

37. Haggblade, Hazell, and Reardon 2007.

38. Christiaensen, Demery, and Kuhl 2011.

39. Hsieh and Klenow 2009.

40. Pagés 2010. Figures are based on physical productivity (or TFPQ), as defined by Foster, Haltiwanger, and Syverson (2008). This factor is a measure of real output per unit of input, which is computed using plant-level price deflators. TFPQ is more precise than TFPR—a revenue proxy for TFPQ that is computed using industry-level price deflators. TFPQ is a preferred measure because TFPR combines the effects of quantities and prices. Quantities and prices are affected by demand factors, quality differences, markups, and potential distortions. A survey of earlier studies based on TFPR did not find a higher dispersion of productivity in developing countries, but those studies are not very informative because they are based on outdated methodologies. See Tybout 2000.

41. Ayyagari, Demirgüç-Kunt, and Maksimovic 2011a.

42. Ayyagari, Demirgüç-Kunt, and Maksimovic 2011a; Haltiwanger, Jarmin, and Miranda 2010.

43. Lin 2012; Wang and Yao 1999.

44. Banerjee and Duflo 2011; Fox and Sohnesen 2012; Schoar 2010; Sutton and Kellow 2010.

45. Fox and Sohnesen 2012.

46. Perry and others 2007.

47. Grimm, Kruger, and Lay 2011; McKenzie and Woodruff 2008.

48. Mertens 2011; *The Economist* 2001; Charoen Pokphand Group, www.cpthailand.com.

49. Kasbekar 2007; Witze 2010.

50. Sonobe, Hu, and Otsuka 2004.

51. Sandefur 2010.

52. Hsieh and Klenow 2011.

53. Liedholm 2002; Mead and Liedholm 1998.

54. Results from 1-2-3 Survey.

55. Grimm, Kruger, and Lay 2011; Kinda and Loening 2008; Loening and Imru 2009.

56. Fajnzylber, Maloney, and Rojas 2006.

57. Bartelsman, Haltiwanger, and Scarpetta 2009a; Haltiwanger 2011; Hsieh and Klenow 2009; Syverson 2011.

58. Banerjee and Duflo 2004; Banerjee and others 2009; de Mel, McKenzie, and Woodruff 2008a; Göbel, Grimm, and Lay 2011; Grimm, Kruger, and Lay 2011; McKenzie and Woodruff 2008.

59. Banerjee and Duflo 2011; Schoar 2010; Sutton and Kellow 2010; Tokman 2007. See de Soto (1989) and Yunus and Jolis (1999) for a more positive view.

60. Fajnzylber, Maloney, and Rojas 2006; results from World Bank's informal enterprise surveys conducted between 2009 and 2010.

61. Djankov and others 2005, 2006b. See also Vivarelli (2012) on the importance of disentangling entrepreneurship drivers to craft policies targeting high potential entrepreneurs.

62. Methodological details of this technique to identify high-potential entrepreneurs can be found in Gindling and Newhouse (2012) for the World Development Report 2013; and Grimm, Knorringa, and Lay (2012) for the World Development Report 2013.

63. Gindling and Newhouse 2012 for the World Development Report 2013.

64. de Mel, McKenzie, and Woodruff 2008b.

65. de Mel, McKenzie, and Woodruff 2009; Sonobe and Otsuka 2006; Sonobe and Otsuka 2011.

66. Bruhn 2008.

67. Baumol 2010; Schoar 2010.

68. Fafchamps and Woodruff 2012.

69. Bloom and others 2011.

70. de Mel, McKenzie, and Woodruff 2010; Fafchamps and others 2011; McKenzie 2010.

71. Gennaioli and others 2011; Kelley, Bosma, and Amorós 2010; van der Sluis, van Praag, and Vijverberg 2005.

72. Bloom and others 2011; Mano and others 2011.

73. Estimate from Brazil's ECINF 2003 survey.

74. Fafchamps and Woodruff 2012; Gindling and Newhouse 2012 for the World Development Report 2013; Grimm, Kruger, and Lay 2011; Otsuka and Sonobe 2011; Sonobe and Otsuka 2006.

75. Sutton and Kellow 2010.

76. Otsuka and Sonobe 2011; Sonobe and Otsuka 2006.

77. Djankov and others 2006a, 2006b.

78. See the initiative by the Inter-American Development Bank, "Bringing Market-Based Solutions to Latin America and the Caribbean to Promote Social Change," http://browndigital.bpc.com/publication/?i=92819.

79. Bennedsen and others 2007; Bloom and others 2011; Bloom, Schweiger, and van Reenen 2011; Bloom and van Reenen 2007, 2010.

80. Drexler, Fischer, and Schoar 2011; Kairiza and Sonobe 2012 for the World Development Report 2013; Mano and others 2011; Valdivia 2011.

81. Karlan, Bruhn, and Schoar 2012.

82. Karlan, Knight, and Udry 2012. In Ghana, the intervention included only a 10-hour consultancy treatment, in contrast to 700 hours provided in a successful Indian program for larger firms that was implemented by Bloom and others (2011).

83. Bloom and van Reenen 2010; Bruhn, Karlan, and Schoar 2010; Bruhn and Zia 2011; de Mel, McKenzie, and Woodruff 2009.

84. Karlan and Valdivia 2010.

85. Valdivia 2011.

86. Berge, Bjorvatn, and Tungodden 2011; Giné and Mansuri 2011.

87. Fafchamps and Woodruff 2012. Alternatively, see the work done by the Entrepreneurial Finance Lab at the Kennedy School (http://www.efinlab .com) on psychometrics tools to uncover successful entrepreneurs.

88. Cho and Honorati 2012 for the World Development Report 2013.

89. Sonobe, Higuchi, and Otsuka 2012 for the World Development Report 2013.

References

The word *processed* describes informally reproduced works that may not be commonly available through libraries.

ADB (Asian Development Bank). 2009. *Enterprises in Asia: Fostering Dynamism in SMEs.* Manila: ADB.

Ayyagari, Meghana, Asli Demirgüç-Kunt, and Vojislav Maksimovic. 2011a. "Firm Innovation in Emerging Markets: The Role of Finance, Governance, and Competition." *Journal of Financial and Quantitative Analysis* 46(6): 1545–80.

———. 2011b. "Small vs. Young Firms across the World: Contribution to Employment, Job Creation, and Growth." Policy Research Working Paper Series 5631, World Bank, Washington, DC.

Baily, Martin Neil, Eric J. Bartelsman, and John Haltiwanger. 1996. "Downsizing and Productivity Growth: Myth or Reality?" *Small Business Economics* 8 (4): 259–78.

Banerjee, Abhijit V., and Esther Duflo. 2004. "Do Firms Want to Borrow More? Testing Credit Constraints Using a Directed Lending Program." Discussion Paper Series 4681, Centre for Economic Policy Research, London.

———. 2011. *Poor Economics: A Radical Rethinking of the Way to Fight Global Poverty.* New York: Public Affairs.

Banerjee, Abhijit V., Esther Duflo, Rachel Glennerster, and Cynthia Kinnan. 2009. "The Miracle of Microfinance? Evidence from a Randomized Evaluation." Massachusetts Institute of Technology, Cambridge, MA. Processed.

Bangladesh Knitwear Manufacturers and Exporters Association. 2012. "History of Development of Knitwear of Bangladesh." Bangladesh Knitwear Manufacturers and Exporters Association, Bangladesh. Processed.

Barrett, Christopher B., Marc F. Bellemare, and Janet Y. Hou. 2010. "Reconsidering Conventional Explanations of the Inverse Productivity–Size Relationship." *World Development* 38 (1): 88–97.

Bartelsman, Eric J., and Mark Doms. 2000. "Understanding Productivity: Evidence from Longitudinal Microdata." *Journal of Economic Literature* (38) 3: 569–94.

Bartelsman, Eric, John Haltiwanger, and Stefano Scarpetta. 2004. "Microeconomic Evidence of Creative Destruction in Industrial and Developing Countries." Discussion Paper Series 1374, Institute for the Study of Labor, Bonn.

———. 2009a. "Cross-Country Differences in Productivity: The Role of Allocation and Selection." Working Paper 15490. National Bureau of Economic Research, Cambridge, MA.

———. 2009b. "Measuring and Analyzing Cross-Country Differences in Firm Dynamics." In *Producer Dynamics: New Evidence from Micro Data*, ed. Timothy Dunne, J. Bradford Jensen, and Mark J. Roberts, 15–82. Cambridge, MA: National Bureau of Economic Research.

Baumol, William J. 2010. *The Microtheory of Innovative Entrepreneurship.* Princeton, NJ: Princeton University Press.

Bennedsen, Morten, Kasper M. Nielsen, Francisco Perez-Gonzalez, and Daniel Wolfenzon. 2007. "Inside the Family Firm: The Role of Families in Succession Decisions and Performance." *Quarterly Journal of Economics* 122 (2): 647–91.

Berge, Lars Ivar Oppedal, Kjetil Bjorvatn, and Bertil Tungodden. 2011. "Human and Financial Capital for Microenterprise Development: Evidence from a Field and Lab Experiment." Discussion Paper 1, Norwegian School of Economics, Bergen, Norway.

Block, Steven. 2012. "The Decline and Rise of Agricultural Productivity in Sub-Saharan Africa." Working Paper Series 16841, National Bureau of Economic Research, Cambridge, MA.

Bloom, Nicholas, Benn Eifert, Aprajit Mahajan, David McKenzie, and John Roberts. 2011. "Does Management Matter? Evidence from India." Policy Research Working Paper Series 5573, World Bank, Washington, DC.

Bloom, Nicholas, Helena Schweiger, and John Van Reenen. 2011. "The Land That Lean Manufacturing Forgot? Management Practices in Transition Countries." Working Paper Series 17231, National Bureau of Economic Research, Cambridge, MA.

Bloom, Nicholas, and John van Reenen. 2007. "Measuring and Explaining Management Practices across Firms and Countries." *Quarterly Journal of Economics* 122 (4): 1351–408.

———. 2010. "Why Do Management Practices Differ across Firms and Countries?" *Journal of Economic Perspectives* 24 (1): 203–24.

Brandt, Loren, Chang-Tai Hsieh, and Xiaodong Zhu. 2008. "Growth and Structural Transformation in China." In *China's Great Economic Transformation*, ed. Loren Brandt and Thomas G. Rawski. Cambridge, U.K.: Cambridge University Press.

Brandt, Loren, and Thomas G Rawski. 2008. *China's Great Economic Transformation.* Cambridge, U.K.: Cambridge University Press.

Brandt, Loren, Johannes van Biesebroeck, and Yifan Zhang. 2012. "Creative Accounting or Creative Destruction? Firm-Level Productivity Growth in Chinese Manufacturing." *Journal of Development Economics* 97 (2): 339–51.

Bruhn, Miriam. 2008. "License to Sell: The Effect of Business Registration Reform on Entrepreneurial Activity in Mexico." Policy Research Working Paper Series 4538, World Bank. Washington, DC.

Bruhn, Miriam, Dean Karlan, and Antoinette Schoar. 2010. "What Capital Is Missing in Developing Countries?" *American Economic Review* 100 (2): 629–33.

Bruhn, Miriam, and Bilal Zia. 2011. "Stimulating Managerial Capital in Emerging Markets: The Impact of Business and Financial Literacy for Young Entrepreneurs." Policy Research Working Paper Series 5642, World Bank, Washington, DC.

Cabral, Luis M. B., and José Mata. 2003. "On the Evolution of the Firm Size Distribution: Facts and Theory." *American Economic Review* 93 (4): 1075–90.

Carletto, Calogero, Sara Savastano, and Alberto Zezza. 2011. "Fact or Artefact: The Impact of Measurement Errors on the Farm Size–Productivity Relationship." Policy Research Working Paper Series 5908, World Bank, Washington, DC.

Cho, Yoonyoung, and Maddalena Honorati. 2012. "A Meta-Analysis of Entrepreneurship Programs in Developing Countries." Background paper for the WDR 2013.

Christiaensen, Luc, Lionel Demery, and Jesper Kuhl. 2011. "The (Evolving) Role of Agriculture in Poverty Reduction—An Empirical Perspective." *Journal of Development Economics* 96 (2): 239–54.

David, Christina C., and Keijiro Otsuka, eds. 1994. *Modern Rice Technology and Income Distribution in Asia.* Boulder, CO: Lynne Rienner.

Davis, Steven J., John C. Haltiwanger, and Scott Schuh. 1996. *Job Creation and Destruction.* Cambridge, MA: MIT Press.

de Mel, Suresh, David J. McKenzie, and Christopher Woodruff. 2008a. "Returns to Capital in Microenterprises: Evidence from a Field Experiment." *Quarterly Journal of Economics* 123 (4): 1329–72.

———. 2008b. "Who Are the Microenterprise Owners? Evidence from Sri Lanka on Tokman v. de Soto." Discussion Paper Series 3511, Institute for the Study of Labor, Bonn.

———. 2009. "Innovative Firms or Innovative Owners? Determinants of Innovation in Micro, Small, and Medium Enterprises." Discussion Paper Series 3962, Institute for the Study of Labor, Bonn.

———. 2010. "Wage Subsidies for Microenterprises." *American Economic Review* 100 (2): 614–18.

de Soto, Hernando. 1989. *The Other Path: The Invisible Revolution in the Third World.* New York: Harper & Row.

Djankov, Simeon, Miguel Edward, Yingyi Qian, Gerard Roland, and Ekaterina Zhuravskaya. 2005. "Who Are Russia's Entrepreneurs?" *Journal of the European Economic Association* 3 (2–3): 1–11.

Djankov, Simeon, Yingyi Qian, Gerard Roland, and Ekaterina Zhuravskaya. 2006a. "Entrepreneurship in China and Russia Compared." *Journal of the European Economic Association* 4 (2–3): 352–65.

———. 2006b. "Who Are China's Entrepreneurs?" *Amercian Economics Review* 96 (2): 348–52.

Drexler, Alejandro, Greg Fischer, and Antoinette Schoar. 2011. "Keeping It Simple: Financial Literacy and Rules of Thumb." MIT Sloan Management, Cambridge, MA. Processed.

Duranton, Gilles. 2007. "Urban Evolutions: The Fast, the Slow, and the Still." *American Economic Review* 97 (1): 197–221.

———. 2012. "Agglomeration and Jobs in Developing Countries." Background paper for the WDR 2013.

Duranton, Gilles, and Diego Puga. 2001. "Nursery Cities: Urban Diversity, Process Innovation, and the Life Cycle of Products." *American Economic Review* 91 (5): 1454–77.

Dutz, Mark A., Ioannis Kessides, Stephen O'Connell, and Robert D. Willig. 2011. "Competition and Innovation-Driven Inclusive Growth." Policy Research Working Paper Series 5852, World Bank, Washington, DC.

Easterly, William. 2002. *The Elusive Quest for Growth Economists' Adventures and Misadventures in the Tropics.* Cambridge, MA: MIT Press.

Evenson, Robert E., and Douglas Gollin. 2003. *Crop Variety Improvement and Its Effect on Productivity: The Impact of International Agricultural Research.* Wallingford, U.K.: CABI Publishing.

Fafchamps, Marcel, David J. McKenzie, Simon Quinn, and Christopher Woodruff. 2011. "When Is Capital Enough to Get Female Microenterprises Growing? Evidence from a Randomized Experiment in Ghana." Working Paper Series 17207, National Bureau of Economic Research, Cambridge, MA.

Fafchamps, Marcel, and Christopher Woodruff. 2012. "Identifying and Relaxing Constraints to Employment Generation in Small-Scale African Enterprises." University of Oxford, Oxford. Processed.

Fajnzylber, Pablo, William Maloney, and Gabriel Montes Rojas. 2006. "Microenterprise Dynamics in Developing Countries: How Similar Are They to Those in the Industrialized World? Evidence from Mexico." *World Bank Economic Review* 20 (3): 389–419.

FAO (Food and Agriculture Organization). 2010. *2000 World Census of Agriculture: Main Results and Metadata by Country (1996–2005).* Rome: FAO.

Foster, Andrew D., and Mark R. Rosenzweig. 2011. "Are Indian Farms Too Small? Mechanization, Agency Costs, and Farm Efficiency." Brown University, Providence, RI. Processed.

Foster, Lucia Smith, John C. Haltiwanger, and Cornell J. Krizan. 2001. "Aggregate Productivity Growth: Lessons from Microeconomic Evidence." In *New Developments in Productivity Analysis*, ed. Charles R. Hulten, Edwin R. Dean, and Michael J. Harper, 303–72. Chicago, IL: University of Chicago Press.

Foster, Lucia Smith, John C. Haltiwanger, and Chad Syverson. 2008. "Reallocation, Firm Turnover, and Efficiency: Selection on Productivity or Profitability?" *American Economic Review* 98 (1): 394–425.

Fox, Louise, and Thomas Sohnesen. 2012. "Household Enterprise in Sub-Saharan Africa: Why They Matter for Growth, Jobs, and Poverty Reduction." Policy Research Working Paper 6184, World Bank, Washington, DC.

Gennaioli, Nicola, Rafael La Porta, Florencio Lopez-de-Silanes, and Andrei Hleifer. 2011. "Human Capital and Regional Development." Working Paper Series 17158, National Bureau of Economic Research, Cambridge, MA.

Ghani, Ejaz, Arti Grover Goswami, and William R. Kerr. 2012. "Is India's Manufacturing Sector Moving Away From Cities?" Working Paper Series 12-090, Harvard Business School, Harvard University, Cambridge, MA.

Gindling, T. H., and David Newhouse 2012. "Self-Employment in the Developing World." Background paper for the WDR 2013.

Giné, Xavier, and Ghazala Mansuri. 2011. "Together We Will: Evidence from a Field Experiment on Female Voter Turnout in Pakistan." World Bank, Washington, DC. Processed.

Göbel, Kristin, Michael Grimm, and Jann Lay. 2011. "Capital Returns, Productivity and Accumulation in Micro and Small Enterprises: Evidence from Peruvian Panel Data." Processed.

Griliches, Zvi, and Haim Regev. 1992. "Productivity and Firm Turnover in Israeli Industry, 1979–1988." *Journal of Development Economics* 65 (1): 175–203.

Grimm, Michael, Peter Knorringa, and Jann Lay. 2012. "Constrained Gazelles: High Potentials in West Africa's Informal Economy." International Institute of Social Studies, Erasmus University–Rotterdam, Rotterdam, Netherlands. Processed.

Grimm, Michael, Jens Kruger, and Jann Lay. 2011. "Barriers to Entry and Returns to Capital in Informal Activities: Evidence from Sub-Saharan Africa." *Review of Income and Wealth* 57 (S1): S27–S53.

Haggblade, Steven, Peter B. R. Hazell, and Thomas Anthony Reardon, eds. 2007. *Transforming the Rural Nonfarm Economy.* Baltimore, MD: Johns Hopkins University Press.

Haltiwanger, John. 2011. "Globalization and Economic Volatility." In *Making Globalization Socially Sustainable*, ed. Marc Bacchetta and Marion Jansen, 119–46. Geneva: International Labour Organization and World Trade Organization.

Haltiwanger, John, Ron S. Jarmin, and Javier Miranda. 2010. "Who Creates Jobs? Small vs. Large vs. Young." Working Paper Series 16300, National Bureau of Economic Research, Cambridge, MA.

Hayami, Yujiro, and Toshihiko Kawagoe. 1989. "Farm Mechanization, Scale Economies and Polarization: The Japanese Experience." *Journal of Development Economics* 31 (2): 221–39.

Hayami, Yujiro, and Keijiro Otsuka. 1993. *The Economics of Contract Choice: An Agrarian Perspective.* New York: Oxford University Press.

Hayami, Yujiro, and Vernon W. Ruttan. 1985. *Agricultural Development: An International Perspective.* Baltimore, MD: Johns Hopkins University Press.

Henderson, Vernon. 2002. "Urbanization in Developing Countries." *World Bank Research Observer* 17 (1): 89–112.

Holden, Stein T., Keijiro Otsuka, and Frank M. Place. 2009. "Land Markets and Development in Africa." In *The Emergence of Land Markets in Africa: Assessing the Impacts on Poverty, Equity, and Efficiency*, ed. Stein T. Holden, Keijiro Otsuka, and Frank M. Place, 3–17. Washington, DC: Resources for the Future.

Hsieh, Chang-Tai, and Peter J. Klenow. 2009. "Misallocation and Manufacturing TFP in China and India." *Quarterly Journal of Economics* 124 (4): 1403–48.

———. 2011. "The Life Cycle of Plants in India and Mexico." Research Paper 11-33, Booth School of Business, University of Chicago, Chicago, IL.

IFC (International Finance Corporation). Forthcoming. *IFC Job Study: Assessing Private Sector Contributions to Job Creation.* Washington, DC: IFC.

Kairiza, Terrence, and Tetsushi Sonobe. 2012. "Are Female Entrepreneurs Less Skillful in Management? A Randomized Experiment in the Garment Industry in Tanzania." Discussion Paper 11-24, National Graduate Institute for Policy Studies, Tokyo.

Karlan, Dean, Miriam Bruhn, and Antoinette Schoar. 2012. "The Impact of Consulting Services on Small and Medium Enterprises: Evidence from a Randomized Trial in Mexico." Working Paper 100, Economics Department, Yale University, New Haven, CT.

Karlan, Dean, Ryan Knight, and Christopher Udry. 2012. "Hoping to Win, Expected to Lose: Theory and Lessons on Micro Enterprise Development." Innovations for Poverty Action, Cambridge, MA. Processed.

Karlan, Dean S., and Martin Valdivia. 2010. "Teaching Entrepreneurship: Impact of Business Training on Microfinance Clients and Institutions." *Review of Economics and Statistics* 93 (2): 510–27.

Kasbekar, Kiron. 2007. *Only the Fittest Survive.* London: Tata Group.

Kelley, Donna, Niels Bosma, and José A. Amorós. 2010. *GEM Global Report.* London: Global Entrepreneurship Monitor.

Kinda, Tidiane, and Josef L. Loening. 2008. "Small Enterprise Growth and the Rural Investment Climate: Evidence from Tanzania." Policy Research Working Paper Series 4675, World Bank, Washington, DC.

Kucera, David, and Leanne Roncolato. 2012. "Structure Matters: Sectoral Drivers of Development and the Labour Productivity–Employment Relationship." International Labour Organization, Geneva. Processed.

Larson, Donald F., Keijiro Otsuka, Tomoya Matsumoto, and Talip Kilic. 2012. "Can Africa's Agriculture Depend on Smallholder Farmers?" Background paper for the WDR 2013.

Liedholm, Carl. 2002. "Small Firm Dynamics: Evidence from Africa and Latin America." *Small Business Economics* 18 (1–3): 227–42.

Lin, Justin Yifu. 2012. *Demystifying the Chinese Economy.* Cambridge, U.K.: Cambridge University Press.

Loening, Josef, and Mikael Imru. 2009. "Ethiopia: Diversifying the Rural Economy. An Assessment of the Investment Climate for Small and Informal Enterprises." Paper 23278, Munich Personal RePEc Archive, Munich.

Mano, Yukichi, Alhassa Iddrisu, Yutaka Yoshino, and Tetsushi Sonobe. 2011. "How Can Micro and Small Enterprises in Sub-Saharan Africa Become More Productive? The Impacts of Experimental Basic Management Training." Policy Research Working Paper Series 5755, World Bank, Washington, DC.

Martin, Will, and Devashish Mitra. 2001. "Productivity Growth and Convergence in Agriculture versus Manufacturing." *Economic Development and Cultural Change* 49 (2): 403–22.

McKenzie, David. 2010. *Impact Assessment in Finance and Private Sector Development: What Have We Learned and What Should We Learn?* Washington, DC: World Bank.

McKenzie, David, and Christopher Woodruff. 2008. "Experimental Evidence on Returns to Capital and Access to Finance in Mexico." *World Bank Economic Review* 22 (3): 457–482.

McMillan, Margaret S., and Dani Rodrik. 2011. "Globalization, Structural Change, and Productivity Growth." Working Paper Series 17143, National Bureau of Economic Research, Cambridge, MA.

Mead, Donald C., and Carl Liedholm. 1998. "The Dynamics of Micro and Small Enterprises in Developing Countries." *World Development* 26 (1): 61–74.

Mertens, Brian. 2011. "Forbes Asia's Businessman of the Year." *Forbes Asia Magazine*, December 5.

Montenegro, Claudio E., and Harry Anthony Patrinos. 2012. "Returns to Schooling around the World." Background paper for the WDR 2013.

Mottaleb, Khondoker A., and Tetsushi Sonobe. 2011. "An Inquiry into the Rapid Growth of the Garment Industry in Bangladesh." *Economic Development and Cultural Change* 60 (1): 67–89.

Nelson, Richard R. 1981. "Research on Productivity Growth and Productivity Differences: Dead Ends and New Departures." *Journal of Economic Literature* 19 (3): 1029–64.

Otsuka, Keijiro, and Frank Place. 2001. *Land Tenure and Natural Resource Management: A Comparative Study of Agrarian Communities in Asia and Africa.* Baltimore, MD: Johns Hopkins University Press.

Otsuka, Keijiro, and Tetsushi Sonobe. 2011. "A Cluster-Based Industrial Development Policy for Low-Income Countries." Policy Research Working Paper Series 5703, World Bank, Washington, DC.

Pagés, Carmen, ed. 2010. *The Age of Productivity: Transforming Economies from the Bottom Up.* New York: Palgrave Macmillan.

Park, Jaegil, Daejong Kim, Yongseok Ko, Eunnan Kim, Keunhyun Park, and Keuntae Kim. 2011. *Urbanization and Urban Policies in Korea.* Korea Research Institute for Human Settlements.

Perry, Guillermo E., William F. Maloney, Omar S. Arias, Pablo Fajnzylber, Andrew D. Mason, and Jaime Saavedra-Chanduvi. 2007. *Informality: Exit and Exclusion.* Washington, DC: World Bank.

Pieper, Ute. 2000. "Deindustrialisation and the Social and Economic Sustainability Nexus in Developing Countries: Cross-Country Evidence on Productivity and Employment." *Journal of Development Studies* 36 (4): 66–99.

Ravallion, Martin. 2005. "Externalities in Rural Development: Evidence for China." In *Spatial Inequality and Development*, ed. Ravi Kanbur and Anthony J. Venables, 137–62. Oxford: Oxford University Press.

Ravallion, Martin, and Shaohua Chen. 2007. "China's (Uneven) Progress against Poverty." *Journal of Development Economics* 82 (1): 1–42.

Rhee, Yung Whee. 1990. "The Catalyst Model of Development: Lessons from Bangladesh's Success with Garment Exports." *World Development* 18 (2): 333–46.

Rijkers, Bob, Hassen Arouri, Caroline Freund, and Antonio Nucifora. 2012. "Which Firms Create

Jobs in Tunisia?" Background paper for the WDR 2013.

Roberts, Mark J. 1996. "Employment Flows and Producer Turnover." In *Industrial Evolution in Developing Countries: Micro Patterns of Turnover, Productivity, and Market Structure*, ed. Mark J. Roberts and James R. Tybout. Oxford: Oxford University Press.

Rutkowski, Jan, Stefano Scarpetta, Arup Banerji, Philip O'Keefe, Gaelle Pierre, and Milan Vodopivec. 2005. *Enhancing Job Opportunities: Eastern Europe and the Soviet Union.* Washington, DC: World Bank.

Sandefur, Justin. 2010. "On the Evolution of the Firm Size Distribution in an African Economy." Centre for the Study of African Economies Working Paper Series 2010-05, Oxford. Processed.

Schoar, Antoinette. 2010. "The Divide between Subsistence and Transformational Entrepreneurship." In *Innovation Policy and the Economy, Volume 10*, ed. Josh Lerner and Scott Stern, 57–81. Cambridge, MA: National Bureau of Economic Research.

Schumpeter, Joseph Alois. 1934. *The Theory of Economic Development: An Inquiry into Profits, Capital, Credit, Interest, and the Business Cycle.* Cambridge, MA: Harvard University Press.

Shiferaw, Admasu, and Arjun S. Bedi. 2010. "The Dynamics of Job Creation and Job Destruction: Is Sub-Saharan Africa Different?" Poverty, Equity and Growth Discussion Paper 22, Courant Research Centre, Göttingen, Germany.

Sonobe, Tetsushi, Yuki Higuchi, and Keijiro Otsuka. 2012. "Productivity Growth and Job Creation in the Development Process of Industrial Clusters." Background paper for the WDR 2013.

Sonobe, Tetsushi, Dinghuan Hu, and Keijiro Otsuka. 2004. "From Inferior to Superior Products: An Inquiry into the Wenzhou Model of Industrial Development in China." *Journal of Comparative Economics* 32 (3): 542–62.

Sonobe, Tetsushi, and Keijiro Otsuka. 2006. *Cluster-Based Industrial Development: An East Asian Model.* New York: Palgrave Macmillan.

———. 2011. *Cluster-Based Industrial Development: A Comparative Study of Asia and Africa.* New York: Palgrave Macmillan.

Sutton, John, and Nebil Kellow. 2010. *An Enterprise Map of Ethiopia.* London: International Growth Centre.

Syverson, Chad. 2011. "What Determines Productivity?" *Journal of Economic Literature* 49: (2), 326–65.

The Economist. 2001. "Face Value: Radicalism, Asian Style." *The Economist Newspaper Limited,* March 22.

Timmer, Marcel P., and Gaaitzen J. de Vries. 2009. "Structural Change and Growth Accelerations in Asia and Latin America: A New Sectoral Data Set." *Cliometrica* 3: 165–90.

Tokman, Victor. 2007. "Modernizing the Informal Sector." Working Paper 42, Department of Economic and Social Affairs, New York, United Nations.

Tybout, James R. 1996. "Heterogeneity and Productivity Growth: Assessing the Evidence." In *Industrial Evolution in Developing Countries: Micro Patterns of Turnover, Productivity, and Market Structure*, ed. Mark J. Roberts and James R. Tybout. Oxford: Oxford University Press.

———. 2000. "Manufacturing Firms in Developing Countries: How Well Do They Do, and Why?" *Journal of Economic Literature* 38 (1): 11–44.

Valdivia, Martin. 2011. "Training or Technical Assistance for Female Entrepreneurship? Evidence from a Field Experiment in Peru." GRADE (Grupo de Análisis para el Desarrollo), Lima. Processed.

van der Sluis, Justin, Mirjam van Praag, and Wim Vijverberg. 2005. "Entrepreneurship Selection and Performance: A Meta-analysis of the Impact of Education in Developing Economies." *World Bank Economic Review* 19 (2): 225–61.

Vivarelli, Marco. 2012. "Entrepreneurship in Advanced and Developing Countries: A Microeconomic Perspective," Discussion Paper Series 6513, IZA, Bonn.

Wang, Yueping, and Yang Yao. 1999. *Market Reforms, Technological Capabilities, and the Performance of Small Enterprises in China.* Washington, DC: World Bank.

Witze, Morgen. 2010. "Case Study: Tata." *Financial Times,* December 29.

World Bank. 2007. *World Development Report 2008: Agriculture for Development.* Washington, DC: World Bank.

———. 2009. *World Development Report 2009: Reshaping Economic Geography.* Washington, DC: World Bank.

———. 2011a. "Brazil Urbanization Review." World Bank, Washington, DC. Processed.

———. 2011b. *Vietnam Urbanization Review: Technical Assistance Report.* Washington, DC: World Bank.

———. Forthcoming. *Planning, Connecting, Financing Cities—Now. Urbanization Review Flagship Report.* Washington, DC: World Bank.

World Bank, and the People's Republic of China Development Research Center of the State Council. 2012. *China 2030: Building a Modern, Harmonious, and Creative High-Income Society.* Washington, DC: World Bank and Development Research Center of the State Council, the People's Republic of China.

Yunus, Muhammad, and Alan Jolis. 1999. *Banker to the Poor: Micro-Lending and the Battle against World Poverty.* New York: Public Affairs.

Jobs and social cohesion

*Jobs can shape social interactions and the ways societies manage
collective decision making. They connect people with others
and can provide access to voice.*

Jobs influence who we are and our relations with others. In most societies, jobs are a fundamental source of self-respect and social identity. Historically, family names in some cultures were associated with specific occupations because people defined themselves by what they did: Miller in English, Hurudza (master farmer) in Shona, and Suthar (carpenters) in Hindi.

Jobs connect people with others through networks. The workplace can be a place to encounter new ideas and information and to interact with people of different ethnicities. The distribution of jobs within society and perceptions about who has access to opportunities and why can shape people's expectations and aspirations for the future, their sense of having a stake in society, and perceptions of fairness.

These individual influences of jobs may have collective consequences. Having or not having a job may affect key elements of social cohesion, the capacity of societies to manage collective decision making peacefully. While the frustration of unemployed youth during the Arab Spring suggests that the lack of jobs can be a source of social unrest, that does not mean that the relationship between jobs and social cohesion is straightforward, immediate, or direct. Rather, the relationship is contextual and shaped by individuals, their values, attitudes, and behaviors, and the institutions that surround them. And it goes both ways: social cohesion can also influence jobs by shaping the context in which entrepreneurs make investment decisions.

Empirical evidence of a connection between jobs and social cohesion is limited by data constraints, the complexity of measuring social interactions, and the multiple factors that can contribute to social cohesion. However, cross-country analysis of values surveys finds that job loss or lack of access to jobs is associated with lower levels of trust and civic engagement. This is not only a rich-country phenomenon, as is often suggested. Unemployment can cause depression, increase mistrust in others, and lead people to drop out of community life. Migrants without social ties may be excluded from job opportunities that would allow them to succeed in their new environments. In extreme cases, if people, particularly youth, lack jobs and hope for the future, they may turn to violent or criminal activity to compensate for the absence of self-esteem and sense of belonging that a job might otherwise provide. Similarly, jobs offering limited opportunities for future growth or lacking access to voice can lead to alienation and frustration.

Some jobs are positively correlated with social cohesion. Jobs that are empowering, build agency, and provide access to voice can increase trust and people's willingness to participate in civil society. Jobs can create economic and social ties and have the potential to build incentives to work across boundaries and resolve conflict.

And people's trust in government and their confidence in institutions may increase if they believe that job opportunities are available to them either now or in the future. Jobs can influence social cohesion through their effects on social identity, networks, and fairness.

Jobs can help manage social tensions

News reports about the financial crisis and the Arab Spring have broadcast a common sentiment that unemployment, especially among young people, can ignite unrest and violence.[1] In September 2010, a *Telegraph* headline reported that the "IMF Fears 'Social Explosion' from World Jobs Crisis" ahead of a summit of the International Monetary Fund and the International Labour Organization (ILO).[2] In 2011, *Le Monde* linked jobs and social unrest in Tunisia to concerns about social justice: "protesters aren't asking the Government to find them a job, but denouncing the lack of transparency and justice in the labor market."[3] The revolution in Tunisia was sparked by the protests of a fruit vendor frustrated by his inability to get a permit to do his job. High levels of youth unemployment were a significant contributing factor to the riots in the United Kingdom in the summer of 2011.[4]

These events suggest that jobs can contribute to social cohesion, including how societies handle differences and manage tensions among different groups, and how they avoid and resolve conflicts. There are many possible ways to define social cohesion (box 4.1). But overall, social cohesion refers to the capacity of societies to peacefully manage collective decision making.[5] Social cohesion thus relates to the processes and institutions that shape how groups interact. It does not follow that collective decision making should be imposed from above, but rather that channels for voice, accountability, and inclusive participation of diverse groups can contribute to a cohesive society.

Trust and civic engagement matter . . .

The capacity of a country to support peaceful collective decision making involves multiple factors including the quality of institutions,

intergroup relations, and the effectiveness of channels for resolving conflicts. Cross-country data on political stability, the absence of violence, and voice and accountability can be used to construct an index of social cohesion at the country level.[6] The Nordic countries, Switzerland, and New Zealand, score high on this index. Although the index is a static measure, the capacity for peaceful decision making can evolve over time as societies change, through urbanization, more female employment, and the growth of a middle class.

The nature of the interactions through jobs affects the degree of social cohesion in communities and societies. Trust and civic engagement are two measurable indicators of social cohesion at the individual level. These indicators are associated with the country-level index of the capacity for peaceful collective decision making (figure 4.1).

Trust refers to the extent to which individuals have confidence in people whom they know personally, including family and neighbors.[7] It can also refer to trust in people met for the first time and in people of different religions and nationalities. Civic engagement captures the extent to which people participate voluntarily in civil society by joining community organizations, unions, political parties, or religious organizations, and by engaging in civic life. These forms of involvement and activism include nonviolent activity, such as participating in protests, that can be constructive for social cohesion. Civic engagement relates to social capital, participation, and the agency that motivates individuals to be part of collective action.

. . . and they are influenced by jobs

Trust and civic engagement can be linked to jobs. Having—or not having—a job may affect the way people view the world by influencing their values and attitudes, including trust in others and in institutions. Jobs can also provide channels for people to interact across diverse groups. Jobs with certain characteristics may contribute more to trust and civic engagement than others.

Not having a job is associated with less self-reported trust in high-income countries (figure 4.2a). The relationship is stronger with civic engagement, where unemployment is linked to

BOX 4.1 *What is social cohesion?*

The concept can be traced as far back as the writings of Ibn Khaldun, a Muslim scholar born in Tunis in the 15th century, whose idea of *asabiyah* is generally translated as "social cohesion." Living during times of manifold conflicts, Khaldun regarded *asabiyah* as the solidarity of small groups (tribes) that has the power to promote broader social integration.[a]

Four centuries later, Emile Durkheim considered cohesion in the context of societal transformation.[b] He was particularly concerned with two different types of solidarity that he observed emerging through industrialization in Europe. Primitive societies, he found, were marked by mechanical solidarity and a strong collective ethos based on relatively homogeneous patterns of life and work. Advanced capitalist society, in contrast, with its complex division of labor, was marked by organic solidarity based on merit, respect for different roles within the labor force, and the need for moral regulation.

More recently, social cohesion has been related to social capital. In the 1990s, Pierre Bourdieu and others focused on the benefits that accrue to individuals through their participation in groups and the need for individuals to invest in these relations. Robert Putnam's analysis of the conditions for creating responsive, effective, and representative institutions builds on this theme. Famously, northern Italy had more of these institutions than southern Italy, and Putnam concluded that the central enabling condition was the existence of more social capital, measured through the density of local associations.[c] Social cohesion can be understood as a broader concept than social capital in that it considers intergroup relations in a wider context. Easterly, Ritzen, and Woolcock define social cohesion (or lack thereof) as "the nature and extent of social and economic divisions within society (income, ethnicity, political party, caste, language)."[d]

Although social cohesion has multiple definitions with differences in focus and emphasis, some common threads emerge:

- Social cohesion is generally viewed as a positive concept. It can be an end in itself, as well as a means. The Organisation for Economic Co-operation and Development describes a cohesive society as one that "works towards the well-being of all its members."[e] The French Commissariat General du Plan defines social cohesion as "a set of social processes that help instill in individuals the sense of belonging to the same community and the feeling that they are recognized as members of the community."[f]

- Social cohesion relates to the interactions among individuals, groups, and societies. These interactions are seen as "the forces holding the individuals within the groupings in which they are" and as linking diverse groups together.[g]

- Social cohesion contributes to sustainable social development. According to the Club de Madrid, "shared societies are stable, safe and just and based on the promotion and protection of all human rights . . . , including disadvantaged and vulnerable groups and persons."[h]

- Last, some definitions of social cohesion relate the concept to processes and institutional characteristics. For example, social cohesion can refer to "the capacity of societies (not just groups, networks) to peacefully manage collective action problems."[i] This definition links social cohesion to participation and civic engagement.

Sources: World Development Report 2013 team based on Norton and de Haan 2012 for the World Development Report 2013; OECD 2011.
a. Weiss 1995.
b. Durkheim 1893.
c. Putnam, Leonardi, and Nanetti 1993.
d. Easterly, Ritzen, and Woolcock 2006, 105.
e. OECD 2011, 17.
f. Jenson 1998, 4.
g. Moreno and Jennings 1937, 371.
h. OECD 2011, 53.
i. Woolcock 2011.

lower participation in associations and demonstrations, and signing petitions (figures 4.2b, c, and d). With the exception of low-income countries, the relationship between unemployment and active membership in an association is significant and negative. The mixed findings on trust and unemployment underscore that unemployment may not always be a meaningful concept in low-income countries. Open unemployment is frequently low in developing countries and is not always concentrated among the worse-off, because most people work to make ends meet in the absence of social safety nets.

In developing countries, the type of job, the opportunities the job provides, and the way jobs connect people may be more relevant for social cohesion.

Further indications of a connection between jobs and social cohesion comes from looking at job characteristics. The 2005 wave of the World Values Survey asks people whether their jobs involve manual or cognitive, routine or creative tasks, and how much independence they have at work. An index of these self-reported characteristics captures how motivating a job is. The index is positively associated with trust

FIGURE 4.1 *Trust and civic engagement go together with peaceful collective decision making*

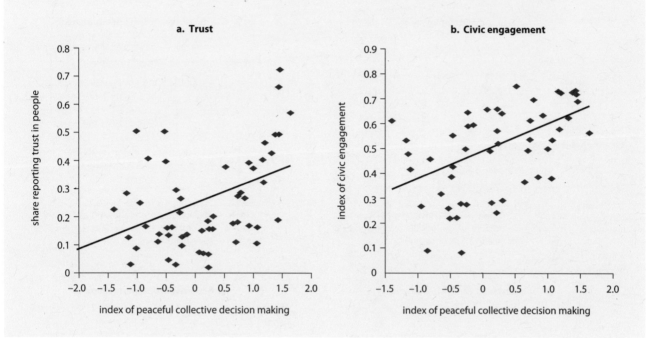

Sources: World Development Report 2013 team, based on World Values Survey 2005 (database), World Values Survey Association, Stockholm; Worldwide Governance Indicators 2005.

Note: The analysis includes 56 countries (panel a) and 49 countries (panel b). "Index of peaceful collective decision making" is an average of indicators of "voice and accountability" and "political stability and the absence of violence" from the Worldwide Governance Indicators. "Index of civic engagement" is the average of responses to questions from the World Values Survey on (a) active membership in associations; (b) whether the respondent participated or would participate in a demonstration; and (c) whether the respondent would sign a petition.

in high- and upper-middle-income countries (figure 4.3a). This relationship is not significant in lower-middle- and low-income countries. Holding a job with perceived cognitive, creative, and autonomous attributes is positively linked with civic engagement indicators in all but low-income countries (figures 4.3b, 4.3c, and 4.3d).[9] Similarly, in surveys conducted in 2012 in China, Colombia, and the Arab Republic of Egypt, workers who perceived that their jobs involved more autonomy and greater creative and cognitive content were more likely to report helping other people.[10]

More than correlations?

As suggestive as they are, these relationships between jobs and social cohesion do not establish causality. While unemployed people may be less likely to trust others or join associations, people with less trust in others may also be more likely to be unemployed or not participate in civil so-

ciety. Moreover, trust and civic participation are influenced by peer and social interaction effects (such as the trust or participation of others), which can make it difficult to draw conclusions.

While the primary focus is on how jobs can contribute to trust and civic engagement, this relationship goes in both directions. There are ways in which social cohesion can affect jobs. Trust and social capital (an element of civic engagement) may create an economic and political environment that is conducive to economic growth.[11] Trust can reduce transaction costs and overcome market failures that arise because of uncertainty; it can reduce costs related to search and information, policing and enforcement, and bargaining and decision making; and it can be the basis for the transmission and exchange of knowledge and allow for innovation, coordination, and cooperation among firms.[12] Meanwhile, factors such as mistrust, discrimination, fragmentation along ethnic lines, or inequality can also influence whether jobs are created, and what kind.

FIGURE 4.2 *People who are unemployed trust and participate less*

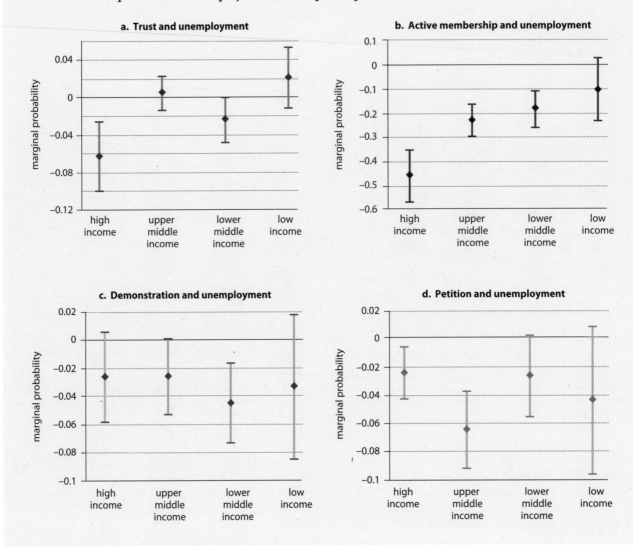

Source: Wietzke and McLeod 2012 for the World Development Report 2013.
Note: The analysis includes 54 countries. The vertical axis shows the marginal probability (d-probit coefficient) of individuals' self-reported trust or civic engagement on being unemployed. The estimates control for the income, education, and demographic characteristics of respondents. Trust is based on the question, "Generally speaking, would you say that most people can be trusted or that you need to be very careful in dealing with people?" Civic engagement variables are (a) whether the respondent is an active member of one or more of nine different associations; (b) whether the respondent attended or would attend a demonstration; or (c) whether the respondent signed or would sign a petition. The line indicates the 95 percent confidence interval of each coefficient. If the line crosses the horizontal axis, the corresponding coefficient is not statistically significant.

Evidence of a directional link between employment status and civic engagement comes from a survey in Indonesia that tracked participation in community meetings and volunteer activities and interviewed the same respondents in 2000 and 2007.[13] On average, participation in community activities increased 8 percent during the period, but it increased at different rates among people with different work histories (figure 4.4).[14]

Controlling for other factors, men and women who were working in 2000 but not in 2007 were less likely to be participating in community activities than others. Conversely, men and women who were not working in 2000 but were working in 2007 were significantly more likely to be involved in community activities than those who were not working in 2007.[15] Reasons not controlled for in the analysis could explain these findings; for example, people who

FIGURE 4.3 *People with motivating jobs trust and participate more*

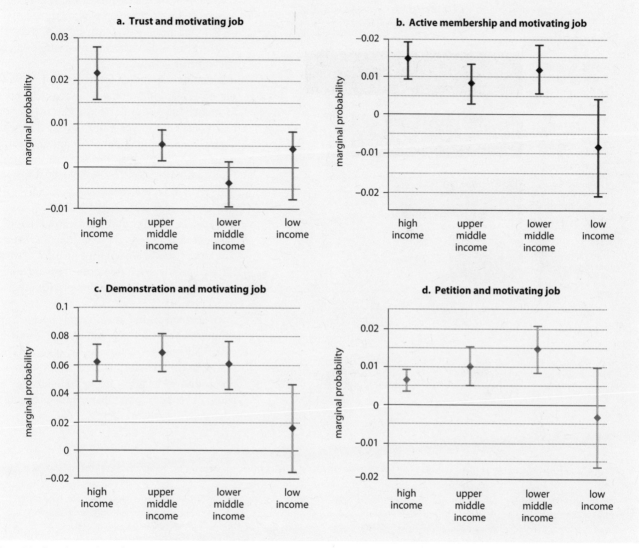

Source: Wietzke and McLeod 2012 for the World Development Report 2013.
Note: The analysis includes 54 countries. The vertical axis shows the marginal probability (d-probit coefficient) of individuals' self-reported trust or civic engagement on an index assessing whether respondents think their job is cognitive, creative, or independent. The estimates control for the income, education, and demographic characteristics of the respondents. Trust is based on responses to the question "Generally speaking, would you say that most people can be trusted or that you need to be very careful in dealing with people?" Civic engagement variables are whether the respondent is an active member of one or more of nine different associations and whether the respondent attended or would attend a demonstration, or signed or would sign a petition. The line indicates the 95 percent confidence interval of each coefficient. If the line crosses the horizontal axis, the corresponding coefficient is not statistically significant.

get sick lose their jobs and their ability to participate in the community. New cross-country analysis from Europe and Latin America suggests a casual relationship between employment status and trust in others and institutions (box 4.2).[16]

The empirical results relating unemployment, trust, and civic engagement imply that losing a job means more than losing income. Job loss can undermine feelings of self-worth and strain family and social relationships. Un-

employment can break economic and social ties, breed mistrust, and damage people's sense of community and hope for the future. Not having a job can mean losing social status as well as not being able to provide income for one's family. A man laid off after 24 years of work in a factory in Serbia explained, "I automatically lost everything. I lost any freedom and power I had. Everything was lost."[17] Ethnographies of communities in Argentina, Bulgaria, and Guyana

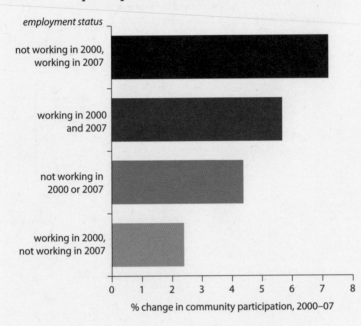

FIGURE 4.4 *Having a job means more community participation in Indonesia*

Source: Indonesia Family Life Survey (database), Rand Corporation, Santa Monica, CA.
Note: Community participation includes joining in a community meeting; cooperative, voluntary labor; neighborhood improvement; neighborhood watch (men); or women's association.

that experienced widespread job losses in contexts of limited new job creation are remarkably consistent in their accounts of the social implications of long-term unemployment (box 4.3).

For communities, job loss appears to foster mistrust not only toward former employers or government authorities suspected of being indifferent or responsible for the lack of employment opportunities but also among neighbors, former colleagues, and friends. This frustration may contribute to general dissatisfaction with the political environment. An empirical study using the World Values Survey in 69 countries finds that joblessness can be linked with negative views about the effectiveness of democracy and preferences for a rogue leader.[18] Insecure jobs or jobs that people find demoralizing can have effects similar to those of unemployment. The lack of status, job security, or voice at work can lead people to feel disempowered and hopeless about the future and to stop participating in social networks.[19]

In extreme cases, unemployment can contribute to violence or social unrest. Youth in particular may turn to gangs or other violent groups to compensate for the lack of ties in economic and social life.[20] A longitudinal study of youth in Ecuador found that members of gangs

---

BOX 4.2 *Do jobs cause trust? Analysis of Eurobarometer and Latinobarómetro Surveys*

An analysis using the Latinobarómetro and Eurobarometer values surveys during the 2000s makes it possible to study the evolution of trust and jobs and links in both directions. The surveys include questions on interpersonal trust and trust in institutions. Cohorts are defined and examined in the different survey years. The analysis looks at how social cohesion and employment conditions for the cohorts evolve over time, controlling for certain country characteristics that could be correlated with both trust and employment status.

The dataset captures important features of the formation of social cohesion, because perceptions of trust and civic participation are highly influenced by peer and social interaction effects. For instance, an individual's propensity to trust other people or the state depends on the perceived or actual trust of others belonging to similar sociodemographic groups.

The model simultaneously allows group level job conditions, including unemployment and self-employment, to influence trust and vice versa. The empirics quantify how earlier changes in group-level employment conditions predict their trust in society and its

institutions over time. The estimated effects measure how a percentage change in, say, the unemployment rate for a cohort in a given year predicts changes in the percentage of individuals of that same cohort reporting to trust in the subsequent year.

This analysis finds that increases in unemployment are followed by increases in trust among Europeans, but the opposite is true among Latin Americans. At the same time, increases in self-employment lead to higher trust in Europe while the opposite is true in Latin America. These results hold in Latin America for trust both in government and in others. Conversely, the analysis finds little evidence of a causal link from trust to jobs, except for a small negative impact of self-employment on trust in government in Latin America. These results may reflect the higher coverage of social protection in Europe and the lower importance of open unemployment in Latin America than in Europe. They are consistent with evidence that in Latin America self-employment, while a last resort for many unable to find wage employment, is valued by some for the independence it provides.[a]

Source: Arias and Sosa 2012 for the World Development Report 2013.
a. Perry and others 2007.

BOX 4.3 *Displacement and unemployment can lead to the erosion of trust and ties*

Downsizing of bauxite mines in Guyana

The downsizing of bauxite mines in the absence of new opportunities has contributed to a deterioration in family and community relationships in Linden, Guyana.[a] Between the early 1970s and the mid-1980s, bauxite mining near Linden was cut by half, and layoffs continued throughout the 1990s. By 1999, formal unemployment in Linden stood at about 40 percent, and residents complained of rising crime.

Once among the best-paid workers, miners were respected for their work and seen as drivers of the economy. People felt particularly demeaned by the downsizing process: "The people off the job don't get any information. They treat us like we don't exist. Yet . . . before we came off, there used to be meetings with us, [about] what was happening."[b]

Material hardship and insecurity took a harsh toll on identity and the relations between men and women. Women directly linked men's inability to retain their authority as breadwinners to domestic violence. "Especially in cases of abuse, you would be surprised that after counseling them, the problem comes right back to the economic situation. The man can't provide adequately for the home."[c] Indigence was linked to shocking forms of child neglect and abuse. Some parents were said to be prostituting their children. The cultivation of cannabis, the use of cocaine, and involvement in the international transshipment of drugs were said to be rapidly increasing among young men.

Downsizing also diminished the economic resources available to community organizations such as churches: "The churches are in crisis also. As individuals, we are part of the crisis, so we carry it into church and it in turn goes into society," one person said.[d]

Regime change and unemployment in Bulgaria

Bulgaria massively downsized its unsustainable state enterprises following the end of the Communist regime. The disappearance of state jobs entailed the loss of numerous benefits, including health care and job security. In focus groups, people linked job loss to poor health, social isolation, and crime. Older men, in particular, lost face when they had to ask young relatives or employers for work.

Unemployment did more than simply weaken social ties; it created distrust and mutual suspicion. The restructuring created winners as well, and they also suffered from the mutual distrust. People who had lost their jobs began to avoid traditional social gatherings because they were unable to afford gifts that they were expected to provide. People felt that security—once linked to good health, the opportunity to pursue personal and professional fulfillment, good personal relations, respect in the community, and social cohesion—had moved out of reach. In communities that were once relatively equal, people identified five or six levels of well-being.

Economic reforms in Argentina

La Matanza is a city of 1.2 million outside Buenos Aires that was once a manufacturing center of textiles, diesel engines, household appliances, and steel. Economic transformations in the 1990s led to increased reliance on technology and skilled workers. Factories in La Matanza closed, and job opportunities became scarce. With mobility low, people had to take up temporary or casual jobs without unemployment or health insurance. Those who managed to find jobs complained of exploitative pay, abusive treatment, and assaults to their dignity.

As elsewhere, job loss affected men and women's relationships. While some men adapted to a more egalitarian role, many responded to the blow to their self-esteem as breadwinners with depression or anger; women complained that violence in the household increased. Men felt joblessness undermined their roles in the family.

Source: Dudwick 2012 for the World Development Report 2013.
a. World Bank 2004a.
b. World Bank 2004a, 26.
c. World Bank 2004a, 29.
d. World Bank 2004a, 53.

involved with drugs and guns had joined "because they were searching for the support, trust, and cohesion—social capital—that they maintained their families did not provide, as well as because of the lack of opportunities in the local context."[21] Similarly, analysis in the United States has found that gangs provide youth with the income, respect, and social ties that they were unable to find in jobs, particularly given the limited opportunities available in cities such as Chicago and New York that had lost stable, unionized manufacturing jobs.[22]

The lack of jobs among dislocated populations, including migrants, refugees, and displaced persons, can be particularly disorienting. It can influence status and identity, for example, for migrants who had better jobs in their places of origin. The social effects of unemployment among dislocated populations may be especially isolating for people lacking family or other ties in their new communities. It can have implications for psychological well-being, as well as the ability to participate in civil society. Even migrants who find work may be vulnerable if their jobs do not provide adequate channels to integrate within the new society or if the migrants lack voice or information about their rights.

Jobs (or the lack of jobs) can shape social interactions

The link between social cohesion and jobs is not necessarily direct or linear. Interactions between jobs and societies are contextual and multidimensional; effects can be positive as well as negative. Having, or not having, a job can influence how people view themselves in relation to others, with implications for values, attitudes, and behaviors. Jobs can connect people with information, economic activities, and other people. And how jobs are allocated can affect whether people think their society is fair and merit-based, believe they have a stake in society, and have expectations and aspirations for the future (Question 4).

Jobs provide social identity

Some jobs can contribute positively to how people view themselves and their relations with others. The identity conveyed by a job can influence the social categories that individuals associate with, their behaviors, and the norms that shape this behavior.[23] In industrial countries, jobs that give people opportunities to learn and develop careers can be motivating and strengthen identity. In the United States, programs that provide skill development and growth opportunities to low-wage workers aim to strengthen self-esteem and motivation.[24] Public and private sector initiatives to establish career ladders in health care, child care, education, biotechnology, and manufacturing define job competencies and give employees the chance to develop skills, participate in training, and increase their responsibility. Results from a program implemented in nursing homes in Massachusetts in the United States found that having opportunities for growth improved communication and teamwork, reduced turnover, and built self-respect and confidence among staff.[25]

Jobs can have similar effects for low-wage workers in developing countries, and these effects can have implications for social cohesion. The growth of the garment sector in Bangladesh brought more than 3 million women into the workplace. Although the factory jobs were physically demanding and poorly paid, they expanded women's autonomy and increased their opportunities to participate in public life.[26] "I am braver now," a 26-year-old worker explained, "I understand more things which I did not before."[27] Observers noted that the sight of women walking back and forth to work changed popular notions about the acceptability of women in the public space and their right to access public institutions.[28] Coworkers travel together, share information about work opportunities, and form savings groups.[29]

The effect of jobs on identity also holds for self-employed workers, including farmers (box 4.4). Jobs that provide access to voice can be empowering and give workers a stake and shared interest in their work.[30] Informal workers lack access to representation on the job and are similarly excluded from local government and economic associations. Associations of self-employed workers and farmers help fill these gaps.[31] A core strategy of the Self Employed Women's Association (SEWA) in India has been to empower its members and partners by increasing their say in communities (box 4.5).

Jobs connect people

Some jobs bring people into contact with others whom they might not otherwise encounter, including people of different ethnicities and social backgrounds (box 4.6). This connecting aspect of jobs can contribute to social cohesion. Jobs can create opportunities for repeated interactions focused on tasks leading to interdependent relationships.[32] A study of political views

---

BOX 4.4 *Jobs, motivation, and identity in Risaralda, Colombia*

David is the owner of a small shop in one of the rural areas of Risaralda. He was born in another part of Colombia but has lived in the region of Risaralda for some years now. He loves living in this area for the safety and peace that exists. He has had his shop, located next to the main street of his village, for around 15 years.

One of the things he loves the most about his job is the deep sense of belonging to the community that it offers. When necessary, people come to his shop and ask for credit for the goods they need. Despite a few unpaid bills some of his customers have left him, he does his best to help the villagers. The income from the shop provides only enough to subsist, and it is necessary for him to engage in other businesses so that he can have an additional income. He feels that his shop is a way of giving back to the community and that by being there, he is able to provide for the needs of his neighbors.

Source: Bjørkhaug and others 2012 for the World Development Report 2013.

BOX 4.5 *Voice can be extended to the self-employed: The case of SEWA*

The Self Employed Women's Association (SEWA) began in 1972 with a small group of migrant women cart pullers in the wholesale cloth market of Ahmedabad City in Gujarat, India. These women worked as head loaders, carrying clothes to and from the wholesale market. They were paid on a per-trip basis, regardless of the distance they traveled or the weight they carried. Often, they were not paid the full amount they were owed because no records were kept. Ela Bhatt, head of the Women's Wing of the Textile Labor Association, helped organize the group and negotiate with the cloth merchants to gain fair treatment.

SEWA is now a member of the International Confederation of Trade Unions and has become a model for associations of informal workers internationally. In 2011, SEWA had more than 1.3 million members across India, of which over 820,000 were in Gujarat, while the rest were in eight other states. The members are drawn from multiple trades and occupations and from all religious and caste groups.

SEWA stresses self-reliance and promotes organizing around the central strategies of work security, income security, food security, and social security. Primarily a trade union, SEWA now engages in a wide range of other areas, including leadership development, collective bargaining, policy advocacy, financial services (savings, loans, and insurance), social services, infrastructure, and training and capacity building.

Of particular concern to SEWA is the fact that the working poor, especially women, do not have a voice in institutions that set the rules that affect them. The association seeks to expand the voice of its members at the local level through representation and by building capacity to participate in local councils; municipal, state, and national planning bodies; tripartite boards; minimum wage and other advisory boards; sector-specific business associations; and local, state, and national labor federations.

Over the past decade, SEWA has also inspired or cofounded national and regional networks of home-workers in other parts of South and Southeast Asia, national networks of street vendors in India and Kenya, and international networks of domestic workers and waste pickers. While some of these networks and organizations remain weak, most have been able to collaborate, leverage resources, and influence policies. The regional and international networks of domestic workers, home-based workers, street vendors, and waste pickers have secured two international conventions (for home-workers and domestic workers) and policies, laws, or legal judgments in several countries.

Source: Chen and others 2012 for the World Development Report 2013.

and the workplace in the United States finds that cross-cutting interactions at work lead to greater awareness of the rationales for views other than one's own and for "exposing people to political dialogue across lines of political difference."[33] In a survey of 200 managers, owners, and sales representatives in Trinidad and Tobago, 81 percent of the interviewees reported that their working lives brought them into contact with people of a wider range of races than did their social lives.[34]

Interactions through jobs can contribute to greater trust and positive interdependence between groups. In the 18th century, Montesquieu wrote that "the natural effect of commerce is to bring peace. Two nations that negotiate between themselves become reciprocally dependent, if one has an interest in buying and the other in selling."[35] Relations through jobs, whether built through trade or other transactions, can influence social relations.

A 2001 study of multiethnic cities in India suggests that economic interdependence, including through jobs, can reduce the incentives for violence between communities.[36] Cities with more interlinked economic relations were less likely to witness ethnic violence, while riots were more frequent in cities with fewer economic ties. The existence of civil society organizations, such as clubs, political parties, labor unions, and business associations, contributed to reducing violence. But economic interests provided a common motivation for community members of both groups to participate in these associations.[37]

Jobs can also play a connecting role outside of urban environments. Studies in Ghana and Uganda illustrate how farmers connected through networks can access information and increase productivity. In Ghana, pineapple farmers adjusted their use of fertilizer in response to the successful or unsuccessful experiences of their neighbors. Farmers who were starting to cultivate pineapples were more likely to make changes based on information they had received from other farmers, showing the potential that on-the-job interactions and learning from others can have.[38] In a qualitative survey, youth in Ghana who were asked about the characteristics that would make a job attractive emphasized the importance of jobs as opportunities to meet new people and build social networks.[39]

BOX 4.6 *Some jobs connect people across ethnic boundaries*

Surveys carried out across the world illustrate the ways jobs can connect people from different backgrounds.

"In Sadakhlo market in Georgia, next to the borders with Armenia and Azerbaijan, one does not hear the virulent expressions of mutual hatred one can hear a few miles away across the border. 'They fight, we don't,' says Mukhta, a trader from Azerbaijan, while putting his arm round his Armenian colleague Ashot."[a]

"According to one of the stallholders at Ergneti market, on the disputed border between South Ossetia and mainland Georgia, 'There are no political questions here. The market has one language: economic. That is it.'"[b]

"In Guinea, members of the Malinke ethnic group are wholesalers in the groundnut market chain, while the primary producers of groundnuts tend to be Guerse. Malinke wholesalers and Guerse farmers are willing to trade with each other. This is helping overcome ethnic and religious tensions. . . . This willingness to trade is due to the mutually recognized possibility of profit."[c]

"In Burma, as in Java, probably the first thing that strikes the visitor is the medley of peoples—European, Chinese, Indians, and native. It is, in the strictest sense, a medley, for they mix but do not combine. Each group holds to its own religion, its own culture and language, its own ideas and ways. As individuals they meet . . . in the market place, in buying and selling."[d]

In ancient Cordoba, Spain, the marketplace represented "the place of encounter over and above the gender, tribal, and faith divides that constituted Islamic urbanization."[e]

"You don't reconcile in a vacuum. There must be a practical programme; there must be something that brings people together. As they work together, cleaning the coffee, they talk together so they start talking business but later they start talking family affairs. It fosters relationships and reconciliation."[f]

"If I wasn't in this job, I might have only Indian friends or African friends," said a sales manager for a processed food manufacturer in Trinidad and Tobago. "But now I have plenty, plenty friends. White friends in Mayaro. Chinese friends in Port-of-Spain. And real close. Closer than if you born with someone, your next-door neighbor. And that's why I wouldn't swap this job for anything else."[g]

Source: Kilroy 2012 for the World Development Report 2013.
a. *The Economist* 2000.
b. Voice of America 2002.
c. Spilsbury and Byrne 2007.
d. Furnivall 1948, 304–12.
e. Vicente-Mazariegos-Eiriz 1985, 763, cited in Briggs 2004, 326.
f. Fatuma Ngangiza, Unity and Reconciliation Commission of Rwanda, quoted in BBC News 2006.
g. Kilroy 2011.

An experiment among farmers in rural Uganda found that subsistence cotton farmers using social networks can change existing social interactions with beneficial results. The randomized intervention compared the impact of training on agricultural productivity with the impact of being paired with another farmer. The pairs were encouraged to discuss farming activities, problems, and solutions and to set a target for increases in cultivation. The intervention encouraged exchanges of information and learning by expanding farmer networks. Farmers who participated in the project, especially women, significantly increased their productivity. Connecting farmers with people outside their established social circles helped spread information that would not otherwise have been shared.[40]

Jobs may not always help overcome differences and tensions between groups. While incentives inherent in jobs can provide people with motives to interact across gender, caste, and ethnic boundaries, these incentives may not be sufficient to build trust or change behaviors and contribute to social cohesion. The literature on prejudice suggests that contact across groups can alter people's perceptions of others.[41] There may also be risks. If cooperation through jobs fails, tensions between groups may flare, particularly if the groups have previously been in conflict and blame each other.[42]

While networks connect people in positive ways, they can also exclude. Surveys in industrial and developing countries consistently find that people obtain jobs through acquaintances. Yet, reliance on networks may have negative social consequences if people and groups who lack such connections are left out. In Morocco, after controlling for education, social status, and other factors, people whose fathers did not have formal sector jobs were significantly less likely to obtain formal sector jobs themselves.[43] In addition to unfairness in access to jobs, family connections can also influence labor earnings. For example, in Brazil, sons' wages are influenced by those of their parents.[44]

The exclusionary nature of networks is highlighted by the experience of migrants moving from rural areas to cities. Migrants often choose destinations where they have connections. But if they do not, they can be uprooted from family and community ties that provide economic and social support, including access to jobs. They may also lack the information needed to integrate into their new destinations. Migrants moving across borders or regions, internally displaced persons or refugees fleeing from conflict or returning after a peace agreement, and soldiers demobilized after conflict may be particularly vulnerable to exclusion from job opportunities. This is a concern in conflict situations as well as in contexts of structural transformation, when massive numbers of people move from rural to urban areas.[45] Networks also do not reach many among the self-employed, especially home-based workers who work in isolation and domestic workers who lack opportunities to interact with others.

Jobs influence aspirations and expectations

The various ways in which jobs are distributed can affect expectations and aspirations and influence whether people believe that they have a stake in society. The jobs that other people have can contribute to an individual's values, attitudes, and behaviors. Children's goals for the future may be influenced by whether their parents have jobs or not, as well as by the types of jobs their parents have. Frustration and even social unrest may develop when education and effort are not rewarded or when people perceive the distribution of jobs to be unfair.

The Arab Spring was as much or more about political voice as it was about jobs. Yet widespread disappointment, especially among youth, about the lack of job opportunities and frustration with the allocation of jobs based on connections rather than merit echoed across countries. A young person in Egypt commented, "To work in a big company, you've got to have *wasta* [connections; literally, a middleman]. Regardless of your qualifications, you must search for someone to secure the job for you. In some cases, you have to pay money."[46] Social assessments in the Republic of Yemen documented frustration with the allocation of jobs based on tribal, family background, or party affiliation.

Respondents at a focus group explained that, "to get jobs, one needs someone to speak for him, particularly from Sana'a." Young people reported that inheriting a civil service post from one's father was not viewed as wrong under the country's civil service rules.[47]

Jobs that are allocated based on connections and other circumstances beyond the control of an individual can influence whether people view society as fair. Recent work on the measurement of inequality of opportunities examines the extent to which access to basic services that are essential for human development, such as education, health, nutrition, and sanitation, is based on circumstances of birth or arises because of inequality within society (box 4.7).[48] Application of this approach to access to jobs considers the extent to which opportunities are related to circumstances at birth, including gender, ethnicity, and parental educational attainment and political affiliation, or to attributes, including educational attainment and age.[49] Results from 29 countries in Europe and Central Asia indicate that inequality across groups based on circumstances and attributes varies between 3 and 20 percent. The share of inequality attributable to circumstances is substantial in most cases, contributing to more than half of the overall inequality (figure 4.5).

Circumstances at birth contribute the most to inequality in Azerbaijan, followed by Uzbekistan, Georgia, Turkey and Albania. In these countries, such factors contribute the most to inequality in access to jobs. Education plays an outsized role in inequality in some countries—Armenia stands out in particular, along with Albania, Bulgaria, and Romania.

Similar analysis for 18 countries in Latin America using the 1990 Latinobarómetro survey confirms these findings. On the whole, the education of the worker and the circumstances he or she was born into play important roles in explaining inequalities in access to jobs, and the role of education is especially important for regular employment in the formal sector.[50]

* * *

The interaction of jobs and social cohesion is not linear or simple to disentangle. This is an emerging area for further research across disciplines. The effect of jobs on trust and civic engagement at the individual level suggests that exchanges

BOX 4.7 *Measuring inequality of opportunities in access to jobs*

The approach

The concept of equality of opportunity, which can be traced back to John Rawls and Robert Nozick,[a] stems from the idea that an individual's chances of success in life should not be caused by circumstances that are beyond the individual's control, such as gender, ethnicity, location of birth, or family background. John Roemer's 1998 work formalized the principle of equality of opportunity and argued that policy should seek to equalize opportunities independent of circumstances.[b] Empirical applications of this concept use different measures of opportunity and estimate the extent to which inequality arises because of circumstances at birth, rather than individual attributes such as effort or talent.[c]

The Human Opportunity Index (HOI) is one approach that is being used across countries and regions to analyze the opportunities available to children in terms of access to basic goods and services such as sanitation, clean water, electricity, and basic education.[d] The HOI captures both the extent to which societies provide these goods and services and how equitably access to them is distributed among groups with different circumstances in a society.

Recent work has tested the application of the HOI methodology to jobs in Europe and Central Asia and Latin America using data from the 2006 Life in Transition Survey and the Latinobarómetro Survey.[e] In this case, opportunity is defined as having a job involving more than 20 hours of work a week; circumstances are the gender of the individual, the educational attainment of the father, parents' past affiliation in the Communist Party (in Europe and Central Asia), and self-reported minority status; and attributes are educational attainment and age. Those lacking opportunity are people working fewer than 20 hours a week, the unemployed, and those who want to work more.

The HOI is the coverage rate of the opportunity, adjusted for inequality between groups defined by circumstances and attributes. Inequality is measured by a "dissimilarity index" (henceforth, D), which reflects the share of available opportunities that would have to be reallocated to achieve the same coverage rate of opportunity across all groups. A decomposition of D indicates how much circumstances contribute to inequality between groups (relative to attri-

butes), and which circumstances contribute the most. Circumstances can affect access to a job involving more than 20 hours of work a week through direct and indirect channels. An example of a direct channel is when belonging to a minority group can affect the chance of getting a job. As for indirect channels, circumstances can influence the education of a person, which, in turn, influence the chance of getting a job. The decomposition of D is intended to measure the direct channel, which is to say the inequality attributable to the predetermined circumstances, net of the effect attributed to differences in education and experience among workers.[f]

Caveats

A number of questions complicate the exercise and act as caveats to the analysis. First, how should opportunity be defined in terms of access to jobs? People have different preferences about jobs, so part of the measured inequality may reflect voluntary choices rather than a lack of access. And people with certain circumstances and attributes may be more (or less) likely to be in the labor force in the first place. Second, which circumstances should be considered? The data only report a limited range of them, and some may simply not be observable. Gender, minority status, and parental education are commonly considered in the literature; and whether parents were affiliated with the Communist Party can be a proxy for social status in the European and Central Asian countries, even many years later. However, parental education may be correlated with unobserved abilities of an individual. Controlling for the individual's education level partially resolves this problem but does not address the possibility that among children who receive the same education, children with educated parents may acquire better skills stemming from unobservable inputs. The methodology makes no assumptions about missing circumstances, which are likely to exist since information on all circumstances is not typically available from the same survey. The inequality or dissimilarity index has the property that the index will always increase with the addition of more circumstances or attributes. Despite these caveats, this approach is a first step in applying the inequality of opportunity analysis to access to jobs.

Source: Abras and others 2012 for the World Development Report 2013.
a. Nozick 1974; Rawls 1971.
b. Roemer 1998.
c. Roemer and others 2003.
d. Paes de Barros and others 2009.
e. Life in Transition Survey I (database), European Bank for Reconstruction and Development, London.
f. Estimating the indirect channel—the effect of circumstances through education—would be difficult because education depends on a host of factors other than the circumstances on which information is available. Moreover, excluding the impact of circumstances through education is justified because we are interested in measuring the extent to which inequality in access to jobs is attributable to circumstances. While circumstances may have influenced educational attainment as well, these effects would have occurred at a much earlier stage of life (primarily in childhood) and therefore do not reflect inequality of opportunities specific to jobs.

and relationships established through jobs can have broader effects on societies, including how they manage tensions between groups and collective decision making. But some jobs may contribute more to social cohesion than others. What matters is not necessarily whether people have a job but whether the job and its characteristics can contribute to social cohesion. In

FIGURE 4.5 *Inequality of job opportunities varies across countries*

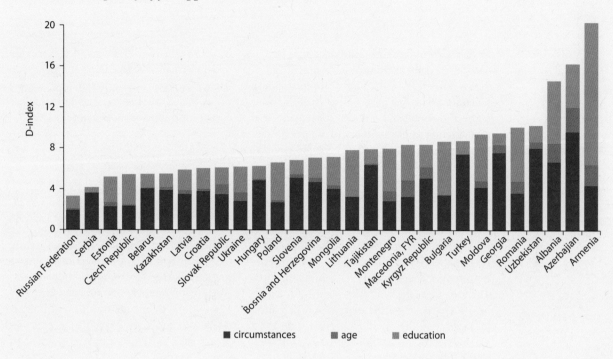

Sources: Abras and others 2012 for the World Development Report 2013; based on the data from the Life in Transition Survey I (database); European Bank for Reconstruction and Development, London.
Note: Opportunity is defined as having a job with 20 or more hours a week. *Circumstances* include gender, ethnicity, and parental education and political affiliation. The *D* Index is the share of available opportunities that would have to be reallocated to achieve the same coverage rate of opportunity across all groups.

certain contexts, jobs can transform societies if they influence social identity and social norms; if they shift bargaining power within households, communities, or society; or if they alter power relations between groups. Jobs that influence identity, connect people through networks, and increase a sense of fairness and meritocracy in access to jobs have the potential to contribute to social cohesion.

In Rabat, Morocco, unemployed college graduates gather daily in front of government buildings to protest the lack of jobs.[51] In Juba, South Sudan, the fledgling government faces the challenge of demobilizing 150,000 combatants and reintegrating large numbers of internally displaced persons after conflict.[52] For policy makers in countries with high youth unemployment and in countries affected by conflict, expanding job opportunities has urgency for social and political reasons, as well as for economic reasons.

In industrial and developing countries alike, the conventional wisdom is that having a job is what matters for social cohesion—how societies peacefully manage collective decision making. The idea that jobs can build identity, or might be associated with trust or more participation in society, is often seen as relevant only for a narrow set of occupations in rich countries. Those jobs are perceived as a luxury that developing countries cannot afford. Even those who concede that some jobs can do more for social cohesion in developing countries are skeptical that policies can do much beyond supporting job creation. Given that most employment is in the private sector, it is unclear how or whether the government could influence the nature of the jobs. Some even doubt that jobs on their own lead to greater social cohesion. They view jobs as only one element that can contribute to changing values, attitudes, and behaviors within a complex web of institutional, historical, political, and social factors. Given this multiplicity of influences, engineering social cohesion through jobs is not an option.

Negative experiences with publicly funded employment programs give some justification to this skepticism. Temporary employment programs that place people into dead-end jobs with no hope for future employment may do more harm than good.[53] Similarly, demobilization programs in post-conflict environments risk exacerbating tensions between former opponents through divisive targeting.[54] Social cohesion is actually undermined when jobs in publicly funded programs are allocated to friends and relatives of government officials, or when the programs themselves are subject to corruption and governance risks. These negative experiences may reveal poor program design, however, rather than prove the impossibility for jobs policies to contribute to social cohesion.

Access to information, rights, and voice

Policies can take social cohesion into account by expanding opportunities for groups who face barriers to getting jobs and increasing access to voice and rights. People may feel frustrated if they perceive that jobs are allocated on the basis of privilege and connections rather than merit and achievement. Increasing fairness and equality of opportunity for jobs involves informing the public about jobs and how to get them, and about the existence of legal mechanisms, such as antidiscrimination laws and affirmative action programs to reduce discrimination and support the inclusion of groups who lack access. But having laws on the books is not enough. Increasing fairness involves institutions for enforcement, and redress mechanisms for accountability. Although such measures can be motivated by multiple objectives, including poverty reduction, they can also be considered from a social cohesion perspective.

Transparency and access to information about jobs can increase fairness and equality of opportunity by ensuring that vacancies are widely publicized, together with information about accessing public employment programs. Access to information about rights is similarly important for ensuring that labor practices are fair. Farmers, self-employed workers, and workers without formal labor contracts are often not knowledgeable about their rights in relation to land owners, traders, local authorities, and employers, or about their options for appeals. Civil society organizations such as cooperatives, associations of informal workers, and trade unions can disseminate information about rights and the channels to voice grievances.[55]

A related challenge is the extension of effective legal protection to those who work outside of legal frameworks. At the international level, the passage of ILO conventions on domestic and home workers has extended coverage for these groups (box 4.8). At the national level, countries such as Zambia and the Philippines include legal protections of informal workers in domestic legislation. Brazil recognizes domestic workers within its constitution and has extended social protection, including leave and maternity benefits to them. The country's National Social Security Institute provides incentives for employers who register domestic workers. Although difficult to enforce in practice, Brazil, the Czech Republic, the Philippines, and South Africa have established minimum wages for domestic workers.[56]

Similarly, migrant workers tend to fall outside legal frameworks. Both sending and receiving countries can adopt measures to extend legal protection. The government of the Philippines has a mechanism to protect its overseas workers. The government provides them with predeparture information and support services; it has also signed bilateral agreements and memoranda of understanding recognizing migrant workers' rights with receiving countries. The government has also promoted voluntary social security schemes for overseas workers.[57]

The existence and quality of institutions for accountability can influence the extent to which rights are enforced in practice.[58] Legal frameworks rely on the ability of labor ministries, inspectorates, and courts to handle disputes and hold the parties accountable. Most countries allow labor disputes to be heard in special labor courts or civil courts. But court proceedings can be lengthy, costly, and cumbersome. In response, some countries have established alternative procedures for dispute resolution, including conciliation, mediation, and arbitration before court hearings.[59] Cambodia introduced an Arbitration Council in 2003 to help manage labor grievances and improve industrial relations in the growing garment sector (box 4.9).

Antidiscrimination policies

Legal mechanisms such as antidiscrimination laws and provisions for affirmative action can facilitate access to jobs for groups who are excluded from opportunities or suffer from stigma. Most countries have equality guarantees within their constitutions, generally covering

---

BOX 4.8 *Domestic workers: The journey to an ILO convention*

Domestic work includes cleaning, cooking, gardening, child care, and elder care. The International Labour Organization (ILO) estimates that there are 52.6 million domestic workers worldwide; other estimates are nearly twice as high. Women, generally from the poorest sections of society, make up over 80 percent of domestic workers.[a] Many are migrants, and child labor is common, especially for girls. Domestic workers, and especially migrants, are excluded from labor and social protection laws in most countries.

Domestic workers have long tried to be recognized and included in the labor laws of their respective countries. In 2006, domestic worker organizations began to organize internationally with the support of international trade unions and nongovernmental organizations representing informal workers. Their main demand was recognition and access to rights, including a campaign for an ILO convention on labor rights for domestic workers.

The campaign involved extensive coordination at the country level to mobilize workers and gain support from labor ministries, trade unions, and employers' associations. As a result of this campaign, the minimum wage for domestic workers was raised by 10 percent in Jamaica, and a memorandum of understanding was signed to improve the conditions of Indonesian domestic workers in Malaysia.

In 2011, the ILO adopted the Domestic Workers Convention and the Domestic Workers Recommendation. The convention states that domestic workers are to be covered under national labor laws and regulations, including those related to social protection programs.

The process of securing an ILO convention contributed to building the capacity of organizations and individual leaders and gained domestic workers associations status with trade unions. It also created better conditions for recognition and enforcement of rights. In March 2012, the government of Singapore announced that it would require employers to give one day a week off to the country's 206,000 domestic workers, most of whom come from Indonesia, the Philippines, Sri Lanka, and India.[b]

Source: Chen and others 2012 for the World Development Report 2013.
a. ILO 2011a.
b. Kennedy 2012.

---

the obligations of the state. Guarantees are often complemented by laws addressing job segregation, unequal pay, prejudice in recruitment, harassment at work, and lack of education and training.[60] Affirmative action programs involve proactive measures for hiring women, minorities, and other groups subject to exclusion.[61] Such programs can be mandatory or voluntary and apply to the public or private sectors.

Affirmative action programs can work, but pitfalls are many. Evaluations yield mixed results.[62] The most extensive research is from the United States; it finds that programs are most effective when they are temporary and combined with improvements in recruitment, train-

BOX 4.9 *From laws on the books to laws in action in Cambodia's garment sector*

The garment industry is Cambodia's largest formal sector employer. By mid-2008, the sector had more than 300 factories, with nearly 340,000 workers, 90 percent of whom were women. Labor conditions including low wages, excessive overtime, poor occupational health and safety, child labor, and antiunion practices emerged as a major issue as the sector expanded. The initial response was passage of a new labor law in 1997. Enforcement was poor, however. The Labor Inspectorate lacked credibility; inspectors were underpaid and underresourced, and were seen as subject to influence. The courts were perceived as corrupt and unresponsive to the needs of workers or employers. As a result, strikes and demonstrations increased, and major international brands raised concerns about the viability of operating in Cambodia.

In this context, Cambodia concluded a 1999 bilateral trade agreement with the United States. Building on a similar clause in other trade deals, the United States agreed to increase Cambodia's import quota for garments if a semiannual review showed that progress had been achieved in adherence to core international labor standards and standards set in Cambodian law. Following the agreement, the United States funded two International Labour Organization (ILO) projects to support the implementation of this clause. The first, which became known as Better Factories Cambodia, involved monitoring working conditions in garment factories.

The second program established an Arbitration Council to prevent and resolve labor disputes. The council's 30 part-time members were nominated through a process facilitated by the ILO and endorsed by unions, employers' organizations, and government. The council conducts mandatory but (generally) nonbinding arbitration of collective labor disputes that cannot be resolved through mediation by the Ministry of Labor. Most disputes handled by the council involve compliance with labor law related to wages, bonuses, benefits, and working conditions. Some cases also relate to rights, including antiunion practices, gender equality, freedom of association, and collective bargaining.

Since its establishment in 2003, the council has heard more than 1,200 disputes, 70 percent of which are reported as successfully resolved. Opinion surveys indicate a high level of confidence in the council's independence and effectiveness. In 2010, the Garment Manufacturers Association of Cambodia and major union federations agreed to switch to the council's arbitration procedures for disputes over existing labor rights. The result has been an upsurge in the rate of awards issued by the council and a decrease in the rate at which parties are filing objections. Strikes per factory have fallen to their lowest level in 10 years.

Source: Adler and Hwang 2012 for the World Development Report 2013.

ing, and on-the-job training.[63] Evidence from developing countries is more limited. In South Africa, affirmative action supporting blacks, women, and people with disabilities was complemented with incentives for firms, including access to licenses and contracts. An evaluation found that programs had limited impact on reducing gaps in employment and wages but narrowed differentials at the top of the wage distribution. This finding suggests that the program might have assisted individuals who were already higher up on the skills ladder but not the average previously disadvantaged individual.[64]

Hiring quotas for underrepresented groups can be enshrined in constitutions, as is the case for Scheduled Castes and Tribes in India and for Bumiputras in Malaysia. Both countries have shown that quotas work well but can become politicized.[65] Quotas supported through specific programs have been successful. In Bangladesh, for instance, where women's employment rates were extremely low, the Employment Generation Program for the Poorest put in place a 30 percent quota for women. This doubled women's participation in the program within a year, with participants reporting a high level of satisfaction.[66]

Jobs policies can shape social identity and connect people

Access to jobs can bolster self-esteem and produce benefits for societies beyond incomes. Programs that support employment for at-risk populations, including youth, can take into account the ways in which jobs affect peoples' attitudes, values, and behaviors and contribute to improved relations between groups. Arguably, in countries with high youth unemployment, targeted training programs have the potential to be designed to strengthen self-esteem, which can lead to greater community involvement and reduced crime and violence. The evidence remains limited and tentative, but emerging findings from some training programs targeted to youth, including those in post-conflict settings are somewhat encouraging.

The Northern Uganda Social Action Fund suggests that combining vocational training, life skills, and counseling can increase community involvement and reduce aggression among youth in a post-conflict setting (box 4.10).[67] A reintegration and agricultural livelihoods program for high-risk Liberian youth led to a modest increase in social engagement and a reduction in illegal activities. Participants were also less interested in recruitment into violent activities in neighboring Côte d'Ivoire. The program had no clear impact on reducing aggression and violence, however.[68] An evaluation of the Juventud y Empleo program in the Dominican Republic found that a combination of vocational and life-skills training for unemployed youth can reduce involvement in gangs and delay teen pregnancy.[69] This is an area for further research; evidence is thin, and few evaluations of employment and training programs incorporate social cohesion outcome measures such as community participation and conflict resolution.

Temporary employment programs can provide skills training and access to employment for youth at risk and vulnerable populations, particularly during crises and after conflicts.[70] These programs have a mixed record in supporting employability, because they generally involve jobs with low status that rarely lead to future earnings opportunities. But there are indications that programs can be designed to invest in skills with benefits for social cohesion. El Salvador's Temporary Income Assistance Program targets women and youth in areas with high rates of violence. Early results suggest that the program has increased the self-esteem of beneficiaries and reduced the recurrence of violence.[71]

Public works programs frequently rely on community participation to identify local projects, providing forums for collective decision making. Community meetings can bring together people affected by conflict and crisis (box 4.10). In Rwanda, meetings for the country's public works program discussed peace building, security, community development, and reconciliation, in addition to project-related issues. In the Republic of Yemen, fuel shortages and price increases in building materials stalled public works activities in 2011. However, communities worked together to find creative solutions to these obstacles, including using local materials and finding alternative modes of transport.[72]

Participatory aspects of programs can provide a channel for voice of excluded groups. In a survey of participants in Ethiopia's Productive Safety Net Program—which at 7.6 million beneficiaries is one of the largest public works programs in the world—two-thirds of respondents said that the project had given them the first opportunity ever to be involved in a local meeting. Many participants had not interacted with local government officials prior to the program.[73]

Employment programs partnering with the private sector can connect people through jobs. A program in Tunisia uses the process of writing an undergraduate thesis to teach students basic

---

BOX 4.10 *In post-conflict settings, well-designed programs reduce social tensions*

Opportunities for youth in Northern Uganda

Two decades of insurgency, instability, and conflict led to high rates of poverty in northern Uganda. By 2005, a measure of peace and stability had returned to the region, allowing for the demobilization and reintegration of former combatants and other war-affected populations. In 2006, the government launched the Youth Opportunities Program to stimulate income generation and employment growth among young adults ages 16 to 35. The program provided cash grants for vocational training and business materials to groups of participants with successful grant proposals. Groups had an average of 22 members, and most expressed interest in tailoring, carpentry, metal works, mechanics, or hairdressing.

An evaluation two years after the intervention found increased investments in skills, participation in skilled work, greater incomes, and higher savings. Grantees were 4 percent more likely to attend community meetings and 9 percent more likely to be community mobilizers. Participants also reported receiving more social support from their family and the community. Furthermore, men who received grants reported a 31 percent decline in aggressive behavior relative to the control group. This finding is consistent with theories that link aggression to stress levels, low social standing, and perceived injustice—all potentially alleviated by higher employment and incomes.

Public works in Sri Lanka's Northern Province

In Sri Lanka, a cash-for-work program initially established to resettle 100,000 returnees following internal conflict actually assisted more than 250,000 returnees and quickly evolved into one of the largest sources of employment in the Northern Province.

Participants noted that in many cases the program meetings were the first community-level gathering that they had attended after having arrived from camps for internally displaced populations. By many accounts, community meetings, shared meals, team work, and the involvement of elders and children as indirect beneficiaries of the program promoted a sense of belonging among the newly resettled families.

Sachchithananthan Subodhini, 36 years old, from Thervipuram in the Puthukkudiyiruppu Division of the Northern Province said that she was "very happy. As a result of cash for work, the whole village is working as one; for our own community and village." Reflecting on her life journey since being displaced in 1995, she said that the program "had helped to bring the community together. . . . [T]he village seemed abandoned but the *shramadana* [volunteer work] helped to get the community back to its original state."

Sources: Blattman, Fiala, and Martinez 2011 (Northern Uganda); Andrews and Kryeziu 2012 for the World Development Report 2013 (Sri Lanka).

---

entrepreneurial skills. Students are mentored by professors and private sector coaches to develop business plans. The initial results of the program show that the program motivated students and gave them confidence to take risks. A male participant from Tunis explained, "I have become more independent. My behavior has changed. I use my new skills, I am more disciplined." Students also explained that the program expanded their professional networks by giving them opportunities to interact with mentors. "I now have a social network. I know whom to consult," explained a female participant.[74]

While not all jobs affect social cohesion, those that shape social identity, build networks, and increase fairness, particularly for excluded groups, can defuse tensions. Increasing fairness in the allocation of jobs and at work can also be important for social cohesion. Measures that support inclusion, extend access to voice and rights, and improve transparency and account-

ability in the labor market can improve equity. They can also increase the extent to which people perceive that they have a stake in society. This perception can be especially critical when risks of social unrest from youth unemployment and conflict are high. While policies with weak governance or divisive targeting can undermine social cohesion, well-designed programs may have positive effects. Jobs policies for youth at risk can incorporate counseling and training in conflict resolution. Public works programs can facilitate community participation and engagement between citizens and local governments.

Shopkeeper and a friend at a foodstuff shop in Mpape, Nigeria

© Ayemoba Godswill / World Bank

Rural migrants working in construction in China

© Curt Carnemark / World Bank

of Female Garment-Factory Workers in Bangladesh." *Studies in Family Planning* 29 (2): 185–200.

Amos, Deborah. 2012. "In Morocco, Unemployment Can Be a Full-Time Job." *National Public Radio*, January 27.

Anarfi, John Kwasi, Nana Akua Anyidoho, and Arjan Verschoor. 2008. "The Economic Empowerment of Young People in Ghana." World Bank, Washington, DC. Processed.

Andrews, Colin, and Adea Kryeziu. 2012. "Public Works and the Jobs Agenda: Pathways for Social Cohesion." Background paper for the WDR 2013.

Arias, Omar, and Walter Sosa. 2012. "Do Jobs Cause Trust? Results from Pseudo-Panel Analysis of Euro and Latino Barometer Surveys." Background paper for the WDR 2013.

Arias, Omar, Gustavo Yamada, and Luis Tejerina. 2004. "Education, Family Background and Racial Earnings Inequality in Brazil." *International Journal of Manpower* 25 (314): 355–74.

Arrow, Kenneth. 1972. "Gifts and Exchanges." *Philosophy and Public Affairs* 1 (4): 343–62.

Austin, William G., and Stephen Worchel. 1979. *The Social Psychology of Intergroup Relations*. Monterey, CA: Brooks/Cole Publishing Company.

Bardhan, Pranab K., Dilip Mookherjee, and Monica L. Parra. 2012. "The Impact of Political Reservations in West Bengal Local Governments on Anti-Poverty Targeting." *Journal of Globalization and Development* 1 (1): 1948–837.

BBC News. 2006. "Coffee Key to Reconciling Rwandans." *BBC World News*, August 30.

Bell, David N. F., and David Blanchflower. 2010. "Youth Unemployment: Déjà Vu?" Discussion Paper Series 4705, Institute for the Study of Labor, Bonn.

Betcherman, Gordon, Karina Olivas, and Amit Dar. 2004. "Impacts of Active Labor Market Programs: New Evidence from Evaluations with Particular Attention to Developing and Transition Countries." Social Protection Discussion Paper Series 0402, World Bank, Washington, DC.

Bjørkhaug, Ingunn, Anne Hatløy, Tewodros Kebede, and Huafeng Zhang. 2012. "Perception of Good Jobs: Colombia." Background paper for the WDR 2013.

Blattman, Christopher, and Jeannie Annan. 2011. "Reintegrating and Employing High Risk Youth in Liberia: Lessons from a Randomized Evaluation of a Landmine Action an Agriculturual Training Program for Ex-Combatants." Policy report 2011.1, Yale University, Innovations for Poverty Action, New Haven, CT.

Blattman, Christopher, Nathan Fiala, and Sebastian Martinez. 2011. "Employment Generation in Rural Africa, Mid-Term Results from an Experimental Evaluation of the Youth Opportunities Program in Northern Uganda." Yale University, Innovations for Poverty Action, New Haven, CT.

Boschma, Ron. 2005. "Social Capital and Regional Development: An Empirical Analysis of the Third Italy." In *Learning from Clusters*, ed. Ron Boschma and Robert Kloosterman, 139–68. Dordrecht: Springer Verlag.

Brand, Jennie, and Sarah Burgard. 2008. "Job Displacement and Social Participation: Findings across the Life Course of a Cohort of Joiners." *Social Forces* 87 (1): 211–42.

Briggs, Xavier de Souza. 2004. "Civilization in Color: The Multicultural City in Three Millennia." *City & Community* 3 (4): 311–42.

Brodmann, Stefanie, Rebekka Grun, and Patrick Premand. 2011. "Can Unemployed Youth Create Their Own Jobs? The Tunisia Business Plan Thesis Competition." Fast Brief 83 (March), MNA Knowledge and Learning, World Bank, Washington, DC.

Burger, Rulof, and Rachel Jafta. 2010. "Affirmative Action in South Africa: An Empirical Assessment of the Impact on Labour Market Outcomes." Working Paper Series 76, Centre for Research on Equality, Human Security and Ethnicity, University of Oxford, Oxford.

Chandra, Kanchan. 2001. "Civic Life or Economic Interdependence?" *Commonwealth and Comparative Politics* 39 (1): 110–18.

Chen, Martha, Chris Bonner, Mahendra Chetty, Lucia Fernandez, Karin Pape, Federico Parra, Arbind Singh, and Caroline Skinner. 2012. "Urban Informal Workers: Representative Voice and Economic Rights." Background paper for the WDR 2013.

Chen, Martha, Renana Jhabvala, Ravi Kanbur, and Carol Richards. 2007. *Membership-Based Organizations of the Poor*. London: Routledge.

Cramer, Christopher. 2010. "Unemployment and Participation in Violence." Background paper for the WDR 2011.

Das, Maitreyi Bordia. 2012. "Stubborn Inequalities, Subtle Processes: Exclusion and Discrimination in the Labor Market." Background paper for the WDR 2013.

Datta, Nonica. 1999. "Backward Caste Movement Gains Ground." *Economic and Political Weekly* 34 (39): 2630–31.

Delhey, Jan, Kenneth Newton, and Christian Welzel. 2011. "How General Is Trust in 'Most People'? Solving the Radius of Trust Problem." *American Sociological Review* 76 (5): 786–807.

Deshpande, Satish. 2008. "Changing Social Composition." *Seminar* 587 (July): 23–26.

Dudwick, Nora. 2012. "The Relationship between Jobs and Social Cohesion: Some Examples from Ethnography." Background paper for the WDR 2013.

Dudwick, Nora, and Radhika Srinivasan, with Jose Cueva and Dorsati Madani. Forthcoming. *Creating Jobs in Africa's Fragile States: Are Value Chains an Answer?* Directions in Development. Washington, DC: World Bank.

Durkheim, Emile. 1893. *The Division of Labor in Society.* New York: Free Press.

Easterly, William, Jozef Ritzen, and Michael Woolcock. 2006. "Social Cohesion, Institutions, and Growth." *Economics and Politics* 18 (2): 103–20.

Eaton, Charles, and Andrew W. Shepherd. 2001. *Contract Farming: Partnerships for Growth.* Rome: Food and Agriculture Organization.

Evans-Pritchard, Ambrose. 2010. "IMF Fears 'Social Explosion' from World Jobs Crisis." *Telegraph*, September 13.

FAFO (Forskningsstiftelsen Fafo [Fafo Research Foundation]). 2012. "Good Jobs Survey." FAFO Institute for Applied International Studies, Oslo.

Fitzgerald, Joan. 2006. *Moving Up in the New Economy: Career Ladders for U.S. Workers.* Ithaca, NY: Cornell University Press.

Feldman, Shelley. 2009. "Historicising Garment Manufacturing in Bangladesh: Gender, Generation, and New Regulatory Regimes." *Journal of International Women's Studies* 11(1): 268–82.

Fredman, Sandra. 2012. "Anti-Discrimination Laws and Work in the Developing World: A Thematic Overview." Background paper for the WDR 2013.

Fukuyama, Francis. 1995. *Trust: The Social Virtues and the Creation of Prosperity.* New York: Free Press.

Funston, John. 2001. "Malaysia: Developmental State Challenged." In *Government and Politics in Southeast Asia*, ed. John Funston, 160–202. Singapore: Institute of Southeast Asian Studies.

Furnivall, John S. 1948. *Colonial Policy and Practice: A Comparative Study of Burma and Netherlands India.* Cambridge, U.K.: Cambridge University Press.

Gatti, Roberta, Diego Angel-Urdinola, Joana Silva, and Andras Bodor. 2012. *Striving for Better Jobs: The Challenge of Informality in the Middle East and North Africa.* Washington, DC: World Bank.

Giles, John, Dimitris Mavridis, and Firman Witoelar. 2012. "Subjective Well-Being, Social Cohesion, and Labor Market Outcomes in Indonesia." Background paper for the WDR 2013.

Gudavarthy, Ajay. 2012. "Can We De-Stigmatize Reservations in India?" *Economic and Political Weekly* 47 (6): 55–62.

Harvey, Philip. 2011. "A Job-Led Recovery Strategy Achieving Economic Recovery through Direct Public Job Creation." Dēmos, NY.

Helliwell, John, and Robert Putnam. 2004. "The Social Context of Well-Being." *Philosophical Transactions of the Royal Society B* 359: 1435–46.

Holzer, Harry, and Robert Lerman. 2009. *The Future of Middle-Skill Jobs.* Washington, DC: Center on Children and Families, Brookings Institute.

Holzer, Harry J., and David Neumark. 2000. "Assessing Affirmative Action." *Journal of Economic Literature* 38 (3): 483–568.

Hossain, Naomi. 2011. "Exports, Equity, and Empowerment: The Effects of Readymade Garments Manufacturing Employment on Gender Equality in Bangladesh." Background paper for the WDR 2012.

Hudson, Maria, Rosemary Davidson, Lucia Durante, Jemma Grieve, and Arjumand Kazmi. 2011. *Recession and Cohesion in Bradford.* York, U.K.: Joseph Rowntree Foundation.

Ibarraran, Pablo, Laura Ripani, Bibiana Taboada, Juan Miguel Villa, and Brigida Garcia. 2012. "Life Skills, Employability and Training for Disadvantaged Youth: Evidence from a Randomized Evaluation Design." IZA Conference Paper, Institute for the Study of Labor, Bonn, May 12.

ILO (International Labour Organization). 2011a. *Global and Regional Estimates on Domestic Workers.* Geneva: ILO.

———. 2011b. *World of Work Report: Making Markets Work for Jobs.* Geneva: ILO.

IOM (International Organization for Migration). 2012. "IOM Tracking of Spontaneous Returns Project: Total Returns to South Sudan Post CPA to June 2009." Geneva, IOM.

Jenson, Jane. 1998. "Mapping Social Cohesion: The State of the Canadian Research." Discussion Paper 3, Canadian Policy Research Networks, Ottawa.

Kaufmann, Daniel, Aart Kraay, and Massimo Mastruzzi. 2010. "The Worldwide Governance Indicators: Methodology and Analytical Issues." Policy Research Working Paper Series 5430, World Bank, Washington, DC.

Kennedy, Alex. 2012. "Singapore to Require One Day Off a Week for Maids." Associated Press, March 5.

Kilroy, Austin. 2011. "Business Bridging Ethnicity." PhD thesis, Massachusetts Institute of Technology, Cambridge, MA.

———. 2012. "Jobs to Social Cohesion: Via Interests, Attitudes, and Identities." Background paper for the WDR 2013.

Knack, Stephen, and Philip Keefer. 1997. "Does Social Capital Have an Economic Payoff? A Cross-Country Investigation." *Quarterly Journal of Economics* 112 (4): 1251–88.

Locke, Richard, Matthew Amengual, and Ashkay Mangla. 2009. "Virtue out of Necessity? Compliance, Commitment and the Improvement of Labor Conditions in Global Supply Chains." *Politics & Society* 37 (3): 319–51.

Marc, Alexandre, Alys Willman, Ghazia Aslam, Michelle Rebosio, with Kanishka Balisuriya. 2012. *Societal Dynamics and Fragility: Engaging Societies in Responding to Fragile Situations*. Washington, DC: World Bank.

Marsden, David. 2000. "A Theory of Job Regulation, the Employment Relationship, and the Organisation of Labour Institutions." *Industrielle Beziehungen* 7 (4): 320–47.

Martin, John P., and David Grubb. 2001. "What Works and for Whom? A Review of OECD Countries' Experiences with Active Labour Market Policies." *Swedish Economic Policy Review* 8 (2): 9–60.

McCord, Anna, and Rachel Slater. 2011. *Overview of Public Works in Sub-Saharan Africa*. London: Overseas Development Institute.

McKenzie, David, Caroline Theoharides, and Dean Yang. 2012. "Distortions in the International Migrant Labor Market: Evidence from Filipino Migration and Wage Responses to Destination Country Economic Shocks." Policy Research Working Paper Series 6041, World Bank, Washington, DC.

Montesquieu, Baron de. 1951. *2 Oeuvres Completes: De l'Esprit des Lois* (2 Complete Works: Spirit of the Laws). Paris: Gallimard/Pleiade.

Montlake, Simon. 2010. "Malaysia Cautiously Challenges Longtime Affirmative Action Policies." *Christian Science Monitor*, March 30.

Moreno, Jacob L., and Helen H. Jennings. 1937. "Statistics of Social Configurations." *Sociometry* 1: 342–74.

Moser, Caroline O. N. 2009. *Ordinary Families, Extraordinary Lives: Assets and Poverty Reduction in Guayaquil, 1978–2004*. Washington, DC: Brookings Institution.

Mutz, Diane, and Jeffery Mondak. 2006. "The Workplace as a Context for Cross-Cutting Political Discourse." *Journal of Politics* 68 (1): 140–55.

North, Douglass C. 1990. *Institutions, Institutional Change and Economic Performance*. New York: Cambridge University Press.

Norton, Andrew, and Arjan de Haan. 2012. "Social Cohesion: Theoretical Debates and Practical Applications with Respect to Jobs." Background paper for the WDR 2013.

Noteboom, Bart. 1999. *Inter-Firm Alliances: Analysis and Design*. London: Routledge.

Nozick, Robert. 1974. *Anarchy, State, and Utopia*. New York: Basic Books.

OECD (Organisation for Economic Co-operation and Development). 2011. *Perspectives on Global Development 2012: Social Cohesion in a Shifting World*. Paris: OECD.

Osterman, Paul. 2005. "Making Bad Jobs Good: Strategies for the Service Section." In *Job Quality and Employer Behaviour*, ed. Stephen Bazen, Claudio Lucifora, and Wiemer Salverda. 237–252. London: Palgrave Macmillan.

Ostrom, Elinor. 1990. *Governing the Commons: The Evolution of Institutions for Collective Action*. Cambridge, U.K.: Cambridge University Press.

Padilla, Felix M. 1992. *The Gang as an American Enterprise*. Piscataway, NJ: Rutgers University Press.

Paes de Barros, Ricardo, Francisco H. G. Ferreira, Jose R. Molinas Vega, Jaime Saavedra Chanduvi. 2009. *Measuring Inequality of Opportunities in Latin America and the Caribbean*. Washington, DC: World Bank.

Perry, Guillermo E., William F. Maloney, Omar S. Arias, Pablo Fajnzylber, Andrew D. Mason, and Jaime Saavedra-Chanduvi. 2007. *Informality: Exit and Exclusion*. Washington, DC: World Bank.

Petesch, Patti. 2012. "The Exponential Clash of Conflict, Good Jobs, and Changing Gender Norms in Four Economies." Background paper for the WDR 2013.

Pettigrew, Thomas F., and Linda R. Tropp. 2011. *When Groups Meet: The Dynamics of Intergroup Contact*. New York: Psychology Press.

Pickering, Paula. 2006. "Generating Social Capital for Bridging Ethnic Divisions in the Balkans: Case Studies of Two Bosniäk Cities." *Ethnic and Racial Studies* 29 (1): 79–103.

Purcell, Julius. 2010. *Individual Disputes at the Workplace: Alternative Disputes Resolution*. Dublin: European Foundation for the Improvement of Living and Working Conditions.

Putnam, Robert. 2000. *Bowling Alone: The Collapse and Revival of American Community*. New York: Simon and Schuster.

Putnam, Robert, Robert Leonardi, and Rafaella Nanetti. 1993. *Making Democracy Work: Civic Traditions in Modern Italy*. Princeton, NJ: Princeton University Press.

Rawls, John. 1971. *A Theory of Justice*. Cambridge, MA: Belknap Press.

Roemer, John E. 1998. *Equality of Opportunity*. Cambridge, MA: Harvard University Press.

Roemer, John E., Rolf Aaberge, Ugo Colombino, Johan Fritzell, Stephen Jenkins, Arnaud Lefranc, Ive Marx, Marianne Page, Evert Pommer, and Javier Ruiz-Castillo. 2003. "To What Extent Do Fiscal Regimes Equalize Opportunities for Income Acquisition among Citizens." *Journal of Public Economics* 87: 539–65.

Singerman, Diane. 2007. "The Economic Imperatives of Marriage: Emerging Practices and Identities among Youth in the Middle East." Middle East Youth Initiative Working Paper 6, Wolfensohn Center for Development, Dubai School of Government at Brookings Institution, Washington, DC.

Solletty, Marion. 2011. "Le Chômage des Diplômés, Moteur de la Révolte Tunisienne." *Le Monde*, January 10.

Spilsbury, John, and Karri Goeldner Byrne. 2007. "Value Chain Activities for Conflict-Affected Populations in Guinea." Micro Report, U.S. Agency for International Development, Washington, DC.

Teoh, Shannon. 2008. "Poll Shows Most Malaysians Want NEP to End." *Malaysian Insider*, October 9.

The Economist. 2000. "An Uncommon Market in the Caucasus." *The Economist*, June 1.

Udry, Christopher, and Timothy G. Conley. 2004. "Social Networks in Ghana." Discussion Paper 888, Economic Growth Center, Yale University, New Haven, CT.

USAID (U.S. Agency for International Development). 2009. *A Guide to Economic Growth in Post-Conflict Countries.* Washington, DC: USAID, Bureau for Economic Growth, Agriculture and Trade.

Varshney, Ashutosh. 2002. *Ethnic Conflict and Civic Life: Hindus and Muslims in India.* New Haven, CT: Yale University Press.

Vasilaky, Kathryn. 2010. "As Good as the Networks They Keep? Expanding Farmer's Social Networks Using Randomized Encouragement in Rural Uganda." Yale University, New Haven, CT. Processed.

Vicente-Mazariegos-Eiríz, José Ignacio. 1985. "La ciudad hispanomusulmana: Organizacíon social y formalizacíon urbana." In *Urbanismo e Historia en el Mundo Hispano*, ed. Antonio Bonet Correa, 2: 749–64. Madrid: Universidad Complutense de Madrid.

Voice of America. 2002. "South Ossetia Market Important for Local Economy." Voice of America, Washington, DC.

Wang, Shing-Yi. 2011. "Marriage Networks, Nepotism and Labor Market Outcomes in China." New York University, New York. Processed.

Weiss, Dieter. 1995. "Ibn Khaldun on Economic Transformation." *International Journal of Middle East Studies* 27 (1): 29–37.

Weisskopf, Thomas. 2004. "Impact of Reservation on Admissions to Higher Education in India." *Economic and Political Weekly* 39 (39): 4339–49.

Welzel, Christian. 2012. "The Contribution of 'Good' Jobs to Development and Cohesion: The Human Empowerment Perspective." Background paper for the WDR 2013.

Wietzke, Frank-Borge, and Catriona McLeod. 2012. "Jobs, Well-Being, and Social Cohesion: Evidence from Value and Perception Surveys." Background paper for the WDR 2013.

Willman, Alys, and Megumi Makisaka. 2010. "Interpersonal Violence Prevention: A Review of the Evidence and Emerging Lessons." Background paper for the WDR 2011.

Wilson, Randall, Susan Eaton, and Amara Kamanu. 2002. "Extended Care Career Ladder Initiative (ECCLI) Round 2: Evaluation Report." Faculty Research Working Paper Series RWP03-006, Harvard University, Cambridge, MA.

Woolcock, Michael. 2011. "What Distinctive Contribution Can Social Cohesion Make to Development Theory, Research, and Policy?" Paper presented at the Organisation for Economic Cooperation and Development International Conference on Social Cohesion and Development, Paris, January 20.

World Bank. 2004a. *Guyana: A Poverty and Social Impact Analysis of Bauxite Mining Reforms in Guyaya.* Washington, DC: World Bank.

———. 2004b. *World Development Report 2005: A Better Investment Climate for Everyone.* New York: Oxford University Press.

———. 2005. *World Development Report 2006: Equity and Development.* New York: Oxford University Press.

———. 2011. *World Development Report 2012: Gender Equality and Development.* Washington, DC: World Bank.

Yadav, Yogendra. 2010. "Why Caste Should Be Counted In." *The Hindu*, May 14.

What are good jobs for development?

Introduction to Part 2

Earnings, benefits (if any), and overall job satisfaction are what matter to individual jobholders. Those earnings and benefits—tangible or otherwise—are the first and most direct measure of the value a job has to society. But jobs may also affect others, positively or negatively. Jobs for women may influence resource allocations at the household level and benefit their children. Jobs connected to world markets may lead to knowledge spillovers and make other workers more productive. Jobs that provide opportunities may convey a sense of fairness to others and help them remain engaged. Spillovers like these have been the focus of recent thinking on development. The analysis may be organized around concepts such as gender, urbanization, or conflict; but much of the action happens through jobs.

Quite often individual and social perspectives on jobs coincide; but not always. For instance, jobs with perks and benefits may be highly coveted by individuals, but they may be less valuable to society if their privileges are supported through government transfers or restrictive regulations, undermining the earnings or job opportunities of others. Because of gaps like these, jobs that look equivalent from an individual perspective may be different from a social perspective. The contributions jobs make to society should be assessed by taking into account the value they have to the people who hold them, but also the potential spillovers on others—positive or negative. Good jobs for development are those with the highest value to society.

Conversely, some forms of work are unequivocally bad. A set of universal rights endorsed by governments, international organizations, and others seeks to eliminate forced labor, harmful forms of child labor, discrimination, and the suppression of voice among workers. These forms of work should not be considered jobs.

How jobs contribute to living standards, productivity, and social cohesion varies with a country's level of development, its demography, its endowments, and its institutions. Jobs agendas are thus inherently country specific. By combining the various features of an economy, however, it is possible to build a typology of jobs challenges. It includes agrarian economies, conflict-affected countries, urbanizing countries, resource-rich countries, small island nations, countries with high youth unemployment, formalizing economies, and aging societies. Because the nature of the challenges varies, what makes a job good for development in one context may not be so relevant in another. And in some circumstances, tradeoffs emerge. The jobs that do the most to defuse tension in the short term may not do much for productivity, or those with the highest productivity impact may not lead to a broad-based improvement in living standards. Identifying good jobs for development helps visualize these tradeoffs.

Different countries face different jobs challenges, but two forces—the migration of people and the migration of jobs—connect their jobs agendas. These two flows have an impact on countries at the sending and the receiving ends. The arrival of migrants or the outsourcing of jobs affects the living standards of both migrants and locals. The availability of foreign workers, the development of migrant networks channeling savings and ideas, and the arrival of multinational firms bringing in more advanced techniques, are all bound to increase productivity. Family structures and community life are also affected by the movement of people and jobs.

CHAPTER 5

Valuing jobs

Jobs are often assessed from an individual perspective. But they can also affect the earnings, productivity, and well-being of others—positively or negatively. These spillovers should be assessed too.

The most important impact of jobs is on the people who hold them. Jobs provide earnings, can give access to benefits and insurance, and are often a source of broader life satisfaction. Development, in large part, consists of increasing these direct effects of jobs on individuals.

Beyond the importance of jobs for those who have them, jobs matter for societies because they can affect the earnings, employment opportunities, and the productivity of others, as well as the collective capacity to manage tensions. Jobs can also contribute to shared social objectives, such as poverty reduction, environmental protection, and fairness. Often, the individual and social values of jobs are similar; but these two perspectives may differ. For instance, Vietnam's poverty rate declined with unprecedented speed in the 1990s when land was redistributed to farmers and agricultural commercialization was liberalized.[1] Albeit increasing individual incomes, farming jobs involved difficult working conditions, substantial variability in earnings, and no formal social protection. But they made a major contribution to the development of Vietnam. Bloated public utilities, on the other hand, often offer a range of privileges to their employees even when the utilities themselves provide only limited coverage of the population and unreliable

services, and are obstacles to economic growth and poverty reduction. Such jobs may look appealing from an individual perspective—but less so from a social perspective. Good jobs for development are those that make the greatest contribution to society, taking into account the value they have to the people who hold them, but also their potential spillovers on others—positive or negative.

Recognizing the multiple effects of jobs is important for understanding the possible tradeoffs they entail. Some jobs greatly contribute to productivity growth but do not lead to poverty reduction in the short run. In other cases, jobs are urgently needed to avoid an unraveling of social cohesion, but the job creation that can be immediately supported using public funds is unlikely to result in rapid productivity growth. An understanding of the various effects of jobs on aggregate well-being, both direct and indirect, may help identify when a virtuous circle of jobs along all three transformations may arise, and when a vicious circle looms.

The value of a job for the person who holds it is a primary indication of its development payoff. But assessing the broader value the job has to society also requires information on the spillovers the job may have on the living standards of others, on aggregate productivity, or on social cohesion. Data from household, plant-level, and values surveys, as well as qualitative assessments, can be used to determine the existence of relevant spillovers. Although quantifying all the gaps between the individual and social values of jobs may not be possible, identifying where these gaps lie can help make policy tradeoffs transparent. The analytical tools to do so can be borrowed from several disciplines in economics and the social sciences. These disciplines often focus on spillovers from jobs, without necessarily calling them that.

While some jobs may contribute more to development than their individual values suggest, some forms of work are likely bad from any point of view. All countries have subscribed to a set of universal rights. Most governments, as well as international organizations and others, have ratified or endorsed standards seeking to eliminate forced labor, harmful forms of child labor, discrimination, and the suppression of voice among workers. Thus, some work activities are widely viewed as unacceptable and should not be treated as jobs.

Rights as the foundation

While jobs can be transformational, some forms of work are harmful. Those that exploit workers, expose them to dangerous environments, or threaten their physical and mental well-being are bad for individuals and societies. Their negative effects can be surprisingly long-lasting. An extreme example is the impact of the Atlantic slave trade on West Africa. A study found that individuals whose ancestors had been threatened by slavery were less likely to trust relatives, neighbors, and local governments even more than 100 years after the end of the slave trade.[2] Today, international norms of human rights and labor standards reject forced labor, harmful forms of child labor, discrimination, and the suppression of voice among workers. Yet close to 21 million people globally are estimated to be victims of bonded labor, slavery, forced prostitution, and other forms of involuntary work.[3] In 2008, 115 million children between the ages of 5 and 17 were involved in hazardous work (box 5.1).[4]

BOX 5.1 *Children do perilous work in artisanal gold mines in Mali*

Much artisanal gold mining in Mali is village based and focused on alluvial deposits that require panning for separation. Although child labor tends to be relatively controlled in Mali, an estimated 20,000 to 40,000 children, some as young as age 6, work in artisanal gold mining.[a] Human Rights Watch has documented the perilous nature of this work:

"They dig shafts and work underground, pull up, carry and crush the ore, and pan it for gold. Many children suffer serious pain in their heads, necks, arms, or backs, and risk long-term spinal injury from carrying heavy weights and from enduring repetitive motion. Children have sustained injuries from falling rocks and sharp tools, and have fallen into shafts. In addition, they risk grave injury when working in unstable shafts, which sometimes collapse."[b]

The work is toxic because miners use mercury to separate the gold from the rock. Mercury poisoning can cause serious neurological disorders, vision impairment, headaches, memory loss, and problems with concentration. Often, the children themselves are aware of the dangers:

"It's my stepmother who makes me work there. I don't want to. My real mother left. My stepmother takes all the money they pay me. . . . I don't get any money from the work. . . . Our work starts at 8 a.m. and continues the whole day. . . . I take the minerals [ore] and pan them. I work with mercury, and touch it. . . . He said mercury was a poison and we shouldn't swallow it, but he didn't say anything else about the mercury. . . . I don't want to work in the mines. I want to stay in school. I got malaria, and I am very tired when I work there [at the mine]."

—Mariam D., estimated age 11, Worognan, Sikasso Region, April 8, 2011[c]

"It's dangerous—there are often collapses. People are injured. Three died in a cave-in. The little children don't come down into the hole. . . . I have had problems since working there—my back hurts and I have problems urinating. No one says anything to me about safety."

—Ibrahim K., age 15[d]

Source: World Development Report 2013 team based on Human Rights Watch 2011.

a. The Government of Mali has taken steps to protect children's rights, including banning hazardous child labor in artisanal mines and adopting a National Action Plan for the Elimination of Child Labor in Mali in June 2011.
b. Human Rights Watch 2011, 6.
c. Human Rights Watch 2011, 29.
d. Human Rights Watch 2011, 31.

At the international level, the United Nation's Universal Declaration of Human Rights of 1948 establishes that "everyone has the right to work, to free choice of employment, to just and favorable conditions of work and to protection against unemployment." These rights are further elaborated in international conventions and regional frameworks and are translated into domestic laws.[5] The global agenda for workers' rights became focused on four fundamental principles and rights in the workplace in 1998. Back then, a vast majority of members of the International Labour Organization (ILO) signed a declaration covering a core set of labor standards on the elimination of forced and compulsory labor, the abolition of child labor, the elimination of discrimination in employment and occupation, and freedom of association and collective bargaining.[6] Other ILO conventions cover a range of related subjects including working time, social security, occupational safety and health, and labor inspections.[7]

International law requires that countries bring their domestic laws into compliance with the international legal instruments the countries have ratified. The core labor standards have a special status among ILO conventions because the 1998 declaration requires all ILO member states to "respect, promote, and realize" the standards, regardless of whether they ratify specific conventions.[8] The standards influence other instruments for protecting workers' rights through references in national and regional legislation, the texts of many bilateral free trade agreements, the procedures of international organizations, and corporate codes of conduct.[9] International legal frameworks arguably do not cover some fundamental rights. The core labor standards, for example, do not directly address working conditions including safety and health.[10]

Gaps remain between rights on paper and implementation in practice (box 5.2). Even in countries that have ratified the core labor standards and have laws on the books, children work in harmful conditions, discrimination happens in access to jobs and in pay, forced labor persists, and freedom of association is limited. Commitments in treaties, conventions, and laws may not change the institutions, practices, and behaviors that affect workers' rights on their own. A key factor driving these gaps is the fact that many workers are not covered by laws. For example:

- Many labor laws and regulations cover only workers in formal employment relationships, limiting the extent to which workers can appeal to legal mechanisms. The growing involvement of agencies in hiring workers complicates legal accountability because temporary workers often have contracts with employment agencies, which, in turn, enter into the contracts with the actual employers. Often, such workers would not count against legal minimum employment levels at which labor rights become binding.[11]

- Some labor laws deliberately exclude domestic workers, family workers, or workers in small enterprises.[12] Exclusions can also apply in export zones and other areas where regulation is suspended to attract investment. Unpaid family workers in agriculture and enterprises, including children on family farms, may also be excluded. Many women perform non-remunerated work of this sort.[13]

- Tensions may also exist between labor rights defined in national and international contexts and customary, religious, and indigenous laws. Many countries are characterized by legal pluralism, whereby multiple legal systems exist side by side. Overlapping jurisdictions are most common in the case of family law relating to marriage, divorce, and inheritance.[14]

Gaps between rights on paper and those in practice underscore a substantial agenda to eliminate unacceptable forms of work. Nonstate actors, including private employers and civil society organizations, are increasingly involved in efforts to improve compliance with labor rights and standards. Multinational corporations and industry associations often adopt codes of conduct, voluntary standards, and monitoring and auditing strategies.[15] Nongovernmental organizations monitor factories and firms, provide training and education to workers, and coordinate domestic and global campaigns. While this heightened involvement in rights and standards does not guarantee that implementation will improve, it provides potential channels and partnerships for increasing accountability for rights at work.

BOX 5.2 *Compliance with core labor standards is partial*

The number of countries that have adopted the eight core labor standards included in the International Labour Organization's 1998 Declaration of the Fundamental Principles and Rights at Work is steadily increasing. But compliance gaps with the four principles—child labor, forced labor, discrimination, and freedom of association and collective bargaining—are still apparent.[a]

Child labor. ILO conventions 138 and 182 require countries to develop and monitor action plans regulating work by children under age 18. Convention 182, covering the most harmful forms of child labor, has been ratified by 175 countries. The largest numbers of children in hazardous work are in East Asia and the Pacific, but across regions there is evidence that progress is being made.[b] Brazil and India are among the countries showing improvements. In Brazil, between 1992 and 2008, employment among 7–15 year olds fell over 10 percentage points, from 18 percent to 7 percent. At the same time, school attendance rose from 85 percent to 97 percent. In India, children's employment fell from 8 percent to nearly 4 percent, and school attendance rose 14 percentage points (from 72 percent to 86 percent).[c]

Forced labor. More countries have ratified conventions 29 and 105, the core standards on forced labor, than the other core standards. An estimated two-thirds of forced labor takes the form of economic exploitation; one-fifth is linked to forced labor imposed by the state or the military; and the remainder involves commercial sexual exploitation. This last form disproportionately affects women and girls.[d] The long-term effects on individuals, families, and communities can be severe. Nongovernmental organizations that rescue victims of forced labor, particularly forced commercial prostitution, find that post-traumatic stress, social stigma, and disease can cripple reentry into society.[e]

Discrimination. Conventions 100 and 111 refer to discrimination by gender, ethnicity, disability, or other status as a source of disparities in access to jobs, segregation within the labor market, pay gaps, and harassment or violence at work. From a legal perspective, discrimination can be understood as inequality before the law within either the formal legal system or customary law. It results from unequal treatment on the grounds of race, gender, religion, political opinion, national extraction, or social origin; or the unequal impact of policies, practices, or rules. Employment outcomes are affected by each of these layers of discrimination.[f] Although progress has been made in removing legal obstacles that affect women's access to jobs, barriers remain.[g] Labor laws in 44 countries restrict the hours that women may work,[h] and 71 countries impose legal limits on the industries in which women may work. Such restrictions have often

deprived women of equal access to jobs. Inequality in laws relating to marriage, inheritance, and property ownership, as well as traditional and customary laws, also affect the access of women to productive assets and business opportunities.

Discrimination in employment may be the outcome of policies not dealing directly with labor issues. For example, in some countries of Central and Eastern Europe, Roma children are often tracked into schools intended for children with special needs, which provide limited opportunities for further advancement in education and subsequent employment. Roma graduates of special schools in the Czech Republic were twice as likely as non-Roma graduates to be out of the labor force.[i] A study of Roma in the Czech Republic found that 19 percent of Roma ages 10–19 had attended a special needs school, while the share in the non-Roma population was 7 percent. The figures in the Slovak Republic were 12 and 8 percent respectively.[j] A 2007 court case involving Roma students in the Czech Republic noted that they were more likely to be placed in schools for the mentally challenged than non-Roma children. The European Court of Human Rights ruled that this overrepresentation violated nondiscrimination protections in the European Convention on Human Rights.[k]

Freedom of association and collective bargaining (FACB). Although conventions 87 and 98 are among the oldest of the core standards, they have been ratified by fewer countries than the others. These conventions cover the right to establish and join organizations and call for mechanisms for negotiations between employers and worker organizations. FACB are "enabling rights" in that they give workers voice to advocate for other aspects of working conditions, including safety and health.[l]

FACB is curtailed in countries where unions and other associations are banned, where associations face restrictions on their activity, or where members are threatened by violence or repression. FACB rights of both workers and employers are monitored by the ILO Governing Body's Committee on Freedom of Association (CFA), a universal monitoring mechanism that functions in addition to the ILO's regular supervisory mechanisms for monitoring ratified conventions. The CFA handles complaints related to civil liberties, including murder, abductions, disappearances, threats, arrests, and detentions of trade union leaders and members, as well as other acts of antiunion harassment and intimidation and violations of freedom of assembly and freedom of expression.[m] Convention 87 protects the rights of all workers, including the self-employed. In practice, however, implementation of FACB is limited because many workers are employed outside traditional employer-employee relationships or do not work in occupations or sectors that are covered by formal unions.

Source: World Development Report 2013 team.

a. ILO 1998; ILO 2012a.
b. Diallo and others 2010.
c. UCW 2010.
d. ILO 2009.
e. Farley 2003.
f. Fredman 2011.
g. World Bank 2011d.
h. World Bank and IFC 2011.
i. World Bank 2008a.
j. World Bank 2012b.
k. European Court of Human Rights 2007.
l. Levi and others 2012 for the World Development Report 2013.
m. ITUC 2011.

The value of jobs to individuals and society

The most obvious outcome of a job is the earnings it provides to the worker. These earnings can be in cash or in kind and may include a range of associated benefits. The earnings the job provides, as well as the output it generates, typically increase with the skills of the worker. Improving skills is thus one of the most direct channels to enhance the value jobs have to individuals and society (question 5). Other characteristics of the job may also matter from the point of view of individual well-being. Stability, voice, and fulfillment at work all play a role in overall job satisfaction, as do any detrimental impacts of jobs on mental and physical health through stress and anxiety.[16]

Several of these dimensions of jobs have been combined into the concept of decent work introduced by the ILO in 1999 (box 5.3). Since then, many governments have used it to articulate their policy agendas on jobs. The concept of decent work has also been embraced by the United Nations and several international organizations and endorsed by numerous global forums.

A job may also matter for others, beyond its holder. When asked about their most preferred jobs, survey respondents from four diverse countries provide different answers from those they offer when asked about the most important jobs to society (figure 5.1). They frequently mention working in the civil service or as a shop owner as the jobs they would prefer for themselves, while identifying teachers and doctors as the most important jobs for societies. China is the only country where a job in civil service is seen as more important for society than for the individual. In the Arab Republic of Egypt, a job as a teacher is more valued individually than socially. And in Sierra Leone, being a farmer is appreciated both individually and socially, while in the other countries it is recognized as socially valuable but is not a preferred job.

This intuition can be developed into a more structured analysis of the reasons why some jobs may be more or less valuable to society than they are to those who hold them. Those reasons can be grouped under three main headings, each corresponding to one of the three development transformations. Individual jobs can improve the living standards of others in society, or they

---

BOX 5.3 *The concept of Decent Work and the Decent Work Agenda*

Decent Work is defined as "opportunities for women and men to obtain decent and productive work in conditions of freedom, equity, security and human dignity."[a] This definition is based on a broad concept of work as encompassing all forms of economic activity.[b] The International Labour Organization has made Decent Work for all the organizing principle for its activities and has set an agenda for incorporating the goal of Decent Work for all into national strategic planning objectives.[c] The ILO's Decent Work Agenda is a policy approach based on four strategic objectives: fundamental principles and rights at work and international labor standards, productive and freely chosen employment, social protection, and social dialogue.

At the global level, the ILO has defined Decent Work indicators to measure the different dimensions of the concept and to track progress over time. In 2010, the United Nations (UN) Summit on the Millennium Development Goals (MDGs) included a new target under Goal 1 (eradicate extreme poverty and hunger): "achieve full and productive employment and Decent Work for all, including women and young people."[d] The Decent Work indicators are being

used to help countries measure progress and establish priorities. A limited set are used to monitor progress toward the MDG target.[e]

The ILO's Decent Work Agenda includes a threshold below which no job should fall. The threshold has four components: productive employment (not simply any job), basic social protection according to national conditions, opportunity for voice and organization, and rights at work. As an incremental agenda, Decent Work indicators can change, depending on the economic, social, and institutional progress of countries.

This ILO agenda has gained considerable traction and international political buy-in over the past decade. First formulated at the International Labour Conference in 1999, it is now part of the ILO constitution and has been endorsed by heads of state at the UN General Assembly, the Group of 20, and regional authorities such as the European Union, the African Union, the Organization of American States, the Association of South East Asian Nations, and the Southern Cone Common Market (Mercosur). Many countries use the Decent Work concept to define development targets, identify policy priorities, and measure progress toward meeting specified goals.

Source: World Development Report 2013 team.
a. ILO 2002.
b. Anker 2003; Ghai 2003; UNECE 2010.
c. "Decent Work Agenda," ILO, Geneva, http://www.ilo.org/global/about-the-ilo/decent-work-agenda/lang--en/index.htm.
d. UN 2011.
e. "Measuring Decent Work," ILO, Geneva, http://www.ilo.org/integration/themes/mdw/lang--en/index.htm.

FIGURE 5.1 *Views on preferred jobs and most important jobs differ*

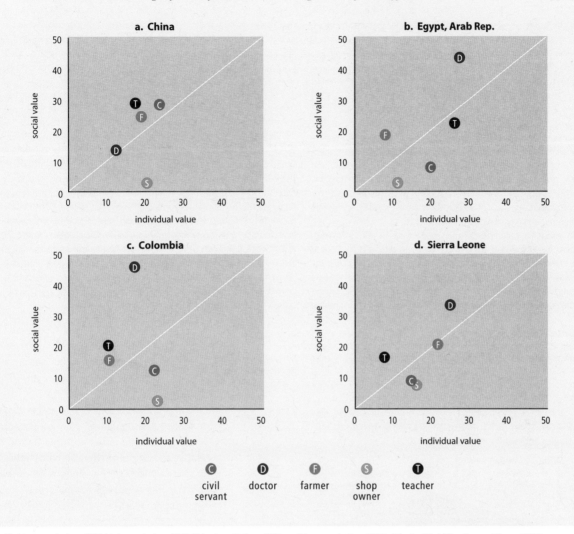

Source: Bjørkhaug and others 2012; Hatløy and others 2012; Kebede and others 2012; and Zhang and others 2012; all for the World Development Report 2013.
Note: The figure shows the share of respondents who would want the job for themselves (individual value) and those who think the job is good for society (social value).

can adversely affect their earnings and employment opportunities. They can help raise the productivity of others, or they can harm them through their environmental impacts. And they can support more peaceful collective decision making, or, alternatively, increase social tensions when they are based on privilege.

Spillovers from jobs

Good jobs for development are those with the highest payoff to society. As a first approximation, the value of the job for the person who holds it provides a good measure of the value of the job to society. But some jobs also have spillovers on the living standards of others, on aggregate productivity, or on social cohesion. When spillovers are positive, the job has a greater value to society than it has to the person who holds it, and the opposite is true when the spillovers are negative. In principle, the spillovers can also be negligible, in which case there is no real distinction between the individual and the social perspective. Nonetheless, the idea that jobs can have sizable spillovers is at the core of several disciplines in the social sciences and has greatly influenced recent development thinking (box 5.4).

BOX 5.4 *Economics and the social sciences deal with spillovers from jobs, under different names*

Several disciplines in economics and in the social sciences focus on the channels through which spillovers from jobs occur, even if they may not articulate it that way. One core focus of *labor economics* is to assess earnings differentials and their causes, including discrimination, uneven bargaining power, regulation, and taxation. The *public finance* literature also evaluates the impact on employment, capital intensity, and earnings of taxes and subsidies, including those used to finance social insurance contributions. *Gender studies* examine the economic, social, and cultural determinants of gender discrimination and their relationships to employment. *Poverty analyses* study the poverty and inequality impact of job distributions and different growth patterns. *Economic geography* uncovers the productivity impact of spatial concentration of jobs. *International economics* analyzes the resource allocation and innovation impetus provided by employment in export sectors and foreign-owned companies. *Environmental economics* measures and values the negative (and positive) impacts of employment in different sectors, or using different techniques, on the natural resource base. *Identity economics* researches how behaviors and norms are influenced by the relationship between people and their peer groups, including through their jobs. The field of *equity analysis* has started to examine

the degree to which job outcomes are shaped by the circumstances in which individuals are born, as opposed to their ability or effort. Finally, *conflict studies* aim to identify the societal conditions that underlie tension not being managed constructively and peacefully, including access to jobs and fairness in their allocation.

These disciplines bring analytical rigor to the assessment of the gaps between the individual and social values of jobs, hence to the identification of good jobs for development.[a]

Although they may not be explicitly articulated around jobs, these disciplines have shaped recent development thinking. The *World Development Report 2007: Development and the Next Generation*[a] shows that opening job opportunities for young people is catalytic for future economic and social development. The *World Development Report 2009: Reshaping Economic Geography* discusses reaping the benefits of agglomeration, which happens through jobs, as a source of economic growth. The *World Development Report 2011: Conflict, Security, and Development* makes the point that jobs are a key element for stabilization in post-conflict societies. And the *World Development Report 2012: Gender Equality and Development* provides evidence that jobs are a medium to promote gender equity and transform it into social and economic progress.

Source: World Development Report 2013 team.
a. As an example, recent World Development Reports on youth (World Bank 2006); geography (World Bank 2009c); conflict (World Bank 2011c); and gender (World Bank 2011d) look at spillovers from jobs in different contexts.

FIGURE 5.2 *Some jobs do more for development*

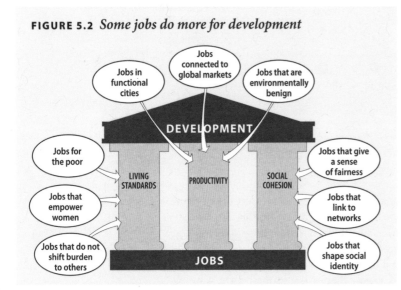

Source: World Development Report 2013 team.

Fully valuing the contribution jobs make to development requires identifying the channels through which the spillovers may occur. Nine of them have received attention as critical for development (figure 5.2):

- *Earnings of others.* Uneven bargaining power or inadequate regulation may result in labor earnings that are either too low or too high relative to the output generated by jobs. This distortion affects the earnings of the employer and the job opportunities of other workers. Taxpayers may also be affected when jobs are supported through transfers. Jobs that do not tax others, literally or figuratively, do more for development.

- *Household allocations.* Having a job and contributing resources to a household's budget can change the status of the jobholder and increase his or her say on how the budget is allocated. If the jobholder is a woman, spending on food and on children may increase, which may result in greater well-being for the children. Jobs that empower women have the potential to generate such positive spillovers.

- *Poverty reduction.* The well-being of others may be affected if they are altruistic and value poverty reduction in general, even when their own earnings do not change. Since jobs are the main avenue out of poverty, there is social value in the availability of jobs that take others out of poverty. Employment opportunities tilted in favor of the poor do more for development.

- *Agglomeration effects.* Productivity depends not only on the internal efficiency of economic units but also on their environment. Learning and imitation through labor turnover and interaction with suppliers, as well as a better matching of skills across a bigger pool of workers, can increase productivity. Hence, jobs in functional cities tend to be good jobs for development. Conversely, negative effects can arise in overcrowded and congested cities.

- *Global integration.* Knowledge spillovers also occur through international trade and participation in global value chains. Firms that engage in export markets tend to become more productive and, in doing so, they push other, less productive firms out of business. Knowledge spillovers from foreign direct investment (FDI) increase aggregate productivity. Jobs that connect to global markets are thus good jobs for development.

- *Environmental effects.* Jobs have negative impacts on aggregate productivity when they damage the environment or lead to an overuse of scarce resources. But they can also have positive effects on the environment, as in the case of jobs to manage forests and other common resources. The social value of a job cannot be assessed without taking into account its environmental impact.

- *Social identity.* Jobs can impact the well-being of others by influencing the values and behavior of those who hold them in ways that affect society at large. Jobs can shape the norms that influence how the jobholder interacts with others, starting with basics such as reliability, punctuality, and courtesy. Depending on their characteristics, jobs can foster civic engagement and result in greater trust.

- *Networks.* Jobs connect people to each other. They convey information among coworkers and society more broadly. They impact the integration of rural migrants in new urban settings. Jobs may also contribute to tolerance when they increase interactions with people from different social and ethnic backgrounds.

- *Sense of fairness.* A perceived absence of fairness in the overall access to job opportunities, beyond one's own job, can undermine the sense of belonging. Job allocations at odds with the idea of equality of opportunity may lead to disengagement from collective decision-making processes. Jobs that live up to standards of transparency and merit contribute to the sense of fairness in society.

Because a job can affect the well-being of others and not only the well-being of the jobholder, two jobs that may appear identical from an individual perspective could still be different from a social perspective. In a society that values poverty reduction, an informal job that takes a household out of poverty should be seen as more valuable to society. A job in a protected industry that needs support through transfers (either by taxpayers or by consumers) is less valuable to society, and even less valuable if the need for protection is associated with the use of outdated technology that results in high environmental costs. The opposite holds for a job in an export industry that contributes to the acquisition of new technical and managerial knowledge from abroad and spreads it through interactions with suppliers; this job is even more valuable to society when the jobholder is a woman and her work status empowers her. And the same is true for a job that gives a young person a sense of belonging in society and conveys to others a sense of opportunity (figure 5.3).

The contribution jobs make to development varies, depending on the circumstances. In low- and middle-income countries, poverty reduction carries significant weight. Productivity effects vary: heavily urbanized and highly connected countries such as Singapore have internalized a large part of these effects already, while urbanizing countries such as Bangladesh and Guatemala are still able to reap significant benefits. Jobs in illegal mining can cause environmental damage, and their net contribution to productivity growth is limited as a result. Jobs in Turkey's wind energy parks, in contrast, likely contribute to all three transformations in a positive way: they offer earnings and job satisfaction to workers; they position Turkey at the forefront of technological developments in new energy; and they often contribute to social cohesion by creating new livelihood opportunities for villages.

FIGURE 5.3 *The individual and social values of jobs can differ*

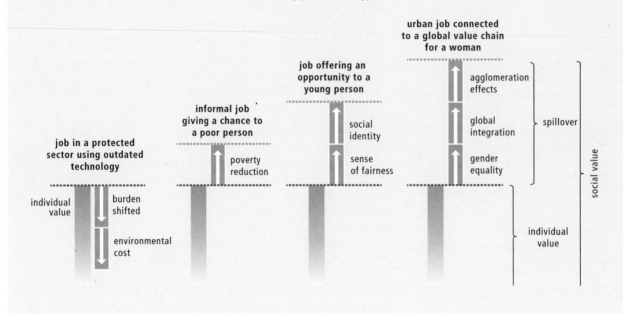

Source: World Development Report 2013 team.

More often than not, however, jobs entail tradeoffs. A specific job can entail positive and negative spillovers simultaneously. Take, for example, a job that requires relatively low-skills but that uses outdated technology and hence causes environmental damage. From a social point of view, such a job has a positive spillover because it leads to poverty reduction, but it also exhibits a negative spillover through its environmental effect. Similar tradeoffs can exist for a job that connects the domestic economy globally but that has been obtained through connections, thereby decreasing the sense that the job market is fair.

Such tradeoffs can take strategic dimensions: in China, the nature and location of investments in roads have different implications for jobs. The investments yield their highest growth returns in the eastern and central regions of China, where the most productive jobs are. But their contribution to poverty reduction is greatest in the western regions, where living standards are lower.[17] In such situations, societal choices are necessary. Assessing and mapping spillovers is an important first step toward informed decision making.

Can the development payoffs from jobs be quantified?

Earnings from labor provide the first and most direct measure of the contribution jobs make to development. But transformations in living standards, productivity, and social cohesion happen at a faster pace when jobs lead to investments in children, give people the possibility to acquire new skills through their work, or engage them more in society. Because these transformational aspects are seldom reflected in labor earnings, good jobs for development may not be as attractive to individuals as they are important to society. This is why, even in a context of full employment, there may not be enough jobs for women in many developing countries, or enough jobs connected to world markets, or enough jobs for idle young men. Spillovers are thus especially relevant in countries where gender equality is far from assured, urbanization and global integration are incipient, and conflict is still a possibility.

Fully valuing the development payoffs from jobs entails assessing the earnings they provide, as well as their possible spillovers. In practice,

BOX 5.5 *Several data sources can be used to quantify the development payoffs from jobs*

Household surveys such as those used for poverty analysis are a critically important input for assessing the contribution jobs make to society. Regular up-to-date, high-quality data on activity, employment, and earnings can be used to understand employment dynamics. Many countries around the world collect household data through living standards surveys and labor force surveys. Social security administrations in countries with a high coverage rate of social programs record information about their contributors. Unfortunately, few countries trace employment histories. Such histories (including employment transitions) are vital to achieving an understanding of how long young jobseekers are unemployed, whether unemployment scars the middle-aged, or how internal migration supports rural families.

Plant-level surveys are another standard input to understand the dynamics of job creation and destruction and their implications for aggregate productivity. Many countries conduct such surveys out of a sampling frame supposed to capture all units in manufacturing; in some cases, the coverage extends to units in other sectors, such as trade. Other countries collect data on production and employment through administrative records; the information is less

detailed on inputs and therefore has limited potential in the estimation of changes in productivity, but it gives a more comprehensive picture of how firms are born, grow, decline and die and how employment evolves as a result. Unfortunately, only a few countries collect information on the myriad microenterprises in the informal sector. This information is vital to understanding where job creation occurs in the economy and where it contributes most to aggregate productivity.

Special household surveys inquiring about values and attitudes, together with qualitative assessments, are important instruments for assessing links between jobs on the one hand and beliefs and behaviors on the other. These surveys often provide information on trust in others and civic participation, and on the characteristics of respondents and their jobs. Information from these surveys can be combined with living standards and labor force surveys to identify population groups at risk, and analyze how jobs are associated with peaceful collective decision making. Observing individual or cohort groups over time allows for an exploration of possible causal links among jobs, trust, behaviors, and attitudes.

Source: World Development Report 2013 team.

this amounts to identifying the gaps between the individual and the social values of jobs (if any) that are relevant in a particular country context. Such an evaluation requires data, some of which many countries are now collecting on a more or less regular basis (box 5.5). Using data to measure the full social value of a job calls for rigorous analysis too. Patterns in the data may result from spurious correlations, and the related conclusions may be tainted if individuals and firms with fundamentally different characteristics selected themselves into specific jobs or activities. Labor economics, productivity studies, and other social sciences have developed analytical tools for the analyses required. Sociological and anthropological methods can provide texture and context missing in quantitative data. In some cases, randomized trials or natural experiments can shed light on the mechanisms at play. But methodological pitfalls abound, so the safest approach is to triangulate the available evidence.

Living standards

Three types of spillovers can enhance or undermine the direct contribution jobs make to living standards: jobs can impact the earnings of others, they can alter the allocation of resources within households in a substantial way, and they can contribute to shared social goals such as poverty reduction.

Earnings of others. Jobs in subsidized firms and in bloated public sector agencies have an impact on the earnings of others, as they lead to an excessive tax burden and a reduction of earnings (or the disappearance of jobs) elsewhere in the economy. Jobs characterized by uneven bargaining power between employers and employees, or discrimination against women or ethnic minority groups, have earnings that are too high or too low relative to the output generated by the job.

The tools of public finance can be used to assess gaps between the individual and the social values of jobs in the case of jobs supported through transfers. Taxation and government spending affect earnings and modify incentives and thus have an impact on resource allocations, including employment. Analyses of the tax burden applying to capital and labor, assessments of cross-subsidization between individuals or firms, or evaluations of the impacts of payroll taxation can identify a gap between the individual value and the social value of a job.

A tax wedge does not necessarily imply that the individual and the social value of a job differ, or that employment effects are large. The methodological pitfall to avoid in this case is to assume that individuals attach no value to the taxes or contributions they pay. If workers value social security contributions as an entitlement to deferred benefits, their net burden is lower than the contribution rate suggests. If they value the contribution in full, there would be no misallocation of resources. In some systems, contributions and benefits are closely linked; in others, the link is looser and redistribution stronger. But even when benefits are low compared to taxes, the effects on employment depend on how much of the taxes employers can pass on to employees through lower wages. In the extreme case, when the number of workers seeking wage employment is fixed, the entire tax is paid by workers, and employment is the same then as without a tax.[18] In Turkey, a reduction in social security taxes would result in higher net wages and lower total labor cost only partially, thereby moderating the change in employment. The effect is somewhat higher, though, for lower-skilled workers earning around the minimum wage.[19]

The tools of labor economics can be used to measure the gaps between the actual earnings of specific groups of workers and the earnings they would have in the absence of uneven bargaining power or discrimination. Earnings functions (a standard tool of labor economics) can provide an estimate of the magnitude of those gaps. Actual earnings are lower than they otherwise would be in the case of women, ethnic minorities, and people working in the agricultural sector; they tend to be higher in the case of union members. Some gaps diminish with economic development, others persist (figure 5.4). On the surface at least, the gender and occupational gaps show no sign of disappearing.

While these exercises are informative, earnings gaps may result from differences in the characteristics of jobs or workers not accounted for in the analysis. Gender gaps can stem from discrimination but also from choices about the work-life balance. Union gaps may signal strong bargaining power but could also reflect higher productivity of organized workers. Rural pay deficits may be affected by unobservable differences between the workers who migrated to the cities and those who stayed behind. So, even when the gaps are rigorously measured, disentangling the reasons behind them is an important step before policy conclusions can be drawn.

Household allocations. Who holds a job can matter for how household earnings evolve and are spent. Job opportunities for youth are particularly important. A difficult transition from school to work can lead to scarring—a negative impact on long-term earnings prospects, hence of future household expenditures. The risk of unemployment later in life is higher for those with difficult school-to-work transitions.[20] Jobs that go to women might also benefit other members of society as well as the woman holding the job. Women generally have lower labor force participation rates than men and typically earn less than their male counterparts, but employment outside the household often empowers them.[21] A body of evidence has found that spending decisions depend on the share of household income contributed by different members of the household. Women's control over household resources leads to more spending on food and children's schooling.

The impact womens' employment has on household allocations can be quantified using standard tools in poverty and gender analyses. In Mexico, for example, higher women's income shares were associated with more food and children's clothing and less alcohol.[22] Similar results were observed in Bangladesh, Côte d'Ivoire, and South Africa.[23] In the Republic of Congo, a higher female share in total household income was associated with significantly higher expenditures on food and significantly lower expenditure on clothing for adults and entertainment (figure 5.5).[24] However, it should not be assumed that impacts are the same everywhere. Providing cash transfers in Burkina Faso boosted routine preventive care for children, regardless of which parent received the money.[25] And evaluations in Ghana and Sri Lanka show that microcredit was invested to a larger extent into a business by men than by women.[26]

Another approach looks directly at the impacts of women's employment on human development outcomes, such as children's educational attainment and health. In a rural setting in southern India, an increase in annual female in-

FIGURE 5.4 *Some earnings gaps decrease with the level of development; some do not*

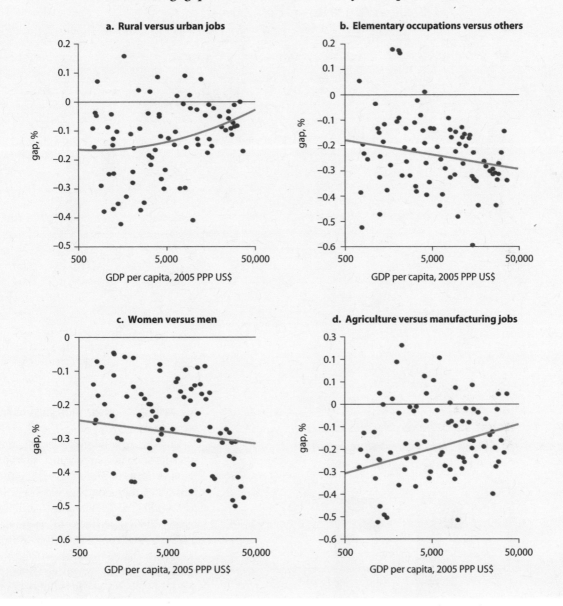

Source: World Development Report 2013 team estimates based on Montenegro and Patrinos 2012 for the World Development Report 2013.
Note: GDP = gross domestic product; PPP = purchasing power parity. Elementary occupations involve simple and routine tasks often requiring considerable physical effort. The vertical axis indicates the difference in earnings between the two groups depicted in each quadrant, controlling for the characteristics of people in the two groups. The *gap measure* is based on country-specific regressions of the logarithms of monthly earnings on years of education, potential years of experience (and its square), and controls for industry, occupation, urban/rural sector, ethnicity, and gender. Each dot represents a country.

come of US$90 increased schooling by 1.6 years for disadvantaged castes.[27] In Mexico, a 10 percent increase in labor demand for adult women raised the chance of having a daughter in good health by 10 percent.[28] In addition, the children of women who found work in export manufacturing thanks to the opening of new factories closer to home were significantly taller.[29]

Poverty reduction. Job opportunities and employment transitions are major determinants of changes in both individual living standards and overall poverty in a country. If societies value poverty reduction, a job lifting an individual or a household out of poverty increases the well-being of others. A spillover exists then, as aggregate welfare increases beyond the increase in

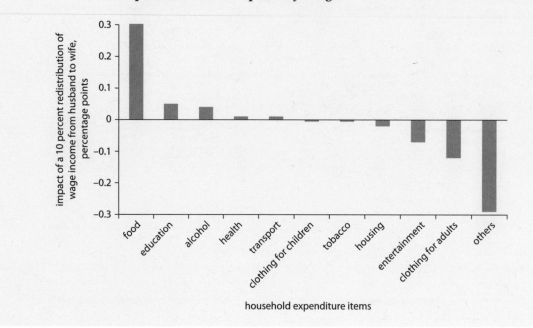

FIGURE 5.5 *A higher women's share of household income raises food expenditures in the Republic of Congo*

Source: Backiny-Yetna and Wodon 2011.

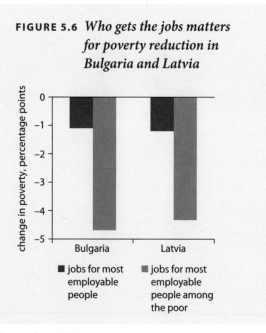

FIGURE 5.6 *Who gets the jobs matters for poverty reduction in Bulgaria and Latvia*

■ jobs for most employable people

■ jobs for most employable people among the poor

Source: World Development Report 2013 team.
Note: Figure is based on microsimulations using data from household surveys. In each country, the employment rate was exogenously increased by 3 percentage points. The baseline scenario allocated the new jobs to those who had the highest likelihood of being employed. Earnings were imputed on the basis of individual characteristics. The alternative scenario brought into jobs all those who had the highest employment likelihood among the poor.

the well-being of the individual or household escaping poverty.

The way new job opportunities are distributed is of major importance for poverty reduction. Poverty profiles, revealing the characteristics of the poor, help identify which types jobs—and in which locations—would make the biggest difference to them. Microsimulations using household survey data allow estimating the impact of changes in employment on poverty rates. For instance, increasing the employment rate is of highest priority in Bulgaria and Latvia, two aging countries. Consider the poverty alleviation effects of raising the employment rate by 3 percentage points depending on who, among those currently not working, gets the additional jobs. If the jobs went to the people whose individual characteristics make them more easily employable, poverty would fall by 1.1 percentage points in Bulgaria and by 1.2 percentage points in Latvia. If new employment opportunities instead went to the most employable among the poor, poverty would fall by 4.7 percentage points in Bulgaria and by 4.1 percentage points in Latvia (figure 5.6).

Productivity

Spillovers from jobs on the productivity of other jobs can happen through three main channels. Jobs in functional cities lead to greater specialization and mutual learning. Jobs connected to global markets allow for the acquisition of more advanced technological and managerial knowledge. And through the production process in which they are embedded, jobs can have negative—or positive—effects on the environment.

Agglomeration effects. The spatial concentration of activity is a strong driver of productivity growth in developing countries. Effects can materialize within sectors (localization economies) or between sectors (urbanization economies). The sharing of inputs, better labor matching, and knowledge spillovers are the main forces behind the geographical concentration of industries and economic activity in urban environments. The sharing of inputs facilitates the emergence of specialized producers of intermediate goods and services. Proximity allows firms to more easily find workers to fill positions. Knowledge spillovers allow firms to learn about new technologies, products, and practices from other firms operating in the vicinity. These agglomeration effects signal a difference between the private and social values of jobs.

The tools of urban economics can be used to assess the potential gains from agglomeration. In industrial countries, as city employment increases by 10 percent, wages and firm productivity in the city grow by 0.2 to 1.0 percent.[30] To give a sense of the magnitudes implied, if wages and productivity were to increase by 0.3 percent, workers moving from a city with 5,000 inhabitants to a metropolis of 5 million would see their earnings increase by 23 percent.[31] Nonetheless, not all workers benefit equally from living and working together in cities, nor do they contribute equally to productivity growth. Workers with better cognitive and social skills tend to benefit more.[32] Workers also enjoy higher wages when they are surrounded by a more educated labor force.[33]

The association between urban scale and productivity has also been documented in many developing economies, including Brazil, China, India, Indonesia, the Republic of Korea, and Turkey.[34] In Taiwan, China, a 10 percent increase in total manufacturing employment in a locality

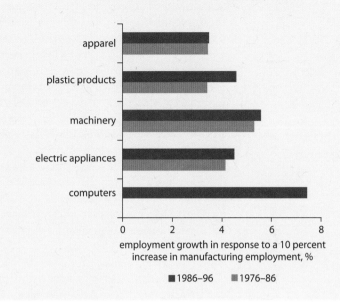

FIGURE 5.7 *Agglomeration effects vary across industrial sectors in Taiwan, China*

employment growth in response to a 10 percent increase in manufacturing employment, %

■ 1986–96   ■ 1976–86

Source: Sonobe and Otsuka 2006b.
Note: The figure shows the increase in the employment of a specific sector in a specific locality when total employment in manufacturing in that locality increases by 10 percent, controlling for other relevant factors.

causes employment in specific industrial sectors to increase between 3.0 and 7.5 percent (figure 5.7).[35] Enterprise surveys also show that firms grow faster in large cities.[36] In many developing countries, however, the poor functionality of cities undermines the potential gains from proximity. Inefficiencies in labor, land, and housing markets may cause poor functionality in cities. Poor functionality may also result from deficits in transportation and communication infrastructure, especially for smaller cities where market access is critical.[37]

But agglomeration can also come with higher costs, from more expensive land to worse congestion and pollution in cities with 1 million to 3 million people. In the United States, between 1980 and 2000, the number of annual hours per person lost to traffic delays increased from 4 to 22.[38] Traffic in central London moves at only 11 miles an hour.[39] In Mexico City, the annual cost of traffic delays amounts to US$580 a person, or 3 percent of annual per capita income.[40] Congestion and pollution limit agglomeration effects.[41] In California, a reduction in ozone concentrations of 10 parts per billion would increase worker productivity by 4.2 percent.[42]

Analytical tools from the management literature can be used to assess the impact of industrial clusters on productivity.[43] In many low-income countries, industrial clusters account for a large share of manufacturing employment, including self-employment.[44] Clustering is more common in light manufacturing industries intensive in unskilled labor, such as garments, footwear, furniture, and metalworking. The formation of a cluster often starts with a pioneer, typically a former trader or engineer who is able to identify a new, profitable business. Success leads to imitation, and a large number of relatively small and similar enterprises emerges in the vicinity. The management literature can help identify dynamic clusters, where jobs have positive spillovers.

Global integration. The fragmentation of production across borders is one of the most notable features of the global economy.[45] Value chains connect firms and jobs across borders, be it through arms-length trade or through intrafirm transactions. Global integration improves domestic resource allocation because it puts greater pressure on firms to be competitive. Exporting allows the most productive firms to grow. But in doing so, they also exert pressure on the least productive ones to contract or exit. Global integration also generates knowledge spillovers. These arise through exposure to new technologies embodied in traded goods or through new management practices in companies receiving FDI. Knowledge spillovers take place horizontally, between competitors, and vertically, through buyer-supplier relationships.

International economics has devoted considerable efforts to quantifying the productivity impacts of global integration. In Colombia, productivity increased faster at the plant level during the trade liberalization period than during the import substitution period.[46] In India, industry restructuring immediately following the trade reforms of 1991, including the entry and exit of firms, contributed significantly to productivity increases.[47] In Brazil, Côte d'Ivoire, and Turkey, the lowering of trade barriers led to a reduction of markups—a sign of intensified competition.[48] Productivity-enhancing effects of exports have been found in China; Indonesia; Korea; Slovenia; and Taiwan, China, as well as at the regional level in East Asia and Sub-Saharan Africa.[49]

A specialized literature focuses on the knowledge spillovers and productivity impacts of multinationals and FDI. In Indonesia, when a plant switched from domestic to foreign ownership, its total factor productivity increased by 13.5 percent within three years. In Brazil, wages of incumbent workers in domestic firms were positively affected by the share of workers who previously worked with multinationals. In Ghana, firms whose owners worked for multinationals in the same industry were more productive than other domestic firms.[50] In developing countries, the knowledge spillovers from FDI may be more important than their impact on resource allocation (figure 5.8).[51]

Research can help assess whether the knowledge spillovers from global integration trickle down to small informal enterprises through value chains. Larger enterprises are more likely to become suppliers to foreign companies or to be directly acquired by multinationals. But they tend to contract out noncore businesses

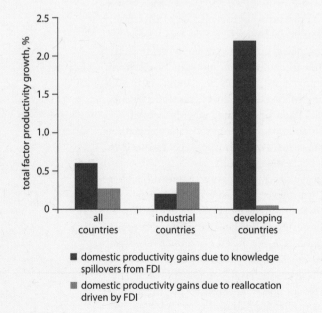

FIGURE 5.8 *Knowledge spillovers from foreign direct investment increase domestic productivity*

■ domestic productivity gains due to knowledge spillovers from FDI

■ domestic productivity gains due to reallocation driven by FDI

Source: Alfaro and Chen 2011.
Note: FDI = foreign direct investment. The figure shows the increase in domestic productivity for different country groups when the probability of entry by new multinational firms doubles. The estimates are based on data from 60 countries.

for cost efficiency, bringing smaller local companies into the value chain. Contracting out provides opportunities for small and microenterprises to also reap the benefits of knowledge spillovers.[52]

Research can also shed light on the obstacles preventing the productivity spillovers from globally integrated jobs from materializing. Cross-country analysis shows that the degree of labor market flexibility, barriers to firm entry, and infrastructure development substantially influence the impact of openness on growth.[53] Knowledge spillovers hinge on the ability of the local economy to absorb them—human capital and research and development capacity are important. Local firms need a certain level of production and technological capabilities to be selected as suppliers by foreign companies. When technology gaps between local firms and foreign companies are large, productivity spillovers are less likely to occur.[54]

Environmental impacts. Jobs that overuse natural resources or damage the environment are less productive than their direct output might suggest. The environmental damage they create imposes a negative spillover on others, resulting in a lower net contribution to aggregate output. Natural resources such as the atmosphere, water, forests, and soil provide services useful for economic activities and necessary for human life, but they are often overused because their cost from a private point of view falls short of their true social cost.[55] The emission of greenhouse gases is an example of a negative spillover.

The tools of environmental economics can be used to quantify the cost of emissions associated with jobs. Worldwide, industry is responsible for over one-fifth of carbon emission.[56] Globally, the average cost from fuel combustion in manufacturing is in the order of US$82 per job per year.[57] However, this average hides an enormous diversity in the emission cost of production across countries, industries, and technologies. Across countries, a negative relation can be observed between the annual emission cost per job and the emission efficiency of production. Richer countries tend to have higher environmental costs associated with one job, but, in parallel, these jobs have a high productivity so that the emission intensity per unit of manufacturing output tends to be relatively low (figure 5.9).

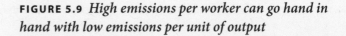

FIGURE 5.9 *High emissions per worker can go hand in hand with low emissions per unit of output*

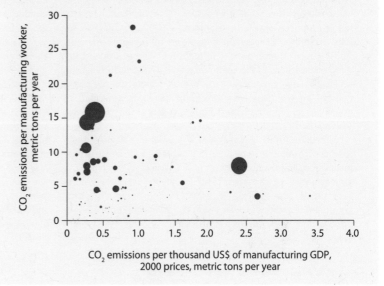

Sources: World Development Report 2013 team estimates based on IEA 2011, International Income Distribution Database (I2D2), and the ILO's Labor Statistics.
Note: CO_2 = carbon dioxide; GDP = gross domestic product. Estimates are based on data from the International Energy Agency and methods and emission factors from the revised 1996 Intergovernmental Panel on Climate Change guidelines for National Greenhouse Gas Inventories. The figure considers only CO_2 emissions from fuel combustion associated with productive activities in the manufacturing and construction sectors. Bubbles represent countries. The size of the bubbles represents the comparable size of manufacturing GDP in constant prices.

Policies to contain carbon emissions and reduce environmental damage rely on price and quantity instruments aimed at transferring the cost to producers. These policies should increase net output per job, accounted for in green terms. However, in the short term, they could result in fewer jobs if natural resources and labor are complements in production.

Policies also try to promote job creation in more environmentally friendly industries. Jobs in enterprises that produce wind mills for electricity generation, construct water and soil conservation systems, and plant and manage trees fall in this category. These are often called green jobs, with different definitions attached to the term. Industries matching the most common definitions of green jobs tend to be relatively small in many developing countries, with Brazil and China notable exceptions (box 5.6).[58]

Pending a precise quantification of environmental spillovers from jobs, it is likely that the activities with the greatest potential to mitigate adverse environmental damage in develop-

---

BOX 5.6 *International definitions of green jobs can be too narrow for developing countries*

While the concept of green growth is well developed, there is less consensus on the concept of green jobs.[a] The Organisation for Economic Co-operation and Development (OECD) uses this label for jobs linked to environmental industries.[b] The European Commission focuses on employment in industries whose products are deemed beneficial to the environment.[c] Examples include jobs in renewable energy sectors and low-carbon manufacturing. Several national governments are developing their own definitions of green jobs, both for statistical purposes as well as to inform policy making.

The United Nations Environment Programme defines green jobs as "positions in agriculture, manufacturing, construction, installation, and maintenance, as well as scientific and technical, administrative, and service-related activities that contribute substantially to preserving or restoring environmental quality."[d] For the United Nations Environment Programme and the International Labour Organization, these jobs must also qualify as Decent Work.

But these definitions can be too narrow. In developing countries, some jobs associated with green growth that have prospects for substantial expansion, such as biofuel and biomass production, may not qualify as Decent Work.[e] Moreover, the focus on renewable energy and low-carbon manufacturing may shift attention away from activities with positive environmental impacts that also provide higher earnings to the poor.

Consider efforts toward reduced forest degradation and sustainable management of trees.[f] Tree resources outside of closed forests are becoming increasingly important to satisfy the demand for charcoal, firewood, timber, and nonwood forest products. Locally managed reforestation and regeneration of degraded landscapes may generate income opportunities for poor people as well as positive environmental impacts. Trees with the capacity to fix nitrogen have been used to improve soil fertility and provide fodder, wood, and fuel. Such enhanced tree management has helped increase sorghum yields by as much as 85 percent in some areas and millet yields by as much as 50 percent.

Source: World Development Report 2013 team.
a. For a detailed discussion, see Bowen 2012.
b. OECD 1999.
c. UNEP and others 2008.
d. UNEP and others 2008, 35–36.
e. Upadhyay and Pahuja 2010.
f. Sander and Dewees 2012 for the World Bank Development Report 2013.

---

ing countries lie outside the modern sector, in areas such as agriculture and forestry management. Agriculture and deforestation account for nearly 30 percent of the greenhouse gas emissions in the world.[59] Low-productivity agriculture leads to deforestation as cultivated areas are expanded.[60] As such, efforts to reduce the environmental spillovers from jobs in developing countries are bound to concern rural areas, affecting farming and rural livelihoods.[61] For example, they may involve community participation in the management of commons such as forests and natural habitats.

Social cohesion

If jobs change values, behaviors, and attitudes of people, they can influence how societies function, specifically, how groups in society are able to resolve tensions and engage in peaceful collective decision making. Three such spillovers from jobs to social cohesion are social identity, networks, and a sense of fairness. The effect of jobs on social identity can be particularly important for youth. Jobs can contribute to socialization and the process of acquiring values and behaviors for the workplace and society.[62]

Social identity. A job can influence the social groups that individuals associate with, their behaviors, and the norms that shape those behaviors.[63] The degree to which a job, or its characteristics, shapes the way individuals perceive themselves in their community and society varies with traditions, culture, and the level of economic development. But when the relationship is significant, a spillover from jobs to social cohesion exists.

Quantifying spillovers from jobs on social cohesion is bound to be more difficult than for living standards or productivity. However, a rough assessment is possible using household surveys as well as qualitative studies. For instance, about half of respondents in China judge their jobs to be somewhat or absolutely meaningful, but in Sierra Leone the share is 90 percent, potentially signaling the social importance of jobs in a low-income and post-conflict setting.

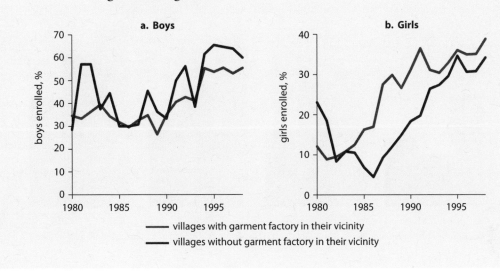

FIGURE 5.10 *Proximity of garment factories stimulates schooling among young girls in Bangladesh*

a. Boys

b. Girls

— villages with garment factory in their vicinity
— villages without garment factory in their vicinity

Source: Heath and Mobarak 2011.

Behaviors and norms can also be changed by perceptions about access to jobs—by raising peoples' expectations and aspirations for the future—and in some cases these changes in perceptions can be gauged as well. For instance, school enrollments in Bangladesh increased among girls after garment factories opened within commuting distance of their villages.[64] No such effect was observed among boys, while some older girls dropped out of school to take up the new job opportunity (figure 5.10). As jobs in the factories became available to women, it is likely that parents saw more employment opportunities for their daughters and realized the importance of education. The women working in these garment factories thus set an example for other women and girls.

Program evaluations are another source of information on the spillovers from jobs on social cohesion. For instance, the Programa Juventud y Empleo (Youth and Employment Program) in the Dominican Republic reaches young people who have not finished secondary school, are unemployed, and are living in poor households. Participants receive a combination of vocational training and training in life skills, including self-esteem, teamwork, and communication skills, followed by internships at private sector firms.[65] The program has led to a decrease in involvement in gangs, violence, and other risky behavior, including drug use and unprotected sex. Participants described the positive impact on their self-esteem and behaviors.

Networks. Jobs can create new contacts and be a vehicle to transmit information. On the negative side, they can also have an exclusionary effect, moving the individual further from the wider society. Positive network effects can give people a stake in their community or society; negative effects can increase social distance.

Again, surveys can inquire about these dynamics as a first entry to gauge whether a spillover exists. In four countries, participants in a survey were asked whether their job was useful or not in establishing contacts with other people, providing information about societal matters or other jobs, or helping with news about good deals (on food, for example). Only a quarter of respondents in China, but fully three-quarters of those in Sierra Leone judged these network effects to be at least somewhat important (figure 5.11). While comparisons across countries need to be interpreted with caution, comparisons across individuals in the same country may be informative.

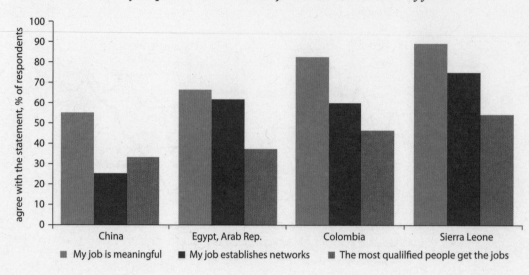

FIGURE 5.11 *Not all jobs provide social identity, networks, or a sense of fairness*

Source: World Development Report 2013 team estimates based on Bjørkhaug and others 2012; Hatløy and others 2012; Kebede and others 2012; and Zhang and others 2012; all for the World Development Report 2013.

Quantitative methods are necessary to contextualize network effects. Surveys in Bosnia and Herzegovina and the former Yugoslav Republic of Macedonia have found that the number of people willing to work or do business with someone of a different ethnicity was greater than the number of people in favor of interethnic cooperation in schools or neighborhoods.[66] Focus groups in Bosnia and Herzegovina in the late 1990s found that the workplace was "the area in which there is the greatest support for ethnic cooperation."[67] Business people working in print and packaging, food and beverages, construction, and retail in Trinidad and Tobago have reported that interactions through work with others of different ethnicities have positively influenced their social life.[68]

Sense of fairness. Whether access to jobs is fair naturally depends on a subjective evaluation. Opinion surveys can provide an assessment of how fair the job market is judged to be, and tracking such evaluations over time can be of guidance to policy makers. About 30 percent of Chinese respondents feel that the most-qualified people get jobs—an indication that rel-

atively few people judge jobs to be distributed on the basis of merit. In Colombia as well as Sierra Leone, the percentages were significantly higher.

Beyond these subjective assessments, fairness in access to jobs can actually be measured rigorously, building on the emerging literature on inequality of opportunity. This literature explores to what degree factors beyond talent and effort matter in accessing jobs. These factors include the circumstances in which a person is born: location, family background, gender, ethnicity, and language.[69] A society that offers equal opportunities would record little influence of these circumstances on job trajectories much later in the life. In some countries, however, the share of inequality that arises from such birth circumstances is large. In this case, the existence of deeply rooted inequities determines the life chances from early on and becomes apparent later on through the access to jobs and the related rewards.[70] The approach can also be used to assess the importance of different factors that contribute to inequality in employment opportunities. Among several countries in Eastern and Central Europe, father's education is a driver for inequity in access to jobs, especially in the Rus-

FIGURE 5.12 *Gender and father's education account for a large share of inequality of opportunity in access to jobs*

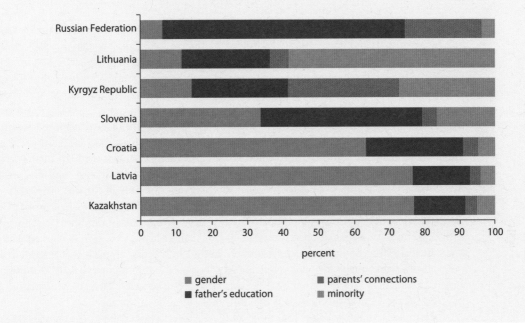

Source: Abras and others 2012 for the World Development Report 2013.
Notes: The figure shows the contribution of each circumstance to an inequity measure, the D-index. The *D-index* is the share of available opportunities that would have to be reallocated to achieve the same coverage rate of opportunity across all groups. *Opportunity* is defined as having a job with 20 or more hours per week. *Parents' connections* refers to parents who were affiliated with the Communist Party. *Father's education* is measured in years of completed schooling.

sian Federation and Slovenia, while gender is predominant in Latvia, Kazakhstan, and Croatia (figure 5.12).

* * *

The assessment of the social value of jobs is important for the identification of what good jobs for development are in a particular country context. Such assessments can be pursued with a variety of means. Some of them allow for an actual quantification, some others for a qualitative treatment of the difference between the individual value and the social value of jobs. Assessing the social value of different types of jobs can inform policy discussions about trade-offs and priorities for developmental policies. The relevant spillovers are bound to be different in countries at different levels of development and with different characteristics, thus leading to diverse jobs agendas.

Since human capital theory first established a link between skills and economic performance, it generally has been held that education and training are wise investments for increasing employment and earnings—and are hence necessary ingredients for growth and job creation. The risk of living in poverty declines with the acquisition of basic cognitive skills, especially numeracy and literacy, and the associated enhancement in earning opportunities. Skills, especially cognitive abilities, are strongly related to productivity growth, more so than school attendance rates.[71] They also are closely associated with structural transformation, especially for low- and lower-middle-income countries where they create opportunities for people outside of agriculture.[72] Across 1,500 subnational regions in 110 countries, education emerges as the critical determinant of knowledge spillovers and entrepreneurship.[73] And skills can shape how jobs link people to neighbors, communities, and societies.[74]

But around the world, available skills are not fitting well with the demands of the economy. Skills mismatches are arguably growing rather than shrinking. Albeit not easy to pinpoint, up to one-third of the employed in countries as diverse as Brazil, Costa Rica, Pakistan, Sri Lanka, and Tanzania are either under- or over-qualified for the work they do.[75] Managers of registered, formal firms around the world judge workforce skills as an obstacle of above-average importance in the production process.[76] In countries at all development levels, skills obstacles are also judged to be more acute now than in the first half of the 2000s (figure 5.13).

Skills shortages are an especially serious constraint for the most dynamic entrepreneurs.[77] Larger as well as younger and growing firms tend to identify skills as a constraint more than medium-sized and smaller firms.[78] Export-oriented firms in Indonesia and the Philippines report skills bottlenecks more than firms producing for the domestic market in those countries.[79] Across 106 developing countries, firms that adopt technology more rapidly and those that are more globally integrated take longer to fill job vacancies through external candidates than other firms—a sign of skill-related constraints being more binding.[80] On the other hand, farmers and entrepreneurs of unregistered firms in both rural and urban environments tend to rate skills bottlenecks as less severe.[81]

The straightforward response to such mismatches would be for private firms or individuals to upgrade skills through further education or training—but several well-known reasons prevent this from occurring. Firms and farms—especially smaller ones—and workers seldom have the necessary funds nor can they borrow for this purpose.[82] Firms are also reluctant to invest in training employees for fear that workers will leave after being trained.[83] And both firms and workers may lack the information needed to identify skills gaps.

Because of such market failures, policy makers often turn to education and training systems to deal with high unemployment or stifled productivity growth. Many countries are currently making a big push to hone the skills of the current and soon-to-be workforce through increased emphasis on on-the-job training and on pre-employment (vocational) education. Turkey's Public Employment Agency has expanded vocational training enrollment almost tenfold since 2007, delivering close to 250,000 courses in 2011. India has launched the National Skills Mission with a stated goal of training 500 million people by 2022.

The pitfalls of skills building

The importance of skills cannot be overstated (box 5.7). But caution is needed before jumping from this recognition to the launching of large skills-building programs. The root cause of skill shortages or mismatches might not lie with the education and training system. Shortages and mismatches may instead result from wrong signals generated by market distortions and institutional failures elsewhere in the economy. If a civil service career pays overly well, young people may study to obtain such jobs, even if they need to queue for them. This can

FIGURE 5.13 *Relative to other obstacles, skills have become a more severe constraint to business*

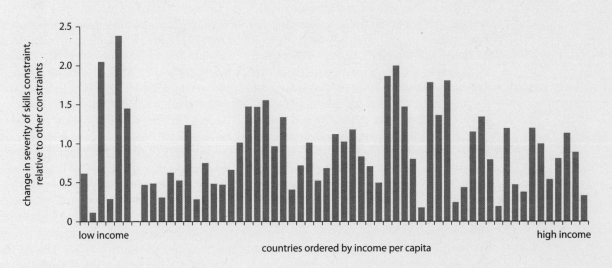

Source: World Development Report 2013 team based on enterprise surveys.
Note: The figure shows the changes in the relative importance of skills obstacles between beginning and end of the 2000s. The relative skill obstacle is defined as the ratio between (a) the share of firm managers saying that lack of skills is a major or severe obstacle and (b) the share of firm managers rating other constraints as major or severe. A positive score indicates that the skills constraint became more severe relative to others.

BOX 5.7 *How skills are formed, and how they can be measured*

Skills are acquired throughout life. People learn, adapt, and form their skills through a multitude of interactions and mechanisms within the household and neighborhood, during the formative years of schooling, at work, and in training. Cognitive skills include verbal ability, working memory, numeracy, and problem-solving abilities. Social skills are based on personality traits that underlie behaviors such as teamwork, reliability, discipline, or work effort.[a] Technical skills enable the performance of specific tasks. Because all jobs require a combination of skills that are formed in multiple ways and in diverse circumstances, policy makers face complex challenges in forging the best path for skills development.

The first months and years of life are the most crucial for skill formation. This is when intelligence and learning abilities, the foundations for the development of core cognitive and social skills, are cemented.[b] Brain maturation occurs in steps, with new skills building on earlier ones. If the foundation is strong, higher-order cognitive and social skills can be added later on. This leads to higher adaptability in rapidly changing job environments and the acquisition of job-specific techniques. In the slums of Mumbai, a special program run in parallel to primary schooling raised children's self-

esteem, self-efficacy, and aspirations, increasing scores on school-leaving examinations and initial labor market outcomes.[c] But while foundations are laid early on, skills are also shaped after childhood and in working life.

Attention to the measurement of skills has gained prominence worldwide. Achievement tests provide information for parents, instructors, and administrators, and enable a better understanding of systemwide performance and achievements. While the skills measured on these tests appear to be purely academic in nature, test scores reflect more than individuals' cognitive skills. A good part of the variation in achievement tests can be attributed to personality traits or social skills as well as to incentive systems. These personality traits and social skills are critical in predicting individuals' life outcomes, including educational attainment and earnings.

More recently, efforts have gone in the direction of assessing adult competencies, by measuring the variety, intensity, and frequency of skills used in the workplace. These measures range from assessing different types of manual and workplace skills of a more routine manner to complex capabilities, such as problem solving abilities.[d]

Source: World Development Report 2013 team.
a. Barrick and Mount 1991.
b. Grantham-McGregor and others 2007; Knudsen and others 2006.
c. Krishnan and Krutikova 2010.
d. OECD 2012; Skills toward Employment and Productivity Measurement Study based on World Bank 2010.

lead to the acquisition of skills that are irrelevant in the private sector and to unrealistic expectations, as was observed, for example, in the Arab Republic of Egypt.[84] Similarly, compressed pay scales reduce the incentives to invest more in education and training.[85] Lack of information about employment opportunities, transportation costs, or housing market failures may be the real reasons why workers do not take available jobs. In all of these cases, constraints that seem to be skills related actually reside outside the education and training system.

Besides, the successful delivery of skills-building services is difficult. Pre-employment and on-the-job training show varying success in the developing world. On-the-job training is consistently found to go hand-in-hand with higher labor earnings and productivity increases, even more so in developing than in industrial countries.[86] But only a fraction of workers have access to it; those with less education and those working in smaller and informal enterprises seldom have the opportunity to benefit from training. Technical and vocational education (TVE) has a mixed record: compared with general education, TVE led to higher earnings in Rwanda, Sri Lanka, and Thailand, more or less equal earnings in Indonesia and India, and lower earnings in Pakistan.[87] The reach of TVE in rural areas is often very limited.[88] In some countries, TVE has actually reinforced socioeconomic inequalities rather than fostered social mobility.[89] Poor quality and inequitable access are key constraints in many countries.

Accountability and governance arrangements are often the weak link of skills-building initiatives, with institutional failures often replacing market failures. On the positive side, modern and flexible skills-development strategies have generally replaced old-fashioned and mechanical manpower planning (box 5.8). Many countries have also created oversight entities, such as the Pakistan Sindh Technical and Vocational Training Authority, to separate quality control and management of providers from financing. In India, the National Skills Development Strategy is based on the principle that the institutions in charge of training, certification, and accreditation should be strictly separated.[90] On the negative side, scattered responsibilities across many ministries, distance from the private sector, slow response to rapidly changing skill needs, and capture by providers continue to plague training programs and pre-employment education around the world.

What is being taught matters as well. Social skills are often the ones missing, but they can rarely be acquired in schools or training centers. In India, employers of engineers stress reliability, willingness to learn, and entrepreneurship as more important than specific technical skills, or the command of mathematics, science, or English.[91] In Botswana, theoretical and practical knowledge of the job, as well as other job-specific skills, are generally considered to be less important than skills such as commitment, communication, and basic problem-solving.[92] In Peru, 40 percent of employers complain about the lack of dependable work ethics and personal qualities such as team work, persistency, ability to reach consensus, or initiative among their employees. This subjective assessment is confirmed by harder evidence showing that returns to the socioemotional trait of perseverance are as high as returns to average cognitive ability.[93]

Learning through jobs

Just as skills are important for jobs, the reverse is true as well. Many technical and social skills can be built through experience in the workplace—shaping skills on the job carries sizable returns. On average across countries, the return to one additional year of work experience in nonagricultural activities is roughly one-half the return to one additional year of education at the beginning of work life.[94] And managers put a premium on experience. In five African countries, managers identified work experience as more important for hiring decisions than technical skills and education.[95]

Apprenticeship programs, fostering the integration of education and learning through jobs, exist in various shapes around the world. They range from the informal model of Sub-Saharan Africa to the dual model of Central Europe. Informal apprenticeship, often the primary mechanism for technical skills to be passed through generations, can be strengthened through its gradual integration into national training systems.[96]

The dual model, deeply rooted in Germany, combines classroom-based schooling—geared to building general and transferable skills—with learning on the job in the training company.[97] In France, Germany, and the Netherlands, the

BOX 5.8 *Manpower planning has given way to dynamic skills development*

Manpower planning, a technique that used macroeconomic and sector forecasts to derive how many workers with specific technical skills would be needed was popular in the 1960s and 1970s. It was successful in a few cases in which it was closely integrated with the overall economic development strategy of the country and benefited from a universal basic education system, as it did in the Republic of Korea.[a] But its rigidity soon became stifling. Manpower planning generally assumed a fixed relationship between labor and outputs, implicitly ruling out technological change. It also emphasized technical skills to the detriment of cognitive and social skills. And it was slow to adapt to rapid changes in the world of work brought by globalization.[b]

Gradually the focus shifted from merely ensuring an adequate supply of skills to delivering demand-responsive, quality-skills development programs. The Republic of Korea stopped developing long-term macroeconomic plans with explicit industrial policies by the mid-1990s. Industrial projections of manpower supply took a backseat to the country's new initiatives emphasizing quality and relevance of education and skills development.[c] The scope became broader and more integrated, replacing mechanistic forecasting. In the 1980s and 1990s, Singapore developed an integrated strategy to upgrade, retrain, and provide lifelong learning for its labor force, especially for those with lower levels of education and skills.

The rapid pace of globalization increasingly requires the private sector to be a driving force in skills development. India's National Association of Software and Service Companies (NASSCOM) developed standardized skills assessments and certification arrangements in 2006. The Korea University of Technology and Education (KUT) established the Bridge Model, a three-way partnership also involving a single major enterprise and clusters of small and medium enterprises (SMEs) that serve as its main subcontractors. The major enterprise contributes technical knowledge, the SMEs bring in the employees to be trained, and KUT supplies the teaching facilities and content.[d] Samsung was the first "bridge'" in 2006; five other major companies have become bridges since then.

Much can be learned from comprehensive skill-building systems, especially from those of East Asia. But these systems require sophisticated institutional mechanisms that may be out of reach in lower-capacity contexts.[e] Over 100 countries have embarked on comprehensive National Qualification Frameworks, built around the definition of competencies, certification, and accreditation. But with exceptions, results and impact are sobering.[f] Often, the administrative capacity available in low- and middle-income countries is overwhelmed, and progress is held back by the lack of strong buy-in from the most important players: parents, teachers, training institutes, and firms. Perhaps the most valuable lesson from East Asian countries is that skills-development systems need to grow organically from below while being coordinated and fostered from above.

Source: World Development Report 2013 team.
a. Kim 2002.
b. Richards 1994.
c. Kim 2002.
d. Lee and others 2008.
e. Nam 2011.
f. ILO 2010b. See also DFID 2010; Gill, Fluitman, and Dar 2000.

dual system is credited with fast and structured employment integration.[98] But the dual system requires more than the right economic incentives—it is based on a social contract between employers (to offer places and invest in the future career of apprentice as a common good), trade unions (to accept below minimum wage payment for trainees), and government (to fund vocational schools and provide quality control).[99] Private sector commitment, including financing of training and continuation even in times of economic downturns, is fundamental. Given such high institutional requirements, attempts to transplant the dual model in its entirety have seen little success.

Building skills on the job is promising, because skills continue to develop and accumulate after formal schooling ends, in teenage years and during working life.[100] Jobs—especially early experiences—can also shape behaviors and attitudes, including the willingness to contribute to society at large.

Importantly, jobs also support the transmission of knowledge through interactions with other people. Knowledge spillovers underlie the agglomeration effects observed in cities and in production clusters.[101] But knowledge spillovers from jobs also occur in rural areas. During the Green Revolution in India, farmers with experienced neighbors made larger profits than those with inexperienced ones.[102] Benefits from social learning at the village level were substantial.[103]

Jobs can also ignite skills building by putting people in contact with the outside world. Working in foreign-owned companies, or in firms integrated in international value chains, allows the acquisition of new technical and managerial skills. This learning then spurs imitation and can have cascading ripple effects.[104] In Singapore, India's Tata group was the first international company to partner with the Economic Development Board in 1972 to establish a company-owned training center for precision engineers. This partnership model was successfully replicated in subsequent years with other foreign companies, eventually leading to the consolidation of various institutions in 1993 to form Singapore's Nanyang Polytechnic. Today, the polytechnic has become a source of international expertise on industry-led training.[105] Intel's decision to establish its semiconductor assembly and test plant in Costa Rica has equally contributed significantly to that country's prospects and skill building system.[106]

Jobs need skills, pull skills, and build skills

Some skills are necessary for productive employment to emerge in the first place. And they cannot be acquired on the job. Without numeracy and literacy skills, the prospects of improving employment opportunities and earnings, whether in agriculture or in urban settings, are thin. Today, more than one-tenth of 15-to-24-year-olds worldwide are functionally illiterate, and that does not bode well for their future.[107] Also, social skills assume an ever more important role as complements to basic cognitive skills. Given that skill building is cumulative, securing the foundation on which much of the later path of skill acquisition follows remains an absolute priority. Many countries are not there yet.

With this foundation in place, jobs can pull skills. Employment opportunities increase the demand for education, which systems then have to meet. The role of policy here is to ensure that signals are adequately transmitted, providing incentives to continue skill accumulation by the young and those of working age alike. In the Dominican Republic, providing students with information about the actual returns to secondary school education led to substantially higher school attendance.[108] In India, informing rural women about job opportunities led to increased schooling for girls and delayed marriage and childbearing for women.[109] On the other hand, privilege in access to jobs distorts the signals. It hurts and discourages, rather than encourages, the building of skills.

Jobs themselves can build skills, especially at entry into the labor market. Given the negative long-term effects of troubled school-to-work transitions, placing emphasis on supporting first-time job-seekers should have significant payoffs.

But jobs may neither pull nor build skills to a significant degree, even if the foundational cognitive skills are in place. This occurs in situations where the benefits from agglomeration and global integration are present but not adequately exploited. Countries undergoing rapid urbanization often have sizable knowledge spillovers to reap but may fail to move up the value-added ladder. If so, they can be caught in traps of low productivity and low skills.[110] Such traps arise when skills are insufficient to spur innovation and the demand for skills is too low to encourage their acquisition. In those cases, more relevant schooling and skill building at the secondary, technical, and likely higher levels are needed as a prerequisite for the creation of good jobs for development.

Notes

1. Glewwe 2004; World Bank 2008b.
2. Nunn and Wantchekon 2011.
3. ILO 2012b.
4. ILO 2010a.
5. United Nations, 1948, The Universal Declaration of Human Rights, United Nations, New York, http://www.un.org/en/documents/udhr/, article 23 (1). Complementing the declaration, international conventions aim to protect the rights of women, children, the disabled, migrants, and others—among these the Convention on the Elimination of All Forms of Discrimination against Women (1979), the Convention on the Rights of the Child (1989), the International Convention on the Protection of the Rights of All Migrant Workers and Members of Their Families (1990), and the Convention on the Rights of Persons with Disabilities (2006). Regional mechanisms that protect labor rights include the European Convention on Human Rights, the European Social Charter, and the Inter-American Convention on Human Rights. Each of these provides explicit protections for a range of labor rights. At the national level, countries include workers' rights in constitutions, national laws, and regulations. National laws clarify details on specific interpretations and applications of international rights and standards.
6. The core international labor standards are the subject of eight conventions covering the four areas: Convention 87 (1948), the Freedom of Association and Protection of the Right to Organize Convention; Convention 98 (1949), the Right to Organize and Collective Bargaining Convention; Convention 29 (1930), the Forced Labor Convention; Convention 105 (1957), the Abolition of Forced Labor Convention; Convention 100 (1951), the Equal Remuneration Convention; Convention 111 (1958), the Discrimination (Employment and Occupation) Convention; Convention 138 (1973), the Minimum Age Convention; and Convention 182 (1999), the Worst Forms of Child Labor Convention. See "Conventions," NORMLEX (Information System on International Labour Standards) database, International Labour Organization, Geneva, http://www.ilo.org/dyn/normlex/en/.
7. For example, Convention 122 covers employment policy, Conventions 81 and 129 address labour inspections (129 for agriculture), and Convention 144 involves tripartite consultations.
8. ILO 1998.
9. Hassel 2008. For example, the safeguard policies of the International Finance Corporation (IFC) are aligned with the core labor standards. See IFC 2012.
10. In theory, freedom of association provides a channel for workers to demand better working conditions. Safety and health are covered by ILO conventions, national laws, and regulations and an increasing number of voluntary private sector codes of conduct.
11. Fredman 2012 for the World Development Report 2013.
12. Family workers hold self-employment positions in market-oriented establishments operated by relatives living in the same households. See ILO 2011a.
13. Sankaran 2007.
14. Fredman 2012 for the World Development Report 2013.
15. Levi and others 2012 for the World Development Report 2013; Newitt 2012 for the World Development Report 2013. These initiatives are supported by international standards and guidelines such as the Performance Standard 2 of the IFC, the Equator Principles for Financial Institutions, and the United Nations Guiding Principles on Business and Human Rights.
16. Clark 2005; Helliwell and Putnam 2004.
17. Fan and Chan-Kang 2008.
18. Summers 1989.
19. World Bank 2009a.
20. Bell and Blanchflower 2010; Bell and Blanchflower 2011.
21. Beegle, Goldstein, and Rosas 2011.
22. Attanasio and Lechene 2002.
23. Hoddinott and Haddad 1995; Quisumbing and Maluccio 2003.
24. Backiny-Yetna and Wodon 2011.
25. Akresh, de Walque, and Kazianga 2012.
26. de Mel, McKenzie, and Woodruff 2009; Fafchamps and others 2011.
27. Luke and Munshi 2011.
28. Kaveh 2012.
29. Atkin 2009.
30. Duranton 2012 for the World Development Report 2013.
31. This example is an illustration of the magnitudes at stake, not a welfare pronouncement. Cities have pecuniary costs, such as higher prices for housing, and nonpecuniary costs, such as worse pollution and more crime. Costs of living also increase with city size. Emerging evidence from industrial countries also shows a wage growth effect, and not only a level effect, in larger cities. See Freedman 2008; Holmlund and Storrie 2002; Wheeler 2006.

32. Bacolod, Blum, and Strange 2009; Glaeser and Resseger 2010; Wheeler 2001.

33. Duranton 2006; Moretti 2004a. Early findings in the literature were generated from U.S. data, but they have been confirmed for most large, developed economies. For transition and developing countries, these findings have been replicated for Chile (Saito and Gopinath 2011), China (Liu 2007), Malaysia (Conley, Flyer, and Tsiang 2003), and the Russian Federation (Muravyev 2008).

34. Duranton 2008; Henderson 2005; Overman and Venables 2005.

35. Sonobe and Otsuka 2006b.

36. IFC, forthcoming.

37. Duranton 2008; Henderson 2005; Overman and Venables 2005; World Bank 2009c.

38. Glaeser and Kohlhase 2004.

39. Santos and Shaffer 2004.

40. Parry and Timilsina 2010.

41. Rappaport 2008. For evidence from the Netherlands, see Broersma and Oosterhaven (2009).

42. Zivin and Neidell 2011.

43. Henderson, Kuncoro, and Turner 1995; Henderson, Lee, and Lee 2001.

44. Long and Zhang 2011; Mano and others, forthcoming; McCormick 1999; Schmitz and Nadvi 1999; Sonobe and Otsuka 2006a.

45. Feenstra 1998; Hummels, Ishii, and Yi 2001; Yeats 2001; Yi 2003.

46. Fernandes 2007.

47. Harrison, Martin, and Nataraj 2011.

48. Harrison 1994; Levinsohn 1993; Muendler 2004.

49. Aw, Chung, and Roberts 2000; Aw, Roberts, and Winston 2007; Blalock and Gertler 2004; De Loecker 2007; Fernandes and Isgut 2007; Hallward-Driemeier, Larossi, and Sokoloff 2002; Lileeva 2004; Matthias Arnold and Javorcik 2009; Park and others 2010; Van Biesebroeck 2005.

50. Aitken, Hanson, and Harrison 1997; Görg and Strobl 2005; Javorcik 2012 for the World Development Report 2013; Kee 2010; Poole, forthcoming.

51. Alfaro and Chen 2011.

52. Unni and Rani 2008.

53. Bolaky and Freund 2004; Chang, Kaltani, and Loayza 2009; DeJong and Ripoll 2006.

54. Blalock and Gertler 2005; Borensztein, De Gregorio, and Lee 1998; Glass and Saggi 2002; Kinoshita 2000; Kokko, Tansini, and Zejan 1996; Javorcik 2012 for the World Development Report 2013.

55. Hallegatte and others 2011.

56. UNEP 2011.

57. This estimate is based on a social cost of a metric ton of carbon of US$20 in 1995 (Fankhauser 1994), converted to 2009 prices using the U.S. GDP deflator. For sources on estimation methodology, see the note for figure 5.9.

58. In contrast, in Europe, the discussion on green growth often focuses on the use of renewable energy and low-carbon manufacturing (GHK 2009; Oral, Santos, and Zhang 2011).

59. IPCC 2007.

60. Stevenson and others 2011.

61. Otsuka and Place 2001; Pingali, Bigot, and Binswanger and Mkhize 1987; Yamano, Otsuka, and Place 2011.

62. Norton and de Haan 2012 for the World Development Report 2013.

63. Akerlof and Kranton 2010.

64. Heath and Mobarak 2011.

65. Ibarraran and others 2012.

66. UNDP 2003a; UNDP 2003b.

67. Dani and others 1999, 3.

68. Kilroy 2011.

69. The circumstances are assumed to be independent of abilities of children at birth.

70. Abras and others 2012 for the World Development Report 2013.

71. Hanushek and Woessmann 2008. Lee and Newhouse (2012, for the World Development Report 2013) extend the analysis by Hanushek and Woessmann (2008) by conducting a cohort analysis, matching achievement test scores to employment outcomes.

72. Lee and Newhouse 2012 for the World Development Report 2013.

73. Gennaioli and others 2011.

74. Welzel 2012 for the World Development Report 2013.

75. World Development Report 2013 team calculations based on national household surveys. Employed are considered overqualified if their education (years of schooling) is one standard deviation above the mean observed for the respective occupation; they are considered underqualified if their education is one standard deviation below the mean observed per occupation. The two-digit ILO definition of occupations is used.

76. This is a comparison of relative constraints. For each country, the percentage of firms that rate skills to be a severe or very severe constraint is divided by the average of such rating for all other obstacles. This allows for a cross-country comparison independent of the level of the subjective answers.

77. Estimating the conditional correlation between the relative skill constraint and a number of variables using the World Bank's enterprise surveys for 105 countries, one finds a significant correlation with firm size (positive), age (negative), exporting activity (positive), innovative

activity (positive), and manufacturing sector (positive).

78. For country examples in Georgia, the former Yugoslav Republic of Macedonia, Poland, and Ukraine, see Rutkowski (2008); Rutkowski (2010); World Bank (2009b); and World Bank (2011a).

79. Di Gropello, Kruse, and Tandon 2011; Di Gropello, Tan, and Tandon 2010.

80. Almeida and Filho 2012.

81. Specialized investment climate surveys of unregistered firms, conducted by the IFC in Afghanistan, Angola, Botswana, Burkina Faso, Cameroon, Cape Verde, the Democratic Republic of Congo, the Arab Republic of Egypt, Mali, and Nepal. Firm owners are asked to single out the most important obstacle to operating their business, with the number of obstacles varying by survey. The highest percentage is recorded in Egypt, where 6 percent of firm owners chose skills as the most important obstacle of a total of 21 choices; the lowest was in Afghanistan, where 5 percent of firm owners named skills among 12 obstacles. Rural investment climate assessments were made in Benin, Burkina Faso, Ethiopia, Indonesia, Mozambique, Nigeria, Tanzania, Sri Lanka, and the Republic of Yemen and returned similar results as to the importance of skills (Sawada 2011).

82. Training funds, set up in many countries and often financed through payroll taxation, as in Brazil, Chile, Mexico, or Singapore, provide financing for training. Almeida, Behrman, and Robalino, 2012.

83. In Latin America, 10 percent of small firms report that this is their major reason for not intensifying in-house training. World Development Report 2013 team calculations based on enterprise surveys of Latin American countries (excluding Brazil).

84. Assaad 1997.

85. See examples for Mediterranean countries in Biavaschi and others (2012 for the World Development Report 2013).

86. Almeida, Behrman, and Robalino 2012.

87. Estimates from studies for specific years. India (2004 data), Pakistan (2004 data), and Sri Lanka (2002 data): Riboud, Savchenko, and Tan (2007); Indonesia (1993, 1997, 2000, 2007 data): Newhouse and Suryadarma (2011); Rwanda (1999–2001 data): Lassibille and Tan (2005); and Thailand (1989–95 data): Moenjak and Worswick (2012).

88. No golden rule exists about how many secondary students should be in the vocational branch. Most advanced countries, with stronger demands—and rewards—for specific technical skills, have between 40 and 50 percent of their students in the vocational track. In the developing world, the average is about 33 percent based on UNESCO statistics (http://www.uis.unesco.org/Pages/default.aspx).

89. See Tan and Nam (2012). For advanced countries, on average, the employability of students graduating from TVE is similar to that of students' graduating from general tracks, but they earn somewhat lower incomes.

90. Indian Planning Commission 2008.

91. Blom and Saeki 2011.

92. World Bank 2012a.

93. World Bank 2011b.

94. WDR 2013 team estimates based on Mincer regressions for 545 household surveys, which include years of education as well as potential work experience (Montenegro and Patrinos 2012, for the World Development Report 2013).

95. McKinsey & Company 2012. Managers were given four choices from which to choose the biggest bottleneck to hiring: education (a school-leaving certificate or degree); technical skills (for instance, welding or accounting) not necessarily taught at school; social skills (for instance, attitude, workplace behavior, arriving on time, trustworthiness); or work experience.

96. ILO 2011b; Nübler 2008. The ILO has also conducted a significant number of school-to-work transition surveys that provide insights into the constraints and options for young people entering the labor market. See, for instance, Matsumoto and Elder (2010).

97. Biavaschi and others 2012 for the World Development Report 2013. Interestingly, for Germany, the initial transition does not hinge on finding employment in the training firm. Even though training and on-the-job learning takes place in a specific firm, skills learned appear to be transferable (Winkelmann 1996).

98. For a literature review, see Biavaschi and others (2012 for the World Development Report 2013).

99. See Biavaschi and others 2012, for the World Development Report 2013.

100. Cunha, Heckman, and Schennach 2010; Heineck and Anger 2010. In the Dominican Republic, early results from a life skills training for poor youths (16 and 29 years of age who had not completed secondary school) show significant results. For young female participants, pregnancy rates are down and employment chances up. For both women and men, job satisfaction and aspirations improved markedly (Ibarraran and others 2012).

101. Glaeser and Mare 2001; Kimura 2011; Mas and Moretti 2009; Peri 2002. Iranzo and Peri (2009) find that in the United States, sizable spill-

overs exist through jobs whose holders have a higher education degree (which is a proxy for advanced skills). One additional year of college education per worker is associated with a spillover—in addition to the effect on the student's income and employment chances—of increasing the respective state's productivity growth by 6 to 9 percent. See also Ciccone and Peri 2006; Moretti 2004a; Moretti 2004b; Moretti 2004c; and Rosenthal and Strange 2008.

102. Foster and Rosenzweig 1996.
103. Yamauchi 2007. See also for Ghana, Conley and Udry 2010.
104. Almeida, Behrman, and Robalino 2012.
105. Lin and Lim 2011; Tan and Nam 2012.
106. World Bank and MIGA 2006.
107. World Development Indicators (database), World Bank, Washington, DC. http://data.world bank.org/data-catalog/world-development-indicators.
108. Jensen 2010.
109. Jensen, forthcoming.
110. For a discussion on low-skill, low-productivity traps, see Acemoglu (1997); Almeida, Behrman, and Robalino (2012); Amjad (2005); Atal and others (2010); Munshi (2011); and Snower (1994). See also, on the relationship between human capital accumulation, product diversification, and attraction of FDI in Central America, Bashir, Gindling, and Oviedo (2012 for the World Development Report 2013).

References

The word *processed* describes informally reproduced works that may not be commonly available through libraries.

Abras, Ana, Alejandro Hoyos, Ambar Narayan, and Sailesh Tiwari. 2012. "Inequality of Opportunities in the Labor Market: Evidence from Life in Transition Surveys in Europe and Central Asia." Background paper for the WDR 2013.

Acemoglu, Daron. 1997. "Technology, Unemployment and Efficiency." *European Economic Review* 41 (3–5): 525–33.

Aitken, Brian, Gordon H. Hanson, and Ann E. Harrison. 1997. "Spillovers, Foreign Investment, and Export Behavior." *Journal of International Economics* 43 (1–2): 103–32.

Akerlof, George A., and Rachel E. Kranton. 2010. *Identity Economics: How Our Identities Shape Our Work, Wages, and Well-Being.* Princeton, NJ: Princeton University Press.

Akresh, Richard, Damien de Walque, and Harounan Kazianga. 2012. "Alternative Cash Transfer Delivery Mechanisms: Impacts on Routine Preventative Health Clinic Visits in Burkina Faso." Policy Research Working Paper Series 5958, World Bank, Washington, DC.

Alfaro, Laura, and Maggie Xiaoyang Chen. 2011. "Selection, Reallocation, and Knowledge Spillovers: Identifying the Impact of Multinational Activity on Aggregate Productivity." Paper presented at the World Bank Conference on Structural Transformation and Economic Growth, Washington, DC, October 6.

Almeida, Rita, Jere R. Behrman, and David A. Robalino, eds. 2012. *The Right Skill for the Job? Rethinking Effective Training Policies for Workers.* Washington, DC: World Bank.

Almeida, Rita, and Jaime Filho. 2012. "Technology Adoption and the Demand for Skills: Learning from the Time to Fill Job Vacancies in LAC." World Bank, Washington, DC. Processed.

Amjad, Rashid. 2005. "Skills and Competitiveness: Can Pakistan Break Out of the Low-Level Skills Trap?" *Pakistan Development Review* 44 (4): 387–409.

Anker, Richard. 2003. "Measuring Decent Work with Statistical Indicators." *International Labour Review* 142 (2): 147–77.

Assaad, Ragui. 1997. "The Effects of Public Sector Hiring and Compensation Policies on the Egyptian Labor Market." *World Bank Economic Review* 11 (1): 85–118.

Atal, Vidya, Kaushik Basu, John Gray, and Travis Lee. 2010. "Literacy Traps: Society-Wide Education and Individual Skill Premia." *International Journal of Economic Theory* 6 (1): 137–48.

Atkin, David. 2009. "Working for the Future: Female Factory Work and Child Health in Mexico." Princeton University, Princeton, NJ. Processed.

Attanasio, Orazio, and Valerie Lechene. 2002. "Tests of Income Pooling in Household Decisions." *Review of Economic Dynamics* 5 (4): 720–48.

Aw, Bee Yan, Sukkyun Chung, and Mark J. Roberts. 2000. "Productivity and Turnover in the Export Market: Micro-Level Evidence from the Republic of Korea and Taiwan (China)." *World Bank Economic Review* 14 (1): 65–90.

Aw, Bee Yan, Mark J. Roberts, and Tor Winston. 2007. "Export Market Participation, Investments in R&D and Worker Training, and the Evolution of Firm Productivity." *World Economy* 30 (1): 83–104.

Backiny-Yetna, Prospere, and Quentin Wodon. 2011. "Gender Labor Income Shares and Human Capital Investment in the Republic of Congo." In *Gender Disparities in Africa's Labor Market*, ed. Jorge Saba-Arbache, Alexandre Kolev, and Ewa Filipiak, 359–80. Washington, DC: World Bank.

Bacolod, Marigee, Bernardo S. Blum, and William C. Strange. 2009. "Skills in the City." *Journal of Urban Economics* 65 (2): 136–53.

Barrick, Murray R., and Michael K. Mount. 1991. "The Big Five Personality Dimensions and Job Performance: A Meta Analysis." *Personnel Psychology* 44 (1): 1–26.

Bashir, Sajitha, T. H. Gindling, and Ana Maria Oviedo. 2012. "Better Jobs in Central America: The Role of Human Capital." Background paper for the WDR 2013.

Beegle, Kathleen, Markus Goldstein, and Nina Rosas. 2011. "A Review of Gender and the Distribution of Household Assets." Background Paper for the WDR 2012, World Bank, Washington, DC. Processed.

Bell, David N. F., and David G. Blanchflower. 2010. "Youth Unemployment: Déjà Vu?" Discussion Paper Series 4705, Institute for the Study of Labor, Bonn.

———. 2011. "The Crisis, Policy Reactions and Attitudes to Globalization and Jobs." Discussion Paper Series 5680, Institute for the Study of Labor, Bonn.

Biavaschi, Costanza, Werner Eichhorst, Corrado Giulietti, Michael J. Kendzia, Alexander Muravyev, Janneke Pieters, Nuría Rodríguez-Planas, Ricarda Schmidl, and Klaus F. Zimmermann. 2012. "Youth Unemployment and Vocational Training." Background paper for the WDR 2013.

Bjørkhaug, Ingunn, Anne Hatløy, Tewodros Kebede, and Huafeng Zhang. 2012. "Perception of Good Jobs: Colombia." Background paper for the WDR 2013.

Blalock, Garrick, and Paul J. Gertler. 2004. "Learning from Exporting Revisited in a Less Developed Setting." *Journal of Development Economics* 75 (2): 397–16.

———. 2005. "Foreign Direct Investment and Externalities: The Case for Public Intervention." In *Does Foreign Direct Investment Promote Development?*, ed. Theodore H. Moran, Edward M. Graham, and Magnus Blomstrom, 73–106. Washington, DC: Peterson Institute for International Economics.

Blom, Andreas, and Hiroshi Saeki. 2011. "Employability and Skill Set of Newly Graduated Engineers in India." Working Paper Series 5640, World Bank, Washington, DC.

Bolaky, Bineswaree, and Caroline Freund. 2004. "Trade, Regulations, and Growth." Policy Research Working Paper Series 3255, World Bank, Washington, DC.

Borensztein, Eduardo, José De Gregorio, and Jong-Wha Lee. 1998. "How Does Foreign Direct Investment Affect Economic Growth?" *Journal of International Economics* 45 (1): 115–35.

Bowen, Alex. 2012. " 'Green' Growth, 'Green' Jobs and Labour Markets." Policy Research Working Paper Series 5990, World Bank, Washington, DC.

Broersma, Lourens, and Jan Oosterhaven. 2009. "Regional Labor Productivity in the Netherlands: Evidence of Agglomeration and Congestion Effects." *Journal of Regional Science* 49 (3): 483–511.

Chang, Roberto, Linda Kaltani, and Norman V. Loayza. 2009. "Openness Can Be Good for Growth: The Role of Policy Complementarities." *Journal of Development Economics* 90 (1): 33–49.

Ciccone, Antonio, and Giovanni Peri. 2006. "Identifying Human-Capital Externalities: Theory with Applications." *Review of Economic Studies* 73 (2): 381–412.

Clark, Andrew. 2005. "What Makes a Good Job? Evidence from OECD Countries." In *Job Quality and Employer Behavior*, ed. Stephen Bazen, Claudio Lucifora, and Wiemer Salverda, 11–30. London: Palgrave Macmillan.

Conley, Timothy G., Fredrick Flyer, and Grace R. Tsiang. 2003. "Spillovers from Local Market Human Capital and the Spatial Distribution of Productivity in Malaysia." *Advances in Economic Analysis and Policy* 3 (1): 1–45.

Conley, Timothy G., and Christopher Udry. 2010. "Learning about a New Technology: Pineapple in Ghana." *American Economic Review* 100 (1): 35–69.

Cunha, Flavio, James J. Heckman, and Susanne Schennach. 2010. "Estimating the Technology of Cognitive and Noncognitive Skill Formation." *Econometrica* 78 (3): 883–931.

Dani, Anis, Sarah Forster, Mirsada Muzur, Dino Djipa, Paula Lytle, and Patrizia Poggi. 1999. *A Social Assessment of Bosnia and Herzegovina*. Washington, DC: World Bank.

De Loecker, Jan. 2007. "Do Exports Generate Higher Productivity? Evidence from Slovenia." *Journal of International Economics* 73 (1): 69–98.

de Mel, Suresh, David J. McKenzie, and Christopher Woodruff. 2009. "Are Women More Credit Constrained? Experimental Evidence on Gender and Microenterprise Returns." *Applied Economics* 1 (3): 1–32.

DeJong, David N., and Marla Ripoll. 2006. "Tariffs and Growth: An Empirical Exploration of Contingent Relationships." *Review of Economics and Statistics* 88 (4): 625–40.

DFID (Department for International Development, United Kingdom). 2010. *Engaging the Private Sector in Skills Development*. London: DFID.

Di Gropello, Emanuela, Aurelien Kruse, and Prateek Tandon. 2011. *Skills for the Labor Market in Indonesia: Trends in Demand, Gaps, and Supply*. Washington, DC: World Bank.

Di Gropello, Emanuela, Hong Tan, and Prateek Tandon. 2010. *Skills for the Labor Market in the Philippines.* Washington, DC: World Bank.

Diallo, Yacouba, Frank Hagemann, Alex Etienne, Yonca Gurbuzer, and Farhad Mehran. 2010. *Global Child Labour Developments: Measuring Trends from 2004 to 2008.* Geneva: International Labour Organization.

Duranton, Gilles. 2006. "Human Capital Externalities in Cities: Identification and Policy Issues." In *A Companion to Urban Economics,* ed. Richard J. Arnott and Daniel P. McMillen, 24–39. Oxford: Blackwell.

———. 2008. "Viewpoint: From Cities to Productivity and Growth in Developing Countries." *Canadian Journal of Economics* 41 (3): 689–736.

———. 2012. "Agglomeration and Jobs in Developing Countries." Background paper for the WDR 2013.

European Court of Human Rights. 2007. D.H. and Others v. The Czech Republic [GC], No. 57325/00. European Court of Human Rights, Strasbourg.

Fafchamps, Marcel, David J. McKenzie, Simon Quinn, and Christopher Woodruff. 2011. "When Is Capital Enough to Get Female Microenterprises Growing? Evidence from a Randomized Experiment in Ghana." Working Paper Series 17207, National Bureau of Economic Research, Cambridge, MA.

Fan, Shenggen, and Connie Chan-Kang. 2008. "Regional Road Development, Rural and Urban Poverty: Evidence from China." *Transport Policy* 15 (5): 305–48.

Fankhauser, Samuel. 1994. "The Economic Costs of Global Warming Damage: A Survey." *Global Environmental Change* 4 (4): 301–9.

Farley, Melissa. 2003. *Prostitution, Trafficking and Traumatic Stress.* Binghamton, NY: Haworth Maltreatment & Trauma Press.

Feenstra, Robert C. 1998. "Integration of Trade and Disintegration of Production in the Global Economy." *Journal of Economic Perspectives* 12 (4): 31–50.

Fernandes, Ana M. 2007. "Trade Policy, Trade Volumes and Plant-Level Productivity in Colombian Manufacturing Industries." *Journal of International Economics* 71 (1): 52–71.

Fernandes, Ana M., and Alberto Isgut. 2007. "Learning-by-Exporting Effects: Are They for Real?" MPRA Paper 3121, Munich Personal RePEc Archive, University Library of Munich, Munich.

Foster, Andrew D., and Mark R. Rosenzweig. 1996. "Technical Change and Human-Capital Returns and Investments: Evidence from the Green Revolution." *American Economic Review* 86 (4): 931–53.

Fredman, Sandra. 2011. *Discrimination Law.* Oxford: Oxford University Press.

———. 2012. "Anti-Discrimination Laws and Work in the Developing World: A Thematic Overview." Background paper for the WDR 2013.

Freedman, Matthew L. 2008. "Job Hopping, Earnings Dynamics, and Industrial Agglomeration in the Software Publishing Industry." *Journal of Urban Economics* 64 (3): 590–600.

Gennaioli, Nicola, Rafael La Porta, Florencio Lopez-de-Silanes, and Andrei Shleifer. 2011. "Human Capital and Regional Development." Working Paper Series 17158, National Bureau of Economic Research, Cambridge, MA.

Ghai, Dharam. 2003. "Decent Work: Concept and Indicators." *International Labour Review* 142 (2): 113–45.

GHK. 2009. "The Impacts of Climate Change on European Employment and Skills in the Short to Medium-Term: A Review of the Literature, Final Report to the European Commission Directorate for Employment." Social Affairs and Inclusion Restructuring Forum No. 2, London.

Gill, Indermit, Fred Fluitman, and Amit Dar. 2000. *Vocational Education and Training Reform: Matching Skills to Markets and Budgets.* Oxford: Oxford University Press.

Glaeser, Edward, and Janet Kohlhase. 2004. "Cities, Regions and the Decline of Transport Costs." *Papers in Regional Science* 83 (1): 197–228.

Glaeser, Edward L., and David C. Mare. 2001. "Cities and Skills." *Journal of Labor Economics* 19 (2): 316–42.

Glaeser, Edward L., and Matthew G. Resseger. 2010. "The Complementarity between Cities and Skills." *Journal of Regional Science* 50 (1): 221–44.

Glass, Amy Jocelyn, and Kamal Saggi. 2002. "Intellectual Property Rights and Foreign Direct Investment." *Journal of International Economics* 56 (2): 387–410.

Glewwe, Paul W. 2004. "An Overview of Economic Growth and Household Welfare in Vietnam in the 1990s." In *Economic Growth, Poverty, and Household Welfare in Vietnam,* ed. Paul Glewwe, Bina Agarwal, and David Dollar, 1–26. Washington, DC: World Bank.

Görg, Holger, and Eric Strobl. 2005. "Spillovers from Foreign Firms through Worker Mobility: An Empirical Investigation." *Scandinavian Journal of Economics* 107 (4): 693–709.

Grantham-McGregor, Sally, Yin Bun Cheung, Santiago Cueto, Paul Glewwe, Linda Richter, Barbara Strupp, and International Child Development Steering Group. 2007. "Development Potential in the First 5 Years for Children in Developing Countries." *Lancet* 369 (9555): 60–70.

Hallegatte, Stephane, Geoffrey Heal, Marianne Fay, and David Treguer. 2011. "From Growth to Green Growth: A Framework." Policy Research Working Paper Series 5872, World Bank, Washington, DC.

Hallward-Driemeier, Mary, Giuseppe Larossi, and Kenneth L. Sokoloff. 2002. "Exports and Manufacturing Productivity in East Asia: A Comparative Analysis with Firm-Level Data." Working Paper Series 8894, National Bureau of Economic Research, Cambridge, MA.

Hanushek, Eric A., and Ludger Woessmann. 2008. "The Role of Cognitive Skills in Economic Development." *Journal of Economic Literature* 46 (3): 607–88.

Harrison, Ann E. 1994. "Productivity, Imperfect Competition and Trade Reform: Theory and Evidence." *Journal of International Economics* 36 (1–2): 53–73.

Harrison, Ann E., Leslie A. Martin, and Shanthi Nataraj. 2011. "Learning Versus Stealing: How Important Are Market-Share Reallocations to India's Productivity Growth?" Working Paper Series 16733, National Bureau of Economic Research, Cambridge, MA.

Hassel, Anke. 2008. "The Evolution of a Global Labor Governance Regime." *Governance: An International Journal of Policy, Administration and Institutions* 21 (2): 231–51.

Hatløy, Anne, Tewodros Kebede, Huafeng Zhang, and Ingunn Bjørkhaug. 2012. "Perception of Good Jobs: Sierra Leone." Background paper for the WDR 2013.

Heath, Rachel, and Mushfiq Mobarak. 2011. "Supply and Demand Side Constraints on Educational Investment: Evidence from Garment Sector Jobs and a Girls' Schooling Subsidy Program in Bangladesh." Yale University, New Haven, CT. Processed.

Heineck, Guido, and Silke Anger. 2010. "The Returns to Cognitive Abilities and Personality Traits in Germany." *Labour Economics* 17 (3): 535–46.

Helliwell, John, and Robert Putnam. 2004. "The Social Context of Well-Being." *Philosophical Transactions of the Royal Society B* 359: 1435–46.

Henderson, J. Vernon. 2005. "Urbanization and Growth." In *Handbook of Economic Growth*, Vol. 1B, ed. Philippe Aghion and Steven Durlauf, 1543–91. Amsterdam: Elsevier.

Henderson, Vernon, Ari Kuncoro, and Matt Turner. 1995. "Industrial Development in Cities." *Journal of Political Economy* 103 (5): 1067–90.

Henderson, Vernon, Todd Lee, and Yung Joon Lee. 2001. "Scale Externalities in Korea." *Journal of Urban Economics* 49 (3): 479–504.

Hoddinott, John, and Lawrence Haddad. 1995. "Does Female Income Share Influence Household Expenditures? Evidence from Côte d'Ivoire." *Oxford Bulletin of Economics and Statistics* 57 (1): 77–96.

Holmlund, Bertil, and Donald Storrie. 2002. "Temporary Work in Turbulent Times: The Swedish Experience." *Economic Journal* 112: 245–69.

Human Rights Watch. 2011. *A Poisonous Mix: Child Labor, Mercury, and Artisanal Gold Mining in Mali.* New York: Human Rights Watch.

Hummels, David, Jun Ishii, and Kei Mu Yi. 2001. "The Nature and Growth of Vertical Specialization in World Trade." *Journal of International Economics* 54 (1): 75–96.

Ibarrarán, Pablo, Laura Ripani, Bibiana Taboada, Juan Miguel Villa, and Brigida Garcia. 2012. "Life Skills, Employability and Training for Disadvantaged Youth: Evidence from a Randomized Evaluation Design." Discussion Paper Series 6617, Institute for the Study of Labor, Bonn.

IEA (International Energy Agency) 2011. *CO_2 Emissions from Fuel Combustion—Highlights.* Organization for Economic Co-operation and Development/IEA: Paris.

IFC (International Finance Corporation). 2012. *IFC's Performance Standard 2.* Washington, DC: IFC.

———. Forthcoming. "Assessing Private Sector Contributions to Job Creation." Jobs Study, IFC, Washington, DC.

ILO (International Labour Organization). 1998. Declaration on Fundamental Principles and Rights at Work. Adopted by the International Labour Conference at its 86th session, ILO, Geneva, June 18.

———. 2002. *Decent Work and the Informal Economy.* Geneva: ILO.

———. 2003. *Safety in Numbers: Pointers for a Global Safety Culture at Work.* Geneva: ILO.

———. 2009. *The Cost of Coercion.* Geneva: ILO.

———. 2010a. *Accelerating Action against Child Labour.* Geneva: ILO.

———. 2010b. *The Implementation and Impact of National Qualification Frameworks: Report of a Study in 16 Countries.* Geneva: ILO.

———. 2011a. *Coverage of Domestic Workers by Key Working Conditions Laws.* Geneva: ILO.

———. 2011b. *Skills for Employment Policy Brief: Upgrading Informal Apprenticeship Systems.* Geneva: ILO.

———. 2012a. *General Survey on the Fundamental Conventions Concerning Rights at Work in Light of the ILO Declaration on Social Justice for a Fair Globalization, 2008.* Geneva: ILO.

———. 2012b. *ILO Global Estimate of Forced Labour: Results and Methodology.* Geneva: ILO.

Indian Planning Commission. 2008. *Eleventh Five Year Plan, 2007–2012.* New Delhi: Oxford University Press and Government of India.

IPCC (Intergovernmental Panel on Climate Change). 2007. *IPCC Fourth Assessment Report: Climate Change 2007 (AR4).* Geneva: IPCC.

Iranzo, Susana, and Giovanni Peri. 2009. "Schooling Externalities, Technology and Productivity: Theory and Evidence from U.S. States." *Review of Economics and Statistics* 91 (2): 420–31.

ITUC (International Trade Union Confederation). 2011. *Annual Survey of Violations of Trade Union Rights, Foreword: 2011 Survey.* Brussels: ITUC.

Javorcik, Beata Smarzynska. 2012. "Does FDI Bring Good Jobs to Host Countries?" Background paper for the WDR 2013

Jensen, Robert. 2010. "The (Perceived) Returns to Education and the Demand for Schooling." *Quarterly Journal of Economics* 125 (2): 515–48.

———. Forthcoming. "Do Labor Market Opportunities Affect Young Women's Work and Family Decisions? Experimental Evidence From India." *Quarterly Journal of Economics.*

Kaveh, Majlesi. 2012. "Labor Market Opportunities and Sex-Specific Investment in Children's Human Capital: Evidence from Mexico." University of Texas at Austin, Austin, TX. Processed.

Kebede, Tewodros, Anne Hatløy, Huafeng Zhang, and Ingunn Bjørkhaug. 2012. "Perception of Good Jobs: Egypt." Background paper for the WDR 2013.

Kee, Hiau Looi. 2010. "Uncovering Horizontal Spillovers: When Foreign and Domestic Firms Share Common Local Input Suppliers." World Bank, Washington DC. Processed.

Kilroy, Austin. 2011. "Business Bridging Ethnicity." PhD thesis, Massachusetts Institute of Technology, Cambridge, MA.

Kim, Gwang-Jo. 2002. "Education Policies and Reform in South Korea." In *Secondary Education in Africa: Strategies for Renewal,* 29–40. Washington, DC: World Bank.

Kimura, Yuichi. 2011. "Knowledge Diffusion and Modernization of Rural Industrial Clusters: A Paper-Manufacturing Village in Northern Vietnam." *World Development* 39 (12): 2105–18.

Kinoshita, Yuko. 2000. "R&D and Technology Spillovers via FDI: Innovation and Absorptive Capacity." Working Paper Series 349, William Davidson Institute, Ann Arbor, MI.

Knudsen, Eric, James Heckman, Judy Cameron, and Jack Shonkoff. 2006. "Economic, Neurobiological, and Behavioral Perspectives on Building America's Future Workforce." *Proceedings of the National Academy of Sciences* 103 (27): 10155–62.

Kokko, Ari, Ruben Tansini, and Mario C. Zejan. 1996. "Local Technological Capability and Productivity Spillovers from FDI in the Uruguayan Manufacturing Sector." *Journal of Development Studies* 32 (4): 602–11.

Krishnan, Pramila, and Sofya Krutikova. 2010. "Skill Formation in Bombay's Slums." Cambridge Working Papers in Economics 1010, University of Cambridge, Cambridge, U.K.

Lassibille, Gerard, and Jee-Peng Tan. 2005. "The Returns to Education in Rwanda." *Journal of African Economies* 14 (1): 92–116.

Lee, Jean, and David Newhouse. 2012. "Cognitive Skills and Labor Market Outcomes." Background paper for the WDR 2013.

Lee, Sing Kong, Chor Boon Goh, Birger Fredriksen, and Jee-Peng Tan. 2008. *Toward a Better Future: Education and Training for Economic Development in Singapore since 1965.* Washington, DC: World Bank; Singapore: National Institute of Education.

Levi, Margaret, Christopher Adolph, Aaron Erlich, Anne Greenleaf, Milli Lake, and Jennifer Noveck. 2012. "Aligning Rights and Interests: Why, When, and How to Uphold Labor Standards." Background paper for the WDR 2013.

Levinsohn, James. 1993. "Testing the Imports-as-Market-Discipline Hypothesis." *Journal of International Economics* 35 (1–2): 1–22.

Lileeva, Alla. 2004. "Import Competition and Selection." York University, Toronto. Processed.

Lin, Cheng Ton, and David Lim. 2011. "Foreign Aid to Expertise Export." In *Heart Work 2: EDB & Partners: New Frontiers for the Singapore Economy,* ed. Chan Chin Bock, 124–29. Singapore: Straits Times Press.

Liu, Zhiqiang. 2007. "The External Returns to Education: Evidence from Chinese Cities." *Journal of Urban Economics* 61 (3): 542–64.

Long, Cheryl, and Xiaobo Zhang. 2011. "Cluster-Based Industrialization in China: Financing and Performance." *Journal of International Economics* 84 (1): 112–23.

Luke, Nancy, and Kaivan Munshi. 2011. "Women as Agents of Change: Female Income and Mobility in India." *Journal of Development Economics* 94 (1): 1–17.

Mano, Yukichi, Alhassa Iddrisu, Yutaka Yoshino, and Tetsushi Sonobe. Forthcoming. "How Can Micro and Small Enterprises in Sub-Saharan Africa Become More Productive? The Impacts of Experimental Basic Management Training." *World Development.*

Mas, Alexandre, and Enrico Moretti. 2009. "Peers at Work." *American Economic Review* 99 (1): 112–45.

Matsumoto, Makiko, and Sara Elder. 2010. "Characterizing the School-to-Work Transition of Young Men and Women: Evidence from the ILO School-to-Work Transition Surveys." Employment Working Paper 51, International Labour Organization, Geneva.

Matthias Arnold, Jens, and Beata S. Javorcik. 2009. "Gifted Kids or Pushy Parents? Foreign Direct Investment and Plant Productivity in Indonesia." *Journal of International Economics* 79 (1): 42–53.

McCormick, Dorothy. 1999. "African Enterprise Clusters and Industrialization: Theory and Reality." *World Development* 27 (9): 1531–51.

McKinsey & Company. 2012. "Survey on African Employment." McKinsey & Company, New York. Processed.

Moenjak, Thammarak, and Christopher Worswick. 2012. "Vocational Education in Thailand: A Study of Choice and Returns." *Economics of Education Review* 22: 99–107.

Montenegro, Claudio E., and Harry Anthony Patrinos. 2012. "Returns to Schooling around the World." Background paper for the WDR 2013.

Moretti, Enrico. 2004a. "Estimating the Social Return to Higher Education: Evidence from Longitudinal and Repeated Cross-Sectional Data." *Journal of Econometrics* 121 (1–2): 175–212.

———. 2004b. "Human Capital Externalities in Cities." In *Handbook of Regional and Urban Economics*, Vol. 4, ed. J. V. Henderson and Jacques Francois Thisse, 2243–92. Amsterdam: Elsevier.

———. 2004c. "Workers' Education, Spillovers, and Productivity: Evidence from Plant-Level Production Functions." *American Economic Review* 94 (3): 656–90.

Muendler, Marc Andreas. 2004. "Trade, Technology, and Productivity: A Study of Brazilian Manufacturers, 1986–1998." Working Paper Series 1148, CESifo, Munich.

Munshi, Kaivan. 2011. "Strength in Numbers: Networks as a Solution to Occupational Traps." *Review of Economic Studies* 78 (3): 1069–101.

Muravyev, Alexander. 2008. "Human Capital Externalities: Evidence from the Transition Economy of Russia." *Economics of Transition* 16 (3): 415–43.

Nam, Chang Chin. 2011. "Equipping the Dream Catchers." In *Heart Work 2: EDB & Partners: New Frontiers for the Singapore Economy*, ed. Chan Chin Bock, 46–54. Singapore: Straits Times Press.

Newhouse, David, and Daniel Suryadarma. 2011. "The Value of Vocational Education: High School Type and Labor Market Outcomes in Indonesia." *World Bank Economic Review* 25 (2): 296–322.

Newitt, Kirsten. 2012. "Private Sector Voluntary Initiatives on Labour Standards." Background paper for the WDR 2013.

Norton, Andrew, and Arjan de Haan. 2012. "Social Cohesion: Theoretical Debates and Practical Applications with Respect to Jobs." Background paper for the WDR 2013.

Nübler, Irmgard. 2008. "Institutions and the Finance of General Skills Training: Evidence from Africa." In *In Defence of Labour Market Institutions: Cultivating Justice in the Developing World*, ed. Janine Berg and David Kucera, 64–79. New York: Palgrave Macmillan; Geneva: International Labour Organization.

Nunn, Nathan, and Leonard Wantchekon. 2011. "The Slave Trade and the Origins of Mistrust in Africa." *American Economic Review* 101 (7): 3221–52.

OECD (Organisation for Economic Co-operation and Development). 1999. *The Environmental Goods and Services Industry: Manual for Data Collection and Analysis.* Paris: OECD.

———. 2012. *Literacy, Numeracy and Problem Solving in Technology-Rich Environments: Framework for the OECD Survey of Adult Skills.* Paris: OECD.

Oral, Isil, Indhira Santos, and Fan Zhang. 2011. "Climate Change Policies and Employment in Eastern Europe and Central Asia." World Bank, Washington, DC. Processed.

Otsuka, Keijiro, and Frank Place. 2001. *Land Tenure and Natural Resource Management: A Comparative Study of Agrarian Communities in Asia and Africa.* Baltimore: Johns Hopkins University Press.

Overman, Henry G., and Anthony J. Venables. 2005. "Cities in the Developing World." Discussion Paper 695, Centre for Economic Performance, London.

Park, Albert, Dean Yang, Xinzheng Shi, and Yuan Jiang. 2010. "Exporting and Firm Performance: Chinese Exporters and the Asian Financial Crisis." *Review of Economics and Statistics* 92 (4): 822–42.

Parry, Ian W. H., and Govinda Timilsina. 2010. "How Should Passenger Travel in Mexico City Be Priced?" *Journal of Urban Economics* 68 (2): 167–82.

Peri, Giovanni. 2002. "Young Workers, Learning, and Agglomerations." *Journal of Urban Economics* 52 (3): 582–607.

Pingali, Prabhu L., Yves Bigot, and Hans P. Binswanger. 1987. *Agricultural Mechanization and the Evolution of Farming Systems in Sub-Saharan Africa.* Baltimore: Johns Hopkins University Press for the World Bank.

Poole, Jennifer P. Forthcoming. "Knowledge Transfers from Multinational to Domestic Firms: Evidence from Worker Mobility." *Review of Economics and Statistics.*

Quisumbing, Agnes R., and John A. Maluccio. 2003. "Resources at Marriage and Intrahousehold Allocation: Evidence from Bangladesh, Ethiopia, Indonesia, and South Africa." *Oxford Bulletin of Economics and Statistics* 65 (3): 283–327.

Rappaport, Jordan. 2008. "A Productivity Model of City Crowdedness." *Journal of Urban Economics* 63 (2): 715–22.

Riboud, Michelle, Yevgeniya Savchenko, and Hong Tan. 2007. *The Knowledge Economy and Education and Training in South Asia.* Washington, DC: World Bank.

Richards, Peter. 1994. "Issues in Manpower Analysis." In *New Approaches to Manpower Planning and Analysis*, ed. Peter Richards and Rashid Amjad, 1–14. Geneva: International Labour Organization.

Rosenthal, Stuart S., and William C. Strange. 2008. "The Attenuation of Human Capital Spillovers." *Journal of Urban Economics* 64 (2): 373–89.

Rutkowski, Jan. 2008. "Labor Market in Georgia: Lack of Jobs or Structural Mismatch?" World Bank, Washington, DC. Processed.

———. 2010. "Demand for Skills in Former Yugoslav Republic of Macedonia." World Bank, Washington, DC. Processed.

Saito, Hisamitsu, and Munisamy Gopinath. 2011. "Knowledge Spillovers, Absorptive Capacity, and Skill Intensity of Chilean Manufacturing Plants." *Journal of Regional Science* 51 (1): 83–101.

Sander, Klas, and Peter A. Dewees. 2012. "Sustainable Management of Trees, Reduction in Forest Degradation, and Job Creation for the Poor." Background paper for the WDR 2013.

Sankaran, Kamala. 2007. *Labour Laws in South Asia: The Need for an Inclusive Approach.* Geneva: International Labour Organization.

Santos, Georgina, and Blake Shaffer. 2004. "Preliminary Results of the London Congestion Charging Scheme." *Public Works Management & Policy* 9 (2): 164–81.

Sawada, Naotaka. 2011. "Improving Rural Investment Climate for Business, Key To Rural Income Generation." World Bank, Washington, DC. Processed.

Schmitz, Hubert, and Khalid Nadvi. 1999. "Clustering and Industrialization." *World Development* 27 (9): 1503–14.

Snower, Dennis J. 1994. "The Low-Skill, Bad-Job Trap." Working Paper Series 94, International Monetary Fund, Washington, DC.

Sonobe, Tetsushi, and Keijiro Otsuka. 2006a. *Cluster-Based Industrial Development: An East Asian Model.* New York: Palgrave Macmillan.

———. 2006b. "The Division of Labor and the Formation of Industrial Clusters in Taiwan." *Review of Development Economics* 10 (1): 71–86.

Stevenson, James, Derek Byerlee, Nelson Villoria, Tim Kelley, and Mywish Maredia. 2011. "Agricultural Technology, Global Land Use, and Deforestation: A Review." Consultative Group on International Agricultural Research Standing Panel on Impact Assessment, Washington, DC. Processed.

Summers, Lawrence H. 1989. "Some Simple Economics of Mandated Benefits." *American Economic Review* 79 (2): 177–83.

Tan, Jee-Peng, and Yoo-Jeung Nam. 2012. "Pre-Employment Technical and Vocational Education and Training: Fostering Relevance, Effectiveness, and Efficiency." In *Right Skills for the Job? Rethinking Training Policies for Workers*, ed. Rita Almeida, Jere R. Behrman, and David Robalino, 67–104. Washington, DC: World Bank.

UCW (Understanding Child Work). 2010. *Child Labor: Trends, Challenges and Policy Responses.* Rome: UCW.

UN (United Nations). 2011. *The Millennium Development Goals Report 2011.* New York: UN.

UNDP (United Nations Development Programme). 2003a. *Early Warning Report: FYR Macedonia.* New York: UNDP.

———. 2003b. *Early Warning System: Bosnia and Herzegovina.* New York: UNDP.

UNECE (United Nations Economic Commission for Europe). 2010. *Measuring Quality of Employment: Country Pilot Reports.* Geneva: United Nations.

UNEP (United Nations Environment Programme). 2011. *Towards a Green Economy: Pathways to Sustainable Development and Poverty Eradication.* St-Martin-Bellevue: UNEP.

UNEP (United Nations Environment Programme), ILO (International Labour Organization), IOE (International Organisation of Employers), and ITUC (International Trade Union Confederation). 2008. *Green Jobs: Towards Decent Work in a Sustainable, Low-Carbon World.* Geneva: UNEP.

Unni, Jeemol, and Uma Rani. 2008. "Sub-Contracting Relationships in the Autocomponents Sector: Do Small Firms and Informal Enterprises Benefit?" In *Flexibility of Labour in Globalizing India*, ed. Jeemol Unni and Uma Rani, 88–126. New Delhi: Tulika Books.

Upadhyay, Himani, and Neha Pahuja. 2010. "Low-Carbon Employment Potential in India: A Climate of Opportunities." Discussion Paper TERI/GCN-2010:1, Centre for Global Climate Research TERI and Global Climate Framework, New Delhi.

Van Biesebroeck, Johannes. 2005. "Exporting Raises Productivity in Sub-Saharan African Manufacturing Firms." *Journal of International Economics* 67 (2): 373–91.

Welzel, Christian. 2012. "The Contribution of 'Good' Jobs to Development and Cohesion: The Human Empowerment Perspective." Background paper for the WDR 2013.

Wheeler, Christopher H. 2001. "Search, Sorting, and Urban Agglomeration." *Journal of Labor Economics* 19 (4): 879–99.

———. 2006. "Cities and the Growth of Wages among Young Workers: Evidence from the NLSY." *Journal of Urban Economics* 60 (2): 162–84.

Winkelmann, Rainer. 1996. "Employment Prospects and Skill Acquisition of Apprenticeship-Trained

Workers in Germany." *Industrial and Labour Relations Review* 49 (4): 658–72.

World Bank. 2006. *World Development Report 2007: Development and the Next Generation.* Washington, DC: World Bank.

———. 2008a. *Czech Republic: Improving Employment Chances of the Roma.* Washington, DC: World Bank.

———. 2008b. *Social Protection: Vietnam Development Report.* Hanoi: World Bank.

———. 2009a. *Estimating the Impact of Labor Taxes on Employment and the Balances of the Social Insurance Funds in Turkey: Synthesis Report.* Washington, DC: World Bank.

———. 2009b. *Ukraine Labor Demand Study.* Washington, DC: World Bank.

———. 2009c. *World Development Report 2009: Reshaping Economic Geography.* Washington, DC: World Bank.

———. 2010. *Stepping Up Skills for More Jobs and Higher Productivity.* Washington, DC: World Bank.

———. 2011a. *Europe 2020: Fueling Growth and Competitiveness in Poland.* Washington, DC: World Bank.

———. 2011b. *Strengthening Skills and Employability in Peru.* Washington, DC: World Bank.

———. 2011c. *World Development Report 2011: Conflict, Security, and Development.* Washington, DC: World Bank.

———. 2011d. *World Development Report 2012: Gender Equality and Development.* Washington, DC: World Bank.

———. 2012a. *Botswana: Skills for Economic Diversification.* Washington, DC: World Bank.

———. 2012b. *Promoting Access to Quality Early Childhood Development for Roma Children in Eastern Europe.* Washington, DC: World Bank.

World Bank and IFC (International Finance Corporation). 2011. *Removing Barriers to Economic Inclusion.* Washington, DC: World Bank.

World Bank and MIGA (Multilateral Investment Guarantee Agency). 2006. *The Impact of Intel in Costa Rica: Nine Years after the Decision to Invest.* Washington, DC: World Bank and MIGA.

Yamano, Takashi, Keijiro Otsuka, and Frank Place. 2011. *Emerging Development of Agriculture in East Africa: Markets, Soil, and Innovations.* Dordrecht: Springer.

Yamauchi, Futoshi. 2007. "Social Learning, Neighborhood Effects, and Investment in Human Capital: Evidence from Green-Revolution India." *Journal of Development Economics* 83: 37–62.

Yeats, Alexander J. 2001. "Just How Big Is Global Production Sharing?" In *Fragmentation: New Production Patterns in the World Economy,* ed. Sven W. Arndt and Henryk Kierzkowski, 108–43. Oxford and New York: Oxford University Press.

Yi, Kei Mu. 2003. "Can Vertical Specialization Explain the Growth of World Trade?" *Journal of Political Economy* 111 (1): 52–102.

Zhang, Huafeng, Ingunn Bjørkhaug, Anne Hatløy, and Tewodros Kebede. 2012. "Perception of Good Jobs: China." Background paper for the WDR 2013.

Zivin, Joshua S., and Matthew J. Neidell. 2011. "The Impact of Pollution on Worker Productivity." Working Paper Series 17004, National Bureau of Economic Research, Cambridge, MA.

CHAPTER 6

Diverse jobs agendas

Countries differ in where the development payoffs from jobs are greatest. These payoffs depend on the country's level of development, demography, endowments, and institutions.

Countries face different jobs challenges as they move along the development path. In *agrarian economies*, most people are still engaged in agriculture and urbanization has not yet picked up. In *urbanizing countries*, productivity growth in agriculture has risen enough to free up large numbers of people to work in cities. *Formalizing countries* generally have more developed economies, where the coverage of social protection systems is large enough to envision extending it to the entire workforce.

In some countries, the jobs challenge is shaped by demography with special circumstances affecting particular groups. In *countries with high youth unemployment*, prolonged joblessness and idleness affect large numbers of young people, with many seeing limited opportunities for the future. *Aging societies* also face generational issues, but these stem from a decreasing share of the working age population and increasing costs related to providing and caring for a growing number of old people.

Natural endowments, including geography, can create unique jobs challenges. *Resource-rich countries* may have substantial foreign exchange earnings, but this wealth often does not translate into employment creation beyond the exploitation of the natural resources. *Small island nations* cannot reap the benefits from agglomeration and global integration because of the size of the population and geographic remoteness.

Finally, the strength of institutions can define a country's jobs challenge. In *conflict-affected countries*, institutions are fragile, private investment is largely out of reach for the time being, and restoring social cohesion through jobs takes on particular importance.

These criteria are not mutually exclusive. A country may be both resource rich and conflict affected, or it may belong to the formalizing group and be characterized by high youth unemployment. Still, focusing on the key features associated with each type of country situation helps to clarify which jobs would make the greatest contribution to development in a particular context. This allows for a richer analysis of the potential tradeoffs among living standards, productivity, and social cohesion in a specific country situation. And it provides clues about the nature of the obstacles to job creation and how they can be removed (question 6).

Agrarian economies

In countries where a majority of the population lives in rural areas, wage employment is not the prevalent form of work. For instance, about half of the employed population in Kenya is engaged in farming, whereas self-employment in nonagricultural household businesses and wage employment in informal enterprises account for slightly more than one-third.[1]

Formal employment, including wage laborers in registered private enterprises and the entire public sector, typically accounts for less than 10 percent of total employment in agrarian economies. The share of wage employment in manufacturing is much smaller. A comparison across several French-speaking Sub-Saharan African countries puts the fraction at less than 5 percent of total employment even in the capital cities—less than 3 percent in Cotonou and Lomé to 8 percent in Yaoundé; only Antananarivo has more than 10 percent.[2] Across Sub-Saharan Africa, one-quarter or less of formal sector workers are women; only in Senegal does the fraction exceed one-third.[3] If anything, employment in the formal sector has trended downward over the past two decades as state-owned enterprises have been privatized and foreign trade has been liberalized.

In this context, the notion of unemployment needs to be interpreted with caution. Unemployment rates can technically be computed, but given the prevalence of poverty in agrarian economies, a substantive share of the labor force is unlikely to remain idle for long. Underemployment and low earnings, rather than open unemployment, are the challenges most people face in agrarian economies. Household survey data from Mozambique show that an astounding 81 percent of those at work were living on less than US$1.25 a day in 2003, and 95 percent were living on less than US$2.00 a day.[4]

In agrarian economies, the main avenues to improving living standards involve increasing productivity in farming, creating a dynamic economic environment in cities, and promoting labor reallocation from rural to urban areas, thereby sparking a positive spiral of productivity growth and improvement in living standards. Together, these approaches should lead to the expansion of off-farm employment opportunities, which are in turn an important driver of poverty reduction.

Mozambique illustrates the jobs challenges faced by agrarian economies.[5] Thanks to important mining discoveries and a commodities boom, as well as Maputo's privileged position as one of the ports closest to Johannesburg, Mozambique has had one of the best growth performances in Sub-Saharan Africa over the past decade. Yet, after falling substantially during the 1990s, probably as a consequence of the end of the civil war, the poverty rate remained basically unchanged between 2003 and 2008, at around 55 percent of the total population.[6]

Agriculture is the locus of much of Mozambique's poverty. Over 80 percent of employment is in agriculture, yet the sector accounts for only 30 percent of gross domestic product (GDP).[7] Value added per hour worked in agriculture is one-seventh that of services and one-twelfth that of manufacturing. Yields have been stagnant over the past decade. About 95 percent of agricultural workers work on small plots, the use of modern technology is low, and access to extension services is minimal.

Evidence suggests that growth in agriculture delivers more poverty reduction than other sectors in lower-income countries, because poor people are concentrated in the sector and because they participate more in the growth in agriculture than in the growth in other sectors.[8] Since 1700, virtually every example of mass poverty reduction has actually begun with an increase in agricultural productivity.[9]

Constraints on agricultural growth vary depending on the availability of land relative to the availability of farm labor. Compared with other areas of the developing world, Sub-Saharan Africa was traditionally seen as a continent of ample land and scarce labor. While that may still be true in some areas, it no longer applies to countries in the south and east of the continent. In Mozambique, the average farm size is less than 1.5 hectares. As the area under cultivation declines relative to the size of the population, producing sufficient food becomes a major issue unless yield-enhancing technological changes take place. In many agrarian economies in Sub-Saharan Africa, these changes have yet to occur. Unlike many parts of Asia, where the Green Revolution has increased cereal yield and the poverty incidence has declined, cereal yield has remained low and poverty incidence high in these Sub-Saharan countries (figure 6.1). Some Asian economies, such as Cambodia, the Lao People's Democratic Republic, and Myanmar, face similar challenges.

Public sector investments are important drivers of productivity growth and intensification of smallholder agriculture. Technology is often a public good. Because farmers can reproduce improved varieties of rice and wheat, private seed companies cannot reap the benefit of in-

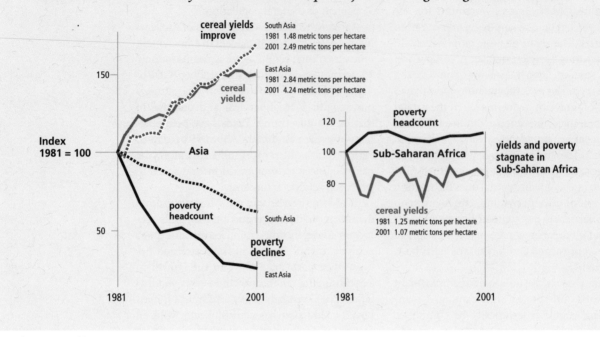

FIGURE 6.1 *In the absence of a Green Revolution, poverty remains high in agrarian economies*

Source: Christiaensen and Demery 2007.

troducing new varieties and so tend not to make the effort. Hybrid seeds of maize, sorghum, and millet cannot be reproduced by farmers, and, hence, the private sector supplies seeds. But even in these cases, basic research is carried out by the public sector. As a result, public support is necessary to develop biological and chemical technologies.

These are enduring collaborations between advanced agricultural research centers and national programs in Sub-Saharan Africa. They have developed improved varieties of cotton and cassava in ways that are reminiscent of the long-term collaboration in rice and wheat research between international agricultural research centers and national programs in Asia.[10] The recent surge in the production of high-value crops for export, including in Mozambique, is also encouraging.[11] Aside from these examples, however, few improved crops appropriate to the African climate have been developed.

Gravity irrigation systems are a local public good as well. Irrigated land accounts for only 5 percent of the total cultivated area in Sub-Saharan Africa. Lowland rice yields in irrigated areas in Sub-Saharan Africa in general

and Mozambique in particular are comparable with yields in Asia.[12] In such areas, improved varieties developed in Asia or crossbred with local varieties have been adopted. This observation suggests that, as far as lowland rice is concerned, Asian technology could be directly transferred to the irrigated areas of Sub-Saharan Africa.

While the intensification of crop-based agriculture has been associated with a significant increase in the use of inorganic fertilizer, the application of fertilizer per hectare is far lower in Sub-Saharan Africa than in any other region of the world. One of the major reasons is the high fertilizer prices relative to grain prices. Fertilizer prices are usually two to three times higher in Sub-Saharan Africa than in Asia and Latin America because of poor infrastructure and trade logistics.[13] Another major constraint on fertilizer application is the lack of credit for smallholders, given that land ownership titles are seldom secured and hence cannot be used as collateral.[14] Therefore, productivity growth in agriculture also requires a favorable investment climate including improved access to infrastructure and credit.[15]

The job structure in the cities is dominated by self-employment, with petty commerce growing quickly. If agriculture matters most for poverty reduction, successful urbanization may hold the key to more rapid productivity and income growth as well as social cohesion. In most of Sub-Saharan Africa, however, urbanization has failed to create the dynamism observed elsewhere in the developing world. Migration from rural to urban areas continues, but migrants are simply swelling the ranks of the self-employed earning subsistence wages. In the absence of dynamic cities, migration is driven by despair, and not hope. In Mozambique, for example, young people are moving to urban areas, but few are moving into regular wage employment. Meanwhile, levels of trust are falling and are lowest among young workers.[16]

Some have argued that the jobs challenge in these urban areas can be addressed through the creation of greater opportunities for self-employment. For example, building space for informal markets around bus stops would allow more rural migrants to make a living. But self-employment of this sort is unlikely to support the agglomeration effects and knowledge spillovers that make cities thrive elsewhere.

An alternative approach is to create conditions for labor-intensive light manufacturing to take off. This approach focuses on identifying activities that may hold latent comparative advantage and on removing the constraints that dissuade private firms from taking up these activities. In fact, there are many informal industrial clusters in urban areas in Sub-Saharan Africa. They produce garments, leather shoes, simple metal products, and furniture, among other things, though seldom for export.[17] These clusters have spontaneously developed, suggesting a potential comparative advantage in these industries. Reducing logistics costs, removing red tape, and addressing coordination issues could create the necessary conditions to attract foreign investors to these clusters, especially at a time when wage increases in coastal China are encouraging the relocation of some industries where low labor costs are a key competitive factor (box 6.1).[18]

Jobs, which start to trigger agglomeration effects and make connections to the global economy, are good jobs for development in agrarian countries. To create more of these jobs and become centers of economic dynamism, cities need to be more functional. But even in the most optimistic scenario, it will take time to complete the urbanization process, so increasing productivity in agriculture is a priority for reducing the high poverty levels.

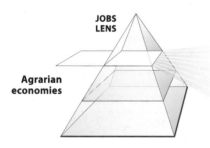

JOBS LENS

Agrarian economies

More productive smallholder farming
Urban jobs connected to global markets

Conflict-affected countries

Jobs are among the most pressing issues in countries in conflict or emerging from it.[19] They are critical for restoring the livelihoods of individuals and families affected by war and violence, reintegrating ex-combatants, and rebuilding everybody's sense of belonging in society. They are also key to jump-start economic activity, reconnect people, and reconstruct networks and the social fabric. Alongside security and justice, jobs are central to breaking cycles of violence, restoring confidence in institutions, and giving people a stake in society.[20]

Yet the obstacles to creating jobs in conflict-affected countries are staggering and confront policy makers with overwhelming questions. How can jobs be generated quickly for demobilized soldiers, displaced persons, and vulnerable groups affected by violence or war? What kinds of government programs can have a quick impact? How can the private sector become an

BOX 6.1 *Can agrarian Ethiopia compete in manufacturing?*

The labor productivity of workers in well-managed firms in Ethiopia is comparable with that in China and Vietnam, although wages are only a quarter of those in China and half those in Vietnam. Ethiopia thus has the potential to compete globally in apparel thanks to a significant and growing labor cost advantage. It is also close to a state-of-the-art and well-located container port in Djibouti and has duty-free access to the markets of the European Union and the United States. The binding constraint on Ethiopia's competitiveness in apparel is poor trade logistics, which wipe out its labor cost advantage and cut the country off from the higher-value time-sensitive segments of the market. Establishing a fast-track channel for moving apparel through customs, providing free and immediate access to foreign exchange, reducing the cost of letters of credit, and setting up an industrial zone closer to Djibouti would alleviate the most important trade logistics bottlenecks. These steps would also put Ethiopia in a position to attract investors to lead the industry in the same way that China and Vietnam have done.

Ethiopia also benefits from an abundance of natural resources. Raw materials such as skins for the footwear industry and hard and soft timber for the furniture industry are available. But they are expensive. A cubic meter of timber costs US$667, compared to US$344 in China and US$246 at most in Vietnam. So urban consumers in Ethiopia buy imported modern furniture, which is cheaper and of better quality. Yet Ethiopia has enormous unexploited potential in timber, particularly bamboo. Reforms could make the country's furniture industry competitive in the domestic market, create more productive jobs, and save foreign exchange.

Source: Dinh and others 2012.

BOX 6.2 *Conflict can increase labor force participation among women*

Out of necessity, women often intensify their economic activity during periods of conflict. Post-conflict programs that target women can help them take advantage of the window of opportunity presented by conflict and assume new roles that contribute meaningfully to local economic recovery. Women in North Maluku, Indonesia, were active participants in the rapid recovery and poverty reduction that occurred in the wake of nearly a year of intensely violent civil strife. "Since 2002, when the conflict ended, I have run a retail shop for extra income to fulfill our family needs. . . . I received support money that I used for my business capital from the Ternate city government. . . . Ten years ago, I was only a housewife because I didn't have the capital to run the business as I do now," a 38-year-old married woman reported.

Source: Petesch 2011.

engine for employment creation? Moreover, countries affected by conflict are often poor to begin with. Their opportunities, resources, and capacity are scarce; data for planning may simply not exist.

Conflict environments range from situations with high levels of criminal violence to civil wars and other forms of internal conflict. Less frequently, they involve hostilities between states. When entire countries are affected by internal or external conflict, the jobs challenge is particularly daunting because of institutional breakdown and fractured connectivity with the outside world. If conflict is localized, constraints are less severe where functioning infrastructure, services, and institutions can be extended to conflict-affected regions once hostilities become manageable. Conflict situations are generally further complicated by large numbers of displaced people. At the end of 2010, an estimated 15.4 million people sought refuge from conflict outside their home countries, and another 27.5 million were displaced internally.[21]

Conflict can fundamentally disrupt jobs by destroying or damaging infrastructure and access to markets, as well as through altering incentives. In Sri Lanka, conflict in the north disrupted economic activity and created favorable conditions for the insurgency to recruit among the newly unemployed.[22]

Even during war, however, people work. Jobs disproportionately involve low-pay or unpaid work, such as subsistence agriculture or petty trading. Youth in rural areas in post-conflict Liberia reported working two to four jobs at a time.[23] Across countries, conflict increases female labor force participation, as women work to help their households cope with income shocks and to compensate for the absence of men who are fighting (box 6.2).[24] In Afghanistan, female employment rates were higher in high-conflict than in low-conflict areas; in Nepal, they increased more than in high-conflict areas.[25]

Some jobs in conflict-affected countries may involve illegal activities that persist in the aftermath of conflict because of weak governance and lack of legal alternatives. Even if these activities are limited in scope, they may undermine the creation of good jobs for development by distorting incentives and generating rents. In Afghanistan, poppy cultivation is an important source of income for rural households.[26] In Somalia, piracy creates jobs for some through the employment of speed boat crews and related land-based operations.[27] In Liberia, young people in rural areas have supplemented their income by working in illegal mining, rubber tapping, and logging.[28]

Jobs are central to recovery in countries emerging from conflict, but the barriers to job creation can be especially steep (box 6.3). Firms in conflict-affected countries report that political instability is the most severe bottleneck to business followed by the lack of electricity (figure 6.2). Simply getting basic services up and running can be a major issue. Corruption and the lack of finance are also among the top constraints. Security risks because of high crime rates or armed conflict reduce returns to investment and can persist even after the armed conflict has officially ended. Firms may need additional funds to hire private security or to pay bribes. The loss of skills because of migration and disruptions in schooling can also create obstacles for firms.

Demobilization and reintegration of former combatants are major challenges for countries emerging from conflict. Although ex-combatants make up a relatively small share of the total population, unemployment and idleness, particularly of young men, are stress factors that can strain and potentially undermine fragile post-conflict environments.[29] Jobs can compensate for the loss of identity and status associated with the dissolution of armed forces and militias and the income lost from theft and looting. Jobs can also help deter further involvement in gangs and violence. Yet not all jobs are alternatives to violence, especially if they provide little income and the work is drudgery.

Most disarmament, demobilization, and reintegration programs include some form of employment support such as emergency temporary jobs, cash for work, public employment services, small grants, or vocational training. Temporary employment programs can play an important bridging role by providing jobs quickly to ex-combatants and other vulnerable populations in the absence of other options. Evidence on whether temporary programs reduce conflict and contribute to rebuilding communities is less clear. Cash-for-work programs can be costly and may strain stretched public budgets, may create poor quality and unsustainable assets, and can be divisive and lead to tensions if they are targeted only at certain groups.

Broadly targeted community-based programs may be more conducive to stability. In the Democratic Republic of Congo, where many ex-combatants have had a difficult time finding jobs, associations of ex-combatants and community members share information about employment opportunities and social support and

also help manage disputes.[30] Programs can be tailored to facilitate the reintegration of youth, particularly young men, who have been involved in conflict. In some cases, such as the Democratic Republic of Congo, Liberia, and Sierra Leone, young ex-combatants have no memory of peaceful times or normal civilian life.

Ultimately, conflict-affected countries need to attract private investment. The state can play an enabling role by strengthening regulations and institutions, rebuilding basic infrastructure, and providing security.[31] Partnerships between the public and private sectors, donors, and civil society can help to rebuild markets and investor confidence. Connecting farmers and entrepreneurs through value chains has the potential to spark innovation and employment growth.[32] Business associations can support entrepreneurship and help solve collective action problems by restoring law and order, roads, and electricity.[33] As security is restored,

---

BOX 6.3 *Solving jobs challenges is urgent in South Sudan*

The Republic of South Sudan, the world's newest country, exemplifies the challenges countries face emerging from conflict. South Sudan has natural resources, including oil, yet more than four-fifths of the population lives in rural areas, and most depend on subsistence farming and cattle raising. Half of the population lives in poverty, which is especially deep in rural areas, according to the 2009 household survey. Only slightly more than one-fourth of the adult population is literate, and prospects for future human capital development are dim: almost half of 10- to 14-year-olds are working, with only slightly more than one-third in school.[a]

The International Organization for Migration estimates that 4 million people were displaced during the Sudanese civil war, and that nearly 1.9 million have returned since the signing of the Comprehensive Peace Agreement in 2005.[b] The return of internally displaced persons creates substantial pressures on already poor communities. The new government of South Sudan is aiming to demobilize 150,000 soldiers over the next six to eight years.[c] Access to land rights and conflict among nomadic groups are also notable challenges for jobs, as is the legacy of overemployment in the public sector, which is not sustainable given severe fiscal pressures.

Creating jobs is one of the most immediate concerns facing the new government—jobs that can contribute to peace and stability, provide sustainable living standards through legal and nonviolent activity, and foster economic recovery. Generating these jobs involves building an enabling environment for private sector investment. That will take time, however, and alternatives are urgently needed for groups whose lack of jobs can threaten stability, including internally displaced persons, ex-combatants, and youth.

Source: World Development Report 2013 team.
a. Guarcello, Rosati, and Lyon 2011.
b. IOM 2009.
c. Republic of South Sudan Disarmament, Demobilisation and Reintegration Commission 2012.

FIGURE 6.2 *Instability and poor infrastructure are severe constraints on business in conflict-affected countries*

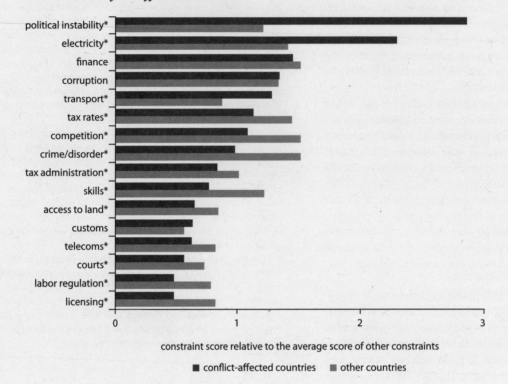

constraint score relative to the average score of other constraints

■ conflict-affected countries ■ other countries

Source: Investment Climate Survey (database), World Bank, Washington, DC.
Note: In this figure, conflict countries include Afghanistan (2008), Bosnia and Herzegovina (2009), Burundi (2006), Chad (2009), the Democratic Republic of Congo (2006 and 2010), Côte d'Ivoire (2009), Georgia (2008), Guinea-Bissau (2006), Kosovo (2009), Liberia (2009), Nepal (2009), Sierra Leone (2009), and Timor-Leste (2009). The horizontal axis measures the ratio of the average score of a constraint to the average score of all other constraints. Asterisks denote statistically significant differences between conflict countries and others at the 1 percent level.

however, the jobs focus can shift from targeted public programs to employment creation in the private sector. But it would be naïve to expect conflict-affected countries to become dynamic economies overnight.

Tackling the jobs challenge faced by conflict-affected countries is a formidable task: it requires creating jobs that contribute to peace and stability, that are an alternative to illegal economic activity and violence, and that start the long process of economic recovery. In conflict settings, jobs can also have development payoffs for social cohesion by involving people in productive activities that strengthen self-esteem and give them a sense of identity and status, by rebuilding networks, and by giving people a sense that opportunities are fairly distributed.

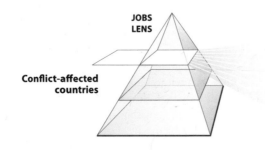

JOBS LENS

Conflict-affected countries

Jobs demobilizing combatants
Jobs reintegrating displaced populations
Jobs providing alternatives to confrontation

Urbanizing countries

Urbanizing countries endowed with abundant unskilled labor have the potential to enter a virtuous jobs circle. The integration of these countries into the world economy can lead to the creation of extensive employment opportunities, especially in light manufacturing. These jobs may involve hard work, relatively low pay, and limited or negligible benefits, but in general they are preferable to jobs in agriculture. They can also be the entry point to a process of economic and technological upgrading that leads to better jobs in the future.[34] Employment opportunities for the unskilled thus provide avenues out of poverty for large numbers of households. In countries in which women's jobs choices have been restricted, new employment opportunities in urbanizing economies can bring about important changes at the household and society levels.

This has been the story of several East Asian countries over the past half century. In many respects, it has also been the recent story of Bangladesh, where industrialization is growing in large cities such as Chittagong and Dhaka. The industrial sector now accounts for nearly 30 percent of value added, up from 20 percent in 1990, and the urbanization rate is approaching 30 percent, double what is was in 1980.[35] Exports as a percentage of GDP tripled between 1990 and 2010, with much of the increase in a thriving ready-made garment industry that is highly intensive in female labor. This structural transformation, along with improvements in agricultural productivity, has had a major impact on living standards. GDP per capita has doubled in the past two decades and the share of the population living below US$1.25 a day fell from 70 percent in 1992 to 43 percent in 2010.[36] Productivity and earnings growth still lag behind some of its neighbors, but Bangladesh's story is remarkable because the country was often held out in the development literature as a hopeless case (box 6.4).

These successes have been built on modernization in the agricultural sector, an industrial sector able to absorb low-skilled surplus farm labor, and supportive social policies.

Faster technology adoption has led to productivity increases in agriculture. Farmers have shifted from growing low-yield, single-crop, deep-water rice to double cropping of short-maturity, high-yield rice. There has also been a pronounced shift away from sharecropping into fixed-rent leasehold tenancy. Landless and marginal farmers have been the major beneficiaries of this change. Simultaneously, credit constraints have been relaxed thanks to the country's well-known microfinance institutions. Access to finance has facilitated human capital accumulation, especially in women's education and health, and promoted investments in microenterprises.

Despite the still considerable labor surplus in rural areas, real wages in agriculture have increased from the monetary equivalent of less than 2.5 kilograms of rice a day in 1983 to more than 6.0 kilograms today. The seasonal hunger associated with the *monga* period—between transplanting and harvesting paddy—is receding. Remittances from women working in factories and from men working in construction have also helped reduce rural poverty.

The movement of labor out of agriculture has been facilitated by close urban proximity, resulting from Bangladesh's high population density. Special links allowed by proximity also may have supported productivity growth among laborers engaged in rural nonfarm sectors. The ready-

---

BOX 6.4 *Development pessimism about Bangladesh was understandable, but has been proven wrong*

In 1975, the first book on the economy of Bangladesh commented: "If the problem of Bangladesh can be solved, there can be reasonable confidence that less difficult problems of development can also be solved. It is in this sense that Bangladesh is to be regarded as the test case of development."[a] In the same spirit, a well-known study on famines concluded that Bangladesh was "below poverty equilibrium."[b]

Such a negative perception of the viability of the Bangladesh economy was conditioned by the adverse initial conditions facing the country after independence—high population density, a limited natural-resource base, underdeveloped infrastructure, frequent natural disasters, and political uncertainty.

This negative perception has given way to optimism in global development circles because of Bangladesh's positive record of socioeconomic development in recent decades. Some countries have done well in human development indicators, and others have done well in economic growth, but Bangladesh belongs to a rather small group of countries that have done well on both fronts, the initial pessimism notwithstanding. This is the crux of the surprise.

Source: Bangladesh country case study for the World Development Report 2013.
a. Faaland and Parkinson 1976, 5.
b. Alamgir 1978.

made garment industry has been an important part of the jobs story in urbanizing Bangladesh. About 3 million women are working in this sector, which has a strong export orientation. Construction has been an important employer for men moving out of rural agriculture. Many low-skilled workers go abroad as well, especially to the Gulf countries. Remittances are growing by about 10 percent every year.[37]

Light manufacturing opens up opportunities for large numbers of workers in urbanizing economies because skill requirements are modest. Firms demand some education but it is generally limited. In Bangladesh, for instance, 87 percent of regular urban wage workers in 2005 had some education but only 28 percent had secondary schooling or more.[38] These education levels are considerably higher, though, than the educational attainment of workers in agriculture, so opportunities in the garment industry stimulate schooling, especially for girls. Urbanization has other beneficial effects on women, as well. Growing labor earnings increase the opportunity cost of raising children, which, in turn, may raise the age of marriage and reduce the birth rate. To the extent that women's educational attainment and labor market participation rise, the status of women in society is enhanced.

On the social policy front, both governmental and nongovernmental organizations have established pro-poor, pro-youth, and pro-women programs. These have been instrumental in reducing population growth and encouraging more effective public and private investments in education and health.

Agricultural modernization, labor migration, and social policies have altered the jobs landscape of Bangladesh, but these transformations have not involved a substantial formalization of the economy. The share of jobs benefitting from legal protection or social insurance has not increased much over the past decade. The booming construction sector remains largely informal. Corporate social responsibility among export-oriented corporations in Bangladesh is making some difference in the ready-made garment sector, but worker unrest has been recurrent. But corporate social responsibility is mainly associated with exports to industrial countries and may become less relevant if the sector diversifies its exports to other developing countries. Corporate social responsibility is unlikely to be a workable option in construction. But while formalization has not advanced, the development of entrepreneurship has been remarkable, leading to the creation of thousands of nationally owned medium and large firms within a mere two decades (box 6.5).

Bangladesh stands out as an intriguing case that is important to understand, especially given its starting point. The government has provided some support, with export processing zones, bonded warehouses, and special treatment of garments at ports. Large infrastructure projects, such as the Jamuna Bridge linking the prosperous eastern and lagging western regions, have made it easier to move around the country. But government has not played the leading role in the transformation. Corruption is a problem and the cost of doing business is high. Power failures are frequent, many roads are unpaved, and those that are paved are highly congested. Despite these obstacles, agricultural modernization has occurred thanks to the Green Revolution associated with the development and diffusion of high-yielding varieties of rice and access to finance. Labor has moved out of agriculture through industrialization, and social policies

---

BOX 6.5 *The entrepreneurs of Bangladesh are local*

The ready-made garment industry in Bangladesh has grown rapidly over the past three decades, and the country now ranks among the largest garment exporters in the world. While the early successes have been attributed to an initial technology transfer from the Republic of Korea, such a one-time infusion of knowledge alone is insufficient to explain the sustained growth. In this respect, the pattern of development in Bangladesh is similar to that in East Asia, where investment in human capital and the importation and assimilation of technological and managerial knowledge from advanced countries played a critical role in promoting industrialization.

Primary data collected from knitwear manufacturers and garment traders can be used to explore the process of the continuous learning of advanced skills and expertise. The data show that the initial infusion of specific human capital attracted highly educated entrepreneurs to the industry, that the division of labor between manufacturers and traders facilitated the expansion of the industry, and that enterprise growth has endured because of the continuous learning from abroad by the highly educated entrepreneurs. These factors, taken together, account for the high profitability of garment manufacturing in Bangladesh.

Sources: Mottaleb and Sonobe 2011; Sonobe and Otsuka 2006.

have been supportive through family planning and social protection.

Urbanizing countries like Bangladesh have the potential to exploit several spillovers. But a key challenge for them is to find a way to move up the value-added chain and diversify manufacturing exports. Apart from ready-made garments, few sectors have grown substantially in Bangladesh.[39] The pharmaceutical industry has developed, and the different pattern of development there relative to that of the garment industry is intriguing. But the high skill levels required by the pharmaceutical sector and other higher value-added export sectors are unlikely to make them a source of jobs for the masses of youth with only primary education.

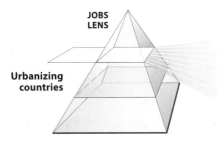

JOBS LENS

Urbanizing countries

Jobs providing opportunities for women
Jobs moving the country up the export ladder
Jobs not leading to excessive congestion
Jobs integrating rural migrants

Resource-rich countries

Investments in extractive industries can represent a sizable fraction of a developing country's GDP and lead to spectacular increases in export revenue, but they do not create many jobs. The number of people at work during the construction phase may be sufficient to generate dynamism at the local level, but once the mines and fields are in operation, employment goes down dramatically. Perhaps the most extreme example is the liquid natural gas project in Papua New Guinea. The investment cost of the project exceeded twice the country's GDP at project start-up, and the project may lead to double-digit growth rates for many years. But it is unlikely to generate more than 1,000 direct jobs in the longer term (table 6.1).

Links to the rest of the economy tend to be weak as well. Port facilities, transport corridors, and logistical, financial, and accounting services are needed. In some cases, oil refining and ore processing can also be carried out within the country. All these services are bound to generate high-value-added jobs in major cities and hubs. But even after including all backward and forward links, the ratio between the total number of jobs generated and the number of direct jobs is likely to remain in the single digits. Taking into account direct and indirect job effects, extractive industries may not account for more than 1 or 2 percent of total employment in resource-rich developing countries.

In addition, extractive industries can have important negative impacts on jobs elsewhere in the economy. These effects are often considered manifestations of Dutch disease, a reference to the experience of the Netherlands after large natural gas fields were discovered in the province of Groningen in the late 1950s. The ensuing export revenue led to strong real exchange rate appreciation, deterioration in competitiveness in sectors exposed to international competition, and a loss of jobs in these tradable sectors.

Some industrial countries confronted with resource booms have successfully protected or fostered the diversification of their economies. Norway offers what may be the most striking example. With strong backing from the labor movement, centralized collective-bargaining agreements ensure that real wages do not grow more rapidly than the productivity of the tradable sectors, excluding oil. Wage moderation supports employment opportunities for everybody, to the point that the unemployment rate remained close to 3 percent during the recent global financial crisis. Oil revenue is used for long-term investments but is not immediately converted into higher labor earnings.

Among oil-rich countries elsewhere, the United Arab Emirates has also managed to diversify its economy through financial and logis-

TABLE 6.1 *Projects in extractive industries are capital intensive and create few jobs*

Country	Project (sector or resource)	Investment, % of 2010 GDP	Direct employment, number
Papua New Guinea	LNG Project (natural gas)	237.0	9,300 during construction; 1,000 afterward
Mongolia	Oyu Tolgoi (copper, gold)	74.2	14,800 during construction; 3,000 to 4,000 afterward
Botswana	Jwaneng Cut 8 Project (diamonds)	20.2	1,000
Papua New Guinea	Ramu Mine (nickel)	19.0	5,000 during construction; 2,000 afterward
Mozambique	Benga Mining (coal)	13.6	currently 150; 4,500 afterward
Tanzania	Mchuchuma (coal)	12.2	5,000
Namibia	Husab Mine (uranium)	11.9	5,200 during construction; 1,200 afterward
Zambia	Lumwana Mine (copper)	9.3	4,700 during construction
Pakistan	Reko Diq Mining (copper, gold)	4.0	2,500 during construction; 200 afterward
Peru	Conga Mine (gold)	2.6	6,000 during construction; 1,700 afterward

Source: World Bank Development Report 2013 team based on project information.
Note: GDP = gross domestic product; LNG = liquid natural gas.

tics services. But overall, in the Gulf states, national citizens have become direct beneficiaries of the oil bonanza through well-paid jobs in the public sector. In the larger countries, these jobs are rationed, with some groups, such as women and youth, having less access than those with good connections. Menial jobs are performed by immigrants on temporary contracts who receive modest pay and benefits. Jobs are a window to rent sharing for some but do not give a stake in society to others.

This tension between jobs for productivity and jobs for social cohesion may be even more difficult to avoid in developing countries, because they lack the institutional strength of Norway or the implementation capacity of the United Arab Emirates. In resource-rich developing countries, the concern is not only about losing competitiveness in tradable sectors but also about missing out on the benefits of urbanization. Indeed, the price of land in major agglomerations becomes prohibitively high in resource-rich developing countries. By one measure, the most expensive city in the world is Luanda (table 6.2). According to this measure, 3 of the top 5, and 9 of the top 50 most expensive cities in the world are in resource-rich developing countries.

Because they do not have the economic density of London, New York, or Tokyo, cities in resource-rich developing countries find it difficult to reap the benefits of agglomeration. Specialization in the production of commodities (including agricultural products such as cocoa) may be an important reason why urbanization has failed to deliver growth in countries in Sub-Saharan Africa.[40] These wealthy consumption agglomerations are nonetheless attracting rural migrants, thereby fueling local inequality, discontent, and crime. None of the cities in resource-rich developing countries among the top 50 in the world according to cost of living is among the top 50 according to quality of life.

While extractive industries fail to create many jobs, they do contribute to the local economy through other channels. A recent survey of employees of large-scale mining projects in Papua New Guinea shows that they make remittances both in kind and in cash to their households. Most remittances in kind were for construction and building materials (41 percent), followed by transport-related items (28 percent).[41] Cash contributions were used most often for school fees (29 percent) and transportation-related items (12 percent). Employees also reported accommodating relatives visiting from rural areas. Some of their guests helped with housework, and some obtained education at the host's expense.[42]

TABLE 6.2 *Cities in resource-rich developing countries are among the most expensive in the world*

Rank in 2011	City	Country
1	Luanda	Angola
2	Tokyo	Japan
3	N'Djamena	Chad
4	Moscow	Russian Federation
5	Geneva	Switzerland
12	Libreville	Gabon
14	Sydney	Australia
18	London	United Kingdom
23	Niamey	Niger
27	Paris	France
29	St. Petersburg	Russian Federation
32	New York	United States
41	Lagos	Nigeria
44	Khartoum	Sudan
48	Baku	Azerbaijan
50	Amsterdam	Netherlands

Source: Mercer 2011.
Note: Cities are ranked from most to least expensive based on the cost of a consumption basket for expatriates. Cities from developing countries are highlighted.

Artisanal mining can flourish in parallel with major investments and raise the living standards of local communities. In Papua New Guinea, the number of grassroots alluvial miners is two to three times greater than the number of people working in the formal extractive industries sector, even if contractors and temporary workers are counted among the latter. Some of the large extractive projects, such as Ok Tedi Mine, happen to be in poor areas. Thus, the artisanal mining taking place around them helps spread the wealth.

But poverty maps show a significant level of spatial dispersion in living standards and a persistence of poverty over the past three decades.[43] The deepest and most persistent rural poverty in Papua New Guinea occurs in areas with no known mineral resources.

When large extractive projects close, artisanal and small-scale mining can also contribute to the local economy by cushioning the decline in earnings. For example, in Misima in Papua New Guinea, local people had become used to making a living around the only large mine project, Misima Mines Limited. When the project closed in 2004, the economy of Misima ground to a halt, and local residents found it hard to make ends meet. Artisanal and small-scale mining provided an avenue for income

for some: each hard rock miner could earn the equivalent of US$50,000–$75,000 a year, and each alluvial miner could make around US$10,000 a year. This income became the main contribution to the local economy, together with remittances sent by those ex-Misima Mines Limited employees who found work in large mines elsewhere.[44]

And even in mining areas, social impacts are more mixed than the positive effect on living standards suggests. The influx of money from mining enclaves has enabled men to pay high prices for brides and marry multiple wives on an unprecedented scale, which might have contributed to a decline in women's status. Around Porgera Mine, the abandonment of older wives and the increasing number of women taken from other tribal groups are considered factors in the increased incidence of domestic violence and tension with neighboring groups. In Lihir, when groups of landowners received compensation and royalty payments, no women were given authority to control the accounts.[45] In addition, children normally help out in artisanal and small-scale mines. In Misima, because of clear restrictions and training by the Wau Small-Scale Mining Center, children are less involved in mining than before, but child labor remains a concern.[46] Finally, land disputes often take place among artisanal miners as people tend to trespass on other's land to find minerals.[47]

Beyond local communities, the boom in extractive industries is affecting jobs in the main agricultural sector of Papua New Guinea. Palm oil exports have been growing steadily in recent years and now exceed the exports of all other agricultural crops combined. Remarkably, the production of palm oil fruit involves 18,000 smallholder blocks around the main plantations.[48] While this sector makes a significant contribution to the economy, improving rural livelihoods and generating employment, the extractive industries boom is undermining the competitiveness of palm oil exports through higher wages for skilled employees and higher logistics costs.

The higher wages paid to skilled workers are also eroding the effectiveness of the public sector. Entire departments in government and in education and training institutions have been depleted because their staff leaves for more attractive opportunities in the extractive industries sector. Mining companies complain about the shortage of skills at the same time as they poach people away from the education and training system, where they could help build skills. For instance, among 181 interviewees in a recent survey on large-scale mining projects, 58 workers (or 32 percent) had at least a university degree.[49] Raising salaries in the public sector may be needed, but that would create other problems. Absenteeism is rife and service delivery is poor. Without strengthened accountability, higher salaries would only transform many public sector jobs into a window for rent sharing.

An encouraging development has been the success of some landowner companies around mining enclaves. These companies may have built up a good work ethic and developed effective business practices in places that were far removed from the modern economy only a few years ago. Not all landowner companies have been successful, however, and this model may fail to spread the wealth from extractive industries beyond the surrounding areas (box 6.6).

The challenge of resource-rich economies is often framed in terms of transparency, which is certainly important for social cohesion. However, accounting for the money involved in extractive industries is only part of the solution. Equally important is ensuring that resources flow from booming enclaves and hubs to the poorer parts of the country, especially in the form of basic infrastructure and service delivery. Focusing the flow of resources on the demand side rather than on the supply side (for example, on health insurance rather than public hospitals) may contribute to productivity rather than to the creation of new windows for rent sharing.

Beyond public finance, the concentration of wealth in mining enclaves and urban hubs requires attention to spatial pricing issues. The benefits of agglomeration cannot be reaped if urban land becomes prohibitively expensive. Active efforts are needed to increase the availability of urban land and keep urban housing affordable. Despite such efforts, the cost of labor is bound to be much higher in mining enclaves and urban hubs. Labor policies need to take these disparities into account and avoid making workers too expensive in poorer and more remote areas through minimum wages or mandated benefits that mimic the wages and benefits available in the booming parts of the country.

The main challenge facing resource-rich countries is to spread the wealth in ways that do not undermine productivity growth and social cohesion spillovers. Good jobs for development in this context are those that generate output (as opposed to just absorbing it) outside the extractive industries sector. Incentives for firms to create jobs and for people to work are important if the economy is going to diversify its export base. The abundance of foreign currency can be a constraint because of exchange rate appreciation. The experience of some countries, most notably Norway, shows how sovereign funds that are used for long-run investments can manage this foreign currency problem.

BOX 6.6 *Landowner companies can build capacity while spreading the wealth*

Firms linked to local landowner groups in Papua New Guinea are developing increasingly diversified businesses and are able to compete regionally, even nationally, thereby generating jobs with a range of skill levels. The origin of these firms is the communal ownership of land in Papua New Guinea, which has meant that mining companies have had to pay compensation for land to communities rather than to individuals. As a result, some of the landowner companies have up to 300,000 shareholders. National agencies negotiate with individual resources projects for local landowning groups to have privileged rights to supply selected services to the project.

The most successful landowner companies, including Trans Wonderland, Anitua, the iPi Group, National Catering, and Star Mountain, are locally managed. Their business activities extend beyond the core job streams of the extractive industries sector in exploration, construction, and extraction. For example, they provide logistical services through a franchise truck-ownership structure and catering services that reach out to all Papua New Guinea including to customers outside the natural resource sectors.

The key to the successes of these companies may be the clear separation between their social roles and their business model, which builds on solid corporate governance. The landowner origins and commercial focus allow them to partner with landowner groups in other resource project areas, which helps them to build scale and management depth. Expatriates with a genuine interest in development seem to have played an important part in achieving the proper balance.

Not all landowner companies have been equally successful. Most exist purely to distribute rents from mines to communities and have no ambitions of building sustainable economic opportunities for their members. Two of four companies established in Central Province never gained a foothold because the funds that were supposed to serve as equity vanished. Even the successful landowner companies may be unsustainable beyond the construction phase of extractive industries, during which the demand for support services is exceptionally high. Skeptics wonder whether building work skills through the development of these businesses is really more valuable than investing in service delivery through local infrastructure.

Source: Blacklock and Bulman 2012.

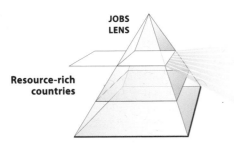

JOBS LENS

Resource-rich countries

Jobs supporting export diversification
Jobs not subsidized through transfers

Small island nations

The jobs agendas of small island nations are shaped by their market size and their geography. Because of their size, these countries cannot exploit economies of scale or reap the benefits of agglomeration or specialization. As islands, many of them are characterized by fragmentation—an already-small population spread thinly over large areas. For example, Fiji has a population of around 860,000 people and a total territory of 18,274 square miles, but this land is fragmented across a total 332 islands. Yet jobs in cities and clusters rely on scale and density to create positive spillovers.

With limited domestic markets, small island nations need to look outward to overcome problems of scale. Exporting to larger foreign markets is difficult, however, as the disadvantage of smallness manifests itself in the form of higher production costs. Given that small countries are price-takers in world markets, these cost premiums are hard to pass on to customers. The only way these economies can export is by accepting lower profits and labor earnings. But in industries such as electronic assembly and clothing, even if capital earns negative returns and wages are zero, the unit cost of production in a tiny economy would still exceed prevailing world prices.[50]

A number of small island nations, especially those located in the Pacific Ocean, are also confronted with the challenge of remoteness. When small islands are located far away from economic centers, the cost of trading with them may become prohibitive. In the case of Pacific island nations, the average GDP-weighted distance to trading partners is about 11,000 kilometers, compared with about 8,000 kilometers for small countries in the Caribbean (figure 6.3).[51] Not surprisingly, these Pacific island nations also trade less relative to other small countries.

Smallness and fragmentation further raise the costs of public services and infrastructure. A road, an energy network, or a government ministry that serves 100,000 people is likely to have a higher cost per user than one serving 10 million people. High fixed costs have to be spread across a smaller number of people, and often across a larger number of locations, which implies higher costs of doing business.

These geographic challenges are fundamental to the economic experience of these small island nations. Unfortunately, policies cannot alter these disadvantages, but they can be partially offset through integration with bigger economies. Canada's seasonal agricultural worker program with Caribbean and Latin American countries is an example. Several other similar bilateral agreements have been introduced.[52] In fact, tighter political relationships with large economic centers are found to be associated with higher income levels among small island nations.[53]

Migration is one of the key channels for economic integration. As workers move to larger economic centers, they gain access to larger markets, cheaper inputs, and more investment. Thus, the labor force is put to more productive use and can earn higher incomes. In turn, remittances from migrants improve living standards at home. Moving labor to larger markets also allows workers and entrepreneurs to interact with more dynamic firms, thus acquiring better and more diversified skills and gaining exposure to new ideas.

Emigrants account for over 20 percent of the total population in a majority of these countries. On average, remittances are responsible for over 8 percent of GDP in Pacific island countries and for 5 percent in other small island nations (figure 6.4). In fact, migration is behind several success stories. Samoa has a long history of migration into New Zealand, through a treaty of friendship in existence for more than 30 years, and the Cook Islands are in a free association with New Zealand. Both have been able to register sustained growth in contrast to the experiences of other Pacific island nations.[54]

It may take time for the benefits from migration to materialize, as a comparison of Tonga and Fiji illustrates. Tonga has more than 40 years of substantial migration and receives large per capita remittance flows. In Fiji, international migration is a much more recent phenomenon. Household surveys show that more than 90 percent of households receive remittances in Tonga, compared with 43 percent of households in Fiji.[55]

The different historical paths influence the impact of migration on the domestic economy. In countries with a more mature migration, household behavior at home is more tilted toward business activities. In both Tonga and Fiji, migration and remittances lead to higher savings, but they have a different impact on household income generation. In Tonga, both the number of emigrants and the level of remittances received are associated with increasing income from business activities. In Fiji, by contrast, remittances do not seem to affect business income and have a negative relationship with wage earnings—as if migration just served as a substitute for wage employment in the domestic economy.[56]

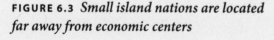

FIGURE 6.3 *Small island nations are located far away from economic centers*

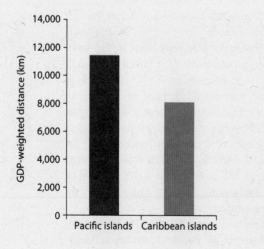

Source: Gibson 2006.

Note: GDP = gross domestic product; km = kilometer. The figure shows the weighted average distance from the islands to 218 other countries, weighted by the GDP of those countries.

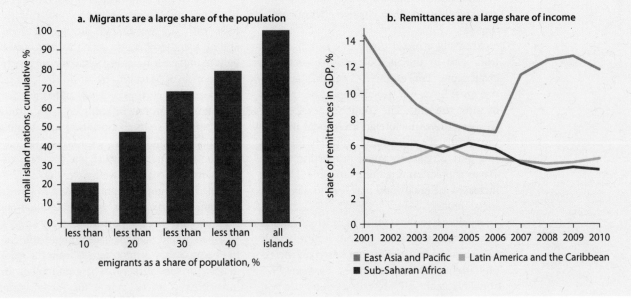

FIGURE 6.4 *Migration matters for small island nations, even more so in the Pacific*

a. Migrants are a large share of the population

b. Remittances are a large share of income

■ East Asia and Pacific   ■ Latin America and the Caribbean
■ Sub-Saharan Africa

Source: World Development Report 2013 team calculations based on World Bank migration database and remittances database.
Note: GDP = gross domestic product. Nineteen small island nations are included in panel a on migration and 15 small island nations in panel b on remittances. The variation of remittances in Pacific Island countries over time is driven by missing data from Samoa.

Migration does not always lead to a win-win situation, however. For example, large remittance flows raise the prospect of Dutch disease—the appreciation of the real exchange rate due to the abundance of foreign currency. Brain drain is also a salient feature in these countries, at least in the short term. Their migrants are more educated than their general population. In 12 of 19 small island nations, more than 30 percent of total emigrants are skilled workers; in 14 of them, skilled emigrants represent more than 40 percent of the domestic skilled population.[57] While these migrants experience large income gains, send substantial remittances back, and do transfer knowledge, they do not appear to trade with their home countries or invest in them to any large degree.[58] In Caribbean countries, the outmigration of health personnel has raised particular concerns because of its negative impact on health systems.

On the other hand, migration and remittances can promote human capital accumulation. The possibility to migrate may motivate greater investments in education, and remittances may finance them. Short-term migration can offer workers better training and education opportunities, which adds to domestic human

capital stock once the migrants return.[59] Evidence from Fiji suggests that migration opportunities increase the probability that household members will acquire tertiary education.[60] Results from qualitative surveys in Fiji also indicate that workers are prompted to acquire special skills for migration.[61]

Viable jobs in small islands are traditionally associated with the exploitation of natural resources including fisheries, forestry, mining, and tourism. When niche opportunities exist, low business costs become less critical for attracting investment. In Fiji, sugar production and tourism are the largest sources of employment. As the most important agribusiness, sugar production contributes about 8 percent of exports and employs over 10 percent of total population. Annually, half a million visitors come to Fiji, while the local population is less than one million. Tourism has become a main source of employment growth in the formal sector.[62]

The reliance on natural resources, however, raises the vulnerability of these countries. These sectors tend to be more susceptible to natural shocks—both natural disasters and volatile rainfall patterns. As with geographical disadvantages, policies cannot eradicate the vulnerability.

But jobs exploiting natural resources should not undermine the fragile ecosystem of the islands. When conducted in a sustainable manner, tourism and fisheries have positive environmental impacts.

Ensuring a broad distribution of the rents from jobs in the natural resource sectors is challenging. For example, Vanuatu's impressive growth has not had an impact on the lives of most residents. The country's development has been driven by foreign investment in tourism, financial services, and land development, and only a relatively small proportion of the urban population is reaping the gains. This has increased inequality and may lead to disruptive social trends.[63]

A closer look at the Mauritius miracle shows how small island nations might be able to diversify into activities not based on the exploitation of natural resources. Between 1977 and 2009, real GDP grew at 5.1 percent a year in Mauritius, compared with 3.2 percent for Sub-Saharan Africa overall. The World Economic Forum ranks Mauritius as the second-most-competitive country in the region. This sustained growth has been accompanied by a profound structural transformation over time. Poor at independence in 1968, Mauritius has transitioned from a sugar economy to manufacturing textiles and apparel to knowledge-intensive services in tourism, finance, and information communication technologies.[64]

Many explanations have been offered for the Mauritius miracle. There is no doubt that the focus on trade and foreign direct investment, and on using export processing zones to target light manufacturing industries, has been a critical element of Mauritius' success. The country also boasts low corruption levels and a favorable regulatory environment, coupled with strong public-private sector cooperation and flexible institutions.[65] But the circumstances that allowed Mauritius to embark on this remarkable development path were exceptional. They included the quota system that used to govern garment exports. Other small island nations may not enjoy such opportunities these days.

Small island nations face unique difficulties because they cannot benefit from the gains of scale or specialization. These difficulties are intensified in places such as the Pacific island countries, which are far from major centers of economic activity. The experience of Mauritius shows what might be possible with strategic policies, strong institution building, and a dose of luck. But for many small island states, establishing links with nearby economic centers, maximizing the benefits of migration, and exploiting niche markets while preserving their fragile ecosystem point the way forward.

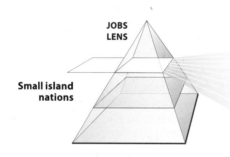

JOBS LENS

Small island nations

Jobs connected to global markets
· Jobs not undermining fragile ecosystems

Countries with high youth unemployment

Young people are much more likely to be unemployed than older adults. In most countries, unemployment rates for youth, defined as 15–24 years old, are usually between two and three times the overall unemployment rate (figure 6.5). And the unemployment rate captures only one aspect of the problems young people face in their transition from school to work. In agrarian countries, for example, open unemployment is low and youth employment difficulties are likely to manifest themselves in poor job quality and low earnings. In countries with high youth unemployment, job quality may be a problem for those young people who do find work. In the Arab Republic of Egypt, informality is two times more common among 15- to 24-year-old workers than among 35- to 54-year-olds.[66] Highly segmented labor markets offer limited scope to make the transition from informal to formal jobs. In Tunisia, even in those sectors that largely employ youth labor, employment is often temporary and informal.[67]

The stakes in youth unemployment are high. Recent events in the Arab world and in southern Europe have highlighted the discontent of educated youth whose employment opportunities are falling short of expectations. The Arab Spring may boost transparency and accountability in the region, but if jobs do not follow, greater instability may result.[68] Youth employment problems have economic costs, not only in the short run but also in the longer term. Unemployment among young people can lead to permanent scarring effects in the form of lower future earnings.[69] The lack of job opportunities may also lead to discouragement. Some of the decline in youth unemployment in the aftermath of the global crisis is actually driven by young people dropping out of the labor force.[70]

Many countries with youth unemployment problems have very large youth cohorts. In Zimbabwe, where 43 percent of the working-age population is between 15 and 24, the youth unemployment rate is three times higher than the overall unemployment rate. The Middle East and North Africa, which has especially high youth unemployment, is an overwhelmingly young region. More than 100 million people are between the ages of 15 and 29, making up 30 percent of the region's population and about 47 percent of the working-age population. Youth cohorts this large are not only likely to face higher unemployment rates but also tend to exert downward pressure on labor earnings.[71]

But demography is far from the whole story. Not all countries with pressing youth employment problems have "youth bulges." In Sri Lanka, less than one-quarter of the working age population is between 15 and 24, but the youth unemployment rate is more than three times the overall rate. And even where youth cohorts are large, young people may encounter other barriers to employment. Poor information on job seekers and on employment opportunities is one reason why young people face more difficulties than adults in finding jobs. Where private and public agencies and other sources of labor market information are not well developed, personal networks are important for match-

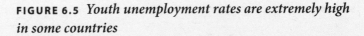

FIGURE 6.5 *Youth unemployment rates are extremely high in some countries*

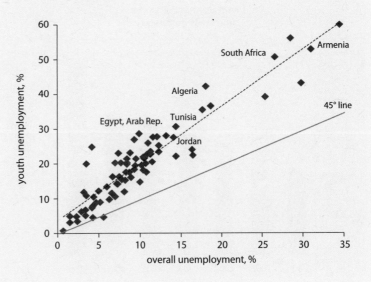

Source: World Development Indicators, World Bank, Washington, DC.
Note: Unemployment rates are averages for 2000–10.

ing people and jobs. A majority of workers in most Middle Eastern and North African countries have found their jobs through family and friends.[72] Adults tend to have better networks than young people going through the transition from education to employment. If a large percentage of a person's network is unemployed, the chances of that person finding a job are low.

A skills mismatch is the other common explanation. Close to 40 percent of the firms surveyed through investment climate assessments in the Middle East and North Africa report that the limited availability of skilled labor is a major constraint on business. Lack of formal schooling, which has increased substantially in the region, is not the cause. In fact, youth unemployment rates tend to rise with educational attainment in many countries. In Morocco, young people with a university education had an unemployment rate in 2009 of 17 percent, 3.7 times the rate for those with primary education or less. In Tunisia, 23 percent of university-educated youth were unemployed in 2010, compared with 11 percent for nongraduates.[73] In Tunisia, it takes graduates 28 months on average to find a job, compared with 19 months for nongraduates.[74] Not only has un-

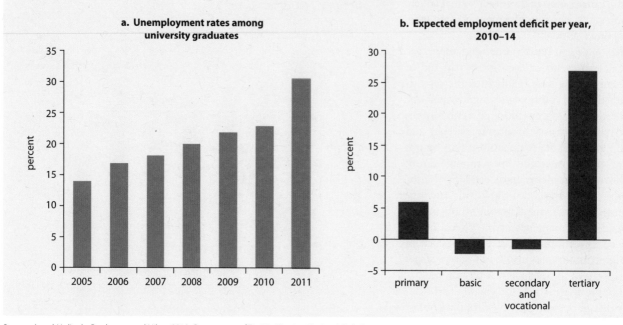

FIGURE 6.6 *Having higher education does not bring better employment chances in Tunisia*

Sources: Angel-Urdinola, Brodmann, and Hilger 2010; Government of Tunisia, L'Institut National de la Statistique.
Note: The employment deficit indicates the difference between predicted annual labor force increase and predicted annual employment increase for the 2010–14 period.

employment been increasing, but the employment deficit is expected to grow more among university graduates than among people with less education (figure 6.6).

The paradox of high unemployment among the highly educated is related to the growth path of countries in the Middle East and North Africa, where the civil service and state-owned enterprises have long been the employers of choice and education systems were built to feed them with staff. Students aspire to public sector jobs, where benefits are generous and employment is stable, and focus on obtaining academic credentials rather than skills that enhance employability.[75] There is a striking difference between the preferred educational path of youth in the region and that of youth in the high-performing East Asian countries. In 2009, one-quarter or less of the university students in Algeria, Lebanon, and Saudi Arabia were majoring in science, technology, or engineering.[76] In some East Asian countries, such as China, the Republic of Korea, and Malaysia, that share was more than two-fifths.[77]

Prescriptions on how to address the jobs challenge in countries with high youth unem-

ployment usually build on these two explanations. The poor flow of information between employers and jobseekers is seen as a justification for active labor market policies that focus on improving the match between labor supply and demand. Counseling can help jobseekers understand what they have to offer and where the opportunities are. Temporary employment programs may provide a first job and make employers realize the value of a young worker. As for skills, the contrast between high educational attainment and high unemployment rates is seen as an indication of a disconnect between the quality and relevance of schooling and the actual needs of the labor market. Improving youth employment prospects, it is argued, will critically depend on restructuring education and training systems to produce marketable skills rather than credentials.[78] In the short term, training programs are indeed the most obvious response to provide unemployed youth with the practical skills employers need.

The potential impact of these prescriptions is limited, however. Better information, counseling, and temporary employment programs can certainly help some jobseekers, but whether they would make a major dent in the aggregate unemployment rate is unclear. Better matches between jobseekers and employment opportunities would result in large increases in total employment only if there were many unfilled vacancies. But that is not the case in the Middle East and North Africa. Part of the high unemployment rate among graduates stems from the fact that the demand for skilled labor derives mainly from public administration, where growth is constrained by budgetary issues, and by increasing privatization and deregulation.[79] Meanwhile, the main sources of private sector growth (such as construction and low-value-added services) demand unskilled workers, for the most part.[80]

The problem is similar with training programs. Educated youth have the capacity to learn quickly. If employers wanted it, they could even provide on-the-job training as needed. But training may not change aspirations.

Despite its diminishing absorption capacity, the public sector in the Middle East and North Africa region remains the main client of the higher education system and thus shapes student expectations and choices. The public sector still accounts for about one-third of overall employment in countries such as the Arab Republic of Egypt, Iraq, Jordan, and the Republic of Yemen.[81] In some of these countries, public sector employment has recorded modest growth in recent years, but budgetary pressures will inevitably result in a severe contraction in the future. Aspirations remain, however, and, for many of the unemployed youth who have pursued university education in the expectation of getting a public sector job, there is a sense of a broken promise.

Information, counseling, and training are unlikely to overcome this frustration. Addressing the jobs challenge of countries with high youth unemployment rates requires a dynamic private sector that can create employment opportunities commensurate with the education and aspirations of new entrants to the labor market.

Growth alone may not be enough. After all, few countries have had a better economic performance than Tunisia, the first country in the Arab world in which jobs discontent erupted into political turmoil. Between 2000 and 2010, its GDP expanded at an average annual rate of almost 5 percent; meanwhile, the overall unemployment rate remained at 14 percent or above, and the rate for university graduates exceeded 30 percent.

The key questions are why growth in Tunisia and other countries with high youth unemployment has not been more labor intensive and why the sectors that have expanded the most rely on unskilled workers. The answers may be in the product market more than in the labor market. Although many countries in the region have implemented reforms to reduce red tape and improve the overall business climate, discretion, arbitrariness, and unequal treatment still hinder competition and private sector development, especially in skills-intensive sectors such as telecommunications. In many countries in the Middle East and North Africa, connections with political power may matter more for success than entrepreneurial capacity.[82] The perks often extend to the workers in these cosseted businesses, under the form of job security and other benefits, adding to the frustration of those left out.

Firm dynamics provide some evidence of the difficulties associated with job creation and employment growth in these countries. Rates of new firm registration are low in most countries in the region.[83] And even when they do get started, small firms face barriers in growing into sizable companies. The vast majority of Tunisian formal firms are small: 86 percent of them are one-person entities, and only 0.4 percent have 100 workers or more. But these large firms account for more than one-third of all jobs, more than all the one-person firms combined. A study of their dynamics over a decade shows that micro- and small firms hardly ever become large firms. Moreover, one-person firms only very rarely graduate into the small size category, and many are likely to shut down.[84]

While countries with high youth unemployment may face a large youth bulge or education quality issues, problems are often on the demand side, with limited competition reducing employment opportunities, especially for highly skilled youth. Many countries in the Middle East and North Africa would have greater scope to generate more jobs for young people if the barriers to firm entry and growth were eased. This prospect is unlikely to materialize, however, as long as political connections remain more important than entrepreneurial capacity to enter into the modern sector. Ending privilege, more than improving labor market matching or upgrading skills, is thus the priority for countries with high youth unemployment. Dynamism in more skills-intensive sectors would lead to faster growth by putting educated youth to work. It would result in higher living standards by reducing the burden protected activities put on others. And it would reinforce a sense of fairness in society—a sense that young people can get ahead by what they know rather than who they know.

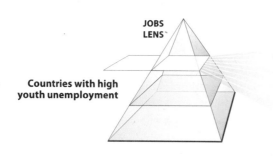

JOBS LENS

Countries with high youth unemployment

Jobs not supported through rents
Jobs not allocated on the basis of connections

Formalizing economies

The challenge of formalization is present in economies where a large share of the labor force is already covered by labor legislation and social protection programs, and reaching universal coverage seems attainable. But going in that direction raises serious tradeoffs. Formalization is often seen as necessary to strengthen social cohesion. It is also bound to increase the living standards of those who get under the purview of labor law and gain access to social protection. But formalization may reduce productivity if it distorts incentives or puts a burden on firms.

Formalizing economies are characterized by already large or growing urban populations where many residents have incomes well above poverty levels, yet where many still work in informal employment. The emerging middle classes in these economies demand advanced public services, including tertiary education, health care, and pensions. They are often frustrated by poor governance. They may perceive taxes and public sector benefits as useless or unfair and resent the weak physical and institutional infrastructure, as well as the excessive regulatory load. These frustrations beget avoidance and evasion of regulations, and, in such a climate, informal jobs not only persist but can even proliferate.[85]

This state of affairs, sometimes described as an informality trap, reflects a weak social contract.[86] That a large share of a country's urban labor force is informal is sometimes interpreted as a sign that the state is unable to enforce regulations and citizens are unwilling to comply with them.[87]

The prevalence of informal employment in these relatively advanced economies can nurture poverty and social exclusion.[88] Almost by definition, informal workers lack legal job protections and social insurance coverage, making them more vulnerable to workplace abuses, health risks, and the vagaries of the business cycle. Informal workers face a higher probability of poverty and often perceive themselves as poor.[89] Men represent a majority of informal workers, but the probability for them to work in the informal sector is generally lower than for women, making informality another source of gender inequality. In Peru, informality rates are 76 and 66 percent for women and men, respectively. In South Africa, the corresponding rates are 37 and 30 percent. The Arab Republic of Egypt is a notable exception, with rates of 23 and 54 percent, respectively.[90]

Informality is also associated with low productivity. Most informal workers are either self-employed or work for small unregistered firms, with low capital per worker, limited technology, and no scale economies. In Turkey, the differential in total factor productivity between formal and informal firms is 19 percent in manufacturing and 62 percent in services.[91] A study in six Latin American countries finds that labor productivity is 30 percent higher in formal firms than in informal firms.[92] The use of public services by the informal sector, without proper tax contributions, puts a burden on formal firms and lowers their productivity as well.[93]

It does not follow that formalization alone would increase productivity. Evidence shows that firms do not become more profitable simply by formalizing.[94] Low productivity may reflect self-selection by workers and firms, who choose whether to formalize depending on the balance between the associated benefits and costs. For many workers, the poor quality of social protection and the possibility of relying on others in case of adverse shocks may make informal sector employment a preferred alternative. An analysis of labor market dynamics in Brazil and Mexico confirms that a substantial part of the informal sector workforce, particularly the self-employed, appears to voluntarily exit from the formal sector.[95] Self-selection also occurs in the case of firms. A business tax reduction and simplification adopted in Brazil in 1996 led to a significant increase in formality among microenterprises.[96] In other cases, workers with limited access to asset accumulation find themselves trapped in low-productivity informal jobs or use this sector as a last resort to escape unemployment. In Colombia and Argentina, evidence shows that a large share of workers, particularly low-skill workers, are systematically less likely to work in the formal sector despite being willing to work in it.[97] In any case, informality is clearly a multilayered phenomenon with some workers trapped in this sector and others self-selecting into it.[98]

Personal views about informality are actually very diverse.[99] For example, some participants in a focus group of young women from a better-off neighborhood in Durban, South Africa, associated good jobs with formal occupations such as doctor, lawyer, teacher, nurse, or police woman: "Being a police-woman is a good way to make a living because they get benefits and they help protect the community." Other participants, from a poorer neighborhood, identified good jobs as those in farming ("because you can sell the veggies") or sewing ("because you can make a lot of money"). But other informal sector jobs were seen as bad because they involved financial precariousness and hard working conditions. Among them were working as a domestic worker ("because you have to go door to door asking people if they have a job for you. . . . [They] would pay you R30 and say because you are just helping") or cutting grass ("because

you have to go around asking people if you can cut their yard . . . and you work in the sun").

In the long run, the informal sector tends to be larger in countries where labor productivity is lower, government services are weaker, and the business environment is less flexible.[100] A controversial question is how much labor market and business regulations actually contribute to informality.[101] Responses by firms surveyed in investment climate assessments suggest that labor legislation is not necessarily the main cause of informality, not because the laws and regulations are irrelevant, but because they are regarded with irreverence. Corruption and taxations are seen as the most vexing obstacles firms face (figure 6.7). Recent research also indicates

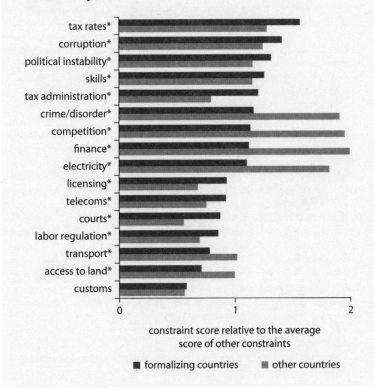

FIGURE 6.7 *Labor regulation may not be the biggest obstacle to formalization*

constraint score relative to the average score of other constraints

■ formalizing countries   ■ other countries

Source: Investment Climate Survey (database), World Bank, Washington, DC.
Note: Formalizing countries in the sample include Albania, Argentina, Armenia, Azerbaijan, Brazil, Cape Verde, Chile, Colombia, Costa Rica, Ecuador, Georgia, Guyana, Kazakhstan, the Kyrgyz Republic, the former Yugoslav Republic of Macedonia, Mauritius, Mexico, Moldova, Mongolia, Panama, Peru, the Philippines, Romania, the Russian Federation, Serbia, Turkey, Ukraine, Uruguay, Vanuatu, and República Bolivariana de Venezuela. The horizontal axis measures the ratio of the average score of a constraint to the average score of all other constraints. The asterisk denotes statistical significance of the difference between formalizing economies and others at the 1 percent level.

BOX 6.7 *The debate on how to reduce informality is intense in Mexico*

Having at least one member working in the formal sector allows Mexican families to have a regular source of income, health coverage for all, and, through these, access to the support of social networks. A case study, based on both ethnographic and statistical evidence, makes the case that households whose members fail to secure formal jobs are more likely to fall into poverty because of the risk of catastrophic health expenses. They are also less likely to secure social support from relatives and neighbors.[a] Formal employment is thus critical for living standards in Mexico.

Despite a GDP per capita around US$14,000 in purchasing power parity terms, Mexico's informal employment has ranged from 50 to 62 percent of total employment depending on the definition used. This rate is considered high given the country's development level and has not shown consistent signs of decline in nearly two decades. Several studies argue that restrictive labor legislation is a factor explaining Mexico's large informal economy.[b] The country has tried unsuccessfully to reform its main labor law, which was enacted in 1973 and which is tied to rights enshrined in the 1917 constitution.

Weak enforcement is another factor behind informality in Mexico. The government announced a doubling of inspectors at the Ministry of Labor in 2012, from 300 to 600. This number still compares unfavorably with other countries.[c] Labor courts are also overstretched: cases may take between three and six years to reach a conclusion.[d]

This stagnation in the reform of legislation and enforcement contrasts with the expansion of a successful cash transfer program, Oportunidades, and a noncontributory social insurance program,

Seguro Popular. Oportunidades covers nearly one-fifth of the total population and nearly all the rural poor, making it one of the best-targeted poverty reduction programs in the country. Seguro Popular is the most rapidly growing program, claiming a coverage of more than 50 million by April 2012.[e] But some preliminary research finds that non-contributory programs in general, and Seguro Popular, in particular, may induce informality or, at least, discourage formal employment.[f]

Meanwhile, the debate about the universalization of health insurance is very much alive in Mexico. Academics and policy makers argue over it, and it is also a topic of political controversy. Much pivots on how much universalization will cost. Estimates vary widely from no incremental costs because of efficiency and tax collection gains to relatively large costs when accounting for long-term demographic changes. These differences originate from different methodologies, which indicate the complexity of the topic and the difficulty in gauging the full implications of the reform.[g]

Mexico's debate on formalization needs to be cast in a broader context. In recent years, poverty and unemployment have increased while real wages have been stagnant. But other measures of well-being, such as access to education, health, and social security, have continued to improve.[h] Average productivity has been growing, but slowly, which can be due to an excessive churning of jobs and firms.[i] Demographic trends still show high fertility rates for a large share of the population, which leads to a social reproduction of poverty and informality.[j] Whether sweeping changes in labor and tax legislation as well as in the organization of social protection would substantially reduce informality is still an open question.

Source: World Development Report 2013 team.

a. Gonzalez de la Rocha 2012.
b. Botero and others 2004; Heckman and Pagés 2004; Levy 2008; Venn 2009.
c. Brazil has 3,000 inspectors, according to Pires (2011); France has 2,100, according to Piore and Schrank (2008). Piore and Schrank (2007) estimate that while Mexico has 1.72 inspectors per 100,000 workers, Brazil has 2.45, Argentina 3.05, and Chile 19.25.
d. Kaplan, Sadka, and Silva-Mendez 2008.
e. http://www.seguro-popular.gob.mx.
f. Aterido, Hallward-Driemeier, and Pagés 2011.
g. Anton, Hernandez, and Levy 2012, Perry and others 2007; Villarreal 2012.
h. Villarreal and Rodriguez-Oreggia 2012.
i. Calderon 2012.
j. Martinez and Aguilera 2012.

that it is business regulations, more than labor regulations, that help explain changes in informality and unemployment.[102]

Addressing the jobs challenge faced by formalizing economies requires extending social protection and the purview of labor laws without choking off economic dynamism. Previous attempts by Latin American countries to formalize through heavy-handed regulation, mandated benefits, and ill-designed social insurance programs led to populist enthusiasm but also to lower productivity and eventually to economic stagnation and poor quality of social protection.

Efforts to reduce informality have taken a new twist in recent years. In several Latin American countries, sweeping changes in the organization of social protection are being implemented or proposed. First, transfer programs have escalated. Brazil and Mexico introduced cash transfer programs in the late 1990s that now cover nearly one-fifth of their populations.[103] Brazil, Chile, and Mexico have also introduced noncontributory programs for senior citizens, and other countries are following suit. More radically, policy makers are debating whether to make the coverage of social insurance universal, moving away from the current contributory systems toward the funding of benefits from general tax revenue.[104] This reform would certainly expand the number of beneficiaries, but whether it would encourage firms to formalize is a matter of intense debate, especially in Mexico (box 6.7).[105]

So far, few countries have managed to substantially reduce informality. Rapid growth and strengthening institutions in Brazil and Chile have made them recent exceptions. In both cases, changes in labor market regulation have had limited effect. Patient accumulation of human capital and sustained growth have paid off. But strengthened rule of law, effective policies, and a better perception of the role of the state have also helped.

Those who see informality as the outcome of a weak social compact argue that the way forward involves a combination of enhanced enforcement of regulations, improved quality of public services, and greater policy coherence.[106] If informality is associated with production units that evade, elude, or stay outside regulation, a three-pronged strategy may be warranted.[107] For those who clearly work outside the purview of regulations, the reach of human development and social protection services and activation policies should be expanded. For those who work in stunted firms that legally avoid becoming formal, regulations should be simplified and their burden eased. Finally, for those in firms that evade regulations, enforcement should be strengthened. For this three-pronged strategy to have a chance of success, workers and employers need to perceive the state as a reliable and fair partner. If the state is not able to generate a sense of trust through the provision of efficient and good-quality services, neither regulatory reform nor increased enforcement will succeed in increasing formalization substantially.

The key is to build formal institutions and programs that are not too costly and that are valued by workers. The jobs agenda of formalizing economies is closely linked, then, to the development of effective regulation and social protection systems.

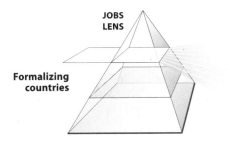

JOBS LENS

Formalizing countries

Jobs with affordable social benefits
Jobs not creating gaps in social protection coverage

Aging societies

Declining fertility rates and, in many countries, rising life expectancy have led to rapidly aging populations in several regions of the world. Today's aging societies are concentrated in industrial countries, in Eastern Europe, and in the Southern Cone of Latin America. China entered the aging phase in 2010; and India, the Islamic Republic of Iran, Singapore, and Thailand will experience significant aging in the relatively near future.[108]

The old-age dependency ratio measures the number of people 65 years or older in relation to the number of people in the working-age population (15 to 64 years). When this ratio is high, the working-age population faces pressure to generate income to meet the needs of the elderly generation. The old-age dependency ratio in the Islamic Republic of Iran and in Singapore will rise almost fivefold between now and 2050. These two countries will have four and six elderly people, respectively, for every ten 15- to 64-year-olds. China's old-age dependency ratio will rise by a factor of almost four. Many already aging societies in Eastern Europe as well as in Argentina, Chile, and Uruguay, will experience a rise in the ratio—a doubling or even more in most cases—between now and 2050.

The reasons for these surges in dependency ratios vary across countries. In most, the elderly live longer; in some, there are fewer people of working age. Low fertility rates in Bulgaria contributed to a population decline of 15 percent

FIGURE 6.8 *The labor force will shrink if age-specific participation rates remain constant*

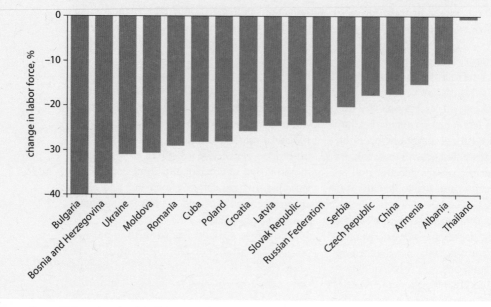

Source: World Development Report 2013 team based on United Nations population statistics.
Note: The simulation assesses the decrease in the total labor force based on the assumption that age-specific labor force participation rates remain constant between 2011 and 2050.

between 1990 and 2010—and by 2050, the country is projected to have lost almost 40 percent of its population compared with its peak in the mid-1980s. Other Eastern European countries, such as Bosnia and Herzegovina, Moldova, Romania, and Ukraine, are expected to follow the same pattern; China's population will be 50 million less in 2050 than it is now. In India and Singapore and in the Southern Cone countries of Latin America, population growth is slowing down and will start to decline by the middle of the century.

If the labor force participation rates of older workers are significant today and if these levels can be maintained, the impact of aging on average income can be cushioned considerably. But that may not be enough. If age-specific participation rates remain constant, some countries, such as Thailand, would be able to limit the absolute decline in its labor force, but many others would not. The impact in many Eastern European countries, Cuba, and China would be stark because of the decline in the size of the working age population. Between 2011 and 2050, Bulgaria would face a 40 percent drop in

its workforce, Poland 28 percent, and China 17 percent (figure 6.8).[109]

Aging affects jobs through several channels.[110] Lower fertility may imply higher numbers of women ready to seek and take up jobs, although little evidence of this has been observed in Eastern Europe over the past 20 years. Smaller cohorts of young people could reduce innovative capacity. Disability rates increase in older age groups and thus further affect the labor supply in aging populations.[111] Understanding how aggregate savings will be affected is also important, given that savings drive investment, growth, and job creation. Savings typically decline among older age groups. This decline could be offset if young people were to build up additional buffers to support their longer life spans, especially if public retirement schemes prove unsustainable or are absent. Expenditure patterns also vary with age. The rapid rise in the long-term care industry in high-income countries is an example. In the United States, the industry now counts more than 3 million formal jobs, and an estimated 10 million Americans 50 years or older (roughly one-quarter of this age group) provide care to one or both of their parents.[112]

Raising productivity is ultimately essential for maintaining living standards in aging societies where fewer people are working. In many Eastern European countries, the productivity gains required would be substantial (figure 6.9). If they do not materialize, falling living standards will threaten those population groups that are vulnerable to poverty.[113]

Through jobs, aging also impacts intergenerational relations and social cohesion. Migration and aging have put stress on the traditional family-based support systems for China's rural elderly, raising the possibility that they will have to continue working at later ages and will not have assistance, financial or otherwise, from their children.[114] The older generation can feel not only neglected, but also excluded. In Poland, a 55-year old man felt that "age is a great barrier. I've submitted my CV and they tell me I am too old, they tell me if you were 35 years old we could hire you. I have 20 years of experience and they expect me to be 35 years old?"[115]

Social security and health systems in many aging middle- and higher-income countries are barely sustainable as currently designed. Systems inspired by the Bismarckian model, where social welfare and insurance are financed through labor taxes on a pay-as-you-go basis, are particularly vulnerable. A decline in the contribution base shrinks the resources available for pensions and health care at the same time that an increasing elderly population makes more claims on both systems. The health care cost for people age 70 years and above, with higher disability prevalence rates, is two to three times higher than the cost for people of prime working age.[116] While education expenditures may fall in many aging countries in the medium term, that in itself will bring about further—and often painful—adjustments as schools close and teachers lose their jobs.

The magnitude of adjustments needed in social welfare systems is daunting. In a representative Eastern European country, the public pension system alone could reach a deficit of almost 7 percent of GDP in 2050 compared with 2 percent today.[117] To balance the accounts, the retirement age would need to increase or the ratio of pension benefits to earnings at retirement would have to be cut, or some combination of the two. Such changes could cause mate-

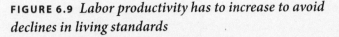

FIGURE 6.9 *Labor productivity has to increase to avoid declines in living standards*

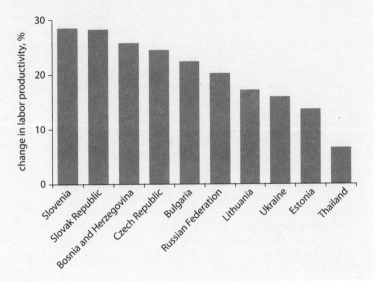

Source: World Development Report 2013 team based on United Nations population statistics and national household surveys.
Note: The simulation assesses the labor productivity increase necessary between 2011 and 2050 to maintain constant gross domestic product per capita given the expected decline in employment rates.

rial hardship for elderly people. The adjustment process itself is likely to be painful economically, socially, and politically. The experience of several high-income countries shows that implementing the necessary reforms can stretch social cohesion to the limit.

Aging also can make a society less mobile, which can have economic consequences. In Ukraine, for example, aging is taking place against a relatively high pre-crisis level of growth with very little creation of jobs. Some firms, though, are desperately looking for workers, both highly skilled and manual. The elderly are usually less mobile than the young, and the housing market makes changing residence difficult. Low internal mobility represents a significant bottleneck to increasing activity and raising productivity (box 6.8).

In aging societies like Ukraine, good jobs for development are those that keep labor force participation rates high, especially for the elderly. These jobs can contain the decline in average income while at the same time protecting the viability of the social insurance system, which, in many countries, is under significant fiscal stress. Through these two channels, such jobs would also contribute to supporting social cohesion.

BOX 6.8 *In Ukraine, the impact of aging is compounded by migration and declining fertility*

Ukraine's population is shrinking. This country, which stretches from the heavily industrialized Russian-speaking east to the more agricultural and predominantly Ukrainian-speaking west, was home to 52 million people when the Soviet Union broke apart. Today, there are 6 million fewer people; by 2050, the population will have fallen to 35 million. Fertility rates are sharply down, from about 2.0 at the end of the 1990s to below 1.5 today, albeit with an upward tick in recent years. The elderly dependency ratio is 22 percent and will reach more than 40 percent over the next 30 years.

The effect of this population aging on jobs is amplified by international migration. Between the turbulent transition years and the middle of the last decade, about 2.5 million Ukrainians emigrated, mainly to the Russian Federation and Western Europe. Every year, around 80,000 people leave the country,[a] and recent studies have shown that the possible positive impacts of migration through remittances, return migration, and diaspora involvement have not (yet) shown their desired impacts.[b] People ages 25–29 years, especially women, are withdrawing in large numbers from the labor market: the female participation rate dropped from 78.1 percent to 70.9 percent between 2001 and 2010.[c]

Achieving high degrees of efficiency in the labor market is key to counterbalancing the impact of aging. But regional labor markets show little integration, as reflected by the high dispersion of unemployment rates. In some parts of the country, employers complain bitterly about the lack of workers with adequate skills, and at the same time they cannot fill available unskilled jobs. Yet, internal mobility is low in Ukraine by international standards and has declined in recent years. The lack of affordable housing has emerged as major barrier to mobility, also hindering registration for benefits in new locations. Rental property is scarce, often expensive, and can absorb up to 50 percent of household incomes in the big cities.[d]

Eventually, Ukraine may face a vicious jobs circle. A declining labor force and a lackluster productivity performance put the social insurance and welfare systems at risk of becoming unsustainable. The inability to provide benefits to an aging population, and the stress that reforming the system could bring about, could become a source of social tension. As participants in focus group discussions mentioned, this tension would be amplified by the perception that the distribution of jobs is unfair and that jobs in the public sector require bribes.[e] The decline in employment rates could also undermine civic engagement. Although low, the level of political and community participation among the employed is about twice as high as among the unemployed and 25 percent higher than among the inactive population.[f]

Source: World Development Report 2013 team.
a. World Population Prospects online database, United Nations, Geneva.
b. Ukraine country case study for the World Development Report 2013.
c. Statistical Service of Ukraine.
d. Komarov 2011.
e. Ukraine country case study for the World Development Report 2013.
f. Ukraine country case study for the World Development Report 2013.

The development of home-care models for the elderly can also support the twin objectives of keeping a high employment rate and containing social insurance costs. Proactively attracting—and integrating—migrants and managing to create virtuous circles with the diaspora promises equally large returns.

Measures such as raising the retirement age can contribute to labor force participation and financing of the welfare system, but not all groups have the same life expectancy. Typically, professional, technical, and skilled workers can expect to live longer than manual workers, especially those in hazardous occupations. Keeping the skilled at work longer is a way to increase average labor productivity and offset the decline in employment rates.

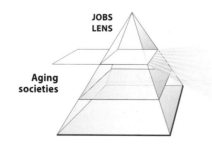

JOBS LENS

Aging societies

Jobs keeping the skilled active for longer
Jobs reducing the cost of services to the elderly

Creating an investment climate conducive to job creation in the private sector is a top policy priority. The question is whether the government should aim for a level playing field or focus its efforts on the specific areas, types of activities, firm sizes, and sectors with the greatest potential to create good jobs for development. Jobs challenges vary depending on a country's level of development, its endowments, its demography, and its institutions. Ensuring free entry and competition across all sectors is a fundamental requisite for growth. But given the often limited fiscal space and administrative capacity of developing countries, creating an enabling business environment across the entire economy can be challenging, and the relevant question is how policy priorities should be set.

The conventional wisdom views targeting with a skepticism that stems from often disastrous experiences with industrial policy. While targeting was common in Latin America during its import substitution phase, by the 1980s the consensus was that interventions favoring specific sectors led to rent seeking, economic stagnation, and external vulnerability. Slow growth in India until the 1990s was also attributed to policies that favored local industrial groups and undermined competition. The success of several East Asian countries in industrializing has reignited the debate on the merits of targeting and the role of the state, but the potential for institutional failures remains the main concern.[118] The dominant view holds that policy makers lack both the information and the capacity to "pick winners" when they select activities to target. In the absence of a solid information base, and taking into account the institutional failures common in developing countries, a risk exists that potential beneficiaries from targeted support could unduly influence the decision process.

Targeting is not necessarily industrial policy

The investment climate is the set of public goods and public policies that shape the opportunities and incentives for firms to invest productively, create jobs, and expand.[119] It encompasses a wide range of policy levers: ensuring stability and security, enhancing financial markets, providing infrastructure services, reducing regulatory and tax burdens, and improving the quality of the workforce. The natural inclination is to equate a targeted investment climate with industrial policy. If some activities result in large productivity spillovers (because of learning-by-doing, for instance, or because of greater specialization and integration), targeting can imply supporting such activities. In recent years, productivity spillovers associated with various activities have been reexamined from different viewpoints, with both academics and practitioners proposing practical approaches for their identification (box 6.9).

The targeting of the investment climate may not necessarily be aimed at industrial sectors, however. Targeting can focus on gender, as when policies aim to increase labor market participation by women, or on spatial concerns, as in urbanization policies or policies for regional development. Or it can focus on firm size, as when policies support the development of small and medium enterprises. Good jobs for development differ across countries. The jobs agenda may involve making smallholder farming more productive in an agrarian economy, preserving international competitiveness in a resource-rich country, or fostering competition in activities employing skilled labor in a country with high youth unemployment. In each case, the logic for targeting lies in tackling market imperfections or government failures that are preventing jobs from contributing more to development.

An example is targeting in the agricultural sector. The underlying logic is based on the notion of public goods. The biggest obstacles to agricultural development are the lack of appropriate technologies and adequate infrastructures. As arable land becomes scarce, the development of yield-enhancing technologies is indispensable.[120] But incentives to generate these technologies are undermined because they can be replicated freely.[121] Thus, public policy plays a role by supporting the development and dissemination of such technologies. Because yield-enhancing technologies are fertilizer intensive

BOX 6.9 *Once again, the debate rages over industrial policy*

Industrial policy is an approach to state economic stewardship in which direct support is given to particular sectors in pursuit of national goals. Industrial policy fell out of favor in the 1980s, but today it is getting recognition again. The emerging views, however, draw criticism and have led to a new round of debate.

Arguments for industrial policy rest on three types of market failures: knowledge spillovers and dynamic scale economies, coordination failures, and information externalities. In the first, industrial policy is derived from the observation that knowledge spillovers and dynamic scale economies differ across industries. Coordination failures arise when markets fail to correctly signal the future payoffs of investment projects, such as large-scale infrastructure projects, and the private sector tends to underinvest on its own. Information externalities exist when knowledge on the profitability of investment opportunities is limited and the risk of free riding discourages investment and innovation.

Building on these rationales, several approaches further develop thinking on industrial policy. The New Structural Economics stresses the shift in comparative advantage that results from changes in endowments. The large productivity spillovers from infrastructure and associated coordination failures justify a leading role for the state. To identify the industries to be supported, this approach proposes to learn from countries with similar endowments but somewhat higher income levels. Exports with a solid track record by these countries indicate which sectors could have a comparative advantage as the economy grows.[a]

A second approach emphasizes the policy process and especially public-private partnerships. In this view, the dialogue between the government and businesses can help to overcome coordination failures and elicit information from the private sector on the most relevant productivity spillovers.[b]

For a third school of thought, what matters is not just any coordination failure or externality, but spillovers of productive knowledge—mastering ways of doing things. Such knowledge is different from codified, public knowledge and is acquired and accumulated through experience. This approach claims that spillovers of productive knowledge associated with different industries can be sizable. To identify industries worth supporting, the approach proposes to rank products by how much productive knowledge is embedded in them and to focus on products that are similar to what is being produced currently but embody a higher knowledge content.[c]

Opponents of industrial policy cast doubts on its alleged rationales, but above all, they question the practicality of its implementation. For instance, while admitting the existence of potentially sizable knowledge spillovers and dynamic scale economies in certain industries, skeptics question the whether the public sector has the capacity to identify these industries. A related concern is the ability of the public sector to make industrial policy a dynamic process: applying credible sunset clauses to old industries, and reallocating resources to new industries. More generally, skeptics believe the knowledge and skill requirements for successful implementation exceed the capacity of the public sector.[d]

Source: World Development Report 2013 team.
a. Lin 2009, 2012; Lin and Monga 2011.
b. Harrison and Rodríguez-Clare 2010 ; Rodrik 2004, 2007.
c. Cimoli, Dosi, and Stiglitz 2009; Hausmann and others 2011; Nuebler 2011 .
d. Noland and Pack 2003; Pack and Saggi 2006.

and sensitive to the availability of water, public investments in infrastructure—including roads and irrigation facilities—are often essential. The Brazilian government, for example, viewed investment in adaptive agricultural research as a prerequisite for development. It therefore supported a research corporation (EMBRAPA) that focused on technology generation and transfer and played a critical role in the success of the Brazilian agribusiness sector.[122]

The emergence of dynamic cities is another case in point. From Dublin to Shanghai, competitiveness initiatives increasingly involve cities, more than countries. This shift is a result of agglomeration effects: the level playing field evokes a flat world, whereas urbanization policies correspond to a world with spikes of economic activity. Dynamic cities may offer more favorable tax treatment, easy access to land, simplified administrative procedures, and sup-

port for public-private partnerships. More efficient logistics and public investments in major infrastructure facilities usually complement the package of incentives. A recent version of spatial targeting is the idea of charter cities: to attract businesses to a country with low credibility in the eyes of foreign investors, sovereignty of a city could be handed over to another country in exchange for the enforcement of a credible set of rules.[123] The objective is to strengthen the investment climate in a small part of the country, potentially providing a demonstration effect for further reforms, while not threatening the rents of powerful local elites elsewhere.

The information base for targeting exists

When there is clarity on the challenges faced by a country, it is also possible to determine which types of jobs would help address these challenges. Thanks to efforts in research and data collection, the information set for deciding whether and how to support the creation of more of those good jobs for development is far from empty.

Consider jobs in farming. Among staple crops, rice, wheat, and maize are more promising than sorghum and millet, but the latter crops are grown in drier and harsher conditions where farmers are particularly poor.[124] Modern cereal varieties are high yielding primarily in favorable rain-fed and irrigated areas.[125] Thus, agricultural policies are bound to affect the well-being of the rural population differently in different regions. The choice depends on the country's natural endowments and societal goals.[126]

In nonagricultural sectors, the main obstacles to job creation can be identified through quantitative and qualitative assessments of the constraints faced by enterprises. While these assessments need to be interpreted with caution, differences in responses across enterprises reveal patterns that can also be used for developing targeted policy interventions (box 6.10).[127]

If creating competitive cities is a feature of a country's jobs agenda, enterprise surveys can provide information on how different the constraints faced by businesses are in cities of different sizes (figure 6.10a). If the jobs agenda requires the inflow of foreign direct investment, enterprise surveys indicate that foreign companies are less concerned about finance, but view customs administration, transportation, and licensing as more severe impediments to firm activity and growth (figure 6.10b). One country may choose to focus on microenterprises, because their success contributes to poverty reduction, and another on young and large firms, because they tend to be the most innovative. In both cases, enterprise surveys can be used to uncover the most relevant constraints (figure 6.10c, 6.10d). For example, shortages of skilled labor, delays in customs, and stringent labor regulations are viewed as more severe constraints by medium and large enterprises than by smaller companies. In contrast, micro- and small enterprises consider access to finance and competition to be more serious obstacles to their growth. Recently, enterprise surveys have been conducted for household enterprises operating in rural areas in selected countries. They can serve as additional tools for countries to foster nonagricultural sectors in rural areas.[128]

The effects of removing those constraints also differ across businesses. Reducing barriers to entry fosters the growth of industries that experience higher natural turnover rates. Improving access to finance stimulates the development

---

BOX 6.10 *Caution is needed when interpreting results from enterprise surveys*

Surveys of entrepreneurs and senior managers can provide feedback on what the private sector sees as significant constraints to private sector development. Some care in interpreting their responses is necessary, however. The respondents will give answers that reflect constraints on their bottom line—without regard to the broader societal or welfare implications. Almost every entrepreneur will complain that taxes and interest rates on loans are too high. But that does not necessarily mean that taxes should be lowered or that interest rates are out of line with risks faced by creditors. Constraints to the individual respondents need to be weighed against the broader social goals.

In addition, enterprise surveys only target incumbent enterprises. The surveys do not reach discouraged entrants and so do not ask about the constraints to entry they could not overcome; nor do they reach those who recently closed down to ask why they are no longer in business. Thus the issues that may have an important role in shaping who is even asked the questions are unlikely to be identified.

Any survey that asks subjective questions has to address issues of comparability of responses. Where possible, more objective questions are preferable. Thus, instead of asking how constraining the supply of electricity is on a scale of one to five, questions can ask for the frequency and length of outages, or the costs of running a generator. These responses can more easily be compared across respondents and over time.

One further complication in interpreting responses from enterprise surveys and linking them to enterprise outcomes is the potential for a two-way causal relationship between them. It could be that more onerous conditions are hindering an enterprise's ability to stay in business. But a firm's poor performance, perhaps stemming from weak management, could also be affecting the degree to which the respondent complains. Performance also affects which dimensions of the investment climate matter the most; for example, the availability of skills may be more constraining to expanding firms, whereas labor regulations may be of greater concern to firms that are contracting and facing the need to shed workers.

Sources: Hallward-Driemeier and Aterido 2009; World Bank 2004b.

FIGURE 6.10 *The assessment of constraints to business varies across enterprises*

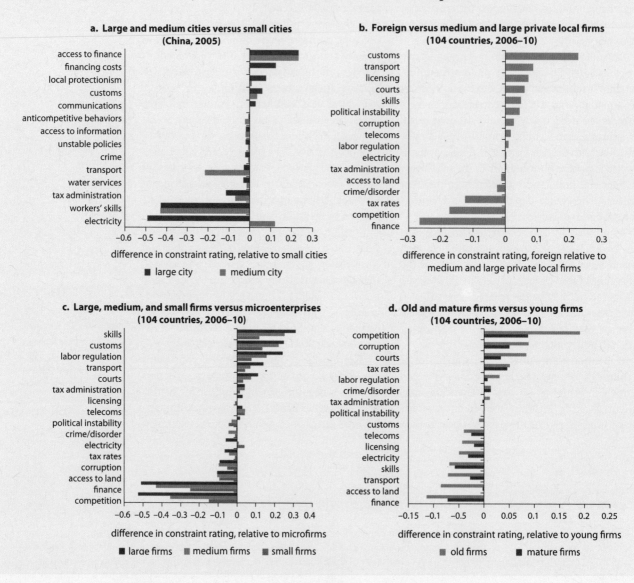

Source: World Development Report 2013 team based on the World Bank's Enterprise Surveys 2006–10.
Note: The analysis is based on a city-level enterprise survey of China in 2005 for panel a, and surveys of more than 60,000 urban enterprises in 104 countries in 2006–10 for other panels. The bars indicate differences in the rating of constraints between firms in two groups. Ratings in the surveys range from 1 (no constraint) to 5 (severe); they are net of the average rating of constraints by each firm, to assess relative severity. The analysis controls for firm age, size, ownership structure, export orientation, industry, and year.

of industries that rely more on external funding. The impact of removing constraints also varies across firm size, age, ownership, and other characteristics.[129] For example, infrastructure bottlenecks tend to stunt the growth of medium and large businesses but do not affect microenterprises significantly. Similarly, when the judiciary system is viewed as a hindrance, foreign companies are more likely to withdraw from the market than private local firms.[130]

Not all targeting is vulnerable to capture by interest groups

Capture by vested interests is arguably the most important concern about targeting. The risk that the potential beneficiaries could unduly influence the decision process is a real one. A too-cozy relationship between businesses and government can make it extremely difficult to remove support, even in the event of a blatant failure. Policy capture by vested interest groups could undermine the often weak capacity of governments in many developing countries.

Targeted activities that involve a large number of beneficiaries are less subject to capture. For example, support for smallholder farming, competitive cities, or female microentrepreneurs is less likely to be influenced by beneficiaries. In every country, thousands, if not millions, of farmers, urban businesses, and female micro-entrepreneurs are all bound to benefit from targeted policies aimed at their group. But individually they do not have the power to influence such policies, and they may not be able to organize as effective interest groups.

Targeted government interventions are justifiable only if they are based on a solid understanding of what good jobs for development are in a particular context and only if they can be designed to be resistant to capture. One example is the involvement of the private sector in the design and management of special economic zones (box 6.11).

BOX 6.11 *Special economic zones have a mixed record*

Special economic zones (SEZs) are demarcated geographic areas within a country's boundaries where the rules of business are different from those that prevail in the national territory. These differential rules principally deal with investment conditions, international trade, and customs. The zones have a business environment that is intended to be more liberal from a policy perspective and more effective from an administrative perspective.

Before the 1970s, most SEZs were operated by developed countries. Then, starting with East Asia and Latin America, developing countries began to use SEZs to attract foreign direct investment, often as a part of export-led growth strategies. The objectives broadened over time, as SEZs became instruments of trade, investment, industrial, spatial, and even broader economic policies. In 1986, there were 176 zones in 47 countries; by 2006, there were 3,500 of them in 130 countries.

SEZs have a mixed record. Their rates of return are still a topic of heated debate among economists. Their performance critically depends on their design and management. SEZs are more likely to be successful when they are an integral component of the country's development strategy, are aligned with the country's comparative advantage, are cluster-based, and establish linkages with the rest of the economy.

For example, in Bangladesh, the SEZ program initially aimed to attract high-technology investments, but the government shifted the focus to garments, where the private sector had shown signs of success. The shift proved to be critical for the performance of the SEZ program. Building effective partnerships with the private sector is an important mechanism through which coordination challenges can be overcome. Institutionally, the partnership can be established through representation of the private sector on the board of the SEZ, as in the Dominican Republic and Lesotho.

A common element of many successful SEZs is the technical competency of the bureaucracy responsible for constructing and implementing them. While this cautions against targeting when government capacity is weak, several Latin American countries have recorded successes by relying on private sector ownership and management. In the Dominican Republic, where public and private zones coexist, there are no clear differences in employment, investment, or exports by zone ownership. But the private zones generally offer higher-quality infrastructure and more value-added services than the government-run ones and, accordingly, charge higher rents.

Sources: Akinci and Farole 2011; Kingombe and te Velde 2012 for the World Development Report 2013.

Farmers in a pomegranate field in Tajikistan
© Gennadiy Ratushenko / World Bank

Street vendor in Kabul, Afghanistan
© Steve McCurry / Magnum Photos

Wage worker at a garment factory in Vietnam
© Lino Vuth / World Bank

Drying peppers in the street in Mexico
© Curt Carnemark / World Bank

Notes

1. Pollin 2009.
2. De Vreyer and Roubaud, forthcoming.
3. Fox and Sekkel Gaal 2008.
4. Altman 2011.
5. Because of new discoveries in the natural resource sector, including natural gas, Mozambique may become a resource-rich country. Yet, raising agricultural productivity and developing light-manufacturing industries will remain key issues in this country, according to the Mozambique country case study for the WDR 2013.
6. Arndt and others 2012; Fox, Bardasi, and Van den Broeck 2005.
7. Mozambique country case study for the WDR 2013.
8. Christiaensen and Demery 2007.
9. Lipton 2005.
10. Otsuka and Larson, forthcoming.
11. Christiaensen, Demery, and Kuhl 2011.
12. Otsuka and Larson, forthcoming.
13. Morris and others 2007.
14. Conning and Udry 2007.
15. Sawada 2012.
16. Mozambique country case study for the WDR 2013.
17. McCormick 1999; Sonobe and Otsuka 2011.
18. Lin 2011b.
19. Surveys conducted for *Moving Out of Poverty* (Narayan and Petesch 2010) identify economic recovery and the restoration of livelihoods as top priorities.
20. World Bank 2010.
21. IDMC and Norwegian Refugee Council 2011; UNHCR 2011.
22. Cramer 2010.
23. Blattman and Annan 2011.
24. Finegan and Margo 1994; Jones and others 2009; Menon and Rodgers 2010; Narayan and Petesch 2010; Schweitzer 1980.
25. Iyer and Santos 2012; World Bank 2011b.
26. World Bank 2005.
27. Shortland 2011.
28. Blattman and Annan 2011.
29. Collier 2007; Collier, Hoeffler, and Rohner 2006; World Bank 2010.
30. Lemasle 2012.
31. World Bank 2010; World Bank 2011b.
32. Dudwick and Srinivasan forthcoming; World Bank 2010.
33. Dudwick and Srinivasan forthcoming.
34. Lin 2011a.
35. World Development Indicators.
36. World Development Indicators; World Bank Poverty and Inequality database.
37. ADB 2012.
38. World Bank 2011b.
39. According to the accepted wisdom, as income increases, the diversity of industrial structure increases before the onset of industrial concentration (Imbs and Wacziarg 2003). Thus, the industrialization process in Bangladesh that has involved a shift toward the monoculture of the garment industry deviates from the general rule.
40. Jedwab 2012.
41. Papua New Guinea country case study for the World Development Report 2013.
42. Papua New Guinea country case study for the World Development Report 2013.
43. Gibson and others 2005.
44. Papua New Guinea country case study for the World Development Report 2013.
45. Macintyre 2011.
46. Papua New Guinea country case study for the World Development Report 2013.
47. Papua New Guinea country case study for the World Development Report 2013.
48. McCrea 2009.
49. Papua New Guinea country case study for the World Development Report 2013.
50. Winters and Martins 2004.
51. Gibson 2006.
52. McKenzie, Martinez, and Winters 2008; World Bank 2006a.
53. Bertram 2004.
54. World Bank 2006a.
55. World Bank 2006a.
56. World Bank 2006a.
57. World Development Report 2013 team calculations based on the World Bank migration database.
58. Gibson and McKenzie 2012.
59. Stillman, McKenzie, and Gibson (2007) also find evidence that migration improves the mental health of workers.
60. World Bank 2006a. Analysis on Tonga suggests an insignificant relationship between migration and tertiary education.
61. World Bank 2011a.
62. https://www.cia.gov/library/publications/the-world-factbook/geos/fj.html.
63. Stefanova 2008.
64. World Bank 2012c; Zafar 2011.
65. Frankel 2010; Roy and Subramanian 2001; Zafar 2011.
66. Gatti and others 2012.
67. Tunisia country case study for the World Development Report 2013; Stampini and Verdier-Choucane 2011.
68. Another social consequence of high levels of youth unemployment is the effect on family formation patterns, and what is referred to as

stalled transitions. In the Middle East and North Africa context specifically, this includes delayed marriage (Wrigley 2010). The rate of marriage has been declining as the age of entry into marriage has increased (Dhillon and Yousef 2009). Adequate employment is necessary for a man to be perceived as an eligible marriage partner.

69. Bell and Blanchflower 2010; Giles, Newhouse, and Witoelar 2010.
70. ILO 2011a.
71. World Bank 2006b; Wrigley 2010.
72. Binzel 2011; Gatti and others 2012; Matsumoto and Elder 2010.
73. World Bank 2012a.
74. Stampini and Verdier-Choucane 2011. These figures are based on data collected in the 2005 and 2006 Labor Force Surveys.
75. According to the 2010 Gallup World Poll, the proportion of young people preferring to work in the public sector ranged from around 40 to 70 percent in countries in the Middle East and North Africa. Only Libya had a significantly lower share.
76. World Bank 2012a.
77. World Bank 2008b.
78. Some call for promoting access to secondary and university education among marginalized groups in the region (see Middle East Youth Initiative 2009).
79. Boughzala 2004; World Bank 2004a.
80. World Bank 2012a.
81. Gatti and others 2012.
82. World Bank 2009.
83. Klapper and Love 2011.
84. Freund and others 2012.
85. Centeno and Portes 2006; Mezzadri 2010; Saavedra and Tommasi 2007.
86. Kanbur 2011.
87. Geertz 1968; North 1991; North 1994; Stiglitz 2000.
88. Some would argue that poverty begets informality because of the constraints that the poor face in finding a formal job (Devicenti, Groisman, and Poggi 2010).
89. Perry and others 2007.
90. ILO 2011b.
91. Taymaz 2009.
92. Perry and others 2007.
93. Loayza 1996; Perry and others 2007.
94. See McKenzie and Seynabou (2010) for recent evidence from Bolivia, and see de Mel, McKenzie, and Woodruff (2008).
95. Bosch and Maloney 2010; Maloney 1999.
96. Fajnzylber, Maloney, and Montes-Rojas 2011.
97. Bernal 2009 for Colombia; Mondragón-Vélez, Peña, and Wills 2010 for Colombia; World Bank 2008a for Argentina.

98. Fields 2005; Perry and others 2007. Gunther and Launov (2012) provide an econometric technique for separating the size of these two components using data on Côte d'Ivoire.
99. Petesch 2012 for the World Development Report 2013.
100. Loayza and Rigolini 2011.
101. Djankov and Ramalho 2009; Heckman and Pagés 2000, 2004; Kaplan 2009. For a more nuanced view from a developed-country perspective, see Boeri and van Ours (2008).
102. Freund and others 2012; Ulyssea 2010.
103. Fiszbein and others 2009.
104. Anton, Hernandez, and Levy 2012; Perry and others 2007.
105. Fields 2005; Kanbur 2009.
106. Almeida and Carneiro 2009; Kan and Lin 2007; Kanbur 2009, 2011; Scarpetta and Tressel 2004.
107. Chen and Doane 2008; Jütting and de Laiglesia 2009; Kanbur 2011.
108. Demographic statistics, including outmigration rates, are based on estimates of the United Nations Population Division.
109. Giles, Wang, and Cai (2011) discuss measures that may facilitate longer working lives as China's population ages.
110. Chawla, Betcherman, and Banerji 2007.
111. WHO and World Bank 2011.
112. Fiegerman 2011.
113. Boersch-Supran 2003.
114. Cai and others 2012.
115. World Bank 2011c.
116. Cotlear 2011; Reinhardt 2003; Werding and McLennan 2011.
117. Schwarz 2009.
118. See Lin and Monga (2011) and Pack and Saggi (2006) for reviews. For detailed discussion, see Cimoli, Dosi, and Stiglitz (2009); Harrison and Rodríguez-Clare (2010); Lin (2012); Porter (1990); Rodrik (2004).
119. World Bank 2004b.
120. Hayami and Ruttan 1985.
121. This is not the case for hybrid seeds, which farmers cannot self-produce, or for mechanical technologies.
122. *The Economist* 2010.
123. Levitt and Dubner 2009; Mallaby 2010; Romer 2010.
124. Otsuka and Larson, forthcoming.
125. Byerlee 1996; David and Otsuka 1994.
126. David and Otsuka 1994; Fan and Hazell 2001; Otsuka and Larson, forthcoming.
127. Aterido, Hallward-Driemeier, and Pagés 2007, 2009; Beck, Demirgüç-Kunt, and Maksimovic 2005; Djankov, Freund, and Pham 2010; Kaufmann and Kraay 2002; Klapper, Laeven, and Rajan 2006; McKenzie 2010.

128. Sawada 2012 for the World Development Report 2013.
129. For example, Aterido, Hallward-Driemeier, and Pagés 2009; Beck, Demirgüç-Kunt, and Maksimovic 2005; Djankov, Freund, and Pham 2010; Haltiwanger, Scarpetta, and Schweiger 2008; Klapper, Laeven, and Rajan 2006; Micco and Pagés 2006; Rajan and Zingales 1998.
130. Aterido, Hallward-Driemeier, and Pagés 2009; Hallward-Driemeier 2009.

References

The word *processed* describes informally reproduced works that may not be commonly available through libraries.

ADB (Asian Development Bank). 2012. *Asian Development Outlook 2012: Confronting Rising Inequality in Asia.* Mandaluyong City, Philippines: ADB.

Akinci, Gokhan, and Thomas Farole. 2011. *Special Economic Zones: Progress, Emerging Challenges, and Future Directions.* Washington, DC: World Bank.

Alamgir, Mohiuddin. 1978. *Bangladesh: A Case of Below Poverty Level Equilibrium Trap.* Dhaka: Bangladesh Institute of Development Studies.

Almeida, Rita, and Pedro Carneiro. 2009. "Enforcement of Labor Regulation and Firm Size." *Journal of Comparative Economics* 37 (1): 28–46.

Altman, Miriam. 2011. *Employment Policy in South Africa and the Region.* Washington, DC: World Bank.

Angel-Urdinola, Diego, Stefanie Brodmann, and Anne Hilger. 2010. "Labor Markets in Tunisia: Recent Trends." World Bank, Washington, DC. Processed.

Anton, Arturo, Fausto Hernandez, and Santiago Levy. 2012. *The End of Informality in Mexico? Fiscal Reform for Universal Social Insurance.* Washington, DC: Inter-American Development Bank.

Arndt, Channing, M. Azhar Hussain, E. Samuel Jones, Nhate Virgulino, Finn Tarp, and James Thurlow. 2012. "Explaining Poverty Evolution: The Case of Mozambique." *American Journal of Agricultural Economics* 94 (4): 854–72.

Aterido, Reyes, Mary Hallward-Driemeier, and Carmen Pagés. 2007. "Investment Climate and Employment Growth: The Impact of Access to Finance, Corruption, and Regulations across Firms." Discussion Paper Series 3138, Institute for the Study of Labor, Bonn.

———. 2009. "Big Constraints to Small Firms' Growth? Business Environment and Employment Growth across Firms." Policy Research Working Paper Series 5032, World Bank, Washington, DC.

———. 2011. "Does Expanding Health Insurance Beyond Formal-Sector Workers Encourage Informality? Measuring the Impact of Mexico's Seguro Popular." Policy Research Working Paper Series 5785, World Bank, Washington, DC.

Beck, Thorsten, Asli Demirgüç-Kunt, and Vojislav Maksimovic. 2005. "Financial and Legal Constraints to Firm Growth: Does Firm Size Matter?" *Journal of Finance* 40 (1): 137–77.

Bell, David N. F., and David Blanchflower. 2010. "Youth Unemployment: Déjà Vu?" Discussion Paper Series 4705, Institute for the Study of Labor, Bonn.

Bernal, Raquel. 2009. "The Informal Labor Market in Colombia: Identification and Characterization." *Desarrollo y Sociedad* 63 (March): 145–208.

Bertram, Geoffrey. 2004. "On the Convergence of Small Island Economies with Their Metropolitan Patrons." *World Development* 32 (2): 343–65.

Binzel, Christine. 2011. "Decline in Social Mobility: Unfulfilled Aspirations among Egypt's Educated Youth." Discussion Paper Series 6139, Institute for the Study of Labor, Bonn.

Blacklock, Carolyn, and Tim Bulman. 2012. *PNG's Maturing Landowner Companies: Telling the Story of the Emerging Group of PNG-Owned-and-Managed Jobs Generators.* Port Moresby: World Bank.

Blattman, Christopher, and Jeannie Annan. 2011. "Reintegrating and Employing High Risk Youth in Liberia: Lessons from a Randomized Evaluation of a Landmine Action Agricultural Training Program for Ex-Combatants." Yale University, Innovations for Poverty Action, New Haven, CT.

Boeri, Tito, and Jan C. van Ours. 2008. *The Economics of Imperfect Labor Markets.* Princeton, NJ: Princeton University Press.

Boersch-Supran, Axel. 2003. "Labor Market Effects of Population Aging." *Review of Labour Economics and Industrial Relations* 17: 5–44.

Bosch, Mariano, and William Maloney. 2010. "Comparative Analysis of Labor Market Dynamics Using Markov Processes: An Application to Informality." *Labour Economics* 17 (4): 621–32.

Botero, Juan C., Simeon Djankov, Rafael La Porta, Florencio Lopez-de-Silanes, and Andres Shleifer. 2004. "The Regulation of Labor." *Quarterly Journal of Economics* 119 (4): 1339–82.

Boughzala, Mongi. 2004. "The Labor Market in Tunisia: Study on the Functioning of the Labor Markets in the Mediterranean Region and the Implications for Employment Policy and Training Systems." University of Tunis, Tunis. Processed.

Byerlee, Derek. 1996. "Modern Varieties, Productivity, and Sustainability: Recent Experience and Emerging Challenges." *World Development* 24 (4): 697–718.

Byrnes, Andrew, and Marsha A. Freeman. 2011. "The Impact of the CEDAW Conventions: Paths to Equality. A Study for the World Bank." Background paper for the WDR 2012.

Cai, Fang, John Giles, Philip O'Keefe, and Dewen Wang. 2012. *The Elderly and Old Age Support in Rural China: Challenges and Prospects.* Washington, DC: World Bank.

Calderon, Alor. 2012. "Employment Outcomes and Firms' Productivity Performance in Mexico. Analysis Based on Economic Census Microdatasets." El Colegio de Mexico, Mexico City. Processed.

Centeno, Miguel Angel, and Alejandro Portes. 2006. "The Informal Economy in the Shadow of the State." In *Out of the Shadows: Political Action and the Informal Economy in Latin America*, ed. Maria Patricia Fernandez-Kelly and Jon Shefner, 1–23. University Park: Pennsylvania State University Press.

Chawla, Mukesh, Gordon Betcherman, and Arup Banerji, eds. 2007. *From Red to Gray: The "Third Transition" of Aging Populations in Eastern Europe and the Former Soviet Union.* Washington, DC: World Bank.

Chen, Martha, and Donna Doane. 2008. "Informality in South Asia: A Review." Background Paper, Swedish International Development Cooperation Agency, Stockholm.

Christiaensen, Luc, and Lionel Demery. 2007. *Down to Earth: Agriculture and Poverty Reduction in Africa.* Washington, DC: World Bank.

Christiaensen, Luc, Lionel Demery, and Jesper Kuhl. 2011. "The (Evolving) Role of Agriculture in Poverty Reduction—An Empirical Perspective." *Journal of Development Economics* 96 (2): 239–54.

Cimoli, Mario, Giovanni Dosi, and Joseph E. Stiglitz, eds. 2009. *Industrial Policy and Development: The Political Economy of Capabilities Accumulation.* Oxford: Oxford University Press.

Collier, Paul. 2007. "Post-Conflict Recovery: How Should Policies Be Distinctive." Centre for the Studies of African Economies, Oxford University, Oxford. Processed.

Collier, Paul, Anke Hoeffler, and Dominic Rohner. 2006. "Beyond Greed and Grievance: Feasibility and Civil War." Working Paper 2006-10, Centre for the Study of African Economies, Oxford University, Oxford.

Conning, Jonathan, and Christopher Udry. 2007. "Rural Financial Markets in Developing Countries." In *Agricultural Development: Farmers, Farm Production and Farm Markets*, Vol. 3 of *Handbook of Agricultural Economics*, ed. Robert Evenson and Prabhu Pingali, 2857–910. Amsterdam: Elsevier.

Cotlear, Daniel, ed. 2011. *Population Aging: Is Latin America Ready?* Washington, DC: World Bank.

Cramer, Christopher. 2010. "Unemployment and Participation in Violence." Background paper for the WDR 2011.

David, Christina C., and Keijiro Otsuka, eds. 1994. *Modern Rice Technology and Income Distribution in Asia.* Boulder, CO: Lynne Rienner.

de Mel, Suresh, David J. McKenzie, and Christopher Woodruff. 2008. "Returns to Capital in Microenterprises: Evidence from a Field Experiment." *Quarterly Journal of Economics* 123 (4): 1329–72.

Devicienti, Francesco, Fernando Groisman, and Ambra Poggi. 2010. "Are Informality and Poverty Dynamically Interrelated? Evidence from Argentina." In *Studies in Applied Welfare Analysis: Papers from the Third ECINEQ Meeting*, ed. John A. Bishop, 79–106. Bingley: Emerald Group Publishing Limited.

De Vreyer, Philippe, and François Roubaud, eds. Forthcoming. *Urban Labour Markets in Sub-Saharan Africa.* Montepellier, France: Institute for Research and Development.

Dhillon, Navtej, and Tarik Yousef. 2009. *Generation in Waiting: The Unfulfilled Promise of Young People in the Middle East.* Washington, DC: Brookings Institution Press.

Dinh, Hinh T., Vincent Palmade, Vandana Chandra, and Frances Cossar. 2012. *Light Manufacturing in Africa: Targeted Policies to Enhance Private Investment and Create Jobs.* Washington, DC: World Bank and L'Agence Française de Développement.

Djankov, Simeon, Caroline Freund, and Cong S. Pham. 2010. "Trading on Time." *Review of Economics and Statistics* 92 (1): 166–73.

Djankov, Simeon, and Rita Ramalho. 2009. "Employment Laws in Developing Countries." *Journal of Comparative Economics* 37 (1): 3–13.

Dudwick, Nora, and Radhika Srinivasan, with Jose Cueva and Dorsati Mandavi. Forthcoming. *Creating Jobs in Africa's Fragile States: Are Value Chains an Answer?* Directions in Development Series. Washington, DC: World Bank.

Faaland, Just, and John Richard Parkinson. 1976. *Bangladesh: The Test Case for Development.* London: C. Hurst & Co. Publishers Ltd.

Fajnzylber, Pablo, William Maloney, and Gabriel V. Montes-Rojas. 2011. "Does Formality Improve Micro-Firm Performance? Evidence from the Brazilian SIMPLES Program." *Journal of Development Economics* 94: 262–76.

Fan, Shenggen, and Peter Hazell. 2001. "Returns to Public Investments in the Less-Favored Areas of India and China." *American Journal of Agricultural Economics* 83 (5): 1217–22.

Fiegerman, Seth. 2011. "Our New Jobs Problem: Aging Americans." *MainStreet*, August 17.

Fields, Gary. 2005. "A Guide to Multisector Labor Market Models." Social Protection Discussion Paper Series 0505, World Bank, Washington, DC.

Finegan, T. Aldrich, and Robert A. Margo. 1994. "Added and Discouraged Workers in the Late 1930s: A Re-examination." *Journal of Economic History* 54 (March): 64–84.

Fiszbein, Ariel, Norbert Schady, Francisco H. G. Ferreira, Margaret Grosh, Nial Kelleher, Pedro Olinto, and Emmanuel Skoufias. 2009. *Conditional Cash Transfers: Reducing Present and Future Poverty.* Washington, DC: World Bank.

Fox, Louise, Elena Bardasi, and Katleen Van den Broeck. 2005. "Poverty in Mozambique: Unraveling Changes and Determinants." Africa Region Working Paper Series 87, World Bank, Washington, DC.

Fox, Louise, and Melissa Sekkel Gaal. 2008. *Working Out of Poverty: Job Creation and the Quality of Growth in Africa.* Washington, DC: World Bank.

Frankel, Jeffrey. 2010. "Mauritius: African Success Story." Working Paper Series 16569, National Bureau of Economic Research, Cambridge, MA.

Freund, Caroline, Antonio Nucifora, Bob Rijkers, Hassen Arouri, and Rim Chabbeh. 2012. "Job Creation: A Big Role for Big Firms? Evidence from Tunisia." World Bank, Washington DC. Processed.

Gatti, Roberta, Diego Angel-Urdinola, Joana Silva, and Andras Bodor. 2012. *Striving for Better Jobs: The Challenge of Informality in the Middle East and North Africa.* Washington, DC: World Bank.

Geertz, Clifford. 1968. *Peddlers and Princes: Social Development and Economic Change in Two Indonesian Towns.* Chicago, IL: University of Chicago Press.

Gibson, John. 2006. "Are the Pacific Islands Economies Growth Failures?" Working Paper 3, Pasifika Interactions Project, Hamilton, New Zealand.

Gibson, John, Gaurav Datt, Allen Bryant, Vicky Hwang, R. Michael Bourke, and Dilip Parajuli. 2005. "Mapping Poverty in Rural Papua New Guinea." *Pacific Economic Bulletin* 20 (1): 27–43.

Gibson, John, and David McKenzie. 2012. "The Economic Consequences of 'Brain Drain' of the Best and Brightest: Microeconomic Evidence from Five Countries." *Economic Journal* 122 (560): 339–75.

Giles, John, David Newhouse, and Firman Witoelar. 2010. "Stuck for Life? The Long-Term Consequences of Initial Informality in Indonesia." Paper presented at the Employment and Development Conference, Cape Town, May 3.

Giles, John, Dewen Wang, and Wei Cai. 2011. "The Labor Supply and Retirement Behavior of China's Older Workers and Elderly in Comparative Perspective." Policy Research Working Paper Series 5835, World Bank, Washington, DC.

Gonzalez de la Rocha, Mercedes. 2012. "Trabajo, Modos de Subsistencia y Vida Social en Mexico." CIE-SAS Guadalajara, Guadalajara. Processed.

Guarcello, Lorenzo, Furio C. Rosati, and Scott Lyon. 2011. "Labour Market in South Sudan." Programme Working Paper, Understanding Children's Work, Rome.

Gunther, Isabel, and Andrey Launov. 2012. "Informal Employment in Developing Countries: Opportunity or Last Resort?" *Journal of Development Economics* 97 (1): 88–98.

Hallward-Driemeier, Mary. 2009. "Who Survives? The Impact of Corruption, Competition, and Property Rights across Firms." Policy Research Working Paper Series 5084, World Bank, Washington, DC.

Hallward-Driemeier, Mary, and Reyes Aterido. 2009. "Comparing Apples with … Apples: How to Make (More) Sense of Subjective Rankings of Constraints to Business." Policy Research Working Paper Series 5054, World Bank, Washington, DC.

Haltiwanger, John, Stefano Scarpetta, and Helena Schweiger. 2008. "Assessing Job Flows across Countries: The Role of Industry, Firm Size, and Regulations." Working Paper Series 13920, National Bureau of Economic Research, Cambridge, MA.

Harrison, Ann, and Andres Rodriguez-Clare. 2010. "Trade, Foreign Investment, and Industrial Policy for Developing Countries." In *Development Economics*, Vol. 5 of *Handbook of Development Economics*, ed. Dani Rodrik and Mark Rosenzweig, 4039–214. Amsterdam: Elsevier.

Hausmann, Ricardo, César Hidalgo, Sebastián Bustos, Michele Coscia, Sarah Chung, Juan Jimenez, Alexander Simoes, and Muhammend A. Yildirim. 2011. *The Atlas of Economic Complexity: Mapping Paths to Prosperity.* Cambridge, MA: Harvard University.

Hayami, Yujiro, and Vernon W. Ruttan. 1985. *Agricultural Development: An International Perspective.* Baltimore, MD: Johns Hopkins University Press.

Heckman, James J., and Carmen Pagés. 2000. "The Cost of Job Security Regulation: Evidence from the Latin American Labor Markets." *Journal of the Latin American and Caribbean Economic Association* 1 (1): 109–54.

———. 2004. "Introduction." In *Law and Employment: Lessons from Latin America and the Caribbean*, ed. James J. Heckman and Carmen Pagés, 1–108. Chicago, IL: University of Chicago Press.

IDMC (Internal Displacement Monitoring Centre) and Norwegian Refugee Council. 2011. *Internal Displacement: Global Overview of Trends and Developments in 2010.* Geneva: IDMC.

ILO (International Labour Organization). 2011a. *Global Employment Trends for Youth.* Geneva: ILO.

———. 2011b. *Statistical Update on Employment in the Informal Economy.* Geneva: ILO.

Imbs, Jean, and Romain Wacziarg. 2003. "Stages of Diversification." *American Economic Review* 93 (1): 63–86.

IOM (International Organization for Migration). 2009. *Total Returns to South Sudan.* Geneva: IOM.

Iyer, Lakshmi, and Indhira Santos. 2012. "Creating Jobs in South Asia's Conflict Zones." Policy Research Working Paper Series 6104, World Bank, Washington, DC.

Jedwab, Remi. 2012. "Why is African Urbanization Different? Evidence from Resource Exports in Ghana and the Ivory Coast." Paper presented at the World Bank Seminar, Washington, DC, February 6.

Jones, Nicola, Rebecca Holmes, Hannah Marsden, Shreya Mitra, and David Walker. 2009. "Gender and Social Protection in Asia: What Does the Crisis Change?" Paper presented at the Asia-wide Regional High-Level Meeting, Hanoi, September 29–30.

Jütting, Johannes P., and Juan R. de Laiglesia, eds. 2009. *Is Informal Normal? Towards More and Better Jobs in Developing Countries.* Paris: OECD Publishing.

Kan, Kamhon, and Yen-Ling Lin. 2007. "The Effects of Employment Protection Legislation on Labor Turnover: Empirical Evidence from Taiwan." *Economic Inquiry* 49 (2): 398–433.

Kanbur, Ravi. 2009. "Conceptualizing Informality: Regulation and Enforcement." *Indian Journal of Labour Economics* 52 (1): 33–42.

———. 2011. "Avoiding Informality Traps." Working Paper Series 06, Charles H. Dyson School of Applied Economics and Management, Ithaca, NY.

Kaplan, David Scott. 2009. "Job Creation and Labor Reform in Latin America." *Journal of Comparative Economics* 37 (1): 91–105.

Kaplan, David Scott, Joyce Sadka, and Jorge Luis Silva-Mendez. 2008. "Litigation and Settlement: New Evidence from Labor Courts in Mexico." *Journal of Empirical Legal Studies* 5 (2): 309–50.

Kaufmann, Daniel, and Aart Kraay. 2002. "Governance Indicators, Aid Allocation, and the Millennium Challenge Account." World Bank, Washington, DC. Processed.

Kingombe, Christian, and Dirk Willem te Velde. 2012. "Structural Transformation and Employment Creation: The Role of Growth Facilitation Policies in Sub-Saharan Africa." Background paper for the WDR 2013.

Klapper, Leora, Luc Laeven, and Raghuram Rajan. 2006. "Entry Regulation as a Barrier to Entrepreneurship." *Journal of Financial Economics* 82 (3): 591–629.

Klapper, Leora F., and Inessa Love. 2011. "The Impact of Business Environment Reforms on New Firm Registration." World Bank, Washington, DC. Processed.

Komarov, Vladyslav. 2011. *Housing Market and Labor Mobility.* Kiev: Bureau of Economic and Social Technologies.

Lemasle, Natacha. 2012. *From Conflict to Resilience: Ex-Combatants Trade Associations in Post-Conflict: Lessons Learned from the Republic of Congo and the Democratic Republic of Congo.* Washington, DC: World Bank.

Levitt, Steven, and Stephen Dubner. 2009. "Can 'Charter Cities' Change the World? A Q&A with Paul Romer." *Freakonomics,* September 29. http://www.freakonomics.com/2009/09/29/can-charter-cities-change-the-world-a-qa-with-paul-romer.

Levy, Santiago. 2008. *Good Intentions, Bad Outcomes, Social Policy, Informality, and Economic Growth in Mexico.* Washington, DC: Brookings Institution Press.

Lin, Justin Yifu. 2009. *Economic Development and Transition: Thought, Strategy and Viability.* Cambridge, U.K.: Cambridge University Press.

———. 2011a. "From Flying Geese to Leading Dragons: New Opportunities and Strategies for Structural Transformation in Developing Countries." Policy Research Working Paper Series 5702, World Bank, Washington, DC.

———. 2011b. "How to Seize the 85 Million Jobs Bonanza." World Bank (blog), Washington, DC. http://blogs.worldbank.org/developmenttalk/node/646.

———. 2012. *New Structural Economics: A Framework for Rethinking Development and Policy.* Washington, DC: World Bank.

Lin, Justin Yifu, and Célestin Monga. 2011. "DPR Debate: Growth Identification and Facilitation: The Role of the State in the Dynamics of Structural Change." *Development Policy Review* 29 (3): 259–310.

Lipton, Richard. 2005. "The Family Farm in a Globalizing World: The Role of Crop Science in Alleviating Poverty." Discussion Paper 40, International Food Policy Research Institute, Washington, DC.

Loayza, Norman. 1996. "The Economics of the Informal Sector: A Simple Model and Some Evidence from Latin America." *Carnegie-Rochester Conference Series on Public Policy* 45: 129–62.

Loayza, Norman, and Jamele Rigolini. 2011. "Informal Employment: Safety Net or Growth Engine?" *World Development* 39 (9): 1503–15.

Macintyre, Martha. 2011. "Modernity, Gender and Mining: Experiences from Papua New Guinea." In *Gendering the Field: Towards Sustainable Livelihoods for Mining Communities,* ed. Kuntala Lahiri-Dutt, 21–32. Canberra: Australian National University.

Mallaby, Sebastian. 2010. "The Politically Incorrect Guide to Ending Poverty." *The Atlantic*, July/August. http://www.theatlantic.com/magazine/archive/2010/07/the-politically-incorrect-guide-to-ending-poverty/8134.

Maloney, William F. 1999. "Does Informality Imply Segmentation in Urban Labor Markets? Evidence from Sectoral Transitions in Mexico." *World Bank Economic Review* 13 (2): 275–302.

Martinez, Gabriel, and Nelly Aguilera. 2012. *The Human Capital Perspective on Employment Policy.* San José, Costa Rica: Inter-American Conference on Social Security.

Matsumoto, Makiko, and Sara Elder. 2010. "Characterizing the School-To-Work Transition of Young Men and Women: Evidence from the ILO School-to-Work Transition Surveys." Employment Working Paper 51, International Labour Organization, Geneva.

McCormick, Dorothy. 1999. "African Enterprise Clusters and Industrialization: Theory and Reality." *World Development* 27 (9): 1531–51.

McCrea, Peter. 2009. "Oil Palm Sector, Situation and Perception Assessment." Report for the World Bank and the Oil Palm Industry Corporation, Port Moresby, Papua New Guinea. Processed.

McKenzie, David. 2010. *Impact Assessment in Finance and Private Sector Development: What Have We Learned and What Should We Learn?* Washington, DC: World Bank.

McKenzie, David, Pilar Garcia Martinez, and L. Alan Winters. 2008. *Who Is Coming from Vanuatu to New Zealand under the New Recognized Seasonal Employer (RSE) Program?* Waikato, New Zealand: University of Waikato.

McKenzie, David, and Sakho Seynabou. 2010. "Does It Pay Firms to Register for Taxes? The Impact of Formality on Firm Profitability." *Journal of Development Economics* 91 (1): 15–24.

Menon, Nidhiya, and Yana van der Meulen Rodgers. 2010. "War and Women's Work: Evidence from the Conflict in Nepal." Working Paper Series 19, Department of Economics and International Business School, Brandeis University, Waltham, MA.

Mercer. 2011. *Worldwide Cost of Living Survey 2011—City Ranking.* London: Mercer.

Mezzadri, Alessandra. 2010. "Globalisation, Informalisation and the State in the Indian Garment Industry." *International Review of Sociology* 20 (3): 491–511.

Micco, Alejandro, and Carmen Pagés. 2006. "The Economic Effects of Employment Protection: Evidence from International Industry-Level Data." Discussion Paper Series 2433, Institute for the Study of Labor, Bonn.

Middle East Youth Initiative. 2009. *Missed by the Boom, Hurt by the Bust: Making Markets Work for Young People in the Middle East.* Washington, DC: Brookings Institution Press; Dubai: Dubai School of Government.

Mondragón-Vélez, Camilo, Ximena Peña, and Daniel Wills. 2010. "Labor Market Rigidities and Informality in Colombia." Documentos CEDE 006717, Universidad de Los Andes, Bogotá.

Morris, Michael, Valerie A. Kelly, Ron J. Kopicki, and Derek Byerlee. 2007. *Fertilizer Use in African Agriculture: Lessons Learned and Good Practice Guidelines.* Washington, DC: World Bank.

Mottaleb, Khondoker A., and Tetsushi Sonobe. 2011. "An Inquiry into the Rapid Growth of the Garment Industry in Bangladesh." *Economic Development and Cultural Change* 60 (1): 67–89.

Narayan, Deepa, and Patti Petesch. 2010. *Moving Out of Poverty: Rising from the Ashes of Conflict.* Washington, DC: Palgrave Macmillan and World Bank.

Noland, Marcus, and Howard Pack, eds. 2003. *Industrial Policy in an Era of Globalization: Lessons from Asia.* Washington, DC: Peterson Institute.

North, Douglass C. 1991. "Institutions." *Journal of Economic Perspectives* 5 (1): 97–112.

———. 1994. "Economic Performance Through Time." *American Economic Review* 84 (3): 359–68.

Nuebler, Irmgard. 2011. "Industrial Policies and Capabilities for Catching Up: Frameworks and Paradigms." Employment Working Paper Series 77, International Labour Organization, Geneva.

Otsuka, Keijiro, and Donald F. Larson, eds. Forthcoming. *An African Green Revolution: Finding Ways to Boost Productivity on Small Farms.* Amsterdam: Springer.

Pack, Howard, and Kamal Saggi. 2006. "The Case for Industrial Policy: A Critical Survey." Policy Research Working Paper Series 3839, World Bank, Washington, DC.

Perry, Guillermo E., William F. Maloney, Omar S. Arias, Pablo Fajnzylber, Andrew D. Mason, and Jaime Saavedra-Chanduvi. 2007. *Informality: Exit and Exclusion.* Washington, DC: World Bank.

Petesch, Patti. 2011. *Women's Empowerment Arising from Violent Conflict and Recovery.* Washington, DC: U.S. Agency for International Development.

———. 2012. "The Exponential Clash of Conflict, Good Jobs, and Changing Gender Norms in Four Economies." Background paper for the WDR 2013.

Piore, Michael, and Andrew Schrank. 2007. "Norms, Regulations and Labour Standards in Central America." *CEPAL–Serie Estudios y Perspectivas* 77: 1–64.

———. 2008. "Toward Managed Flexibility: The Revival of Labour Market Inspection in the Latin World." *International Labour Review* 147 (1): 1–23.

Pires, Roberto Rocha. 2011. "Governing Regulatory Discretion: Innovation and Accountability in Two Models of Labour Inspection Work." In *Regulating for Decent Work: New Directions in Labour Market Regulation*, ed. Sangheon Lee and Deirdre McCann, 313–38. Geneva: International Labour Organization.

Pollin, Robert. 2009. "Labor Market Institutions and Employment Opportunities in Kenya." University of Massachusetts-Amherst, Amherst. Processed.

Porter, Michael E. 1990. *The Competitive Advantage of Nations.* New York: The Free Press.

Rajan, Raghuram, and Luigi Zingales. 1998. "Financial Dependence and Growth." *American Economic Review* 88 (3): 559–86.

Reinhardt, Uwe. 2003. "Does the Aging of the Population Really Drive Up Demand for Health Care?" *Health Affairs* 22: 27–39.

Republic of South Sudan Disarmament, Demobilisation and Reintegration Commission. 2012. *Republic of South Sudan Disarmament, Demobilisation and Reintegration Commission.* Juba: Republic of South Sudan.

Rodrik, Dani. 2004. "Industrial Policy for the Twenty-First Century." Discussion Paper Series 4767, Centre for Economic Policy Research, London.

———. 2007. *One Economics, Many Recipes: Globalization, Institutions, and Economic Growth.* Princeton, NJ: Princeton University Press.

Romer, Paul. 2010. *Technologies, Rules, and Progress: The Case for Charter Cities.* Washington, DC: Center for Global Development.

Roy, Devesh, and Arvind Subramanian. 2001. "Who Can Explain the Mauritian Miracle: Meade, Romer, Sachs, or Rodrik?" Working Paper Series 01/116, International Monetary Fund, Washington, DC.

Saavedra, Jaime, and Mariano Tommasi. 2007. "Informality, the State and the Social Contract in Latin America: A Preliminary Exploration." *International Labour Review* 146 (3–4): 279–309.

Sawada, Naotaka. 2012. "Providing Business Services for Rural Income Generations: Using the Rural Investment Climate Survey Data." Background paper for the WDR 2013.

Scarpetta, Stefano, and Thierry Tressel. 2004. "Boosting Productivity via Innovation and Adoption of New Technologies: Any Role for Labor Market Institutions?" Policy Research Working Paper Series 3273, World Bank, Washington, DC.

Schwarz, Anita M. 2009. "Pensions in Crisis: Europe and Central Asia Regional Policy Note." World Bank, Washington, DC.

Schweitzer, Mary M. 1980. "World War II and Labor Force Participation Rates." *Journal of Economic History* 40 (1): 89–95.

Shortland, Anja. 2011. "'Robin Hook': The Developmental Effects of Somali Piracy." Discussion Paper Series 1155, German Institute for Economic Research, Berlin.

Sonobe, Tetsushi, and Keijiro Otsuka. 2006. *Cluster-Based Industrial Development: An East Asian Model.* New York: Palgrave Macmillan.

———. 2011. *Cluster-Based Industrial Development: A Comparative Study of Asia and Africa.* New York: Palgrave Macmillan.

Stampini, Marco, and Audrey Verdier-Choucane. 2011. "Labor Market Dynamics in Tunisia: The Issue of Youth Unemployment." Discussion Paper Series 5611, Institute for the Study of Labor, Bonn.

Stefanova, Milena. 2008. *The Price of Tourism: Land Alienation in Vanuatu.* Washington, DC: World Bank.

Stiglitz, Joseph E. 2000. "Formal and Informal Institutions." In *Social Capital: A Multifaceted Perspective*, ed. Partha Dasgupta and Ismael Serageldin, 59–68. Washington, DC: World Bank.

Stillman, Steven, David McKenzie, and John Gibson. 2007. "Migration and Mental Health: Evidence from a Nature Experiment." Policy Research Working Paper Series 4138, World Bank, Washington, DC.

Taymaz, Erol. 2009. "Informality and Productivity: Productivity Differentials between Formal and Informal Firms in Turkey." Working Papers in Economics 09/01, European Research Council, Ankara.

The Economist. 2010. "Brazilian Agriculture: The Miracle of the Cerrado." *The Economist*, August 26.

Ulyssea, Gabriel. 2010. "Regulation of Entry, Labor Market Institutions and the Informal Sector." *Journal of Development Economics* 91: 87–99.

UNHCR (Office of the United Nations High Commissioner for Refugees). 2011. *UNHCR Statistical Yearbook 2010.* 10th ed. Geneva: UNHCR.

Venn, Danielle. 2009. "Legislation, Collective Bargaining and Enforcement." Social, Employment and Migration Working Paper Series 89, Organisation for Economic Co-operation and Development, Paris.

Villarreal, Hector J. 2012. *El Cambio Demográfico y las Finanzas Públicas de Mexico.* Mexico, D.F.: Centre de Investigación Económica y Presupuestaria.

Villarreal, Hector J., and Eduardo Rodriguez-Oreggia. 2012. "Precarious Labor Markets and the Evolution of Poverty: The Mexican Experience." Instituto Tecnológico de Monterrey, Monterrey, Mexico. Processed.

Werding, Martin, and Stuart McLennan. 2011. "International Portability of Health-Cost Coverage: Concepts and Experience." Social Protection Discussion Paper Series 1115, World Bank, Washington, DC.

WHO (World Health Organization) and World Bank. 2011. *World Report on Disability.* Washington, DC: WHO and World Bank.

Winters, Alan, and Pedro Martins. 2004. "When Comparative Advantage Is Not Enough: Business Costs in Small Remote Economies." *World Trade Review* 3 (3): 347–83.

World Bank. 2004a. *Republic of Tunisia Development Policy Review: Making Deeper Trade Integration Work for Growth and Jobs.* Washington, DC: World Bank.

———. 2004b. *World Development Report 2005: A Better Investment Climate for Everyone.* New York: Oxford University Press.

———. 2005. *Afghanistan: Poverty, Vulnerability and Social Protection: An Initial Assessment.* Washington, DC: World Bank.

———. 2006a. *At Home and Away: Expanding Job Opportunities for Pacific Islanders through Labour Mobility.* Washington, DC: World Bank.

———. 2006b. *World Development Report 2007: Development and the Next Generation.* Washington, DC: World Bank.

———. 2008a. *Argentina Labor Market Study: Informal Employment in Argentina: Causes and Consequences.* Washington, DC: World Bank.

———. 2008b. *The Road Not Travelled: Education Reform in the Middle East and North Africa.* Washington, DC: World Bank.

———. 2009. *From Privilege to Competition: Unlocking Private-Led Growth in the Middle East and North Africa.* Washington, DC: World Bank.

———. 2010. *World Development Report 2011: Conflict, Security, and Development.* Washington, DC: World Bank.

———. 2011a. *Defining Gender in the 21st Century: Talking with Women and Men around the World, A Multi-Country Qualitative Study of Gender and Economic Choice.* Washington, DC: World Bank.

———. 2011b. *More and Better Jobs in South Asia.* Washington, DC: World Bank.

———. 2011c. *World Development Report 2012: Gender Equality and Development.* Washington, DC: World Bank.

———. 2012a. *Bread, Freedom, and Dignity: Jobs in the Middle East and North Africa.* Washington, DC: World Bank.

———. 2012b. *Gender Equality and Development in the Middle East and North Africa Region.* Washington, DC: World Bank.

———. 2012c. "Ten Things You Didn't Know About Mauritius." World Bank, Washington, DC. Processed.

Wrigley, Patrick. 2010. "Youth 'Bulges' in the Middle East and North Africa: Risk or Asset?" MENA Knowledge and Learning Fast Brief Series 74, World Bank, Washington DC.

Zafar, Ali. 2011. "Mauritius: An Economic Success Story." In *Yes Africa Can: Success Stories from a Dynamic Continent,* ed. Punam Chuhan-Pole and Manka Angwafo, 91–106. Washington, DC: World Bank.

Connected jobs agendas

*The migration of people matches opportunities across borders.
Globalization is leading to a growing international migration of jobs
not only in manufacturing but also, increasingly, in services.*

Different countries face different jobs challenges, but their jobs agendas are interconnected by two forces—the migration of people and the migration of jobs. These two flows have consequences for living standards, productivity, and social cohesion in sending and receiving countries. The arrival of migrants or the outsourcing of jobs abroad affects the living standards of both migrants and locals. The availability of foreign workers, the development of migrant networks channeling savings and ideas, and the arrival of multinational firms bringing more advanced techniques are all bound to increase productivity. But family structures as well as community life are affected by the movement of people and jobs. The potential gains are considerable, but there are also tradeoffs.

Even if development strategies succeed in addressing jobs challenges at the country level, mismatches between employment opportunities at home and abroad are bound to occur, encouraging people to leave their communities and try their chances elsewhere. Almost inevitably, the international migration of people will be one of the policy levers to consider in South Asia and in Sub-Saharan Africa, given the projected rapid growth in the labor force in these regions over the coming decades. Migration trends will be driven not only by demographic pressures but also by cultural and geographic proximity, as well as economic factors.

Jobs agendas are also connected through the international migration of jobs. The splintering of production tasks has facilitated their delocalization and outsourcing to developing countries, resulting in greater trade volumes and lower prices of final goods. But it has also led to a global redistribution of jobs in manufacturing, and the same trend is increasingly visible in services as well. So far, the migration of jobs out of industrial countries has mainly affected blue-collar workers, but white-collar jobs are following. These are not once-and-for-all moves. Growing labor costs in Asia may open up opportunities for other developing countries to jump-start industrialization.

Migration of workers

Precise figures on the global number of international migrants are not available, an unsurprising fact given that a number of them cross borders illegally or do not return once their visas and permits expire. That is why estimates tend to rely on population censuses and household surveys. Even then, differences across countries in the way that data are gathered, and in the way legislation defines nationality and migratory status, make accurate counts difficult.[1] The orders of magnitude are relatively uncontroversial, however. There are more than 200 million migrants worldwide, and 90 million of them are workers. Migrants represent between 2.5 and 3 percent of the world's population and the global labor force.[2] Many are temporary or seasonal workers and return to their home country.

Global patterns of migration

Global figures hide important differences across countries. Some countries are mainly recipients, while others are sources, and yet others neither host nor send significant numbers of migrants (map 7.1). In a few relatively small recipient countries, the foreign-born population makes up more than 40 percent of the total population. Israel, Jordan, Kuwait, Qatar, and Singapore are in this group. Among bigger recipient countries, those with the largest share of immigrants in their population are Saudi Arabia (27.8 percent), Canada (21.3 percent), Australia (21.0 percent), and the United States (13.5 percent). In absolute numbers, the United States is the largest recipient of migrants, with 42.8 million,

MAP 7.1 *Only in some countries are migrants a substantial share of the population*

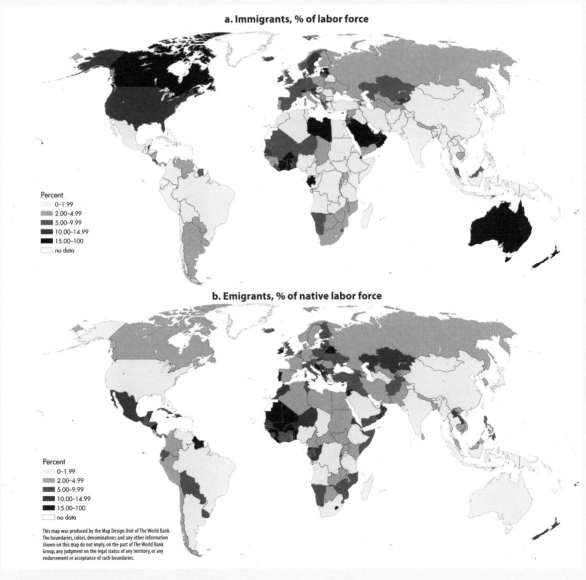

Source: World Development Report 2013 team based on Özden and others 2011 and Artuc and others 2012, using census data from around 2000.

followed by the Russian Federation (12.3 million), and Germany (10.8 million). Among the sending countries, those with the largest numbers of migrants are Mexico (10.1 million), India (9.1 million), and Bangladesh (6.0 million).[3] Russia is so high on the list, because many ethnic Russians live in countries that were formerly part of the Soviet Union.

Political turmoil and globalization accelerated migration flows in the first half of the 20th century. The partition of Bangladesh, India, and Pakistan involved large numbers of people living in countries different from their birthplace. The decline of transportation costs, the growth of Persian Gulf economies following surges in oil prices, and the entry into world markets of developing countries with large populations have all stimulated a surge of migrant workers worldwide.

Differences in expected earnings between the country of origin and the country of destination are an important reason for people to migrate. Earnings gains, however, are offset to varying degrees by the direct costs of migration (such as transportation fees and intermediation services) as well as by indirect costs associated with the difficulties of adapting to a different culture and society and leaving family and friends behind. These costs also help explain aggregate migration flows. For many migrants, physical and cultural proximity (including a common language, religion, or way of life) are important when choosing a host country. Concerns about employment opportunities and personal safety in the sending countries are other important, sometimes crucial, drivers of migration. More than 10 million migrants are refugees, and nearly 2 million are asylum seekers.[4]

The growth rate in the global number of migrant workers peaked between 2005 and 2008 and then decelerated because of the impact of the global economic crisis. During previous decades, the growth in migration flows came primarily from South-North flows; that is, from developing to developed countries. South-South migration, although numerically larger, remained stable over that period.[5]

Skilled workers represent a growing share of international migration. Developed countries increasingly implement policies to attract talent. Between 1990 and 2000, the share of workers with at least some tertiary education among immigrants increased from 15 to 25 percent in the United Kingdom, and from 25 to 30 percent in the United States. Stark country differences are also present in skilled labor migration. Some developing countries explicitly promote emigration of skilled workers, while others complain about "brain drain." More than 70 percent of citizens with tertiary education in Haiti, Jamaica, and Trinidad and Tobago live abroad. The share of skilled workers among migrants is particularly high in African countries (map 7.2).[6]

Highly skilled migrants fall into a range of categories including technology and business creators, scientists, scholars, students, and health and cultural workers. At 10 percent, their share of total migration is still relatively small, but 90 percent of them live in industrial countries.[7] In some occupations, the concentration of skilled migrants is substantial: 27 percent of all physicians in the United States, 21 percent in Australia, and 20 percent in Canada are foreign-trained.[8]

Impacts on sending and receiving countries

The most direct impact of international migration is on living standards. Through their work in receiving countries, and through remittances to sending countries, migrants increase their incomes and those of their families. Migrants also contribute to global output if their productivity abroad is higher than it was at home, which may often be the case. They can even contribute to output in the sending country, as networks of migrants and returnees serve as channels for investment, innovation, and expertise. Social effects are mixed, however. On the positive side, migration connects people from different cultures in ways bound to widen their horizons. On the negative side, separation from family and friends can be a source of distress and isolation in the recipient country. Large numbers of immigrants can also exacerbate frustration among vulnerable groups in recipient countries, if foreigners are seen as competitors for jobs and public services.

The increase in earnings from migration may amount to tens of thousands of dollars per worker per year. After controlling for worker

MAP 7.2 *Many migrants are highly skilled*

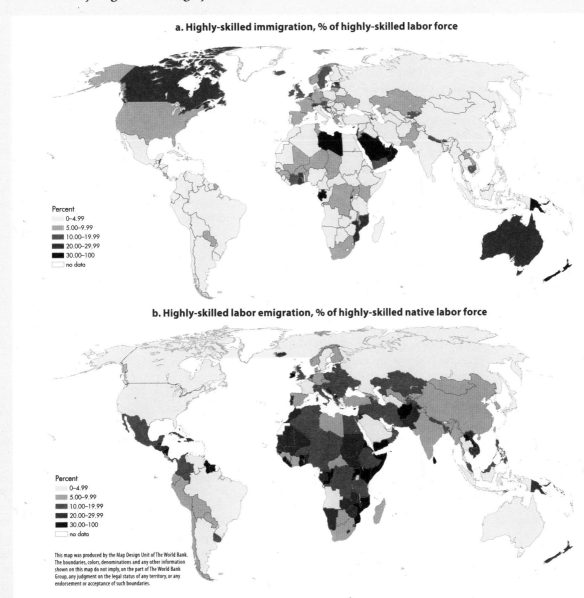

a. Highly-skilled immigration, % of highly-skilled labor force

Percent
- 0–4.99
- 5.00–9.99
- 10.00–19.99
- 20.00–29.99
- 30.00–100
- no data

b. Highly-skilled labor emigration, % of highly-skilled native labor force

Percent
- 0–4.99
- 5.00–9.99
- 10.00–19.99
- 20.00–29.99
- 30.00–100
- no data

This map was produced by the Map Design Unit of The World Bank. The boundaries, colors, denominations and any other information shown on this map do not imply, on the part of The World Bank Group, any judgment on the legal status of any territory, or any endorsement or acceptance of such boundaries.

Source: World Development Report 2013 team based on Özden and others 2011 and Artuc and others 2012.
Note: Highly-skilled migrants are those with at least some tertiary education.

characteristics, the gain may range from 50 percent to more than double the difference in income per capita between the host and the sending countries.[9,10] Transportation costs and rents taken by intermediaries can reduce these gains, however. In some cases, these intermediaries are part of illegal organizations linked to trafficking of people and criminal abuses, making migrants a particularly vulnerable group. In others, intermediaries are informal agents who provide market-priced migration services in the absence of other formal mechanisms to address the existence of demand and supply for migration.[11] Migrants also face psychological and physical health risks, often without access to health insurance.[12] The persistent flows of migration would indicate, though, that the large gains, actual and expected, more than compensate for the costs.

Evidence on the impact of migration on labor outcomes in sending countries is scattered. If employment opportunities for those who migrate were limited, earnings and employment would remain unaltered. If they were plentiful, earnings rise and the participation rates of previously inactive persons would increase. Studies for Mexico, Pakistan, and the Philippines show that out-migration did affect wages and unemployment rates in the sending country, but no discernable effects on labor outcomes have been found in Bangladesh, India, and Sri Lanka.[13]

The net effects of migration flows on employment opportunities and labor earnings depend on the skills and the jobs of those who move abroad. A recent study using data for high- and middle-income economies shows that immigration of high-skill workers has positive effects on wages of both high- and low-skill local workers. On the other hand, emigration of more educated workers is associated with declines in wages for both low- and high-skill workers who remain in the country of origin.[14]

Remittances are an important source of income for households in sending countries, although they do not necessarily reach the poorest of the poor. In different countries, an increase in international remittances is associated with declines in the share of people living in poverty.[15] Remittances also increase savings and investment in recipient families.[16] And they are more resilient than is generally believed. Recent studies show that despite tougher conditions for migrants during the 2009 recession, remittances dipped only slightly.[17] Results are mixed on the impact of remittances on income inequality. Some studies find that migrants come from the middle of the income (or wealth) distribution and that, in the short term, remittances leave overall inequality unaltered. Others show that in the medium term inequality decreases, because of the higher economic activity in localities with migrants.[18] Most studies also report that remittances reduce labor force participation among migrants' relatives.[19]

The growing migration trend among the highly skilled raises concerns about the implications for developing countries. Some fear a brain drain, whereby developing countries would suffer from the loss of valuable human resources.[20] According to this view, developing countries put considerable fiscal resources into the education of these workers, with the intention of enhancing their productivity and creating an elite of innovators, thinkers, and administrators. Thus the migration of skilled workers not only creates a fiscal and distributive concern in the short term, but it also impairs the growth capacities of the country in the long term. In this view, developing countries should create incentives for skilled workers to return to their home country, for example, through financial reforms of secondary and tertiary education.

Others, however, see a "brain gain," whereby developing countries benefit from networks, return migration, and the incentives for young people to improve their skills. Returning migrants bring home entrepreneurial and technical capacities that enhance productivity in sending countries. Experience acquired abroad has been found to induce higher wages among salaried workers and higher productive efficiency among entrepreneurs in several countries.[21] Beyond the individual benefits are societal benefits that may extend to the proliferation of a whole industry and the creation of new jobs in an entire locality. Bangalore and Hyderabad in India illustrate this point: returning migrants set up information technology and communication companies to take advantage of their previous experience and their links with international companies.[22] The presence of highly qualified Indian engineers and executives in U.S. corporations paved the way for the rise of the Indian software industry.[23] The activities of migrant networks are not restricted to skilled migrants or corporate activities. Networks of Mexican low-skill workers in the United States have worked with the Mexican government to redirect and enhance public investment in infrastructure in their communities of origin.[24]

Networks of migrants can also be important sources of foreign direct investment and know-how, both of which promote productivity growth in sending countries. It is estimated that Chinese migrants contributed more than half of all foreign direct investment in China.[25] The impact of returning migrants on their communities may be more modest in smaller countries that lack the scale for the development of new vibrant businesses.[26]

The increase in talent migration may also bring a brain gain through its impact on human capital accumulation in sending countries. The prospect of migration raises the returns to education and, thus, fosters investment in human capital. However, these positive effects depend on the size of skill migration and the relative size of the country. Recent evidence indicates that large countries with low rates of high-skill emigration experience a net gain in human capital. In contrast, small countries with high rates of high-skill emigration suffer a net loss.[27]

Social impacts are more diverse. In sending countries, researchers find changes in gender and family relations as well as in political attitudes. But the nature of these changes depends on the country. In some cases, women and children are empowered by the migration of spouses and parents; in others, they become more vulnerable.[28] Migrants to societies that value liberty and democracy come to appreciate these values, whereas those in more traditional host countries may become more traditional themselves.[29]

In host countries, most studies have concentrated on the influence of migrants on the employment and earnings of locals, as well as on the fiscal consequences of migrant inflows. The majority of these studies finds either no effect or a very small negative effect on the average labor earnings of the locals. But the composition of employment between locals and migrants shifts, creating winners and losers.[30] The fiscal consequences for host countries depend on the characteristics of the migrants. The younger and more skilled they are, the higher the tax revenues. The impact of government spending in host countries varies, depending on the duration of migration and the family composition of the migrants. Computations of the net effect on the welfare systems of recipient countries are sensitive to hypotheses and estimation methods.[31]

Last but not least, migration may also bring racial prejudice and exacerbate social tensions in host countries. This happens when migrants are secluded in segregated occupations or neighborhoods, preventing their genuine integration in society.[32] It may also occur when migrants are perceived as competing for "nonmigrant" jobs. Prejudice and tensions may result in distrust of migrants and lead to the hardening of legal requirements for entering the host country, forced repatriations, and even the building of physical walls to prevent migration. These policies may not ease tensions unless a more comprehensive approach is adopted. Irregular or undocumented migration is growing, partly in reaction to the lack of legal alternatives to migration given the mounting mismatches between employment opportunities in sending and receiving countries.[33]

Migration of jobs

Quantifying the international migration of jobs is even more difficult than estimating the global number of international migrants. The past four decades have been marked by the delocalization and outsourcing of manufacturing tasks from industrial countries to the developing world, especially to East Asia. More recently, the same pattern is observed for tasks in the services sector. In fact, exports of services are the fastest-growing component of global trade. And the share originating in developing countries has been growing steadily over the past two decades. But counting how many jobs are affected globally is not feasible, because the process involves job destruction in some countries and job creation in others, in ways that cannot be easily matched with each other.

Global trends

The share of manufacturing in total employment in industrial countries declined by roughly one-third between 1970 and 2008, as did its share in gross domestic product (GDP) (figure 7.1).[34] Although starting from higher levels, the pattern was the same in Japan as in Europe and North America. The Republic of Korea industrialized in the 1970s and 1980s, but the share of manufacturing in its employment and GDP started declining in 1992. Meanwhile,

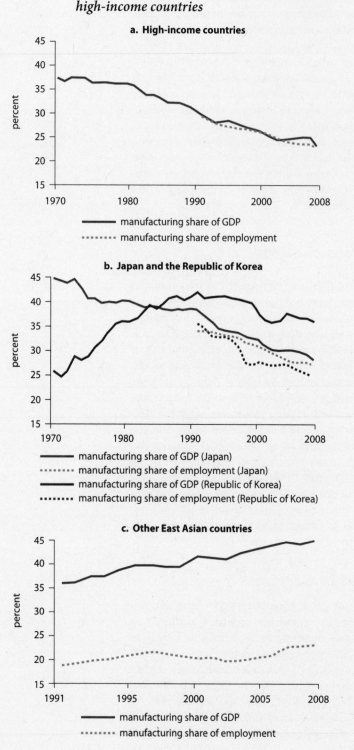

FIGURE 7.1 *Manufacturing jobs have migrated away from high-income countries*

a. High-income countries

— manufacturing share of GDP
······· manufacturing share of employment

b. Japan and the Republic of Korea

— manufacturing share of GDP (Japan)
······· manufacturing share of employment (Japan)
— manufacturing share of GDP (Republic of Korea)
······· manufacturing share of employment (Republic of Korea)

c. Other East Asian countries

— manufacturing share of GDP
······· manufacturing share of employment

Source: World Development Report 2013 team estimates based on data from the United Nations Industrial Development Organization (UNIDO) database and United Nations Statistics Division.
Note: Japan is not included in panel a. GDP = gross domestic product.

the share of manufacturing in total employment increased steadily in other East Asian countries, including China, for four decades. In South Asia and Sub-Saharan Africa, the share has been low and stagnant, whereas it has declined in Latin America and increased in Eastern Europe and Central Asia. The overall pattern is one where manufacturing jobs migrated primarily from Western Europe and the United States to Northeast Asia and then to the rest of East Asia.

The East Asian trends are consistent with the "flying geese" pattern of development, where economic transformation is consistent with dynamic changes in comparative advantage. Industrialization in East Asian countries began with the development of labor-intensive sectors, gradually shifted to capital-intensive sectors, and then to knowledge-intensive activities. In parallel, wages rose and skills increased.[35] First Japan, then Korea, and more recently China followed a similar pattern. As labor costs increase further, light manufacturing jobs are likely to migrate away from coastal China, where most industries have concentrated. By some estimates, nearly 100 million jobs are at stake.[36]

The migration of light manufacturing jobs out of coastal China could open a once-in-a-generation opportunity for countries in Sub-Saharan Africa and South Asia to jump-start their industrialization. But some observers predict that the migration will go mainly to the inland areas in China, where wage rates are lower than on the coast. This would be consistent with the patterns of industrialization in Japan; Korea; Taiwan, China; and the United States, where the initial geographical concentration of industries was followed by dispersion within the same country.[37] However, China's labor market is relatively integrated to the point where even unskilled wage rates in rural areas have been increasing rapidly.[38] Therefore, an overall decline in the manufacturing share of GDP in China might be unavoidable, opening up the opportunity for labor-intensive industrialization in other developing countries.[39]

The rapid growth of labor productivity in manufacturing is resulting in the stagnation or even the decline of the number of manufacturing jobs worldwide (figure 7.2). Global employment in manufacturing increased by only 30 percent from 1990 to 2008, with most of the expansion taking place in Asia, especially in China. Given that manufacturing jobs connect to ex-

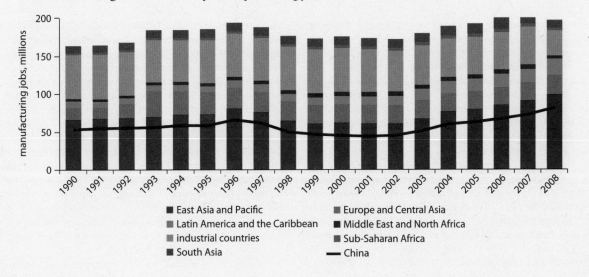

FIGURE 7.2 *The global number of manufacturing jobs has not varied much*

Legend:
- East Asia and Pacific
- Europe and Central Asia
- Latin America and the Caribbean
- Middle East and North Africa
- industrial countries
- Sub-Saharan Africa
- South Asia
- China

Sources: World Development Report 2013 team based on ILO 2010; Industrial Statistics Database: INDSTAT2-2011 Edition, United Nations Industrial Development Organization, Vienna, and World Development Indicators.

port markets and global value chains more than other jobs and are thus more likely to generate productivity externalities, this stagnation or decline raises the prospect of a fierce international competition ahead (question 7). If aggregate numbers of manufacturing jobs are bound to remain relatively stable, successful industrialization in one region may come at the expense of industrial employment in another region.

Manufacturing could take off in South Asia or Sub-Saharan Africa if technology and management knowledge were transferred there. Such a transfer, however, is not simple: fostering entrepreneurship, nurturing a more skilled workforce, creating a stronger investment climate, and establishing a more favorable institutional environment would be necessary. There is also a risk of focusing on industries that are not in line with the potential comparative advantage of these regions.[40] Combined with poor logistics and weak government capacity, that could mean that few manufacturing jobs would actually migrate to these regions. Studies on the locational decisions of multinational corporations show that many factors come into play (box 7.1).

Services were once regarded largely as non-tradable, but this is no longer the case. Both country-specific and global trends show a grow-ing share of employment and GDP in services, some of which are sold across borders.[41] New ways of delivering services, often broken down into small tasks and driven by information and communication technology (ICT), are transforming where service activities can be located (box 7.2). The world share of developing countries in global exports of services increased from 11 percent in 1990 to 21 percent in 2008. Services are now the main contributor to economic growth in many developing countries, including India.[42]

The rapid expansion of trade in services is bound to increase productivity on a global scale. But it also is raising fears in developed countries that service sector jobs will migrate to developing countries through offshoring or international outsourcing, much the same as manufacturing jobs did over the past four decades.

A telltale sign of the potential for offshoring and outsourcing is the substantial number of service sector tasks already being performed remotely within industrial countries.[43] In the United States, service occupations that are tradable by nature, such as computer systems design and management consulting, display a heavy geographic concentration. This concentration results partly from agglomeration economies,

BOX 7.1 *Why do multinationals locate where they do?*

Where multinationals locate provides insights into the critical characteristics in a host country that firms want or need. Traditionally, foreign direct investment (FDI) was categorized either as horizontal—multinationals seeking better access to larger markets overseas—or vertical—multinationals moving part of their production to a lower-cost location. As trade barriers and transportation costs have fallen and supply chains involve ever more specialized tasks, the importance of locating near the final market has diminished. But the empirical patterns show that "costs" need to be determined over a range of dimensions.

The location-decision question has been examined empirically by looking at how the characteristics of host countries predict the inflow of FDI and entry of multinationals. Significant macroeconomic instability or conflict disqualifies most locations. Low wages can be attractive, but given that labor is often a small share of overall manufacturing costs, they are often not the predominant consideration. And labor costs cannot be evaluated separately from the quality of skills; developed countries remain significant destinations of FDI in part because of their highly skilled workforces. Access to land, particularly in parts of Africa and Asia where land access is more regulated, can be a significant consideration. Poor or inconsistent public services, including electricity, security, and transportation infrastructure, can quickly raise costs—through delays, lost production, and the expense of privately providing these services.

Costs associated with complying with business regulations and with taxes can also be important, as are the reliability and cost of contract enforcement institutions. The literature shows that the relative importance of these dimensions often varies by different types of sectors, the degree of capital intensity, and technological sophistication. The presence of other firms is also a consideration. Quick and reliable access to suppliers can reduce costs and delays.

In addition to the academic literature, a number of consulting firms provide analysis and rankings of the attractiveness of countries based on the views of top executives of multinationals. A.T. Kearney has published a Foreign Direct Investment Index since 1998. Three dimensions emerge as critical in its analysis: well-functioning financial markets, a strong business environment, and strong labor skills. A separate index for the location of services also emphasizes skills, particularly language skills, and the degree of global integration. Labor typically accounts for a larger share of overall costs in services than in manufacturing.

The evolution of supply chains into more specialized tasks operating across more diverse locations can offer opportunities for an increasing number of developing countries. Multinationals are not looking for a strong business environment across the board; they care about inputs and services that are specific to their needs and thus are location-specific.

Sources: World Development Report 2013 team based on Alfaro and Chen 2011, Helpman 2006, and Harrison and Rodríguez-Clare 2009.

BOX 7.2 *E-links create job opportunities in developing countries, but the scale is still modest*

Internet services are becoming ever more accessible, including in the developing world. Crowdsourcing tools help businesses to break up larger tasks into many smaller discrete steps. These are then offered to a global online community through competition. The platform TopCoder, for example, brings together close to 400,000 programmers globally.

A special type of online outsourcing, branded impact sourcing by some, aims to bring employment and supplementary income to low-income areas. Impact sourcing is estimated to represent 4 percent of the entire business process outsourcing industry, accounting for US$4.5 billion in total revenues and employing around 140,000 people around the globe. Samasource is a nonprofit organization based in San Francisco, working with major technology clients. It splits large projects into "micro work"—small tasks that can be done online using inexpensive computers—and distributes the tasks largely to women working with partner service providers in the poorest parts of the world, including remote villages, slums, and refugee camps in countries, such as Haiti, Pakistan, Uganda, and others. Data workers develop skills in English, computers, and a variety of project-specific tasks. Samasource has reached 1,600 women and youth over the past three years.

Similarly, RuralShores aims to bring rural India into the global knowledge world. It provides remote processing of noncritical business transactions such as data entry, simple bookkeeping, expenses handling, and document digitalization and archiving. RuralShores runs 10 centers in 7 Indian states, employing about 1,000 people. The centers, run as for-profit entities, are all located in remote Indian villages. While most employees are high-school graduates, the company gives preference to people with disabilities and young jobseekers from poor, agrarian families. Impact sourcing does face challenges that include access to clients and contracts, sustainable demand, robust infrastructure, effective recruitment, and identification of investors.

Sources: World Development Report 2013 team based on Monitor Inclusive Markets 2011 and Selim 2012 for the World Development Report 2013.

supporting specialization. But simple geographic imbalances between the local supply and demand for services also contribute to remote provision.

Trade in services can be expected to expand rapidly in the coming years. Until recently, it was thought that only labor-intensive tasks would be relocated to developing countries, allowing production in industrial countries to focus on capital- or skill-intensive tasks.[44] However, developing countries are now exporting not only traditional services, such as transportation and tourism, but also modern and skill-intensive services, such as financial intermediation, computer and information services, and legal and technical support.[45] Skilled jobs performed by accountants, programmers, designers, architects, medical diagnosticians, and financial and statistical analysts are increasingly outsourced by firms in industrial countries.[46] In India, the number of such skilled white-collar jobs has grown rapidly.[47] However, some of the service jobs seen as skilled in developing countries are considered unskilled in industrial countries.[48]

India was a developing world pioneer in building a modern export-oriented services sector, but other countries—Brazil, Chile, China, and Malaysia, to name a few—have also seized the opportunity.[49] But outsourcing does not only happen between industrial and developing countries. In the United States (the largest offshoring economy), 85 percent of the service trade is with other industrial countries.[50] Two-thirds of service sector exports from developing countries are actually South-South trade.[51]

Developing countries tend to specialize in certain activities within the services sector. For example, Brazil, Costa Rica, and Uruguay are strong in professional and ICT-related services; Chile in distribution and transportation services; Mexico in communication and distribution services; and Sub-Saharan African countries in professional services.[52] This diversity in specialization will likely lead to both competition and cooperation, involving different segments of the services sector, rather than a head-on collision between industrial and developing countries.

This new phase of globalization is bound to influence views and interpretations about structural transformation and the migration of jobs.

Some researchers claim that a "revolution" is under way that is turning services sectors into the main engine of economic growth in developing countries.[53] Others argue that developing countries such as India and the Philippines are successful in exporting relatively skill-intensive services not because of their comparative advantage in such services but because of policies preventing their manufacturing sectors from taking off.[54] Given the stagnation of global employment in manufacturing and the growing trade in services, a relevant question is whether developing countries can successfully skip the industrialization phase of development.

Winners and losers

The obvious winners of globalization are the workers and entrepreneurs in countries to which industries and splintered tasks have migrated. Outsourcing and offshoring, along with the attendant transfer of new technologies and advanced management methods, contributes to productivity growth and improvements in living standards. The development of more efficient industries and services encourage a reallocation of labor toward more productive uses. It also stimulates the subsequent development of other interrelated industries and sectors through backward and forward linkages. The development of a modern services sector can lead to greater coordination in value chains and make a further subdivision of tasks and the reorganization of production possible, leading to economies of scale.[55] Multiple actors—including multinationals, civil society organizations and consumers in industrial countries—are increasingly active in efforts to improve working conditions and workers' rights in developing countries. To the extent that such efforts bear fruit, enhanced export opportunities improve workers' well-being.[56] In all these ways, significant trickle-down effects can have widespread benefits for recipient countries.

The hidden winners from the migration of jobs are consumers at large. The improved international division of labor expands the global availability of goods and services, improving living standards around the world.[57] This point can be easily understood by thinking how the world would look if China and India could not provide cheap goods and services to the rest of the world.

The obvious losers are those who have lost their jobs because of the declining competitiveness of the industries and services where they used to work. While skilled workers may easily find similar occupations in other industries without a loss in salary, many low-skilled workers are not so fortunate. Low-skilled workers or those with industry- or occupation-specific skills that are no longer in demand are more likely to be forced to accept lower-paying jobs in different industries or remain unemployed.[58] Job losses could become a serious issue not only in industrial countries but also in dynamically growing developing countries, such as China, as their labor costs increase.

There are also hidden losers. These are the workers and entrepreneurs in countries which have failed to develop new industries and services connected to world markets and the jobs that go with them.[59] Workers in those countries, however, may not perceive the lost employment opportunities.[60]

One way to mitigate the welfare losses from globalization, both apparent and hidden, is through the international migration of workers. Income differentials across countries, which reflect differences in the growth rates of different economies, are important drivers of this migration. By reallocating workers from stagnant or slowly growing economies to rapidly growing ones, the international migration of workers contributes to the reduction in the income gap created by the international migration of jobs. But jobs tend to migrate more easily than people.

* * *

The migration of people and the migration of jobs make clear that jobs challenges, despite being country specific, can also be global in scope. Both sending and recipient countries can benefit from these international movements in a variety of ways, from higher labor earnings to remittances, from greater productivity to broader networks. Consumers worldwide also benefit from less expensive consumer goods. Tensions and costs are associated with these two migrations, however. Migrant workers may suffer discrimination and segregation or lose their family and cultural connections and identity, disrupting not only their own sense of well-being but also have an impact on communities in origin and host countries.

The migration of people and the migration of jobs may transform entire communities, creating winners and losers. Many see their lives improve, but those who lose their jobs to outsourcing and offshoring may experience permanent declines in well-being, especially if they are unskilled. These spillovers, positive and negative, are powerful motivators for the political and social groups that promote or oppose the migration of people and of jobs. But these spillovers are international in nature, so coping with them only through national policy instruments may prove unsatisfactory.

Many developing countries face a jobs agenda. In some, it involves offering avenues to rural populations to move out of poverty. In others, it aims at leveraging the gains from urbanization and from integration in global markets. Yet in others, the goal is to prevent youth from becoming disenfranchised or to reduce the risk of conflict. These agendas are addressed through national policies that stimulate job creation by the private sector, especially in the areas and activities where development payoffs are highest. But jobs agendas of individual countries are connected through globalization: trade in goods and services, investment flows, and migration of workers. This begs the question: if jobs can migrate from one country to another, do policies to support job creation in one country become policies affecting jobs in other countries—policies competing for jobs globally?

Among economists, the conventional wisdom is that the number of jobs is not determined by international trade and investment but by the total number of people in the labor force. And in general, openness to international trade and foreign direct investment is beneficial for all the countries involved. Thus, globalization is not a zero-sum game. From this point of view, policies to support job creation are not policies competing for jobs, even as they may alter the global flows of trade, investment, and workers.

The general public seems to have a less sanguine view of the situation. Representative public opinion polls show that firm relocation and tasks outsourced abroad are seen as a threat to employment in industrial countries (box 7.3). Globalization is perceived as a head-to-head competition in which employment gains in one country can be achieved only at the expense of jobs in other countries.

There is merit to both views. Past the short-term impact of outsourcing and delocalization, the total number of jobs in one country should not be substantially affected by policy decisions in other countries. Some firms may close or start activities, others may expand or contract their business, but total employment will be roughly

determined by the size of the labor force. However, the composition of employment is bound to change. The concern is that the share of good jobs for development may decline in one country and increase in another. Whether that happens depends on the nature of good jobs for development and the types of national policies being adopted to support job creation. While the public's concern is legitimate, not all measures to support job creation amount to a beggar-thy-neighbor policy.

Not a competition for total employment but for its composition

International trade and investment can be expected to lead to greater prosperity. Globalization, including firm relocation and outsourcing, may result in job losses at home in the short term, but the demand for labor should increase in the longer run, as specialization generates efficiency gains in both industrial and developing countries.[61] Lower prices for goods and services, and a growing consumption demand from emerging countries as they prosper, can only reinforce the upward trend in the global demand for labor.

Empirical evidence to a large extent confirms this upbeat assessment. Labor earnings and working conditions improve as countries grow richer, and global integration has been good for growth. Across developing countries, a 1 percent increase in a country's openness, measured as the share of its foreign trade in its output, has been associated with a 1 percent increase in GDP per capita.[62] Gains may reach up to 1.5 percentage points on average in the case of openness in financial services and telecommunications.[63] Even in Sub-Saharan Africa, where trade liberalization was viewed with skepticism, the increase in output growth rates could be in the range of 0.5 to 0.8 percent.[64] Evidence also shows that firms engaged in global markets pay higher wages. This is true of exporting firms from Colombia to Morocco and from Mexico to Korea. It is also true of foreign-owned companies, whether they operate in Cameroon or

BOX 7.3 *Globalization is often viewed as jobs migrating abroad*

Across European countries, popular perceptions can be inferred from the Eurobarometer surveys. One of its questions is the following: "What comes first to mind when you hear the word 'globalization'?" The options for answering this question are opportunities for domestic companies in terms of new outlets; foreign investments in the country; relocation of some companies to countries where labor is cheaper; increased competition for the country; and other. The third option reflects perceived job insecurity. Even before the global crisis and the European debt crisis, when concerns about unemployment were not exacerbated, about one-third to one-half of respondents see globalization as a relocation of companies abroad. The survey also asked: "Which of the following two propositions is the one which is closest to your opinion with regard to globalization?" Possible answers included good opportunity for domestic companies; threat to employment and companies; and "do not know." With the exception of Denmark, where only a small minority chose the second

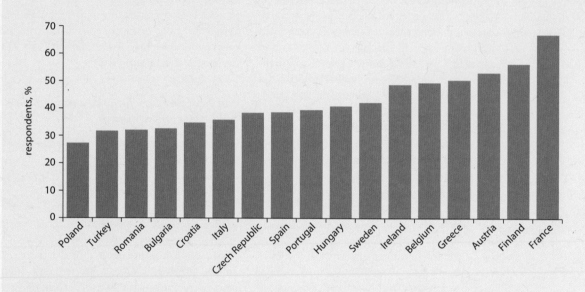

Note: The figure is based on the following question and answer: *Question:* "There are multiple consequences of the globalization of trade. When you hear the word 'globalization,' what comes first to mind?"; and *Answer:* "Relocation of some companies to countries where labor is cheaper." Data are from surveys conducted in 2008.

option, between one-third and three-quarters of the respondents saw globalization as a threat to jobs.

Based on opinion polls, policies for jobs are often perceived as a zero-sum game in which gains for one country can be achieved only at the expense of others. The chairman and CEO (Chief Executive Officer) of Gallup put it as follows: "If you were to ask me, from all the world polling Gallup has done for more than 75 years, what would fix the world—what would suddenly create worldwide peace, global well-being, and the next extraordinary advancements in human development, I would say the immediate appearance of 1.8 billion jobs—formal jobs." In his view, "this raises an important distinction—not only do we need to create more jobs, we need to increase the number of good jobs. And we can't see that quest for good jobs as an internal skirmish between warring political ideologies. It's an international war."[a]

Sources: Clifton 2011; Eurobarometer Surveys (database) 2010, European Commission, Brussels.
a. Interview given in connection with the book launch.

República Bolivariana de Venezuela, Indonesia or Zambia.[65]

Admittedly, the dispersion of earnings within countries has also increased, for instance in the form of higher returns to education, and it is tempting to attribute this trend to globalization. Low-skill jobs in industrial countries are often high-skill jobs from the perspective of developing countries, and exporting itself is a skill-intensive activity. Therefore, international trade and offshore outsourcing can be expected to increase the relative demand for skills at both ends, favoring better-off workers. The empirical results on this possible effect vary widely, however.[66] For sure, all policies create winners and losers, and the distribution of labor earnings has widened in parallel with globalization, but a causal relationship is difficult to establish. Overall, widening disparities may have more to do with technological progress and financial liberalization than with globalization.

A different perspective arises when considering the composition of employment, rather than the level or dispersion of labor earnings. Globalization provides developing countries with the opportunity to connect to world markets and derive productivity spillovers boosting their economic growth. Manufacturing jobs integrated in global value chains, as well as jobs in technologically advanced services and in finance, are often seen as tickets to rapid development. However, rapid technological progress and economies of scale may mean the global number of some of these jobs will not increase much. For jobs in manufacturing, the experience of the last few decades has shown a relative stability of their global numbers together with a dramatic change in their spatial distribution. If so, policies for job creation could lead to a competition not for the level of employment but for the jobs with the highest development payoffs.

The experience of Japan and the United States illustrates the point. In the 1950s, Japan exported cheap labor-intensive products in exchange for goods embedded with more advanced knowledge and technology. This strategy generated much needed revenue for Japan's post–World War II recovery. More importantly, it contributed to Japan's productivity growth and built the foundation for the production of more sophisticated goods. In the 1970s and 1980s, Japan not only began exporting steel, semiconductors, and automobiles but turned into a leading supplier. As the major exporter of these products, the United States suffered from Japan's expansion.[67] The United States had been characterized by its fluid labor markets. Yet, the potential welfare loss from the decline of Pittsburgh, Detroit, and other industrial centers could be substantial, even if labor was reallocated smoothly.[68] This competition was resolved by "voluntary export restraints"—a special form of quota that actually granted all quota rents to Japan but prevented a complete decline of such employment in the United States, indicating the importance attributed to these industries.[69]

Concerns are similar for developing countries nowadays. Consider the opportunities opened by the increase in labor earnings in the coastal areas of China.[70] Some labor-intensive manufacturing jobs connected with global value chains will migrate out of China in search of lower production costs. Given rapid technological progress, the global number of jobs in light manufacturing is unlikely to increase much. Low-income countries in both Sub-Saharan Africa and South Asia aspire to attract some of those jobs, so a competition is involved. Tension is not limited to labor-intensive manufacturing jobs. A similar logic underlies government efforts to attract high-tech companies, as Costa Rica successfully did with Intel.[71] This is also the logic behind government efforts to foster services exports, exemplified by the success of Brazil, Chile, India, Malaysia, and the Philippines.[72]

Because technological progress and globalization connect markets to an unprecedented level, they also result in competition over other types of jobs with high development payoffs. Jobs located in a global hub can generate large productivity spillovers. London stands as one of the most economically vibrant cities in Europe largely because it serves as an international financial center. The financial industry entails scale economies and is supported by density. Therefore, the number of global financial centers is limited, and their formation is shaped by location, history, and national policies. Similar logic applies to international transportation hubs such as Singapore, clusters of information and computer technology–related industries such as Silicon Valley and Bangalore, and so on.

Policies for jobs: Different degrees of competition

Even if globalization may result in a competition for good jobs for development, not all efforts to support job creation amount to beggar-thy-neighbor policies. Whether they do so depends on the type of instruments used and the nature of the spillovers from jobs.[73]

Because globalization involves international trade and foreign direct investment, it is natural to first consider trade- and investment-related instruments. Some of them, such as import tariffs, export subsidies, and local content requirements, are ruled out by multilateral trade agreements; others, such as improving access to credit for private exporters and identifying and removing specific constraints faced by foreign investors, are not. But in reality these are just a narrow subset of policies for jobs. When bidding to attract foreign direct investment, governments can compete directly through tax holidays or through dedicated physical infrastructure and human resources. They can also compete indirectly, as when they take actions that appeal to both local entrepreneurs and foreign investors. For example, they can contain increases in the cost of labor by keeping mandated benefits affordable. Or they can improve the availability and quality of factors of production, such as worker skills and public infrastructure. In South Asia, for example, the quality of physical infrastructure and the education of the workforce are the strongest predictors of entry of new firms.[74]

When considering good jobs for development more generally, and not just jobs connected to world markets, the set of policy options is even broader. Urban policies are another important instrument to stimulate job creation by the private sector. Given the potential agglomeration of economies, relatively small interventions can have large effects.[75] In low-income countries, enhancing extension services may have a large impact on farm productivity and, thus, on poverty reduction. Whether this broader set of policies leads to a competition for jobs depends on whether policies in one country have a positive or an adverse effect on the social welfare of another country.

A key question to ask is what purpose policies serve (figure 7.3). For instance, policies for jobs may aim to improve compliance with rights, prosecuting forced labor and harmful forms of child labor. Because fundamental labor rights and principles have been endorsed by most countries, promoting compliance with rights amounts to providing a global public good. Thus, interventions against human trafficking or child prostitution in one country are unlikely to have adverse effects in other countries and do not lead to a competition for jobs.

In the absence of a global public good dimension, the second question is what market imperfection or institutional failure is being addressed by the policy intervention. Tackling the institutional failures that lead to conflict, discrimination, or lack of voice might have an effect on the international flows of goods, services, and finance, but only indirectly. The risk that government interventions in these areas will result in a competition for jobs with other countries is limited. The risk is also limited in the case of interventions aimed at providing jobs opportunities for the poor. In all of these cases, there should be gains in well-being in the developing country, and no substantial loss in well-being in other countries. Therefore, jobs policies focused on strengthening social cohesion and improving living standards should be acceptable as well.

The answer is less clear when government interventions aim at enhancing productivity spillovers from jobs. These interventions typically include urban development policies, investments in infrastructure and skills, or the promotion of entrepreneurship. Because these interventions are likely to affect the international flows of goods, services, and finance, the range of possible outcomes is broader. While no general rule is available, interventions that undermine an open trading system most likely reduce aggregate well-being—probably more at home than abroad. On the other hand, interventions aligned with a country's dynamic comparative advantage could result in mutual gains. Admittedly, assessing what "aligned" means in practice is bound to involve an element of judgment.[76]

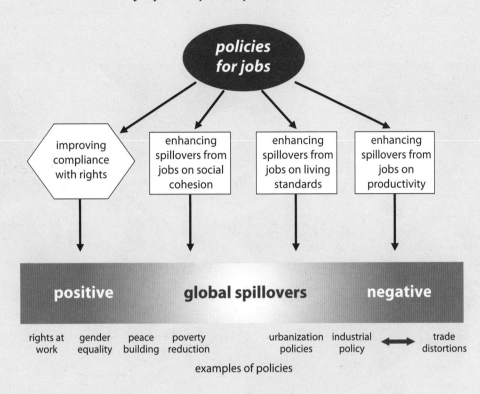

FIGURE 7.3 *Policies for jobs may or may not harm other countries*

Source: World Development Report 2013 team.

But the East Asian experience, with jobs in manufacturing migrating from Japan to Korea and Taiwan, China, and subsequently to China, and then to Vietnam, provides some hints. As these countries followed their dynamic comparative advantage under the "flying geese" pattern of development, there were few instances of an open competition for jobs between them.

Employees at a call center in Poland

© Piotr Malecki / Panos Pictures

Notes

1. Özden and others 2011.
2. IOM 2008; Lucas 2005.
3. IOM 2010.
4. See IOM 2010; UNHCR 2010.
5. This finding discounts the effect of political changes in South Asia and the former Soviet Union. See Özden and others 2011.
6. Docquier and Marfouk 2006.
7. Docquier and Marfouk 2006; Solimano 2010.
8. Bach 2008.
9. Docquier, Özden, and Peri 2011.
10. For the case of migration to New Zealand from Tonga, McKenzie, Gibson, and Stillman (2006) find that migration leads to a 263 percent increase in income. Clemens, Montenegro, and Pritchett (2008) find an annual gain in wages close to US$10,000 for migration from Mexico to the United States and about US$18,000 for migration from the Arab Republic of Egypt, Haiti, India, and Nigeria.
11. Chin 1999; Di Nicola 1999.
12. Hanson 2006; Spener 2009.
13. See Lucas 2005, chapter 3. See also Docquier, Özden, and Peri 2010. For a cross country analysis of this topic, see Hovhannisyan 2012 for the World Development Report 2013.
14. Lucas 2005, 267–69; Priebe and others 2011. The connection between health and migration is still a growing area of research. Gibson, McKenzie, and Stillman (forthcoming) find—using data on migrants from Tonga to New Zealand—that migration leads to improvements in mental health, whereas McKenzie, Gibson, and Stillman (2006) find that migration leads to significant and persistent increases in blood pressure.
15. Gupta, Patillo, and Wagh 2009; Lokshin, Bontch-Osmolovski, and Glinskaya 2010.
16. Anzoategui, Demirgüç-Kunt, and Martinez-Peria 2011.
17. Sirkeci, Cohen, and Ratha 2012.
18. See Shen, Docquier, and Rapoport (2010) for a theoretical explanation of the difficulties in explaining the link between remittances and inequality. Empirical studies include Acosta and others (2007); Adams (1989); Adams (1992); Adams (2004); Adams (2006); McKenzie and Rapoport (2007); and Milanovic (1987).
19. Adams 2011.
20. A related problem is the case of "brain waste": skilled workers who perform low-skilled jobs in either sending countries (because of stagnant growth) or in host countries (because of occupational segregation). In both cases, productivity is hindered because of underuse of these resources. See Özden and Schiff 2006.
21. See Wahba (2007) on Egypt; Thomas (2009) on Uganda and South Africa; and De Vreyer, Gubert, and Robilliard (2010) on the countries of the West African Economic and Monetary Union.
22. Chacko 2007. See also Saxenian 2004.
23. Pandey and others 2006.
24. Cordova 2009; Garcia Zamora 2005; McKenzie and Rapoport 2007; Torres and Kuznetsov 2006.
25. Gibson and McKenzie 2012.
26. Kuznetsov and Sabel 2006.
27. Beine, Docquier, and Rapoport 2011; Lucas 2010.
28. For Mexico, see Heymann and others (2009). For Albania, see de Soto and others (2002).
29. Some, including Keddie (1998), argue that migrants bring political radicalization, whereas others, such as Pérez-Armendáriz and Crow (2010), say migrants bring democracy.
30. For evidence in the United States, see Abowd and Freeman (1991); Borjas (2003); Card (2001); and LaLonde and Topel (1997). Qualitatively similar results are in Giuletti (2012), Hunt (1992), and Pischke and Velling (1997) for the cases of France and Germany; in Friedberg (2001) for Israel; in Carrasco, Jimeno, and Ortega (2008) for Spain; and in Dustmann, Fabbri, and Preston (2005) for the United Kingdom. See Chiswick and Miller 2009.
31. Lucas 2005, 285–86. For the complex political economy links between attitudes toward migration and the welfare state, see Koopmans (2010) and Razin, Sadka, and Suwankiri (2011).
32. Dingeman and Rumbaut 2010.
33. Despite the difficulties in measuring irregular migration, there is a consensus that the number of irregular migrants was growing in the years before the Great Recession of 2009. New sources for measuring irregular migration include administrative records and regularization programs. Other experiences include the IOM (International Organization for Migration) Counter-Trafficking Module (CTM), the CIREFI (Centre for Information, Discussion, and Exchange on the Crossing of Frontiers and Immigration), or EIL (Enforcement of Immigration Legislation) statistics collected by the European Commission. See IOM 2010.
34. Because of limited availability of data, figure 7.1 shows the gross domestic product share of the industrial sector, which consists of the manufacturing and the construction and mining sectors.
35. Akamatsu 1962; Lin 2011.
36. Lin 2011; Lin 2012.
37. Glaeser and others 1992; Henderson, Lee, and Lee 2001; Mano and Otsuka 2000; Sonobe and Otsuka 2006.

38. Rozelle and Huang 2012 for the World Development Report 2013.
39. See, in particular, Dinh and others 2012.
40. Lin 2012; Lin and others 2010.
41. Measuring the net effect of offshoring is complex, and different methodologies have been proposed. From a theoretical point of view, the net effect in a given country is ambiguous because offshoring may reduce employment in the short term, but the resulting specialization can induce productivity gains that increase employment in the long term, although with a change in the share of different types of labor and occupations within the total. The Organisation for Economic Cooperation and Development (OECD 2007) and the United Nations Conference on Trade and Development (UNCTAD 2004) indicate that offshoring is not necessarily a zero-sum game and that short-term job losses may be more than compensated for by job gains, although with variations across industries and sectors.
42. Ghani 2010.
43. Jensen 2011.
44. See, for example, Görg 2011.
45. Goswami, Mattoo, and Sáez 2011.
46. Millberg and others 2007.
47. See, for example, Suri 2007.
48. Goldberg and Pavcnik 2007.
49. Goswami, Mattoo, and Sáez 2011.
50. Ebenstein and others 2009.
51. Goswami, Mattoo, and Sáez 2011.
52. Goswami, Mattoo, and Sáez 2011.
53. Ghani 2010.
54. Goswami, Mattoo, and Sáez 2011; Jensen 2011.
55. François and Hoekman 2010.
56. Elliott and Freeman 2003; Newitt 2012 for the World Development Report 2013.
57. Bhagwati, Panagariya, and Srinivasan 2004.
58. Ebenstein and others 2009.
59. There is evidence that China's increasing exports affected the export patterns of other Asian countries. See Eichengreen, Rhee, and Tong 2007; Greenaway, Mahabir, and Milner 2008.
60. Blomström and Kokko 2009.
61. See, for example, Bhagwati, Panagariya, and Srinivasan 2004; François and Hoekman 2010; and Grossman and Rossi-Hansberg 2008.
62. Noguer and Siscart 2005.
63. Mattoo and Rathindran 2006.
64. Brückner and Lederman 2012.
65. See Aw, Chung, and Roberts (2000) and Clerides, Lach, and Tybout (1998) for exporting firms. See Aitken, Harrison, and Lipsey (1996); Velde and Morrissey (2003); and Görg, Strobl, and Walsh (2007) for foreign-owned companies.
66. For general reviews, see Goldberg and Pavcnik (2007); Jansen, Ralf, and Manuel (2011); New-

farmer and Sztajerowska (2012); Rama (2003); and Robertson and others (2009).
67. See, for example, McKinnon and Ohno 1997.
68. Gomory and Baumol 2001.
69. See, for example, Feenstra 1984 and Hymans and Stafford 1995.
70. Lin 2012.
71. Rodríguez-Clare 2001.
72 Goswami, Mattoo, and Sáez 2011.
73. Levy 2012 for the World Development Report 2013.
74. Ghani, Kerr, and O'Connell 2011.
75. Glaeser and Gottlieb 2008.
76. Lin (2012) proposes to use as a reference the trade patterns of countries whose endowments are similar but whose income per capita is moderately higher than in the country under consideration.

References

The word *processed* describes informally reproduced works that may not be commonly available through libraries.

Abowd, John M., and Richard B. Freeman. 1991. *Immigration, Trade, and the Labor Market.* Chicago, IL: University of Chicago Press.

Acosta, Pablo, César Calderón, Pablo Fajnzylber, and J. Humberto Lopez. 2007. "What Is the Impact of International Remittances on Poverty and Inequality in Latin America?" Policy Research Working Paper Series 4249, World Bank, Washington, DC.

Adams, Richard H. 1989. "Worker Remittances and Inequality in Rural Egypt." *Economic Development and Cultural Change* 38 (1): 45–71.

———. 1992. "The Effects of Migration and Remittances on Inequality in Rural Pakistan." *Pakistan Development Review* 31 (4 Pt. 2): 1189–203.

———. 2004. "Remittances and Poverty in Guatemala." Policy Research Working Paper Series 3418, World Bank, Washington, DC.

———. 2006. "Remittances and Poverty in Ghana." Policy Research Working Paper Series 3838, World Bank, Washington, DC.

———. 2011. "Evaluating the Economic Impact of International Remittances on Developing Countries Using Household Surveys: A Literature Review." *Journal of Development Studies* 47 (6): 809–28.

Aitken, Brian, Ann Harrison, and Robert E. Lipsey. 1996. "Wages and Foreign Ownership: A Comparative Study of Mexico, Venezuela, and the United States." *Journal of International Economics* 40 (3–4): 345–71.

Akamatsu, Kaname. 1962. "A Historical Pattern of Economic Growth in Developing Countries." *Developing Economies* 1 (Suppl. s1): 3–25.

Alfaro, Laura, and Maggie Xiaoyang Chen. 2011. "Selection, Reallocation, and Knowledge Spillovers: Identifying the Impact of Multinational Activity on Aggregate Productivity." Paper presented at the World Bank Conference on Structural Transformation and Economic Growth, Washington, DC, October 6.

Anzoategui, Diego, Asli Demirgüç-Kunt, and Maria Soledad Martinez-Peria. 2011. "Remittances and Financial Inclusion: Evidence from El Salvador." Policy Research Working Paper Series 5839, World Bank, Washington, DC.

Artuc, Erhan; Frederic Docquier, Caglar Özden and Chris Parsons. 2012. "Education Structure of Global Migration Patterns: Estimates Based on Census Data." World Bank, Washington DC. Processed.

Aw, Bee Yan, Sukkyun Chung, and Mark J. Roberts. 2000. "Productivity and Turnover in the Export Market: Micro-level Evidence from the Republic of Korea and Taiwan (China)." *World Bank Economic Review* 14 (1): 65–90.

Bach, Stephen. 2008. "International Mobility of Health Professionals: Brain Drain or Brain Exchange?" In *The International Mobility of Talent*, ed. Andrés Solimano, 202–34. Oxford: Oxford University Press.

Beine, Michel, Frédéric Docquier, and Hillel Rapoport. 2011. "Brain Drain and Human Capital Formation in Developing Countries: Winners and Losers." *Economic Journal* 118 (4): 631–52.

Bhagwati, Jagdish, Arvind Panagariya, and T. N. Srinivasan. 2004. "The Muddles over Outsourcing." *Journal of Economics Perspectives* 18 (4): 93–114.

Blomström, Magnus, and Ari Kokko. 2009. "The Economics of Foreign Direct Investment Incentives." In *Foreign Direct Investment in the Real and Financial Sector of Industrial Countries*, ed. Heinz Hermann and Robert Lipsey, 37–56. Heidelberg, Germany, and New York: Springer.

Borjas, George J. 2003. "The Labor Demand Curve Is Downward Sloping: Reexamining the Impact of Immigration on the Labor Market." *Quarterly Journal of Economics* 118 (4): 1335–74.

Brückner, Markus, and Daniel Lederman. 2012. "Trade Causes Growth in Sub-Saharan Africa." Policy Research Working Paper Series 6007, World Bank, Washington, DC.

Card, David. 2001. "Immigrant Inflows, Native Outflows, and the Local Labor Market Impacts of Higher Immigration." *Journal of Labor Economics* 19 (1): 22–64.

Carrasco, Raquel, Juan F. Jimeno, and Anna Carolina Ortega. 2008. "The Effect of Immigration on the Labor Market Performance of Native-Born Workers: Some Evidence for Spain." *Journal of Population Economics* 21 (3): 627–48.

Chacko, Elizabeth. 2007. "From Brain Drain to Brain Gain: Reverse Migration to Bangalore and Hyderabad, India's Globalizing High Tech Cities." *Geo Journal* 68 (2–3): 131–40.

Chiswick, Barry R., and Paul W. Miller. 2009. "Earnings And Occupational Attainment among Immigrants." *Industrial Relations: A Journal of Economy and Society* 48 (3): 454–65.

Chin, Ko-Lin. 1999. *Smuggled Chinese: Clandestine Immigration to United States*. Philadelphia: Temple University Press.

Clemens, Michael A., Claudio E. Montenegro, and Lant Pritchett. 2008. "The Place Premium: Wage Differences for Identical Workers across the U.S. Border." Policy Research Working Paper Series 4671, World Bank, Washington, DC.

Clerides, Sofronis K., Saul Lach, and James R. Tybout. 1998. "Is Learning by Exporting Important? Micro-dynamic Evidence from Colombia, Mexico and Morocco." *Quarterly Journal of Economics* 113 (3): 903–47.

Clifton, Jim. 2011. *The Coming Jobs War: What Every Leader Must Know about the Future of Job Creation*. New York: Gallup Press.

Cordova, Karina. 2009. "Collective Remittances in Mexico: Their Effect on the Labor Market for Males." Paper presented at the Second Conference on International Migration and Development, World Bank Migration and Development Program, Washington, DC, September 10.

de Soto, Hermine, Peter Gordon, Ilir Gedeshi, and Zamira Sinoimeri. 2002. "Poverty in Albania: A Qualitative Assessment." Europe and Central Asia Environmentally and Socially Sustainable Development Series 520, World Bank, Washington, DC.

De Vreyer, Philippe, Flore Gubert, and Anne-Sophie Robilliard. 2010. "Are There Returns to Migration Experience? An Empirical Analysis Using Data on Return Migrants and Non-Migrants in West Africa." *Annales d'Économie et de Statistique* 97–98 (January/June): 307–28.

Dingeman, Kathleen M., and Ruben G. Rumbaut. 2010. "The Immigration-Crime Nexus and Post-Deportation Experiences: Encountering Stereotypes in Southern California and El Salvador." *University of La Verne Law Review* 31 (2): 363–402.

Dinh, Hinh T., Vincent Palmade, Vandana Chandra, and Frances Cossar. 2012. *Light Manufacturing in Africa: Targeted Policies to Enhance Private Investment and Create Jobs*. Washington, DC: World Bank and Agence Française de Développement.

Di Nicola, Andrea. 1999. "Trafficking in Immigrants: A European Perspective." Research Centre on Transnational Crime, University of Trento.

Docquier, Frédéric, and Abdeslam Marfouk. 2006. "International Migration by Education Attainment, 1990–2000." In *International Migration, Remittances, and the Brain Drain*, ed. Çaglar Özden and Maurice Schiff, 151–99. New York: Palgrave Macmillan.

Docquier, Frédéric, Çaglar Özden, and Giovanni Peri. 2010. "The Wage Effects of Immigration and Emigration." Working Paper Series 116646, National Bureau of Economic Research, Cambridge, MA.

———. 2011. "The Labor Market Effects of Immigration and Emigration in OECD Countries." Discussion Paper Series 6528, Institute for the Study of Labor, Bonn.

Dustmann, Christian, Francesca Fabbri, and Ian Preston. 2005. "The Impact of Immigration on the British Labour Market." *Economic Journal* 115 (507): F324–41.

Ebenstein, Avraham, Ann Harrison, Margaret McMillan, and Shannon Phillips. 2009. "Estimating the Impact of Trade and Offshoring on American Workers Using the Current Population Surveys," Working Paper Series 15107, National Bureau of Economic Research, Cambridge, MA.

Eichengreen, Barry, Yeongseop Rhee, and Hui Tong. 2007. "China and the Exports of Other Asian Countries." *Review of World Economics* 143 (2): 201–26.

Elliott, Kimberly A., and Richard B. Freeman. 2003. *Can Labor Standards Improve under Globalization?* Washington, DC: Institute for International Economics.

Feenstra, Robert C. 1984. "Voluntary Export Restraint in U.S. Autos, 1980–81: Quality, Employment and Welfare Effects." In *The Structure and Evolution of Recent U.S. Trade Policy*, ed. Robert E. Baldwin and Anne O. Kruger, 35–66. Chicago: University of Chicago Press.

François, Joseph F., and Bernard Hoekman. 2010. "Services Trade and Policy." *Journal of Economic Literature* 48 (3): 642–92.

Friedberg, Rachel M. 2001. "The Impact of Mass Migration on the Israeli Labor Market." *Quarterly Journal of Economics* 116 (4): 1373–408.

Garcia Zamora, Rodolfo. 2005. "Mexico: International Migration, Remittances and Development." In OECD (Organisation for Economic Co-operation and Development), *Migration, Remittances and Development*, 81–87. Paris: OECD.

Ghani, Ejaz. 2010. *The Services Revolution in South Asia*. New York: Oxford University Press.

Ghani, Ejaz, William R. Kerr, and Stephen D. O'Connell. 2011. "Who Creates Jobs?" *Economic Premise* 2011 (70): 1–7.

Gibson, John, and David McKenzie. 2012. "The Economic Consequences of 'Brain Drain' of the Best and Brightest: Microeconomic Evidence from Five Countries." *Economic Journal* 122 (560): 339–75.

Gibson, John, David McKenzie, and Steven Stillman. Forthcoming. "Selectivity and the Estimated Impact of Emigration on Incomes and Poverty in Sending Areas: Evidence from the Samoan Quota Migration Lottery." *Economic Development and Cultural Change*.

Giuletti, Corrado. 2012. "Jobs, Migration, and Social Inclusion—Empirical Evidence." In *Federal Ministry for Economic Cooperation and Development 2012: Moving Jobs Center Stage*. Berlin: Berlin Workshop Series.

Glaeser, Edward L., and Joshua D. Gottlieb. 2008. "The Economics of Place-Making Policies." Working Paper Series 14373, National Bureau of Economic Research, Cambridge, MA.

Glaeser, Edward L., Hedi D. Kallal, Jose A. Scheinkman, and Andrei Shleifer. 1992. "Growth in Cities." *Journal of Political Economy* 100 (6): 1126–52.

Goldberg, Pinelopi Koujianou, and Nina Pavcnik. 2007. "Distributional Effects of Globalization in Developing Countries." *Journal of Economic Literature, American Economic Association* 45 (1): 39–82.

Gomory, Ralph E., and William J. Baumol. 2001. *Global Trade and Conflicting National Interests*. Cambridge, MA: MIT Press.

Görg, Holger. 2011. "Globalization, Offshoring and Jobs." In *Making Globalization Socially Sustainable*, ed. Marc Bacchetta and Marion Jansen, 21–47. Geneva: World Trade Organization and International Labour Organization.

Görg, Holger, Eric Strobl, and Frank Walsh. 2007. "Why Do Foreign-Owned Firms Pay More? The Role of On-the-Job Training." *Review of World Economics* 143 (3): 464–82.

Goswami, Arti Grover, Aaditya Mattoo, and Sebastián Sáez, eds, 2011. *Exporting Services: A Developing Country Perspective*. Washington, D.C: World Bank.

Greenaway, David, Aruneema Mahabir, and Chris Milner. 2008. "Has China Displaced Other Asian Countries' Exports?" *China Economic Review* 19 (2): 152–69.

Grossman, Gene M., and Esteban Rossi-Hansberg. 2008. "Trading Tasks: A Simple Theory of Offshoring." *American Economic Review* 98 (5): 1978–97.

Gupta, Sanjeev, Catherine A. Patillo, and Smita Wagh. 2009. "Effect of Remittances on Poverty and Financial Development in Sub-Saharan Africa." *World Development* 37 (1): 104–15.

Hanson, Gordon H. 2006. "Illegal Migration from Mexico to the United States." *Journal of Economic Literature* 44 (4): 869–924.

Harrison, Ann, and Andrés Rodríguez-Clare. 2009. "Trade, Foreign Investment, and Industrial Policy for Developing Countries." In *Development Economics*, vol. 5 of *Handbook of Development Economics*, ed. Dani Rodrik and Mark Rosenzweig, 4039–214. Amsterdam: Elsevier.

Helpman, Elhanan. 2006. "Trade, FDI, and the Organization of Firms." *Journal of Economic Literature* 44 (3): 589–630.

Henderson, Vernon, Todd Lee, and Yung Joon Lee. 2001. "Scale Externalities in Korea." *Journal of Urban Economics* 49 (3): 479–504.

Heymann, Jody, Francisco Flores-Macias, Jeffrey A. Hayes, Malinda Kennedy, Claudia Lahaie, and Alison Earle. 2009. "The Impact of Migration on the Well-being of Transnational Families: New Data from Sending Communities in Mexico." *Community, Work and Family* 12 (1): 91–103.

Hovhannisyan, Shoghik. 2012. "Labor Market and Growth Implications of Emigration: Cross-Country Evidence." Background paper for the World Development Report 2013.

Hunt, Jennifer. 1992. "The Impact of the 1962 Repatriates from Algeria on the French Labor Market." *Industrial and Labor Relations Review* 45 (3): 556–72.

Hymans, Saul H., and Frank P. Stafford. 1995. "Divergence, Convergence, and the Gains from Trade." *Review of International Economics* 3 (1): 118–23.

ILO (International Labour Organization). 2010. *Key Indicators of the Labour Market.* Geneva: ILO.

IOM (International Organization for Migration). 2008. *World Migration Report 2008: Managing Labour Mobility in the Evolving Global Economy.* Geneva: IOM.

———. 2010. *World Migration Report 2010—The Future of Migration: Building Capacities for Change.* Geneva: IOM.

Jansen, Marion, Peters Ralf; and Jose Manuel, eds. 2011. *Trade and Employment: From Myths to Facts.* Geneva: International Labour Organization.

Jensen, J. Bradford. 2011. *Global Trade in Services.* Washington, DC: Peter G. Peterson Institute for International Economics.

Keddie, Nikki R. 1998. "The New Religious Politics: Where, When and Why Do 'Fundamentalisms' Appear?" *Comparative Studies in Society and History* 40 (4): 696–723.

Koopmans, Rudd. 2010. "Trade-Offs between Equality and Difference: Immigrant Integration, Multiculturalism and the Welfare State in Cross-National Perspective." *Journal of Ethnic and Migration Studies* 36 (1): 1–26.

Kuznetsov, Yevgeny, and Charles Sabel. 2006. "International Migration of Talent, Diaspora Networks, and Development: Overview of Main Issues." In *Diaspora Networks and International Migration of Skills: How Countries Can Draw on Their Talent Abroad*, ed. Yevgeny Kuznetsov, 3–20. Washington, DC: World Bank.

LaLonde, Robert, and R Topel. 1997. "Economic Impact of International Migration and the Economic Performance of Migrants." In *Handbook of Population and Family Economics*, ed. Mark R. Rozenweig and Oded Stark, 799–850. Amsterdam: Elsevier.

Levy, Philip. 2012. "Potential for International Rivalry as Governments Pursue Jobs." Background paper for the WDR 2013.

Lin, Justin Yifu. 2011. "From Flying Geese to Leading Dragons: New Opportunities and Strategies for Structural Transformation in Developing Countries." Policy Research Working Paper Series 5702, World Bank, Washington, DC.

———. 2012. *New Structural Economics: A Framework for Rethinking Development and Policy.* Washington, DC: World Bank.

Lin, Justin Yifu, Célestin Monga, Dirk Willem te Velde, Suresh D. Tendulkar, Alice Amsden, K. Y. Amoako, Howard Pack, and Wonhyuk Lim. 2010. "Growth Identification and Facilitation: The Role of the State in the Dynamics of Structural Change." *Development Policy Review* 29 (3): 259–310.

Lokshin, Michael, Mikhail Bontch-Osmolovski, and Elena Glinskaya. 2010. "Work-Related Migration and Poverty Reduction in Nepal." *Review of Development Economics* 14 (2): 323–32.

Lucas, Robert E. B. 2005. *International Migration and Economic Development: Lessons from Low-Income Countries.* Cheltenham, U.K.: Edward Elgar.

———. 2010. "Migrant Sending Countries, the Internationalization of Labor Markets and Development." In *The Internationalization of Labor Markets*, ed. Christiane Kuptsch, 63–87. Geneva: International Labour Organization.

Mano, Yukichi, and Keijiro Otsuka. 2000. "Agglomeration Economies and Concentration of Industries: A Case Study of Manufacturing Sectors in Postwar Japan." *Journal of Japanese and International Economies* 14 (3): 189–203.

Mattoo, Aaditya, and Randeep Rathindran. 2006. "Measuring Services Trade Liberalization and Its Impact on Economic Growth: An Illustration." *Journal of Economic Integration* 21 (1): 64–98.

McKenzie, David, John Gibson, and Steven Stillman. 2006. "How Important Is Selection? Experimental versus Non-experimental Measures of the Income Gains from Migration." *Journal of the European Economic Association* 8: 913–45.

McKenzie, David J., and Hillel Rapoport. 2007. "Network Effects and the Dynamics of Migration and Inequality: Theory and Evidence from Mexico." *Journal of Development Economics* 84 (1): 1–24.

McKinnon, Ronald, and Kenichi Ohno. 1997. *Dollar and Yen: Resolving Economic Conflict between the United States and Japan.* Cambridge, MA: MIT Press.

Milanovic, Branko. 1987. "Remittances and Income Distribution." *Journal of Economic Studies* 14 (5): 24–37.

Millberg, William, Melissa Mahoney, Markus Schneider, and Rudy von Arnim. 2007. "Dynamic Gains from U.S. Services Offshoring." In *Global Capitalism Unbound: Winners and Losers from Offshoring,* ed. Eva Paus, 77–94. New York: Palgrave MacMillan.

Monitor Inclusive Markets. 2011. *Job Creation through Building the Field of Impact Sourcing.* Mumbai: Monitor Inclusive Markets.

Newfarmer, Richard, and Monika Sztajerowska. 2012. *Trade and Employment in a Fast-Changing World.* Paris: Organisation for Economic Co-operation and Development.

Newitt, Kirsten. 2012. "Private Sector Voluntary Initiatives on Labour Standards." Background paper for the WDR 2013.

Noguer, Marta, and Marc Siscart. 2005. "Trade Raises Income: A Precise and Robust Result." *Journal of International Economics* 65 (2): 447–60.

OECD (Organisation for Economic Co-operation and Development). 2007. *Offshoring and Employment: Trends and Impacts.* Paris: OECD.

Özden, Çaglar, and Maurice Schiff. 2006. *International Migration, Remittances, and the Brain Drain.* New York: Palgrave Macmillan and World Bank.

Özden, Çaglar, Christopher Parsons, Maurice Schiff, and Terrie L. Walmsley. 2011. "Where on Earth Is Everybody? The Evolution of Global Bilateral Migration 1960–2000." *World Bank Economic Review* 25 (1): 12–56.

Pandey, Abhishek, Alok Aggarwal, Richard Devane, and Yevgeny Kuznetsov. 2006. "The Indian Diaspora: A Unique Case?" In *Diaspora Networks and the International Migration of Skills,* ed. Yevgeny Kuznetsov, 71–98. Washington, DC: World Bank.

Pérez-Armendáriz, Clarisa, and David Crow. 2010. "Do Migrants Remit Democracy? International Migration, Political Beliefs, and Behavior in Mexico." *Comparative Political Studies* 43 (1): 119–48.

Pischke, Jörn-Steffen, and Johannes Velling. 1997. "Employment Effects of Immigration to Germany: An Analysis Based on Local Labor Markets." *Review of Economics and Statistics* 79 (4): 594–604.

Priebe, Stefan, Sima Sandhu, Sónia Dias, Andrea Gaddini, Tim Greacen, Elisabeth Ioannidis, Ulrike Kluge, Allan Krasnik, Majda Lamkaddem, Vincent Lorant, Rosa Puigpinósi Riera, Attila Sarvary, Joaquim JF Soares, Mindaugas Stankunas, Christa Strafsmayr, Kristian Wahlbeck, Marta Welbel, and Marija Bogic. 2011. "Good Practice in Health Care for Migrants: Views and Experiences of Care Professionals in 16 European Countries." *BMC Public Health* 11 (187): 1471–2458.

Rama, Martín. 2003. "Globalization and the Labor Market." *World Bank Research Observer* 18 (2): 159–86.

Razin, Assaf, Efraim Sadka, and Benjarong Suwankiri. 2011. *Migration and the Welfare State Political-Economy Policy Formation.* Cambridge, MA: MIT Press.

Robertson, Raymond, Drusilla Brown, Gaelle La Borgne Pierre, and Maria Laura Sanchez-Puerta, eds. 2009. *Globalization, Wages, and the Quality of Jobs: Five Country Studies.* Washington, DC: World Bank.

Rodríguez-Clare, Andrés. 2001. "Costa Rica's Development Strategy Based on Human Capital and Technology: How It Got There, the Impact of Intel, and Lessons for Other Countries." *Journal of Human Development and Capabilities* 2 (2): 311–24.

Rozelle, Scott, and Jikun Huang. 2012. "China's Labor Transition and the Future of China's Rural Wages and Employment." Background paper for the WDR 2013.

Saxenian, Annalee. 2004. "The Bangalore Boom: From Brain Drain to Brain Circulation." In *IT Experience in India: Bridging the Digital Divide,* ed. Kenneth Keniston and Deepak Kumar, 169–81. New Delhi: Sage Publications.

Selim, Nadia. 2012. "Innovation for Job Creation." Background paper for the WDR 2013.

Shen, I-Ling, Frédéric Docquier, and Hillel Rapoport. 2010. "Remittances and Inequality: A Dynamic Migration Model." *Journal of Economic Inequality* 8: 197–220.

Sirkeci, Ibrahim, Jeffrey Cohen, and Dilip Ratha, eds. *Migration and Remittances during the Global Financial Crisis and Beyond.* Washington, DC: World Bank.

Solimano, Andrés. 2010. *International Migration in the Age of Crisis and Globalization: Historical and Recent Experiences.* New York: Cambridge University Press.

Sonobe, Tetsushi, and Keijiro Otsuka. 2006. *Cluster-Based Industrial Development: An East Asian Model.* New York: Palgrave Macmillan.

Spener, David. 2009. *Clandestine Crossings: Migrants and Coyotes on the Texas-Mexico Border.* Ithaca, NY: Cornell University Press.

Suri, Navdeep. 2007. "Offshoring Outsourcing of Services as a Catalyst of Economic Development: The Case of India." In *Global Capitalism Unbound: Winners and Loser from Offshoring,* ed. Eva Paus, 163–80. New York: Palgrave MacMillan.

Thomas, Kevin J. A. 2009. "The Human Capital Characteristics and Household Living Standards of Returning International Migrants in Eastern and Southern Africa." *International Migration* 50 (4): 85–106.

Torres, Federico, and Yevgeny Kuznetsov. 2006. "Mexico: Leveraging Migrants' Capital to Develop Hometown Communities." In *Diaspora Networks and the International Migration of Skills*, ed. Yevgeny Kuznetsov, 99–128. Washington, DC: World Bank.

UNCTAD (United Nations Conference on Trade and Development). 2004. *World Investment Report.* New York: United Nations.

UNHCR (United Nations High Commissioner for Refugees). 2010. *Global Appeal 2010–2011: Real People, Real Needs.* Geneva: UNHCR.

Velde, Dirk Willem te, and Oliver Morrissey. 2003. "Do Workers in Africa Get a Wage Premium if Employed in Firms Owned by Foreigners?" *Journal of African Economies* 12 (1, Special Issue): 41–73.

Wahba, Jackline. 2007. "Return to Overseas Work Experience: The Case of Egypt." In *International Migration, Economic Development and Policy*, ed. Çaglar Özden and Maurice Schiff, 235–58. Washington, DC: World Bank.

World Bank. 2011. *World Development Indicators 2011.* Washington, DC: World Bank.

Policies through the jobs lens

Introduction to Part 3

Most jobs are created by the private sector. While public works and targeted employment programs are justified in certain situations, the primary role of government is not to directly provide employment. It is to set the conditions for job creation by the private sector, and especially to remove the obstacles to the creation of more of the jobs with the highest development payoffs, given the circumstances of the country.

When faced with jobs challenges, policy makers tend to look first at labor policies as either the solution or the problem. It is important, then, to understand the role and the impacts of policies and institutions like labor market regulation, collective bargaining, active labor market programs, and social insurance. But the main constraints to the job creation often lie outside the labor market, and a clear approach is needed to support appropriate policy responses.

- *Fundamentals* are necessary for growth and are a precondition for strong job creation by the private sector. Macroeconomic stability, an enabling business environment, human capital, and the rule of law, including the progressive realization of rights, are the key policy fundamentals.

- *Labor policies* need to be adequate for growth to translate into jobs. Policies should seek to avoid the distortive interventions that stifle labor reallocation and undermine the creation of jobs in functional cities and global value chains. But policies should also

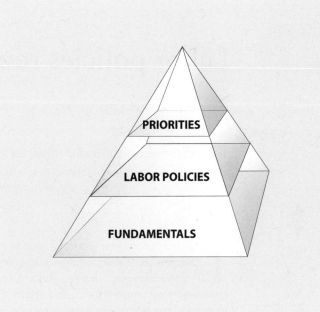

Source: World Development Report 2013 team.

ensure voice and social protection, especially for the most vulnerable.

- *Policy priorities* have to be established in support of good jobs for development. Ideally, policies should aim at removing the market imperfections and institutional failures preventing the private sector from creating more of those jobs. If the constraints cannot be easily singled out or are difficult to remove, offsetting policies may be considered.

CHAPTER 8

Labor policies revisited

Labor policies can address labor market imperfections. But interventions can hinder dynamism in some cases, while the lack of mechanisms for voice and social protection affects the most vulnerable.

Labor markets have imperfections in the form of inadequate information, uneven bargaining power, limited ability to enforce long-term commitments, and insufficient insurance mechanisms against employment-related risks. Imperfections like these create gaps between the individual and the social value of jobs. They can thus result in a level and composition of employment that are not optimal from a social point of view.

Labor policies and institutions—regulations, collective representation, active labor market programs, and unemployment insurance—can in principle be used to address these imperfections. Other policies, such as pensions and other forms of social insurance, address imperfections elsewhere in the economy but can have important implications for the functioning of the labor market.

Labor policies and institutions are bundled in different ways in different countries (figure 8.1).[1] Their configuration tends to vary by level of development, with policies and institutions generally more developed in industrial countries. This is especially so for institutions providing a vehicle for collective voice, such as bargaining between employers and employees, and for social insurance. But the nature of the labor policies and institutions in any country is affected by more than just the level of development and must be seen in the context of the country's legal traditions, politics, and social norms and values.

The impact of labor policies is often the subject of heated debates. In the past decade, improved data and methods have generated a great deal of new information not only in industrial countries but increasingly in developing countries as well. The analyses of these data have led to fresh insights. Estimated effects prove to be relatively modest in most cases—certainly more modest than the intensity of the debate would suggest. Excessive or insufficient interventions can certainly have detrimental effects on productivity. But in between these extremes lies a "plateau" where effects enhancing and undermining efficiency can be found side by side and most of the impact is redistributive. Overall, labor policies and institutions are neither the major obstacle nor the magic bullet for creating good jobs for development in most countries.

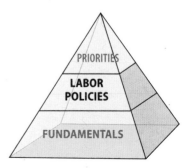

PRIORITIES

LABOR POLICIES

FUNDAMENTALS

FIGURE 8.1 *The mix of labor policies and institutions varies across countries*

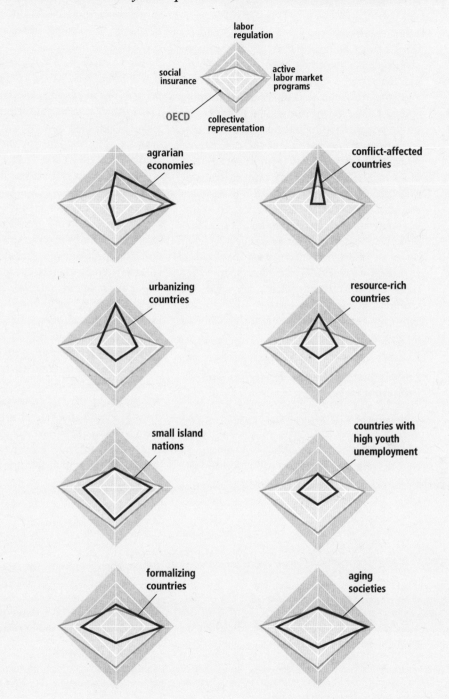

Sources: World Development Report 2013 team estimates based on Eurostat Public Expenditure on Labour Market Policy (LMP) Interventions (database), European Commission; Institutional Characteristics of Trade Unions, Wage Setting, State Intervention and Social Pacts (ICTWSS) (database), Amsterdam Institute for Advanced Labour Studies, Amsterdam; Pallares-Miralles, Romero, and Whitehouse 2012; Public Expenditure and Participant Stocks on Labour Market Programmes (database), Organisation for Economic Co-operation and Development, Paris; Robalino, Newhouse, and Rother, forthcoming; and World Bank, forthcoming.
Note: OECD = Organisation for Economic Co-operation and Development. Figures are averages across OECD member countries. *Labor regulation* indicates the ratio of minimum to average wage. *Active labor market programs* is the share of gross domestic product spent on them. *Collective representation* is the coverage of collective bargaining agreements divided by the labor force. *Social insurance* indicates workers contributing toward old-age pensions as a percentage of the labor force. Countries were classified in the eight groups by the World Development Report 2013 team. One country can belong to several groups. The figure shows unweighted averages across countries.

Labor regulations: A "plateau" effect

Labor regulations can be designed to address labor market failures that result in inefficient or inequitable outcomes. Difficulties in enforcing long-term contracts between employers and employees may lead to excessive churning and underinvestment in training. Inefficiencies in the organization of insurance schemes may leave workers unprotected in the case of dismissal, which could force them to curtail their job search before finding the right match. Uneven market power can enable firms to set wages that are lower than would be agreed upon under more competitive conditions. Discriminatory practices can have the same effect. Uneven power or incomplete information may lead to an unsafe workplace. These market imperfections and institutional failures can affect job creation and lead to gaps between what workers gain from employment and the social value of their jobs.

Employment protection legislation and minimum wages

Employment protection legislation (EPL) and minimum wages have been widely adopted to address some of these failures. EPL consists of rules governing hiring and termination and de-fining the degree to which job security is guaranteed (box 8.1). Virtually all countries regulate hiring and termination in some way—severance payments, for example, are mandated by law or through collective agreements in 170 countries.[2] Similarly, more than 100 countries have ratified International Labour Organization (ILO) conventions regarding minimum wages, and many others have established minimum wages even though they have not ratified these conventions.[3] However, the specific nature of labor regulations reflects the society for which they are written. Important determinants include a country's legal tradition, as well as civic attitudes toward solidarity, inequality, and trust.[4] The content, as well as the impact of regulations, is also influenced by interactions with other potentially complementary institutions such as collective representation and social insurance.

Views on labor regulations can be polarized, with contrasting implications for policy making. Fundamental questions, such as whether labor policies should protect jobs or workers, often spark heated debates (question 8).

For some, these regulations provide necessary guarantees for workers against economic volatility and the strong bargaining power of firms.[5] EPL can offer job security, deterring precarious forms of employment. Minimum wages can prevent extreme poverty among workers and address the inefficiencies that stem from

---

BOX 8.1 *Employment protection legislation covers more than firing rules*

Employment protection legislation, or EPL, can be classified into two main groups of rules, one pertaining to hiring, the other to termination. Rules on hiring dictate what types of labor contracts are permissible under what conditions—for instance, open-ended, fixed-term, part-time, and apprenticeship contracts. Rules on termination govern the ending of contracts including causes (voluntary and involuntary, justified or unfair), end-of-service compensation (severance pay), and procedures (for instance, third-party notification or approval, advance notice, and vesting periods). The mix and stringency of these rules result in a continuum of regulation across countries, which has been subject to different measurement efforts.[a]

Other types of labor policies can also have implications for job security. Some regulations set specific conditions for the employment of women and young workers. They include maternity leave, the need for child care facilities, first-contract waivers, or reduced minimum wage for apprentices. The aim of these policies is to facilitate the participation of more vulnerable population groups and to protect them once they are employed. Antidiscrimination regulations address socially unaccepted differences in the treatment of workers, with the goal to reduce inequality and enhance social cohesion and fairness in employment.

Source: World Development Report 2013 team.
a. Measures attempting to summarize EPL include those proposed by Botero and others 2004; Employment Protection indicators (database), Organisation for Economic Co-operation and Development, Paris; and Doing Business Indicators (database), World Bank, Washington, DC.

noncompetitive labor markets.[6] By establishing a reference wage, minimum wages can even benefit uncovered workers through the so-called lighthouse effect.[7] EPL and minimum wages are also seen as creating the conditions for human capital accumulation and associated productivity gains.[8]

Critics of strong EPL and minimum wages hold that they tend to reduce employment, hinder productivity growth, and can lead to divisions in society between those who benefit from the regulations and those who do not. According to this view, to the extent that EPL and minimum wages raise labor costs, they can increase poverty by pushing low-skilled workers, young people, and women into unemployment or into informal sector jobs.[9] Hiring and termination restrictions can slow down labor reallocation and hence constrain productivity growth. Finally, because they are often perceived as part of the social contract, labor market regulations can be difficult to reform, when circumstances change, generating discord and even conflict.[10]

Modest impacts overall . . .

New data and more rigorous methodologies have spurred a wave of empirical studies over the past two decades on the effects of labor regulation.[11] These studies examine the influence of EPL and minimum wages on employment, wages, the distribution of wages, and to a lesser extent, productivity. Few have looked at wider impacts on social cohesion.

Based on this wave of new research, the overall impact of EPL and minimum wages is smaller than the intensity of the debate would suggest (tables 8.1 and 8.2).[12] Most estimates of the impacts on employment levels tend to be insignificant or modest.[13] Studies of EPL in Latin America and the Caribbean, for example, report mixed results: negative employment effects of job security rules have been found in Argentina, Colombia, and Peru, while no significant effect was evident in Brazil and some Caribbean countries. Different studies for Chile have reached both results.[14] Overall, the ma-

TABLE 8.1 *There is a wave of new empirical evidence on the impacts of EPL*

Dimension	Indicator	Findings	Comments
Living standards	Aggregate employment and unemployment	Either no impact or modest negative (positive) impact on employment (unemployment)	Evidence for both industrial and developing countries (largely Latin America) Results tend not to be robust.
	Employment for particular groups	Prime-age males favorably affected Youth, women, and low-skilled unfavorably affected	Partial reforms for two-track labor markets lead to more precarious employment for affected groups.
	Employment dynamics	Longer durations in employment, unemployment, and out of the labor force Smaller flows between different types of work status	
	Adjustments to shocks	Increases in negative impact of shocks	Consensus not strong
	Wage distribution	Reduces wage dispersion	
Productivity	Labor and multifactor productivity growth	No consistent conclusion	Very little evidence for developing countries
	Training	Positive effect	Longer-duration employment spells and greater human capital investments
	Technological change	Negative effect	Few studies
	Reallocation of labor	Negative effect because smaller labor flows	
Social cohesion	Fairness	Signals social responsibility of employers	Depends on enforcement and coverage "Two-track" regulations can be seen as unfair.
	Security	Positive because of longer tenure	Depends on enforcement and coverage
	Equality	Greater wage equality has modest equalizing effect on income distribution.	Evidence mostly for industrial countries

Source: Betcherman 2012 for the World Development Report 2013 based on a review of empirical studies of EPL.
Note: EPL = employment protection legislation.

TABLE 8.2 *The impacts of minimum wages are a favorite research topic in labor economics*

Dimension	Indicator	Findings	Comments
Living standards	Aggregate employment	Either no impact or modest negative impact	Both industrial and developing countries Some studies show positive employment effect.
	Employment for particular groups	Negative employment impacts concentrated on youth and low-skilled	Some studies show positive employment effect.
	Wages	Positive effect	Effect strongest around minimum wage Some evidence of positive effect in informal sector
	Wage distribution	Reduces wage inequality	
	Poverty	Reduces poverty	Some studies find no effect.
Productivity	Labor and total factor productivity	No consistent conclusion	Rarely analyzed
Social cohesion	Fairness	Provides "decent" wage	Depends on enforcement and coverage

Source: Betcherman 2012 for the World Development Report 2013 based on a review of empirical studies of minimum wages.

jority of minimum wage studies do find negative employment effects, especially on young workers. But magnitudes tend to be small and a number of studies report no effect, or in some cases, even positive effects.[15] EPL and minimum wages can shift employment away from young people, women, and the less-skilled and toward prime-age men and the better educated.[16] Their effects can vary within a country. In Indonesia, increasing minimum wages during the 1990s had a negative effect on employment among small firms but not on large firms.[17] Across countries, both EPL and minimum wages are associated with a reduction in wage inequality.[18]

EPL has clear dynamic effects, reducing labor market flows and increasing durations in both employment and unemployment.[19] In this way, strong job security rules slow down labor reallocation and limit the efficiency gains from creative destruction. Studies on the overall impact of EPL on productivity are mixed, however, with some finding negative productivity impacts and others finding positive or no significant effects.[20] This mix of findings may be caused by other influences of job security rules, such as incentives to invest in training, which can counteract the lower rates of labor reallocation. Some countries have tried to reduce EPL by implementing partial ("dual-track") reforms that increase the scope for nonpermanent employment. However, unless accompanied by reductions in the protection of permanent jobs, this approach seems to result in the more vulnerable groups ending up in more precarious employment.[21]

In many developing countries with large informal sectors, the generally modest impacts of EPL and minimum wages may stem in part from poor coverage and weak enforcement. In Brazil, employment effects of strong job security provisions were negative in municipalities where enforcement was strong.[22] Mechanisms for voice and representation and the capacity of government to effectively administer regulations influence the effectiveness of enforcement. Certainly, poor rules coupled with weak enforcement are not a desirable combination to address labor market imperfections.

But many countries appear to set EPL and minimum wages in a range where impacts on employment or productivity are modest. Within that range, or "plateau," effects enhancing and undermining efficiency can be found side by side, and most of the impact is redistributive. The distributional effects tend to be equalizing among those who are covered by these regulations, but divisions can be accentuated between those covered and those who are not. With efficiency effects relatively modest on the plateau, countries can choose where they want to be depending on their normative preferences for redistribution.

. . . but cliffs at the edge of the plateau

However, when the edge of the plateau is reached (either on the too-strict or too-loose side), impacts are more negative. Some studies have found that Indian states with more restrictive EPL have significantly lower employment and output, and this effect is strongest where dispute resolution is ineffective or costly.[23] Large increases in the minimum wage in Colombia in the late 1990s led to significant employment losses, exacerbated by weak labor demand at the time.[24] At this edge of the plateau, which can vary according to the country situation, labor regulations can slow down job creation in cities, or in global value chains, and can cause countries to miss out on jobs supporting agglomeration effects and knowledge spillovers. Forgoing the development payoffs from urbanization and global integration would be one way to fall off the cliff.

It does not follow that minimal regulation is the answer. If rules are too weak, or not enforced, the problems of poor information, unequal bargaining power, or inadequate risk management remain unaddressed. This cliff may be less visible than excessive labor market rigidity, but it is no less real.

The main challenge is to set EPL and minimum wages so that they address the imperfections in the labor market without falling off the plateau. The edges of the plateau vary across countries and even within countries over time, as conditions change. In Brazil, for example, minimum wages had negative impacts on employment in the 1990s but not over the past decade, even though they were increasing relative to average wages.[25] It is important, then, to monitor impacts closely and reflect on the design and implementation of regulations and their interaction with other institutions.[26] Although EPL and minimum wages may not address labor market imperfections effectively, in most countries good jobs for development are lacking for other reasons.

Collective representation: New forms of voice

Collective bargaining and other forms of "voice" can address information failures at the workplace in ways that enhance productivity as well as employment security and earnings. For instance, workers may have knowledge about the details of production and operations that those making decisions do not have. Employers are likely to be informed about certain aspects of the business that would be relevant and useful for workers. Information sharing can generate additional efficiency gains by providing a mechanism for resolving conflicts and reducing wasteful turnover.

Collective representation and bargaining can also address problems of uneven market power whereby firms may be able to impose lower wages or inferior working conditions on individual workers than would be the case under competitive conditions.

Bargaining between firms and workers

The coverage of unions and collective bargaining varies considerably around the world (figure 8.2). Coverage rates are generally low in developing countries, where few workers out of the civil service or protected sectors belong to a trade union. In most countries where regular data are available, the coverage of collective bargaining agreements has declined during the past two decades.[27] The shift of employment toward the services sector, globalization, technological progress, evolving social values, and legislative changes have all been advanced as causes of this decline.[28]

The vast majority of the evidence confirms the existence of a wage premium in favor of union members and other workers covered by collective agreements. Estimates of the adjusted union wage effect (controlling for other factors) range from around 5 percent in Japan and the Republic of Korea, up to 15 percent in countries as varied as Brazil, Canada, Germany, Malaysia, Mexico, and the United States.[29] South Africa stands at the upper end, although there is controversy on how high the union wage effect actually is (box 8.2). Wage effects tend to be strongest for women and in countries where union membership is high. It is also clear that unions and collective bargaining have an equalizing effect on earnings distributions by compressing wage differentials. Research has shown that wage inequality falls during periods when union density is increasing and rises when union membership is in decline.[30] Little evidence exists on the impact of unions on poverty.

One relevant question is whether union wage gains come at the expense of reduced employment. Unfortunately, few studies have addressed this question in developing countries. In in-

FIGURE 8.2 *The coverage of collective bargaining is low in developing countries*

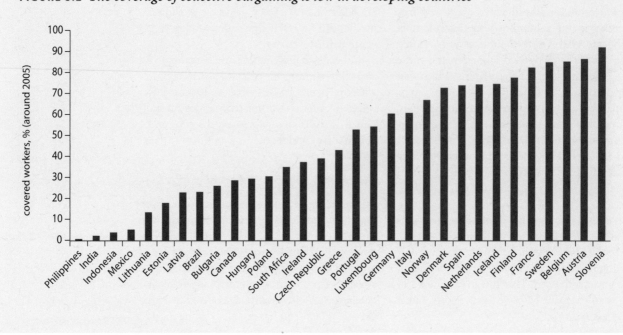

Sources: World Development Report 2013 team based on ICTWSS database, Visser 2011, and World Bank 2011b.
Note: The reported variable is either union membership or collective bargaining coverage as a share of total employment.

dustrial countries, studies are divided between those finding that unions reduce employment (or increase unemployment) and those finding no significant effect. Where negative impacts are found, the magnitude is modest. The most recent estimates by the Organisation for Economic Co-operation and Development (OECD) find that a 10 percentage point decline in union coverage is associated with an increase in employment of 0.8 percentage points.[31]

Industrial relations and productivity

The impact of collective bargaining on productivity reflects the balance of two opposing forces. On the one hand, voice may lead to better information sharing, while higher labor costs under unionization may encourage management to invest more on training and technology, leading to higher productivity. On the other hand, unions may also be able to negotiate restrictions in hours worked and pay rules that reduce effort, hindering productivity. The net effect of these forces is then an empirical mat-

ter. The evidence collected on productivity in the United States and Europe is not conclusive.[32] In developing countries, effects are positive in Malaysia, Mexico, and Uruguay, but negative in Brazil.[33] Findings suggest that unionized firms undertake more training than nonunionized firms. But differences in the introduction of new technologies are not significant.

The institutional structure for collective bargaining can differ considerably across countries, especially in the degree of centralization and coordination. Arrangements vary from firm-level bargaining with no influence on other firms to industry-based bargaining to centralized bargaining with national coverage. Prior to the 1990s, researchers found that both centralized and decentralized bargaining led to better employment performance. Analysis has been less conclusive since then, however.[34]

With policy changes, some developing countries and emerging economies have extended worker representation and are seeing new forms of collective bargaining. In China, for example, a number of legislative reforms appear to have

BOX 8.2 *Are bargaining councils the cause of unemployment in South Africa?*

With unemployment rates well above 20 percent, the South African labor market is very different from that of other developing countries, usually characterized by low or moderate levels of open unemployment. Diverse explanations have been put forward, including growth concentrated in low-labor-intensity sectors, skills deficits, work disincentives created by social benefits, and various legacies of apartheid. South Africa's distinct collective bargaining arrangements are also frequently mentioned as a possible explanation for the lack of jobs.

Since the 1920s, bargaining over wages and working conditions in most of South Africa's manufacturing sector has taken place through industrial councils, now known as bargaining councils. Bargaining councils can request that agreements be extended to their entire sector, including to employers and workers who did not participate in the negotiations. Extensions are common but vary considerably across sectors and areas. Firm-level bargaining also occurs. It has been argued that sectorwide extensions of bargaining council agreements impose a heavy labor cost burden on small firms, undermining employment creation.[a]

Estimates of wage premiums as high as 60 percent for union members appeared to provide some credence to this argument.[b] A substantial part of this wage effect was associated with industries that could possibly reflect the influence of the councils. Subsequent research using more recent data and better methodologies has concluded that early studies overestimated the real wage effect of the bargaining council agreements. The latest research suggests the wage premium is in the 10–20 percent range.[c] This level is signifi-

cant but more in line with union wage differentials observed in other countries. Evidence also suggests that bargaining council extensions do have effects as well, adding around 10 percent to the wages of nonunion workers within the bargaining council system.[d]

These results imply that the South Africa's wage-setting institutions do have some employment effects, especially among small firms, whose contribution to total job creation is small by international standards. Bargaining councils are estimated to be associated with 8–13 percent lower employment in the firms they cover directly and with 7–16 percent lower employment in small firms.[e]

While these effects are not trivial, bargaining councils can explain only a small part of South Africa's unusually high unemployment rates. Given the number of workers employed in industries covered by collective agreements, eliminating the employment effect of bargaining councils would reduce the unemployment rate by 1.5 percentage points, at the most.[f] So the main constraints to job creation may lie elsewhere.

One clue is the relatively small size of the informal sector compared to other countries at a similar development level. South Africa is different from these countries in other ways, too. During the apartheid period, slum clearance, harsh licensing, and strict zoning regulations rid cities of black-dominated informal sector niches. Two decades after the end of apartheid, spatial segregation remains, and investment in black-dominated areas is low.[g] The legacy of separation also results in high transportation costs for the unemployed, who tend to live far from where the jobs are. So South Africa's job creation problems may stem primarily from urban issues.

Source: World Development Report 2013 team.
a. Butcher and Rouse 2001.
b. Schultz and Mwabu 1998.
c. Magruder 2010.
d. Bhorat, Goga, and van der Westerhuizen 2011.
e. Magruder 2010.
f. Godfrey and others 2010; Magruder 2010.
g. Banerjee and others 2007; Kingdon and Knight 2004.

opened the door to a proliferation of unions and collective bargaining agreements (box 8.3).

Voice beyond the firm

Employers' organizations and unions also play roles as social and political agents. They may influence the laws that regulate labor markets and even policies beyond the sphere of labor relations. The nature of such involvement depends on the norms and institutional framework in the society in which they operate. Historically, labor unions have contributed to the establishment of social and labor rights, as well as to political change, in many countries. For instance,

Solidarność, a Polish trade union federation, was prominent in the fight against Communist rule, while the Confederation of South African Trade Unions played a leading role in the fight against apartheid.

In some countries, especially developing countries, the political involvement of unions can overshadow their activities at the workplace.[35] Because their membership is strong in the civil service and in protected sectors, unions have often opposed reforms involving fiscal consolidation, privatization, or liberalization. A comparison of economic performances in times of reform shows that developing countries with higher union membership and higher shares of

BOX 8.3   *New forms of collective bargaining are emerging in China*

Since the turn of the century, China has undergone important changes in labor policies, including enactment of new laws regarding trade unions (in 2001) and employment promotion, labor contracts, and labor dispute mediation and arbitration (in 2007). These changes have been accompanied by rapid growth in the number of unionized workers and workers covered by wage or collective agreements (more than 150 million at present). In addition to the spread of unionization and collective agreements, the International Labour Organization (ILO) has documented the gradual spread in the direct election of union representatives by workers. Such changes reflect a policy shift that "is intended to bring better protection of workers' rights, to create a new balance between flexibility and security and to facilitate a dialogue between employers and workers on issues of mutual concern."[a]

Another notable change over the past decade has been the introduction of local, sectoral-based collective bargaining agreements. The first of these agreements was negotiated in 2003 in the wool-sweater manufacturing industry in the Xinhe district of Wenling in Zhejiang province.[b] This is a district known as an example of transparency and local democracy. Since then, these agreements have been most prominent in Zhejiang, but have also spread to some other coastal provinces.[c] For the most part, local, sectoral-based bargaining has emerged where industries cluster around a district or village. By the end of 2010, this form of bargaining covered over 5 million workers through 73,000 agreements.[d]

The spread of local, sectoral collective bargaining agreements has occurred against the backdrop of a vibrant private sector increasingly facing labor shortages and an inadequately regulated labor market that has led to many disruptive labor disputes. In some cases, these agreements appear to protect workers' rights more effectively.[e] At the same time, the private sector can also benefit from a more stable relationship with workers, a more reliable supply of labor, and more regular and transparent changes in labor costs.

The forms of collective representation in China are diversifying, with government encouragement. Although evidence is only gradually emerging about the consequences of these changes, some research suggests that sectoral bargaining at the district or local level holds the most promise.[f] Centralized "top-down" efforts have been made to spur the proliferation of these agreements, with limited success. But the spontaneous spread of this spatial organization of collective bargaining suggests that it matches well the interest of the private sector in coordinating the operation of industrial clusters with the interest of workers to have voice in the workplace.

Source: World Development Report 2013 team.
a. Lee and Liu 2011a; 2011b, 8.
b. Wei and others 2009.
c. The Xinhe district of Wenling has also led the country in increasing transparency in local budgeting through introducing public deliberation in the process. See Ministry of Finance of the People's Republic of China 2011.
d. workercn.cn 2011.
e. Liu 2010.
f. Liu 2010.

employment in the public sector (where most unionized workers are) experienced deeper declines in economic activity before the adoption of major reforms and slower recoveries afterward.[36] This finding is consistent with the reforms being adopted late, and their implementation being watered-down. On the other hand, the level of minimum wages and social security benefits did not affect performance, suggesting that trade unions made a difference because of their political activities, more than because of their impact on labor costs.

Trade unions organized around the employer-employee relationship are less suited to providing voice to those who do not work for a wage. The high incidence of self-employment in most developing countries, and the persistence of informality more generally, have created impetus for innovative institutions for collective representation. These institutions are different from traditional unions because the market imperfec-

tions and institutional failures they address do not involve conventional employer-employee relationships or workplace-based production structures. They are often organized to represent members' interests with a particular municipal authority or local government.

Associations of self-employed workers are emerging as a vehicle to demand and protect their members' rights and improve their working conditions. Some of them have drawn their inspiration from India's Self Employed Women's Association (SEWA), which was created 40 years ago. In many cases, groups such as street vendors in Lima, Peru, or garbage collectors in Pune, India, may not only negotiate with government authorities but also resort to litigation in the courts. Waste pickers in Bogotá, Colombia, organized to defend their right to provide services to municipalities (box 8.4). Street vendors associations in Durban, South Africa, filed cases in court against the construction of malls

BOX 8.4 Recicladores *forced changes in Bogotá's solid waste management policies*

Waste pickers, or *recicladores*, in Colombia's capital earn a living by recycling metals, cardboard, paper, plastic, and glass and selling them through intermediaries. Efficiency considerations aside, their experience shows how associations of informal workers can use legal frameworks to access rights.

When reforms for the tendering of public services allowed municipal governments to give exclusive contracts to private companies for collecting, transporting, and disposing waste and recyclables, the *recicladores* organized and filed legal claims. Organizations such as the Asociación de Recicladores de Bogotá (ARB), an umbrella association of groups representing more than 25,000 waste pickers, played a key role in aggregating claims and taking cases forward. In making its case, the ARB appealed to the constitution's provision of the "right to equality," arguing that waste pickers

need preferential treatment and judicial affirmative action in the tendering and bidding process for government contracts to manage waste.

In 2003, the Constitutional Court ruled that the municipal government's tendering process for sanitation services had violated the basic rights of waste pickers. Subsequent cases have referred to constitutional provisions including the "right to survival" as an expression of the "right to life." Article 11 of the constitution was invoked to argue the right to pursue waste picking as a livelihood and the "right to pursue business and trade." Article 333 was invoked to argue that cooperatives of waste pickers, not just corporations, can compete in waste recycling markets. The most recent case in December 2011 halted a US$1.37 billion contract for the collection and removal of waste in the city.

Source: Chen and others 2012 for the World Development Report 2013.

and against harassment and confiscation of their inventories of goods by municipal authorities.[37]

These nontraditional workers' organizations are increasingly participating in global institutions such as the ILO. For instance, the International Domestic Workers Network attended the International Labour Conference in 2009 in order to prepare for discussion and vote on a new ILO convention on domestic work at the International Labour Conferences in 2010 and 2011.[38]

Active labor market programs: Effective within limits

Active labor market programs (ALMPs) can improve the efficiency of job matching by transmitting information on job openings and worker characteristics between employers and jobseekers. They can fill the gap when employers or workers underinvest in training because of various market failures, and they can mitigate the impacts of economic downturns by providing workers with temporary employment or creating incentives for employers to hire. ALMPs are politically attractive for governments eager to do something about job creation.

The most common active labor market programs are job search assistance, wage subsidies, training, and public works.[39] In terms of size, interventions range from huge public

works programs such as the Mahatma Gandhi National Rural Employment Guarantee Act (MGNREGA), offering work to millions in rural India, to tailor-made life-skill courses for small groups of young participants in the Dominican Republic. All ALMPs strive to foster new job opportunities, often for those with the fewest chances in the labor market.

A panorama of programs

Job search assistance. These are services providing information on job vacancies and jobseekers and offering counseling and placement support. Evaluations indicate that job search assistance can improve employment and earnings at a low cost—but only when job vacancies exist. By providing information and making the labor market more meritocratic, more effective matching can have positive productivity effects. But job search assistance is less relevant in countries where a majority of the workers are farmers and self-employed.

In many high-income and some middle-income countries with largely formal labor markets, job search services have been overhauled in the past 10 years. Although public financing remains the norm, private provision of services has become more common. Performance contracts are being used to create incentives for providers. These contracts must ensure that providers reach those in most need and do not concentrate only on those who are easy to place.[40] Job search support is increasingly being integrated with a range of complementary services such as profiling to assess opportunities, life skills, or other training. "Activation" strategies requiring job seekers to be brisk, are also becoming more common. Ultimately, the success of job search services depends on the capacity of providers to reach out to employers' needs.[41]

Potentially game-changing technological innovations are now extending the reach of traditional intermediation.[42] Mobile phones and the Internet have opened up possibilities for inclusive information access, connecting unregistered firms and hard-to-reach youth. New actors, including both businesses and nonprofit organizations, have emerged and run services in various country settings (box 8.5).

Wage subsidies. These are direct transfers to employers or reductions in their taxes or social contributions to encourage them to hire new workers or to keep employees who might otherwise be laid off. Wage subsidies work best when they are targeted to particular groups, such as young people who need an opportunity to demonstrate their skills, or the long-term unemployed who are at risk of suffering "scarring" effects.[43] But many studies show that they often do not have their intended effect of creating new jobs in a cost-effective fashion.[44]

The real costs of wage subsidies are often hard to calculate; the direct toll on the public purse is only part of the story. To access the subsidies, firms might replace ineligible workers with eligible ones or dismiss and then hire the same worker under the subsidy program. If firms would have hired anyway, the employment effect of a subsidy is zero. Design can help increase cost-effectiveness. Improvements in the targeting and other features of a subsidy program in Turkey reduced this "deadweight loss," although somewhere between 25 and 50 percent of all subsidized jobs would have still been created without the subsidy.[45] Proper cost accounting can reduce the estimated employment impact of wage subsidies by up to 90 percent.[46] Aggregate employment effects are hence low at best. Alternative designs, especially to reach the young and low-skilled, can include a wage subsidy linked to other active labor market programs such as training.[47] The Jóvenes programs and similar in-

---

BOX 8.5 *E-links to jobs: New technologies open new frontiers*

New technologies are revolutionizing how people connect with jobs. Mobile phones have spread widely and have penetrated low-income households around the world. Over 4 billion people have cell phone access, and 1.5 billion have regular access to the Internet.

Text messaging, voice, and mobile applications give jobseekers and employers access to information and job counseling services that improve résumés and interview skills and establish networks. Voice-based services are particularly important for illiterate jobseekers. Companies or nonprofit organizations such as Souktel, Assured Labor, Babajob, and Labournet, operating in places as diverse as Latin America, India, and the Middle East, have established thriving job matching networks. Souktel, for example, has 17,000 jobseekers and 600 companies registered in West Bank and Gaza alone. Sixty percent of registered employers reported they had cut recruiting time and costs by more than 50 percent.

Some organizations, such as Assured Labor, specifically focus on services for middle- to low-wage workers, most without college degrees. Currently, Assured Labor has 150,000 registered jobseekers and 2,000 employers in Mexico. Similarly, Babajob and Labournet in India serve 200,000 and 100,000 jobseekers who can search for employment in databases containing 40,000 and 45,000 employers, respectively. Labournet is unique in that it serves the informal labor market, focusing on sectors such as construction and facility management.

While these companies and organizations have been successful, others such as Konbit in Haiti and PULS in Pakistan had to overcome significant difficulties. Challenges have included attracting sufficient numbers of jobseekers and employers, building trust among users, and ensuring adequate assurance on the quality of jobseekers. In response, Konbit has tried to increase the number of users by partnering with a locally famous radio disk jockey and mobile phone provider to advertise its service. Through these efforts, the company was successful in attracting 10,000 jobseekers in one month.

The Internet also brings together jobseekers and employers through online platforms. The large and fast growing oDesk connects about 350,000 companies (mainly small and medium enterprises) with individual contractors worldwide. From April to June 2012, oDesk posted online close to 450,000 jobs and more than 280,000 job applications. Jobs range from typing, web research, and translation to software development and back-office legal services. Wages range from US$1 to several hundred US$ per hour. While this new phenomenon has the potential to create many new jobs and generate substantial new wealth, online platforms generally serve people with specialized and technical skills, and as such, reach few of the most vulnerable.

Sources: Based on Selim 2012 for the World Development Report 2013 and Monitor Inclusive Markets 2011.

terventions in several Latin American countries have employed this model with positive results.[48]

The impact of wage subsidies tends to rise with tight targeting and the extent of the disadvantage of the beneficiary group. In Morocco, the Idmaj youth wage subsidy effectively eased labor market entry for beneficiaries.[49] Argentina provided wage subsidies to employers hiring former participants in large public works programs. These workers exerted more effort in searching for jobs and were perceived as more trustworthy than other similar workers. That was true especially for women and young participants.[50] But the narrower the focus, the higher the potential stigma effects. In Poland, men eligible for the wage subsidies were actually less likely to be employed.[51]

Training for jobseekers. Training is the most widely used active labor market program. The growing body of impact evaluations underlines the importance of aligning the skills taught with labor demand. These evaluations show that positive benefits are not guaranteed and program costs can be substantial. When programs are well conceived and implemented, however, they can benefit those furthest from jobs the most. In Latin American countries, and in transition economies such as Romania, youth and women record significantly higher success rates from training than do middle-aged men.[52]

Some design features are critical for success. Integrated programs that include both on-the-job and classroom components pay off. Especially in developed and Latin American countries, training for job seekers now often follows this integrated model, sometimes with complementary services such as life skills training and counseling. Such combinations increase success rates (figure 8.3).[53] The Jóvenes programs in Latin America, which combine life-skills and technical training with work experience, are a case in point. In Colombia, Jóvenes en Acción has increased employability of trainees, with an estimated rate of return of 13.5–25 percent for female participants.[54]

In addition, providers need incentives to ensure that the training they offer is relevant for the needs of employers. Public training agencies often respond too slowly to changing demands from firms and jobseekers alike. Where a country's institutional capacity and supply of training

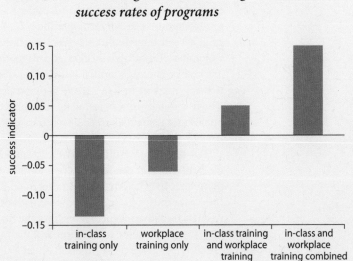

FIGURE 8.3 *Combining work and training increases the success rates of programs*

Source: Fares and Puerto 2009.
Note: The figure shows the correlation coefficient between type of training and reported success of a program, with success defined as improving employment or earnings and being cost-effective.

organizations allows, public training funds can be directed to private and nonprofit providers in competitive terms. Performance-based tendering can create incentives for more relevant training, while contracting can be designed so that the toughest-to-reach groups do not lose out. In Bulgaria, Hungary, Romania, Serbia, and Slovenia, public employment services purchase training programs from various providers through public tenders.

Research shows that at least some training programs help build trust and civic engagement, but information about how that happens is scant. In Tunisia, the inclusion of entrepreneurship training in education curricula reform improved participants' optimism about the future.[55] In the Dominican Republic, participants in the Juventud y Empleo program were more likely to have higher expectations for the future, higher job satisfaction, and more intensive search attitudes.[56] In northern Uganda, participation in a comprehensive intervention that combined grants, vocational training, life skills, and psychosocial counseling was successful in increasing community participation.[57]

Public works. These programs offer short-term employment for wages or food. The evidence from impact evaluations shows that public works programs can be useful as a safety net, especially when targeted toward those in the greatest need.[58] Careful setting of the wage level can be a self-targeting tool as has been done in Colombia's Empleo en Acción and Argentina's Trabajar programs. A similar targeting approach is being used in India's MGNREGA program, which is notable not only for its scale and cost but also for its rights-based approach in guaranteeing employment (box 8.6).

But seldom are public works a springboard for better jobs in the future. There is little evidence that they help participants get a job after they leave the program.[59] Compared with other ALMPs, public works programs have the lowest placement rates after completion and the highest costs per placement (figure 8.4). In Poland and Romania, public works have even adversely affected employability.[60] Their productivity impact, hence, tends to be very low at best.

To become a jobs ladder, public works programs need to go beyond poverty relief—a route some countries already are taking. In El Salvador and Papua New Guinea, participants in public works programs obtain additional technical and life-skills support. In Sierra Leone, the package comes with compulsory literacy and numeracy training, and in Liberia with life-skills training. In Bangladesh, the beneficiaries of a rural employment scheme were referred to microfinance institutions; three years after the program closed, almost 80 percent were still self-employed in microenterprise activities.[61] But overall, very few public works programs succeed in improving the long-run employability of participants.

Public works have the potential to contribute to social cohesion though, especially in conflict-affected countries. Soon after the conflict ended in Sierra Leone, a workfare program was launched to help rebuild infrastructure and provide short-term employment opportunities to the poor and ex-combatants. Public works programs have also been launched and scaled up in Guinea, Guinea-Bissau, Liberia, and the Republic of Yemen. In Serbia, participants felt socially more included as a result of a public works program.[62]

Striving to deliver better outcomes

While many programs have met expectations in countries with very different job challenges, many others have not succeeded in improving outcomes for participants. Moreover, while some programs are affordable, others are expensive. Outcomes for ALMPs depend on their design but also on the institutional capacity of the country to provide services on a national scale and on a continuous basis.

Program and policy design has been revamped in many countries in recent years to achieve better performance. Public funds increasingly finance private or nonprofit provision. In aging and formalizing countries, a forthcoming attitude by jobseekers is increasingly required for them to remain eligible for unemployment and other social benefits. Such activation measures create incentives for job search through participation in training or education courses, counseling and other employment services, or public works.

Many industrial countries are implementing such policies through "one-stop shops" for the administration of both social benefits and ALMPs. Germany's Jobcenter and the United Kingdom's JobCentre Plus are examples. This integrated approach can in principle help workers maintain or create links in society, albeit evidence here is scant.[63] The one-stop-shop model is gaining momentum in a number of developing countries as varied as Argentina, Azerbaijan, and Bulgaria.

Another important delivery reform is the growing investment in identifying the employment constraints faced by jobseekers. Obstacles to finding jobs may range from inadequate skills to health issues to difficulties balancing family responsibilities with work. Statistical profiling, where individual characteristics of beneficiaries are linked with likely constraints and appropriate remedies, has become an important tool, especially in countries with significant institutional capacity.[64] Comprehensive programs like Chile Solidario invest heavily in linking beneficiaries to the most appropriate programs depending on their constraints.

In sum, ALMPs can make a difference, but they need to be well aligned to the needs of the labor market and designed to address the market imperfections and institutional failures that hinder desired employment outcomes. Overall, evaluations of programs with youth participants show that developing countries have better results than industrial countries in fostering employability.[65] The time horizon also matters:

BOX 8.6 *The Mahatma Gandhi National Rural Employment Guarantee Act launched the biggest public works program in the world*

Public works programs have been actively used in India since the 1950s. Yet no scheme has had a scope or budget on the scale of the Mahatma Gandhi National Rural Employment Guarantee Act (MGNREGA). Launched in 2006 and implemented in three rollout phases, this program guarantees jobs to all districts with rural populations. The program aims to provide wage employment, improve the purchasing power of the rural poor, create assets for the community, strengthen natural resource management, and foster social and gender equality.[a]

The program guarantees up to 100 days of employment a year to rural households with adult members willing to do unskilled work at a wage that is roughly the state statutory minimum wage.[b] Rural households wanting to participate in the program are required to register with their respective village council (*gram panchayats*) and are issued a free job card with photographs of all members living in it. A job card holder may apply for employment and the government must provide it within 15 days. If the government fails to do so, in principle a daily unemployment allowance must be given to the applicant. Each household decides how to distribute employment among its members. Daily wages are based on the amount of work done and are paid directly into post office or bank accounts. The program includes some provision for adequate worksite facilities, including access to safe drinking water, shade, a first aid kit in case of accident, and crèches for women to leave their children. The program encourages the participation of women through a mandate that they should account for 33 percent of employed workers. In addition, wages have to be equal for men and women, work has to be provided within five kilometers of the applicant's village, and gender discrimination of any type is forbidden.[c]

Most of the public works carried out under MGNREGA are labor intensive; contractors and machines are not allowed on work sites. Projects are meant to be chosen in open village meetings (*gram sabhas*) to reflect village priorities, and local councils play a substantive role in planning, implementing, and monitoring them. The projects mainly focus on developing and maintaining community assets such as water conservation and water harvesting, irrigation channels, and rural roads. Drought proofing, flood control, and land development are also supported by the program. The central government bears 90 percent of the total cost, covering participants' wages in full and 75 percent of materials and administrative expenses.[d] State governments pay for 25 percent of materials and administrative costs, the daily unemployment allowance, and the expenses of the state employment guarantee council. The act also calls for accountability through the use of information and communication technology, social audits, and third-party monitoring.[e]

During the program's first phase in 2006–07, the budget outlay was US$2.49 billion. The program issued 37 million job cards and provided on average 43 person-days of work to 21 million households, totaling 0.9 billion person-days of work. Since then, the program has expanded substantially in its coverage and budget. During fiscal year 2010–11, 55 million households were provided an average of 47 person-days of work, totaling 2.5 billion person-days at a cost of US$8.7 billion (0.51 percent of GDP).[f] That makes MGNREGA the largest workfare program in the world. Participation of the poor and vulnerable has been quite significant according to administrative data.

Critics argue that MGNREGA may be affecting the functioning of rural labor markets. By setting the wage paid by the program at roughly Rs 100 (US$1.80) a day, it may help to enforce a sort of minimum wage for all casual rural work. If that is above the normal wage offered, the program may be altering the supply of casual labor and crowding out private employers.[g] It may also be constraining the process of labor reallocation out of agriculture and into more productive sectors.

The program has received considerable media attention because of alleged corruption, leakage, inadequate implementation, and the like. But few studies have attempted to assess its impact on rural households, rural labor markets, and productivity in a systematic way. Among the emerging evidence, a striking finding is that participation rates in areas where the program is most needed are not the highest.[h] Household surveys show evidence of rationing and unmet demand, limiting the poverty alleviation impact of the program. Yet, despite the rationing, the program is reaching poor people and attracting women and disadvantaged castes into the workforce.[i] One study in the state of Andhra Pradesh suggests the program increases expenditure on food and nonfood goods.[j] Evidence of effects on wage levels in rural labor markets and on labor reallocation is still inconclusive. Studies on non-labor-market effects of the program are scant.

Several challenges face the MGNREGA program. Addressing leakage and transparency is one. The government has taken this challenge seriously, for example, through the adoption of biometric-unique identification cards. Improving the quality and relevance of the communal assets to generate wider and long-term effects is another challenge. But the biggest one is ensuring that demand for work is met, and that wages are paid fully and on time. Also, if the program's objective is to lift the poorest, the program should accommodate those whose physical conditions do not allow them to perform hard manual work.[k]

Source: World Development Report 2013 team.
Notes: GDP = gross domestic product.
a. Ministry of Rural Development 2012; World Bank 2011d.
b. Ministry of Rural Development 2012. Initially, the statutory minimum wage varied across states. But in 2009, the central government delinked MGNREGA wages from the state-level statutory minimum and established a uniform daily wage of Rs. 100, which is adjustable for state-specific inflation.
c. Ministry of Rural Development 2008; World Bank 2011d.
d. World Bank 2011b.
e. Ministry of Rural Development 2008.

f. World Bank 2011b. In terms of budget as a percent of GDP, the MGNREGA is comparable to the largest cash transfers programs such as PROGRESA/Oportunidades (0.4 percent GDP in Mexico) or Bolsa Família (0.36 percent GDP in Brazil). Yet in terms of household coverage, the massive scale of the MGNREGA stands out.
g. Basu 2011; Basu, Chau, and Kanbur 2009; Dutta and others 2012; World Bank 2011b.
h. Dutta and others 2012.
i. Dutta and others 2012.
j. Ravi and Engler 2009.
k. World Bank 2011d.

FIGURE 8.4 *In Romania, public works programs have the lowest placement rate and highest placement costs*

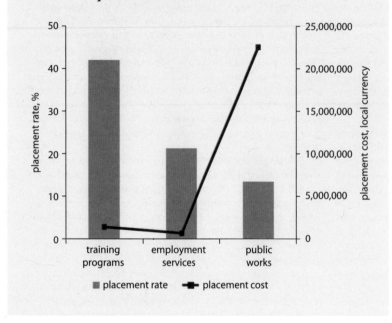

Source: Rodriguez-Planas and Benus 2010.
Note: The placement rate is the percentage of program participants who get a job.

in industrial countries, training programs show their real value only in the medium to longer run.[66] But a thorough understanding of the jobs challenge faced and a good sense of institutional capacities are critical when deciding whether a specific ALMP could be part of the solution.

Even with these innovations, expectations for active labor market programs need to be kept in check. Job search and intermediation can work only if firms are creating jobs. Short training courses cannot solve a fundamental problem in the education system. Activation incentives will be fruitless if deep-rooted discrimination causes people to withdraw from a job search.

Social insurance: The challenge of expanding coverage

Many people are unable or unwilling to save against major risks such as job loss, disability, the death of a breadwinner, or aging without resources. Because insurers cannot accurately assess individual risk (adverse selection) and be-

cause individuals can influence that level of risk (moral hazard), markets do not provide adequate risk pooling. Social insurance is a package of programs that can potentially address market failures such as these. But social insurance programs are also shaped by history, values, and politics, so their design is not exclusively aimed at improving efficiency.

Some countries have introduced public unemployment insurance systems to help workers mitigate the risk of job loss. Many have disability insurance to cover situations where illness or injury affects employment opportunities. Most countries also have social safety nets that, while not directly tied to employment status, can provide a coping mechanism when earnings are insufficient to meet a basic living standard.

Other social insurance programs not directly related to labor market risks are often tied to the jobs that people have or to their employment status. The most important of these are old-age pensions and health insurance programs that are financed by payroll taxes (social security contributions) from employers, employees, or both. These benefits are publicly provided because of imperfections in the insurance market, not in the labor market. However, they can have important consequences for the types of jobs that are created and thus for productivity. Financing them through payroll taxes can affect labor demand and employer choices on whether to provide insurance coverage as part of the employment contract. It can also influence workers' behavior, including their incentives to take, keep, and switch jobs, to work in the formal or the informal sector, and to engage in work with higher risks and returns.

From a jobs perspective, the major questions are twofold: how to manage labor market risks and how to design the financing of other types of social insurance to have the most favorable impact on employment.

Managing labor market risks

In low-income countries, managing income loss is more important than managing the loss of a job. When most people are engaged in subsistence agriculture or are self-employed, open unemployment is not a common occurrence. In these contexts, social safety nets, including noncontributory cash transfers and public works programs, can be critically important to cope with adverse shocks.[67]

However, when wage employment is more prevalent, unemployment insurance may be a higher priority. Unemployment insurance can provide income support to workers who lose their jobs and prevent individuals and households from falling into poverty. By supporting a job search, it can result in better matches and efficiency gains. Effective coverage is far from complete, however; according to the ILO, only 15 percent of the unemployed worldwide received benefits during the recent financial crisis.[68] Another concern with unemployment benefit systems is that they may reduce incentives to keep jobs, look for jobs, or accept a job offer. Most of the evidence on the incentive effects of unemployment benefits comes from industrial countries and is mixed. Some studies find that more generous benefits—either through higher benefit levels, or longer duration of benefits—can increase either the length of unemployment or the unemployment rate.[69] Exits from unemployment typically increase when benefits expire.[70]

Over the past decade, unemployment insurance eligibility and benefits have been reformed in a number of countries to reduce job search disincentives. While some disincentive effects are inherent in any unemployment insurance system, recent studies for Denmark, France, Germany, Ireland, Italy, and Spain found that even if workers remain unemployed for a longer period of time, they are eventually able to find more stable jobs.[71] Studies of unemployment insurance in Brazil found that benefits did not affect the duration of unemployment, except when workers were moving from unemployment to self-employment. In this case the transition period was shorter, suggesting that benefits may have made it possible to start a new business.[72]

Concerns about job search disincentives and hidden redistribution have led to some interest in unemployment insurance savings accounts. While the design can vary, workers make contributions to the accounts and can draw money from them during unemployment spells. Any remaining balance is paid out when the worker retires and can be used as a pension top-up. Some countries, mainly in Latin America but also Austria and Jordan, have adopted these savings accounts as an alternative approach to insurance-based programs. But insurance savings accounts do not allow for risk pooling, so that young workers and workers with frequent unemployment spells may not have adequate savings. To address this concern, some plans have a redistribution feature. For example, Chile's program includes a Solidarity Fund to support workers whose account balances are too low to provide adequate income support during unemployment.

In all countries, disability is an important labor market risk. According to recent estimates, the prevalence of disability is about 15 percent of the adult population. Rates are higher in low-income countries and in aging societies.[73] Although many people with disabilities do work, inactivity rates among them are significantly higher than for the overall population. In industrial countries, the inactivity rate for persons with disabilities is about 2.5 times higher than it is for those without disability.[74]

Disability benefits can provide important income protection, but costs have mounted in some countries and the benefits can create work disincentives among the general population. Accommodation of workplaces to persons with disabilities is an important strategy to encourage them to seek employment. Benefit systems can be adjusted to this end as well. In-work payments, time-limited benefits, and working tax credits are all being tested in the European Union.[75] Countries without disability benefits need to emphasize accommodation and rely on social safety nets where disability is associated with poverty.

Financing social insurance

A salient feature of social insurance programs in developing countries is their low coverage.[76] Across the world only 30 percent of workers have access to social insurance; in Africa and Asia, the share is less than 25 percent (map 8.1). On average, coverage rates are highest in aging societies and formalizing countries and lowest in conflict-affected countries and agrarian economies, where less than 10 percent of the working population is enrolled in pension programs. In general, low-income workers are the least likely to be covered. In most countries in Latin America, coverage rates are below 10 percent in the bottom income quintile but above 50

MAP 8.1 *Coverage of social insurance remains low in many countries*

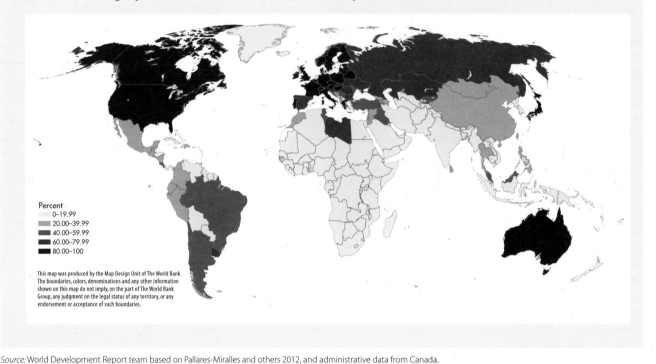

Percent
- 0–19.99
- 20.00–39.99
- 40.00–59.99
- 60.00–79.99
- 80.00–100

This map was produced by the Map Design Unit of The World Bank. The boundaries, colors, denominations and any other information shown on this map do not imply, on the part of The World Bank Group, any judgment on the legal status of any territory, or any endorsement or acceptance of such boundaries.

Source: World Development Report team based on Pallares-Miralles and others 2012, and administrative data from Canada.
Note: Coverage refers to number of people who have contributed (at least for one month in the reference year) to an earnings-related mandatory pension scheme, measured as a percentage of the labor force.

percent in the top quintile.[77] Even if workers are covered on paper by social insurance, they may not necessarily receive benefits. Effective coverage can be reduced by fiscal pressures and low implementation capacity.

Coverage is low for multiple reasons, including limited fiscal space to finance programs, low institutional capacity to manage the administration and delivery of benefits, fragmented schemes that cover certain groups and not others, and program design providing weak incentives to participate. In many developing countries, workers and firms in the informal sector generally fall outside the scope of programs. Reaching the self-employed, farmers, and migrants is particularly difficult. Social insurance laws in many countries do not cover micro- and small enterprises, or these firms and farms opt out because they cannot afford minimum contribution costs.[78] Weak enforcement capacity also contributes to low coverage.

Payroll taxes (including contributions for social programs) have been the dominant means of financing social insurance in most countries. But whether payroll taxes are the optimal model, especially for developing countries, is increasingly being questioned.[79] Financing social insurance through payroll taxes may exacerbate the coverage problem by creating disincentives for the creation of formal sector jobs.

Studies in countries such as Colombia, Turkey, and some transition countries in Eastern Europe and Central Asia have found that increases in the levels of social insurance contributions decreased formal employment, by varying amounts.[80] By contributing to the "tax wedge" (the gap between total labor costs and take-home pay), payroll taxes to fund social insurance can discourage both labor demand and the willingness to work. The size of this tax wedge varies considerably across countries. It is most significant in industrial countries, aging societies, and formalizing countries (figure 8.5).

However, a complete assessment needs to take into account the value that workers place on access to social insurance. Social contributions should not be seen as a pure tax when contributors attach value to the attendant benefits. And the evidence largely suggests that they do.[81] When asked to name the essential elements of a good job, people in China, Colombia, the Arab Republic of Egypt, and Sierra Leone rated access to pensions and health insurance equally with good wages. In those countries, workers who participate in social insurance systems indicated that they would require substantial income increases to compensate for losing access to social insurance. At the same time, workers outside these systems would be willing to contribute a significant portion of their pay to participate (figure 8.6).[82] But design and implementation matter, because the value attached to participation depends to a significant degree on the adequacy of benefits relative to contributions and the efficiency and transparency of benefits administration. The long-term credibility of the social insurance system is also a critical factor, especially in aging societies.

In trying to extend the coverage of social protection in developing countries, two important issues need to be addressed. The first one is which risks are the priorities to address. In low-income countries, pensions for old-age and disability and basic health insurance are more important than unemployment insurance.

The second issue is how to extend the priority programs to workers in the informal sector. Some countries are using technology in innovative ways to make participation by informal sector workers easier (box 8.7). But technology alone cannot overcome the market imperfections and institutional failures that result in low social protection coverage. For instance, mobile phones may make it easier for farmers to pay contributions toward health insurance, but those less prone to be ill may still choose not to enroll. This is why extending social protection coverage requires adequate regulations and resources, in addition to modern "technology."

One approach is to run a parallel system for informal sector workers in conjunction with the contributory system. This approach addresses the coverage gap, but if the parallel system is funded out of general tax revenue, it discourages enrollment in the contributory system and can hinder the development of the formal sector. These problems could be addressed to some

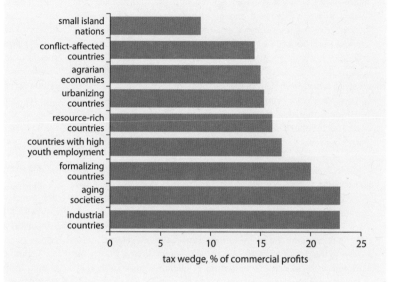

FIGURE 8.5 *Labor taxes and social contributions vary across countries facing different jobs challenges*

Source: World Bank 2011a.
Note: Labor tax and contributions measured as the amount of taxes and mandatory contributions on labor paid by businesses.

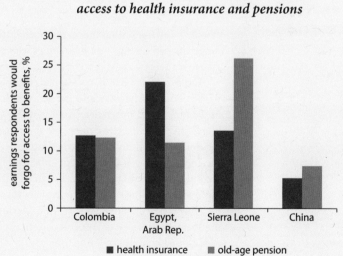

FIGURE 8.6 *Workers are willing to give up earnings for access to health insurance and pensions*

Sources: Bjørkhaug and others 2012; Hatløy and others 2012; Kebede and others 2012; and Zhang and others 2012; all for the World Development Report 2013.
Note: Data are for wage workers who do not receive health insurance or pension benefits paid by their employer. The figure shows the maximum amount (percentage of typical monthly income) they were willing to give up to receive benefits.

BOX 8.7 *Modern technology can reduce social protection costs, leakage, and corruption*

Innovative technology-based approaches are transforming the ways in which insurance and other cash benefits are provided. India's new health insurance scheme for the poor uses biometric smart cards both to verify that households are eligible and to keep track of hospital procedures not involving cash payments. Almost 30 million households now hold these smart cards. According to a recent report from the U.K. Department for International Development, "evidence from South Africa, India, Kenya, and Liberia has demonstrated that electronic payment systems involving smart cards or mobile phones can significantly reduce costs and leakage."[a] Another report, by the Consultative Group to Assist the Poor, finds significant reductions in transaction costs through electronic payments in Brazil and Colombia. These "front-end" applications help overcome several problems that have plagued service delivery in the past, including the need for beneficiaries to go long distances to obtain benefits and for middlemen to fill out forms.

Many developing countries lack robust systems for identifying people, allowing fraud of various kinds, and preventing many among the poor from accessing social programs. In the Dominican Republic, for example, one-quarter of eligible beneficiaries for a poverty program could not participate because they lacked proper documents. Poor identification also hampers efforts to coordinate across government and donor-sponsored programs and leads to duplication of costs. To confront this challenge, a growing number of countries is moving to biometric technology. India's unique identification program, known as Aadhaar, is the most ambitious so far, having collected digital fingerprints and iris scans for close to 200

million people. Applications such as mobile phones with fingerprint readers that would allow online verification of identity acceptable to service providers are now being piloted.

Less glamorous, but just as important, is the "back-end" part of social protection systems, which allows tracking of transactions on a regular basis and generation of key indicators and reports. The Management Information Systems (MIS) are arguably even more important for complex social insurance programs, especially as populations age and noncommunicable diseases become more prevalent. Keeping track of work histories allows for a better alignment of pension benefits and social security contributions. Databases of medical histories support a more efficient design of health protocols and payments to health care providers.

Information is no longer the sole domain of those administering the program, however. One of the applications of modern technology with the most potential impact is citizen reporting of acts of corruption and negligence through social media. Massive mobile phone penetration has been an especially empowering tool.

Technology is not a panacea, however, and failed projects are common. In most cases, the technology is not matched with a reengineering of the processes involved. Other common problems include poor planning and procurement practices, asymmetric information between government and vendors, and lack of trained personnel to operate the systems after they are in place. Despite these problems, the future of social protection will inevitably include creative ways of applying new technology.

Sources: World Development Report 2013 team based on Bold, Porteous, and Rotman 2012; Devereux and others 2007; DFID 2011; Gelb and Decker 2011; Palacios, Das, and Sun 2011.
a. DFID 2011, 9.

extent by differentiating the level of benefits between the two systems and financing the parallel system on at least a partially contributory basis.[83]

Another approach is to partially subsidize participation by farmers and the self-employed in general social insurance programs. In Vietnam, those classified as poor get their health insurance cards fully paid by the budget, while the "near poor" get a 50 percent subsidy.[84] This second approach may look similar to the previous one, as funding relies on general tax revenue too. But it has the advantage of not discouraging formalization. From a social cohesion point of view it also allows building universal systems, rather than two-tier systems.

Well-designed social insurance and social protection systems have the potential to enhance the three transformations. Mitigating labor market distortions and covering priority risks can compensate for lost income; it can also contribute to subjective well-being by reducing uncertainty. Portability of benefits from one job to another and the capacity of systems to manage transitions can help workers move to higher-productivity jobs and encourage risk taking. And extending coverage can contribute to social cohesion through its role in building an encompassing social contract.[85]

Policies that protect people are usually hailed as being better than policies that protect jobs. Providing income support prevents large drops in consumption and mitigates the risk of poverty among households affected by unemployment, underemployment, or loss of labor earnings. Relying on transitional income support and, in some cases retraining programs, rather than measures to protect jobs allows for the reallocation of labor, keeping up the process of creative destruction. Resources are thus allocated more efficiently and economic growth is enhanced. Preserving jobs that are no longer economically viable through government transfers and employment protection legislation prolongs an inefficient allocation of resources.

Moreover, job protection also entails a high risk of capture. It runs the danger of becoming permanent rather than temporary, creating enduringly unproductive, subsidized jobs. The development experience is full of examples in which explicit job protection has led to little other than large rents for business owners and workers in the sectors that benefited from it, stifling technological advance, structural change, and growth.

The conventional wisdom, then, argues against the protection of jobs. But in times when many jobs are lost or threatened at once and few are being created, such conventional wisdom needs to be revisited. The productivity of a protected job can still be higher than that of the alternative jobs the displaced worker may find. And the productivity gap may exceed the costs of keeping the job alive. This is likely to be the case when the alternative after displacement is to be jobless for a long period of time. In this case, in addition to the immediate loss in output, prolonged unemployment can depreciate skills and undermine social cohesion.

Importantly, it is the overall productivity of the job that needs to be considered, including its possible spillovers on the productivity of others. When people work together, or when they are connected through broader value chains, the loss of a large number of jobs may have ripple effects on productivity. In areas or activities where jobs have important productivity spillovers, the aggregate loss of output is then more than the sum of the losses in individual earnings. Massive job losses can then lead to ghost towns and depressed regions, and this prospect suggests that the conventional wisdom may not always be right.

Turnover versus decoupling

Every day, jobs are created and destroyed. Workers are hired and dismissed, or they quit their jobs and start their own businesses; meanwhile some firms close and others are born. In industrial countries, this process of creative destruction affects around 15 percent of all jobs every year.[86] In normal times, the probability of job loss for an individual is largely independent of the probability of job loss for another. And the probability of landing another job is also independent of what happens to other workers. The employment shock is then what economists call "idiosyncratic."

But there are exceptional times, when employment shocks are systemic. Then, a sustained decoupling of the normal process of job creation and job destruction occurs: jobs are lost in large numbers but not created at the same pace. This is what occurs in times of severe economic crises, when a decline in economic activity affects a broad swath of firms and industries. Job destruction accelerates, often sharply, and job creation levels off or even decreases (figure 8.7). This decoupling leads to unemployment in formalized economies and under-employment in less formalized ones.[87] In many countries, droughts, floods, or other natural disasters can have a similar impact. After the sources of the crisis dissipate, job creation picks up and unemployment or underemployment declines. The longer it takes for job creation to recover, the longer unemployment or underemployment lasts.

Decoupling can also occur in times of massive structural change brought about by rapid technical progress (for example, the introduction of computers) or policy reforms (for exam-

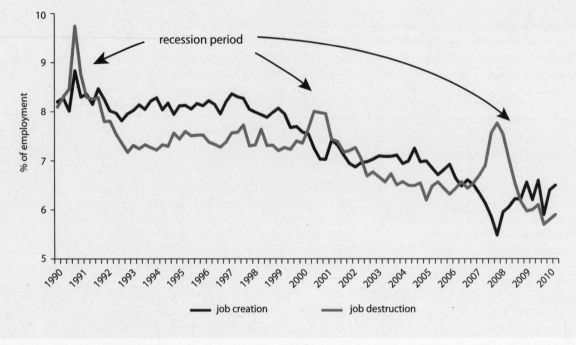

FIGURE 8.7 *Decoupling between job creation and job destruction was massive in the United States during recessions*

Source: Davis, Faberman, and Haltiwanger 2012.

ple, trade liberalization). Structural change can affect entire industries. In transition economies, such changes were enormous, as entire sectors economies had to cope with uncertainty and adapt to new incentives. Public sector restructuring or the privatization of state-owned enterprises can cause a similar shock. In all these cases, unemployment and underemployment can be large and long-lasting.

Losses in earnings and output are more pervasive with systemic shocks than with idiosyncratic shocks. But sometimes these two types of employment shocks can overlap. The recent financial crisis has led to an unusually deep recession in many countries. In the United States, high unemployment rates have persisted, unemployment spells have lasted longer than usual, and new job creation is still sluggish four years after the beginning of the crisis.[88] Some argue that the crisis is not a regular cyclical perturbation but the manifestation of a more enduring shift caused by technological change and globalization.[89]

Decoupling hurts

Protecting people should have primacy if shocks are idiosyncratic—if the employment dislocation is limited and if turnover continues to be the norm. A variety of social protection mechanisms exist that support people in their transition from one job to another. They concentrate on sustaining standards of living through unemployment benefits and public transfers. Learning new skills or relocating to where job opportunities are can also play a role. By moving from an adversely affected activity to another job, there is a gain in output that over time outweighs the cost of the support mechanisms. Protecting people is thus good for individuals and for society.

If massive decoupling occurs—through either a wider crisis or large-scale structural change—protecting workers will rarely be enough. Intermediation services falter because jobs are simply not available. Training may help individual workers land a job, but it does not create many jobs at the aggregate level, because it does not address the cyclical or structural causes of the employment shock. Income support through unemployment benefits and public transfers may suffer from inadequate funds or seriously affect fiscal accounts. Only sustained job creation can deal with the effects of decoupling, but even under the best of circumstances it may take several years to offset the employment decline from a systemic shock. The question then is whether providing income support on a large scale for long periods of time is preferable to temporarily supporting employment, while job creation picks up.

The long-term consequences and costs of decoupling can be higher than is usually thought. During periods of massive structural change, the reallocation of workers out of declining industries can lead to large output losses because little alternative employment is available. The productivity of jobs in declining industries may be low, but it can still be higher than the alternatives. Similarly, during crises, firms might not be insolvent but rather illiquid. Death of inherently solvent firms could cause loss of firm-specific human capital and intangible assets, disruption of value chains, and damage to surrounding communities. While the provision of credit would be the preferred solution, identifying insolvent firms might not always be feasible and could be marred by transparency problems. Temporary job protection policies can be a workable alternative to provide a lifeline for struggling, but inherently solvent, firms.

Long-term unemployment can also erode skills and workforce attachment. Aptitudes and attitudes to perform a given occupation can be lost.[90] "Scarring" can occur, with long-run consequences for finding employment with similar earnings.[91] Human capital and skills depreciate. Regardless of whether decoupling is the result of severe downturns or major structural changes, workers may enter a spiral of unappealing jobs and lower living standards. The potential costs might be particularly disruptive to social cohesion. Social networks can be undone in ways that make it more difficult for the dislocated to reengage in work and even in other forms of social activity.[92] Prolonged periods of high unemployment are of particular concern because they can affect young people's transition from school to work, and may lead to disenfranchisement from society.[93]

In some circumstances, then, job protection can be considered. What is meant by that is not permanent restrictions on hiring and firing through employment protection legislation, but rather time-bound policy measures that mitigate job destruction. In other words, these are selectively used active labor market policies that promote job creation or sustain existing jobs. Several countries adopted policies of this sort during the recent recession; Germany, which has a long tradition with such policies, averted job losses through a coordinated reduction of hours of work (box 8.8). The United States also took measures to protect jobs during the recent recession, most notably by salvaging its auto industry. But the United States relied mostly on aggregate demand stimulation and on extensions of unemployment insurance to protect workers, rather than on measures to protect jobs. In relative terms, changes in employment and unemployment in the United States were much larger than in Germany.[94]

The pitfalls of protecting jobs

There are examples in developing countries as well. Chile and Mexico introduced work-sharing policies and compensatory subsidies to moderate the impact of the crisis. But these policies had a limited impact in their case. Given their novelty, they required new procedures that were difficult to implement quickly, resulting in very low take-up rates. More important, these policies are not well suited to countries where a large share of employment is informal, because they fail to reach the vast majority of employers. The experiences of Chile and Mexico, two countries with relatively high administrative capacity that have made progress in formalization, suggest that the usefulness of work-sharing policies is limited in developing "countries."

There are positive examples as well. The different ways in which China and many Latin American countries handled the restructuring of their economies through the 1980s and 1990s are telling. At the beginning of its reform process, China had hundreds of thousands of uncompetitive state-owned enterprises (SOEs). But large-scale labor retrenchment would have pushed workers into even less productive jobs until the private sector developed sufficiently to absorb them. China thus supported its ail-

BOX 8.8 *Kurzarbeit has become a new word in labor market policies*

Kurzarbeit (which translates to "short work" or "reduced working hours") has been used in Germany for a century. Under this program, employees in participating firms can be asked to cut down on working hours with a commensurate reduction in compensation. The German government, through the Federal Employment Agency, covers a percentage of the ensuing wage loss. Participation of the firm is tied to the consent of the workers affected.[a] Thus there is an emphasis on social dialogue in the implementation of the program. During economic downturns, German employers tend to respond by reducing the number of hours worked, thereby mitigating the loss in jobs.

More than a dozen countries have adopted programs for reduced working hours based on the general *kurzarbeit* model but involving a variety of designs and regulations.[b] The countries where these programs were in place before the global economic crisis experienced substantial increases in take-up rates during the 2008–09 period.

As a response to the crisis, several countries implementing a work-share program increased the percentage of wages covered, extended benefit duration, and relaxed the criteria for qualifying for the program. In Germany, the period during which firms could request subsidies was extended from 6 to 24 months; the government coverage of social insurance costs was increased to 50 percent; temporary help workers were made eligible; and the program was allowed to cover up to 67 percent of wage losses incurred by affected employees.[c] It is estimated that more than 1 percent of permanent jobs were saved in Germany through *kurzarbeit*.[d] In 2009, more than 3 percent of the labor force was covered by the program.

The program is touted as beneficial in that it is less expensive for government to contribute funds toward paying the lost hours of work to the employee than to pay unemployment benefits. From the point of view of the employer, it helps retain skilled staff and reduces churning and retraining costs, thus maintaining firm productivity. From the perspective of the employee, the scheme prevents unemployment and the problems that come with it such as loss of income, depreciation of skills, decrease in life satisfaction, and insecurity. From the societal perspective, it cushions the impact of the economic downturn and spreads it more evenly across the labor force.

However, work-share programs only benefit formal sector employees, and not even all of them. The *kurzarbeit* is effective in saving permanent jobs but has no significant impact on temporary employment or on the hours worked by temporary workers.[e] Work-share programs are also more effective in countries with less flexible labor market regulations, where take-up rates are higher.[f] Furthermore, long-term reliance on this type of program can lead to significant delays in necessary labor reallocation and therefore could hinder growth and productivity in the medium term.

Source: World Development Report 2013 team.

a. If the adoption of the work-share program was foreseen in a collective agreement, the consent of the employees is not necessary; see Eurofound 2009.
b. These are Argentina, Belgium, Canada, Colombia, the Czech Republic, Denmark, Finland, Italy, Japan, Luxembourg, Mexico, New Zealand, Norway, Poland, and Turkey. See Hijzen and Venn 2011
c. Burda and Hunt 2011.
d. Cahuc and Carcillo 2011.
e. Cahuc and Carcillo 2011.
f. Robalino and Banerji 2009.

ing SOEs through access to banking credit while rapidly modernizing its economy, preventing social disruptions in the process.[95] Latin American countries also embarked on the dismantling of inefficient industries that had developed under import substitution policies. But they did so more abruptly. Sudden downsizing may have caused a more durable rise in informality and led to slower productivity growth.[96]

The risk with job protection policies is that they can create permanent inefficiency, especially in countries with weak institutions. Job protection policies involve firms or even whole industries that can coordinate to engage in rent seeking to secure permanent government support. If such policies are adopted, it is necessary to establish and enforce trigger rules and sunset clauses that define the extent and size of the protection. If the institutional prerequisites to ensure that support is temporary do not exist, or are not credible, job protection policies can be dangerous indeed. And they should not be considered at all if job losses do not result from a systemic employment shock, involving a large decoupling of job creation and job destruction.

Notes

1. A particular country can be included in more than one group. Country types have been classified according to the following definitions. *Agrarian economies*: a rural share of population of 60 percent or above in 2010 (World Development Indicators [WDI], World Bank, Washington, DC, http://data.worldbank.org/data-catalog/world-development-indicators); *conflict-affected countries*: derived from a combination of two sources: (i) countries in the Uppsala Conflict Data Program database with at least 1,000 battle deaths in an internal or internationalized internal conflict in 2010, or (ii) with UN peace keeping and peace building missions (2012 World Bank fragility list); *urbanizing economies*: with 65 percent or less of the population living in urbanized areas in 2000, and with an increase of 4.5 percentage points by 2010 (WDI); *resource-rich countries*: with mineral exports accounting for at least 20 percent of total exports over 2005–10 (World Integrated Trade Solution); *countries with high youth unemployment*: with a "youth bulge index" score of 0.90 or above. The youth bulge index is calculated as total youth employment (2010) times youth unemployment rate (mean, 2001–10) divided by total population (2010, WDI); *formalizing economies*: pension contributors representing between 25 and 75 percent of the total labor force (PDB Provisional Pension Database, February 2012); *aging societies*: an elderly population (aged 65 or above) that is more than 8 percent of the working-age group (15-to-64-year-olds) (WDI); *small island nations*: island nations with a population of less than 2 million (UN Office of the High Representative for the Least Developed Countries, Landlocked Developing Countries and Small Island Developing States and WDI).

2. Holzmann and Vodopivec 2012.

3. One hundred sixteen countries have ratified conventions 26 and 131, which are related to the minimum wage. The World Bank's *Doing Business Indicators 2012* report informs that 147 countries, of a sample of 182, have a minimum wage defined for a 19-year-old worker or apprentice.

4. Aghion, Algan, and Cahuc 2011; Aghion and others 2010; Alesina and others 2010; Botero and others 2004.

5. This applies to other areas of regulation as well. For example, restrictions of night and overtime work; provisions for sickness, vacation, and maternity leave; and health and safety regulations all establish a "floor" for workers.

6. Boeri and van Ours 2008; Eyraud and Saget 2008.

7. The term *lighthouse effect* was introduced by Souza and Baltar (1980). See also Boeri, Garibaldi, and Ribeiro 2011; Neri, Gonzaga, and Camargo 2001.

8. Acemoglu 2001.

9. For more on the channels through which the minimum wage can influence poverty, see Fields and Kanbur (2007).

10. Cahuc and Kramarz 2004.

11. See Boeri, Helppie, and Macis (2008) and Freeman (2009) for reviews of many of these studies.

12. Betcherman 2012 for the World Development Report 2013.

13. For EPL, negative impacts on employment are found by Nickell and Layard (1999) for OECD countries; Heckman and Pagés (2000), but not Heckman and Pagés (2004), for OECD and Latin American countries; Mondino and Montoya (2004) for Argentina; Micco and Pagés (2006) for Chile; Kugler (2004) for Colombia; Ahsan and Pagés (2009) and Gupta, Hasan, and Kumar (2008) for India; Saavedra and Torero (2004) for Peru; Djankov and Ramalho (2009) for a large set of developing countries; and Kaplan (2009) for Latin America. In contrast, Baccaro and Rei (2007) and Bassanini and Duval (2006) for OECD countries; Paes de Barros and Corseuil (2004) for Brazil; Downes, Mamingi, and Antoine (2004) for three Caribbean countries; and Petrin and Sivadasan (2006) for Chile find no significant effect of EPL upon employment or unemployment. For minimum wages, among those who find negative employment effects are Fajnzylber (2001), Lemos (2004), and Neumark, Cunningham, and Siga (2006) for Brazil; Arango and Pachón (2004), Bell (1997), and Maloney and Núñez Méndez (2003) for Colombia; Kertesi and Kollo (2003) for Hungary; Alatas and Cameron (2003), Rama (2001), and SMERU Research Institute (2001) for Indonesia; and Strobl and Walsh (2003) for Trinidad and Tobago. Among those who find no effect are Lemos (2007) for Brazil; Gindling and Terrell (2007) for Costa Rica; and Bell (1997) and Feliciano (1998) for Mexico.

14. Micco and Pagés 2006; Petrin and Sivadasan 2006.

15. Card and Krueger 1995.

16. Although some studies have found that youth employment can be positively affected by minimum wage increases (for example, Card and Krueger 1995), most studies have found negative employment effects, although the magnitude is typically modest (for example, Montenegro and Pagés 2004 for Chile; Arango and Pachón 2004 for Colombia; SMERU Research Institute 2001 for Indonesia; and Neumark and Nizalova 2007

for the United States). Employment of women has been found to fall in several cases as a result of minimum wage increases (for example, Feliciano 1998 for Mexico and Arango and Pachón 2004 for Colombia), although Pagés and Montenegro (2007) identified a shift in employment toward women in Chile. Where researchers have looked at employment effects of minimum wage increases on the less skilled, they typically find negative effects (for example, Arango and Pachón 2004; Kertesi and Kollo 2003; Montenegro and Pagés 2004; and SMERU Research Institute 2001). In general, workers in small firms are most likely to be affected by employment losses caused by increases in the minimum wage (Kertesi and Kollo 2003; Rama 2001). Regarding EPL, Montenegro and Pagés (2004) found that the introduction of more protective rules in Chile had adverse effects for women relative to men, for youth relative to the more experienced, and for the skilled relative to the less skilled. Similarly, cross-country analysis by the Organisation for Economic Co-operation and Development (OECD 2004) identified negative impacts of EPL on women and youth.

17. Alatas and Cameron 2003; Rama 2001.

18. For minimum wages, a number of studies in Latin America find increased wage equality (for example, Fajnzylber 2001 for Brazil; Gindling and Terrell 1995 for Costa Rica; and Bosch and Manacorda 2010 for Mexico). OECD (2011) identifies declining real minimum wages and less restrictive EPL as factors behind increasing inequality in many countries.

19. See Messina and Vallanti (2007) for European countries; Eslava and others (2004) for Colombia; Haltiwanger, Scarpetta, and Schweiger (2008) for OECD and Latin American countries; Bentolila and others (2011) for OECD countries; and Caballero (2004) for 60 developing and developed countries. Eichhorst and others (2010), however, found no systematic difference in adjustment to shocks by EPL differences for a sample of 20 OECD countries.

20. Belot, Boone, and van Ours (2007) find positive effects, but only in environments where workers invested in firm-specific skills. Koeniger (2005) and Nickell and Layard (1999) find positive productivity effects, but results depended on estimation specifications. Autor, Kerr, and Kugler (2007) find that increases in employment protection had a negative effect on total factor productivity but a positive one on labor productivity. In contrast, Bassanini and Venn (2008) and Cingano and others (2010) find negative impacts. Bassanini, Nunziata, and Venn (2009) find that dismissal regulations have a depressing effect on labor but restrictions on the use of temporary

employment do not. All of these studies are based on data from industrial countries. In a study of developed and developing countries, Micco and Pagés (2006) conclude that labor regulations do not robustly affect labor productivity. In a study of Asian and Latin American countries, DeFreitas and Marshall (1998) find that job security protections have a positive productivity effect in some situations and a negative effect in others. Bassanini and Venn (2007) find a positive effect of minimum wages on productivity in OECD countries.

21. Blanchard and Landier 2002; Dolado, García-Serrano, and Jimeno 2002; OECD 2004.

22. Almeida and Carneiro 2009.

23. Ahsan and Pagés 2009; World Bank 2011b.

24. Kucera and Roncolato 2008.

25. Berg 2011; Fajnzylber 2001; Foguel, Ramos, and Carneiro 2001; Lemos 2004; Neumark, Cunningham, and Siga 2006.

26. For an analytical discussion on the need for joint design of labor market institutions, see Blanchard and Tirole (2008). For a discussion of the design of labor market institutions in a developing country setting, see Blanchard (2005).

27. The share of workers covered by a collective agreement is generally larger than the union membership rates. The reason is that agreements negotiated between unions and employers are sometimes extended to other workplaces not involved in the bargaining.

28. Hayter 2011. Recent changes in legislation are summarized in ILO and International Institute for Labour Studies (2012).

29. For summaries of the evidence on the union wage effect, see Aidt and Tzannatos (2002) and Freeman (2009).

30. DiNardo, Fortin, and Lemieux 1996.

31. This is based on regressions using panel data for 22 OECD countries from 1985 to 2007. For details, see OECD (2011).

32. Aidt and Tzannatos 2002.

33. Freeman 2009.

34. Aidt and Tzannatos 2002.

35. Betcherman 2012 for the World Development Report 2013.

36. Forteza and Rama 2006.

37. Chen and others 2012 for the World Development Report 2013.

38. Chen and others 2012 for the World Development Report 2013.

39. Small-business development and microcredit generally do not fall under this category because they aim to foster entrepreneurship.

40. Almeida and others 2012.

41. Kuddo 2009.

42. Information provision can help bring people to available jobs. Information will not solve the

signaling insufficiency of the market, however, if employers cannot judge the full capabilities and abilities of applicants.

43. Bell and Blanchflower 2010.

44. Betcherman, Olivas, and Dar (2004) find that most evaluated wage subsidies do not improve employment or earnings of participants.

45. Betcherman, Daysal, and Pagés 2010.

46. Calmfors 1994; Martin and Grubb 2001.

47. For evidence on the positive impact of these combined programs, see Cockx, van der Linden, and Karaa (1998) and Katz (1996). Robalino and Sanchez-Puerta (2008) also provide a review.

48. Almeida and others 2012.

49. World Bank 2011c.

50. Galasso, Ravallion, and Salvia 2004.

51. Kluve, Lehmann, and Schmidt 1999; Kluve, Lehmann, and Schmidt 2008.

52. Rodriguez-Planas and Benus 2010.

53. Almeida, Behrman, and Robalino 2012. For OECD countries, see Almeida and Carneiro (2009); Heckman, Stixrud, and Urzua (2006); and Holzer and Lerman (2009).

54. Attanasio, Kugler, and Meghir 2008.

55. Premand and others 2011.

56. Acevedo Alameda, Garcia, and Martinez 2011; World Bank 2008.

57. Blattman, Fiala, and Martinez 2011.

58. del Ninno, Subbarao, and Milazzo 2009.

59. The evidence on the ineffectiveness of public works has been widely documented; see, for example, Betcherman, Olivas, and Dar (2004) and Martin and Grubb (2001) for reviews, and Card, Kluve, and Weber (2010) and Kluve (2010) for metastudies. Carling and Richardson (2004) and Sianesi (2008) conclude that the closer a policy is to regular work, the better its longer-term employability effects on participants.

60. Kluve, Lehmann, and Schmidt 2008 for Poland; Rodriguez-Planas 2010 for Romania.

61. Hashemi and Rosenberg 2006.

62. Bonin and Rinne 2006. The Beautiful Serbia program combined vocational training and public works in the construction sector for disadvantaged unemployed in Serbia and Montenegro in 2004 and 2005. The positive effect of this program was much stronger for subjective well-being than for labor market outcomes—the latter were insignificant.

63. Almeida and others 2012; de Koning, Kotzeva, and Tsvetkov 2007.

64. Almeida and others 2012 for the World Development Report 2013.

65. Kluve and others, forthcoming.

66. Card, Kluve, and Weber 2010; Hotz, Imbens, and Klerman 2006; Lechner, Miquel, and Wunsch 2005.

67. Grosh, del Ninno, and Ouerghi 2008.

68. ILO 2010b.

69. Boeri and van Ours 2008; Holmlund 1998; Margolis, Navarro, and Robalino 2011; Olinto and others 2007; Vodopivec, Worgotter, and Raju 2005.

70. van Ours and Vodopivec 2006.

71. Tatsiramos 2009.

72. Ribe, Robalino, and Walker 2011.

73. WHO and World Bank 2011.

74. OECD 2010.

75. OECD 2010.

76. Dorfman and Palacios 2012; Holzmann, Robalino, and Takayama 2009; ILO 2010b; Robalino and others 2012.

77. Ribe, Robalino, and Walker 2011.

78. Cho and others 2012; Rutkowski and others 2005.

79. Bird and Smart 2012; Levy 2008.

80. Betcherman, Daysal, and Pagés 2010; Kugler and Kugler 2003; Rutkowski and others 2005.

81. These observations are based on the FAFO survey conducted for the World Development Report 2013.

82. Bärnighausen and others (2007) provide corroborating evidence for China, finding that informal sector workers were willing to pay nearly 5 percent of their income for access to basic health insurance.

83. Some examples of these sorts of approaches are being implemented in South Asian countries. See World Bank 2011d.

84. Lieberman and Wagstaff 2009.

85. Babajanian 2012; Almeida and others 2012 for the World Development Report 2013.

86. Cahuc and Zylberberg 2006 for France; Davis, Haltiwanger, and Schuh 1996 for the United States. There are similar rates for Mexico although with much more churning, reported by Kaplan, Martínez González, and Robertson (2007).

87. See Bosch, Goni, and Maloney (2007) for Brazil, and Bosch and Maloney (2006) and Kaplan, Martínez González, and Robertson (2007) for Mexico.

88. Haltiwanger 2012; Haltiwanger, Jarmin, and Miranda 2011; Herkenhoff and Ohanian 2011.

89. Stiglitz 2009; Gatti and others 2011.

90. Pissarides 1992.

91. "Scarring" refers to an increasing probability of unemployment and lower earnings among those who have suffered unemployment previously. It implies that the negative effects of unemployment extend beyond the period of unemployment; see Arulampalam, Gregg, and Gregory (2001). The term is also used to describe the psychological impacts of unemployment and its duration even after unemployment spells conclude; see Clark, Georgellis, and Safney (2001); Knabe and Ratzel (2009).

92. Biewen and Steffes (2010), Bramoullé and Saint-Paul (2010), and Calvó-Armengol and Jackson (2004) are modern accounts of the role of being connected to social networks to find a job. Wahba and Zenou (2005) find evidence of network effects among high- and low-skill workers in Egypt; Munshi (2003) finds that immigrants with larger networks are more likely to be hired in higher-paying nonagricultural jobs.

93. Bell and Blanchflower 2011; Cramer 2010; Fougère, Kramarz, and Pouget 2009; World Bank 2006.

94. Burda and Hunt 2011; Cazes, Verick, and Al Hussami 2011; Farber 2011; Ohanian 2010.

95. Fang, Park, and Zhao 2008.

96. Hirschmann 1987.

References

The word *processed* describes informally reproduced works that may not be commonly available through libraries.

Acemoglu, Daron. 2001. "Good Jobs Versus Bad Jobs." *Journal of Labor Economics* 19 (1): 1–21.

Acevedo Alameda, Paloma, Brigida Garcia, and Sebastian Martinez. 2011. *Informe de Linea de Base de la Evaluación de Impacto del Banco Mundial del Programa Juventud y Empleo en República Dominicana.* Washington, DC: World Bank.

Aghion, Philippe, Yann Algan, and Pierre Cahuc. 2011. "Civil Society and the State: The Interplay between Cooperation and the Minimum Wage Regulation." *Journal of the European Economic Association* 9 (1): 3–42.

Aghion, Philippe, Yann Algan, Pierre Cahuc, and Andrei Shleifer. 2010. "Regulation and Distrust." *Quarterly Journal of Economics* 125 (3): 1015–49.

Ahsan, Ahmad, and Carmen Pagés. 2009. "Are All Labor Regulations Equal? Evidence from Indian Manufacturing." *Journal of Comparative Economics* 37 (1): 62–75.

Aidt, Toke, and Zafiris Tzannatos. 2002. *Unions and Collective Bargaining: Economic Effects in a Global Environment.* Washington, DC: World Bank.

Alatas, Vivi, and Lisa Ann Cameron. 2003. "The Impact of Minimum Wages on Employment in a Low Income Country: An Evaluation Using the Difference-in-Differences Approach." Policy Research Working Paper Series 2985, World Bank, Washington, DC.

Alesina, Alberto, Yann Algan, Pierre Cahuc, and Paola Giuliano. 2010. "Family Values and the Regulation of Labor." Working Paper Series 15747, National Bureau of Economic Research, Cambridge, MA.

Almeida, Rita, Juliana Arbelaez, Maddalena Honorati, Arvo Kuddo, Tanja Lohmann, Mirey Ovadiya, Lucian Pop, Maria Laura Sanchez-Puerta, and Michael Weber. 2012. "Improving Access to Jobs and Earnings Opportunities: The Role of Activation and Graduation Policies in Developing Countries." Social Protection and Labor Discussion Paper Series 1204, World Bank, Washington, DC.

Almeida, Rita, Jere R. Behrman, and David A. Robalino, eds. 2012. *The Right Skills for the Job? Rethinking Training Policies for Workers.* Washington, DC: World Bank.

Almeida, Rita, and Pedro Carneiro. 2009. "Enforcement of Labor Regulation and Firm Size." *Journal of Comparative Economics* 37 (1): 28–46.

Almeida, Rita, David Margolis, David Robalino, and Michael Weber. 2012. "Facilitating Labor Market Transitions." Background Paper for the WDR 2013.

Arango, Carlos, and Angelica Pachón. 2004. "Minimum Wages in Colombia: Holding the Middle with a Bite on the Poor." Borradores de Economía Serie 280, Banco de la República de Colombia, Bogotá.

Arulampalam, Wiji, Paul Gregg, and Mary Gregory. 2001. "Unemployment Scarring." *Economic Journal* 111 (475): 577–84.

Attanasio, Orazio, Adriana Kugler, and Costas Meghir. 2008. "Training Disadvantaged Youth in Latin America: Evidence from a Randomized Trial." Working Paper Series 13931, National Bureau of Economic Research, Cambridge, MA.

Autor, David H., William Kerr, and Adriana D. Kugler. 2007. "Do Employment Protections Reduce Productivity? Evidence from U.S. States." *Economic Journal* 117 (6): 189–217.

Babajanian, Babken. 2012. *Social Protection and Its Contribution to Social Cohesion and State-Building.* London: Overseas Development Institute.

Baccaro, Lucio, and Diego Rei. 2007. "Institutional Determinants of Unemployment in OECD Countries: A Time-Series Cross-Section Analysis (1960–1998)." *International Organization* 160: 527–69.

Banerjee, Abhijit V., Sebastian Galiani, Jim Levinsohn, Zoë McLaren, and Ingrid Woolard. 2007. "Why Has Unemployment Risen in the New South Africa?" *Economics of Transition* 16 (4): 715–40.

Bärnighausen, Till, Yuanli Liu, Xinping Zhang, and Rainer Sauerborn. 2007. "A Contingent Valuation Study of Willingness to Pay for Health Insurance among Informal Sector Workers in Urban China." *BMC Health Services Research* 7 (114): 2–16.

Bassanini, Andrea, and Romain Duval. 2006. "Employment Patterns in OECD Countries: Reassessing the Role of Policies and Institutions." Working Papers Series 486, Economic Department, Organisation for Economic Co-operation and Development, Paris.

Bassanini, Andrea, Luca Nunziata, and Danielle Venn. 2009. "Job Protection Legislation and Productivity Growth in OECD Countries." *Economic Policy* 58 (April): 349–402.

Bassanini, Andrea, and Danielle Venn. 2007. "Assessing the Impact of Labour Market Policies on Productivity: A Difference-in-Differences Approach." Social, Employment and Migration Working Papers Series 54, Organisation for Economic Co-operation and Development, Paris.

———. 2008. "The Impact of Labour Market Policies on Productivity in OECD Countries." *International Productivity Monitor, Centre for the Study of Living Standards* 17: 3–15.

Basu, Arnab. 2011. "Impact of Rural Employment Guarantee Schemes on Seasonal Labor Markets: Optimum Compensation and Workers' Welfare." Discussion Paper Series 5701, Institute for the Study of Labor, Bonn.

Basu, Arnab, Nancy Chau, and Ravi Kanbur. 2009. "A Theory of Employment Guarantees: Contestability, Credibility and Distributional Concerns." *Journal of Public Economics* 99 (3-4): 482–97.

Bell, David N. F., and David G. Blanchflower. 2010. "Youth Unemployment: Déjà Vu?" Discussion Paper Series 4705, Institute for the Study of Labor, Bonn.

———. 2011. "Youth Unemployment in Europe and the United States." Discussion Paper Series 5673, Institute for the Study of Labor, Bonn.

Bell, Linda A. 1997. "The Impact of Minimum Wages in Mexico and Colombia." *Journal of Labor Economics* 15 (3): S102–35.

Belot, Michèle, Jan Boone, and Jan van Ours. 2007. "Welfare-Improving Employment Protection." *Economica* 74 (295): 381–96.

Bentolila, Samuel, Pierre Cahuc, Juan Dolado, and Thomas Le Barbanchon. 2011. "Why Have Spanish and French Unemployment Rates Differed So Much during the Great Recession?" *VOX*, January 22.

Berg, Janine. 2011. "Laws or Luck? Understanding Rising Formality in Brazil in the 2000s." In *Regulating for Decent Work, New Directions in Labour Market Regulation*, ed. Sangheon Lee and Deirdre McCann, 123–50. Basingstoke, U.K.: Palgrave Macmillan; Geneva: International Labour Organization.

Betcherman, Gordon. 2012. "Labor Market Institutions: A Review of the Literature." Background paper for the World Development Report 2013.

Betcherman, Gordon, N. Meltem Daysal, and Carmen Pagés. 2010. "Do Employment Subsidies Work? Evidence from Regionally Targeted Subsidies in Turkey." *Labor Economics* 17 (4): 710–22.

Betcherman, Gordon, Karina Olivas, and Amit Dar. 2004. "Impacts of Active Labor Market Programs: New Evidence from Evaluations with Particular Attention to Developing and Transition Countries." Social Protection Discussion Paper Series 0402, World Bank, Washington, DC.

Bhorat, Haroon, Sumayya Goga, and Carlene van der Westerhuizen. 2011. "Institutional Wage Effects: Revisiting Union and Bargaining Council Wage Premia in South Africa." Working Paper Series 11/146, Development Policy Research Unit, School of Economics, University of Cape Town, Cape Town, South Africa.

Biewen, Martin, and Susanne Steffes. 2010. "Unemployment Persistence: Is There Evidence for Stigma Effects?" *Economic Letters* 106 (3): 188–90.

Bird, Richard M., and Michael Smart. 2012. "Financing Social Expenditures in Developing Countries: Payroll or Value Added Taxes?" International Center for Public Policy Working Paper Series 1206, Andrew Young School of Policy Studies, Georgia State University, Atlanta.

Blanchard, Olivier. 2005. "Designing Labor Market Institutions." In *Labor Markets and Institutions*, ed. Jorge Restrepo, and Andrea R. Tokman, 367–81. Santiago: Banco Central de Chile.

Blanchard, Olivier, and Augustin Landier. 2002. "The Perverse Effects of Partial Labour Market Reform: Fixed-Term Contracts in France." *Economic Journal* 112 (480): 214–44.

Blanchard, Olivier J., and Jean Tirole. 2008. "The Joint Design of Unemployment Insurance and Employment Protection: A First Pass." *Journal of the European Economic Association* 6 (1): 45–77.

Blattman, Christopher, Nathan Fiala, and Sebastian Martinez. 2011. *Employment Generation in Rural Africa, Mid-Term Results from an Experimental Evaluation of the Youth Opportunities Program in Northern Uganda*. New Haven, CT: Yale University, Innovations for Poverty Action.

Boeri, Tito, Pietro Garibaldi, and Marta Ribeiro. 2011. "The Lighthouse Effect and Beyond." *Review of Income and Wealth* 57: S54–78.

Boeri, Tito, Brooke Helppie, and Mario Macis. 2008. "Labor Regulations in Developing Countries: A Review of the Evidence and Directions for Future Research." Social Protection Discussion Paper Series 0833, World Bank, Washington, DC.

Boeri, Tito, and Jan C. van Ours. 2008. *The Economics of Imperfect Labor Markets*. Princeton, NJ: Princeton University Press.

Bold, Chris, David Porteous, and Sarah Rotman. 2012. *Social Cash Transfers and Financial Inclusion: Evidence from Four Countries*. Washington, DC: Consultative Group to Assist the Poor.

Bonin, Holger, and Ulf Rinne. 2006. "Beautiful Serbia." Discussion Paper Series 2533, Institute for the Study of Labor, Bonn.

Bosch, Mariano, Edwin Goni, and William F. Maloney. 2007. "The Determinants of Rising Informality in Brazil: Evidence from Gross Worker Flows." Discussion Paper Series 2970, Institute for the Study of Labor, Bonn.

Bosch, Mariano, and William Maloney. 2006. "Gross Worker Flows in the Presence of Informal Labor Markets: The Mexican Experience 1987–2002." Discussion Paper Series 2864, Institute for the Study of Labor, Bonn.

Bosch, Mariano and Marco Manacorda. 2010. "Minimum Wages and Earnings Inequality in Urban Mexico." Discussion Paper 7882, Centre for Economic Policy Research, London.

Botero, Juan C., Simeon Djankov, Rafael La Porta, Florencio Lopez-de-Silanes, and Andres Shleifer. 2004. "The Regulation of Labor." *Quarterly Journal of Economics* 119 (4): 1339–82.

Bramoullé, Yann, and Gilles Saint-Paul. 2010. "Social Networks and Labor Market Transitions." *Labour Economics* 17 (1): 188–95.

Burda, Michael C., and Jennifer Hunt. 2011. "What Explains the German Labor Market Miracle in the Great Recession?" Working Paper Series 17187, National Bureau of Economic Research, Cambridge, MA.

Butcher, Kristin F., and Cecilia Elena Rouse. 2001. *Wage Effects of Unions and Industrial Councils in South Africa.* Washington, DC: World Bank, Poverty and Human Resources.

Caballero, Ricardo J. 2004. "Effective Labor Regulation and Microeconomic Flexibility." Working Paper Series 10744, National Bureau of Economic Research, Cambridge, MA.

Cahuc, Pierre, and Stéphane Carcillo. 2011. "Is Short-Time Work a Good Method to Keep Unemployment Down?" Discussion Paper Series 5430, Institute for the Study of Labor, Bonn.

Cahuc, Pierre, and Francis Kramarz. 2004. *De la Précarité à la Mobilité: Vers une Sécurité Sociale Professionnelle.* Paris: Ministère de l'Economie, des Finances et de l'Industrie.

Cahuc, Pierre, and André Zylberberg. 2006. *The Natural Survival of Work: Job Creation and Job Destruction in a Growing Economy.* Cambridge, MA: MIT Press.

Calmfors, Lars. 1994. *Active Labour Market Policy and Unemployment: A Framework for the Analysis of Crucial Design Features.* Paris: Organisation for Economic Co-operation and Development.

Calvó-Armengol, Antoni, and Matthew O. Jackson. 2004. "The Effects of Social Networks on Employment and Inequality." *American Economic Review* 94 (3): 426–54.

Card, David, Jochen Kluve, and Andrea Weber. 2010. "Active Labour Market Policy Evaluations: A Meta-Analysis." *Economic Journal* 120 (11): 452–77.

Card, David, and Alan Krueger. 1995. *Myth and Measurement: The New Economics of the Minimum Wage.* Princeton, NJ: Princeton University Press.

Carling, Kenneth, and Katarina Richardson. 2004. "The Relative Efficiency of Labor Market Programs: Swedish Experience from the 1990s." *Labour Economics* 11 (3): 335–54.

Cazes, Sandrine, Sher Verick, and Fares Al Hussami. 2011. "Diverging Trends in Unemployment in the United States and Europe: Evidence from Okun's Law and the Global Financial Crisis." Employment Working Paper Series 106, Employment Sector, International Labour Organization, Geneva.

Chen, Martha, Chris Bonner, Mahendra Chetty, Lucia Fernandez, Karin Pape, Federico Parra, Arbind Singh, and Caroline Skinner. 2012. "Urban Informal Workers: Representative Voice and Economic Rights." Background paper for the WDR 2013.

Cho, Yoonyoung, David Margolis, David Newhouse, and David A. Robalino. 2012. "Labor Markets in Middle and Low Income Countries: Trends and Implications for Social Protection and Labor Policies." Social Protection Discussion Paper Series 67613, World Bank, Washington, DC.

Cingano, Federico, Marco Leonardi, Julian Messina, and Giovanni Pica. 2010. "The Effects of Employment Protection Legislation and Financial Market Imperfections on Investment: Evidence from a Firm-Level Panel of EU Countries." *Economic Policy* 25 (61): 117–63.

Clark, Andrew, Yannis Georgellis, and Peter Safney. 2001. "Scarring: The Psychological Impact of Past Unemployment." *Economica* 68 (May): 221–41.

Cockx, Bart, Bruno van der Linden, and Adel Karaa. 1998. "Active Labour Market Policies and Job Tenure." *Oxford Economic Papers* 50: 685–708.

Cramer, Christopher. 2010. *Unemployment and Participation in Violence.* Washington, DC: World Bank.

Davis, Steven J., R. Jason Faberman, and John Haltiwanger. 2012. "Labor Market Flows in the Cross-Section and Over Time." *Journal of Monetary Economics* 59: 1–18.

Davis, Steven J., John C. Haltiwanger, and Scott Schuh. 1996. *Job Creation and Destruction.* Cambridge, MA: MIT Press.

de Koning, Jaap, Mariana Kotzeva, and Stoyan Tsvetkov. 2007. "Mid-Term Evaluation of the Bulgarian Programme 'From Social Assistance to Employment.'" In *Employment and Training Policies in Central and Eastern Europe: A Transitional Labour Market Perspective*, ed. Jaap de Koning. 103–31. Amsterdam: Dutch University Press.

DeFreitas, Gregory, and Adriana Marshall. 1998. "Labour Surplus, Worker Rights and Productivity Growth: A Comparative Analysis of Asia and Latin America." *Labour* 12 (3): 515–39.

del Ninno, Carlo, Kalanidhi Subbarao, and Annamaria Milazzo. 2009. "How to Make Public Works Work: A Review of Experiences." Social Protection

Discussion Paper Series 905, World Bank, Washington, DC.

Devereux, Stephen, Catherine Mthinda, Fergus Power, Patrick Sakala, and Abigail Suka. 2007. *An Evaluation of Concern Worldwide's Dowa Emergency Cash Transfer Project (DECT) in Malawi, 2006/07*. Lilongwe: Concern Worldwide.

DFID (Department for International Development). 2011. *DFID Cash Transfers Evidence Paper*. London: DFID Policy Division.

DiNardo, John E., Nicole M. Fortin, and Thomas Lemieux. 1996. "Labor Market Institutions and the Distribution of Wages, 1973–1992: A Semiparametric Approach." *Econometrica* 64 (5): 1001–44.

Djankov, Simeon, and Rita Ramalho. 2009. "Employment Laws in Developing Countries." *Journal of Comparative Economics* 37 (1): 3–13.

Dolado, Juan J., Carlos García-Serrano, and Juan F. Jimeno. 2002. "Drawing Lessons from the Boom of Temporary Jobs in Spain." *Economic Journal* 112 (480): 270–95.

Dorfman, Mark, and Robert Palacios. 2012. *The World Bank in Pensions: A Background Paper for the Social Protection Strategy*. Washington, DC: World Bank.

Downes, Andrew S., Nlandu Mamingi, and Rose-Marie Belle Antoine. 2004. "Labor Market Regulation and Employment in the Caribbean." In *Law and Employment: Lessons from Latin America and the Caribbean*, ed. James J. Heckman and Carmen Pagés, 517–52. Chicago: University of Chicago Press.

Dutta, Puja, Rinku Murgai, Martin Ravallion, and Dominique van del Walle. 2012. "Does India's Employment Guarantee Scheme Guarantee Employment?" Policy Research Working Paper Series 6003, World Bank, Washington, DC.

Eichhorst, Werner, Veronica Escudero, Paul Marx, and Steven Tobin. 2010. *The Impact of the Crisis on Employment and the Role of Labour Market Institutions*. Geneva: International Labour Organization.

Eslava, Marcela, John C. Haltiwanger, Adriana Kugler, and Maurice Kugler. 2004. "The Effects of Structural Reforms on Productivity and Profitability Enhancing Reallocation: Evidence from Colombia." *Journal of Development Economics* 75 (2): 333–71.

Eurofound (European Foundation for the Improvement of Living and Working Conditions). 2009. *Eurofound European Industrial Relations Dictionary*. Dublin: Eurofound.

Eyraud, François, and Catherine Saget. 2008. "The Revival of Minimum Wage-Setting Institutions." In *In Defence of Labour Market Institutions: Cultivating Justice in the Developing World*, ed. Janine Berg and David Kucera, 100–18. New York: Palgrave Macmillan and International Labour Organization.

Fajnzylber, Pablo. 2001. "Minimum Wage Effects throughout the Wage Distribution: Evidence from Brazil's Formal and Informal Sectors." Working Paper Series 151, Centro de Desenvolvimento e Planejamento Regional, Belo Horizonte, Brazil.

FAFO. 2012. "Household Survey on Good Jobs." Fafo Institute for Applied International Studies, Oslo. Background work for the World Development Report 2013.

Fang, Cai, Albert Park, and Yaohui Zhao. 2008. "The Chinese Labor Market in the Reform Era." In *China's Great Economic Transformation*, ed. Loren Brandt and Thomas G. Rawski, 167–214. Cambridge, U.K.: Cambridge University Press.

Fang, Tony, and Ying Ge. 2011. "Unions and Firm Innovation in China: Synergy or Strife?" *China Economic Review* 23 (1): 170–80.

Farber, Henry S. 2011. "Job Loss in the Great Recession: Historical Perspective from the Displaced Workers Survey, 1984–2010." Discussion Paper Series 5696, Institute for the Study of Labor, Bonn.

Fares, Jean, and Olga Susana Puerto. 2009. "Towards Comprehensive Training." Social Protection Discussion Paper Series 0924, World Bank, Washington, DC.

Feliciano, Zadia. 1998. "Does the Minimum Wage Affect Employment in Mexico?" *Eastern Economic Journal* 24 (2): 165–80.

Fields, Gary, and Ravi Kanbur. 2007. "Minimum Wages and Poverty with Income-Sharing." *Journal of Economic Inequality* 5 (2): 135–47.

Foguel, Miguel Natan, Lauro Ramos, and Francisco Galrao Carneiro. 2001. "The Impact of the Minimum Wage on the Labor Market, Poverty and Fiscal Budget in Brazil." Discussion Paper Series 839, Institute of Applied Economic Research, Brasilia.

Forteza, Alvaro, and Martín Rama. 2006. "Labor Market 'Rigidity' and the Success of Economic Reforms across More Than 100 Countries." *Journal of Policy Reform* 9 (1): 75–105.

Fougère, Denis, Francis Kramarz, and Julien Pouget. 2009. "Youth Unemployment and Crime in France." *Journal of European Economic Association* 7 (5): 909–38.

Freeman, Richard. 2009. "Labor Regulations, Unions, and Social Protection in Developing Countries: Market Distortions or Efficient Institutions?" In *Handbook of Development Economics*, Vol. 5, ed. Dani Rodrik and Mark Rosenzweig, 4657–702. Amsterdam: Elsevier.

Galasso, Emanuela, Martin Ravallion, and Agustin Salvia. 2004. "Assisting the Transition from Workfare to Work: A Randomized Experiment." *Industrial and Labor Relations Review* 58 (1): 128–42.

Gatti, Domenico Delli, Mauro Gallegati, Bruce C. Greenwald, Alberto Russo, and Joseph E. Stiglitz. 2011. "Sectoral Imbalances and Long Run Crises."

Paper presented at the International Economic Association Meeting, Beijing, July 4.

Gelb, Alan, and Caroline Decker. 2011. "Cash at Your Fingertips: Biometric Technology for Transfers in Developing and Resource-Rich Countries." Working Paper Series 253, Center for Global Development, Washington, DC.

Gindling, T. H., and Katherine Terrell. 1995. "The Nature of Minimum Wages and Their Effectiveness as a Wage Floor in Costa Rica, 1976–91." *World Development* 23 (8): 1439–58.

———. 2007. "The Effects of Multiple Minimum Wages throughout the Labor Market: The Case of Costa Rica." *Labour Economics* 14 (3): 485–511.

Godfrey, Shane, Johann Maree, Darcy Du Toit, and Jan Theron. 2010. *Collective Bargaining in South Africa: Past, Present and Future.* Cape Town: Juta.

Grosh, Margaret, Carlo del Ninno, and Azedine Ouerghi. 2008. *For Protection and Promotion: The Design and Implementation of Effective Safety Nets.* Washington, DC: World Bank.

Gunther, Isabel, and Andrey Launov. 2012. "Informal Employment in Developing Countries: Opportunity or Last Resort?" *Journal of Development Economics* 97 (1): 88–98.

Gupta, Poonam, Rana Hasan, and Utsav Kumar. 2008. "What Constrains Indian Manufacturing?" Working Paper Series 119, Economics and Research Department, Asian Development Bank, New Delhi.

Haltiwanger, John. 2012. "Job Creation and Firm Dynamics in the U.S." In *Innovation Policy and the Economy,* Vol. 12, ed. Josh Lerner and Scott Stern, 17–38. Chicago: University of Chicago Press.

Haltiwanger, John, Ron S. Jarmin, and Javier Miranda. 2011. *Business Dynamics Statistics Briefing: Historically Large Decline in Job Creation from Startup and Existing Firms in the 2008–2009 Recession.* Kansas City: Euwing Marion Kauffman Foundation.

Haltiwanger, John, Stefano Scarpetta, and Helena Schweiger. 2008. "Assessing Job Flows across Countries: The Role of Industry, Firm Size and Regulations." Working Paper Series 13920, National Bureau of Economic Research, Cambridge, MA.

Hashemi, Syed, and Richard Rosenberg. 2006. *Graduating the Poorest into Microfinance: Linking Safety Nets and Financial Services.* Washington, DC: Consultative Group to Assist the Poor.

Hayter, Susan, ed. 2011. *The Role of Collective Bargaining in the Global Economy.* Geneva: Edward Elgar.

Heckman, James J., and Carmen Pagés. 2000. "The Cost of Job Security Regulation: Evidence from the Latin American Labor Markets." *Journal of the Latin American and Caribbean Economic Association* 1 (1): 109–54.

Heckman, James J., and Carmen Pagés. 2004. *Law and Employment: Lessons from Latin America and the Caribbean.* Cambridge, MA: NBER Books.

Heckman, James J., Jora Stixrud, and Sergio Urzua. 2006. "The Effects of Cognitive and Noncognitive Abilities on Labor Market Outcomes and Social Behavior." *Journal of Labor Economics* 24 (3): 411–82.

Herkenhoff, Kyle F., and Lee E. Ohanian. 2011. "Labor Market Dysfunction during the Great Recession." Working Paper Series 17313, National Bureau of Economic Research, Cambridge, MA.

Hijzen, Alexander, and Danielle Venn. 2011. "The Role of Short-Time Work Schemes during the 2008–09 Recession." Social, Employment and Migration Working Papers Series 115, Organisation for Economic Co-operation and Development, Paris.

Hirschmann, Albert O. 1987. "The Political Economy of Latin American Development: Seven Exercises in Retrospection." *Latin American Research Review* 22 (3): 7–36.

Holmlund, Bertil. 1998. "Unemployment Insurance in Theory and Practice." *Scandinavian Journal of Economics* 100 (1): 113–41.

Holzer, Harry, and Robert Lerman. 2009. *The Future of Middle-Skill Jobs.* Washington, DC: Center on Children and Families, Brookings Institutution.

Holzmann, Robert, David Robalino, and Noriyuki Takayama. 2009. *Closing the Coverage Gap: The Role of Social Pensions and Other Retirement Income Transfers.* Washington, DC: World Bank.

Holzmann, Robert, and Milan Vodopivec, eds. 2012. *Reforming Severance Pay: An International Perspective.* Washington, DC: World Bank.

Hotz, V. Joseph, Guido Imbens, and Jacob Alex Klerman. 2006. "Evaluating the Differential Effects of Alternative Welfare-to-Work Training Components: A Re-Analysis of the California GAIN Program." *Journal of Labor Economics* 24: 521–66.

Ibarrarán, Pablo, and David Rosas Shady. 2008. *Evaluating the Impact of Job Training Programs in Latin America: Evidence from IDB Funded Operations.* Washington, DC: Inter-American Development Bank.

ILO (International Labour Organization). 2010a. *Accelerating Action against Child Labour.* Geneva: ILO.

———. 2010b. *World Social Security Report 2010/11: Providing Coverage in Times of Crisis and Beyond.* Geneva: ILO.

ILO and International Institute for Labour Studies. 2012. *Better Jobs for a Better Economy.* Geneva: ILO.

Kaplan, David Scott. 2009. "Job Creation and Labor Reform in Latin America." *Journal of Comparative Economics* 37 (1): 91–105.

Kaplan, David Scott, Gabriel Martínez González, and Raymond Robertson. 2007. "Mexican Employment Dynamics: Evidence from Matched Firm-Worker Data." Policy Research Working Paper Series 4433, World Bank, Washington, DC.

Katz, Lawrence. 1996. "Wage Subsidies for the Disadvantaged." Working Paper Series 5679, National Bureau of Economic Research, Cambridge, MA.

Kertesi, Gabor, and Janos Kollo. 2003. "The Employment Effects of Nearly Doubling the Minimum Wage: The Case of Hungary." Working Papers 6, Hungarian Academy of Sciences, Budapest.

Kingdon, Geeta Gandhi, and John Knight. 2004. "Unemployment in South Africa: The Nature of the Beast." *World Development* 32 (3): 391–408.

Kluve, Jochen. 2010. "The Effectiveness of European Active Labor Market Programs." *Labour Economics* 17 (6): 904–18.

Kluve, Jochen, Hartmut Lehmann, and Christoph Schmidt. 1999. "Active Labor Market Policies in Poland: Human Capital Enhancement, Stigmatization or Benefit Churning." *Journal of Comparative Economics* 1 (27): 61–89.

———. 2008. "Disentangling Treatment Effects of Active Labor Market Policies: The Role of Labor Force Status Sequences." *Labour Economics* 15 (6): 1270–95.

Kluve, Jochen, Friederike Rother, Susana Puerto-Gonzalez, Michael Weber, and David Robalino. Forthcoming. *Youth Employment Inventory (YEI) Synthesis Report: New Evidence on Employment Interventions for Young People.* Washington, DC: World Bank.

Knabe, Andreas, and Steffen Ratzel. 2009. "Scarring or Scaring? The Psychological Impact of Past Unemployment and Future Unemployment Risk." *Economica* 78: 283–93.

Koeniger, Winfried. 2005. "Dismissal Costs and Innovation." *Economics Letters* 88 (1): 79–84.

Kucera, David, and Leanne Roncolato. 2008. "Informal Employment: Two Contested Policy Issues." *International Labour Review* 147 (4): 321–48.

Kuddo, Arvo. 2009. "Employment Services and Active Labor Market Programs in Eastern European and Central Asian Countries." Social Protection Discussion Paper Series 0918, World Bank, Washington, DC.

Kugler, Adriana. 2004. "The Effect of Job Security Regulations on Labor Market Flexibility: Evidence from the Colombian Labor Market Reform." In *Law and Employment: Lessons from Latin America and the Caribbean,* ed. James J. Heckman and Carmen Pagés, 2004, 183–228. Chicago: University of Chicago Press.

Kugler, Adriana, and Maurice Kugler. 2003. "The Labor Market Effects of Payroll Taxes in a Middle-Income Country." Discussion Papers Series 4046, Centre for Economic Policy Research, London.

Lechner, Michael, Ruth Miquel, and Conny Wunsch. 2005. "The Curse and Blessing of Training the Unemployed in a Changing Economy: The Case of East Germany after Unification." Discussion Paper Series 5171, Center for Economic and Policy Research, Washington, DC.

Lee, Hee Chang, and Mingwei Liu. 2011a. "Collective Bargaining in Transition: Measuring the Effects of Collective Voice in China." In *The Role of Collective Bargaining in the Global Economy: Negotiating for Social Justice,* ed. Susan Hayter, 205–26. Cheltenham, U.K.: Edward Elgar.

———. 2011b. "Measuring the Effects of the Collective Voice Mechanism and the Labour Contract Law: A Survey of Labour Relations and Human Resource Management Practices in China." International Labour Organization, Geneva.

Lemos, Sara. 2004. "Minimum Wage Policy and Employment Effects: Evidence from Brazil." *Economía* 5 (1): 219–66.

———. 2007. "A Survey of the Effects of the Minimum Wage in Latin America." Discussion Papers in Economics 07/04, University of Leicester, U.K.

Levy, Santiago. 2008. *Good Intentions, Bad Outcomes, Social Policy, Informality, and Economic Growth in Mexico.* Washington, DC: Brookings Institution Press.

Lieberman, Samuel S., and Adam Wagstaff. 2009. *Health Financing and Delivery in Vietnam: Looking Forward.* Health, Nutrition, and Population Series. Washington, DC: World Bank.

Liu, Mingwei. 2010. "Union Organizing in China: Still a Monolithic Labor Movement?" *Industrial & Labor Relations Review* 64 (1): 30–52.

Magruder, Jeremy R. 2010. "Intergenerational Networks, Unemployment, and Persistent Inequality in South Africa." *Applied Economics* 2 (1): 62–85.

Maloney, William F., and Jairo Núñez Méndez. 2003. "Measuring the Impact of Minimum Wages: Evidence from Latin America." Working Paper Series 9800, National Bureau of Economic Research, Cambridge, MA.

Margolis, David, Lucas Navarro, and David Robalino. 2011. "Unemployment Insurance, Job Search and Informal Employment." Discussion Paper Series 6660, Institute for the Study of Labor, Bonn.

Martin, John P., and David Grubb. 2001. "What Works and for Whom? A Review of OECD Countries' Experiences with Active Labour Market Policies." *Swedish Economic Policy Review* 8 (2): 9–60.

Messina, Julián, and Giovanna Vallanti. 2007. "Job Flow Dynamics and Firing Restrictions Evidence from Europe." *Economic Journal* 117 (521): F279–301.

Micco, Alejandro, and Carmen Pagés. 2006. "The Economic Effects of Employment Protection: Evidence from International Industry-Level Data." Discussion Papers Series 2433, Institute for the Study of Labor, Bonn.

Ministry of Finance. 2011. "How to Promote Public Deliberation in Budgeting." (Chinese). People's Republic of China.

Ministry of Rural Development. 2008. *The National Rural Employment Guarantee Act 2005 (NREGA):*

Operational Guidelines 2008. New Delhi: Department of Rural Development, Government of India.

————. 2012. *Report to the People*. New Delhi: Department of Rural Development, Government of India.

Mondino, Guillermo, and Silvia Montoya. 2004. "The Effect of Labor Market Regulations on Employment Decisions by Firms: Empirical Evidence for Argentina." In *Law and Employment: Lessons from Latin American and the Caribbean*, ed. James J. Heckman and Carmen Pagés, 351–400. Chicago: University of Chicago Press.

Monitor Inclusive Markets. 2011. *Job Creation through Building the Field of Impact Sourcing*. Mumbai: Monitor Inclusive Markets.

Montenegro, Claudio E., and Carmen Pagés. 2004. "Who Benefits from Labor Market Regulations? Chile, 1960–1998." In *Law and Employment: Lessons from Latin American and the Caribbean*, ed. James J. Heckman and Carmen Pagés, 401–34. Chicago: University of Chicago Press.

Munshi, Kaivan. 2003. "Networks in the Modern Economy: Mexican Migrants in the United States Labor Market." *Quarterly Journal of Economics* 118 (2): 549–99.

Neri, Marcelo, Gustavo Gonzaga, and José Márcio Camargo. 2001. "Salário Mínimo, Efeito Farol e Pobreza." *Revista de Economia Política* 21 (2): 79–90.

Neumark, David, Wendy V. Cunningham, and Lucas Siga. 2006. "The Effects of the Minimum Wage in Brazil on the Distribution of Family Incomes: 1996–2001." *Journal of Development Economics* 80 (1): 136–59.

Neumark, David, and Olena Nizalova. 2007. "Minimum Wage Effects in the Longer Run." *Journal of Human Resources* 42 (22): 435–52.

Nickell, Stephen, and Richard Layard. 1999. "Labor Market Institutions and Economic Performance." In *Handbook of Labor Economics*, Vol. 3, ed. Orley Ashenfelter and David Card, 3029–84. Amsterdam: Elsevier.

OECD (Organisation for Economic Co-operation and Development). 2004. *OECD Employment Outlook: 2004*. Paris: OECD.

————. 2006. *OECD Employment Outlook: 2006*. Paris: OECD.

————. 2010. *Sickness, Disability, and Work: Breaking the Barriers. A Synthesis of Findings across OECD Countries*. Paris: OECD.

————. 2011. *Divided We Stand*. Paris: OECD.

Ohanian, Lee E. 2010. "The Economic Crisis from a Neoclassical Perspective." *Journal of Economic Perspectives* 24 (4): 45–66.

Olinto, Pedro, Kathy Lindert, Rita Almeida, Jason Hobbs, and Rodrigo G. Verdú. 2007. *The Impacts of Public Transfers on Labor Supply in Brazil and Abroad: A Review of the Evidence*. Washington, DC: World Bank.

Paes de Barros, Ricardo, and Carlos Henrique Corseuil. 2004. "The Impact of Regulations on Brazilian Labor Market Performance." In *Law and Employment: Lessons from Latin America and the Caribbean*, ed. James J. Heckman and Carmen Pagés, 273–350. Chicago: University of Chicago Press.

Pagés, Carmen, and Claudio E. Montenegro. 2007. "Job Security and the Age Composition of Employment: Evicence from Chile." *Estudios de Economía* 34 (2): 109–39.

Palacios, Robert, Jishnu Das, and Changqing Sun. 2011. *India's Health Insurance Scheme for the Poor: Evidence from the Early Experience of the Rashtriya Swasthya Bima Yojana*. New Delhi: Centre for Policy Research.

Pallares-Miralles, Montserrat, Carolina Romero, and Edward Whitehouse. 2012. "International Patterns of Pension Provision II: A Worldwide Overview of Facts and Figures." Social Protection Discussion Paper Series 1211, World Bank, Washington, DC.

Petrin, Amil, and Jagadeesh Sivadasan. 2006. "Job Security Does Affect Economic Efficiency: Theory, A New Statistic, and Evidence from Chile." Working Paper Series 12757, National Bureau of Economic Research, Cambridge, MA.

Pissarides, Christopher A. 1992. "Loss of Skill during Unemployment and the Persistence of Employment Shocks." *Quarterly Journal of Economics* 107 (4): 1371–91.

Premand, Patrick, Stefanie Brodmann, Rita Almeida, and Barouni Mahdi. 2011. *Entrepreneurship Training and Self-Employment among University Graduates: Evidence from a Randomized Evaluation in Tunisia*. Washington, DC: World Bank.

Rama, Martín. 2001. "The Consequences of Doubling the Minimum Wage: The Case of Indonesia." *Industrial and Labor Relations Review* 54 (4): 864–81.

Ravi, Shamik, and Monika Engler. 2009. "Workfare in Low Income Countries: An Effective Way to Fight Poverty? The Case of India's NREGS." Working Paper, Indian School of Business, Hyderabad.

Ribe, Helena, David A. Robalino, and Ian Walker. 2011. *Achieving Effective Social Protection for All in Latin America and the Caribbean: From Right to Reality*. Washington, DC: World Bank.

Robalino, David, and Arup Banerji. 2009. "Addressing the Employment Effects of the Financial Crisis." Employment Policy Primer Note 14, World Bank, Washington, DC.

Robalino, David, David Newhouse, and Friederike Rother. Forthcoming. "Labor and Social Protection Policies during the Crisis and Recovery." In *Labor Markets in Developing Countries during the Great Recession: Impacts and Policy Responses*, ed. Arup Banerji, David Newhouse, David Robalino, and Pierella Paci. Washington, DC: World Bank.

Robalino, David, Aleksandra Posarac, Friederike Rother, Michael Weber, Arvo Kuddo, and Kwabena Otoo. 2012. "Towards Smarter Worker Protection Systems: Improving Labor Regulations and Social Insurance Systems While Creating (Good) Jobs." Social Protection Discussion Paper Series 1212, World Bank, Washington, DC.

Robalino, David A., and Maria Laura Sanchez-Puerta. 2008. *Managing Labor Market Risks and Creating Better Jobs: Alternative Designs for Income Protection and Active Labor Market Policies.* Washington, DC: World Bank.

Rodriguez-Planas, Nuria. 2010. "Channels Through Which Public Employment Services and Small Business Assistance Programs Work." *Oxford Bulletin of Economics and Statistics* 72 (4): 458–85.

Rodriguez-Planas, Nuria, and Jacob Benus. 2010. "Evaluating Active Labor Market Programs in Romania." *Empirical Economics* 38 (1): 65–84.

Rutkowski, Jan, Stefano Scarpetta, Arup Banerji, Philip O'Keefe, Gaelle Pierre, and Milan Vodopivec. 2005. *Enhancing Job Opportunities: Eastern Europe and the Soviet Union.* Washington, DC: World Bank.

Saavedra, Jaime, and Maximo Torero. 2004. "Labor Market Reforms and Their Impact over Formal Labor Demand and Job Market Turnover: The Case of Peru." In *Law and Employment: Lessons from Latin America and the Caribbean,* ed. James J. Heckman and Carmen Pagés, 131–82. Chicago: University of Chicago Press.

Schultz, T. Paul, and Germano Mwabu. 1998. "Labor Unions and the Distribution of Wages and Employment in South Africa." *Industrial and Labor Relations Review* 51 (4): 680–703.

Selim, Nadia. 2012. "Innovation for Job Creation." Background paper for the World Development Report 2013.

Sianesi, Barbara. 2008. "Differential Effects of Active Labour Market Programs for the Unemployed." *Labour Economics* 15 (3): 370–99.

SMERU Research Institute. 2001. *Wage and Employment Effects of Minimum Wage Policy in the Indonesian Urban Labor Market.* Jakarta: SMERU Research Institute.

Souza, Paulo R., and Paulo E. Baltar. 1980. "Salario Minimo e Taxa de Salarios no Brasil." *Pesquisa e Planejamento Economico* 10: 1045–58.

Stiglitz, Joseph E. 2009. "The Current Economic Crisis and Lessons for Economic Theory." *Eastern Economic Journal* 35: 281–96.

Strobl, Eric, and Frank Walsh. 2003. "Minimum Wages and Compliance: The Case of Trinidad and Tobago." *Economic Development and Cultural Change* 51 (2): 427–50.

Tatsiramos, Konstantinos. 2009. "Geographic Labour Mobility and Unemployment Insurance in Europe." *Journal of Population Economics* 22 (2): 267–83.

van Ours, Jan C., and Milan Vodopivec. 2006. "Shortening the Potential Duration of Unemployment Benefits Does Not Affect the Quality of Post-Unemployment Jobs: Evidence from a Natural Experiment." Discussion Paper Series 5741, Centre for Economic Policy Research, London.

Visser, Jelle. 2011. "ICTWSS: Database on Institutional Characteristics of Trade Unions, Wage Setting, State Intervention and Social Pacts in 34 Countries between 1960 and 2007." University of Amsterdam, Amsterdam. Processed.

Vodopivec, Milan, Andreas Worgotter, and Dhushyanth Raju. 2005. "Unemployment Benefit Systems in Central and Eastern Europe: A Review of the 1990s." *Comparative Economic Studies* 47 (4): 615–51.

Wahba, Jacqueline, and Yves Zenou. 2005. "Density, Social Networks and Job Search Methods: Theory and Application to Egypt." *Journal of Development Economics* 78: 443–73.

Wei, Weiwei, Jianqiang Ping, Min Zhao, Shasha Liao, and Xeurong Wang. 2009. "Sectoral Collective Bargaining: Sectoral Collective Bargaining of the Wool-Sweater Manufacturing Industry at Xinhe District of Wenling." China Institute of Industrial Relations. Processed (in Chinese).

WHO (World Health Organization) and World Bank. 2011. *World Report on Disability.* Washington, DC: WHO and World Bank.

workercn.cn. 2011. "Zhejiang: The Implications of Harmonizing the Management-Union Relationship in a Labor Abundant Province." April 6 (in Chinese).

World Bank. 2006. *World Development Report 2007: Development and the Next Generation.* Washington, DC: World Bank.

———. 2008. *Nota Conceptual de la Evaluación de Impacto del Banco Mundial del Programa Juventud y Empleo en República Dominicana.* Washington, DC: World Bank.

———. 2011a. *Doing Business 2012: Doing Business in a More Transparent World.* Washington, DC: World Bank.

———. 2011b. *More and Better Jobs in South Asia.* Washington, DC: World Bank.

———. 2011c. *Program Document for Morocco First Skills and Employment Development Policy Loan.* Washington, DC: World Bank.

———. 2011d. *Social Protection for a Changing India.* Washington, DC: World Bank.

———. Forthcoming. *Doing Business 2013: Past, Present, and Future of Business Regulation.* Washington, DC: World Bank.

CHAPTER 9

Beyond labor policies

Fundamentals need to be in place, and constraints to the creation of jobs with high development payoffs need to be removed or offset. Policy coordination across borders can help.

A prerequisite for improved living standards is a policy environment conducive to private-sector-led job creation. Macroeconomic stability, an enabling business environment, human capital, and the rule of law are all necessary ingredients. Adequate macroeconomic policies mitigate aggregate fluctuations and keep key relative prices aligned. The business environment provides the basic public goods needed for the private sector to operate: infrastructure, access to finance, and sound regulation. Human capital is formed through good nutrition, health, and education that builds human skills. The rule of law ensures the enforcement of contracts; it also includes the progressive realization of rights to avoid a situation where growth coexists with unacceptable forms of work. These are the fundamentals on which policies for jobs rest (figure 9.1).

Fundamentals alone may not be enough to facilitate job creation and address the jobs challenges faced by many developing countries. Labor policies need to be set within a sensible range—a *plateau* that avoids two cliffs: one is the misguided intervention that clogs the creation of jobs in cities and in global value chains; the other, the lack of voice and social protection especially for the most vulnerable.

Markets might work without much friction but that may not be sufficient to make smallholder farming more productive in agrarian economies, or to generate enough employment opportunities for young men in conflict-affected countries.

An active role of government, however, needs to be carefully considered. Jobs are mainly created by the private sector with government intervention justified when individual incentives are misaligned with social goals—when, for example, employment is not rewarding for women, when young people are "queuing" to be civil servants, when cities are too congested to productively absorb more rural migrants, or when logistics costs are too high for domestic firms to engage in international trade. In these cases, government policy should aim to remove the constraints that prevent individuals, farms, and firms from making the best choices for society. If constraints cannot be precisely identified, or reforms are not politically feasible, policies can aim at offsetting the constraints rather than relieving them directly. In most cases, the policies to create good jobs for development lie outside of the labor market.

Domestic policies for jobs are part of the solution, but there is also scope for international coordination. Rights are a global public good—their violation in one country harms the world. But policies for job creation in one country can affect employment and earnings in another, positively or negatively, while migration policies can generate opportunities abroad or shut them down. Labor standards, rules for international trade and foreign direct investment (FDI), and migration agreements are among the instruments available to manage these international spillovers. International organizations have a role to play in coordinating the important global project of producing and using high-quality data on jobs, on which sound policy making must rest.

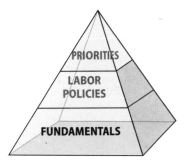

Establishing the fundamentals

A vast majority of jobs are created by the private sector—in formal sector firms as well as in microenterprises and farms. The relevant conditions for private sector investment and job creation are macroeconomic stability, an enabling business environment, human capital, and the rule of law.

Macroeconomic stability

In its assessment of the policy ingredients of growth strategies across 13 successful developing countries, the Commission on Employment and Growth noted: "No economy can flourish in the midst of macroeconomic instability. Wild fluctuations in the price level, the exchange rate, the interest rate, or the tax burden serve as a major deterrent to private investment, the proximate driver of growth."[1] Macroeconomic instability also affects employment and earnings in the short run. According to a recent estimate, a 1 percent decline in gross domestic product (GDP) is associated with an increase in the unemployment rate of 0.19 percentage point in Japan, 0.45 in the United States, and 0.85 in Spain.[2]

In developing countries, where income support mechanisms are more limited, the short-term impact of macroeconomic instability is often not so much on open unemployment as it is

on the composition of employment. Economic downturns lead to transitions to informal employment or to household-based activities, and not necessarily to joblessness. Hence, research focuses on how macroeconomic fluctuations affect the share of informal employment, rather than the unemployment rate.[3] Country case studies of the impact of the global crisis have confirmed the resilience of employment in developing countries. But macroeconomic stability is not less relevant there: while aggregate fluctuations do not greatly affect the number of workers employed, they do affect the earnings of those at work as well as their access to basic social protection instruments.[4]

Macroeconomic instability is often the outcome of unsustainable budget deficits and lax monetary policy. In the 1980s, Brazil plunged into a debt and high-inflation crisis that slashed its economic growth and halved the share of exports in its GDP. Triggered by high international interest rates in the late 1970s, the crisis then was compounded by the difficulty of keeping spending by subnational governments in check. Tight budgets and rigid monetary policy rules may not be a magic wand, however. Budget deficits are more or less worrisome depending on how quickly an economy is growing, whereas

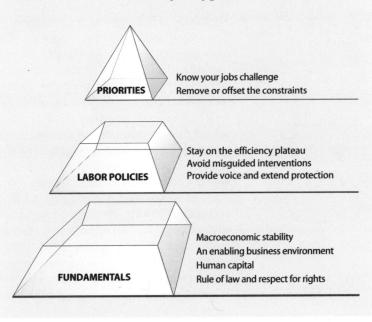

FIGURE 9.1 *Three distinct layers of policies are needed*

PRIORITIES
Know your jobs challenge
Remove or offset the constraints

LABOR POLICIES
Stay on the efficiency plateau
Avoid misguided interventions
Provide voice and extend protection

FUNDAMENTALS
Macroeconomic stability
An enabling business environment
Human capital
Rule of law and respect for rights

Source: World Development Report 2013 team.

the independence of central banks needs to be weighed against the overall coherence of a development strategy. An assessment of the soundness of macroeconomic management requires taking account of the impact of fiscal and monetary policies on economic growth.[5]

Not all macroeconomic instability is self-inflicted, however. Turbulence may result from shocks over which countries have little control, from natural disasters to crises originating abroad. Precautionary policies can be adopted to cushion those shocks if and when they occur. But most often there is a need to respond with short-term stimulus or adjustment packages. The effectiveness of these responses is a matter of controversy. A recent study based on the experience of 29 aid-dependent countries estimates that GDP increases by close to 0.5 percentage points for every percentage point of GDP in additional government spending. This so-called multiplier effect is substantially lower than in the United States, where a range between 0.8 and 1.5 is considered plausible.[6]

Wild fluctuations are only one way in which the macroeconomic context can adversely affect employment and earnings. The misalignment of key relative prices is another. Surges in a country's foreign exchange earnings often lead to an overvaluation of its currency, making imports more affordable and exports less competitive. Resource-rich countries in the developing world face similar currency appreciation pressures.[7] The commodity booms of the last few years have only strengthened these pressures. Currency overvaluation can also happen in countries where large volumes of foreign assistance are needed to jump-start development, cope with natural disasters, or facilitate recovery after a conflict. In Afghanistan, for instance, civilian aid from multilateral and bilateral donors was estimated at around 40 percent of GDP in 2010/11.[8] Currency overvaluation is a concern for many other countries where foreign aid does not reach the levels in Afghanistan but still funds a significant fraction of the budget. An analysis of 83 developing countries between 1970 and 2004 confirms that aid fosters growth (albeit with decreasing returns) but induces overvaluation and has a negative impact on export diversification.[9]

Avoiding exchange rate misalignment is necessary to sustain a vibrant export sector and hence create jobs that are connected to international markets and global value chains.[10] A case has even been made in favor of currency undervaluation, on the grounds that the export sectors of developing countries suffer disproportionately from institutional failures and market imperfections.[11] However, not all countries in the world can simultaneously have an undervalued currency. And while the argument that jobs integrated with world markets have positive growth spillovers is sensible, these jobs are not necessarily the ones with the highest development payoffs. Different countries have different jobs agendas, from creating employment opportunities for women to supporting the development of jobs in cities. The exchange rate is only one instrument and would seldom be able to deliver on such diverse agendas.

An enabling business environment

Across firms and countries at varying levels of development, the most important constraints on formal private sector businesses are remarkably consistent: access to finance, infrastructure, and aspects of regulation including taxation and unfair competition (figure 9.2). Skills shortages are also key, but mainly in the case of large firms and especially in richer countries.

Access to finance provides firms with the ability to expand, to invest in new technologies, or to smooth cash flow over time.[12] Financial markets also play an important role in the allocation of resources toward more productive uses.[13] Transparency within the financial sector avoids resources being channeled to those with political connections or economic power, and it also supports financial inclusion. Expanded credit registries keeping track of positive as well as negative episodes in debtors' histories help people demonstrate that they are creditworthy. But regulatory oversight is needed to ensure transparency and competition in the allocation of funds. The financial crisis of 2008 has reopened heated debates about the appropriate level of regulation of the financial sector and the need to balance prudence and stability with innovation and inclusion.

Access to affordable infrastructure of reasonable quality is, often, another top constraint to firm growth and job creation. Electricity enables the use of more sophisticated technology. It also frees up time from domestic chores; in

FIGURE 9.2 *Finance and electricity are among the top constraints faced by formal private enterprises*

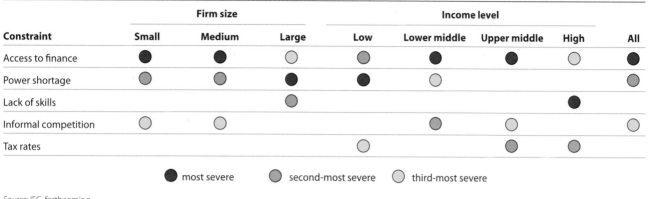

| | Firm size | | | Income level | | | | |
Constraint	Small	Medium	Large	Low	Lower middle	Upper middle	High	All
Access to finance	●	●	○	◐	●	●	○	●
Power shortage	◐	◐	●	●	○			◐
Lack of skills				◐			●	
Informal competition	○	○			◐	○		○
Tax rates				○		◐	○	

● most severe   ◐ second-most severe   ○ third-most severe

Source: IFC, forthcoming.
Note: The analysis is based on World Bank enterprise surveys covering 46,556 enterprises in 106 countries. Small firms have fewer than 20 employees, medium firms have 21–99, and large firms 100 and more.

rural areas, it can significantly increase women's employment.[14] Telecommunications allows for better information flows among suppliers, producers, and customers, and the Internet and mobile technology facilitate the spread of new ideas. Roads provide greater access to markets, as do ports and airports.[15]

In many low-income countries, poor-quality infrastructure is an especially severe challenge. Part of the problem stems from how infrastructure services are regulated, however, and not only from insufficient resources to build additional facilities and roads. By one estimate, improved infrastructure was responsible for more than half of Sub-Saharan Africa's recent growth.[16] But efficiency improvements stemming from better management of spending and maintenance, pricing policies, and regulations would be needed to close a significant portion of the remaining gap in infrastructure services. In many countries and infrastructure sub-sectors, monopolies—based on political connections— have resulted in lower quantities of services being provided, at higher prices and of lower quality than in areas where competition has been allowed to thrive.[17]

Regulation is another area that influences the opportunities for businesses to grow. Some regulations determine the rules of the game, encouraging—or discouraging—certain activities. Others affect firms at various stages of their life cycle, from getting started, to enforcing contracts, to closing down.[18] Regulations impact on the cost of doing business, both in monetary terms and in time needed to comply. Steps taken to meet requirements or to pay fees are a burden to businesses, as are delays in receiving permits or licenses. The time it takes to comply with regulations or to receive permits varies greatly across firms in the same location, suggesting discretionary power and corruption.[19] Beyond these broader cost measures, regulations affect the types of opportunities that are available and how widely they are available. Regulations can relieve or exacerbate uncertainty and corruption, but they can also have a deeper influence on the degree of competition and thus the structure of industries in the economy.

Because business regulations affect the degree of competition, they shape the pressures to innovate and increase productivity. Competition contributes to the reallocation of resources from inefficient activities to more productive ones. Regulations that serve to protect an industry or deter new entrants can be particularly costly in terms of forgone output and employment growth.[20] Across countries, regulations on business entry are inversely correlated with productivity and firm creation, with stronger effects in sectors that tend to have higher turnover rates.[21] Easing entry requirements helped increase business registration and employment and drove down prices for consumers in Mexico. The effect was achieved largely through creation of new firms rather than formalization of existing informal firms.[22] Combining relaxed entry requirements with other regulatory reforms, such as investment promotion and trade logistics, tends to be more effective than simply easing entry.[23]

Human capital

Good nutrition, health, and education outcomes are development goals in themselves, because they directly improve people's lives. But they also equip people for productive employment and open job opportunities—and through this employment channel, human capital drives economic and social advances. According to the Commission on Growth and Development, "every country that sustained high growth for long periods put substantial efforts into schooling its citizens and deepening its human capital."[24]

Connections between human capital and jobs are manifold. There is robust evidence from around the world that each additional year of schooling raises labor earnings substantially, and that this earnings premium reflects the higher productivity of more educated workers.[25] Together, nutrition, health, and education form skills and abilities that have been clearly linked to productivity growth and poverty reduction in the medium to longer run.[26] Better health also brings, directly, higher labor productivity. For example, where malaria is endemic, workers can expect to suffer an average of two bouts of fever each year, losing 5 to 10 working days each time.[27] In rural Ethiopia, onchocercal skin disease lowers the earnings of affected workers by 10 to 15 percent.[28] As such, human capital becomes a fundamental ingredient for desirable job outcomes.

Human capital formation is cumulative. It is a life-cycle process that proceeds in consecutive stages, each of them building on the previous one. Of crucial importance are adequate health and nutrition during the first 1,000 days of life, from inception to two years of age. Brain development in this period affects physical health, learning abilities, and social behavior throughout life.[29] In the early years, a child develops all the basic brain and physiological structures upon which later growth and learning depend. Stunting in early childhood has been proven to have a significant negative effect on cognitive development; iodine deficiency can lead to poor brain development; and insufficient cognitive stimulation reduces learning abilities. Ensuring adequate nutrition, health, and cognitive

stimulation through a nurturing environment from the womb through the first years of life raises significantly the returns to later education investments.[30] Supporting young children born into poverty during these crucial development phases can significantly improve equality of opportunities. The later the support, the more difficult and costly it is to put that child back on a normal developmental trajectory. In Romania, during the early transition years, the cognitive performance of orphans was lower the older they were when they left state orphanages. Social, emotional, and cognitive isolation was common in these facilities.[31]

While foundations are laid early on, human capital and skills continue to be formed throughout childhood, young adulthood, and working life. Schooling is fundamental for the further development of cognitive and social skills until the end of adolescence, but learning abilities continue to be shaped by physical and mental health. Social skills remain malleable through adolescence and early adult years.[32] Young adults can continue into more specialized skill-building, including at tertiary levels, but their success depends on whether they have acquired the generic skills needed to learn and adapt to different tasks and problem-solving environments. These abilities are especially important in more dynamic economies.

Unfortunately, the evidence shows that many countries are falling short in building up the human capital of their children and youth. The quality of delivery systems has often failed to keep pace with the expansion of access to basic social services. In education, for example, by 2010, the net primary school enrollment rate in low-income countries had reached 80 percent, primary school completion was at 68 percent, and gross lower secondary school enrollment exceeded 50 percent.[33] But learning outcomes were clearly lagging behind. In a large majority of developing countries that took part in the Programme for International Student Assessment (PISA) in 2009, at least 20 percent of 15-year-old students were functionally illiterate. For a number of countries, including Indonesia, the Kyrgyz Republic, Panama, Peru, Qatar, Tunisia, and the two Indian states that participated in the PISA, more than 60 percent of 15-year-old students failed to reach this level. Similarly, early reading tests taken at the end of second grade revealed that, in diverse countries, a significant share of students were unable to read a single word: around 30 percent in Honduran rural schools, 50 percent in The Gambia and more than 80 percent in Mali.[34] Enrollment numbers, hence, do not necessarily signal actual learning and skill building.

The rule of law and respect for rights

Across countries, the presence of institutions that uphold the rule of law is associated with higher levels of development (figure 9.3).[35] Clear property rights and institutional mechanisms that strengthen governance can create a climate in which firms are willing to make investments, enter into contracts, and create new jobs. In such a climate, individuals may be more inclined to take the risks needed to set up new businesses and become entrepreneurs.[36]

The link between respect for property and development is well established.[37] Property rights foster private sector growth by allowing firms to invest without fearing that their assets will be stolen or confiscated. The ability to enforce contracts widens the circle of potential suppliers and customers, as personal connections become less important in establishing trust.[38] Entrepreneurs who believe their property rights are secure reinvest more of their profits than those who do not.[39] Increasing the security of property rights often involves setting up effective titling and registration processes. Mechanisms for valuing and protecting other types of property, including legislation governing intellectual property, are also important.

Rampant crime and violence can be devastating for development and for job creation.[40] Lawlessness can drive firms away and discourage domestic and foreign investment. Across countries, investment climate surveys consistently find crime and corruption to be obstacles to conducting business.[41] Inclusive and responsive institutions, which lead to a reduction of violent behavior, increase safety and security. Strengthening efforts to detect and prosecute white-collar crime and malfeasance can reduce corruption.

An effective judicial system is a key ingredient for enforcing property rights and reducing crime and corruption. An independent, accountable, and fair judiciary can contribute to private sector growth and job creation by en-

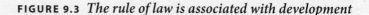

FIGURE 9.3 *The rule of law is associated with development*

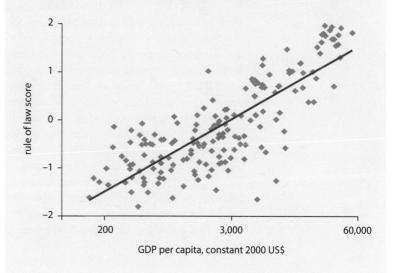

Sources: World Development Indicators 2010 (database) World Bank, Washington, DC; World Governance Indicators 2010.

Note: GDP = gross domestic product. The rule of law score is a measure of the extent to which agents have confidence in the rules of society, including the quality of contract enforcement, property rights, the police, and the courts, as well as the likelihood of crime and violence.

forcing the rules that govern transactions and helping ensure that the costs and benefits of growth are fairly distributed.[42] The justice system can enforce contracts, reduce transaction costs for firms, and create a safe and more predictable business environment.[43] The presence of effective courts increases the willingness of firms to invest.[44]

An institutional environment that respects rights is another integral part of the rule of law. The International Labour Organization's core labor standards provide guidance on what is unacceptable in the areas of child labor, forced labor, discrimination, and freedom of association and collective bargaining.[45] Health and safety at work also necessitate attention by governments and employers. Ensuring that standards are enforced in practice requires providing access to information to workers and employers. Information can increase the extent to which workers are able and willing to hold employers and intermediaries accountable. It can also help ensure that all parties involved are aware of their obligations. Strengthening institutions for enforcement and grievance redress is another necessary building block.

Ensuring that rights and standards are upheld requires a focus not only on implementing acquired rights but also on expanding their reach to workers in jobs that fall outside of formal laws and regulations. Associations of informal workers can play a key role in informing them, helping them access legal mechanisms, and offering them collective voice. But often, information alone is not enough: garment workers in the Lao People's Democratic Republic reported that they were told about their basic conditions of employment, but they did not always understand the details, nor how to enforce their rights.[46] Not only can organizations of informal workers support workers in learning about and accessing rights and standards, but they can also bring cases to court on behalf of individuals and groups.[47]

The quality of institutions for accountability affects the extent to which labor rights are enforced in practice.[48] Because court proceedings are often lengthy and costly, alternative mechanisms for resolving disputes, including conciliation, mediation, and arbitration prior to court hearings can expand access to justice and grievance redress.[49] These alternative mechanisms are especially valuable to workers who cannot access the court system due to high costs or other barriers.

Setting policy priorities for jobs

In addition to ensuring that the fundamentals are in place and that labor policies are set in a sensible range, decision makers can help realize the development payoffs that come from jobs. Some jobs do more than others for living standards, productivity, and social cohesion. What those jobs are depends on the country context—its level of development, demogra-

phy, endowments, and institutions. In some circumstances, there are no constraints to the emergence of good jobs for development and no specific policy is needed. In others, governments can support the private sector in creating more of these jobs. Sometimes removing existing constraints that impede the creation of jobs with high development payoffs is possible. In other cases, policies may need to circumvent the constraints.

A simple approach to setting policy priorities follows a series of steps. First, the country context must be assessed and the particular jobs challenge or challenges it faces must be identified. The second step is examining whether the jobs with the highest development payoffs are really the most attractive to individuals or the most profitable for firms. When incentives are aligned—with the individual and social value of jobs equal—there should be no shortage of good jobs for development and intervention is not needed. The third step is determining whether the institutional failures and market imperfections leading to misaligned incentives can be pinpointed or not. The fourth step is understanding whether politically feasible reforms can remove or correct those failures and imperfections. If not, the last step involves assessing whether incentives should be realigned through other policies (figure 9.4).

Step one: What are good jobs for development? Assessing the development payoffs from jobs in a particular country context is an important first step in identifying priorities. The nature of the jobs with the greatest payoffs varies with the characteristics of the country, including its phase of development, endowments, and institutions. Jobs challenges differ in agrarian economies, conflict-affected countries, resource-rich countries, and countries with high youth unemployment, as well as in other settings. And the jobs with the greatest development impact differ as well, resulting in diverse jobs agendas.

Step two: Are there enough of these jobs? A country may or may not face constraints in creating good jobs for development. For example, light manufacturing can offer employment opportunities for women, with significant impacts on reducing poverty. If a boom is under way, the development payoff of new manufacturing jobs

FIGURE 9.4 *A decision tree can help set policy priorities*

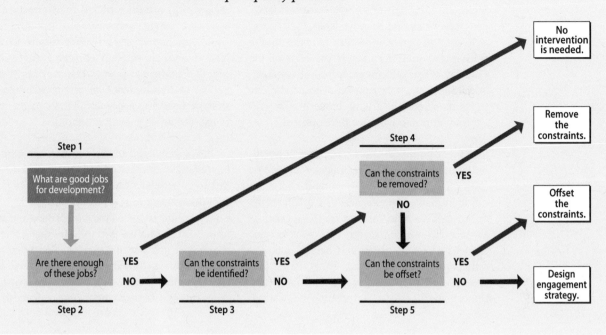

Source: World Development Report 2013 team.

might materialize. If so, it is difficult to justify government interventions beyond establishing the fundamentals and adopting adequate labor policies.

Misaligned incentives exist when good jobs for development are not rewarding enough to individuals or profitable enough to farms and firms. Data and analysis can be used to identify gaps between the individual and the social value of jobs. Arguably, many key areas in development economics deal with these gaps. For instance, the tools of public finance can be applied to measure the tax burden on capital and labor and to assess the extent of cross-subsidization between individuals or firms. Labor economics methods can be used to uncover gaps between the actual earnings of specific groups of workers and their potential earnings. Poverty analyses help in identifying the kinds of jobs that are more likely to provide opportunities to the poor, or the locations where job creation would have a greater impact on poverty reduction. Productivity studies can help quantify the spillovers from employment in FDI companies, in firms connected to global markets, or in functional cities. Environmental studies shed light on the carbon footprint and pollution created by various types of jobs. And analysis of values surveys can discover which types of jobs link to networks and provide social identity.

Step three: Can the constraints be identified? Understanding why the individual and social values of specific types of jobs differ is next. Gaps of this sort indicate the presence of unexploited spillovers from jobs. The gaps typically arise from market imperfections and institutional failures that cause people to work in jobs that are suboptimal from a social point of view, lead firms to create jobs that are not as good for development as they could be, or connect people less through jobs than would be socially desirable. But identifying where those constraints are is not always easy. For instance, a broad set of cultural, social, and economic forces may result in insufficient employment opportunities for women. Similarly, it may be difficult to pinpoint whether the key obstacles to making cities functional lie in the land market, or in the institutional arrangements to coordinate urban development, or in the ability to raise revenue to finance infrastructure.

Step four: Can the restraints be removed? If the institutional failures and market imperfections leading to misaligned incentives can be identified, reforms should be considered. It is a good economic principle to target reforms to the failures and imperfections at the root of the problem. Where reforms are technically and politically feasible, policy makers should directly tackle the major constraints hindering the creation of more good jobs for development.

Step five: Can the constraints be offset? Reforms might not be feasible, technically or politically. Or perhaps the constraints for jobs are not identifiable. An alternative is to enact offsetting policies that can restore the incentives for job creation. For instance, if a diffuse but entrenched set of priors and beliefs makes it difficult for women to work, efforts could aim at increasing their employability through targeted investments and interventions in social

and physical infrastructure (box 9.1). Similarly, if politically charged regulations slow the reallocation of labor toward more productive activities, urban infrastructure and logistics could enhance the attractiveness of jobs in cities and jobs connected to world markets (question 9). But there are cases when constraints can neither be removed nor offset. An engagement strategy involving a deeper analysis of the options and buy-in by key stakeholders is needed then.

Policy making to remove or offset constraints has to be selective and supported by good public finance principles. The costs and benefits of policy options need to be assessed, but the calculations are different when the overall development impact is the guiding objective. But they are also more difficult. For instance, an employment program for ex-combatants in a conflict-affected country could be assessed in terms of whether the earnings gains of participants justify the pro-

---

BOX 9.1 *How does women's labor force participation increase?*

Some developing countries have experienced important increases in women's labor force participation over a relatively short period of time. Nowhere has the change been faster than in Latin America. Since the 1980s, more than 70 million women have entered the labor force, raising the women's labor participation rate from 36 percent to 43 percent. In Colombia, the rate increased from 47 percent in 1984 to 65 percent in 2006. By contrast, in the Middle East and North Africa, women's labor force participation has only grown by 0.17 percentage points per year over the last three decades.

Recent research attributes this rapid transformation to increases in labor force participation among married or cohabiting women with children, rather than to demographics, education or business cycles. Changes in social attitudes contributed to the transformation, but this is a complex area with limited scope—and justification—for direct policy intervention. For instance, women's participation rates are very low in the West Bank and Gaza, particularly among married women. But this cannot be mechanically attributed to religion, as countries like Indonesia have high participation rates. Other social norms and regulations prevent women from participating, despite their willingness and capacity to do so.

While the scope to influence social attitudes is limited, evidence suggests that public policies and programs in other areas have an important role to play. It also suggests that a combination of targeted investments and interventions in social and physical infrastructure can modify women's labor force participation and the

returns to their earnings. These investments and interventions can be categorized into three groups. They can address shortages in the availability of services (such as lack of electricity or daycare facilities) that force women to allocate large amounts of time to home production. They can make it easier for women to accumulate productive assets, such as education, capital, and land, facilitating their entry into high-productivity market activities. And they can remove norms or regulations that imply biased or even discriminatory practices, preventing women from having equal employment opportunities.

There are successful experiences with targeted investments and interventions of these three sorts. Public provision or subsidization of child care can reduce the costs women incur at home when they engage in market work. Examples include Estancias Infantiles in Mexico, Hogares Comunitarios in Colombia, and similar programs in Argentina and Brazil. Improvements in infrastructure services—especially in water and electricity—can free up women's time spent on domestic and care work. Electrification in rural South Africa, for instance, has increased women's labor force participation by about 9 percent. Correcting biases in service delivery institutions, such as the workings of government land distribution and registration schemes, allows women to own and inherit assets. Finally, the use of active labor market policies, the promotion of networks, and the removal of discriminatory regulations, are important to make work more rewarding for women.

Source: World Development Report 2013 team based on Amador and others 2011, Chioda 2012, and World Bank 2011i.

gram costs. But a full accounting would need to incorporate the potentially positive effects on peace building. In the Democratic Republic of Congo, the cost of a reintegration program for ex-combatants was about US$800 per beneficiary.[50] Such a program would likely be judged as cost inefficient by traditional standards. Whether or not it is still worth implementing depends on the implicit value policy makers attach to its social cohesion benefits. These spillovers from jobs may not be measured precisely, but at least they should be stated, for policy decisions to be transparent.

Diverse jobs agendas, diverse policy priorities

Following a protocol to identify constraints to the creation of good jobs for development, and then remove or offset them, may sound abstract. But some countries have successfully done this in practice, and it is possible to learn directly from their experiences (box 9.2). The stories of Vietnam, Rwanda, Chile, and Slovenia, show that policy can effectively support the creation of jobs with high development payoffs. Each of these countries faced a different jobs challenge, so their policy choices are relevant for other countries confronted with similar jobs agendas. Getting the fundamentals right by ensuring macroeconomic stability, improving the business environment, and adhering to the rule of law, featured prominently in all four cases. All four countries also embraced labor policies and institutions within a reasonable range. But it is telling that the main constraints they targeted were not in the labor market.

Agrarian economies: Vietnam

Increasing productivity in agriculture, thereby freeing up labor to work in rural off-farm employment and to eventually migrate to cities, is the main challenge facing agrarian economies. At the beginning of its economic reform process, in the late 1980s and early 1990s, Vietnam was a clear illustration of this challenge. In 1993, the first year for which reliable data exist, over 70 percent of employment was in agriculture, 58 percent of the population lived in poverty,

and famine was not a distant possibility.[51] Two decades later, Vietnam is the world's second-largest exporter of rice after Thailand; the second-largest exporter of coffee after Brazil; the largest exporter of pepper; and a top exporter of rubber, cashew nuts, and seafood products. The poverty rate declined to 16 percent by 2006, the fastest reduction in poverty ever recorded. These two decades of accelerated progress took Vietnam out of the least-developed-country category and made it a lower-middle-income economy with upbeat growth prospects.

Vietnam's transformation from an inefficient agrarian economy into an export powerhouse started with land reform. In the late 1980s and early 1990s, the country abandoned collectivization by initially allowing local authorities to reallocate communal land to individual households and subsequently extending land-use rights to them. The devolution of land to rural households was remarkably egalitarian, especially in the north.[52] By 1993, land-use rights could be legally transferred and exchanged, mortgaged, and inherited. Land reform was part of a broader package of reforms, or *Doi Moi*, which took Vietnam from central planning to a market economy with a socialist orientation.[53] The package included the gradual removal of barriers to entry in most sectors, including the commercialization of agricultural products. Competition brought farmgate prices much closer to international prices. Combined with a strong emphasis on agricultural extension, land reform and deregulation led to rapidly growing agricultural productivity on very small farm plots.

In parallel, policies aimed to create employment opportunities outside agriculture. Vietnam opened to foreign investors, first in selected sectors such as natural resource exploitation and light manufacturing, and then more broadly in the context of its accession to the World Trade Organization (WTO) in 2007. Registered FDI increased fourfold in just two years, from 1992 to 1994; by 2007, FDI inflows were consistently exceeding 8 percent of GDP.[54] Initially investors partnered with state-owned enterprises (SOEs), because of the complexity of a legal system still in transition. But SOEs had gradually been given the flexibility to make their own business decisions, and many were

BOX 9.2 *There have been successes in tackling jobs challenges around the world*

The Republic of Korea effectively used policies to bring out the agglomeration and integration benefits of an *urbanizing country*.[a] Almost three-quarters of the population was rural in 1960, but by 2000, four-fifths were urban. Seoul, which has grown to more than 10 million people today, was a motor for the country's overall growth, especially from the late 1980s until the mid-1990s. Many industrial clusters were established in close proximity to the capital city. Carefully designed and phased urban development policies accompanied the transition from jobs in agriculture to jobs in light manufacturing and then to jobs in industries with higher value added. Land development programs were established first, followed by a land-use regulation system, and then by comprehensive urban planning. Housing and transportation policies held the diseconomies of urbanization in check. The global integration of Korea's urban hubs was a core driver of its growth dynamic. The country invested massively in skills to support its structural transformation. The mean years of education of the adult population increased from 4.3 in 1960 to 11.8 in 2010. International test scores now place Korea at the top of Organization of Economic Cooperation and Development (OECD) countries in reading, mathematics, and science outcomes for 15-year-olds.

Small island nations are characterized by their size, isolation, and exposure to climatic risks. In these circumstances, reaping the productivity gains from agglomeration and global integration is especially challenging. Tonga is using migration as an active instrument to connect to the world economy.[b] Approximately 100,000 Tongans live abroad, almost as many as at home. Remittances account for an estimated 32 percent of GDP and reach 80 percent of households, raising the education levels and productive investments. Migration agreements also reach poorer and less-skilled workers. In 2007, New Zealand launched the Recognized Seasonal Employer (RSE) program, which provides temporary opportunities for seasonal workers from the Pacific to work in horticulture and viticulture. For the households of participants, the program has led to income gains of up to 38 percent, more purchases of durable goods, and a broader improvement in well-being. In addition to income, RSE workers brought home their newly acquired knowledge of agricultural techniques, computer literacy, and English-language skills.

Formalizing countries can envision increasing the coverage of their social protection systems to levels typical of industrial countries. But costs are high, as is the risk of distoring incentives and undermining productivity. Brazil is one country that has been able to not only grow quickly but expand the formal sector in the process.[c] Benefiting from a booming global commodities market and a competitive exchange rate, its economy was growing at around 5 percent a year before the 2008 financial crisis. But unlike other rapidly growing countries, Brazil's job creation in the formal sector was three times as high as in the informal sector. Just in the five years leading up to the crisis, the formal share of total employment increased by about 5 percentage points. In some ways, Brazil is an unlikely "formalizer"—it has a heavily regulated business sector and a costly labor system. Although its rapid formalization is too recent to be fully explained yet, it appears efforts to simplify and extend the reach of programs and regulations have been contributing factors. The government has expanded the coverage of its social protection system through noncontributory programs. It has also simplified tax rules for small businesses, increased incentives for firms to formalize their workers, and improved enforcement of tax and labor regulations.

In *aging societies* the increase in the old-age dependency ratio reduces the average productivity per person, while the growing costs of caring for the elderly undermine living standards. But the reforms needed to address these challenges are politically difficult to implement and often involve hard tradeoffs. Poland is an example of a country that has taken several successful steps.[d] By the turn of the century, labor force participation rates were declining due to the growing incidence of early retirement and disability pensions. But several reforms that reduced the inflows of new beneficiaries led to an increase in the employment-to-population ratio from 60 percent in 2006 to 65 percent in 2009. Changes in the application of eligibility rules of disability pensions, enacted in 2005, sharply reduced the intake of new beneficiaries. In 2009, a pension reform tackled early retirement options. This reform is such that old-age pension benefits adjust downward as life expectancy increases. Hence, the country is expected to have a fiscally sustainable pension system in the long run. That sustainability came at a cost: benefits as a percentage of earnings at retirement became significantly lower than the average in the European Union. In 2012, a new wave of pension reforms raised the retirement age to 67 for men and women from the current 65 for men and 60 for women. This increase should help to raise the benefit level without adversely affecting fiscal sustainability. Policies and programs to ease labor market entry for the inactive and unemployed of all ages remain modest, however, and their impact still needs to be determined. Also, long-term health care continues to rely largely on informal arrangements, but reforms are now publicly debated.

Source: World Development Report 2013 team.
a. Park and others 2011; Yusuf and Nabeshima 2006.
b. Gibson, McKenzie, and Rohorua 2008; World Bank 2010a.
c. Fajnzylber, Maloney, and Montes-Rojas 2011; OECD and ILO 2011.
d. Styczynska 2012; World Bank 2011b.

totally or partially sold to private investors. By the turn of the century, greenfield FDI investments had become the norm, especially in sectors such as garments, footwear, appliances, and consumer electronics.[55] Firms in these sectors are employing workers in large numbers. Important challenges remain, but Vietnam is by now a rapidly urbanizing economy, which is a testimony to its success.

Conflict-affected countries: Rwanda

Rwanda today seems far removed from the war and genocide of the mid-1990s, and jobs contributed to such a remarkable turnaround. The conflict has had a severe impact on society and the economy, with massive loss of life, destruction of infrastructure, a crisis of state institutions, and a drop in GDP that exceeded 50 percent.[56] The cessation of conflict and an aggressive package of reforms allowed Rwanda's economy to rebound to pre-crisis levels by 2000.[57] Growth has continued, reaching an estimated 8.8 percent in 2011, and the poverty rate fell by 12 percentage points between 2005 and 2010.[58]

A precondition for sustainable job creation in countries emerging from conflict is securing peace and reducing risks of recurring violence.[59] In the wake of the conflict, the Rwandan government supported the reintegration and demobilization of more than 54,000 former combatants. Ex-combatants received a combination of cash assistance, counseling, vocational training, education, support for income-generating activities, and social reintegration activities involving community members.[60] More than a decade after the end of conflict, most former combatants were participating in vocational training or working, mainly in subsistence agriculture and self-employment, similar to the rest of Rwanda's population.[61] Although many ex-combatants continued to experience social and psychological hardships, their relations with their neighbors were reportedly good, and trust was improving. In 2012, 73 percent of ex-combatants expressed satisfaction with their social integration, and 85 percent of community members felt that there was trust between the two groups.[62]

While the number of ex-combatants only represents a small share of Rwanda's total population of 10 million, reintegration through jobs had social cohesion payoffs, which established a basis for the country to move forward. Rwanda has built on this start by rejuvenating the private sector through reforms to institutions and business regulations.[63] A good example of the government's private sector development strategy was its decision to revitalize its coffee industry through deregulation and investments in new technology, a decision that has led to new job creation.[64] Rwanda still faces serious jobs challenges. More than 80 percent of the population works in subsistence agriculture and household enterprises, where productivity needs to be improved. Also, opportunities for off-farm employment need to expand, and growth in the currently small manufacturing sector would

help.[65] But the economic reintegration and social cohesion through jobs have established a basis for future progress.[66]

Resource-rich countries: Chile

While many countries rich in resources seem unable to diversify and are beset by poor governance, Chile's savvy management of its copper riches makes it a notable exception. In 2010, Chile was home to 28 percent of the world's copper reserves and about one-third of world copper production; for the past two decades, it has accounted for 17 percent of world copper exports.[67] But despite the prominence of copper in its economy, Chile has been able to diversify its exports and its economy while effectively managing resource-related risks such as currency appreciation and macroeconomic turbulence. Nonmineral exports increased significantly as a share of total exports after the 1980s, before retreating somewhat during the global commodities boom after 2007 (figure 9.5). Employment in the nonmining sectors has grown strongly at more than 2 percent annually over the past two decades.[68] The unemployment rate has averaged around 8 percent over the past decade, a far cry from the record 20 percent of the early 1980s.[69]

A set of macroeconomic, institutional, export-diversification, and skill-building policies contributed to this broad-based job creation path. Chile combines the use of a resource stabilization mechanism (since 1987, with the current framework adopted in 2006) with a transparent fiscal rule (since 1999) that jointly regulate how copper extraction rents are used.[70] A structural surplus target is the anchor for determining inflows and outflows into two funds, one for pensions and other long-term government liabilities, the other for short-term stabilization purposes. The funds are authorized to invest their portfolio fully abroad, relieving pressures on the exchange rate.[71] In parallel, governance reforms over the past decades in all areas of public sector management have led to significant success: Chile climbed 5 percentiles in its voice and accountability rating between 1996 and 2009 and also improved its political stability and control of corruption ratings.[72]

Further, Chile adopted an active export-oriented growth policy, opening up to trade and welcoming direct foreign investment,

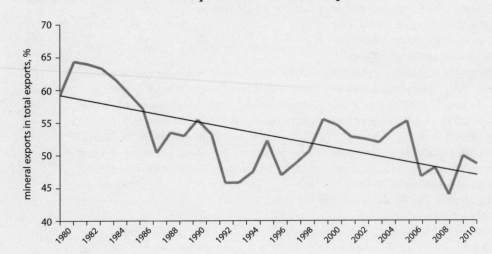

FIGURE 9.5 *Chile reduced its dependence on mineral exports*

Source: World Development Report 2013 team, based on export values data from Chile's Central Bank and copper price index from IMF's International Financial Statistics database.
Note: The figure shows the share of mineral exports in total exports, measured at constant 1990 prices. Total exports and mineral export values were deflated using the export price index and the copper price index, respectively.

thereby enhancing the productivity spillovers from global integration. An ambitious innovation strategy to raise competitiveness was developed.[73] Public funds were used specifically to boost education expenditures, which almost doubled in real terms between 1990 and 2009.[74] While quality as well as equity in the education system are much debated today, the share of low-skilled workers declined in all economic sectors.[75]

Countries with high youth unemployment: Slovenia

Slovenia has made inroads into the problem of high youth unemployment (figure 9.6). Throughout the first decade after the breakup of the former Yugoslavia, young people were three times as likely as adults to be unemployed. By 2010, this ratio had fallen to two to one.[76] The youth employment rate, which was 10 percentage points above the European Union (EU) average in 2000, was lower than the EU average in 2010.[77] By then, the share of Slovenia's youth not in education, employment, or training was just 7.5 percent among the 15- to 24-year age group, well below the EU average of 11.2 percent.[78] While the crisis has certainly been felt by

young people, European Commission President José Manuel Barroso recently highlighted Slovenia as an example of best practice in the employment of youth.[79]

Slovenia's relative success in reducing youth unemployment does not strictly follow traditional recipes. Its spending on active labor market policies is about average for transition countries. Although some reforms have been made to liberalize the rules for contract and temporary work, Slovenia's labor regulations remain more restrictive than the Organisation for Economic Co-operation and Development (OECD) average, a policy stance that is usually associated with reduced job opportunities for young people. Minimum wages—also frequently cited as a barrier for youth employment—are on the high side. But potential distortions from these policies seem to be somewhat offset by a model of consensus-based decision making. In Slovenia, trade unions and employers' organizations, both with broad coverage, set wages that respond well to macroeconomic trends and sectoral productivity patterns.[80]

Sustained growth supported by increased competition in product markets, is ultimately responsible for much of Slovenia's decrease in youth unemployment. Taking advantage of

European integration, the economy successfully restructured its export sector to access EU markets. Very good infrastructure and a fairly skilled workforce helped as well. This dynamism, requiring the use of more advanced production and management techniques in modern sectors, was especially well-suited for youth. While the story is a good one in many ways, further policy reforms could help Slovenia realize more of the development payoffs that flow from jobs for young people. Some of these reforms are in the labor market, such as removing the incentives created by employment protection laws that tilt job creation for youth toward contract and temporary work. But others are outside the labor market, such as introducing measures to encourage more FDI.[81]

Connected jobs agendas: Global partnerships for jobs

Policies for jobs in one country can have spillovers on other countries, both positive and negative. An important issue is whether international coordination mechanisms could influence the decisions that governments make, enhancing the positive spillovers and mitigating the negative ones. Several areas lend themselves to coordination. Promoting compliance with rights and labor standards, a global public good, is the most obvious one, but the effectiveness of the mechanisms for doing so is limited. Measures to facilitate FDI flows, especially in services, would have substantial effects on productivity in developing countries but they may also have social implications. Migration has impacts on both sending and recipient countries, suggesting that bilateral agreements could lead to better outcomes for both parties.

Rights and standards: Pressure goes only so far

Several mechanisms operating across borders exist to set standards and provide channels for improving workers' rights and their working conditions. They include the issuance and ratification of ILO conventions, bilateral and multilateral trade agreements, and initiatives involving the private sector, civil society, and other stakeholders. These mechanisms operate either

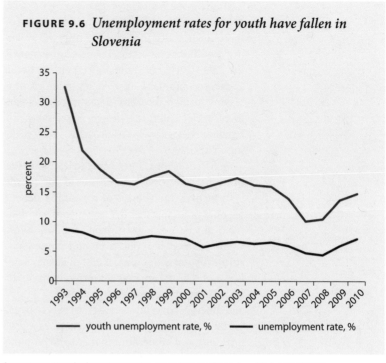

FIGURE 9.6 *Unemployment rates for youth have fallen in Slovenia*

Source: International Labour Organization, Key Indicators of the Labour Market (KILM) 2011.
Note: The youth unemployment rate refers to the 15-to-24 age group, whereas the general unemployment rate is for people aged 15 and above.

through peer pressure or by providing positive incentives for governments and firms to comply. But it is not certain that these kinds of pressures and incentives actually change working conditions on the ground, and the risk that improvements come at the expense of job creation cannot be ruled out.

ILO conventions provide a framework for rights, standards, and conditions at work. At the country level, conventions can influence domestic legislation if countries do align their laws with global standards. They can be a channel for voice and coordination internationally, as demonstrated by the adoption of conventions for home-based and domestic workers.[82] Evidence from the ratification of the eight conventions included in the ILO's 1998 Declaration on Fundamental Rights and Principles at Work (the core labor standards) suggests that countries respond to pressure from the international community.[83] Yet, the persistence of forced labor, children working in hazardous conditions, discrimination, and lack of voice also suggests that ratification on its own is not sufficient.

Trade agreements have also been used with the intent of supporting workers rights. Some of them incorporate incentives to improve working conditions and access to voice. For instance, the 1999 bilateral trade agreement between Cambodia and the United States included provisions to increase Cambodia's quota for garment imports into the United States market if regular reviews showed improvements in working conditions.

Whether labor clauses actually lead to better outcomes for workers on either side of a trade agreement is the subject of a running debate. Skeptics point out that the agreements, on their own, can be weak instruments for improving rights and working conditions and cannot substitute for adequate enforcement of domestic labor laws.[84] There are also concerns about political capture and pressures from interest groups and uneven bargaining power between treaty parties.[85] Labor clauses could be used as a protectionist tool, undermining trade and employment opportunities in developing countries. Supporters claim that labor clauses in trade agreements not only improve the enforcement of existing labor and employment standards but also lead to increased FDI to developing countries, thus benefiting workers in developing countries in both direct and indirect ways.[86]

Linking rights to trade agreements may have an impact on working conditions if complemented by investments in capacity for enforcement and compliance at the country level. After it signed the Central America Free Trade Agreement, the Dominican Republic increased the number of labor inspectors and invested in capacity building.[87] And after it entered the bilateral trade agreement with Cambodia, the United States funded two ILO projects there. One of them, Better Factories Cambodia, involved building capacity for compliance and monitoring of working conditions in garment factories. The other supported an arbitration council to resolve collective labor disputes.[88] Subsequent reviews have found improvements in working conditions and collective rights.[89]

Beyond the initiatives of governments through conventions and trade agreements, there has been a growing emphasis on private sector accountability. Under the broader corporate social responsibility (CSR) agenda, companies voluntarily assume social and en-

vironmental concerns into their operations.[90] While some develop their own codes of conduct, collective initiatives are increasingly important for improving working conditions in global supply chains. Shared codes enable companies to collaborate with other businesses in industry-led platforms, and with trade unions and nongovernmental organizations in multistakeholder initiatives (sometimes with government observers).[91]

Almost all such initiatives have defined standards of practice, but they differ substantially in their governance structures, in their procedures for implementation, monitoring, and verification, and in whether they involve certification and labeling.[92] CSR initiatives focused on labor issues are generally concentrated in sectors relying on global supply chains that are exposed to reputational risk, such as garments, sportswear, food and, increasingly, electronics.[93] Codes of conduct are most frequently adopted by companies based in the European Union and North America, which then make compliance with labor standards a condition for doing business with them. A small number of voluntary initiatives have also emerged in developing countries, although these are generally a response to external pressure more than a reaction to campaigning by local consumers.[94]

There is limited evidence to demonstrate how far CSR initiatives go beyond good intentions to result in tangible and sustainable improvements in rights and working conditions. The clearest impacts are found in the area of health and safety and, to a lesser extent, in regularization of working hours. Improvements on freedom of association and discrimination are much less likely. Overall, the benefits are more pronounced for permanent workers than for migrants, agency workers, and seasonal and temporary workers.[95] Codes do not operate in a vacuum, so the capacity of local actors and the quality of domestic laws and institutions are critical to the effectiveness of the efforts.[96]

These findings stress the need for approaches to improving working conditions that extend to sectoral and national-level engagement with governments, employers, trade unions, and civil society organizations. Voluntary labor initiatives cannot substitute for domestic efforts to set up adequate legal protections and put in place institutions to support compliance and provide av-

---

BOX 9.3 *Improving business practices facilitates compliance with labor standards*

The Better Work program seeks to improve compliance with international labor standards and national laws, while promoting business competitiveness. The program operates through partnerships with governments, employer and worker organizations, and international buyers. It currently includes global garment brands and retailers with supply chains outsourcing production to Cambodia, Haiti, Indonesia, Jordan, Lesotho, Nicaragua, and Vietnam.

The program involves thorough workplace assessments that examine compliance with international labor standards and national labor law, as well as advisory services to help employers and workers jointly create and implement improvement plans. Tailored training services support workplace cooperation and address specific issues, such as supervisory skills, human resource systems, and occupational safety and health. The program undertakes public reporting, which presents aggregate noncompliance data from all participating factories in a country and allows comparisons across countries according to specific indicators. A Better Work global team ensures quality, consistency, and effective knowledge management, supporting country teams with tools for advisory services, monitoring and evaluation, and impact assessment.

Better Work is modeled on the Better Factories Cambodia program, which was introduced in conjunction with the bilateral trade agreement between Cambodia and the United States. Results of evaluations of Better Factories Cambodia, covering more than 90 percent of participating factories, found that compliance on occupational safety and health improved 20 percent. Correct payment of wages, overtime, and benefits increased 37 percent. Initially, incentives to improve working conditions were driven by the quota increases called for under the trade agreement; however, with the expiration of the Multi-Fiber Arrangement (MFA), quota increases were no longer possible. Nevertheless, the Cambodian garment industry has continued to invest in monitoring, having identified labor compliance as an important part of its claim to a niche in the global garment industry. This niche exists despite the expiration of the MFA largely because of the role that reputation plays in the supply chain.

Sources: World Development Report 2013 team based on Better Work Programme, International Finance Corporation, Washington, DC, and International Labour Organization, Geneva; Robertson and others 2009; and Adler and Hwang 2012 for the World Development Report 2013.

---

enues for redress. The public and private sectors can work together, as in Brazil, where in 2003 the Ministry of Labor began publishing lists of companies found to be using forced labor. The increased public awareness led companies to subscribe to a National Pact to Combat Slave Labor, with civil society organizations establishing a committee to monitor the pact.[97]

While most jobs in developing countries fall outside the scope of CSR initiatives, these efforts have the potential for a wider influence if they can be expanded to include workers, mainly women, who do not have formal contracts. At the same time, local governance and institutions could be boosted through activities to strengthen the capacity of actors and institutions and improve processes of dialogue and cooperation. Demonstration effects may also occur at the country level if CSR efforts increase the visibility of activities to improve rights and working conditions, and if labor inspectorates and third-party monitoring bodies gain experience and capacity. The potential benefits of local capacity building are illustrated by the experience of Better Work, a partnership program between the ILO and the International Finance Corporation (IFC) aimed at improving compliance with labor standards in the garment sector (box 9.3).[98]

Further liberalizing trade, but managing the tradeoffs

International trade in goods has been gradually liberalized, and the notion that freer trade is mutually beneficial for the transacting parties is now widely shared. Various mechanisms have been used in the liberalization process, including multilateral, regional, and bilateral agreements, as well as unilateral commitments. At the multilateral level, liberalization has been achieved through negotiations under the framework of the General Agreement on Tariffs and Trade (GATT) first, and then of its successor, the WTO. The most recent round of multilateral negotiations, the Doha Development Agenda, aims for better market access for the exporting industries of developing countries. Average bound tariffs would fall from 40 to 30 percent for agricultural products, and from 10 to 5 percent for manufactures. Actual tariffs could fall by 11 to 14 percentage points for the former, and by 2 to 3 percentage points for the latter. Cuts could be much sharper in sectors such as textiles and clothing. The least-developed countries could even benefit from duty-free quota access on almost all of their exports to industrial countries.[99] For developing countries, the success of the Doha Round could therefore have a substantive impact on the creation of jobs connected to global value chains, which are typically good jobs for development. But the Doha negotiations are in limbo.

Despite the progress in trade liberalization, many developing countries still lack the competitiveness to harness the benefits from global integration. Providing them with direct assistance to reduce logistics costs and improve the competitiveness of firms and farms is thus a priority. The Aid for Trade initiative aims to increase aid to developing countries so that they can tap existing market opportunities. Aid for Trade has increased substantially and now accounts for about a third of total aid to developing countries. To date, most of the resources have been channeled to infrastructure investments and trade facilitation. But the assistance could be made more effective by focusing on the export activities most suited to addressing the specific jobs challenges facing recipient countries. Increasing the involvement of the private sector would also enhance the effectiveness of the assistance provided.[100]

In contrast to trade in goods, services liberalization has made slow progress, at both the multilateral and the regional levels. Services are subject to more pervasive regulations, because they are characterized by well-known market imperfections. These range from natural monopolies in the distribution of electricity to network externalities in telecommunications, and from asymmetric information and moral hazard in finance to market power in retail trade. While the liberalization of trade in goods is associated with domestic liberalization, the liberalization of trade in services usually requires domestic regulation. Setting up markets for electricity, ensuring universal service in telecommunications, adopting appropriate banking supervision, and managing the social impacts of large distributors on retail trade are challenging tasks.[101]

Not surprisingly, liberalization in services is much less advanced in developing countries than in industrial countries. The former are also reluctant to make additional commitments. Neither existing agreements under General Agreement on Trade in Services (GATS) nor proposals in the Doha agenda and in regional trade discussions offer prospects for significant liberalization (figure 9.7).[102]

However, the productivity gains from services liberalization would be substantial. Electricity, finance, telecommunications, and trade have a direct impact on production and transaction costs, making downstream sectors more competitive. By boosting job creation and raising labor earnings, these productivity gains should also lead to improved living standards. Social impacts can be more mixed. They are clearly positive when cell phones connect people (especially the poor) to markets for their products, to employment opportunities, or to government services. They can be negative when the disappearance of retail trade leads to the decline of traditional urban areas and affects the livelihoods of older shopkeepers who may not find alternative employment easily.

An adequate sequencing of services liberalization and domestic regulation can help manage these tradeoffs and, in doing so, address the concerns of developing countries. For instance, in telecommunications, enhanced domestic competition improves welfare more than handing over existing providers to better-performing foreign operators. Evidence from 86 developing countries between 1985 and 1999 suggests that both competition and liberalization can independently improve performance. But penetration of telecommunications services, measured by main-line access, is lower if competition is introduced after liberalization, rather than at the same time.[103]

A careful design of liberalization, can also cushion social impacts. For instance, in its preferential trade agreement with the United States, Oman chose a sequential approach for the liberalization of its retail trade. Foreign nationals were initially permitted to own up to 100 percent of the equity in established retail enterprises valued at more than US$5 million, with the threshold subsequently declining to US$1 million. This agreement allowed for gradual adjustment. At the same time, it was generous in relation to foreign ownership, which is restricted to 49 percent in Oman's prevailing multilateral agreements.[104] Similarly, concerns about the impact of liberalization on urban centers are addressed through land-zoning restrictions, as some industrial countries do. But these restrictions can also be used as entry de-

FIGURE 9.7 *Offers to liberalize services are generally modest*

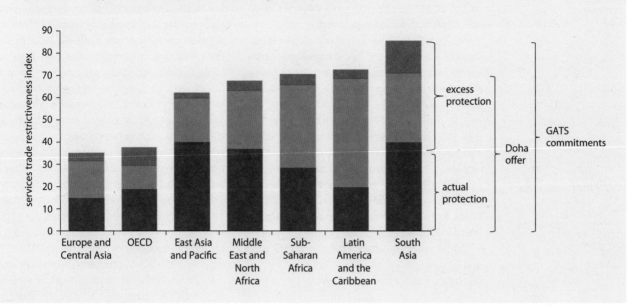

Source: Borchert, Gootiiz, and Mattoo 2010.
Note: GATS = General Agreement on Trade in Services; OECD = Organisation for Economic Co-operation and Development. The figure compares the applied trade policies in major services sectors with countries' commitments under GATS and the best offers that they have made in the Doha negotiations. The figure is based on data from 62 countries. The country services trade restrictiveness index is a weighted average of a country's policies or commitments to market access by foreigners in financial, retailing, telecommunication, transportation and selected professional services sectors. Weights are sectoral gross domestic product shares. The regional index is a simple average of country indices.

terrents, reducing competition and undermining job creation.[105]

The limited traction in services liberalization is due largely to the potential tradeoffs involved. Developing countries may lack knowledge on the gains from opening markets, the on preconditions for realizing such gains in light of existing tradeoffs, and on the policy options available for maximizing the gains and handling the tradeoffs. Similar to the case of trade in goods, many countries also lack the ability to implement policies and agreements. International collaboration is thus needed to address such knowledge gaps and facilitate implementation.[106]

International agreements can also be used to promote global public goods. One case in point is gender equality. Trade is not gender neutral. Its liberalization, including services trade, changes women's access to jobs. Traditionally men were more likely to have "brawn jobs," involving stronger physical requirements. But "brain jobs" involving dexterity, attention, or communication—from stitching garments to processing data—present more opportunities for women. In Delhi and Mumbai, call centers employ more

than 1 million people, most of them women. Preferential access for developing country imports from sectors with more "brain jobs" can thus be used to create employment opportunities for women in countries where gender equality is far from being attained.[107] However, as countries move up the ladder of global value chains, women may also lose job opportunities. This was the case in Malaysia, where the share of women working in manufacturing declined in the mid-1980s.[108]

Migration policies: Toward bilateral agreements

Movements of people across borders have elicited diverse policy reactions by recipient countries over the course of history. These have included physical walls that keep foreigners away, policies preventing forced and bonded labor across oceans, and policies of open migration. In addition, there has been a range of specific measures including amnesties for irregular migrants, statutes controlling entry by refugees, and complex systems for granting visas. In most cases, these policies have been introduced unilaterally by the recipient country and have involved little or no international dialogue or cooperation with sending countries.

In contrast to the movement of goods and services across borders, few international agreements concern migration in general and migration of workers in particular. Those in existence have limited coverage. ILO Conventions 97 and 143, in force since 1952 and 1978, respectively, seek to protect migrants from discrimination and abuse, and call for penalties and sanctions against those who promote clandestine or illegal migration. But these conventions have been ratified by only 49 and 23 countries, respectively. Mode 4 of GATS covers exports of services conducted through individuals present in another WTO member country.[109] It entered into force in 1995 and covers all signatories to the WTO, but only a limited number of services have been liberalized by either developed or developing countries, with very few moving ahead in sensitive areas like health services. Finally, the United Nations International Convention on the rights of all migrant workers and members of their families aims to "contribute to the harmonization of the attitudes of States through the acceptance of basic principles concerning the treatment of migrant workers and members of their families." This convention entered into force in 2003 but has been ratified by only 22 countries, mostly sending countries.

Growing differences in ages, incomes, skills and economic perspectives between countries are likely to create mounting pressures for migration. Despite the interest of both industrial and developing countries in "talent" migration, low-skill migrants will still account for the bulk of cross-border flows in the years to come.[110] But readiness to make the most of these growing differences between countries, and manage migration in a mutually beneficial way, is limited. Multicountry agreements have been slow to develop. Bilateral agreements that take into consideration geographical and historical trends, protect basic rights of workers, and take into account the social impacts of migration, could benefit both host and sending countries.

Migration is an area where a global perspective is warranted, but views on what needs to be done are quite diverse. One view focuses on the large earnings differentials between countries, suggesting that the free movement of labor would accelerate global productivity growth and poverty reduction enormously.[111] Another perspective focuses on national security and the protection of communities and their cultures, implying the need for barriers to contain migration. Yet another highlights the moral imperative to protect the human rights of migrants, no matter their legal status, and to give shelter to those who suffer any form of persecution.[112] None of these views suffices, because none of them alone can address the complex tradeoffs that migration poses for policy design.

There are many examples of such tradeoffs. The more that is spent in protecting the welfare of migrants, which sending countries and concerned citizens everywhere demand, the more expensive the use of migrant labor will become, and the fewer the number of workers who will be hired. The more that is done to assimilate and integrate the migrants, which some host-country groups favor, the less likely migrants will be to return to their home countries. The more active the policies to attract "talent" migrants, the greater the "brain drain" concerns among sending countries. The higher the protection of sectors such as agriculture by industrial countries, the more likely are migrants from developing countries to work in those sectors. Conditioning foreign aid on banning migration seems unacceptable and would affect fundamental rights of workers by constraining their freedom to move. Stern visa restrictions and deportations usually backfire and may turn overstayers into irregular migrants. These examples indicate that unilateral policies cannot address all these dilemmas. However, the adoption of global agreements setting the conditions of migration and superseding country legislation, seems unlikely. This is why an intermediate solution can be more effective.

In many instances, both sending and host countries can benefit from migration through a collaborative approach. Most abuses perpetrated by traffickers, firms, or workers are associated with illegal migrant flows. The formalization of these flows is a basic tool for protecting the rights of migrant workers, while at the same time having them honor the terms under which they were welcomed. This formalization, however, is difficult to enforce without the cooperation of institutions in both sending and receiving countries.[113] Bilateral agreements can include provisions regarding quotas by occupation, industry, region, and duration of stay. They can distinguish between temporary movements of workers and steps to permanent migration, with conditions and protocols for moving from one country to another and regulation of recruitment agencies and intermediaries. They can include considerations about taxation and social security, including on benefits to be provided, portability of contributions, and cost-sharing arrangements. These agreements can design incentives so that firms, worker associations, and governments in both sending and receiving countries have an interest in enforcing the provisions.[114]

Formalizing and extending temporary migration agreements could capture part of the wage gain from migration that is currently absorbed by intermediaries, to the benefit of both migrants and their employers. Agreements in the financial sector could lower the cost of remittances to migrants and avoid the prevalence of illegal transactions. Reconsidering the financing of higher education in both developing and developed countries could favor a more balanced sharing of the returns to investments in the case of talent migrants. More generally, bilateral coordination is a sensible way to manage migration and ensure mutual benefits for sending and recipient countries.

Jobs are center stage, but where are the numbers?

Policies for jobs need to be based on reliable data and rigorous analysis.[115] Given that a large share of the people at work in developing countries are not wage employees, and that even a larger share lacks social security coverage, the measurement of employment must look beyond whatever formal employment data the country gathers. Determining which jobs have the greatest payoffs for poverty reduction requires linking information on a household's income or consumption with information on the employment of its members. Understanding which firms create more jobs, or whether labor reallocation leads to substantial growth rather than just churning, requires information on the inputs and outputs of very diverse production units, including microenterprises. Assessing whether employment experiences affect trust and willingness to engage in society requires information on individual values and behaviors. Such information is necessary to tackle an emerging research agenda on jobs and development (box 9.4).

However, the paucity of empirical analyses on the employment impact of the global crisis in developing countries and the difficulty of comparing measures of informal employment across countries suggest that data quality and availability are limited. Much effort goes into measuring unemployment rates, even with a relatively high frequency.[116] But open unemployment is not a very telling indicator in countries where an important fraction of the labor force is not salaried. Four indicators are listed to monitor progress toward the employment target under the Millennium Development Goal (MDG) on eradicating poverty. This target calls for "achieving full and productive employment and decent work for all, including women and young people." But the four indicators considered only partially capture advances in the quantity and quality of jobs in the developing world.[117] Many available employment figures are actually inferred through interpolation between years and extrapolation using data from "similar" countries, but how reliable these methods are remains an open question.

These remarks are not meant to criticize statistical agencies at the country level or data collection efforts at the international level. Their efforts are filling important gaps and mobilizing expertise to improve definitions, reach agreements on best practices, and provide technical assistance to those generating primary data.[118] Despite the limitations, data on informal employment, the unemployment rate, or the MDG employment target serve an important objective, namely, increasing awareness on the importance of jobs for promoting development. However, moving jobs center stage could remain an aspirational statement in the absence of a sustained effort to improve the amount and comparability of data.

Today's challenges regarding labor statistics can be regrouped into three key areas: data gaps; data quality issues; and planning, coordination, and communication issues. In some countries, labor statistics do not exist at all or are collected

BOX 9.4 *Knowledge gaps on jobs and development chart the research agenda*

Increased reliance on disaggregated survey data, together with rigorous program evaluation and controlled experiments, has pushed the knowledge frontier on jobs and development in recent years. On almost all relevant issues a substantive body of evidence already exists. Current efforts of the research community promise its expansion in the coming years, in ways that should contribute to better informed policy making. However, knowledge gaps remain in several areas.

Jobs and living standards. An abundance of high-quality work has been done on the measurement of poverty and the assessment of poverty alleviation programs. Less is known on how employment dynamics affect household living standards and movements in and out of poverty. Research on transitions between different employment statuses, occupations, industries, and types of jobs can shed light on incentives to work and formalize, as well as on impacts of jobs on household well-being. Knowledge is also limited on the subjective value workers attach to various characteristics of their jobs, including to social security benefits such as old-age and disability pensions.

Jobs and productivity. Many studies are available on firm dynamics, including births, growth, and deaths. There is also a growing literature on the impacts of trade liberalization and foreign direct investment on productivity and earnings at the plant level. Much of this research focuses on formal sector firms, however. Much less research is available on the dynamics of micro- and small enterprises in the informal sector, despite their importance for employment. There is also some disconnect between studies based on plant-level surveys and the growing literature on the effects of urbanization. The dialogue between these different literatures is in part hampered by different visions of production processes on issues such as returns to scale or externalities.

Jobs and social cohesion. Research in this area is tentative and the empirical evidence is scarce. The importance of the topic and the paucity of robust results mean that the payoffs to high-quality research in this area could be very high. Natural experiments combined with longitudinal data spanning relatively long periods of time may shed light on the links between jobs and behaviors. Interdisciplinary research could provide insights on the broader relationship between jobs and institutional development processes. Anthropological approaches may provide insights on the mechanisms at play; for instance on how jobs affect perceptions on fairness and the willingness to trust others.

Spillovers from jobs. Research on the magnitude of spillovers from jobs is patchy. The agenda is long, but a promising area concerns the impact of jobs on the acquisition of cognitive and noncognitive skills, and how this impact varies depending on the characteristics of the job and those of the person who holds it. Evidence on agglomeration effects across cities with different characteristics is also scarce, as are estimates of the environmental impacts of different types of jobs.

Labor policies. A growing number of empirical studies focus on the impact of labor policies and institutions, and many of these studies are very rigorous. However, a careful review suggests that the relationship between policies and institutions on the one hand, and outcomes on the other, is not linear. Rather, it evokes a "plateau" of modest effects, but with "cliffs" at both ends where the impacts on efficiency and the distribution of jobs can be sizeable. Empirical work to determine where these cliffs lie and how to identify the institutional characteristics that demarcate the limits of the plateau would be of much value for policy makers.

Connected jobs agendas. More research is needed on how international trade, investment at both ends, and migration affect the composition of employment across countries. Knowledge gaps are common in all of these areas. The ability of national policies and supranational mechanisms such as trade agreements to affect jobs in different countries is only partially understood. More solid knowledge on the right sequencing of international commitments and domestic policies related to services could address the reluctance of developing countries to make further progress in the direction of liberalization. Rigorous evaluations of migration policies would also be helpful.

Source: World Development Report 2013 team.

only sporadically. Where labor statistics do exist, data quality is a concern throughout the statistical production chain, from the use of appropriate definitions to questionnaire design, from sampling frames to interviewing protocols, and from data entry and coding to verification and estimation procedures. Planning, coordination, and communication issues are exacerbated when different institutions are responsible for collecting and disseminating the data.[119] The most urgent priorities are to standardize the employment modules attached to the household surveys used for poverty analysis, and to ensure that establishment surveys include informal firms and microenterprises.

A quarter of a century ago, a renewed emphasis on poverty reduction as the key objective of development policy launched a long-term data effort. Across the world, information on household living standards was collected through standardized surveys, the sampling methods and the variable definitions used were duly documented, and the data and documentation were made available to researchers and practitioners whenever possible. A similar approach should be envisioned to move jobs center stage.

How to accelerate labor reallocation?

Creative destruction, the mainstay of economic growth, happens to a large extent through labor reallocation. As workers move from jobs in low-productivity farms and obsolete firms to jobs in more dynamic economic units, output increases and the economy moves closer to the efficiency frontier. Differences in productivity across economic units underlie this creative destruction process. Such differences can reflect a healthy ecosystem driven by competition which offers the basis for efficiency-enhancing job reallocation. Market imperfections and government failures may hinder labor reallocation, however, resulting in a wider dispersion of productivity and many missed opportunities for growth.[120]

Stringent regulations that obstruct the movement of workers from low- to high-productivity areas or that prevent their separation from obsolete firms are a case in point. These regulations may stem from good intentions, such as containing congestion in cities or providing earnings stability to workers. But their cost in productivity growth can be substantial. Regulations of this kind do not sit on the efficiency "plateau" where labor policies are mainly redistributive; they are rather on the cliff, and have unambiguously negative effects on economic efficiency.

India is arguably an example of a country whose complex and cumbersome labor policies have pushed it off the "plateau." The country has more than 40 national and state-level labor laws. Most of them apply to the organized (or formal) sector and to firms above a certain size. As firms' employment increases, they fall under the purview of a growing number of regulations.[121] The Industrial Disputes Act (IDA) of 1947 is particularly restrictive. Governing employee-employer relationships, the IDA makes it extremely difficult for firms to terminate employment.[122]

The stringency of labor regulations is consistent with the "missing middle" phenomenon, characteristic of India and other developing countries, where medium-size businesses make up a disproportionately small share of the total. Also consistent with the stringency of labor regulations is the substantial dispersion of productivity. If the dispersion observed within each industry narrowed to the point of matching the dispersion observed in the United States, India's average productivity in manufacturing could increase by more than half.[123] Instead, despite India's buoyant economic growth during the past two decades, the performance of the labor-intensive manufacturing sector has been sluggish.[124] The bulk of the growth in nonfarm employment has been in the informal sector.

The conventional wisdom, when a country is riddled with misguided labor regulations, is to repeal them. This repeal may be easier said than done, however. India's complex labor regulatory system has been in place for 60 years; even the ambitious reform program triggered by the balance-of-payment crisis of 1991 left labor regulations largely untouched.[125] The IDA of 1947 has been amended at the state level but not always toward the plateau. Between 1958 and 1992, seven states amended the IDA to give employers more latitude in labor decisions. These states subsequently experienced higher growth in output, employment, investment, and productivity in their formal manufacturing sector. But six other states changed the IDA in the opposite direction, which resulted in a worsening in firm performance and an expansion of the informal sector.[126] Overall, the dispersion of productivity in India's manufacturing sector remained stable, or even increased, between 1987 and 1994.[127]

From bypassing regulatory obstacles . . .

India's response to these regulatory obstacles has been to learn how to live with them, and this has been achieved through widespread noncompliance.[128] For example, large firms rely on contractors, who in turn hire workers; thus total employment is "sliced" into smaller packages, each escaping the most stringent labor market regulations. Short-term contracts and temporary employment agencies are other mechanisms used to circumvent the regulations. The propensity of firms to hire contract workers has increased over time for all firms employing 10 or more workers and is highest among medium-

FIGURE 9.8 *Is there a "missing middle" in the distribution of manufacturing firms in India?*

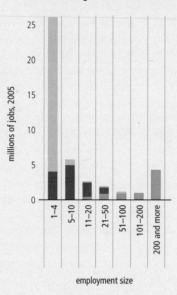

a. Including own-account firms

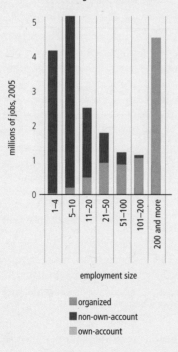

b. Excluding own-account firms

■ organized
■ non-own-account
■ own-account

Source: Hasan and Jandoc 2010.
Note: Data for the organized, or formal, sector are from the Annual Survey of Industries (ASI) conducted by India's Central Statistical Organisation; data for the unorganized or informal sector are from the National Sample Survey Organisation (NSSO) Survey of Unorganized Manufacturing Enterprises. Own-account manufacturing enterprises are those operating without hired workers employed on a regular basis.

sized firms (50–99 workers).[129] A 10-year study of 1,300 firms also finds insignificant differences between medium and larger firms in their hiring of manual workers.[130] The share of informal workers in total employment in organized firms grew from 32 percent in 2000 to 52 percent in 2005 to 68 percent in 2010.[131]

Consistent with noncompliance, the distribution of firms by size does not show substantial discontinuities around the threshold levels where regulations become more stringent. Considering the entire distribution, including informal firms, the biggest discontinuity is between firms employing up to 4 workers and those employing 5 to 10 (figure 9.8a). However, there is no 5-worker threshold in the applicable labor market regulations. On the other hand, there is no discontinuity in the distribution when crossing the 50-worker cutoff point, despite it being the threshold above which firms fall under the purview of the IDA (figure 9.8b).

Admittedly, other factors could influence India's distribution of firms by size.[132] But overall, these patterns are consistent with firms bypassing labor regulations.

… to actively offsetting them …

While India has learned how to live with cumbersome regulatory obstacles, other developing countries with similar constraints have accomplished more efficiency-enhancing labor reallocation. Sri Lanka inherited the same labor regulations from the British colonial administration as India did. Without reaching the extremes in India, many Latin American countries face similar regulatory obstacles. Although China's labor regulations were less stringent until the 1990s, its household registration (*hukou*) system represented the ultimate obstacle to labor reallocation.[133] Yet, all of these countries have managed to spur growth in high-productivity sectors and locations.

Sri Lanka gradually liberalized many of its markets during the 1980s and 1990s but did not reform its complicated and costly employment protection legislation. Under the Termination of Employment of Workman Act (TEWA) of 1971, firms with 15 or more employees cannot lay off workers without official authorization and are liable for termination payments of up to four years of salary, depending on the employee's length of service. Yet the country's garment industry was a runaway success. Replacing tea as the country's major source of export revenue, the industry now accounts for half of Sri Lanka's sales abroad, up from almost nothing in the 1970s. It also accounts for much of the increase in employment in manufacturing.[134] The success of the garment industry has been a magnet for rural migrants, with 45 percent of them moving to the western provinces where the garment industry is concentrated.

Restrictive labor market regulations are a common feature of many Latin American countries too. In Brazil, after years of economic reforms, hiring workers remains as burdensome as ever. If anything, the sustained increase in formalization over the past decade has made compliance with labor regulations more common. Yet, Brazil's labor market has been characterized by massive internal migration and remarkably high labor turnover rates. Lifetime interstate migration is estimated to have doubled between the 1980s and the 1990s, reaching two-fifths of the population by 1999. In the 1990s, one-third of the workers who changed jobs in Brazil's formal sector had migrated

across state borders to find employment. And an estimated two-fifths to one-half of formal sector workers change jobs every year.[135]

Nowhere is the extent of labor reallocation more striking than in China, and much of it happened under the *hukou* system. Since its introduction in the 1950s, this system governed where people could live, effectively preventing rural-to-urban labor flows and reserving employment in cities for their residents (box 9.5). With market-oriented reforms, the system was gradually liberalized, and many restrictions on internal migration were lifted. But the *hukou* system has not been completely abolished; even today it may still inhibit migrant flows and reduce the incidence of workers moving with dependents. Despite this barrier to labor mobility, China experienced phenomenal growth in labor-intensive manufacturing, involving massive internal migration from the hinterland to coastal areas, and from villages to towns and urban centers. This geographically concentrated development absorbed an important share of rural surplus labor, while integrating China into international value chains and making it the "world's factory."[136]

BOX 9.5 *China's* hukou *system has been partially liberalized*

A *hukou* is analogous to an internal passport. Legal residency in a city, town, or village is determined by an individual's birth place. Rural and urban populations are registered separately. The *hukou* system regulates many social entitlements of citizens, including education, housing, utilities subsidies, and social protection. Together with other policies such as urban food rationing during the period under central planning the *hukou* system prevented the rural labor force from moving out of agriculture. It maintained an exclusive urban labor market with basic social welfare, and supported industrial policy, effectively creating rural-urban segmentation.

At the beginning of the reform process, cities and towns could afford basic social welfare only for a limited population. Inflows of rural workers were therefore seen as a double-edged sword that could increase the well-being of rural residents but also lead to congestion and overcrowded infrastructure. After reforms in urban areas were under way in the mid-1980s, and the growth of township and village enterprises stagnated, farmers were allowed to work in small and medium cities—but only on the condition that they continued to be self-sufficient in terms of staples, in accordance with

the food ration scheme that was still in force. Restrictions were not lifted until the mid-1990s, when reforms were well under way. By then, the fast growth of labor-intensive and export-oriented sectors and the dramatic surge of private sector activities in urban areas generated a substantial demand for low-skilled labor. Only at that point was the *hukou* system substantially liberalized.

The implementation of this liberalization process has been conducted in a decentralized way. Most medium and large cities have gradually lowered the criteria for migrants to change *hukou* identities, and hence their accompanying entitlements. However, the criteria remain exceptionally strict in major cities and in cities with high income levels, including Shanghai, Beijing, and Guangzhou. For example, Shanghai was the first city to make the residence permit system open to all, but its qualifying conditions are among the strictest. Shanghai's system favors immigrants with college degrees or special talents, and those who do business or invest. It also requires seven years of social insurance contributions before applying. In addition, the city has a tight overall quota on *hukou* conversions, and the actual number of conversions has to date been very low.

Sources: World Development Report 2013 team based on Cai, Du, and Meiyan 2002; Cai and Meiyan 2011; Cai, Park, and Zhao 2008; Chaudhuri and Datt 2009; and Giles, Wang, and Park 2012.

... through productivity spillovers

These examples point to a successful second-best approach to offset regulatory obstacles. Instead of trying to avoid or evade labor regulations, this approach involves actively taking advantage of productivity spillovers from jobs in industrial clusters, dynamic cities, or global value chains to make the regulations less relevant in practice.

In Sri Lanka, the development of export processing zones (EPZs) drove the takeoff of the garment industry. These economic enclaves offered better infrastructure and a more favorable regulatory environment than the rest of the economy. As a result, they attracted large inflows of FDI and became the source of a large fraction of Sri Lanka's exports (figure 9.9).[137] Local producers in these zones were able to benefit from cluster effects. Outperforming competitors in many other developing countries, the industry has managed to move up the value chain, transforming factories into design centers.

In Brazil, the surge of internal migration is closely associated with the country's continuing integration into the global economy and a development policy that favors agglomeration effects. In the 1990s, Brazil implemented major trade liberalization measures, gradually relaxed restrictions on FDI, and devalued its currency. In this context, development policy was increasingly left to subnational governments, emphasizing the importance of regional hubs and facilitating a location-specific policy agenda built on local strengths. These efforts supported the relocation of industries toward previously less-favored regions. While local policies were largely targeted at fostering small and medium firms, they also attracted bigger firms and multinational companies. The impact on internal migration was significant. A 1 percent increase in the concentration of FDI in a particular location was associated with a 0.2 percent increase in the location's immigration rate. And a 1 percent increase in employment in export sectors was associated with a 0.3 percent reduction in outmigration.[138]

In China, labor reallocation is rooted in the development of competitive cities. The urban share of the population jumped from just 27 percent in 1990 to almost 50 percent in 2010. This transformation is unprecedented, with the urban population increasing from 170 million in 1978 to 456 million in 2000 and 665 million today. The increase was supported through a phenomenal expansion of commercial power supply, urban infrastructure, highways, and ports. In 1988, China had barely 100 kilometers of expressways; 10 years later, the total length

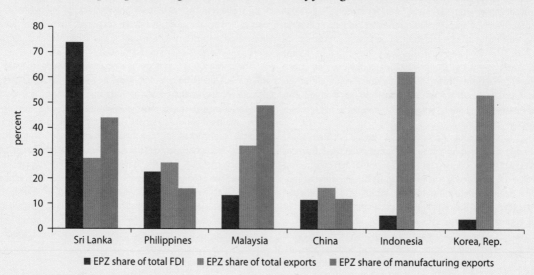

FIGURE 9.9 *Export processing zones were a driver of foreign direct investment in Sri Lanka*

■ EPZ share of total FDI   ■ EPZ share of total exports   ■ EPZ share of manufacturing exports

Source: Jayanthakumaran 2003.
Note: EPZ = Export Processing Zone; FDI = foreign direct investment. The figure summarizes EPZ activities during the 1980s.

FIGURE 9.10 *Restrictions to* hukou *conversion increase with city size and income*

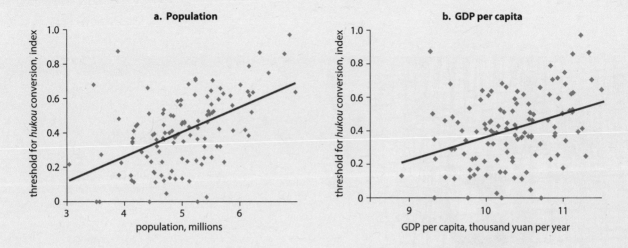

Source: Wang, Song, and O'Keefe 2012 for the World Development Report 2013.
Note: GDP = gross domestic product. The index measuring the threshold for *hukou* conversion takes into account requirements on investment, employment and family reunion. Each dot represents one of 120 cities in 30 provinces.

was second to the United States; and by 2009, more than 60,000 kilometers were in use.[139]

Regional competition and experimentation in part underpin these successes. In China, local governments have substantial autonomy to raise fiscal and nonfiscal resources. They thus have considerable scope to take responsibility for local development. The Chinese Communist Party also rewards local officials based on local performance, prompting them to actively engage in economic competition.[140]

This decentralized institutional setting allowed cities in China to experiment with reforms to the *hukou* system as a tool for urbanization. It has been argued that a large fraction of cities in China are too small because of it.[141] But the decentralized implementation of the system allowed major globalizing cities to use the *hukou* system as a screening tool to select more skilled migrants and enhance the productivity spillovers from jobs. Most medium and large cities have gradually eased the criteria for migrants to change *hukou* identities. However, bigger and richer globalizing cities have embraced a more skill-intensive pattern of growth, putting more weight on productivity growth than on poverty reduction (figure 9.10).[142] Ac-

cordingly, the criteria for changing *hukou* identities in these cities are generally defined by skills, investments, income, and residence requirements. The numbers of migrants meeting these criteria have been small.[143]

Back to India, then, where the slow pace of urbanization is even more striking than the rigidity of its labor regulations. In 1990, the share of India's population living in cities was the same as China's: 27 percent. Two decades later, it had grown only to 30 percent.[144] The functionality of the cities also poses severe challenges. For instance, large swaths of Delhi or Mumbai have access to no more than four to five hours of water supply a day. Energy shortfalls have increased in recent years and are perceived as the top constraint for doing business. A company can expect 17 power shutdowns a month. The cost imposed on firms by the power problem is among the highest in the world.[145] Judging from the experiences of Brazil, China, and Sri Lanka, and after 60 years of partial success in making labor regulations more flexible, the key for India to accelerate labor reallocation and thereby realize its development potential may lie in its urbanization policy.

Worker at a construction site in Jakarta, Indonesia

© Sebastião Salgado / Amazonas—Press Images

Notes

1. Commission on Growth and Development 2008, 53.
2. Ball, Leigh, and Loungani, forthcoming.
3. Bosch and Maloney 2010; Fiess, Fugazza, and Maloney 2010.
4. World Bank 2012b, various issues.
5. Commission on Growth and Development 2008.
6. Kraay 2012.
7. Frankel 2012.
8. World Bank 2012a.
9. Elbadawi, Kaltani, and Soto 2009.
10. Options to cope with the abundance of foreign exchange earnings include creating professionally managed sovereign funds to smooth the impact of surges in earnings, adopting countercyclical fiscal policy to stabilize aggregate demand, and targeting monetary policy on a rate of inflation more directly influenced by the abundance of foreign exchange than the change in the consumer price index. Arezki, Sy, and Gylfason 2012.
11. Rodrik 2008.
12. IFC, forthcoming.
13. King and Levine 1993; Levine 2005.
14. Dinkelman 2011.
15. IFC, forthcoming.
16. Foster and Briceño-Garmendia 2010.
17. Foster and Briceño-Garmendia 2010.
18. World Bank (2011a) measures 11 areas of business regulations across 183 economies.
19. Hallward-Driemeier, Khun-Jush, and Pritchett 2010.
20. Ramachandran, Gelb, and Shah 2009; World Bank 2009a.
21. Klapper, Laeven, and Rajan 2006.
22. Bruhn 2008.
23. IFC, forthcoming.
24. Commission on Growth and Development 2008, 37.
25. Montenegro and Patrinos 2012 for the World Development Report 2013; Psacharopoulos and Patrinos 2004.
26. See, for example, Hanushek and Woessmann (2008) on the productivity link. Structural change and poverty links are explored in Lee and Newhouse (2012) for the World Development Report 2013.
27. Bloom and Canning 2008.
28. Kim, Tandon, and Hailu 1997.
29. Engle and others 2007; Grantham-McGregor and others 2007; Heckman 2008; Walker and others 2007; Young and Richardson 2007.
30. Engle and others 2007.
31. O'Connor and others 2000.
32. Cunha, Heckman, and Schennach 2010; Heineck and Anger 2010.
33. Data from Education Statistics (Edstats), World Bank, Washington, DC. http://web.worldbank .org/WBSITE/EXTERNAL/TOPICS/EXTED UCATION/EXTDATASTATISTICS/EXTEDST ATS/0,,menuPK:3232818~pagePK:64168427~ piPK:64168435~theSitePK:3232764,00.html
34. Gove and Cvelich 2010.
35. IMF 2003; Rodrik 2000.
36. World Bank 1997; World Bank 2004b; World Bank 2011h.
37. Keefer 2009; North 1981, 1990.
38. Acemoglu, Johnson, and Robinson 2001; North 1990; Rodrik, Subramanian, and Trebbi 2004.
39. World Bank 2004b.
40. World Bank 2011h.
41. World Bank 2004b.
42. World Bank 2012e.
43. World Bank 2004b.
44. Laeven and Woodruff 2007.
45. ILO 1998.
46. World Bank 2012c.
47. Chen and others 2012 for the World Development Report 2013.
48. Locke, Amengual, and Mangla 2009.
49. Purcell 2010.
50. World Bank 2010b. Note that this unit cost is the aggregate cost of the Multi-Country Demobilization and Reintegration Program, including all forms of reintegration support, not only employment.
51. Glewwe 2004.
52. Ravallion and van de Walle 2008.
53. Rama 2009.
54. World Bank 2012f.
55. World Bank 2009b; World Bank 2011e.
56. Up to 800,000 lives were lost from civil war and genocide. About 3.8 million people were displaced, of whom about 2 million fled to refugee camps in the Democratic Republic of the Congo and Tanzania. World Bank 2007.
57. World Bank 2007.
58. World Bank 2012d.
59. World Bank 2011h.
60. MDRP 2008.
61. The exception was female ex-combatants, who had unemployment rates higher than the rest of the population. Consia Consultants 2007; Stavrou, Jorgensen, and O'Riordan 2007; MDRP 2010; Mehreteab 2005.
62. Rwanda Demobilization and Reintegration Commission 2012.
63. Rwanda was named a top reformer in 2010 by *Doing Business* (http://www.doing business.org/ reforms/top-reformers-2010/).

64. Dudwick and Srinivasan, forthcoming; World Bank 2011h.
65. World Bank 2011d.
66. A study of farmers and workers in coffee enterprises found that interactions through these jobs were associated with improved attitudes toward interethnic collaboration as well as less distrust and positive views about reconciliation. Tobias and Boudreaux 2011.
67. United States Geological Survey, http://minerals.usgs.gov/minerals/pubs/commodity/copper/mcs-2012-coppe.pdf; UNCTAD Statistics, http://unctadstat.unctad.org/.
68. BADECEL (database), Economic Commission for Latin America, Santiago, http://websie.eclac.cl/badecel/badecel_new/index.html.
69. World Bank 2012f.
70. Sinnott, Nash, and de la Torre 2010. At the outset of the international financial crisis, Chile's stabilization fund accounted for US$20 billion (or 12 percent of GDP) in 2008, permitting the country to finance a substantial countercyclical expansion of expenditures.
71. Sinnott, Nash, and De la Torre 2010. After the Asian financial crisis of 1997, the government adopted a free floating exchange rate policy and introduced instruments to mitigate exchange rate risk. World Bank 2006.
72. Worldwide Governance Indicators. See Kaufmann, Kraay, and Mastruzzi 2010.
73. Consejo Nacional de Innovación 2008; World Bank 2008.
74. World Bank 2011f.
75. World Bank 2006.
76. OECD Scoreboard for Youth, http://www.oecd.org/document/31/0,3746,en_2649_37457_46328479_1_1_1_37457,00.html.
77. OECD 2010.
78. OECD 2010.
79. EU Press Release, http://www.eu-skladi.si/information-and-publicity/news-on-cohesion-policy-implementation/latest-news/barroso-slovenia-example-of-best-practice-in-youth-employment#c1=News%20Item&c1=novica.
80. OECD 2009.
81. OECD 2011.
82. ILO 1996; ILO 2011.
83. Chau and Kanbur (2001) find evidence of a peer effect whereby ratification depends on the number of similar countries that have already ratified the convention.
84. Aaronson and Zimmerman 2008; Elliott and Freeman 2003.
85. Hafner-Burton 2009.
86. Mosley 2011.
87. Schrank 2009.

88. Adler and Hwang 2012 for the World Development Report 2013.
89. Berik and Rodger 2010; Polaski 2006.
90. Levi and others 2012 for the World Development Report 2013; Newitt 2012 for the World Development Report 2013.
91. Examples of multistakeholder initiatives include the U.K.-based Ethical Trading Initiative, http://www.ethicaltrade.org/; the U.S.-based Fair Labor Association, http://www.fairlabor.org/; and Social Accountability International, http://www.sa-intl.org/.
92. Levi and others 2012 for the World Development Report 2013; Newitt 2012 for the WDR 2013; UNCTAD 2011.
93. Newitt 2012 for the World Development Report 2013.
94. These include the Wine Industry Ethical Trade Association in South Africa, http://wieta.org.za.www34.cpt3.host-h.net/; and Fibre Citoyenne, a multistakeholder initiative in the Moroccan garment sector, http://www.fibrecitoyenne.org/.
95. Barrientos and Smith 2007.
96. Locke, forthcoming; Locke, Quin, and Brause 2007.
97. Maranhao Costa and Trindade 2009.
98. See "Better Work," International Finance Corporation, Washington, DC; International Labour Organization, Geneva, http://www.betterwork.org/EN/Pages/newhome.aspx.
99. Laborde and Martin 2011a; Laborde and Martin 2011b.
100. Hoekman 2011.
101. François and Hoekman 2010; Hoekman and Mattoo 2011.
102. Hoekman and Mattoo 2011.
103. Fink, Mattoo, and Rathindran 2003; François and Hoekman 2010.
104. Roy 2008.
105. Bertrand and Kramarz 2002; Wrigley and Lowe 2010.
106. Hoekman and Mattoo 2011.
107. Randriamaro 2007.
108. World Bank 2011g.
109. See World Trade Organization, "Movement of National Pensions," http://www.wto.org/english/tratop_e/serv_e/mouvement_persons_e/mouvement_persons_e.htm.
110. Solimano 2008.
111. See, for instance, Winters and others (2002) and World Bank (2005).
112. See, for instance, EFRA (2011), and Angenendt (2012).
113. Regional agreements also exist, for example, for the European Union's Schengen area.
114. For a discussion on these issues, see Pritchett (2006).
115. Kanbur and Svejnar 2009.

116. Around the world, 65 countries produce monthly or quarterly labor force surveys, whereas 116 produce annual surveys.
117. The four indicators are GDP per employed person (a measure of productivity), the employment-to-population rate, the proportion of the employed population living on less than US$1.25 per day (the so-called working poor), and the proportion of own-account and unremunerated workers in employed population (also called vulnerable workers). United Nations Development Group 2010.
118. International standards on labor statistics are of two types: those outlined in Conventions and Recommendations adopted by the ILO International Labour Conference, and the Resolutions and Guidelines adopted by the International Conference of Labour Statisticians (ICLS). The first type of standards is part of the international labor code and is legally binding in ratifying countries, whereas standards adopted by the ICLS are intended to provide guidance to countries, promote international comparability of labor statistics, and encourage coherence in concepts and methods across sources and domains.
119. ILO 2012.
120. Bartelsman, Haltiwanger, and Scarpetta 2011; Hsieh and Klenow 2009, 2011; McMillan and Rodrik 2011; McMillan and Verduzco for the World Development Report 2013; Pagés 2010.
121. For example, once employment in a firm using power reaches 10 workers (20 for firms that do not use power), the firm enters the organized sector and becomes subject to the Factories Act of 1948. Once it reaches 50 workers, it is subject to the IDA of 1947 and must offer mandatory health insurance under the Employee State Insurance Act of 1948. Once it reaches 100 workers, it effectively loses the rights to terminate workers.
122. Panagariya 2008.
123. Hsieh and Klenow 2009.
124. Panagariya 2008. The entire decline in the share of agriculture since 1990–91 has been absorbed by services. Agriculture as a share of GDP fell from 46 percent in 1970–71 to 27 percent in 1990–91 and to 21 percent in 2004–05; industry's share of GDP rose from 22 percent in 1970–71 to 27 percent in 1990–91 and remained at the same level through 2004–05; the share of manufacturing, consequently, rose from 13 percent in 1970–71 to 17 percent in 1990–91 through 2004–05.
125. The reforms focus on the liberalization of trade and foreign investment and the dismantling of the License Raj system introduced in 1951 to impose central control over entry and production in the organized manufacturing sector.
126. Ahsan and Pagés 2009; Besley and Burgess 2004. Also see Bhattacharjea (2006) for concerns about the evidence presented by Besley and Burgess (2004) because of the interpretation and enforcement of the amendments to the IDA of 1947.
127. Hsieh and Klenow 2009.
128. Bhattacharjea 2006.
129. Hasan and Jandoc 2012.
130. Deshpande and others 2004.
131. Preliminary estimates by Santosh Mehrotra (Planning Commission of India).
132. Hasan and Jandoc 2012.
133. Several labor laws have been enacted in China since 2000, including a revision to the Trade Union Law in 2001; the Labor Contract Law, the Employment Promotion Law, and the Labor Dispute Mediation and Arbitration Law in 2008; and the Social Insurance Law in 2011. The implementation of these regulations may lead to lower flexibility in the labor market.
134. World Bank 2004a.
135. More interesting, the migration flows of formal sector workers were directed toward unconventional destinations: a few states in Brazil's Center-West, North, and Northeast. These flows contradict the assertion that the typical migrant flow runs from the low-income North to the higher-income South. Aguayo-Tellez, Muendler, and Poole 2010.
136. World Bank 2009c; Lin 2012.
137. Jayanthakumaran 2003.
138. Aguayo-Tellez, Muendler, and Poole 2010; Amaral-Filho 2003; Lastres, Cassiolato, and Campos 2006.
139. Bardhan 2010.
140. Bardhan 2010
141. Au and Henderson 2006.
142. Wang, Song, and O'Keefe 2012 for the World Development Report 2013.
143. Cai 2011; Cai, Du, and Meiyan 2002; Cai, Park, and Zhao 2008; Chaudhuri and Datt 2009; Giles, Wang, and Park 2012.
144. World Bank 2012f.
145. Bardhan 2010; World Bank 2011c.

References

The word *processed* describes informally reproduced works that may not be commonly available through libraries.

Aaronson, Susan, and Jamie Zimmerman. 2008. *Trade Imbalance: The Struggle to Weigh Human*

Rights Concerns in Trade Policymaking. New York: Cambridge University Press.

Acemoglu, Daron, Simon Johnson, and James A. Robinson. 2001. "The Colonial Origins of Comparative Development: An Empirical Investigation." *American Economic Review* 91 (5): 1369–401.

Adler, Daniel, and Hans Hwang. 2012. "From Law on the Books to Law in Action: A Note on the Role of Regulation in the Production of Good Jobs in Cambodia's Garment Sector." Background paper for the WDR 2013.

Aguayo-Tellez, Ernesto, Marc-Andres Muendler, and Jennifer P. Poole. 2010. "Globalization and Formal Sector Migration in Brazil." *World Development* 38 (6): 840–56.

Ahsan, Ahmad, and Carmen Pagés. 2009. "Are All Labor Regulations Equal? Evidence from Indian Manufacturing." *Journal of Comparative Economics* 37 (1): 62–75.

Amador, Diego, Raquel Bermal, and Ximena Peña. 2011. "The Rise in Female Participation in Colombia: Fertility, Mental Status, or Education?" Background Paper for the World Development Report 2012.

Amaral-Filho, Jair. 2003. "Ajustes Estruturais, Novas Formas de Intervencao Publica e Regime de Crescimento, Economico no Ceara." In *Regiões e Cidades, Cidades nas Regiões: O Desafio Urbano-Regional*, ed. Maria Flora Gonçalves, Carlos Antônio Brandão, and Antônio Carlos Galvão, 367–85. São Paolo: Universidade Estadual Paulist.

Angenendt, Steffen. 2012. "Migration and Social Inclusion—Looking through the Good Jobs Lens." In *Moving Jobs to Center Stage*. Berlin: BMZ (Bundesministerium fuer Wirtschaftliche Zussamenarbeit), Berlin Workshop Series.

Arezki, Rabah, Amadou Sy, and Thorvaldur Gylfason. 2012. *Beyond the Curse: Policies to Harness the Power of Natural Resources*. Washington, DC: International Monetary Fund.

Au, Chun Chung, and J. Vernon Henderson. 2006. "Are Chinese Cities Too Small?" *Review of Economic Studies* 73 (3): 549–76.

Ball, Laurence, Daniel Leigh, and Prakash Loungani. Forthcoming. "Okun's Law: Fit at 50?" Working Paper, International Monetary Fund, Washington, DC.

Bardhan, Pranab K. 2010. *Awakening Giants, Feet of Clay: Assessing the Economic Rise of China and India*. Princeton, NJ: Princeton University Press.

Barrientos, Stephanie, and Sally Smith. 2007. "Do Workers Benefit from Ethical Trade? Assessing Codes of Labour Practice in Global Production Systems." *Third World Quarterly* 28 (4): 713–29.

Bartelsman, Eric, John Haltiwanger, and Stefano Scarpetta. 2011. "Cross-Country Differences in Productivity: The Role of Allocation and Selection." University of Maryland, College Park, MD. Processed.

Berik, Gunseli, and Yana van der Meulen Rodger. 2010. "Options for Enforcing Labour Standards: Lessons from Bangladesh and Cambodia." *Journal of International Development* 22 (1): 56–85.

Bertrand, Marianne, and Francis Kramarz. 2002. "Does Entry Regulation Hinder Job Creation? Evidence from the French Retail Industry." *Quarterly Journal of Economics* 117 (4): 1369–413.

Besley, Timothy, and Robin Burgess. 2004. "Can Labor Regulation Hinder Economic Performance? Evidence from India." *Quarterly Journal of Economics* 119 (1): 91–134.

Bhattacharjea, Aditya. 2006. "Labour Market Regulation and Industrial Performance in India." Working Papers 141, Centre for Development Economics, Delhi School of Economics, New Delhi.

Bloom, David E., and David Canning. 2008. "Population Health and Economic Growth." Working Paper 24, Commission on Growth and Development. Washington DC.

Borchert, Ingo, Batshur Gootiiz, and Aaditya Mattoo. 2010. "Restrictions on Services Trade and FDI in Developing Countries." World Bank, Washington, DC. Processed.

Bosch, Mariano, and William Maloney. 2010. "Comparative Analysis of Labor Market Dynamics Using Markov Processes: An Application to Informality." *Labour Economics* 17 (4): 621–32.

Bruhn, Miriam. 2008. "License to Sell: The Effect of Business Registration Reform on Entrepreneurial Activity in Mexico." Policy Research Working Paper Series 4538, World Bank, Washington, DC.

Cai, Fang. 2011. "Hukou System Reform and Unification of Rural-Urban Social Welfare." *China and World Economy* 19 (3): 33–48.

Cai, Fang, Yang Du, and Wang Meiyan. 2002. "What Determine Hukou System Reform? A Case of Beijing." Working Paper Series 15, Chinese Academy of Social Sciences, Beijing.

Cai, Fang, and Wang Meiyan. 2011. "Labor Market Changes, Labor Disputes and Social Cohesion in China." Working Paper Series 307, Organisation for Economic Co-operation and Development, Paris.

Cai, Fang, Albert Park, and Yaohui Zhao. 2008. "The Chinese Labor Market in the Reform Era." In *China's Great Economic Transformation*, ed. Loren Brandt and Thomas G. Rawski, 167–214. New York: Cambridge University Press.

Chau, Nancy H., and Ravi Kanbur. 2001. "The Adoption of International Labor Standards Conventions: Who, When and Why?" In *Brookings Trade Forum: 2001*, ed. Nancy H. Chau, Ravi Kanbur,

Ann E. Harrison, and Peter Morici, 113–56. Washington, DC: Brookings Institution.

Chaudhuri, Shubham, and Gaurav Datt. 2009. *From Poor Areas to Poor People: China's Evolving Poverty Agenda, An Assessment of Poverty and Inequality in China.* Washington, DC: World Bank.

Chen, Martha, Chris Bonner, Mahendra Chetty, Lucia Fernandez, Karin Pape, Federico Parra, Arbind Singh, and Caroline Skinner. 2012. "Urban Informal Workers: Representative Voice and Economic Rights." Background paper for the WDR 2013.

Chioda, Laura. 2012. *Work and Family: Latin American and Caribbean Women in Search of a New Balance.* Washington, DC: World Bank.

Commission on Growth and Development. 2008. *The Growth Commission Report: Strategies for Sustained Growth and Inclusive Development.* Washington, DC: Commission on Growth and Development.

Consejo Nacional de Innovación. 2008. *Hacia una Estrategia Nacional de Innovación para la Competitividad.* Santiago: Consejo Nacional de Innovación.

Consia Consultants. 2007. *Second External Annual Independent Evaluation of the Rwanda Demobilization and Reintegration Program (RDRP).* Copenhagen: Consia Consultants.

Cunha, Flavio, James J. Heckman, and Susanne Schennach. 2010. "Estimating the Technology of Cognitive and Noncognitive Skill Formation." *Econometrica* 78 (3): 883–931.

Deshpande, Lalit K., Alakh N. Sharma, Anup K. Karan, and Sandip Sarkar. 2004. *Liberalisation and Labour: Labour Flexibility in Indian Manufacturing.* New Delhi: Manohar Publishers and Distributors.

Dinkelman, Taryn. 2011. "The Effects of Rural Electrification on Employment: New Evidence from South Africa." *American Economic Review* 101 (7): 3078–108.

Dudwick, Nora, and Radhika Srinivasan, with Jose Cueva and Dorsati Mandavi. Forthcoming. *Creating Jobs in Africa's Fragile States: Are Value Chains an Answer?* Directions in Development Series. Washington, DC: World Bank.

EFRA (European Union Agency for Fundamental Rights). 2011. *Fundamental Rights of Migrants in an Irregular Situation in the European Union.* Luxembourg: Publications Office of the European Union.

Elbadawi, Ibrahim, Linda Kaltani, and Raimundo Soto. 2009. *Aid, Real Exchange Rate Misalignment and Economic Performance in Sub-Saharan Africa.* Santiago: Universidad Católica de Chile.

Elliott, Kimberly A., and Richard B. Freeman. 2003. *Can Labor Standards Improve under Globalization?* Washington, DC: Peterson Institute, Institute for International Economics.

Engle, Patrice L., Maureen M. Black, Jere R. Behrman, Meena Cabral de Mello, Paul J. Gertler, Lydia Ka-

piriri, Reynaldo Martorell, Mary Eming Young, and the International Child Development Steering Group. 2007. "Strategies to Avoid the Loss of Developmental Potential in More Than 200 Million Children in the Developing World." *Lancet* 369: 229–42.

Fajnzylber, Pablo, William Maloney, and Gabriel V. Montes-Rojas. 2011. "Does Formality Improve Micro-Firm Performance? Evidence from the Brazilian SIMPLES Program." *Journal of Development Economics* 94: 262–76.

Fiess, Norbert, Marco Fugazza, and William Maloney. 2010. "Informal Self-Employment and Macroeconomic Fluctuations." *Journal of Development Economics* 91 (2): 211–26.

Fink, Carsten, Aaditya Mattoo, and Randeep Rathindran. 2003. "An Assessment of Telecommunications Reform in Developing Countries." *Information Economics and Policy* 15 (4): 443–66.

Foster, Vivien, and Cecilia Briceño-Garmendia, eds. 2010. *Africa's Infrastructure: A Time for Transformation.* Washington, DC: World Bank.

François, Joseph F., and Bernard Hoekman. 2010. "Services Trade and Policy." *Journal of Economic Literature* 48 (3): 642–92.

Frankel, Jeffrey. 2012. "The Natural Resource Curse: A Survey of Diagnoses and Some Prescriptions." Paper presented at the International Monetary Fund High-Level Seminar, "Commodity Price Volatility and Inclusive Growth in Low-Income Countries," Washington, DC, September 21.

Gibson, John, David McKenzie, and Halahingano Rohorua. 2008. "How Pro-Poor Is the Selection of Seasonal Migrant Workers from Tonga under New Zealand's Recognized Seasonal Employer Program." Policy Research Working Paper Series 4698, World Bank, Washington, DC.

Giles, John, Dewen Wang, and Albert Park. 2012. "Expanding Social Insurance Coverage in Urban China: Understanding the Evolutions of Policy and Participation." World Bank, Washington, DC. Processed.

Glewwe, Paul W. 2004. "An Overview of Economic Growth and Household Welfare in Vietnam 1990s." In *Economic Growth, Poverty and Household Welfare in Vietnam*, ed. Paul Glewwe, Nisha Agarwal, and David Dollar, 1–26. Washington, DC: World Bank.

Grantham-McGregor, Sally, Yin Bun Cheung, Santiago Cueto, Paul Glewwe, Linda Richter, Barbara Strupp, and the International Child Development Steering Group. 2007. "Development Potential in the First 5 Years for Children in Developing Countries." *Lancet* 369: 60–70.

Gove, Amber, and Peter Cvelich. 2010. *Early Reading: Igniting Education for All.* Research Triangle Park, NC: Research Triangle Institute.

Hafner-Burton, Emilie. 2009. *Forced to be Good: Why Trade Agreements Boost Human Rights.* Ithaca, NY: Cornell University Press.

Hallward-Driemeier, Mary, Gita Khun-Jush, and Lant Pritchett. 2010. "Deals Versus Rules: Policy Implementation Uncertainty and Why Firms Hate It." Working Paper Series 16001, National Bureau of Economic Research, Cambridge, MA.

Hanushek, Eric A., and Ludger Woessmann. 2008. "The Role of Cognitive Skills in Economic Development." *Journal of Economic Literature* 46 (3): 607–88.

Hasan, Rana, and Karl Jandoc. 2010. "The Distribution of Firm Size in India: What Can Survey Data Tell Us?" Working Paper Series 213, Asian Development Bank, Manila.

———. 2012. "Labor Regulations and the Firm Size Distribution in Indian Manufacturing." In *Reforms and Economic Transformation in India*, ed. Jagdish Bhagwati and Arvind Panagariya. New York: Oxford University Press.

Heckman, James J. 2008. "The Case for Investing in Disadvantaged Young Children." In *Big Ideas for Children: Investing in Our Nation's Future*, 49–58. Washington, DC: First Focus.

Heineck, Guido, and Silke Anger. 2010. "The Returns to Cognitive Abilities and Personality Traits in Germany." *Labour Economics* 17 (3): 535–46.

Hoekman, Bernard. 2011. "Aid for Trade: Why, What, and Where Are We?" In *Unfinished Business? The WTO's Doha Agenda*, ed. Will Martin and Aaditya Mattoo, 233–54. London: London Publishing Partnership.

Hoekman, Bernard, and Aaditya Mattoo. 2011. "Services Trade Liberalization and Regulatory Reform: Re-invigorating International Cooperation." Policy Research Working Paper Series 5517, World Bank, Washington, DC.

Hsieh, Chang-Tai, and Peter J. Klenow. 2009. "Misallocation and Manufacturing TFP in China and India." *Quarterly Journal of Economics* 124 (4): 1403–48.

———. 2011. "The Life Cycle of Plants in India and Mexico." Chicago Booth Research Paper Series 11-33, University of Chicago, IL.

IFC (International Finance Corporation). Forthcoming. *IFC Job Study: Assessing Private Sector Contributions to Job Creation.* Washington, DC: IFC.

ILO (International Labour Organization). 1996. C177 Home Work Convention (Entry into force: 22 April 2000). Adopted by the International Labour Conference at its 83rd session, ILO, Geneva, June 20.

———. 1998. Declaration on Fundamental Principles and Rights at Work. Adopted by the International Labour Conference at its 86th session, ILO, Geneva, June 18.

———. 2011. C189 Domestic Workers Convention. Adopted by the International Labour Conference at its 100th session, ILO, Geneva, June 16.

———. 2012. "What Are the Key Challenges Facing Labour Statistics Today?" ILO, Geneva. Processed.

IMF (International Monetary Fund). 2003. "Growth and Institutions." In *World Economic Outlook: April 2003; Growth and Institutions*, 95–128. Washington, DC: IMF.

Jayanthakumaran, Kankesu. 2003. "Benefit-Cost Appraisals of Export Processing Zones: A Survey of the Literature." *Development Policy Review* 21 (1): 51–65.

Kanbur, Ravi and Jan Svejnar. 2009. "Overview." In *Labor Markets and Economic Development*, ed. Ravi Kanbur and Jan Svejnar, 1–12. New York: Routledge.

Kaufmann, Daniel, Aart Kraay, and Massimo Mastruzzi. 2010. "The Worldwide Governance Indicators: Methodology and Analytical Issues." Policy Research Working Paper Series 5430, World Bank, Washington, DC.

Keefer, Philip. 2009. "Governance." In *The SAGE Handbook of Comparative Politics*, ed. Todd Landman and Neil Robinson, 439–62. London: SAGE Publications.

Kim, Aehyung, Ajay Tandon, and Asrat Hailu. 1997. "Health and Labor Productivity: The Economic Impact of Onchocercal Skin Disease." Policy Research Working Paper Series 1836, World Bank, Washington, DC.

King, Robert, and Ross Levine. 1993. "Finance and Growth: Schumpeter Might Be Right." *Quarterly Journal of Economics* 108 (3): 717–37.

Klapper, Leora, Luc Laeven, and Raghuram Rajan. 2006. "Entry Regulation as a Barrier to Entrepreneurship." *Journal of Financial Economics* 82 (3): 591–629.

Kraay, Aart. 2012. "How Large Is the Government Spending Multiplier? Evidence from World Bank Lending." *Quarterly Journal of Economics* 127 (2): 1–59.

Laborde, David, and Will Martin. 2011a. "Agricultural Market Access." In *Unfinished Business? The WTO's Doha Agenda*, ed. Will Martin and Aaditya Mattoo, 35–54. London: London Publishing Partnership.

———. 2011b. "Non-agricultural Market Access." In *Unfinished Business? The WTO's Doha Agenda*, ed. Will Martin and Aaditya Mattoo, 55–68. London: London Publishing Partnership.

Laeven, Luc, and Christopher Woodruff. 2007. "The Quality of the Legal System, Firm Ownership, and Firm Size." *Review of Economics and Statistics* 89 (4): 601–14.

Lastres, Helena M. M., Cassiolato Jose E., and Renato Campos. 2006. "Arranjos e Sistemas Produtivos e Inovativos Locais: Vantagens e Enfoque." In *Es-*

trategias para o Desenvolvimento: Um Enfoque sobre Arranjos Produtivos Locais do Norte, Nodeste e Centro-Oeste Brasileiro, ed. Helena M. M. Lastres and Jose E. Cassiolato, 13–28. Rio de Janeiro: Instituto de Economia da Universidade Federal do Rio de Janeiro.

Lee, Jean, and David Newhouse. 2012. "Cognitive Skills and Labor Market Outcomes." Background paper for the WDR 2013.

Levi, Margaret, Christopher Adolph, Aaron Erlich, Anne Greenleaf, Milli Lake, and Jennifer Noveck. 2012. "Aligning Rights and Interests: Why, When, and How to Uphold Labor Standards." Background paper for the WDR 2013.

Levine, Ross. 2005. "Finance and Growth: Theory and Evidence." In *Handbook of Economic Growth*, ed. Philippe Aghion and Steven Durlauf, 865–934. Amsterdam: Elsevier.

Lin, Justin Yifu. 2012. *Demystifying the Chinese Economy*. Cambridge, U.K.: Cambridge University Press.

Locke, Richard. Forthcoming. *Beyond Compliance: Promoting Labor Justice in a Global Economy*. New York: Cambridge University Press.

Locke, Richard, Matthew Amengual, and Ashkay Mangla. 2009. "Virtue out of Necessity? Compliance, Commitment and the Improvement of Labor Conditions in Global Supply Chains." *Politics & Society* 37 (3): 319–51.

Locke, Richard, Fei Quin, and Alberto Brause. 2007. "Does Monitoring Improve Labor Standards? Lessons from Nike." *Industrial and Labor Relations Review* 61 (1): 3–31.

Maranhao Costa, Patricia Trindade. 2009. *Fighting Forced Labour: The Example of Brazil*. Geneva: International Labour Organization.

McMillan, Margaret S., and Dani Rodrik. 2011. "Globalization, Structural Change and Productivity Growth." Working Paper Series 17143, National Bureau of Economic Research, Cambridge, MA.

MDRP (Multi-Country Demobilization and Reintegration Program). 2008. *The Rwanda Demobilization and Reintegration Program: Reflections on the Reintegration of Ex-Combatants*. Washington, DC: MDRP.

———. 2010. *Final Report Overview of Program Achievements*. Washington, DC: MDRP.

Mehreteab, Amanuel. 2005. *Rwanda Demobilization and Reintegration Program: Tracer Study*. Kigali: Rwanda Demobilization and Reintegration Commission.

Montenegro, Claudio E. and Harry Anthony Patrinos. 2012. "Returns to Schooling around the World." Background paper for the WDR 2013.

Mosley, Layna. 2011. *Labor Rights and Multinational Production*. New York: Cambridge University Press.

Newitt, Kirsten. 2012. "Private Sector Voluntary Initiatives on Labour Standards." Background paper for the WDR 2013.

North, Douglass C. 1981. *Structure and Change in Economic History*. New York: W. W. Norton.

———. 1990. *Institutions, Institutional Change and Economic Performance*. Cambridge, U.K.: Cambridge University Press.

O'Connor, Thomas, Michael Rutter, Celia Beckett, Lisa Keaveney, Jana Kreppner, and the English and Romanian Adoptees Study Team. 2000. "The Effects of Global Severe Privation on Cognitive Competence: Extension and Longitudinal Follow-up." *Child Development* 71 (2): 376–90.

OECD (Organisation for Economic Co-operation and Development). 2009. *OECD Reviews of Labour Market and Social Policies: Slovenia*. Paris: OECD.

———. 2010. *Off to a Good Start? Jobs for Youth*. Paris: OECD.

———. 2011. *OECD Economic Surveys: Slovenia*. Paris: OECD.

OECD and ILO (International Labour Organization). 2011. *G20 Country Policy Briefs: Brazil— Share of Formal Employment Continues to Grow*. Paris: OECD and ILO.

Pagés, Carmen, ed. 2010. *The Age of Productivity: Transforming Economies from the Bottom Up*. New York: Palgrave Macmillan.

Panagariya, Arvind. 2008. *India: The Emerging Giant*. New York: Oxford University Press.

Park, Jaegil, Daejong Kim, Yongseok Ko, Eunnan Kim, Keunhyun Park, and Keuntae Kim. 2011. *Urbanization and Urban Policies in Korea*. Korea Research Institute for Human Settlements.

Polaski, Sandra. 2006. "Combining Global and Local Forces: The Case of Labor Rights in Cambodia." *World Development* 34 (5): 919–32.

Pritchett, Lant. 2006. *Let Their People Come: Breaking the Gridlock on Global Labor Mobility*. Washington, DC: Center for Global Development.

Psacharopoulos, George, and Harry Patrinos. 2004. "Returns to Investment in Education: A Further Update." *Education Economics* 12 (2): 111–34.

Purcell, Julius. 2010. *Individual Disputes at the Workplace: Alternative Disputes Resolution*. Dublin: European Foundation for the Improvement of Living and Working Conditions.

Rama, Martín. 2009. "Making Difficult Choices: Vietnam in Transition." Working Paper Series 40, Growth and Development Commission, World Bank, Washington, DC.

Ramachandran, Vijaya, Alan Gelb, and Manju Kedia Shah. 2009. *Africa's Private Sector: What's Wrong with the Business Environment and What to Do About It*. Washington, DC: Center for Global Development.

Randriamaro, Zo. 2007. *Gender and Trade: Overview Report (2006).* Brighton, U.K.: BRIDGE.

Ravallion, Martin, and Dominique van de Walle. 2008. *Land in Transition: Reform and Poverty in Rural Vietnam.* Washington, DC: World Bank.

Robertson, Raymond, Drusilla Brown, Gaëlle La Borgne Pierre, and Maria Laura Sanchez-Puerta, eds. 2009. *Globalization, Wages, and the Quality of Jobs: Five Country Studies.* Washington, DC: World Bank.

Rodrik, Dani. 2000. "Institutions for High-Quality Growth: What They Are and How to Acquire Them." *Studies in Comparative International Development* 35 (3): 3–31.

———. 2008. "The Real Exchange Rate and Economic Growth." *Brookings Papers on Economic Activity* 39 (2): 365–439.

Rodrik, Dani, Arvind Subramanian, and Francesco Trebbi. 2004. "Institutions Rule: the Primacy of Institutions over Geography and Integration in Economic Development." *Journal of Economic Growth* 9 (2): 131–65.

Roy, Martin. 2008. "Out of Stock or Just in Time? Doha and the Liberalization of Distribution Services." In *Opening Markets for Trade in Services: Countries and Sectors in Bilateral and WTO Negotiations,* ed. Juan Marchetti and Martin Roy, 224–63. Geneva: World Trade Organization; New York: Cambridge University Press.

Rwanda Demobilization and Reintegration Commission. 2012. *Tracer: Community Dynamics and Payment Verification Study.* Kigali: Rwanda Demobilization and Reintegration Commission.

Schrank, Andrew. 2009. "Professionalization and Probity in a Patrimonial State: Labor Inspectors in the Dominican Republic." *Latin America Politics and Society* 51 (2): 91–114.

Sinnott, Emily, John Nash, and Augusto de la Torre. 2010. *Natural Resources in Latin America and the Caribbean. Beyond Booms and Busts?* Washington, DC: World Bank.

Solimano, Andres. 2008. *The International Mobility of Talent: Types, Causes and Development Impact.* New York: Oxford University Press.

Stavrou, Aki, Rasmus Jorgensen, and Jennifer O'Riordan. 2007. *Beneficiary Impact Assessment and Tracer Study.* Taastrup, Denmark: Nordic Consulting Group.

Styczynska, Izabela. 2012. *Provision of Long Term Care for the Elderly in Poland in Comparison to Other European Countries.* Prague: Policy Association for an Open Society.

Tobias, Jutta, and Karol Boudreaux. 2011. "Entrepreneurship and Conflict Reduction in the Post-Genocide Rwanda Coffee Industry." *Journal of Small Business and Entrepreneurship* 24 (2): 217–42.

UNCTAD (United Nations Conference on Trade and Development). 2011. *World Investment Report 2011: Non-Equity Modes of International Production and Development.* New York and Geneva: UNCTAD.

United Nations Development Group. 2010. *Thematic Paper on MDG1: Eradicate Extreme Poverty and Hunger, Review of Progress.* New York: United Nations.

Walker, Susan, Theodore Wachs, Julie Meeks Gardner, Betsy Lozoff, Gail Wassermann, Ernesto Pollitt, Julie Carter, and the International Child Development Steering Group. 2007. "Child Development: Risk Factors for Adverse Outcomes in Developing Countries." *Lancet* 369: 145–57.

Wang, Dewen, Jin Song, and Philip O'Keefe. 2012. "Understanding the Hukou System through Quantifying Hukou Thresholds: Methodology and Empirical Findings." Background paper for the WDR 2013.

Winters, Alan, Terrie Walmsley, Zhen Kun Wang, and Roman Grynberg. 2002. "Negotiating the Liberalization of the Temporary Movement of Natural Persons." University of Sussex Discussion Paper 87, Sussex, U.K.

World Bank. 1997. *World Development Report 1997: The State in a Changing World.* New York: Oxford University Press.

———. 2004a. *Sri Lanka: Reshaping Economic Geography; Connecting People to Prosperity.* Washington, DC: World Bank.

———. 2004b. *World Development Report 2005: A Better Investment Climate for Everyone.* New York: Oxford University Press.

———. 2005. *Global Economic Prospects: Economic Implications of Remittances and Migration.* Washington, DC: World Bank.

———. 2006. *Chile Development Policy Review.* Washington, DC: World Bank.

———. 2007. *Rwanda: Toward Sustained Growth and Competitiveness, Vol. I, Synthesis and Priority Measures.* Washington, DC: World Bank.

———. 2008. *Chile: Toward a Cohesive and Well Governed National Innovation System.* Washington, DC: World Bank.

———. 2009a. *From Privilege to Competition: Unlocking Private-Led Growth in the Middle East and North Africa.* Washington, DC: World Bank.

———. 2009b. *Vietnam Development Report 2009: Capital Matters.* Washington, DC: World Bank.

———. 2009c. *World Development Report: Reshaping Economic Geography.* Washington, DC: World Bank.

———. 2010a. *Country Assistance Strategy for the Kingdom of Tonga.* Washington, DC: World Bank.

———. 2010b. *MDRP (Multi-Country Demobilization and Reintegration Program) Report.* Washington, DC: World Bank.

———. 2011a. *Doing Business 2012: Doing Business in a More Transparent World.* Washington, DC: World Bank.

———. 2011b. *Fueling Growth and Competitiveness in Poland Through Employment, Skills, Innovation, Technical Report.* Washington, DC: World Bank.

———. 2011c. *More and Better Jobs in South Asia.* Washington, DC: World Bank.

———. 2011d. *Rwanda Economic Update: Resilience in the Face of Economic Adversity.* Washington, DC: World Bank.

———. 2011e. *Vietnam Development Report 2012: Market Economy for a Middle-Income Country.* Washington, DC: World Bank.

———. 2011f. *World Development Indicators 2011.* Washington, DC: World Bank.

———. 2011g. *World Development Report 2012: Gender Equality and Development.* Washington, DC: World Bank.

———. 2011h. *World Development Report 2011: Conflict, Security, and Development.* Washington, DC: World Bank.

———. 2011i. "Capabilities, Opportunities, and Participation: Gender Equality and Development in the Middle East and North Africa Region." Companion report to the World Development Report 2012.

———. 2012a. *Afghanistan in Transition: Looking Beyond 2014.* Washington, DC: World Bank.

———. 2012b. *Job Trends.* Washington, DC: World Bank.

———. 2012c. *Labor Practices in Lao PDR.* Washington, DC: World Bank.

———. 2012d. "Rwanda Ninth Poverty Reduction Support Financing." Program Information Document, World Bank, Washington, DC.

———. 2012e. *The World Bank: New Directions in Justice Reform.* Washington, DC: World Bank.

———. 2012f. *World Development Indicators 2012.* Washington, DC: World Bank.

Wrigley, Neil, and Michelle Lowe. 2010. *The Globalization of Trade in Retail Services.* Paris: Organisation for Economic Co-operation and Development.

Young, Mary Eming, and Linda Richardson. 2007. *Early Child Development: From Measurement to Action.* Washington, DC: World Bank.

Yusuf, Shahid, and Kaoru Nabeshima. 2006. *Post-Industrial East Asian Cities: Innovation for Growth.* Palo Alto, CA: Stanford University Press.

работа
swyxli
وظائف
Pekerjaan
TRABAHO
Nitsumo
küdawün
Darbo vietos
kop 일
starf
ori
就业
Emplois
Työ
mahi asa
Tembiapo
Tiro
Traballo
Θέσεις εργασίας
Werk
काज
Jobs
ise
Зайнятість
naqawi Emprego
Tsi Nikaio'tenhsero:ten's
வேலை
Basa
আচাঁশ
Empregos
Posao
praca
काम
Banen
Muncă
Imirimo
işं
仕事
Unsebenzi
việc làm
arbeten
Занятость
KAZI punë
thi Empleo
Postanna
Arbeitsplätze
Llamkay
ian
a lavur
luoi chokol

Glossary

JOBS

Jobs: While precise definitions vary, jobs are labor activities that generate income, monetary or in kind, without violating fundamental rights and principles at work. Jobs can take the form of wage employment, self-employment, and farming. They can be formal or informal.

Good jobs for development: These are jobs that contribute the most to societal goals. The development payoff of a job is the sum of the value it has to the worker and its spillovers (if any) on others. The individual value is the first-order measure of the development payoff, but spillovers can be substantial.

Jobs lens: Strategies, policies, and programs adopt a jobs lens if they take into account the development payoffs from jobs. The jobs lens involves aims at realizing the untapped development payoffs by addressing the constraints that prevent the private sector from creating more good jobs for development.

SKILLS

Cognitive skills: They include verbal ability, working memory, numeracy, and problem-solving abilities. They are the foundation for the acquisition and building of other skills throughout life.

Social skills: They facilitate interaction and communication with others. They are based on personality traits that underlie behaviors such as teamwork, reliability, discipline, or work effort.

Technical skills: They enable the performance of specific tasks. They take the form of knowledge that is specific to a particular occupation or group of occupations.

Entrepreneurship: It is the combination of innovative capacity to put new ideas into effect with managerial capacity to increase a firm's efficiency within the limits of known technology.

TRANSFORMATIONS

Living standards: They encompass the material and subjective aspects of well-being. Jobs contribute to living standards through earnings opportunities that lift people out of poverty, make them less vulnerable, motivate them, and contribute to their broader happiness and satisfaction with life.

Bibliographical note

This Report draws on a wide range of background papers commissioned by the team, as well as on contributions by numerous colleagues inside and outside of the World Bank. The team gratefully acknowledges the papers, notes, presentations, and data analyses by:

Ana Abras, Daniel Adler, Christopher Adolph, Cristian Aedo, Alpasan Akay, Yilmaz Akyuz, Rita Almeida, Miriam Altman, Uma Rani Amara, Colin Andrews, Steffen Angenendt, Omar Arias, Hassen Arouri, Javier Arias-Vasquez, Gabriela Armenta, Ragui Assaad, João Pedro Azevedo, Elisabeth Baehr, Aminata Bakouan, Sajitha Bashir, Daniel Berliner, Janine Berg, M. Inés Berniell, Haroon Bhorat, Constanza Biavaschi, Ingunn Bjørkhaug, David Blanchflower, Erik Bloom, Nicholas Bloom, Chris Bonner, Alessio Brown, Drusilla Brown, Tilman Brueck, Martha Chen, Mahendra Chetty, Yoonyoung Cho, Hayat Chowdhury, Sarah Cook, Katia Covarrubias, Hai-Anh Dang, Maitreyi Bordia Das, Benjamin Davis, Arjan de Haan, Joost de Laat, Rajeev Dehejia, Peter Dewees, Stefania Di Giuseppe, Rafael Díez de Medina, Susanne Dorasil, Nora Dudwick, Gilles Duranton, Werner Eichhorst, Aaron Erlich, Jonna Estudillo, Christine Evans-Klock, Paolo Falco, Lucia Fernandez, Gary Fields, Sandra Fredman, Richard Freeman, Caroline Freund, Leonardo Garrido, John Giles, T. H. Gindling, Corrado Giulietti, Anne Greenleaf, Michael Grimm, Lorenzo Guarcello, John Haltiwanger, Anne Hatløy, Ricardo Hausmann, Yuki Higuchi, Margo Hoftijzer, Maddalena Honorati, Shoghik Hovhannisyan, Alejandro Hoyos, Jikun Huang, Steffen Hummelsheim, Hans Hwang, Gabriela Inchauste, Beata Javorcik, Johannes Jütting, Tewodros Kebede, Jennifer Keller, Michael Kendzia, Niny Khor, Talip Kilic, Austin Kilroy, Christian Kingombe, Johannes Koettl, Irina Kovrova, Adea Kryeziu, David Kucera, Nandika Kumanayake, Milli Lake, Peter Lanjouw, Donald Larson, Jean Lee, Hartmut Lehman, Margaret Levi, Philip Levy, Richard Locke, Javier Luque, Scott Lyon, William Maloney, Ghazala Mansuri, David Margolis, Pedro Martins, Tomoya Matsumoto, Dimitris Mavridis, Catriona McLeod, Margaret McMillan, Johan Mistiaen, Martin Moreno, Marc-Andreas Muendler, Alexander Muravyev, Yoo-Jeung Nam, Ambar Narayan, David Newhouse, Kirsten Newitt, Andrew Norton, Jennifer Noveck, Antonio Nucifora, Philip O'Keefe, Sergio Olivieri, Remco Oostendorp, Ana Maria Oviedo, Caglar Özden, Pierella Paci, Karin Pape, Federico Parra, Harry Anthony Patrinos, Patti Petesch, Janneke Pieters, Uma Rani, Marco Ranzani, Bob Rijkers, David Robalino, Raymond Robertson, Nuría Rodríguez-Planas, Paul Romer, Furio Camillo Rosati, Friederike Rother, Scott Rozelle, Jaime Saavedra Chanduvi, Klas Sander, Mauricio Sarrias, Naotaka Sawada, Ricarda Schmidl, Helmar Schneider, Nadia Selim, Binayak Sen, Slesh Shrestha, Arbind Singh, Caroline Skinner, Jin Song, Tetsushi Sonobe, Walter Sosa, Dirk Willem te Velde, Sailesh Tiwari, Ihnsan Tunali, Erol Tymaz, Zia Uddin, Inigo Verduzco, Marco Vivarelli, Jacqueline Wahba, Dewen Wang, Michael Weber, Christian Welzel, Frank-Borge Wietzke, Hernan Winkler, Firman Witoelar, Monica Yanez-Pagans, Huafeng Zhang, and Klaus Zimmerman.

Many people inside and outside of the World Bank gave comments to the team and supported the preparation of the Report in various ways:

Paloma Acevedo, Cristian Aedo, Junaid Kamal Ahmad, Ahmad Ahsan, Rita Almeida, Tilman Altenburg, Colin Andrews, Omar Arias, Gabriela Armenta, Erhan Artuc, Orazio

Attanasio, Ajita Berar Awad, João Pedro Azevedo, Peter Bakvis, Elena Bardasi, Nicholas Barr, Andrew Beath, Deepak Bhattasali, Benu Bidani, Erik Bloom, Richard Blundell, Carlos Braga, Milan Brahmbhatt, Hana Brixi, Miriam Bruhn, Sharan Burrows, Wei Ca, Sandrine Cazes, Barry Chiswick, Luc Christiansen, Michael Cichon, Tito Cordella, Paulo Correa, Wendy Cunningham, Karen Curtis, Mahesh Dahal, Andrea Mario Dall'Olio, Maitreyi Das, Joost de Laat, Augusto de la Torre, Gabriel Demombynes, Stefan Dercon, Shanta Devarajan, Peter Dewees, Charles di Leva, Carolina Diaz-Bonilla, Nancy Donaldson, Nora Dudwick, Olivier Dupriez, Friedel Eggelmeyer, Philippe Egger, Marcelo Jorge Fabre, Gabriel Alejandro Faccini Palma, Marcel Fafchamps, Marianne Fay, Juan Feng, Colin Fenwick, Manuela Ferro, Deon Filmer, Georg Fischer, Ciprian Fisiy, Ariel Fiszbein, Roberto Foa, Louise Fox, Caroline Freund, Bernard Funck, Leonardo Garrido, Roberta Gatti, Varun Gauri, Steve Gibbons, Indermit Gill, Delfin Go, Pablo Gottret, Timo Graf von Koenigsmarck, Duncan Green, Mary Hallward-Driemeier, Mark Hanush, Bernard Harborne, Niels Harild, Rana Hasan, Susan Hayter, James Heckman, Rasmus Heltberg, Bernard Hoekman, Bert Hofman, Robin Horn, James Howard, Chang-Tai Hsieh, Elisabeth Huybens, Herwig Immervoll, Gabriela Inchauste, Selina Jackson, Steen Lau Jorgensen, Roy Katayamà, Philip Keefer, William James Kemp, Austin Kilroy, Elizabeth King, Leora Klapper, Judith Klemmer, Jeni Klugman, Kalpana Kochhar, Markus Kostner, Aphichoke Kotikula, Rachel Kranton, Arvo Kuddo, Somik Lall, Esperanza Lasagabaster, Daniel Lederman, Philippe Leite, Jeffrey Lewis, Eduardo Ley, Michael Lipton, Gladys López-Acevedo, Malte Luebker, Amy Luinstra, Mattias Lundberg, Xubei Luo, Nora Lustig, Larissa Luy, Ghazala Mansuri, Alexandre Marc, Andrew Mason, Elizabeth Mata Lorenzo, Aaditya Mattoo, Piotr Mazurkiewicz, Siobhan McInerney-Lankford, David McKenzie, Gerard McLinden, Julian Messina, Roland Michelitsch, Pradeep Mitra, Layna Mosley, Rose Mungai, Ana Maria Muñoz Boudet, Reema Nanavaty, Urvashi Narain, Ambar Narayan, Reema Nayar, David Newhouse, Philip O'Keefe, Anna Olefir, Israel Osorio-Rodarte, Caglar Özden, Pierella Paci, Howard Pack, Truman Packard, Carmen Pagés, Robert Palacios, Montserrat Pallares-Millares, Pia Peeters, Nicola Pontara, Aleksandra Posarac, Peter Poschen, Patrick Premand, Menachem Prywes, Stephen Pursey, Rita Ramalho, Martin Ravallion, Michelle Rebosio, Ritva Reinikka, Jose Guilherme Reis, Ana Revenga, Carolyn Reynolds, Francesca Riccardone, Jamele Rigolini, Bob Rijkers, David Robalino, Nigel Roberts, Halsey Rogers, Mark Rosenzweig, Friederike Rother, Robert Francis Rowe, Jan Rutkowski, Jaime Saavedra Chanduvi, Frank Sader, Juan Sebastián Saez, Jamil Salmi, Carolina Sánchez Paramo, Maria Laura Sanchez Puerta, Justin Sanderfur, Prem Sangraula, Indhira Santos, Sigrid Schenk-Dornbusch, Grit Schmalisch, Anita Schwarz, Sudhir Shetty, Saurabh Shome, Sandor Sipos, Radhika Srinivasan, Stavros Stavrou, Henriette Strothmann, Manami Suga, Naotaka Sugawara, Victor Sulla, Jee-Peng Tan, Afia Tasneem, Ehab Tawfik, Graham Teskey, Manuela Tomei, Carrie Turk, Alexandria Valerio, Bernice Van Bronkhurst, Aleem Walji, David Warren, Michael Weber, Deborah Welzel, Jill Wilkins, Alys Willman, Doris Witteler-Stiepelmann, Michael Woolcock, Colin Xu, Xiao Ye, Nobuo Yoshida, and Anders Zeijlon.

The World Development Report 2013 team benefited from close collaboration with the team preparing the International Finance Corporation's Jobs Study: "Assessing Private Sector Contributions to Job Creation," led by Roland Michelitsch. The team also benefited from the interaction with the Jobs Knowledge Platform, which was launched during the preparation of the report under the guidance of Mary Hallward-Driemeier, Gladys López-Acevedo, David Robalino, and Claudia Sepulveda.

The team also engaged closely with the Implementation Task Force for the Report convened by Mahmoud Mohieldin, led by Tamar Manuelyan Atinc and Arup Banerji, and including Omar Arias, Najy Benhassine, Mary Hallward-Driemeier, Roland Michelitsch, Pierella Paci, and Idah Pswarayi-Riddihough.

Background papers and notes

Abras, Ana, Alejandro Hoyos, Ambar Narayan, and Sailesh Tiwari. 2012. "Inequality of Opportunities in the Labor Market: Evidence from Life in Transition Surveys in Europe and Central Asia."

Adler, Daniel, and Hans Hwang. 2012. "From Law on the Books to Law in Action: A Note on the Role of Regulation in the Production of Good Jobs in Cambodia's Garment Sector."

Almeida, Rita, David Margolis, David Robalino, and Michael Weber. 2012. "Facilitating Labor Market Transitions and Managing Risks."

Aedo, Cristian, Jesko Hentschel, Javier Luque, and Martin Moreno. 2012. "Skills Around the World: Structure and Recent Dynamics."

Andrews, Colin, and Adea Kryeziu. 2012. "Public Works and the Jobs Agenda: Pathways for Social Cohesion."

Arias, Omar, and Walter Sosa. 2012. "Do Jobs Cause Trust? Results from Pseudo-Panel Analysis of Euro and Latino Barometer Surveys."

Arias-Vasquez, Javier, Jean N. Lee, and David Newhouse. 2012. "The Role of Sectoral Growth Patterns in Labor Market Development."

Azevedo, João Pedro, Gabriela Inchauste, Sergio Olivieri, Jaime Saavedra Chanduvi, and Hernan Winkler. 2012. "Is Labor Income Responsible for Poverty Reduction? A Decomposition Approach."

Bashir, Sajitha, T. H. Gindling, and Ana Maria Oviedo. 2012. "Better Jobs in Central America: The Role of Human Capital."

Betcherman, Gordon. 2012. "Labor Market Institutions: A Review of the Literature."

Bhorat, Haroon. 2012. "Temporary Employment Services in South Africa."

Biavaschi, Costanza, Werner Eichhorst, Corrado Giulietti, Michael J. Kendzia, Alexander Muravyev, Janneke Pieters, Nuría Rodríguez-Planas, Ricarda Schmidl, and Klaus F. Zimmermann. 2012. "Youth Unemployment and Vocational Training."

Bjørkhaug, Ingunn, Anne Hatløy, Tewodros Kebede, and Huafeng Zhang. 2012. "Perception of Good Jobs: Colombia."

Chen, Martha, Chris Bonner, Mahendra Chetty, Lucia Fernandez, Karin Pape, Federico Parra, Arbind Singh, and Caroline Skinner. 2012. "Urban Informal Workers: Representative Voice and Economic Rights."

Cho, Yoonyoung, and Maddalena Honorati. 2012. "A Meta-Analysis of Entrepreneurship Programs In Developing Countries."

Covarrubias, Katia, Benjamin Davis, Aminata Bakouan, and Stefania Di Giuseppe. 2012. "Household Income Generation Strategies."

Das, Maitreyi Bordia. 2012. "Stubborn Inequalities, Subtle Processes: Exclusion and Discrimination in the Labor Market."

Dehejia, Rajeev, Drusilla Brown, and Raymond Robertson. 2012. "Life Satisfaction, Mental Well-Being and Workplace Characteristics: Evidence from Vietnam, Jordan, and Haiti."

Dudwick, Nora. 2012. "The Relationship Between Jobs and Social Cohesion: Some Examples from Ethnography."

Duranton, Gilles. 2012. "Agglomeration and Jobs in Developing Countries."

Estudillo, Jonna P., Tomoya Matsumoto, Hayat Chowdhury, Zia Uddin, Nandika Kumanayake, and Keijiro Otsuka. 2012. "Labor Markets, Occupational Choice, and Rural Poverty in Selected Countries in Asia and Sub-Saharan Africa."

Falco, Paolo, William Maloney, Bob Rijkers, and Mauricio Sarrias. 2012. "Subjective Well-Being, Informality, and Preference Heterogeneity in Africa."

Fredman, Sandra. 2012. "Anti-Discrimination Laws and Work in the Developing World: A Thematic Overview."

Giles, John, Dimitris Mavridis, and Firman Witoelar. 2012. "Subjective Well-Being, Social Cohesion, and Labor Market Outcomes in Indonesia."

Gindling, T. H., and David Newhouse. 2012. "Self-Employment in the Developing World."

Hatløy, Anne, Tewodros Kebede, Huafeng Zhang, and Ingunn Bjørkhaug. 2012. "Perception of Good Jobs: Sierra Leone."

Hovhannisyan, Shoghik. 2012. "Labor Market and Growth Implications of Emigration: Cross-Country Evidence."

Inchauste, Gabriela. 2012. "Jobs and Transitions Out of Poverty: A Literature Review."

Inchauste, Gabriela, Sergio Olivieri, Jaime Saavedra Chanduvi, and Hernan Winkler. 2012. "Decomposing Recent Declines in Poverty: Evidence from Bangladesh, Peru, and Thailand."

Javorcik, Beata Smarzynska. 2012. "Does FDI Bring Good Jobs to Host Countries?"

Kebede, Tewodros, Anne Hatløy, Huafeng Zhang, and Ingunn Bjørkhaug. 2012. "Perception of Good Jobs: Egypt."

Kilroy, Austin. 2012. "Jobs to Social Cohesion: Via Interests, Attitudes, and Identities."

Kingombe, Christian, and Dirk Willem te Velde. 2012. "Structural Transformation and Employment Creation: The Role of Growth Facilitation Policies in Sub-Saharan Africa."

Kovrova, Irina, Scott Lyon, and Furio Camillo Rosati. 2012. "NEET Youth Dynamics in Indonesia and Brazil: A Cohort Analysis."

Larson, Donald, Keijiro Otsuka, Tomoya Matsumoto, and Talip Kilic. 2012. "Can Africa's Agriculture Depend on Smallholder Farmers?"

Lee, Jean N., and David Newhouse. 2012. "Cognitive Skills and Labor Market Outcomes."

Levi, Margaret, Christopher Adolph, Aaron Erlich, Anne Greenleaf, Milli Lake, and Jennifer Noveck. 2012. "Aligning Rights and Interests: Why, When, and How to Uphold Labor Standards."

Levy, Philip. 2012. "Potential for International Rivalry as Governments Pursue Jobs."

Lyon, Scott, Furio Camillo Rosati, and Lorenzo Guarcello. 2012. "At the Margins: Young People Neither in Education nor in Employment."

Mansuri, Ghazala, Slesh Shrestha, Hernan Winkler, and Monica Yanez-Pagans. 2012a. "A Plot of My Own: Land Titling and Economic Mobility in Rural Uganda."

———. 2012b. "Health or Wealth? Income Earner Death and Economic Mobility in Rural Pakistan."

Martins, Pedro. 2012. "Growth, Employment and Poverty in Africa: Tales of Lions and Cheetahs."

McMillan, Margaret S., and Inigo Verduzco. 2012. "Measuring the Impact of Structural Change on Labor's Share of Income."

Montenegro, Claudio E., and Harry Anthony Patrinos. 2012. "Returns to Schooling around the World."

Newitt, Kirsten. 2012. "Private Sector Voluntary Initiatives on Labour Standards."

Norton, Andrew, and Arjan de Haan. 2012. "Social Cohesion: Theoretical Debates and Practical Applications with Respect to Jobs."

Oostendorp, Remco. 2012. "The Occupational Wages around the World (OWW) Database: Update for 1983–2008."

Petesch, Patti. 2012. "The Exponential Clash of Conflict, Good Jobs, and Changing Gender Norms in Four Economies."

Ranzani, Marco, and Furio Camillo Rosati. 2012. "The NEET Trap: A Dynamic Analysis for Mexico."

Rijkers, Bob, Hassan Arouri, Caroline Freund, and Antonio Nucifora. 2012. "Which Firms Create Jobs in Tunisia?"

Rozelle, Scott, and Jikun Huang. 2012. "China's Labor Transition and the Future of China's Rural Wages and Employment."

Sander, Klas, and Peter A. Dewees. 2012. "Sustainable Management of Trees, Reduction in Forest Degradation, and Job Creation for the Poor."

Sawada, Naotaka. 2012. "Providing Business Services for Rural Income Generations: Using the Rural Investment Climate Survey Data."

Selim, Nadia. 2012. "Innovation for Job Creation."

Sonobe, Tetsushi, Yuki Higuchi, and Keijiro Otsuka. 2012. "Productivity Growth and Job Creation in the Development Process of Industrial Clusters."

Wang, Dewen, Jin Song, and Philip O'Keefe. 2012. "Understanding the Hukou System through Quantifying Hukou Thresholds: Methodology and Empirical Findings."

Welzel, Christian. 2012. "The Contribution of 'Good' Jobs to Development and Cohesion: The Human Empowerment Perspective."

Wietzke, Frank-Borge, and Catriona McLeod. 2012. "Jobs, Well-Being, and Social Cohesion: Evidence from Value and Perception Surveys."

Zhang, Huafeng, Ingunn Bjørkhaug, Anne Hatløy, and Tewodros Kebede. 2012. "Perception of Good Jobs: China."

Selected indicators

TABLE 1 *Labor force*

	Population (millions) Total			Working age population (%) Total			Participation rate (%) Total			Unemployment rate (%) Total		
	1995	2005	2010	1995	2005	2010	1995	2005	2010	1995	2005	2010
Afghanistan	22.5	29.9	34.4		48.7			65.2			8.5	
Albania	3.1	3.1	3.2	61.7	69.1		68.1	57.8			13.5	13.8
Algeria	28.3	32.9	35.5							27.9	15.3	11.4
Angola	12.1	16.5	19.1									
Argentina	34.8	38.6	40.5	61.0	64.7	65.6	63.5	69.0	67.8	18.8	10.6	8.6
Armenia	3.2	3.1	3.1		66.6			54.3		36.4	28.4	28.6
Australia	18.1	20.4	22.3	66.6	67.3	67.6	74.1	75.4	76.5	8.5	5.0	5.2
Austria	8.0	8.2	8.4	67.1	67.9	67.5	71.5	72.4	75.1	3.7	5.2	4.4
Azerbaijan	7.7	8.4	9.0	63.2			48.0				8.1	6.0
Bangladesh	117.5	140.6	148.7		59.0	60.5			60.0	2.5	4.3	5.0
Barbados	0.3	0.3	0.3	83.9			73.2			19.7	9.1	8.1
Belarus	10.2	9.8	9.5		70.0			70.3				
Belgium	10.1	10.5	10.9	66.2	65.6	65.9	62.1	66.7	67.7	9.3	8.4	8.3
Belize	0.2	0.3	0.3	52.8			58.1				3.1	4.0
Benin	5.7	7.6	8.8		50.4			78.6				
Bhutan	0.5	0.7	0.7		61.7			68.8		12.5	11.0	8.2
Bolivia	7.5	9.1	9.9	55.7	57.2	59.6	71.4	71.8	74.7	3.6	5.4	
Bosnia and Herzegovina	3.3	3.8	3.8		80.9			58.5			31.8	27.2
Botswana	1.6	1.9	2.0			59.9			68.5	21.5	17.6	
Brazil	161.8	186.0	194.9	62.1	66.6	67.9	72.1	74.0	73.9	6.0	9.3	8.3
Bulgaria	8.4	7.7	7.5	67.0	69.0	68.9	68.7	62.1	66.5	15.7	10.1	10.2
Burkina Faso	10.7	14.2	16.5	48.3	50.5		86.8	86.7		2.6	2.7	
Burundi	6.1	7.3	8.4									
Cambodia	11.2	13.4	14.1	56.3	62.1	63.4	77.0	84.6	84.8			1.7
Cameroon	13.9	17.6	19.6	51.4	89.7		69.4	67.5		8.1	4.4	
Canada	29.4	32.3	34.1	67.6	69.2	69.4	74.7	77.7	77.8	9.5	6.7	8.0
Central African Republic	3.3	4.0	4.4		51.3			75.4				
Chad	7.0	9.8	11.2		49.0					0.7		
Chile	14.4	16.3	17.1	63.8	67.1	68.7	59.1	59.3	64.8	4.7	8.0	8.1
China	1211.2	1307.6	1340.9	66.7	71.4	74.5		71.7	71.0	2.9	2.7	2.9
Colombia	36.5	43.0	46.3	53.9	62.8	64.5	56.0	69.3	71.9	8.7	11.3	11.6
Congo, Dem. Rep.	44.1	57.4	66.0		50.1			70.9				
Congo, Rep.	2.7	3.5	4.0		57.3			66.0				
Costa Rica	3.5	4.3	4.7	60.5	65.9	68.5	61.7	65.5	65.3	5.2	6.6	7.8
Côte d'Ivoire	14.7	18.0	19.7									
Croatia	4.7	4.4	4.4		66.9	67.2		63.3	61.5	10.0	12.6	11.8
Cuba	10.9	11.3	11.3							8.3	1.9	1.6
Czech Republic	10.3	10.2	10.5	68.0	71.0	70.6		70.4	70.2	4.0	7.9	7.3
Denmark	5.2	5.4	5.5	67.4	66.2	65.6	72.3	79.8	79.4	7.0	4.8	7.5
Dominican Republic	7.9	9.3	9.9	58.5	61.9	63.5	63.1	58.2	59.4	15.8	18.0	14.2
Ecuador	11.4	13.4	14.5	58.0	61.1	62.5	72.1	73.4	66.8	6.9	7.7	6.5
Egypt, Arab Rep.	62.1	74.2	81.1	56.2	63.2		48.5	59.8		11.3	11.2	8.7
El Salvador	5.7	6.1	6.2	56.5	58.7	61.1	62.9	63.5	64.8	7.6	7.2	7.3
Eritrea	3.2	4.5	5.3									
Estonia	1.4	1.3	1.3	65.8	68.0	67.8		70.1	73.8	9.7	7.9	16.9
Ethiopia	57.0	74.3	82.9	49.2	49.4		70.4	84.4		3.1	5.4	
Fiji	0.8	0.8	0.9	61.2		65.7	48.9		54.6	5.4	4.6	
Finland	5.1	5.2	5.4	66.8	66.7	66.4	72.1	74.7	74.5	15.3	8.4	8.4
France	59.4	63.0	64.9	65.3	65.0	64.8	67.6	69.9	70.5	11.8	8.9	9.4
Gabon	1.1	1.4	1.5		58.5			58.4		17.8		
Gambia, The	1.1	1.5	1.7									
Georgia	4.7	4.4	4.5		66.5	67.6			64.2		13.8	16.5
Germany	81.6	82.5	81.7	68.3	66.9	65.9	70.5	73.8	76.6	8.1	11.1	7.1
Ghana	17.0	21.6	24.4		55.3			75.6			3.6	
Greece	10.6	11.1	11.3	67.5	67.5	66.7	60.4	66.8	68.2	9.1	9.8	12.5
Guatemala	10.0	12.7	14.4		53.8			68.0			3.1	
Guinea	7.6	9.0	10.0	49.4			83.6			3.1		
Guinea-Bissau	1.1	1.4	1.5									
Haiti	7.9	9.3	10.0									
Honduras	5.6	6.9	7.6	52.2	55.4	58.2	60.6	63.6	63.2	3.2	4.2	
Hungary	10.3	10.1	10.0	67.6	68.7	68.6	58.9	61.3	62.4	10.2	7.2	11.2
India	932.2	1094.6	1170.9	59.9	61.8	64.5	62.0	62.2	56.6	2.2	4.4	3.6
Indonesia	199.4	227.3	239.9	61.9	66.0	65.4	63.8	64.8	61.6	4.4	11.2	7.9
Iran, Islamic Rep.	59.8	69.7	74.0		65.9			49.0		9.1	12.1	10.5
Iraq	20.9	27.6	32.0	48.6	57.4		43.5	41.5			18.0	
Ireland	3.6	4.2	4.5	64.0	68.2	67.3	61.6	70.8	69.8	12.0	4.3	13.6
Israel	5.5	6.9	7.6	60.9	61.7	62.2	60.8	62.4	64.5	6.9	9.0	6.6
Italy	56.8	58.6	60.5	68.8	66.4	65.7	57.6	62.5	62.2	11.7	7.7	8.4
Jamaica	2.5	2.7	2.7	60.1			86.3			16.2	10.9	11.4
Japan	125.4	127.8	127.5	69.5	66.1	63.8	71.5	72.6	74.0	3.2	4.4	5.0
Jordan	4.2	5.4	6.0		56.0			47.5		14.6	12.4	12.9
Kazakhstan	15.8	15.1	16.3	63.8	70.3		55.9	64.3		11.0	8.1	6.6
Kenya	27.4	35.6	40.5	51.4	53.8		58.7	60.6				
Kiribati	0.1	0.1	0.1		58.4			66.5				
Korea, Rep.	45.1	48.1	48.9	70.7	71.7	73.2	64.9	66.3	65.8	2.1	3.7	3.7
Kosovo	2.0	1.8	1.8		62.5			46.5			41.4	
Kyrgyz Republic	4.6	5.1	5.4	57.9			57.4				8.1	8.2
Lao PDR	4.8	5.8	6.2	52.0		59.5			87.7	2.6	1.4	

TABLE 1 *Labor force,* continued

	Population (millions) Total			Working age population (%) Total			Participation rate (%) Total			Unemployment rate (%) Total		
	1995	2005	2010	1995	2005	2010	1995	2005	2010	1995	2005	2010
Latvia	2.5	2.3	2.2	65.7	68.7	68.9	.	69.6	73.2	20.2	8.9	18.7
Lebanon	3.5	4.1	4.2		64.7			47.9		8.5	7.9	
Lesotho	1.8	2.1	2.2							39.3		25.3
Liberia	2.1	3.2	4.0		55.6			73.1			5.6	3.7
Libya	4.8	5.8	6.4									
Lithuania	3.6	3.4	3.3	65.9	67.8	68.9		68.4	70.5	17.1	8.3	17.8
Macedonia, FYR	2.0	2.0	2.1	66.6	69.1	70.6		62.2	64.2	36.0	37.3	32.0
Madagascar	13.1	17.9	20.7	51.8	51.0		89.1				2.6	
Malawi	9.9	12.8	14.9	53.5	49.9			89.2			7.8	
Malaysia	20.7	26.1	28.4							3.1	3.5	3.7
Mali	9.8	13.2	15.4	62.2	50.7		83.4	57.3		3.3	8.8	
Mauritania	2.3	3.0	3.5			52.2			83.1		33.0	
Mauritius	1.1	1.2	1.3		68.8	69.9		63.6	62.2	5.8	9.6	7.7
Mexico	92.3	106.5	113.4	59.3	63.5	65.9	61.5	61.9	63.7	6.9	3.5	5.2
Moldova	3.7	3.6	3.6		67.6			73.5			7.3	7.4
Mongolia	2.3	2.5	2.8			68.4			68.1		3.3	
Montenegro	0.6	0.6	0.6		68.7			56.9			30.3	
Morocco	26.9	30.4	32.0	55.9	61.7		52.2	54.3		22.9	11.0	10.0
Mozambique	15.9	20.8	23.4	51.6	50.2	48.2	79.9	83.1	91.2	2.2		
Myanmar	42.1	46.3	48.0									
Namibia	1.7	2.1	2.3	52.2			56.9			19.4	21.9	37.6
Nepal	21.6	27.3	30.0	55.0	55.7	57.4	62.3	81.3	75.7	4.5		2.7
Netherlands	15.5	16.3	16.6	68.4	67.5	67.1	69.2	76.9	78.2	7.2	4.7	4.5
New Zealand	3.7	4.1	4.4	65.4	66.4	66.5	74.5	77.3	77.5	6.5	3.8	6.5
Nicaragua	4.6	5.4	5.8	51.6	59.1		65.6	67.3		16.9	5.6	
Niger	9.2	13.0	15.5	47.6			59.2			5.1		
Nigeria	110.0	139.8	158.4	53.3	63.3		62.7	63.7				
Norway	4.4	4.6	4.9	64.6	65.5	66.2		78.3	78.1	4.9	4.6	3.6
Oman	2.2	2.4	2.8				76.8					
Pakistan	127.3	158.6	173.6		53.7	55.3		56.7	55.2	5.0	7.4	5.0
Panama	2.7	3.2	3.5	60.7	62.7	62.6	62.2	67.3	68.4	14.0	9.8	6.5
Papua New Guinea	4.7	6.1	6.9	55.7	56.2			70.5				
Paraguay	4.8	5.9	6.5	53.1	58.9	61.6	79.7	73.5	72.0	3.4	5.8	5.6
Peru	23.8	27.6	29.1	59.3	61.3	61.0	74.3	74.4	78.0	7.1	11.4	6.3
Philippines	69.3	85.5	93.3	58.3	60.7	62.4	64.1	62.1	63.7	8.4	7.7	7.5
Poland	38.6	38.2	38.2	65.9	70.1	71.3	67.4	64.4	65.6	13.3	17.7	9.6
Portugal	10.0	10.5	10.6	67.3	67.3	66.9	67.4	73.4	74.0	7.2	7.6	10.8
Romania	22.7	21.6	21.4	67.3	69.5	69.9	71.5	62.3	63.6	8.0	7.2	7.3
Russian Federation	148.1	143.2	141.8		52.4					9.4	7.2	7.5
Rwanda	5.6	9.2	10.6	51.9	53.5		76.3	85.7		0.6		
Saudi Arabia	18.5	24.0	27.4								6.3	5.4
Senegal	8.4	10.9	12.4	58.7	53.7		59.3	51.6			10.0	
Serbia	7.7	7.4	7.3			64.5			59.1		20.8	16.6
Sierra Leone	3.9	5.2	5.9		52.6			67.1			3.4	
Singapore	3.5	4.3	5.1							2.7	5.6	5.9
Slovak Republic	5.4	5.4	5.4	66.3	71.3	72.4	69.3	68.9	68.7	13.1	16.2	14.4
Slovenia	2.0	2.0	2.1	69.4	70.3	69.4	66.3	70.7	71.5	7.2	6.5	7.2
Somalia	6.5	8.4	9.3									
South Africa	39.1	47.2	50.0	62.3	62.6		57.6	68.2		16.9	23.8	24.7
Spain	39.4	43.4	46.1	68.0	68.7	68.2	60.6	69.7	73.4	22.7	9.2	20.1
Sri Lanka	18.2	19.8	20.9	65.3	67.3	66.9	60.8	58.8	59.1	12.2	7.7	4.9
Sudan	30.1	38.4	43.6									
Swaziland	1.0	1.1	1.2	57.1			61.8			21.7		
Sweden	8.8	9.0	9.4	63.7	65.2	65.3	77.7	78.7	79.5	9.1	7.7	8.4
Switzerland	7.0	7.4	7.8	67.7	67.9	68.0	79.1	80.9	82.4	3.3	4.4	4.5
Syrian Arab Republic	14.2	18.5	20.4		57.5			51.1		7.2	8.2	8.4
Tajikistan	5.8	6.5	6.9		57.0			54.4				
Tanzania	29.9	38.8	44.8	48.8	51.3	50.5	77.4	91.4	78.4		4.3	
Thailand	59.7	66.7	69.1	74.1	66.3	67.5	80.7	82.1	81.5	1.1	1.3	1.2
Timor-Leste	0.9	1.0	1.1		53.7	53.3		63.3	43.0			
Togo	4.1	5.4	6.0		55.1			82.8				
Tonga	0.1	0.1	0.1	55.7			60.6			13.3	1.1	
Trinidad and Tobago	1.3	1.3	1.3							17.2	8.0	4.6
Tunisia	9.0	10.0	10.5	61.0			51.4			15.9	14.2	14.2
Turkey	58.9	68.1	72.8	63.0	65.5	67.0	56.8	49.8	51.9	7.6	10.6	11.9
Turkmenistan	4.2	4.7	5.0									
Uganda	20.8	28.4	33.4		51.4			85.7			2.0	4.2
Ukraine	51.5	47.1	45.9		67.8			68.3		5.6	7.2	8.8
United Kingdom	58.0	60.2	62.2	64.7	66.0	66.1	74.7	75.4	75.5	8.6	4.7	7.8
United States	266.3	295.8	309.1	65.4	67.0	66.8	76.9	75.4	73.9	5.6	5.1	9.6
Uruguay	3.2	3.3	3.4	62.4	61.6	62.9	71.7	72.7	75.0	10.2	12.2	7.6
Uzbekistan	22.8	26.2	28.2									
Venezuela, RB	22.0	26.6	28.8	59.8	63.6		64.0	69.2		10.2	11.4	7.6
Vietnam	72.0	82.4	86.9	61.9	68.3	69.0	84.4	80.5	79.6	1.9	2.1	2.4
West Bank and Gaza	2.5	3.6	4.2	51.9		55.6	45.1	42.6	43.0			
Yemen, Rep.	15.1	20.6	24.1		52.1					8.3	16.1	14.6
Zambia	8.9	11.5	12.9		62.3			64.2		15.3	15.9	
Zimbabwe	11.7	12.6	12.6							5.0	4.2	

TABLE 1 *Labor force, continued*

	Population (millions) Men			Working age population (%) Men			Participation rate (%) Men			Unemployment rate (%) Men		
	1995	2005	2010	1995	2005	2010	1995	2005	2010	1995	2005	2010
Afghanistan	11.6	15.5	17.8		47.9			85.2			7.6	
Albania	1.6	1.6	1.6	61.0	69.4		73.5	65.8			14.4	12.2
Algeria	14.3	16.6	17.9							26.0	14.9	10.0
Angola	6.0	8.2	9.4									
Argentina	17.1	18.9	19.8	61.8	64.2	65.4	80.4	81.7	81.0	16.5	9.2	7.8
Armenia	1.5	1.4	1.4		65.6			64.6		38.0	21.9	
Australia	9.0	10.1	11.1	67.4	67.9	68.1	83.9	82.6	82.9	8.8	4.9	5.1
Austria	3.8	4.0	4.1	69.9	70.0	69.4	80.8	79.3	80.9	3.1	4.9	4.6
Azerbaijan	3.8	4.1	4.5	62.1				57.9			8.0	5.2
Bangladesh	60.3	71.9	75.3		58.5	59.1			89.0	2.7	3.4	4.2
Barbados	0.1	0.1	0.1	85.6				79.7		16.6	7.3	6.8
Belarus	4.8	4.6	4.4		72.3			72.0				
Belgium	5.0	5.1	5.3	68.2	67.4	67.6	72.3	73.9	73.4	7.3	7.6	8.1
Belize	0.1	0.1	0.2	51.9			81.9				2.9	2.6
Benin	2.7	3.7	4.4		47.9			77.4				
Bhutan	0.3	0.3	0.4		60.3			76.1		10	7.5	
Bolivia	3.7	4.6	5.0	54.4	55.8	58.9	83.1	82.1	84.5	3.3	4.5	
Bosnia and Herzegovina	1.6	1.8	1.8		84.5			73.7			29.5	25.6
Botswana	0.8	0.9	1.0			59.0			74.7	19.4	15.3	
Brazil	80.2	91.7	95.9	61.5	66.3	67.5	87.7	85.6	85.1	5.1	7.1	6.1
Bulgaria	4.1	3.8	3.6	67.8	70.7	70.9	71.7	67.0	70.8	15.5	10.3	10.9
Burkina Faso	5.2	7.0	8.2	45.8	47.9		92.2	91.7			2.9	
Burundi	3.0	3.5	4.1									
Cambodia	5.4	6.5	6.9	54.0	60.7	62.1	80.7	90.8	89.1			1.5
Cameroon	6.9	8.8	9.8	49.4	90.5		76.8	70.0		9.5	4.2	
Canada	14.5	16.0	16.9	68.7	70.3	70.3	81.5	82.5	81.5	9.8	7.0	8.7
Central African Republic	1.6	2.0	2.2		49.5			76.6				
Chad	3.5	4.9	5.6		46.9					1.1		
Chile	7.1	8.1	8.5	64.0	67.6	69.2	80.7	76.7	77.8	4.4	7.0	7.2
China	618.1	673.8	687.5		70.5	74.1		78.6	78.2		2.4	2.6
Colombia	18.0	21.2	22.8	52.4	61.9	63.6	80.7	84.1	84.8	6.8	8.7	9.1
Congo, Dem. Rep.	21.8	28.5	32.8		48.9			72.2				
Congo, Rep.	1.4	1.8	2.0		55.7			68.0				
Costa Rica	1.8	2.2	2.4	59.3	65.4	67.6	86.4	84.0	82.1	4.6	5.0	6.6
Côte d'Ivoire	7.6	9.2	10.1									
Croatia	2.3	2.1	2.1		69.2	69.5		70.0	67.2	9.5	11.6	11.4
Cuba	5.5	5.7	5.7							5.4	1.8	1.4
Czech Republic	5.0	5.0	5.2	69.9	73.1	72.7	80.6	78.4	78.6	3.4	6.5	6.4
Denmark	2.6	2.7	2.7	69.3	67.5	66.7	85.6	83.6	82.6	5.6	4.4	8.4
Dominican Republic	4.0	4.7	5.0	57.4	61.9	63.1	85.1	75.6	75.3	10.2	11.1	8.5
Ecuador	5.7	6.7	7.2	56.9	60.4	61.8	89.3	86.6	81.8	5.5	5.6	5.2
Egypt, Arab Rep.	31.2	37.3	40.7	56.7	62.8		80.7	78.6		7.6	7.1	5.9
El Salvador	2.8	2.9	2.9	54.2	56.3	59.1	84.5	81.9	82.6	8.7	8.9	9.0
Eritrea	1.6	2.2	2.6									
Estonia	0.7	0.6	0.6	67.9	70.9	70.9	79.9	73.6	76.8	10.5	8.8	19.5
Ethiopia	28.3	36.9	41.3	47.8	47.3		90.4	91.6		3.0	2.7	
Fiji	0.4	0.4	0.4	60.8		65.3	72.1		75.1	4.8	4.1	
Finland	2.5	2.6	2.6	69.3	68.9	68.4	74.8	76.6	76.4	15.4	8.1	9.0
France	28.9	30.6	31.6	66.9	66.5	66.2	74.9	75.2	74.9	10.0	8.0	9.0
Gabon	0.5	0.7	0.8		59.1			66.2		19.1		
Gambia, The	0.6	0.7	0.9									
Georgia	2.2	2.1	2.1		66.0	68.4			71.9		14.8	16.8
Germany	39.7	40.3	40.0	71.6	69.3	67.9	79.6	80.6	82.3	7.2	11.3	7.5
Ghana	8.6	11.0	12.4		53.9			76.4			3.5	
Greece	5.2	5.5	5.6	68.3	68.7	68.2	77.2	79.2	78.9	6.2	6.1	9.9
Guatemala	5.0	6.2	7.0		51.2			90.9			2.8	
Guinea	3.8	4.6	5.0	45.8			85.7			4.6		
Guinea-Bissau	0.6	0.7	0.8									
Haiti	3.9	4.6	5.0									
Honduras	2.8	3.4	3.8	50.6	53.6	56.4	87.6	85.9	85.8	3.2	3.2	
Hungary	4.9	4.8	4.8	69.3	71.1	71.3	67.9	67.9	68.3	11.3	7.0	11.6
India	484.0	566.6	604.8	59.3	61.1	63.7	85.7	85.1	82.1	2.4	4.1	3.3
Indonesia	99.7	113.5	119.6	60.9	65.6	64.7	89.1	84.4	83.0	3.8	9.5	7.5
Iran, Islamic Rep.	30.1	35.5	37.5		64.6			79.3		8.5	10.5	9.1
Iraq	10.4	13.8	16.1	48.6	56.1		78.0	72.4			19.2	
Ireland	1.8	2.1	2.2	64.7	68.9	67.7	76.1	80.6	77.4	11.9	4.6	16.8
Israel	2.7	3.4	3.8	61.1	62.0	62.4	69.0	66.8	68.2	5.6	8.5	6.8
Italy	27.5	28.5	29.6	70.5	68.4	67.6	73.2	74.6	73.3	9.1	6.2	7.6
Jamaica	1.2	1.3	1.3	61.4			87.7			10.8	7.4	8.5
Japan	61.5	62.4	62.1	71.2	68.0	65.9	84.5	84.4	84.8	3.1	4.6	5.4
Jordan	2.2	2.8	3.1		55.8			71.8		12.1	11.8	10.3
Kazakhstan	7.6	7.2	7.8	63.2	70.3			62.7			6.7	5.6
Kenya	13.7	17.8	20.2	50.1	53.0		68.3	68.7				
Kiribati					58.2			70.4				
Korea, Rep.	22.6	24.0	24.4	71.3	72.7	74.7	78.7	78.2	77.1	2.3	4.0	4.0
Kosovo					61.9			63.9			32.9	
Kyrgyz Republic	2.3	2.5	2.6	57.9				69.4			7.4	7.3
Lao PDR	2.4	2.9	3.1	50.8		58.3			90.3	2.6	1.3	

TABLE 1 *Labor force,* continued

	Population (millions) Men			Working age population (%) Men			Participation rate (%) Men			Unemployment rate (%) Men		
	1995	2005	2010	1995	2005	2010	1995	2005	2010	1995	2005	2010
Latvia	1.2	1.1	1.0	68.0	71.9	72.5		74.4	75.8	20.6	9.1	21.7
Lebanon	1.7	2.0	2.1		63.3			74.5			7.3	
Lesotho	0.9	1.0	1.1							30.7		23.0
Liberia	1.0	1.6	2.0		54.2			77.1			6.8	3.4
Libya	2.5	2.9	3.2									
Lithuania	1.7	1.6	1.5	67.5	70.1	71.8		72.1	72.4	15.3	8.2	21.2
Macedonia, FYR	1.0	1.0	1.0	66.7	69.7	71.4		75.0	77.7			
Madagascar	6.6	8.9	10.3	51.1	49.5		91.6				1.7	
Malawi	4.9	6.4	7.5	53.3	49.7			91.3			5.4	
Malaysia	10.5	13.3	14.4							2.8	3.4	3.6
Mali	4.9	6.6	7.7	60.3	48.1		88.0	68.0		3.3	7.2	
Mauritania	1.1	1.5	1.7			48.3			89.5			
Mauritius	0.6	0.6	0.6		69.3	70.2		81.9	79.3	4.6	5.8	4.6
Mexico	45.7	52.6	55.9	58.8	62.9	65.4	85.7	83.1	83.0	6.0	3.4	5.2
Moldova	1.8	1.7	1.7		67.8			79.0			8.7	9.1
Mongolia	1.1	1.3	1.4			67.2			73.0		3.0	
Montenegro	0.3	0.3	0.3		69.2			64.2			26.2	
Morocco	13.4	15.0	15.7	54.6	60.9			84.7	83.7	18.7	10.8	9.8
Mozambique	7.6	10.0	11.4	49.8	48.0	46.4	79.6	82.3	90.6	3.4		
Myanmar	20.9	22.9	23.6									
Namibia	0.8	1.0	1.1	50.7			64.6			17.9	19.4	32.5
Nepal	10.8	13.5	14.9	54.4	52.6	53.7	64.2	88.1	81.0			3.1
Netherlands	7.6	8.1	8.2	70.3	69.0	68.3	79.9	83.7	83.7	6.1	4.4	4.4
New Zealand	1.8	2.0	2.1	65.9	66.6	66.5	83.7	84.4	83.6	6.4	3.5	6.2
Nicaragua	2.3	2.7	2.9	50.3	58.3		87.3	88.1	75.0	15.9	5.4	
Niger	4.6	6.5	7.8	47.3			65.7				3.6	
Nigeria	55.4	70.7	80.2	50.2	60.9		82.0	74.2				
Norway	2.2	2.3	2.4	66.4	67.1	67.7	81.2	81.6	80.6	5.1	4.8	4.1
Oman	1.3	1.3	1.6									
Pakistan	65.5	81.0	88.2		52.7	54.0		85.1	83.2	3.7	6.2	4.0
Panama	1.4	1.6	1.8	60.5	61.5	61.9	83.1	84.2	85.3	10.8	7.6	5.3
Papua New Guinea	2.4	3.1	3.5	54.2		55.2			70.0			
Paraguay	2.4	3.0	3.3	52.7	59.1	61.7	93.7	87.7	86.5	3.1	4.8	4.4
Peru	12.0	13.8	14.6	58.4	61.1	60.6	86.0	84.3	86.2	6.0	9.6	4.4
Philippines	35.0	43.0	46.8	57.9	60.6	62.3	80.5	77.6	76.6	7.7	7.7	7.5
Poland	18.8	18.5	18.4	67.2	72.0	73.3	73.9	70.8	72.4	12.1	16.6	9.3
Portugal	4.8	5.1	5.2	68.3	68.7	68.5	76.4	79.0	78.2	6.4	6.7	9.8
Romania	11.1	10.5	10.4	68.3	71.0	71.6	77.7	69.4	71.5	7.5	7.8	7.9
Russian Federation	69.4	66.4	65.6		47.9					9.7	7.3	8.0
Rwanda	2.7	4.5	5.2	49.8	51.8		75.4	83.7		0.9		
Saudi Arabia	10.3	13.5	15.2								4.7	3.5
Senegal	4.2	5.4	6.2	58.2	50.9		77.8	71.5			7.9	
Serbia	3.8	3.7	3.6			65.9			67.4		16.8	15.3
Sierra Leone	1.9	2.5	2.9		50.0			66.8			4.5	
Singapore	1.8	2.1	2.6							2.6	5.6	5.4
Slovak Republic	2.6	2.6	2.6	67.3	73.0	74.4	77.3	76.5	76.1	12.6	15.4	14.2
Slovenia	1.0	1.0	1.0	71.7	73.0	72.3	71.1	75.1	75.4	7.4	6.1	7.4
Somalia	3.2	4.1	4.6									
South Africa	19.3	23.3	24.8	61.3	61.4		68.0	72.3		14.4	20.0	22.6
Spain	19.3	21.4	22.8	69.4	70.4	69.9	75.5	80.9	80.7	17.8	7.0	19.7
Sri Lanka	9.2	9.8	10.3	64.3	66.5	65.5	82.1	80.2	80.9	9.0	5.6	3.5
Sudan	15.2	19.3	21.9									
Swaziland	0.5	0.5	0.6	57.0			71.3			20.4		
Sweden	4.4	4.5	4.7	65.4	66.8	66.7	79.6	80.9	82.3	9.8	7.8	8.5
Switzerland	3.4	3.6	3.8	69.5	69.5	69.5	90.0	87.4	88.3	2.9	3.9	4.2
Syrian Arab Republic	7.1	9.4	10.3		56.6			81.3		5.5	5.3	5.7
Tajikistan	2.9	3.2	3.4		56.0			63.5				
Tanzania	14.8	19.4	22.4	46.5	50.1	50.3	83.6	92.0	91.7		2.8	
Thailand	29.7	32.8	34.0	73.5	65.4	66.8	89.8	88.4	88.0	1.0	1.5	1.2
Timor-Leste	0.4	0.5	0.6		53.5	53.3		77.5	57.9			
Togo	2.0	2.7	3.0		53.6			82.2				
Tonga	0.0	0.1	0.1	54.7			77.6				3.6	
Trinidad and Tobago	0.6	0.6	0.7							15.2	5.8	3.5
Tunisia	4.5	5.0	5.3	60.4			77.2			15.5	13.1	
Turkey	29.4	34.0	36.3	63.1	65.9	67.4	81.1	73.0	74.5	7.8	10.4	11.4
Turkmenistan	2.1	2.3	2.5									
Uganda	10.3	14.2	16.7		52.9			87.9			1.8	3.1
Ukraine	23.9	21.7	21.1		69.7			75.8		6.3	7.5	6.6
United Kingdom	28.2	29.5	30.6	66.3	67.1	67.1	83.3	82.0	81.7	10.0	5.0	8.6
United States	130.2	145.6	152.5	66.5	68.0	67.8	84.3	81.8	79.6	5.6	5.1	10.5
Uruguay	1.6	1.6	1.6	62.7	62.3	63.2	86.4	82.9	84.5	8.0	9.5	5.4
Uzbekistan	11.3	13.0	14.0									
Venezuela, RB	11.1	13.4	14.5	59.7	63.6		84.1	83.5		9.0	10.3	7.2
Vietnam	35.3	40.6	43.0	60.4	68.6	69.6	85.9	82.3	81.9	2.2	1.9	
West Bank and Gaza	1.3	1.8	2.1	52.1		56.6	79.0	70.0	65.9			
Yemen, Rep.	7.6	10.4	12.1		50.5					9.3	11.9	11.5
Zambia	4.4	5.7	6.5		61.3			62.5		14.9		
Zimbabwe	5.8	6.2	6.2							6.8	4.2	

TABLE 1 *Labor force,* continued

	Population (millions) Women			Working age population (%) Women			Participation rate (%) Women			Unemployment rate (%) Women		
	1995	2005	2010	1995	2005	2010	1995	2005	2010	1995	2005	2010
Afghanistan	10.8	14.4	16.6		49.6			45.1			9.5	
Albania	1.6	1.6	1.6	62.4	68.7		62.3	49.2			12.2	15.9
Algeria	14.0	16.3	17.6							38.4	17.5	20.0
Angola	6.1	8.3	9.6									
Argentina	17.7	19.7	20.7	61.0	62.8	63.8	47.7	57.2	55.5	22.3	12.4	9.8
Armenia	1.7	1.6	1.7		67.6			45.0		34.4	35.0	
Australia	9.1	10.3	11.2	65.7	66.8	67.1	64.2	68.2	70.0	8.1	5.2	5.4
Austria	4.1	4.2	4.3	64.5	66.0	65.8	62.3	65.6	69.3	4.3	5.5	4.2
Azerbaijan	3.9	4.3	4.6	64.2			39.3				8.3	6.9
Bangladesh	57.2	68.7	73.4		59.5	61.8			31.0	2.2	7.0	7.4
Barbados	0.1	0.1	0.1	82.4			67.3			22.7	10.9	9.4
Belarus	5.4	5.2	5.1		68.1			68.9				
Belgium	5.2	5.4	5.5	64.3	63.8	64.3	51.7	59.5	61.8	12.2	9.5	8.5
Belize	0.1	0.1	0.2	53.6			34.8				3.3	5.3
Benin	2.9	3.9	4.5		53.1			79.8				
Bhutan	0.3	0.3	0.3		62.9			62.1		17.9	17.2 .	
Bolivia	3.8	4.6	5.0	57.0	58.5	60.3	60.5	62.4	65.8	4.0	6.5	
Bosnia and Herzegovina	1.7	2.0	2.0		77.5			43.3			35.7	30.0
Botswana	0.8	0.9	1.0			60.7			63.0	23.9	19.9	
Brazil	81.7	94.3	99.0	62.6	67.0	68.4	57.4	63.1	63.5	7.2	12.2	11.0
Bulgaria	4.3	4.0	3.9	66.3	67.5	67.1	65.8	57.3	62.3	15.8	9.8	9.5
Burkina Faso	5.4	7.2	8.3	50.7	53.0		82.0	82.4			1.7	
Burundi	3.1	3.7	4.3									
Cambodia	5.8	6.8	7.2	58.4	63.3	64.6	74.0	79.2	80.8			1.8
Cameroon	7.0	8.8	9.8	53.3	89.0		62.7	65.0		6.5	4.6	
Canada	14.8	16.3	17.2	66.6	68.2	68.5	67.8	72.9	74.2	9.1	6.5	7.2
Central African Republic	1.7	2.0	2.2		53.1			74.5				
Chad	3.5	4.9	5.6		51.0					0.3		
Chile	7.3	8.2	8.7	63.6	66.7	68.1	37.4	42.3	51.8	5.3	9.8	9.6
China	593.1	633.8	653.4		72.3	74.9		64.8	63.7		3.1	3.2
Colombia	18.4	21.8	23.5	55.3	63.8	65.3	33.2	55.4	59.8	11.3	14.9	15.0
Congo, Dem. Rep.	22.2	28.9	33.2		51.3			69.6				
Congo, Rep.	1.4	1.8	2.0		58.8			64.2				
Costa Rica	1.7	2.1	2.3	61.7	66.4	69.3	37.7	47.5	49.2	6.6	9.6	9.9
Côte d'Ivoire	7.1	8.8	9.7									
Croatia	2.4	2.3	2.3		64.8	65.0		56.7	55.9	10.5	13.8	12.2
Cuba	5.4	5.6	5.6							13.0	2.2	2.0
Czech Republic	5.3	5.2	5.4	66.3	69.1	68.5		62.4	61.5	4.8	9.8	8.5
Denmark	2.6	2.7	2.8	65.6	64.8	64.5	64.1	75.9	76.0	8.6	5.3	6.5
Dominican Republic	3.9	4.6	4.9	59.6	61.9	63.9	73.3	40.7	44.0	26.2	28.8	22.8
Ecuador	5.7	6.7	7.2	59.6	61.8	63.1	55.3	60.4	52.5	8.8	10.8	8.4
Egypt, Arab Rep.	30.9	36.9	40.4	55.7	63.6		15.3	40.7		24.1	25.1	19.2
El Salvador	3.0	3.2	3.3	58.6	60.9	62.9	44.5	48.2	49.7	5.9	4.8	4.9
Eritrea	1.6	2.3	2.7									
Estonia	0.8	0.7	0.7	64.0	65.6	65.1		66.9	71.0	8.9	7.1	14.3
Ethiopia	28.7	37.3	41.7	50.5	51.5		66.5	78.0		3.3	8.2	
Fiji	0.4	0.4	0.4	61.5		66.0	25.3		33.9	7.8	5.9	
Finland	2.6	2.7	2.7	64.4	64.6	64.4	69.4	72.8	72.5	15.1	8.7	7.7
France	30.5	32.4	33.3	63.8	63.6	63.5	60.6	64.7	66.1	14.1	9.8	9.7
Gabon	0.5	0.7	0.8		57.9			50.7		16.1		
Gambia, The	0.6	0.8	0.9									
Georgia	2.5	2.3	2.4		67.1	67.0			57.2		12.7	16.1
Germany	41.9	42.1	41.7	65.2	64.6	63.9	61.3	66.9	70.8	9.4	10.9	6.6
Ghana	8.4	10.6	12.0		56.6			74.9			3.6	
Greece	5.4	5.6	5.7	66.7	66.2	65.2	44.3	54.5	57.6	13.8	15.3	16.2
Guatemala	5.0	6.5	7.4		56.3			49.0			3.7	
Guinea	3.7	4.5	4.9	52.8			81.8				1.7	
Guinea-Bissau	0.6	0.7	0.8									
Haiti	4.0	4.7	5.0									
Honduras	2.8	3.4	3.8	53.8	57.2	59.9	35.9	44.0	43.6	3.4	6.2	
Hungary	5.4	5.3	5.3	66.1	66.6	66.3	50.3	55.1	56.7	8.7	7.5	10.7
India	448.1	528.0	566.1	60.5	62.4	65.5	37.2	38.7	30.1	1.7	5.1	4.5
Indonesia	99.7	113.8	120.2	62.8	66.4	66.1	39.6	45.4	40.9	5.5	14.2	8.5
Iran, Islamic Rep.	29.7	34.2	36.4		67.3			19.5		13.4	18.2	16.8
Iraq	10.5	13.8	16.0	48.5	58.6		9.3	12.8			14.2	
Ireland	1.8	2.1	2.2	63.3	67.5	67.0	47.1	60.8	62.2	12.1	4.0	9.6
Israel	2.8	3.5	3.9	60.7	61.5	61.9	52.7	58.1	60.9	8.6	9.5	6.5
Italy	29.3	30.2	30.9	67.1	64.5	64.0	42.4	50.4	51.1	16.1	10.1	9.7
Jamaica	1.3	1.3	1.4	58.8			84.8			22.5	15.3	14.8
Japan	64.0	65.4	65.4	67.9	64.2	61.8	58.4	60.8	63.2	3.3	4.2	4.5
Jordan	2.0	2.6	2.9		56.1			21.6		29.9	16.5	24.1
Kazakhstan	8.2	7.9	8.5	64.8	70.3		49.7	58.0			9.6	7.5
Kenya	13.8	17.8	20.3	52.7	54.5		49.9	53.0				
Kiribati					58.6			62.7				3.3
Korea, Rep.	22.5	24.1	24.5	70.2	70.7	71.8	51.4	54.5	54.5	1.7	3.4	
Kosovo					63.0			28.3			60.5	9.4
Kyrgyz Republic	2.3	2.6	2.7	58.1			46.0				9.1	
Lao PDR	2.4	2.9	3.1	53.3		60.6			85.3	2.6	1.4	15.7

TABLE 1 *Labor force,* continued

	Population (millions) Women			Working age population (%) Women			Participation rate (%) Women			Unemployment rate (%) Women		
	1995	2005	2010	1995	2005	2010	1995	2005	2010	1995	2005	2010
Latvia	1.4	1.2	1.2	63.7	65.9	65.8		65.1	70.7	19.8	8.7	
Lebanon	1.8	2.1	2.2		66.1			22.9			9.5	
Lesotho	0.9	1.1	1.1							47.1		28.0
Liberia	1.1	1.6	2.0		56.9			69.4			4.2	4.1
Libya	2.3	2.8	3.1									
Lithuania	1.9	1.8	1.8	64.5	65.8	66.5		64.9	68.8	15.9	8.3	14.4
Macedonia, FYR	1.0	1.0	1.0	66.4	68.5	69.9		49.2	50.4	40.8	38.4	32.2
Madagascar	6.6	9.0	10.4	52.5	52.5		86.6				3.5	
Malawi	5.0	6.4	7.4	53.6	50.0		87.3				10.0	
Malaysia	10.2	12.8	14.0							3.8	3.7	3.8
Mali	5.0	6.6	7.7	64.1	53.1		79.2	47.8		3.3	10.9	
Mauritania	1.1	1.5	1.7		55.7			72.7				
Mauritius	0.6	0.6	0.6		68.3	69.7		45.3	45.2	8.2	16.5	12.8
Mexico	46.6	53.9	57.5	59.7	64.1	66.5	39.5	43.2	46.3	8.6	3.6	5.2
Moldova	1.9	1.9	1.9		67.4			69.0			6.0	5.7
Mongolia	1.2	1.3	1.4			69.4			63.5		3.6	
Montenegro	0.3	0.3	0.3		68.3			50.0			35.5	
Morocco	13.5	15.4	16.3	57.1	62.5		21.4	26.4		32.2	11.5	10.5
Mozambique	8.3	10.7	12.0	53.3	52.3	49.9	80.0	83.7	91.8	1.3		
Myanmar	21.2	23.4	24.3									
Namibia	0.8	1.1	1.1	53.1			50.4			21.1	25.0	43.0
Nepal	10.8	13.7	15.1	55.6	58.5	60.5	60.3	75.6	70.9			2.4
Netherlands	7.8	8.2	8.4	66.6	66.1	65.9	58.3	70.0	72.6	8.7	5.1	4.5
New Zealand	1.9	2.1	2.2	64.9	66.3	66.4	65.6	70.6	71.8	6.5	4.1	6.8
Nicaragua	2.3	2.7	2.9	52.9	59.8		45.2	47.8	31.1	19.3	6.0	
Niger	4.6	6.5	7.7	47.9			52.6			8.1		
Nigeria	54.6	69.1	78.2	56.5	65.8		44.9	53.1	75.5			
Norway	2.2	2.3	2.4	62.8	64.0	64.8	72.3	74.9	75.5	4.6	4.4	3.0
Oman	0.9	1.1	1.1									
Pakistan	61.9	77.7	85.4		54.8	56.6		28.2	26.8	14.0	13.0	8.7
Panama	1.3	1.6	1.7	61.0	63.8	63.3	41.5	50.9	52.1	20.1	13.3	8.5
Papua New Guinea	2.3	3.0	3.4	57.4				71.1				
Paraguay	2.4	2.9	3.2	53.6	58.6	61.5	66.0	59.2	57.2	3.7	7.2	7.5
Peru	11.9	13.7	14.5	60.2	61.5	61.4	63.4	64.9	70.2	8.7	13.7	8.8
Philippines	34.3	42.5	46.5	58.8	60.7	62.4	47.9	46.4	50.6	9.4	7.8	7.4
Poland	19.8	19.7	19.8	64.7	68.4	69.4	55.3	58.1	59.0	14.7	19.1	10.0
Portugal	5.2	5.4	5.5	66.5	66.1	65.5	59.1	67.9	69.9	8.2	8.7	11.9
Romania	11.6	11.1	11.0	66.4	68.1	68.3	65.4	67.9	55.0	8.6	6.4	6.5
Russian Federation	78.8	76.7	76.2		56.0			56.3		9.2	7.0	6.9
Rwanda	2.9	4.7	5.4	53.7	54.9		77.0	87.4		0.4		
Saudi Arabia	8.2	10.6	12.3								14.7	15.9
Senegal	4.2	5.5	6.3	59.3	56.3		43.2	35.0			13.6	
Serbia	3.9	3.8	3.7			63.1			50.9		26.2	18.4
Sierra Leone	2.0	2.6	3.0		55.0			67.3			2.3	
Singapore	1.8	2.1	2.5							2.8	6.2	6.5
Slovak Republic	2.8	2.8	2.8	65.3	69.7	70.5	61.4	61.5	61.3	13.8	17.2	14.6
Slovenia	1.0	1.0	1.0	67.3	67.7	66.7	61.5	66.1	67.4	6.8	7.0	7.0
Somalia	3.3	4.2	4.7									
South Africa	19.8	23.9	25.2	63.2	63.7		48.5	64.4		20.0	28.2	27.3
Spain	20.1	22.0	23.3	66.6	67.0	66.6	45.8	58.3	65.9	30.8	12.2	20.5
Sri Lanka	9.1	10.0	10.6	66.3	67.9	68.2	40.4	39.3	39.7	18.7	11.9	7.7
Sudan	15.0	19.1	21.6									
Swaziland	0.5	0.6	0.6	57.2			52.8			23.2		
Sweden	4.5	4.6	4.7	61.9	63.6	64.0	75.9	76.3	76.7	8.2	7.6	8.2
Switzerland	3.6	3.8	4.0	65.9	66.3	66.6	68.3	74.3	76.4	3.8	5.1	5.0
Syrian Arab Republic	7.0	9.1	10.1		58.4			20.5		14.2	23.8	22.5
Tajikistan	2.9	3.3	3.5		58.0			45.6				
Tanzania	15.1	19.5	22.4	51.1	52.5		72.0	90.9	76.2		5.8	
Thailand	30.0	33.9	35.1	74.8	67.1	68.1	72.2	76.4	75.7	1.1	1.2	1.1
Timor-Leste	0.4	0.5	0.6		53.9	53.4		48.7	27.9			
Togo	2.1	2.7	3.0		56.6			83.4				
Tonga	0.0	0.1	0.1	56.7			43.7					
Trinidad and Tobago	0.6	0.7	0.7							20.6	11.0	6.2
Tunisia	4.5	5.0	5.3	61.5			25.5			17.3	17.3	
Turkey	29.5	34.1	36.5	62.8	65.2	66.7	32.7	25.2	29.6	7.3	11.2	13.0
Turkmenistan	2.1	2.4	2.6									
Uganda	10.5	14.3	16.7		50.1			83.5			2.2	5.1
Ukraine	27.6	25.4	24.8		66.3			61.5		4.9	6.8	6.1
United Kingdom	29.8	30.7	31.6	63.2	64.8	65.0	66.0	68.8	69.4	6.8	4.2	6.7
United States	136.1	150.1	156.6	64.4	66.2	66.3	69.7	69.7	68.4	5.6	5.1	8.6
Uruguay	1.7	1.7	1.7	62.1	61.1	62.7	58.5	63.6	66.4	13.2	15.3	10.1
Uzbekistan	11.5	13.2	14.2									
Venezuela, RB	10.9	13.2	14.4	59.9	63.6		43.6	54.7		12.8	13.0	8.1
Vietnam	36.7	41.8	44.0	63.3	67.9	68.5	83.1	78.8	77.3	1.7	2.4	
West Bank and Gaza	1.2	1.8	2.0	51.6		54.5	9.9	14.2	18.2			
Yemen, Rep.	7.5	10.3	11.9		53.7					3.9	46.3	40.9
Zambia	4.5	5.7	6.4		63.2			65.9		15.9		
Zimbabwe	5.9	6.3	6.4							3.0	4.1	

TABLE 1 *Labor force,* continued

| | Participation rate (%) Ages 15 to 24 | | | | | | Participation rate (%) Ages 25 to 64 | | | | | |
| | Men | | | Women | | | Men | | | Women | | |
	1995	2005	2010	1995	2005	2010	1995	2005	2010	1995	2005	2010
Afghanistan		72.3			36.7			92.3			49.3	
Albania	52.3	39.6		50.9	33.8		82.6	76.8		67.2	55.7	
Algeria												
Angola												
Argentina		54.7	50.1		36.5	32.4		92.7	92.6		64.5	63.4
Armenia		30.2			25.6			79.1			53.4	
Australia	73.8	72.0	69.8	69.8	69.6	67.3	86.9	85.4	86.5	62.6	67.9	70.7
Austria	64.6	63.6	63.6	58.9	54.8	54.1	84.5	82.7	84.6	63.1	67.9	72.6
Azerbaijan	27.4			26.0			70.1			45.0		
Bangladesh												
Barbados	62.0			50.5			85.6			72.3		
Belarus		31.2			29.5			87.3			79.9	
Belgium	36.0	37.6	35.2	31.7	32.3	29.8	81.1	82.2	82.1	56.5	65.5	68.9
Belize	62.3			28.0			93.8			38.6		
Benin		46.3			61.8			93.8			88.0	
Bhutan		45.9			46.7			90.3			70.1	
Bolivia	59.1	55.5	59.0	45.2	44.2	46.1	95.2	95.6	96.7	68.0	71.2	75.2
Bosnia and Herzegovina		52.3			32.7			79.5			46.1	
Botswana			45.2			37.4			88.6			74.0
Brazil	78.5	74.7	71.3	51.8	55.9	54.0	91.9	90.2	90.1	59.7	65.9	66.6
Bulgaria	40.9	31.1	33.5	38.4	24.5	24.2	80.4	76.1	79.5	72.8	65.2	70.6
Burkina Faso	86.1	83.0		77.6	77.5		96.0	97.1		84.3	85.3	
Burundi												
Cambodia	58.7	81.1	78.4	68.3	75.7	75.0	92.3	96.4	95.5	76.6	81.0	83.7
Cameroon	51.7	71.8		43.8	63.2		92.6	69.9		73.7	65.1	
Canada	64.9	66.0	64.4	61.3	65.7	64.6	85.8	86.6	85.6	69.4	74.6	76.5
Central African Republic		72.1			73.7			79.2			75.0	
Chad												
Chile	49.1	38.2	43.8	26.3	24.4	30.4	91.9	90.9	90.5	41.3	48.1	58.6
China		60.4	59.6		58.7	55.1		90.5	90.8		74.5	74.1
Colombia		62.5	61.9		42.8	43.4		93.4	94.2		60.5	65.9
Congo, Dem. Rep.		37.5			47.8			91.3			82.0	
Congo, Rep.		40.5			41.7			84.3			76.4	
Costa Rica	71.7	61.1	57.8	35.1	36.4	36.1	93.3	94.5	93.1	38.9	52.1	54.2
Côte d'Ivoire												
Croatia		43.0	40.2		32.9	27.6		77.0	74.0		62.2	62.0
Cuba												
Czech Republic	58.7	38.9	36.2	42.0	28.9	25.3	87.9	87.7	87.8	70.9	69.9	69.1
Denmark	77.0	70.0	67.6	69.4	66.2	67.4	87.7	86.3	86.1	74.3	77.9	78.0
Dominican Republic	67.9	51.5	49.0	38.6	26.2	26.5	95.2	87.5	87.9	44.1	47.0	51.8
Ecuador	78.1	66.7	55.4	45.1	45.6	33.8	95.1	96.4	94.5	60.9	66.8	59.9
Egypt, Arab Rep.		51.1			25.9			95.0			48.7	
El Salvador	69.8	63.0	62.8	31.9	31.6	31.6	94.0	92.2	93.2	51.5	55.6	57.8
Eritrea												
Estonia	58.3	39.7	42.3	39.7	29.5	34.3	86.1	84.2	86.3	73.1	77.0	79.9
Ethiopia	81.3	81.7		48.0	72.3		96.4	97.2		53.6	81.3	
Fiji	49.7		44.1	21.2		23.8	82.5		88.0	27.2		37.3
Finland	51.1	50.9	49.4	48.1	50.4	49.3	79.9	82.2	82.4	73.8	77.9	77.7
France	37.3	41.8	42.8	33.8	34.3	35.5	84.0	83.4	82.5	67.4	71.9	73.0
Gabon		26.4			22.2			86.8			68.4	
Gambia, The												
Georgia			41.8			23.6			81.8			67.3
Germany	54.6	52.4	53.7	50.3	46.7	48.9	84.4	86.7	88.2	63.3	71.2	75.2
Ghana		43.6			44.3			94.8			89.6	
Greece	41.3	37.0	33.4	32.5	30.4	27.2	86.3	88.0	87.1	47.3	59.5	63.0
Guatemala		80.0			40.9			97.2			53.5	
Guinea	67.9			74.2			95.1			84.8		
Guinea-Bissau												
Haiti												
Honduras	75.7	73.4	71.9	28.1	33.1	29.5	95.6	94.5	95.3	40.5	50.6	51.6
Hungary	44.6	30.3	27.7	31.9	23.8	22.1	75.4	76.9	77.4	55.5	62.0	63.9
India	66.0	63.3	52.1	29.1	27.6	19.1	94.9	94.8	95.1	40.7	43.4	34.4
Indonesia	65.7	59.5	47.5	35.1	37.9	26.9	98.9	93.9	94.6	41.5	48.1	45.2
Iran, Islamic Rep.		58.7			16.9			93.2			21.1	
Iraq		51.4			4.7			83.1			16.7	
Ireland	48.3	56.6	43.1	41.4	49.9	41.5	86.5	87.7	85.0	49.1	63.9	66.8
Israel	35.1	30.4	28.9	34.6	34.4	33.7	83.4	80.3	81.6	59.8	66.3	69.7
Italy	43.9	38.7	33.2	33.6	28.7	23.4	80.6	81.4	80.8	44.6	54.3	56.0
Jamaica	62.6			58.7			97.9			94.9		
Japan	48.0	44.5	42.3	47.2	45.0	44.0	94.7	92.6	92.9	61.4	63.9	66.7
Jordan												
Kazakhstan	33.1	32.4		26.5	25.1		74.7	89.6		57.8	70.0	
Kenya	42.6	40.6		35.3	29.2		83.3	88.7		58.6	69.0	
Kiribati		60.0			55.6			75.5			65.8	
Korea, Rep.	31.2	26.7	20.2	41.8	39.0	30.4	92.6	88.8	88.2	54.7	58.2	59.7
Kosovo		46.8			31.8			72.8			26.7	
Kyrgyz Republic	52.1			32.3			78.1			53.2		
Lao PDR			78.5			80.6			96.2			87.7

TABLE 1 *Labor force,* continued

| | Participation rate (%) Ages 15 to 24 | | | | | | Participation rate (%) Ages 25 to 64 | | | | | |
| | Men | | | Women | | | Men | | | Women | | |
	1995	2005	2010	1995	2005	2010	1995	2005	2010	1995	2005	2010
Latvia		43.8	43.0		31.3	37.7		84.0	85.2		74.3	79.0
Lebanon		43.7			17.8			88.4			24.9	
Lesotho												
Liberia		58.5			58.0			87.8			75.8	
Libya												
Lithuania		29.5	32.8		20.5	26.3		85.4	84.5		77.0	80.1
Macedonia, FYR		42.0	42.2		29.3	24.0		85.0	87.9		55.0	57.7
Madagascar	83.1			80.2			96.9			90.4		
Malawi		80.3			78.7			97.9			93.0	
Malaysia												
Mali	80.6	53.5		75.5	42.5		92.1	78.1		81.0	50.9	
Mauritania			81.3			59.9		92.0				78.6
Mauritius		53.3	45.7		35.6	31.4		90.7	89.8		48.2	49.2
Mexico	71.8	61.3	61.8	37.3	33.3	33.2	92.6	92.8	92.3	40.6	47.3	51.4
Moldova		50.9			41.7			87.9			76.9	
Mongolia			41.2			30.7			89.4			80.4
Montenegro		39.3			27.6			73.0			56.8	
Morocco												
Mozambique	59.2	56.1	76.1	68.8	70.0	82.8	91.5	96.7	98.0	86.4	91.9	96.6
Myanmar												
Namibia	37.8			34.3			83.6			61.1		
Nepal	50.0	76.4	58.0	53.5	69.1	52.7	72.1	93.9	91.5	64.1	78.9	80.3
Netherlands	62.2	71.2	68.6	61.8	70.8	69.4	84.1	86.4	87.1	57.4	69.8	73.3
New Zealand	71.2	65.6	62.2	63.0	59.4	58.5	87.5	89.7	89.9	66.4	73.5	75.3
Nicaragua	73.7	76.8		33.1	34.9		95.8	95.9		52.4	54.9	
Niger	54.5			45.6			71.2			55.8		
Nigeria	47.3	30.9		27.2	23.7		97.6	91.0		52.9	64.0	
Norway	54.3	60.5	56.6	55.4	60.1	56.8	87.9	86.1	86.4	76.8	78.1	80.0
Oman												
Pakistan		70.8	64.9		25.5	23.8		93.9	94.5		29.8	28.4
Panama	62.5	62.1	62.8	28.4	35.3	32.4	92.6	93.1	93.7	47.3	56.8	59.2
Papua New Guinea			68.3			68.4			70.8			72.4
Paraguay	86.8	73.5	70.0	56.8	45.0	43.6	96.8	95.2	94.5	70.3	66.3	63.3
Peru	67.4	64.9	67.2	51.8	51.8	54.6	95.8	93.6	94.7	69.3	70.5	76.4
Philippines	56.0	52.1	50.3	32.6	31.6	31.9	93.1	90.4	89.5	55.1	53.8	59.4
Poland	43.9	39.5	39.1	35.6	31.8	29.7	82.2	80.1	80.6	67.9	65.5	65.7
Portugal	47.2	46.9	38.6	38.9	38.9	34.8	86.4	86.6	86.2	65.0	74.2	76.5
Romania	50.1	35.9	36.2	42.3	26.5	26.1	86.5	79.1	80.5	72.6	63.3	62.9
Russian Federation												
Rwanda	65.1	69.5		66.7	73.5		84.2	95.4		84.7	97.4	
Saudi Arabia												
Senegal	60.0	53.8		25.9	24.8		88.6	83.4		55.4	41.4	
Serbia			34.6			21.2			75.0			57.0
Sierra Leone		35.2			46.5			85.1			77.5	
Singapore												
Slovak Republic	52.0	40.7	36.4	40.4	32.4	25.5	86.2	87.4	86.4	68.3	69.9	70.1
Slovenia	44.6	44.5	44.4	40.7	36.3	34.8	79.1	82.4	82.0	67.7	73.0	73.7
Somalia												
South Africa	30.3	42.5		26.8	43.0		86.5	87.4		58.8	74.1	
Spain	44.6	52.3	45.1	38.6	42.9	40.1	85.4	87.2	87.3	48.1	61.5	70.5
Sri Lanka	57.9	53.7	50.8	36.8	32.9	28.1	92.7	89.5	90.8	41.9	41.3	43.3
Sudan												
Swaziland	39.4			37.4			90.8			62.4		
Sweden	44.2	49.1	52.1	46.8	51.3	51.4	88.3	88.4	90.1	82.9	82.1	83.1
Switzerland	65.0	66.6	69.1	62.1	64.7	66.5	95.5	91.9	92.5	69.6	76.2	78.5
Syrian Arab Republic		63.3			18.9			93.7			21.5	
Tajikistan		43.8			37.0			75.9			50.9	
Tanzania	58.9	80.2	57.0	55.2	81.2	55.3	97.8	97.6	95.3	82.5	95.5	87.8
Thailand	71.8	58.4	56.0	64.8	45.2	39.9	96.2	95.7	95.4	74.8	83.0	83.0
Timor-Leste		47.6	17.5		37.8	10.5		94.4	79.8		54.2	36.8
Togo		63.1			68.8			92.8			90.4	
Tonga	53.9			29.7			91.4			51.1		
Trinidad and Tobago												
Tunisia	50.0			27.3			91.0			24.6		
Turkey	63.7	51.7	49.8	34.2	24.5	25.5	89.1	83.3	82.3	37.0	75.5	31.0
Turkmenistan												
Uganda		75.4			70.0			95.2			92.9	
Ukraine		40.6			29.6			86.0			69.2	
United Kingdom	67.9	65.3	61.8	59.2	56.4		87.1	86.1	86.5	67.6	71.0	72.4
United States	70.2	62.9	56.7	62.3	58.6	53.5	87.8	86.4	85.1	71.5	71.6	71.8
Uruguay	72.6	60.3	61.3	52.5	45.8	44.5	91.5	90.9	92.5	60.5	68.9	72.8
Uzbekistan												
Venezuela, RB	64.0	60.1		29.3	35.1		93.9	93.9		50.3	63.1	
Vietnam	79.7	57.6	56.3	80.1	53.8	49.5	89.1	94.9	93.9	84.4	89.2	87.9
West Bank and Gaza		43.0	42.5		7.2	7.7		86.8	85.8		18.4	26.0
Yemen, Rep.												
Zambia		43.1			55.3			74.4			72.5	
Zimbabwe												

TABLE 2 *Skills*

	Average schooling (years) Total			Average schooling (years) Men			Average schooling (years) Women			Skills as a constraint (%) Total	
	1995	2005	2010	1995	2005	2010	1995	2005	2010	2005	2010
Afghanistan	2.2	3.4	4.2	3.4	5.5	6.7	0.9	1.1	1.5		18
Albania	9.4	10.3	10.3	9.8	10.5	10.4	9.1	10.1	10.1	10	
Algeria	6.3	7.7	8.3	7.7	8.8	9.1	4.8	6.7	7.5		
Angola										21	26
Argentina	8.6	9.1	9.3	8.5	9.0	9.1	8.7	9.3	9.5	49	57
Armenia	10.4	10.4	10.4	10.5	10.1	9.8	10.3	10.6	11.0	2	23
Australia	11.7	11.9	12.1	11.5	11.5	11.7	11.9	12.2	12.5		
Austria	8.5	9.3	9.5	9.5	10.3	10.3	7.6	8.4	8.8		
Azerbaijan										2	15
Bangladesh	3.7	5.2	5.8	4.3	5.5	6.0	3.1	4.8	5.6	25	
Barbados	8.8	9.3	9.5	8.8	9.2	9.2	8.7	9.5	9.8		
Belarus										7	61
Belgium	9.9	10.5	10.5	10.0	10.6	10.7	9.8	10.4	10.4		
Belize	8.8	9.3	9.5	8.8	9.4	9.5	8.7	9.3	9.5		
Benin	2.6	3.6	4.2	3.6	4.8	5.5	1.6	2.4	2.9	26	26
Bhutan											13
Bolivia	7.8	9.4	9.9	8.6	10.1	10.5	6.9	8.7	9.3	28	37
Bosnia and Herzegovina										4	19
Botswana	8.2	9.2	9.6	8.3	9.4	9.8	8.2	9.1	9.4	20	32
Brazil	5.4	7.2	7.5	5.3	7.1	7.4	5.4	7.3	7.7	40	69
Bulgaria	9.1	9.7	9.9	9.2	9.7	9.8	9.0	9.7	9.9	10	21
Burkina Faso										13	37
Burundi	2.2	2.9	3.3	2.7	3.4	3.9	1.6	2.3	2.7	12	
Cambodia	5.6	5.9	6.0	6.1	6.2	6.3	5.3	5.6	5.8	7	
Cameroon	5.0	5.8	6.1	5.8	6.5	6.8	4.1	5.0	5.4	8	38
Canada	10.8	12.1	12.1	10.8	12.1	12.0	10.7	12.2	12.1		
Central African Republic	3.0	3.5	3.6	4.1	4.7	4.8	1.9	2.4	2.6		
Chad											53
Chile	8.8	9.7	10.2	8.9	9.8	10.3	8.7	9.6	10.1	42	41
China	6.4	7.6	8.2	6.9	8.2	8.7	5.9	7.0	7.6		
Colombia	6.5	7.0	7.7	6.6	7.0	7.7	6.4	7.1	7.7	29	45
Congo, Dem. Rep.	3.2	3.5	3.5	4.6	4.7	4.6	2.0	2.3	2.4	13	65
Congo, Rep.	5.7	5.9	6.0	6.4	6.7	6.9	5.1	5.1	5.2		51
Costa Rica	7.6	8.1	8.7	7.6	8.0	8.6	7.5	8.1	8.8	13	38
Côte d'Ivoire				4.2	5.2	5.5					27
Croatia	8.1	8.7	9.0	8.7	9.2	9.4	7.5	8.3	8.6	7	
Cuba	9.5	10.1	10.6	9.7	10.3	10.7	9.3	10.0	10.5		
Czech Republic	11.4	12.7	12.1	11.6	12.9	12.3	11.2	12.6	12.0	12	29
Denmark	9.7	9.9	10.1	9.9	10.1	10.2	9.5	9.7	9.9		
Dominican Republic	6.3	7.0	7.4	6.5	7.0	7.3	6.1	7.0	7.5	31	
Ecuador	7.2	7.6	8.1	7.4	7.8	8.3	7.1	7.5	7.9	36	34
Egypt, Arab Rep.	5.1	6.6	7.1	6.1	7.5	7.9	4.0	5.6	6.3	30	
El Salvador	5.6	7.3	8.0	5.8	7.7	8.3	5.4	7.0	7.7	32	30
Eritrea											1
Estonia	10.4	11.6	11.8	10.3	11.3	11.5	10.5	11.8	12.1	7	30
Ethiopia											
Fiji	10.1	9.4	10.0	10.3	9.4	9.9	9.9	9.3	10.0		14
Finland	9.1	9.8	10.0	9.2	9.7	9.9	9.0	9.8	10.1		
France	8.6	9.9	10.5	8.8	10.2	10.7	8.3	9.6	10.4		
Gabon	6.2	7.7	8.4	5.5	7.1	7.9	7.0	8.2	8.8		43
Gambia, The	2.5	3.1	3.5	3.2	3.8	4.2	1.7	2.3	2.9	12	
Georgia										14	26
Germany	9.2	11.8	11.8	9.9	12.2	12.1	8.4	11.5	11.6	7	
Ghana	6.1	6.8	7.1	7.6	7.7	7.8	4.6	5.8	6.4	5	
Greece	8.7	9.9	10.7	9.2	10.2	10.9	8.2	9.6	10.5	9	
Guatemala	3.9	4.0	4.8	4.3	4.4	5.3	3.5	3.6	4.4	29	33
Guinea										12	
Guinea-Bissau										12	
Haiti	4.0	4.8	5.2	5.6	6.8	7.3	2.6	3.0	3.1		
Honduras	5.6	6.8	7.5	5.7	7.0	7.6	5.4	6.7	7.4	23	28
Hungary	10.4	11.5	11.7	10.7	11.6	11.8	10.2	11.4	11.5	13	6
India	3.8	4.7	5.1	4.9	5.8	6.1	2.6	3.6	4.1	14	
Indonesia	4.7	5.7	6.2	5.4	6.4	6.9	3.9	5.1	5.6	19	4
Iran, Islamic Rep.	6.1	8.1	8.6	7.3	9.3	9.6	4.9	6.8	7.5		
Iraq	4.9	5.4	5.8	6.0	6.4	6.8	3.7	4.4	4.9		
Ireland	10.7	11.3	11.6	10.6	11.1	11.5	10.8	11.4	11.7	16	
Israel	10.9	11.3	11.3	10.9	11.2	11.2	10.8	11.3	11.5		
Italy	8.3	9.1	9.5	8.6	9.5	9.9	7.9	8.8	9.2		
Jamaica	8.1	9.6	9.9	7.9	9.4	9.7	8.3	9.8	10.0	42	20
Japan	10.6	11.3	11.6	11.0	11.6	11.8	10.2	11.0	11.4		
Jordan	7.4	8.7	9.2	8.3	9.4	9.8	6.4	8.0	8.6		
Kazakhstan	8.8	10.1	10.4	9.0	10.2	10.5	8.6	10.0	10.3	9	50
Kenya	6.2	7.1	7.3	6.9	7.7	7.8	5.4	6.5	6.8	3	
Kiribati											
Korea, Rep.	10.6	11.5	11.8	11.4	12.1	12.4	9.7	10.8	11.3	7	
Kosovo											10
Kyrgyz Republic	8.4	8.6	8.7	8.6	8.6	8.7	8.3	8.6	8.8	19	28
Lao PDR	3.9	4.7	5.1	4.8	5.4	5.7	3.0	3.9	4.5	11	19

TABLE 2 *Skills,* continued

	Average schooling (years) Total			Average schooling (years) Men			Average schooling (years) Women			Skills as a constraint (%) Total	
	1995	2005	2010	1995	2005	2010	1995	2005	2010	2005	2010
Latvia	8.9	10.2	10.6	9.1	10.2	10.6	8.8	10.2	10.6	18	39
Lebanon										38	
Lesotho	5.1	6.0	6.6	4.1	4.9	5.5	5.9	7.0	7.5	30	17
Liberia	3.0	4.2	5.4	4.3	5.7	7.0	1.8	2.8	3.9		5
Libya	5.7	7.2	7.9	6.1	6.9	7.4	5.3	7.6	8.3		
Lithuania	9.2	10.4	10.9	9.5	10.5	10.9	8.9	10.3	10.9	15	40
Macedonia, FYR										6	15
Madagascar										30	17
Malawi	3.1	4.4	4.7	3.8	5.1	5.2	2.3	3.7	4.2	50	22
Malaysia	8.4	9.7	10.1	8.9	10.0	10.4	7.9	9.4	9.9		
Mali	1.0	1.5	2.0	1.3	1.9	2.3	0.7	1.2	1.7	8	12
Mauritania	3.1	4.1	4.6	4.0	5.1	5.6	2.3	3.1	3.7	23	
Mauritius	6.8	7.3	7.9	7.4	7.7	8.2	6.3	6.9	7.5	43	46
Mexico	7.1	8.4	9.1	7.4	8.7	9.4	6.8	8.1	8.8	10	31
Moldova	8.8	9.4	9.7	9.2	9.6	9.7	8.5	9.2	9.6	12	41
Mongolia	7.8	8.0	8.4	7.8	7.8	8.3	7.7	8.1	8.5	29	15
Montenegro										20	7
Morocco	3.5	4.4	5.0	4.5	5.5	6.1	2.5	3.4	4.0	21	
Mozambique	0.9	1.2	1.8	1.3	1.7	2.3	0.6	0.8	1.2	19	
Myanmar	3.1	4.1	4.6	3.1	4.1	4.8	3.1	4.0	4.5		
Namibia	6.1	5.9	6.0	6.1	5.6	5.5	6.1	6.1	6.4	20	
Nepal	2.6	3.4	4.0	3.7	4.1	4.4	1.6	2.7	3.5		6
Netherlands	10.5	10.8	11.0	10.8	11.1	11.2	10.2	10.6	10.8		
New Zealand	12.0	12.4	12.7	12.1	12.5	12.7	11.8	12.3	12.6		
Nicaragua	4.8	6.1	6.7	5.8	6.9	7.5	3.9	5.3	6.0	23	24
Niger	1.2	1.5	1.8	1.8	2.1	2.4	0.6	0.9	1.2	18	37
Nigeria										6	
Norway	11.0	12.3	12.3	11.2	12.3	12.2	10.8	12.4	12.4		
Oman										35	
Pakistan	3.4	4.9	5.6	4.6	6.2	6.8	2.1	3.6	4.3		
Panama	8.4	9.3	9.6	8.3	9.1	9.3	8.5	9.5	9.8	14	19
Papua New Guinea	3.3	3.9	4.1	4.0	4.6	4.7	2.6	3.2	3.4		
Paraguay	6.3	7.6	8.5	6.4	7.7	8.6	6.2	7.5	8.5	36	51
Peru	7.8	8.7	9.0	8.3	9.2	9.4	7.4	8.2	8.6	32	28
Philippines	7.9	8.6	9.0	7.9	8.4	8.7	8.0	8.9	9.2	12	8
Poland	9.2	9.7	9.9	9.2	9.7	9.8	9.1	9.7	10.0	15	36
Portugal	7.0	7.6	8.0	7.3	7.8	8.1	6.7	7.4	7.8	12	
Romania	9.6	10.1	10.4	10.0	10.4	10.6	9.2	9.8	10.1	14	43
Russian Federation	10.2	11.3	11.5	10.5	11.5	11.7	9.9	11.1	11.3	13	57
Rwanda	2.6	3.6	3.9	3.0	3.8	4.1	2.3	3.4	3.8	12	
Saudi Arabia	6.3	7.7	8.5	7.1	8.0	8.7	5.1	7.2	8.2		
Senegal	3.8	4.7	5.2	4.9	5.8	6.3	2.8	3.6	4.1	10	
Serbia	8.5	9.0	9.2	9.0	9.4	9.4	7.9	8.7	8.9	20	17
Sierra Leone	2.6	3.4	3.7	3.5	4.3	4.6	1.8	2.5	2.8		16
Singapore	7.4	8.5	9.1	7.8	9.0	9.5	7.0	7.9	8.8		
Slovak Republic	11.0	11.1	11.2	11.4	11.0	11.0	10.7	11.1	11.3	8	30
Slovenia	11.0	11.5	11.7	11.2	11.6	11.7	10.9	11.4	11.6	5	15
Somalia											
South Africa	8.3	8.3	8.6	8.2	8.3	8.4	8.3	8.3	8.7	9	
Spain	8.2	9.7	10.4	8.5	9.9	10.5	8.0	9.5	10.3	14	
Sri Lanka	9.7	10.8	11.1	9.9	10.9	11.1	9.5	10.7	11.0	21	
Sudan	2.5	3.0	3.3	3.1	3.5	3.7	1.9	2.5	2.8		
Swaziland	6.3	7.3	7.6	5.9	7.1	7.4	6.7	7.5	7.8	13	
Sweden	10.8	11.5	11.6	10.5	11.3	11.4	11.1	11.7	11.7		
Switzerland	9.6	9.7	9.9	10.3	10.3	10.4	8.9	9.1	9.4		
Syrian Arab Republic	4.5	4.8	5.3	5.2	5.2	5.5	3.9	4.5	5.0	36	
Tajikistan	9.6	9.3	9.3	9.9	8.8	8.6	9.3	9.8	10.0	5	34
Tanzania	4.4	5.0	5.5	5.1	5.6	6.0	3.7	4.5	5.1	20	
Thailand	5.9	6.8	7.5	6.2	7.0	7.7	5.6	6.6	7.3	30	
Timor-Leste											19
Togo	4.5	5.4	5.9	6.3	7.3	7.9	2.8	3.6	4.0		17
Tonga	9.2	9.2	9.4	9.3	9.3	9.5	9.1	9.2	9.2		59
Trinidad and Tobago	8.5	9.3	9.6	8.5	9.1	9.5	8.6	9.5	9.8		
Tunisia	5.1	6.6	7.3	6.1	7.4	8.0	4.1	5.7	6.6		
Turkey	5.4	6.5	7.0	6.5	7.4	7.9	4.4	5.6	6.1	33	25
Turkmenistan											
Uganda	4.0	4.9	5.4	4.8	5.6	5.9	3.2	4.2	4.8	10	
Ukraine	10.4	10.9	11.1	10.7	11.0	11.2	10.2	10.7	11.0	20	42
United Kingdom	8.6	9.3	9.8	8.4	9.1	9.5	8.7	9.5	10.0		
United States	12.6	12.9	13.1	12.7	12.9	13.0	12.6	12.9	13.2		
Uruguay	7.6	8.0	8.6	8.2	7.8	8.3	7.1	8.2	8.8	25	31
Uzbekistan										5	35
Venezuela, RB	5.5	6.4	7.0	5.5	6.3	7.0	5.5	6.5	7.0	28	25
Vietnam	4.6	5.7	6.4	4.9	6.0	6.6	4.3	5.5	6.3	14	9
West Bank and Gaza											
Yemen, Rep.	1.6	3.0	3.7	2.6	4.2	5.0	0.7	1.7	2.4		24
Zambia	6.0	6.5	7.0	6.2	7.0	7.4	5.9	6.0	6.5	8	
Zimbabwe	6.7	7.5	7.7	7.4	7.8	7.9	6.0	7.1	7.4		

TABLE 2 *Skills, continued*

	Educational attainment Reading			Educational attainment Mathematics			Educational attainment Science		
	2003	2006	2009	2003	2006	2009	2003	2006	2009
Afghanistan									
Albania			385			377			391
Algeria					387*			408*	
Angola									
Argentina		374	398		381	388		391	401
Armenia				478*	499*		461*	488*	
Australia	525	513	515	524	520	514	525	527	527
Austria	491	490	470	506	505	496	491	511	494
Azerbaijan		353	362		476	431		382	373
Bangladesh									
Barbados									
Belarus									
Belgium	507	501	506	529	520	515	509	510	507
Belize									
Benin									
Bhutan									
Bolivia									
Bosnia and Herzegovina					456*			466*	
Botswana				366*	364*		365*	355*	
Brazil	403	393	412	356	370	386	390	390	405
Bulgaria		402	429	476*	413	428	479*	434	439
Burkina Faso									
Burundi									
Cambodia									
Cameroon									
Canada	528	527	524	532	527	527	519	534	529
Central African Republic									
Chad									
Chile		442	449	387*	411	421	413*	438	447
China									
Colombia		385	413		370	381		388	402
Congo, Dem. Rep.									
Congo, Rep.									
Costa Rica									
Côte d'Ivoire									
Croatia		477	476		467	460		493	486
Cuba									
Czech Republic	489	483	478	516	510	493	523	513	500
Denmark	492	494	495	514	513	503	475	496	499
Dominican Republic									
Ecuador									
Egypt, Arab Rep.				406*	391*		421*	408*	
El Salvador					340*			387*	
Eritrea									
Estonia		501	501	531*	515	512	552*	531	528
Ethiopia									
Fiji									
Finland	543	547	536	544	548	541	548	563	554
France	496	488	496	511	496	497	511	495	498
Gabon									
Gambia, The									
Georgia					410*			421*	
Germany	491	495	497	503	504	513	502	516	520
Ghana				276*	309*		255*	303*	
Greece	472	460	483	445	459	466	481	473	470
Guatemala									
Guinea									
Guinea-Bissau									
Haiti									
Honduras									
Hungary	482	482	494	490	491	490	503	504	503
India									
Indonesia	382	393	402	360	391	371	395	393	383
Iran, Islamic Rep.				411*	403*		453*	459*	
Iraq									
Ireland	515	517	496	503	501	487	505	508	508
Israel		439	474	496*	442	447	488*	454	455
Italy	476	469	486	466	462	483	486	475	489
Jamaica									
Japan	498	498	520	534	523	529	548	531	539
Jordan		401	405	424*	384	387	475*	422	415
Kazakhstan			390			405			400
Kenya									
Kiribati									
Korea, Rep.	534	556	539	542	547	546	538	522	538
Kosovo									
Kyrgyz Republic		285	314		311	331		322	330
Lao PDR									

*An asterisk denotes data from TIMSS. All other data are from PISA.

TABLE 2 *Skills,* continued

	Educational attainment Reading			Educational attainment Mathematics			Educational attainment Science		
	2003	2006	2009	2003	2006	2009	2003	2006	2009
Latvia	491	479	484	483	486	482	489	490	494
Lebanon				433*	449*		393*	414*	
Lesotho									
Liberia									
Libya									
Lithuania		470	468	502*	486	477	519*	488	491
Macedonia, FYR				435*			449*		
Madagascar									
Malawi									
Malaysia				508*	474*		510*	471*	
Mali									
Mauritania									
Mauritius									
Mexico	400	411	425	385	406	419	405	410	416
Moldova				460*			472*		
Mongolia									
Montenegro		392	408		399	403		412	401
Morocco				387*	381*		396*	402*	
Mozambique									
Myanmar									
Namibia									
Nepal									
Netherlands	513	507	508	538	531	526	524	525	522
New Zealand	522	521	521	523	522	519	521	530	532
Nicaragua									
Niger									
Nigeria									
Norway	500	484	503	495	490	498	484	487	500
Oman					372*			423*	
Pakistan									
Panama			371			360			376
Papua New Guinea									
Paraguay									
Peru			370			365			369
Philippines				378*			377*		
Poland	497	508	500	490	495	495	498	498	508
Portugal	478	472	489	466	466	487	468	474	493
Romania		396	424	475*	415	427	470*	418	428
Russian Federation	442	440	459	468	476	468	489	479	478
Rwanda									
Saudi Arabia				332*	329*		398*	403*	
Senegal									
Serbia	412	401	442	437	435	442	436	436	443
Sierra Leone									
Singapore			526	605*	593*	562	578*	567*	542
Slovak Republic	469	466	477	498	492	497	495	488	490
Slovenia		494	483	493*	504	501	520*	519	512
Somalia									
South Africa				264*			244*		
Spain	481	461	481	485	480	483	487	488	488
Sri Lanka									
Sudan									
Swaziland									
Sweden	514	507	497	509	502	494	506	503	495
Switzerland	499	499	501	527	530	534	513	512	517
Syrian Arab Republic					395*			452*	
Tajikistan									
Tanzania									
Thailand	420	417	421	417	417	419	429	421	425
Timor-Leste									
Togo									
Tonga									
Trinidad and Tobago			416			414			410
Tunisia	375	380	404	359	365	371	385	386	401
Turkey	441	447	464	423	424	445	434	424	454
Turkmenistan									
Uganda									
Ukraine					462*			485*	
United Kingdom		495	494		495	492		515	514
United States	495		500	483	474	487	491	489	502
Uruguay	434	413	426	422	427	427	438	428	427
Uzbekistan									
Venezuela, RB									
Vietnam									
West Bank and Gaza				390*			435*		
Yemen, Rep.									
Zambia									
Zimbabwe									

*An asterisk denotes data from TIMSS. All other data are from PISA.

TABLE 3 *Employment structure*

	Employment in primary sector (%)			Employment in secondary sector (%)			Employment in tertiary sector (%)			Employment in civil service (%)		
	1995	2005	2010	1995	2005	2010	1995	2005	2010	1995	2005	2010
Afghanistan		59.1			12.5			28.4		1.8	3.3	3.2
Albania	3.0	47.1		40.2	20.5		56.8	32.4		15.9	11.2	
Algeria												
Angola												
Argentina	7.3	6.7	5.8	34.6	30.3	29.4	58.1	63.0	64.8	8.7	9.0	
Armenia										10.4	16.5	15.6
Australia	5.0	3.6	3.3	22.8	21.3	21.1	72.2	75.1	75.5	13.4	14.0	14.6
Austria	7.4	5.5	5.2	32.0	27.5	24.9	60.6	66.9	69.9	14.9	11.8	11.5
Azerbaijan	24.8			18.2			57.0			21.7	15.4	14.3
Bangladesh			39.0			21.0			40.0		2.2	
Barbados												
Belarus										22.1	24.4	
Belgium	2.7	2.0	1.4	28.3	24.7	23.4	69.1	63.3	65.3	18.9	18.7	18.8
Belize	29.7			18.7			51.6			12.6		
Benin		45.1			9.2			45.7		1.4		
Bhutan		69.1			7.2			23.7		8.8		
Bolivia	43.8	40.0	35.6	18.2	18.9	18.8	38.1	41.1	45.6	6.2		
Bosnia and Herzegovina		30.4			40.5			29.1				
Botswana			25.5			18.1			56.5	16.0	15.5	15.2
Brazil	26.3	20.5	17.0	19.8	21.4	22.2	53.9	58.1	60.9	8.9	10.6	11.0
Bulgaria	23.9	8.9	6.8	33.5	34.2	33.3	42.6	56.6	59.9	18.0	16.3	13.9
Burkina Faso	89.1	88.0		2.7	2.8		8.2	9.2				
Burundi												
Cambodia	72.5	62.3	60.1	7.4	12.3	13.1	20.1	25.3	26.8			
Cameroon	68.7			6.1			25.1					
Canada	4.1	2.7	2.4	22.0	22.0	21.5	74.0	75.3	76.5	19.4	17.8	18.6
Central African Republic		66.9			9.2			23.9				
Chad												
Chile	15.7	13.2	11.2	26.1	23.0	23.2	58.2	63.9	65.6	8.1	8.5	9.3
China	52.2	44.8	36.7	23.0	23.8	28.7	24.8	31.4	34.6	5.4		
Colombia	27.0	20.7	18.5	21.8	20.0	19.8	51.2	59.3	61.7	3.2	6.1	5.3
Congo, Dem. Rep.		71.5			8.0			20.6				
Congo, Rep.		36.4			23.9			39.7		7.6		
Costa Rica	7.2	15.2	11.9	28.8	21.6	20.0	64.0	63.1	68.1	13.3	11.3	11.7
Côte d'Ivoire												
Croatia	19.9	17.3	14.9	29.1	28.6	27.3	50.9	54.0	57.6	15.9	16.1	15.5
Cuba										37.1	41.6	42.5
Czech Republic	6.6	4.0	3.1	41.8	39.5	38.0	51.5	56.5	57.9		14.0	13.4
Denmark	4.4	2.8	2.4	27.0	23.4	19.6	68.6	73.5	77.7	30.4	30.6	30.7
Dominican Republic	16.8	14.8	14.6	23.7	22.3	18.1	59.4	63.0	67.4	9.7		
Ecuador	38.1	31.3	28.4	17.3	17.5	18.6	44.6	51.3	53.0	9.0	7.5	7.9
Egypt, Arab Rep.	33.3	39.1		22.8	18.8		44.0	42.1			22.8	23.6
El Salvador	27.0	20.2		26.3	22.1		46.7	57.7		7.2		
Eritrea												
Estonia	10.2	5.2	4.2	34.2	33.8	30.1	55.6	61.1	65.1	24.2	20.8	22.8
Ethiopia	81.9	82.8		3.5	6.0		14.5	11.2		1.3	1.7	
Fiji	32.9		26.1	20.5		17.5	46.6		56.4	11.1	11.9	11.4
Finland	8.0	4.8	4.4	26.8	25.6	23.2	64.9	69.5	71.9	24.3	23.1	22.0
France	4.9	3.6	2.9	26.9	23.7	22.2	68.1	72.4	74.5		22.8	
Gabon		23.8			21.2			55.0		13.4		
Gambia, The												
Georgia			53.3			9.7			37.0			
Germany	3.2	2.3	1.6	36.0	29.7	28.4	60.8	67.9	70.0	13.1	11.6	11.2
Ghana		57.4			14.2			28.5				
Greece	20.4	12.4	12.5	23.2	22.4	19.7	56.3	65.1	67.7	6.8	7.6	8.2
Guatemala		33.8			22.6			43.6		4.3	4.5	
Guinea											1.7	2.1
Guinea-Bissau												
Haiti												
Honduras	37.4	34.3	37.1	25.0	23.0	20.3	37.6	42.7	42.5	6.2	6.2	
Hungary	8.0	5.0	4.5	32.6	32.4	30.7	59.4	62.6	64.9	21.9	22.1	22.0
India	61.9	56.1	51.2	15.8	19.0	22.3	22.3	24.9	26.4	2.8	2.3	
Indonesia	45.3	45.7	37.1	17.3	17.7	18.7	37.3	36.7	44.1	4.9	3.7	
Iran, Islamic Rep.		20.8			32.7			46.5			11.7	10.6
Iraq		2.9			29.8			67.3				
Ireland	9.1	5.9	4.6	29.3	27.9	19.5	61.5	65.5	75.5	17.5	15.5	18.4
Israel	2.9	2.0	1.7	28.7	21.4	20.4	67.7	75.7	77.1	19.0	17.2	17.0
Italy	6.6	4.2	3.8	33.7	30.8	28.8	59.8	65.0	67.5	18.3	16.0	15.1
Jamaica	19.5			17.9			62.6					
Japan	5.7	4.4	3.7	33.6	27.9	25.3	60.4	66.4	69.7	8.0	7.0	7.1
Jordan		3.8			22.8			73.4		16.1	14.9	16.2
Kazakhstan												
Kenya	67.9	72.3		4.6	7.9		27.5	19.8		4.3		
Kiribati		3.4			6.3			90.3				
Korea, Rep.	12.4	7.9	6.6	33.3	26.8	17.0	54.3	65.2	76.4	4.3		
Kosovo		17.3			26.7			56.0				
Kyrgyz Republic	51.3			10.2			38.5			18.3	14.3	
Lao PDR			71.3			10.7			18.1			

TABLE 3 *Employment structure,* continued

	Employment in primary sector (%)			Employment in secondary sector (%)			Employment in tertiary sector (%)			Employment in civil service (%)		
	1995	2005	2010	1995	2005	2010	1995	2005	2010	1995	2005	2010
Latvia	17.3	12.1	8.8	27.2	25.8	24.0	55.4	61.8	66.9	24.4	22.7	23.2
Lebanon		7.3			54.6			38.1				
Lesotho												
Liberia		44.2			1.9			53.8				
Libya										36.4		
Lithuania	20.7	14.0	9.0	28.5	29.1	24.4	50.8	56.9	66.2	21.4	23.4	25.0
Macedonia, FYR		19.5			32.3			48.2				
Madagascar	70.1			3.9			26.0			2.0	· 2.1	
Malawi		84.9			4.6			10.5		2.7		
Malaysia												
Mali	70.7	58.0		6.6	12.2		22.8	29.8				
Mauritania			25.2			9.7			65.2			
Mauritius		12.0	11.5		32.4	31.4		55.6	57.1	14.0	14.7	13.8
Mexico	23.8	14.9	13.1	21.5	25.5	25.5	54.2	59.0	60.6	12.4	8.9	8.8
Moldova		48.7			15.8			35.5			19.3	17.9
Mongolia			40.5			16.8			42.7			
Montenegro												
Morocco	39.2	34.9		24.3	24.8		36.6	40.3			7.5	7.7
Mozambique	87.2	81.2	83.5	3.9	3.2	3.8	8.8	15.6	12.7			
Myanmar												
Namibia	44.5			12.7			42.8					
Nepal		80.1	76.3		8.1	10.5		11.8	13.2			
Netherlands	3.7	3.2	2.8	22.6	19.6	15.9	70.6	72.4	71.6	13.8	12.8	12.5
New Zealand	9.7	7.1	6.6	25.1	22.0	20.9	65.2	70.7	72.5	12.4	10.2	10.7
Nicaragua	43.8	35.9	31.7	14.7	18.8	18.3	41.4	45.2	50.0	5.4		
Niger												
Nigeria	68.1			2.7			29.2					
Norway	5.4	3.3	2.5	23.0	20.8	19.7	71.3	75.7	77.6	30.9	30.1	30.8
Oman										14.0		
Pakistan		41.8	43.4		21.3	21.2		36.9	35.5			
Panama	21.3	19.9	18.1	17.9	16.9	18.5	60.7	63.3	63.4	8.8	7.9	
Papua New Guinea			25.2			6.8			68.8			
Paraguay	40.8	32.4	25.8	16.5	15.7	19.2	42.7	51.9	54.9	5.1	6.6	
Peru	31.7	37.5	31.7	15.7	13.7	16.4	52.6	48.8	51.9		8.2	9.5
Philippines	40.2	38.7	33.5	17.1	16.0	14.5	42.7	45.3	52.0	7.4	7.1	7.8
Poland	22.6	17.4	12.8	32.0	29.2	30.2	45.3	53.4	56.9	16.2	11.4	10.6
Portugal	11.5	11.8	10.9	32.2	30.6	27.7	56.3	57.5	61.4		13.6	12.5
Romania	40.3	32.1	30.1	31.0	30.3	28.7	28.7	37.5	41.2	13.1	13.9	13.0
Russian Federation										20.1	21.5	
Rwanda	88.6	78.0		1.7	5.0		9.7	17.0				
Saudi Arabia												
Senegal	5.1	36.2		29.7	14.5		65.2	49.3		2.9	2.7	
Serbia		22.9				24.9		52.2				14.2
Sierra Leone		70.8			5.5			23.7				
Singapore										5.4	5.0	5.0
Slovak Republic	9.2	4.7	3.2	38.9	38.8	37.1	51.9	56.3	59.6	30.7	16.0	14.8
Slovenia	10.1	8.8	8.8	43.1	37.2	32.5	46.4	53.3	58.3	11.6	15.5	16.0
Somalia												
South Africa	14.3	7.8		27.9	25.5		57.9	66.6		12.8	8.9	
Spain	9.0	5.3	4.3	30.2	29.7	23.1	60.8	65.0	72.6	14.8	14.1	15.5
Sri Lanka	38.8	30.9	31.6	20.9	26.4	26.3	40.3	42.7	42.1	8.2	10.7	
Sudan												
Swaziland	16.3			19.0			64.7					
Sweden	3.1	2.0	2.1	25.9	22.0	19.9	71.0	75.7	77.7	30.3	28.0	
Switzerland	4.4	3.8	3.3	28.6	23.7	21.1	67.0	72.5	70.9	11.8	12.4	12.1
Syrian Arab Republic		25.4			26.6			47.9			20.7	19.8
Tajikistan		67.0			4.5			28.5				
Tanzania		75.8	78.5		4.5	2.7		19.7	18.8			
Thailand	28.9	44.3	42.1	24.5	19.9	20.0	46.6	35.8	38.0		6.7	7.3
Timor-Leste			50.5			9.8			39.7		3.0	
Togo		59.1			8.6			32.3				
Tonga	33.1			26.0			40.9					
Trinidad and Tobago										24.3	21.2	21.1
Tunisia	21.8			37.2			41.0					
Turkey	43.4	29.5	23.7	22.3	24.8	26.2	34.3	45.8	50.1	9.8	11.2	12.8
Turkmenistan												
Uganda		73.1			6.4			20.5		1.8		
Ukraine		9.6			31.9			58.6		22.4	19.5	20.3
United Kingdom	2.0	1.3	1.2	27.3	22.2	19.1	70.2	76.3	78.9	17.0	19.7	19.6
United States	2.9	1.6	1.6	24.3	20.6	16.7	72.9	77.8	81.2	15.0	15.0	15.6
Uruguay	5.2	4.6	11.6	21.0	21.9	21.4	73.9	73.5	67.0	14.1	11.2	12.5
Uzbekistan												
Venezuela, RB	14.2	10.4		24.0	21.7		61.9	67.8				
Vietnam	61.8	52.3	54.0	14.8	20.0	20.4	23.4	27.8	25.7		4.3	4.4
West Bank and Gaza	11.0	6.9	26.3	41.7	38.2	32.8	47.3	54.9	40.9		23.6	23.8
Yemen, Rep.											8.5	
Zambia		72.1			6.4			21.5				
Zimbabwe										5.9		

TABLE 4 *Living standards*

| | Wages in selected occupations (2005 US$ per year) | | | | | | | | | | | |
| | Accountant | | | Chemical engineer | | | Bus driver | | | Sewing machine operator | | |
	1995	2005	2008	1995	2005	2008	1995	2005	2008	1995	2005	2008
Afghanistan												
Albania												
Algeria												
Angola	7,139						1,989					
Argentina					10,849	17,214	9,581			2,948		
Armenia												
Australia	32,498	40,267		39,694	59,054		28,065	29,331		22,418	21,019	
Austria	57,907			38,574			27,954			19,402		
Azerbaijan		2,769	7,483	454	1,785	6,544						
Bangladesh	1,548			1,201			578	1,077		584		
Barbados	32,772						13,553			4806		
Belarus				1,188	2,657					761	1,133	
Belgium										22,692	22,093	
Belize												
Benin												
Bhutan	25028						5967			4989		
Bolivia	12,745			5,159			1,173			2,134		
Bosnia and Herzegovina												
Botswana		1,528										
Brazil		20,045						3,134				
Bulgaria												
Burkina Faso	3,516											
Burundi												
Cambodia	293						225			707		
Cameroon												
Canada	25,459	37,540	41,143	37,116	60,033		20,146	21,033	27,400	12,253	13,125	13,159
Central African Republic	21,735			10,284			1,028			799		
Chad												
Chile		12,951									5,184	
China	1,096	2,913		874	2,538		501			891	1,327	
Colombia												
Congo, Dem. Rep.												
Congo, Rep.												
Costa Rica	10,761	8,998	12,518		9,078	12,011	5,198	3,993	5,973	3,475	2,541	2,579
Côte d'Ivoire												
Croatia	8,955			6,953			5,424			6,281		
Cuba												
Czech Republic		14,387	23,583	5,918	14,559	22,528	4,024	8,478	12,911	3,133	4,383	
Denmark		123,067			116,081			51,740			47,102	
Dominican Republic	2,561									2,561		
Ecuador												
Egypt, Arab Rep.	2,778			4,469			1,041			615		
El Salvador	16,107	15,103	17,006	12,547	12,267	16,327	2,688	2,906	4,083	2,053	2,496	2,079
Eritrea	3,077						1,518			615		
Estonia	8,180			5,166			3,593			2,011		
Ethiopia												
Fiji												
Finland	42,583	59,695		44,183	55,887		30,885	32,263		23,362	24,554	
France												
Gabon	12,045									2,725		
Gambia, The												
Georgia												
Germany	68,538	63,483	71,989	78,873	73,544	86,265	48,206	41,013	44,482	29,536	26,388	31,576
Ghana	5,589	1,516		2,298	519		760			867	562	
Greece												
Guatemala										1,476		
Guinea												
Guinea-Bissau												
Haiti												
Honduras	3,206			32,684			2,304			953		
Hungary	4,548	24,679		10,439	28,345		4,514	8,987				
India	3,261						912			800		
Indonesia					2,533			818			731	
Iran, Islamic Rep.												
Iraq												
Ireland												
Israel												
Italy	55,684	52,973	58,298	30,449	34,726	40,328	20,270	21,559	24,880	17,366	18,269	20,791
Jamaica												
Japan							50,366	30,710	30,452	29,592	19,914	19,836
Jordan	8,320	8,163		3,580	4,925		3,830	2,488		1,757	2,945	
Kazakhstan		5,965			3,269			2,165			957	
Kenya												
Kiribati												
Korea; Rep.	22,122	38,755		20,206	29,415		14,914	14,647		13,291	13,698	
Kosovo												
Kyrgyz Republic	605									251		
Lao PDR												

TABLE 4 *Living standards,* continued

	Accountant			Chemical engineer			Bus driver			Sewing machine operator		
	Wages in selected occupations (2005 US$ per year)											
	1995	2005	2008	1995	2005	2008	1995	2005	2008	1995	2005	2008
Latvia	8,347	12,686		3,837	10,368		2,763	5,877		2,181	3,066	
Lebanon												
Lesotho												
Liberia												
Libya												
Lithuania	3,939	11,976					2,864	5,228		2,030	4,155	
Macedonia, FYR												
Madagascar	1,205						466	488		424		
Malawi	16,360						1,106			389		
Malaysia										1,673		
Mali												
Mauritania												
Mauritius	17,701	16,091	19,100				3,465	2,826	3,622	2,330	1,895	2,369
Mexico		3,319	3,220		11,355		1,796	2,623	2,682	1,552	2,115	2,158
Moldova	1,130	1,644	3,693		1,436	2,345		588	1,535	377	1,040	1,691
Mongolia												
Montenegro												
Morocco												
Mozambique												
Myanmar	4,880	11,869		4,164	16,617		2,733	10,575		2,082	7,985	
Namibia	19,393											
Nepal												
Netherlands												
New Zealand												
Nicaragua	3,891			11,728			1,327					
Niger												
Nigeria	4,472			21,678			3,012			944		
Norway							24,680	28,863	36,446			
Oman												
Pakistan		3,193			2,182			1,230			851	
Panama												
Papua New Guinea	16,770			23,560			5,500			3,779		
Paraguay												
Peru	17,836	24,789	23,679				1,543	2,181	5,702	2,516	2,474	2,579
Philippines	5,853	3,951		6,513	3,408		2,640	1,919		2,314	1,653	2,159
Poland	7,068	12,502		5,867	12,150		3,869	7,961		3,656	7,059	
Portugal	19,084	23,948		32,444	34,440		8,653	9,039		6,259	5,940	
Romania	4,773	9,876	15,849	3,476	5,661	10,681	2,754	3,395	6,386	1,549	2,082	3,805
Russian Federation				2,288	2,780			2,922		759	1,542	
Rwanda												
Saudi Arabia												
Senegal												
Serbia												
Sierra Leone	5,782			29,164	27,275		463			449		
Singapore	44,523	28,089		29,164	27,275		10,665	9,229		9,005	6,424	
Slovak Republic	4,394	7,829		2,753	7,315		2,027	5,963		2,053	2,583	
Slovenia	11,945			19,381			12,974			6,153		
Somalia												
South Africa												
Spain												
Sri Lanka							1,101			1,054		
Sudan	11,213			14,663			7,095			4,341		
Swaziland	16,472									8,697		
Sweden	37,390			33,607			24,762			28,083		
Switzerland												
Syrian Arab Republic												
Tajikistan	288			357			108			338		
Tanzania												
Thailand	14,657	13,861		7,118	16,327		4,072	3,291		4,343	2,562	
Timor-Leste												
Togo	11,021											
Tonga												
Trinidad and Tobago							7,777			1,903		
Tunisia				4,911			4,702			2,849		
Turkey		14,624		16,305	17,410			5,823		3,140	5,648	
Turkmenistan												
Uganda	3,784			1,235			866			237		
Ukraine				1,909						767		
United Kingdom	46,991	60,352	56,524		33,624		21,452	30,880	32,388		22,402	23,513
United States	43,432	50,457		67,014	82,647		27,533	30,958		18,100	18,515	
Uruguay							10,389			4,782		
Uzbekistan												
Venezuela, RB	7,857			7,275			2,205			1,924		
Vietnam												
West Bank and Gaza												3,464
Yemen, Rep.	7,572			9,466			5,429			3,360		
Zambia	2,758							522		781	304	
Zimbabwe												

TABLE 4 *Living standards,* continued

	Working poor (% below $1.25 PPP US$ a day)			Satisfied with life (% in latest survey)			Labor share (% of national income)			Gender gap in earnings (women/men)		
	1995	2005	2010	Employed	Unemployed	Out of labor force	1995	2005	2010	1995	2005	2010
Afghanistan												
Albania				46.3	33.3	35.5						
Algeria				55.4	39.3	57.5	29.9	22.8				
Angola												
Argentina	0.0	5.0	1.0	87.1	71.6	90.4	37.8	34.8			0.90	0.96
Armenia		11.0					39.4	42.6	43.9			
Australia				86.9	65.6	81.5	54.3	52.8	52.5			
Austria							59.6	54.5	54.2		0.87	0.88
Azerbaijan	16.0						24.5	24.4	18.9			
Bangladesh				40.4	41.5	42.4					0.68	
Barbados												
Belarus	1.0						45.7	52.9	55.5			
Belgium							56.9	56.5	57.2		0.93	0.85
Belize	12.0											
Benin		47.0					18.3					
Bhutan		10.0						89.5	88.9			
Bolivia	17.0	18.0	16.0				37.5	37.6	31.5		0.76	
Bosnia and Herzegovina				58.7	38.2	49.1		54.3	59.9			
Botswana							31.9					
Brazil	11.0	9.0	6.0	85.6	74.2	82.3	48.8	46.7	49.1	0.84	0.88	0.89
Bulgaria	2.0	0.0		51.9	31.3	38.3	38.9	40.7	42.5		0.93	0.82
Burkina Faso	71.0	57.0		48.7	37.1	47.1		24.9	22.0	0.80		
Burundi	86.0							40.7				
Cambodia		32.0	23.0								1.05	0.99
Cameroon		10.0					22.5	20.0	20.8			
Canada				91.4	78.7	90.7	55.8	54.3				
Central African Republic		62.0						20.7				
Chad							18.8					
Chile	3.0	1.0	1.0	80.1	73.2	74.6	40.5	39.8	42.3	0.96	0.93	0.86
China				72.5	65.8	74.9						
Colombia		13.0	8.0	91.3	84.1	89.9	36.0	35.1	35.0			0.91
Congo, Dem. Rep.											0.89	
Congo, Rep.												
Costa Rica	0.0	4.0	3.0				50.0	51.9	55.4			
Côte d'Ivoire							24.1					
Croatia		0.0					56.9	57.0			0.93	
Cuba							48.5	46.2	44.5			
Czech Republic							47.5	48.0	49.2		1.01	0.99
Denmark							60.4	62.9	66.5			
Dominican Republic	5.0	6.0	2.0				37.7					
Ecuador	14.0	9.0	5.0									
Egypt, Arab Rep.		2.0		52.2	42.9	54.6	24.4	27.2	26.1		0.59	
El Salvador	10.0	12.0	9.0	82.3	75.6	78.0						
Eritrea												
Estonia		0.0					59.6	49.9	59.7		0.77	0.69
Ethiopia	61.0			40.2	38.2	47.5					0.84	
Fiji							39.0					
Finland				94.4	69.9	87.4	56.7	56.4	56.6			
France				80.8	63.5	71.6	58.0	58.0	58.4		0.77	0.88
Gabon		5.0						22.3				
Gambia, The	66.0											
Georgia				42.8	28.4	33.8		19.2	33.3			0.60
Germany				86.0	50.6	78.1	59.7	55.9	54.7		0.99	
Ghana	39.0			63.3	59.7	64.9					0.77	
Greece							34.9	38.7	39.3		0.89	0.93
Guatemala		14.0		88.1	89.3	82.4		34.4	32.6			
Guinea												
Guinea-Bissau												
Haiti												
Honduras	27.0	26.0	18.0				47.7	48.7	49.5			
Hungary	0.0	0.0					54.4	54.5	54.6		1.01	
India				38.9	51.2	39.0	30.5	29.1	30.0	0.68	0.73	0.73
Indonesia	47.0	22.0	18.0	73.3	69.3	77.4					0.86	
Iran, Islamic Rep.				63.3	60.7	66.9	23.4	21.8			0.70	
Iraq				31.4	22.1	31.3	6.7	14.7	21.9			
Ireland							50.3	46.2	48.8		0.93	1.02
Israel				80.7	71.9	67.6	56.6	54.1	53.3			
Italy				85.7	69.4	80.6	45.8	45.3	46.4		1.12	0.90
Jamaica								48.5	51.0	0.98		
Japan				80.9	70.6	85.2	52.1	49.5				
Jordan				47.7	40.2	50.6	45.0	42.0	44.0			
Kazakhstan							39.0	34.4	34.4			
Kenya		43.0					35.1	41.4	40.4		0.81	
Kiribati												
Korea, Rep.				72.5	55.0	71.2	51.5	51.1	51.6			
Kosovo												
Kyrgyz Republic				64.9	73.4	64.7	40.0	27.2	32.0			
Lao PDR	49.0		34.0									

TABLE 4 *Living standards,* continued

	Working poor (% below $1.25 PPP US$ a day)			Satisfied with life (% in latest survey)			Labor share (% of national income)			Gender gap in earnings (women/men)		
	1995	2005	2010	Employed	Unemployed	Out of labor force	1995	2005	2010	1995	2005	2010
Latvia		0.0	0.0				50.0	47.3	47.9		0.74	0.67
Lebanon							35.5					
Lesotho							57.4	48.8	48.4			
Liberia		84.0										
Libya												
Lithuania			0.0				41.6	45.1	49.5		0.69	0.71
Macedonia, FYR							51.1	43.9	44.0			
Madagascar	72.0											
Malawi												
Malaysia				79.6	75.0	81.2						
Mali	86.0			58.2	53.1	54.5				0.49		
Mauritania								25.2				
Mauritius							43.3	38.7	38.4		0.76	
Mexico	6.0	5.0	4.0	89.2	83.5	89.5	32.3	30.4		0.94		
Moldova	27.0	12.0		52.1	49.1	42.6	50.6	49.9	57.5		0.85	
Mongolia							27.5	26.1	33.8			0.77
Montenegro												
Morocco				36.7	20.0	52.2		37.4	34.2			
Mozambique							16.9	27.7	27.3	1.09		0.93
Myanmar												
Namibia	49.0						47.6	46.4	44.4			
Nepal		53.0	25.0									0.72
Netherlands				96.4	76.6	93.4	56.5	55.8	55.8			
New Zealand							37.0	40.6				
Nicaragua	21.0	15.0										
Niger							17.1	17.0	15.8			
Nigeria				71.4	76.7	80.6	17.3	5.2	4.1			
Norway				94.5	58.3	89.4	54.2	46.8	46.7			
Oman							33.4	26.4	32.5			
Pakistan				26.6	29.2	29.1					0.63	0.36
Panama	16.0	9.0	6.0				39.2	34.5	31.4			
Papua New Guinea							26.0	17.3				
Paraguay	12.0	7.0	7.0				35.2	36.9	37.1			
Peru	14.0	9.0	5.0	75.5	68.5	74.7	27.9	25.3	23.8	0.71	0.82	0.81
Philippines		23.0	18.0	67.4	69.5	64.9	25.3	27.7	27.9		0.89	
Poland	0.0	0.0	0.0	82.2	64.5	71.4	45.1	40.7	42.4		0.89	0.96
Portugal							54.7	58.2	58.2		0.83	0.90
Romania	5.0	1.0	0.0	67.4	25.7	45.6	39.6	44.3	47.1	0.86	0.81	0.89
Russian Federation				59.5	41.2	59.6	48.5	49.9	52.1			
Rwanda				42.2		44.7				0.93	0.90	
Saudi Arabia				77.2	67.1	78.6	35.1	28.1				
Senegal		34.0					17.6	24.1	21.6			
Serbia			0.0	70.9	55.9	53.1	65.7	56.6	53.6			
Sierra Leone		53.0										
Singapore				83.3	71.6	83.9	43.9	42.1	44.3			
Slovak Republic		0.0	0.0				65.1	58.1	60.9			
Slovenia				85.0	65.5	72.5						
Somalia												
South Africa				81.9	63.4	77.7	54.9	49.9	49.8		0.85	
Spain				93.4	94.5	83.6	53.0	52.9	53.3		0.80	0.83
Sri Lanka							46.4	57.3	57.3		0.86	0.80
Sudan							37.1	25.1	25.1			
Swaziland	79.0											
Sweden				92.4	77.1	88.6	60.2	62.0	61.1		1.06	0.91
Switzerland				93.7	75.6	90.7	64.1	65.8				
Syrian Arab Republic		2.0									1.08	
Tajikistan		35.0						15.9	15.7		0.66	
Tanzania				23.5	22.1	27.2					0.79	
Thailand	4.0	1.0	0.0	84.5	72.1	91.3	32.3	32.9	33.2	0.89	0.89	0.95
Timor-Leste		37.0										
Togo		39.0										
Tonga												
Trinidad and Tobago				82.5	71.6	79.8	46.2	30.6	33.0			
Tunisia							41.8	35.8	36.1			
Turkey				85.9	70.4	84.3	22.2	27.1			0.96	0.96
Turkmenistan	25.0											
Uganda				49.6	31.2	49.6						
Ukraine		0.0		60.1	57.3	48.4	53.2	55.7	56.3			
United Kingdom				89.8	79.6	91.8	58.2	60.1			0.98	
United States				85.9	81.0	87.8	57.2	56.2	56.0		0.85	
Uruguay	1.0	1.0	0.0	88.9	80.2	86.8	43.0	38.5			0.99	
Uzbekistan												
Venezuela, RB	10.0	13.0		80.8	75.0	76.6	35.6	30.6		0.93	0.94	
Vietnam	50.0	21.0	17.0	82.6	46.3	82.2				0.94	0.89	0.80
West Bank and Gaza			0.0								0.77	0.73
Yemen, Rep.	13.0										0.70	
Zambia	56.0	65.0		64.3	56.2	64.5					0.89	
Zimbabwe				25.0	25.1	28.1						

TABLE 5 *Productivity*

| | Value added per worker (2005 US$ per year) | | | | | | | | |
| | Primary sector | | | Secondary sector | | | Tertiary sector | | |
	1995	2005	2010	1995	2005	2010	1995	2005	2010
Afghanistan									
Albania	2,409	2,622	3,885	6,602	10,419	8,110	3,031	13,496	14,021
Algeria		5,364			23,962			6,979	
Angola									
Argentina	169,887	115,095	134,720	30,924	18,165	24,822	27,453	8,976	14,530
Armenia		2,452	4,636		15,285	28,403		4,803	10,819
Australia	40,133	61,462	70,416	73,971	95,996	90,412	55,153	70,239	89,745
Austria	32,626	22,953	26,250	83,512	89,626	99,691	95,032	88,496	84,955
Azerbaijan	903	909	1,627	1,915	18,994	44,847	1,115	1,939	6,286
Bangladesh	394	398		2,406	1,720		1,914	1,348	
Barbados	25,047	24,469		19,951	19,992		22,501	23,701	
Belarus	3,261			4,693			5,595		
Belgium	51,682	40,155	67,238	103,700	93,212	91,242	104,053	99,852	99,674
Belize	7,302	7,920		12,726	10,017		12,421	11,235	
Benin		1,066			1,960			1,684	
Bhutan		1,474	1,017		6,136	25,363		2,837	4,794
Bolivia	22,960	827		3,106	3,780		1,971	2,861	
Bosnia and Herzegovina									
Botswana	2,562	858		20,939	47,317		7,425	12,354	
Brazil	2,764	2,618	5,048	17,135	13,428	18,599	15,379	10,798	16,888
Bulgaria	3,536	10,254	11,062	4,412	8,675	13,748	7,076	11,058	15,240
Burkina Faso	207	348		3,803	6,551		2,813	3,125	
Burundi									
Cambodia			615			3,359			2,762
Cameroon									
Canada	42,189	46,905	84,494	81,109	112,454	129,063	52,079	67,069	76,038
Central African Republic									
Chad	316			5,679			2,875		
Chile	8,839	7,230	7,742	20,778	32,805	39,481	14,640	18,340	21,281
China	576	912	1,649	3,077	6,683	10,799	1,972	4,425	7,788
Colombia	143,353	3,298	5,171	9,289	13,472	23,951	7,423	8,389	12,101
Congo, Dem. Rep.									
Congo, Rep.		626			16,495			2,705	
Costa Rica	6,904	6,367	7,964	13,678	14,495	16,232	11,644	11,324	13,886
Côte d'Ivoire									
Croatia	5,509	8,061	12,516	16,501	26,744	34,397	18,959	33,420	39,446
Cuba	2,778	2,396	2,848	7,880	8,687	12,553	10,416	10,477	12,875
Czech Republic	10,589	21,146	30,708	13,520	26,449	38,029	17,605	31,396	41,145
Denmark	78,444	46,179	65,098	83,948	107,422	120,024	93,598	95,626	108,138
Dominican Republic	4,614	5,113	4,814	10,323	14,995	17,142	6,144	10,549	11,879
Ecuador	17,147	1,428	1,942	6,974	13,671	14,885	4,995	7,264	8,338
Egypt, Arab Rep.	2,299	2,125	2,759	6,839	7,234	10,894	5,391	4,543	7,308
El Salvador	3,217	4,267	4,839	6,845	10,911	10,641	7,131	8,254	8,561
Eritrea									
Estonia	286	1,122	1,831	477	1,338	1,992	538	1,770	2,157
Ethiopia	264	216		1,986	678		1,619	1,136	
Fiji									
Finland	44,202	46,796	63,793	97,244	105,407	111,333	75,501	78,173	83,346
France	61,774	51,238	59,087	84,530	77,422	83,291	98,683	95,476	107,508
Gabon	4,968	4,517		92,742	113,418		24,212	11,700	
Gambia, The	665			2,418			7,841		
Georgia		1,091			10,531			5,537	
Germany	39,654	37,059	35,975	83,494	83,183	82,362	102,070	87,032	82,997
Ghana		1,204			3,353			3,797	
Greece									
Guatemala	2,485	2,226		5,193	7,885		10,519	7,908	
Guinea	434			6,850			4,665		
Guinea-Bissau									
Haiti									
Honduras	1,441	1,373		3,167	5,364		3,032	5,649	
Hungary	15,389	24,218	22,162	13,658	27,139	31,452	16,227	30,227	31,631
India	530	620	1,154	1,919	2,733	4,089	2,395	3,917	6,775
Indonesia	1,223	947	2,527	7,292	7,779	15,500	3,393	3,462	5,637
Iran, Islamic Rep.	9,417	3,798		16,510	13,886		14,977	9,339	
Iraq									
Ireland	53,117	27,237	22,334	88,974	127,274	172,844	60,801	100,012	103,349
Israel									
Italy	36,317	49,362	41,152	68,402	77,744	75,596	85,677	98,654	93,103
Jamaica	2,865	3,409	3,123	13,424	14,414	13,113	6,946	10,989	11,501
Japan	32,158	28,324	30,531	116,579	93,297	115,414	131,008	99,791	107,592
Jordan		10,358	27,585		13,865	26,114		9,033	13,463
Kazakhstan		1,725	3,016		18,115	28,778		8,638	13,905
Kenya		644			3,941			2,425	
Kiribati									
Korea, Rep.	15,783	15,431	14,515	37,835	51,736	91,830	28,615	33,609	30,423
Kosovo									
Kyrgyz Republic	1,035	921	1,550	1,274	1,399	2,183	1,125	1,166	2,142
Lao PDR	690			5,064			2,400		

TABLE 5 *Productivity,* continued

	Value added per worker (2005 US$ per year)								
	Primary sector			Secondary sector			Tertiary sector		
	1995	2005	2010	1995	2005	2010	1995	2005	2010
Latvia	3,207	5,585	11,889	7,771	14,025	23,498	8,546	20,297	28,582
Lebanon									
Lesotho	652			6,868			2,365		
Liberia		888	879		1,717	489		1,146	526
Libya									
Lithuania	4,290	6,692	10,421	8,886	22,045	31,384	9,674	21,276	27,697
Macedonia, FYR		6,775	8,551		9,675	14,199		13,631	17,705
Madagascar		207			2,309			2,047	
Malawi									
Malaysia	9,322	7,825	11,257	18,628	23,171	26,866	13,692	10,460	12,878
Mali		881			6,310			2,198	
Mauritania									
Mauritius	8,652	7,300	6,256	9,137	10,423	14,876	13,003	13,840	17,007
Mexico	2,494	5,183	6,269	13,386	27,286	27,497	13,003	22,058	21,103
Moldova	929	1,055	1,468	2,606	2,262	3,040	1,148	3,305	6,502
Mongolia	1,779	1,355	1,825	4,588	5,234	8,190	2,048	2,385	3,915
Montenegro									
Morocco	13,450	1,949	2,764	5,359	8,431	10,669	4,611	9,749	11,517
Mozambique		188			4,724			1,556	
Myanmar	4,933			4,676			6,976		
Namibia	2,600	3,717	8,562	18,084	22,451	30,857	11,804	12,665	11,758
Nepal									
Netherlands	71,226	56,148	54,577	97,454	97,381	124,750	79,808	82,539	86,039
New Zealand	36,258	45,578		52,576	67,432		49,929	57,782	
Nicaragua	1,506	1,539		5,147	3,503		3,252	2,359	
Niger									
Nigeria		1,796			8,285			1,333	
Norway	56,806	72,622	85,197	138,356	290,065	318,919	82,263	105,301	118,318
Oman	9,161			158,023			14,500		
Pakistan	1,139	1,139	1,187	2,564	3,092	3,519	2,929	3,172	3,968
Panama	3,933	4,407	4,143	10,280	11,691	13,451	12,711	14,334	18,196
Papua New Guinea									
Paraguay	2,743	2,149	5,335	7,104	4,204	6,493	6,952	3,642	6,241
Peru	58,831	46,902	61,865	7,986	9,308	12,014	5,533	5,007	6,279
Philippines	1,860	1,197	1,724	7,581	7,197	9,750	4,380	3,716	5,093
Poland	4,038	5,933	7,196	12,748	23,585	27,886	14,647	27,215	30,078
Portugal	15,813	9,349	9,359	30,226	32,333	34,814	40,227	50,158	51,660
Romania	2,410	3,564	4,085	6,205	13,115	15,498	5,560	16,253	27,896
Russian Federation	2,951	5,713	7,744	7,167	14,600	19,908	7,369	10,919	16,432
Rwanda		295			2,134			1,698	
Saudi Arabia		33,414	30,025		146,499	120,850		19,343	20,513
Senegal		857			3,030			3,406	
Serbia		5,228	5,949		10,346	16,543		11,991	18,115
Sierra Leone		395			2,099			750	
Singapore	9,160	3,408	2,873	67,962	90,290	87,976	61,005	55,810	64,964
Slovak Republic	256	539	45,309	377	691	33,247	422	790	35,907
Slovenia	53	51	11,699	99	156	41,034	161	202	48,714
Somalia									
South Africa		6,241	10,725		22,418	22,059		18,468	16,554
Spain	32,396	41,405	48,517	63,427	64,101	80,812	70,171	66,716	69,968
Sri Lanka	1,545	1,366	2,015	2,866	4,160	6,217	3,686	5,467	7,548
Sudan									
Swaziland									
Sweden	84,800	57,864	93,839	98,760	119,616	135,069	78,875	87,010	94,173
Switzerland	61,238	34,325	48,439	124,652	122,634	166,833	120,305	106,178	130,553
Syrian Arab Republic	17,111	34,206	61,887	9,922	44,830	40,385	17,821	31,138	38,924
Tajikistan	245	355		923	1,624		379	1,648	
Tanzania		303			4,392			1,888	
Thailand	1,294	1,252	1,934	14,421	11,532	15,349	12,577	6,490	8,209
Timor-Leste									
Togo		619			2,450			1,119	
Tonga									
Trinidad and Tobago	3,466	3,403	3,883	28,504	54,117	82,586	12,489	17,024	24,172
Tunisia									
Turkey	4,162	7,974	10,596	16,599	25,270	27,153	16,311	29,236	33,775
Turkmenistan									
Uganda		293	395		3,951	4,542		1,655	1,870
Ukraine	1,405	2,366	3,997	3,199	5,825	11,824	6,283	4,419	7,756
United Kingdom	55,402	58,380	56,013	68,950	92,373	88,189	57,625	86,429	75,957
United States	41,807	57,756	59,247	85,509	100,647	118,051	77,029	93,562	97,669
Uruguay	35,312	26,313		21,948	15,641		18,551	10,712	
Uzbekistan	1,312			2,437			1,900		
Venezuela, RB	4,708	5,358		20,515	36,656		10,073	7,370	
Vietnam	351	538		2,391	2,846		1,979	1,862	
West Bank and Gaza									
Yemen, Rep.	6,093			30,134			19,342		
Zambia		534			7,446			3,541	
Zimbabwe		285			2,776			3,404	

TABLE 5 *Productivity,* continued

	Value added per worker (2005 US$ per year)			Employment in micro-enterprises (% of non-agricultural employment)			Informal employment (% of non-agricultural employment)		
	1995	2005	2010	1995	2005	2010	1995	2005	2010
Afghanistan									
Albania	2,935	6,784	8,379						
Algeria		11,055							
Angola									
Argentina	29,815	12,243	17,954		57.7	55.9	44.0		49.7
Armenia		5,399	11,088						49.6
Australia	58,730	75,297	89,305		31.7	30.7			
Austria	86,977	85,765	85,704		32.1	34.6			
Azerbaijan	1,026	3,584	9,545						26.5
Bangladesh	967	948							
Barbados	19,868	20,723							
Belarus	4,565								
Belgium	102,383	96,998	96,414		25.3	24.0			
Belize	11,094	10,353							
Benin		1,429							
Bhutan		2,798	3,525						
Bolivia	2,720	2,242			79.3	80.5		75.1	
Bosnia and Herzegovina									
Botswana	10,235	14,150							
Brazil	12,450	9,633	15,252	60.0	57.0	55.3	47.3		42.2
Bulgaria	5,391	10,176	14,455		25.2	22.9			
Burkina Faso	523	868							
Burundi									
Cambodia			1,270						
Cameroon					95.3				
Canada	58,070	76,449	88,633						
Central African Republic									
Chad	807								
Chile	15,308	20,223	23,977	52.1	44.9	44.7	33.1		
China	1,500	3,386	6,145						
Colombia	9,380	8,253	13,223			70.0	53.4	63.5	59.6
Congo, Dem. Rep.									
Congo, Rep.		4,819							
Costa Rica	11,089	10,938	13,136	52.1	51.5	47.9	39.6	39.9	43.8
Côte d'Ivoire									
Croatia	15,556	27,173	34,043						
Cuba	7,923	8,521	10,912						
Czech Republic	15,574	29,321	39,648		31.6	30.7			
Denmark	90,386	96,856	109,655						
Dominican Republic	6,918	10,290	11,621						48.5
Ecuador	6,160	6,486	7,810		42.2	45.5		71.3	60.9
Egypt, Arab Rep.	4,658	4,431	6,677						51.2
El Salvador	6,000	8,041	8,216						66.4
Eritrea									
Estonia	492	1,591	2,073		21.4	21.1			
Ethiopia	404	366							
Fiji									
Finland	78,868	84,467	88,167						
France	93,016	89,373	100,485		28.7	29.2			
Gabon	24,595	22,182							
Gambia, The	2,773								
Georgia		3,530							
Germany	93,510	84,878	81,878		26.2	22.6			
Ghana		2,257							
Greece					56.8	54.3			
Guatemala	5,276	6,028							
Guinea	1,581								
Guinea-Bissau									
Haiti									
Honduras	2,475	3,921		58.7	60.6	66.3	49.0	54.6	73.9
Hungary	15,312	28,939	31,419		37.3	35.8			
India	1,163	1,846	3,318		79.4	77.8		83.5	
Indonesia	3,140	3,176	6,273					63.2	61.6
Iran, Islamic Rep.	13,874	9,318							
Iraq					72.4				
Ireland	68,280	103,279	113,892		34.5	41.1			
Israel									
Italy	77,205	90,200	86,879		47.7	47.8			
Jamaica	7,303	10,241	10,099						
Japan	120,171	93,118	105,389						
Jordan		10,087	16,149						
Kazakhstan		8,132	13,573						
Kenya		1,445							
Kiribati									
Korea, Rep.	29,831	37,049	39,749						
Kosovo									
Kyrgyz Republic	1,108	1,124	1,949						
Lao PDR	1,053								

TABLE 5 *Productivity,* continued

	Value added per worker (2005 US$ per year)			Employment in micro-enterprises (% of non-agricultural employment)			Informal employment (% of non-agricultural employment)		
	1995	2005	2010	1995	2005	2010	1995	2005	2010
Latvia	7,344	16,901	25,859		29.9	26.8			
Lebanon									
Lesotho	2,064								34.9
Liberia		650	696						60.0
Libya									
Lithuania	8,412	19,457	26,750		20.2	17.5			
Macedonia, FYR		10,994	14,788		29.0				12.6
Madagascar		585						73.6	
Malawi									
Malaysia	14,397	13,983	16,556						
Mali		1,576						81.8	
Mauritania									
Mauritius	10,838	12,093	15,443		35.5				
Mexico	10,565	20,886	20,837	71.0	59.8	63.4		54.8	53.7
Moldova	1,273	2,216	4,249						15.9
Mongolia	2,381	2,457	3,720						
Montenegro									
Morocco	5,349	5,975	7,741						
Mozambique		543							
Myanmar	5,406								
Namibia	9,068	11,449	14,685						43.9
Nepal						93.0			
Netherlands	81,927	80,589	83,545						
New Zealand	49,224	59,050							
Nicaragua	2,639	2,350						58.8	65.7
Niger									
Nigeria		2,362							
Norway	93,069	143,121	158,628						
Oman	25,608								
Pakistan	2,047	2,282	2,627		94.2	96.2			78.4
Panama	10,430	11,998	14,765	44.8	50.5	45.1	33.7	44.1	43.8
Papua New Guinea						78.3			
Paraguay	5,294	3,254	6,106						70.7
Peru	6,704	6,508	8,211					78.0	70.6
Philippines	3,783	3,404	4,612						70.1
Poland	11,599	22,272	26,446		43.0	43.5	12.7		
Portugal	34,097	40,237	42,290		43.7	43.0			
Romania	4,500	11,251	17,157		20.2	19.4			
Russian Federation	6,594	11,503	16,536						
Rwanda		607							
Saudi Arabia		45,337	40,961						
Senegal		1,972							
Serbia		9,975	14,802			47.8			6.1
Sierra Leone		607			85.3				
Singapore	63,970	62,872	69,405						
Slovak Republic	389	738	35,205		42.7	43.7			
Slovenia	122	170	42,848		23.9	25.6			
Somalia									
South Africa		18,701	17,639		46.2				32.7
Spain	64,748	64,666	71,604		41.1	42.6			
Sri Lanka	2,484	3,583	5,238						62.1
Sudan									
Swaziland									
Sweden	84,223	93,600	102,345						
Switzerland	119,203	108,315	129,181						
Syrian Arab Republic	15,173	35,585	43,556						
Tajikistan	376	920							
Tanzania		768				87.6			76.2
Thailand	7,079	5,246	7,083						42.3
Timor-Leste					96.6	100.0			
Togo		931							
Tonga									
Trinidad and Tobago	15,785	27,808	42,053						
Tunisia									
Turkey	10,987	22,158	26,490		54.6	46.6			30.6
Turkmenistan									
Uganda		789	1,057						68.5
Ukraine	2,099	4,322	8,090						
United Kingdom	60,062	86,592	77,322		27.6	28.2			
United States	78,008	95,269	100,365						
Uruguay	20,492	12,684			54.5	51.3		44.6	39.8
Uzbekistan	1,666								
Venezuela, RB	11,929	13,319			60.3				47.5
Vietnam	885	1,370							68.2
West Bank and Gaza									57.2
Yemen, Rep.	13,181								
Zambia		1,649							69.5
Zimbabwe		945						51.6	

TABLE 6 *Social cohesion*

	Trust (% in latest survey)			Civic participation (% in latest survey)			Wage inequality (90%/10% ratio)		
	Employed	Unemployed	Out of labor force	Employed	Unemployed	Out of labor force	1995	2005	2010
Afghanistan								2.5	
Albania	22.4	27.5	26.8				2.6	3.9	
Algeria	10.1	10.6	13.9						
Angola									
Argentina	19.9	10.1	15.5	32.4	32.0	28.7		5.8	5.5
Armenia									
Australia	49.2	38.5	41.2	64.9	28.7	55.0		10.3	8.8
Austria				41.9				4.4	5.2
Azerbaijan							10.0		
Bangladesh	24.8	24.6	23.7					3.8	3.8
Barbados							6.1		
Belarus								4.7	
Belgium				29.5				2.9	3.0
Belize							5.7		
Benin				39.5	37.7	37.7			
Bhutan									
Bolivia	21.6	16.3	21.9	31.2	29.3	30.9	10.0	8.5	7.5
Bosnia and Herzegovina	13.9	16.1	18.0						
Botswana	17.3	12.3		55.0	42.3	55.3			28.3
Brazil	8.4	11.3	10.4	66.8	50.0	72.8	10.4	7.4	6.0
Bulgaria	21.3	23.0	22.9	11.4	6.6	5.8		3.6	4.5
Burkina Faso	12.3	13.3	17.5	43.7	35.2	33.0			
Burundi									
Cambodia							20.0	6.9	8.6
Cameroon								10.4	
Canada	44.9	36.5	40.3	72.4	46.6	63.4			
Central African Republic									
Chad									
Chile	14.1	18.5	10.2	45.5	44.2	42.2	7.0	5.5	5.5
China	52.7	43.1	53.0	15.7	26.0	23.5		5.6	4.0
Colombia	16.0	12.5	11.4	36.2	33.1	39.1		6.5	6.6
Congo, Dem. Rep.									
Congo, Rep.									
Costa Rica	10.1	4.6	6.9	30.9	20.3	28.0			
Côte d'Ivoire									
Croatia								2.9	
Cuba									
Czech Republic									
Denmark				47.3					
Dominican Republic									
Ecuador	12.2	8.7	11.6	19.8	0.0	16.8	6.5	6.6	4.9
Egypt, Arab Rep.	16.9	17.3	20.0	11.8	4.6	3.0			
El Salvador	15.8	12.2	13.7	34.1	35.9	27.3			
Eritrea									
Estonia								4.3	4.3
Ethiopia	21.4	27.2	26.9	49.5	36.5	52.6		11.8	
Fiji									
Finland	65.9	44.5	52.6	54.4	42.3	43.0			
France	19.4	18.5	17.7	43.6	27.5	34.7		4.7	4.9
Gabon								10.7	
Gambia, The									
Georgia	21.2	10.4	21.7	7.4	4.7	3.5			7.4
Germany	40.6	22.6	34.1	47.1	25.5	44.6		6.3	
Ghana	8.7	8.0	8.7	81.7	76.2	81.2		9.1	
Greece				8.8				4.3	4.2
Guatemala	17.5	24.1	10.6	35.9	32.0	35.0		6.2	
Guinea									
Guinea-Bissau									
Haiti									
Honduras	18.2	13.8	16.4	51.0	59.3	49.8	6.6	9.7	8.8
Hungary								4.2	
India	23.4	19.1	27.1	54.2	40.6	34.6	12.1	11.4	10.7
Indonesia	45.7	25.0	40.7	60.6	51.2	58.9	10.4	4.2	8.6
Iran, Islamic Rep.	11.2	10.3	10.0	50.0	43.4	33.5			
Iraq	36.7	46.0	43.2					4.4	
Ireland				34.7				5.8	5.6
Israel	27.5	17.6	18.1						
Italy	31.3	26.3	26.1	44.4	22.8	35.7		3.4	3.2
Jamaica							5.7		
Japan	39.3	12.5	40.3	34.1	31.3	39.7			
Jordan	33.6	27.1	23.9						
Kazakhstan									
Kenya				73.3	74.3	70.1		13.3	
Kiribati									
Korea, Rep.	30.0	40.3	25.6	36.4	23.6	33.5			
Kosovo								3.5	
Kyrgyz Republic	17.6	12.4	17.4						
Lao PDR									

TABLE 6 *Social cohesion,* continued

	Trust (% in latest survey)			Civic participation (% in latest survey)			Wage inequality (90%/10% ratio)		
	Employed	Unemployed	Out of labor force	Employed	Unemployed	Out of labor force	1995	2005	2010
Latvia						4.7	6.1		
Lebanon									
Lesotho	3.3	4.0		44.6	44.6	44.9			
Liberia				83.8	78.5	80.6			
Libya									
Lithuania								4.9	4.3
Macedonia, FYR	11.7	14.7	15.0	12.3				2.7	
Madagascar				12.5	10.3	9.4			
Malawi	44.4	45.3		75.3	62.9	61.7		10.1	
Malaysia	9.5	9.6	7.7	29.4	21.2	28.0			
Mali	16.6	20.0	17.1	65.6	59.4	51.6	24.4		
Mauritania									
Mauritius								5.8	6.7
Mexico	17.5	15.1	12.8	64.6	50.5	59.7	8.4		6.5
Moldova	16.0	14.6	22.3	36.0	18.9	33.9		8.1	
Mongolia									3.6
Montenegro								2.9	
Morocco	12.3	20.8	17.5	17.0	8.7	11.1			
Mozambique				62.8	58.1	52.6	6.7		10.5
Myanmar									
Namibia	33.3	36.2		35.2	33.4	39.1			
Nepal									6.0
Netherlands	47.0	25.8	42.7	60.3	31.3	57.0			
New Zealand									
Nicaragua	21.5	24.2	20.5	46.8	42.7	42.7	6.8	5.8	
Niger							7.0		
Nigeria	24.9	27.2	26.3	63.8	60.0	61.1	5.0	28.8	
Norway	77.4	66.7	66.3	58.3	45.5	46.6			
Oman									
Pakistan	32.5	25.4	29.7					6.3	6.4
Panama	27.6	12.5	21.7	25.6	34.9	22.9	7.6	6.7	5.5
Papua New Guinea									10.9
Paraguay	5.5	9.3	6.3	45.1	52.2	38.8	6.8	6.5	5.3
Peru	5.7	9.0	7.1	54.7	36.4	42.6	6.3	6.8	6.1
Philippines	8.1	12.4	6.8					6.1	6.3
Poland	19.3	21.8	18.9	28.2	15.6	27.7		5.4	5.2
Portugal				8.2				4.9	4.3
Romania	18.7	14.3	22.1	19.6	6.7	8.4	3.2	5.5	3.7
Russian Federation	26.7	18.1	26.7	13.2	6.6	17.7			
Rwanda	4.0		8.4	70.8		70.8	37.8	31.3	
Saudi Arabia	52.6	62.7	52.4						
Senegal				50.3	42.9	40.0			
Serbia	15.9	11.1	15.8	18.6	15.1	9.8			3.8
Sierra Leone								4.7	
Singapore	15.8	16.7	18.7						
Slovak Republic								3.0	
Slovenia	17.7	13.3	19.2	51.4	32.6	38.6		3.2	3.2
Somalia									
South Africa	16.1	21.6	19.3	66.3	52.9	66.2		14.0	
Spain	22.0	23.8	17.4	28.4	24.9	22.2		4.5	4.2
Sri Lanka								6.2	5.7
Sudan									
Swaziland									
Sweden	72.3	43.8	60.4	63.7	52.3	59.9		4.3	3.8
Switzerland	59.4	7.5	45.6	69.5	51.2	64.0			
Syrian Arab Republic								3.3	
Tajikistan								15.0	
Tanzania	7.6	9.3	6.7	79.9	75.1	74.8		12.9	13.3
Thailand	42.7	32.4	44.4	35.4	24.7	37.9	8.9	10.8	9.6
Timor-Leste								8.5	5.5
Togo								14.6	
Tonga									
Trinidad and Tobago	3.8	3.0	4.1	59.0	56.0	63.6			
Tunisia									
Turkey	4.8	3.3	5.1	13.8	6.6	4.0		4.0	4.2
Turkmenistan									
Uganda	7.0	4.7	9.6	60.4	55.2	54.3		13.6	
Ukraine	29.1	35.7	25.3	19.2	22.1	13.9		4.7	
United Kingdom	31.0	19.5	32.0	66.2	38.2	57.5		5.3	
United States	40.2	36.5	40.7	66.1	47.0	63.2		12.5	
Uruguay	30.2	15.7	29.4	29.5	29.8	30.9	6.0	6.4	5.8
Uzbekistan									
Venezuela, RB	16.9	16.7	13.4	33.7	27.3	30.5	4.6	5.5	
Vietnam	51.9	52.2	53.7	49.6	51.5	59.0	7.7	8.0	8.7
West Bank and Gaza								3.8	4.0
Yemen, Rep.	42.4								
Zambia	11.5	12.5	10.6	81.0	70.3	78.7		11.1	
Zimbabwe	13.9	10.4	5.3	59.4	61.3	65.4			

TABLE 6 *Social cohesion,* continued

| | Youth unemployment (% of youth labor force) | | | | | | Youth not in school or at work (% of youth cohort) | | | | | |
| | Men | | | Women | | | Men | | | Women | | |
	1995	2005	2010	1995	2005	2010	1995	2005	2010	1995	2005	2010
Afghanistan								8.2			50.0	
Albania		22.8	26.2		16.6	28.3	50.2	33.7		41.7	35.1	
Algeria		42.8			46.3							
Angola												
Argentina	29.9	21.6	18.8	37.6	28.0	24.7		14.7	14.8		24.8	24.8
Armenia		47.2	37.4		69.4	54.7		52.2			67.2	
Australia	15.9	10.9	11.9	14.8	10.4	11.1		15.3	18.1		18.5	19.0
Austria	4.8	10.7	8.9	5.6	9.9	8.8		14.5	18.5		14.5	20.0
Azerbaijan		18.2	13.4		10.4	15.5	49.3			57.8		
Bangladesh	8.0	8.0			5.7	13.6						
Barbados	33.3	24.1		42.4	28.7		23.1			28.9		
Belarus								53.4			60.3	
Belgium	19.7	21.0	22.4	23.7	22.1	22.4		10.6	12.7		15.1	11.6
Belize	19.1	13.8		31.7	28.8		26.6			69.2		
Benin								14.9			20.1	
Bhutan		5.5	10.7		7.2	14.7		17.7			22.8	
Bolivia	5.2				7.0		3.5	5.5	15.8	17.0	18.3	18.5
Bosnia and Herzegovina		60.4	44.7		65.6	51.9		32.0			33.7	
Botswana	33.5			42.4					25.7			38.9
Brazil	9.7	15.3	13.9	14.1	24.9	23.1	10.4	11.5	12.1	28.2	26.0	24.8
Bulgaria		23.4	24.1		21.0	21.7	33.5	29.3	17.4	36.0	32.3	29.6
Burkina Faso		4.6			2.9		5.8	5.7		17.5	15.0	
Burundi												
Cambodia		3.5				3.3	7.9	4.0	3.6	15.2	11.5	10.6
Cameroon							20.0	7.8		34.2	19.6	
Canada	16.3	14.2	17.1	13.2	10.6	12.4						
Central African Republic								26.4			27.0	
Chad												
Chile	10.8	17.3	16.6	12.7	23.8	21.7	11.6	13.5	17.6	30.4	24.5	26.8
China								9.8	12.8		9.4	11.0
Colombia	15.6	17.9	18.2	21.8	28.3	29.9		16.9	14.5		38.4	33.3
Congo, Dem. Rep.								13.2			23.1	
Congo, Rep.								6.0			13.4	
Costa Rica	10.2	11.3	9.6	13.0	21.5	13.4	11.5	9.3	12.8	37.5	28.2	27.1
Côte d'Ivoire												
Croatia		30.2	31.1		35.1	35.0		20.8			20.5	
Cuba		3.5	2.8		4.4	3.5						
Czech Republic	7.2	19.4	18.3	8.7	19.1	18.5		11.5	9.6		15.3	12.3
Denmark	7.8	8.6	16.1	12.3	8.6	11.8		9.5	11.9		15.1	14.5
Dominican Republic	20.9	21.2		41.5	44.5		10.6	14.5	14.1	31.7	28.8	28.1
Ecuador	13.0	12.2	11.7	18.6	20.6	18.1	6.8	7.9	8.3	31.1	27.6	23.6
Egypt, Arab Rep.		23.3			62.2			15.2			45.7	
El Salvador	13.4	11.3		13.0	8.4		13.0	14.1	13.5	41.7	39.3	36.7
Eritrea												
Estonia	21.0	16.6	35.4	15.4	15.1	30.0		16.0	10.6		13.3	11.2
Ethiopia		4.1			11.2		7.5	1.8		43.6	10.9	
Fiji	11.3			16.8			24.0		19.6	49.9		36.7
Finland	25.7	18.4	21.6	28.7	19.4	18.9		20.2	17.2		15.1	13.1
France	23.7	19.5	22.2	30.6	21.9	23.7		8.6	10.5		12.7	10.5
Gabon	41.7			40.2				20.0			31.3	
Gambia, The												
Georgia		26.8	32.4		30.6	40.7						
Germany	8.3	16.1	10.4	8.0	14.0	8.8		15.3	13.0		9.0	8.5
Ghana								12.9			20.8	
Greece	19.4	18.7	26.7	37.7	34.8	40.6		17.3	16.1		21.3	20.2
Guatemala								4.6			40.7	
Guinea							6.6			16.9		
Guinea-Bissau												
Haiti												
Honduras	4.3	5.2		6.9	11.2		9.3	10.2	10.0	51.7	43.0	42.7
Hungary	20.7	19.7	27.9	15.6	19.1	24.9		13.6	13.1		12.4	19.4
India	8.3	9.9	9.9	8.0	10.3	11.3	9.7	10.0	10.0	56.1	51.8	50.5
Indonesia	14.3	28.8	21.6	17.0	37.7	23.0	19.3	23.3	13.8	45.1	44.0	33.6
Iran, Islamic Rep.		21.2	20.2		34.0	33.9		21.6			55.1	
Iraq								25.6			75.6	
Ireland	20.3	9.1	34.0	17.4	7.9	21.5		9.9	17.0		11.8	17.1
Israel	12.8	17.0	14.5	17.1	18.6	12.9						
Italy	29.8	21.5	26.8	38.2	27.4	29.4		20.5	20.7		22.6	20.6
Jamaica	25.1	22.0	22.5	44.6	36.3	33.1	20.5			44.0		
Japan	6.1	9.9	10.4	6.1	7.4	8.0						
Jordan		23.7	22.6		47.9	45.9						
Kazakhstan		13.1	6.8		15.7	8.2	54.0	13.8		56.9	14.9	
Kenya							24.5	16.3		36.8	31.6	
Kiribati								21.8			22.4	
Korea, Rep.	7.8	12.2	11.2	5.3	9.0	9.0						
Kosovo								37.7			59.3	
Kyrgyz Republic		13.3			16.2		24.9			36.7		
Lao PDR	6.4			3.9					2.1			5.3

TABLE 6 *Social cohesion,* continued

| | Youth unemployment (% of youth labor force) | | | | | | Youth not in school or at work (% of youth cohort) | | | | | |
| | Men | | | Women | | | Men | | | Women | | |
	1995	2005	2010	1995	2005	2010	1995	2005	2010	1995	2005	2010
Latvia	34.2	11.7	35.4	34.1	16.1	33.5		10.2	11.8		14.0	15.8
Lebanon		20.3			19.0			18.1			33.3	
Lesotho	37.9		29.0	58.5		41.9						
Liberia		5.7	3.4		3.7	6.6		6.8			15.2	
Libya												
Lithuania	28.5	16.0	38.4	21.7	15.3	30.8		11.9	8.0		12.3	3.6
Macedonia, FYR		63.0	53.8		62.1	53.4						
Madagascar		1.7			2.8		8.8			12.2		
Malawi							19.4	5.4		44.9	11.1	
Malaysia		10.5	10.3		11.5	11.8			12.2			21.4
Mali							10.2	26.7		19.8	47.6	
Mauritania									23.9			34.6
Mauritius	21.4	20.5	19.4	28.1	34.3	29.0		27.6	26.1		45.7	39.0
Mexico	9.2	6.1	9.0	15.3	7.4	10.1	11.3	10.9	12.0	41.9	34.3	33.7
Moldova		19.1	20.1		18.3	15.0		5.8			6.6	
Mongolia		19.5			20.7				14.0			16.9
Montenegro								32.3			24.9	
Morocco		16.2	22.8		14.4	19.4						
Mozambique							15.3	9.0	5.9	19.7	11.5	8.3
Myanmar												
Namibia	29.6	36.7	54.6	33.8	47.0	63.8	20.4			29.2		
Nepal							33.5	8.4	8.3	36.2	19.6	15.4
Netherlands	11.5	8.0	8.8	12.7	8.4	8.6		8.3	11.9		10.7	12.8
New Zealand	12.3	9.4	16.8	12.2	10.1	17.4						
Nicaragua	22.4	8.1		24.7	9.7		20.9	10.5		52.3	39.4	
Niger							15.2			45.3		
Nigeria							7.2	22.2		43.4	36.1	
Norway	11.9	12.5	10.9	11.8	11.5	7.7		7.4	17.8		6.1	20.5
Oman												
Pakistan	7.6	11.0	7.0	18.1	14.9	10.5		11.4	9.9		65.8	59.6
Panama	23.0	18.5	11.7	35.6	29.6	21.1	15.4	11.8	10.6	36.4	30.1	30.8
Papua New Guinea									17.3			18.7
Paraguay	5.5	12.1	8.7	7.3	20.5	16.8	6.3	9.7	9.9	27.7	29.7	28.3
Peru	9.8	16.2	12.5	13.6	17.4	15.6	11.9	15.4	11.7	25.3	28.7	21.6
Philippines	14.4	14.9	16.2	19.1	18.9	19.3	10.6	10.7	19.9	24.9	27.4	31.9
Poland	29.0	36.7	22.4	33.8	39.2	25.4		16.4	8.5		17.7	12.3
Portugal	14.1	13.7	21.1	17.7	19.1	23.7		12.3	13.4		13.3	15.2
Romania	18.8	21.5	22.3	23.1	18.4	21.8	30.8	2.0	11.3	32.8	6.3	16.7
Russian Federation	17.8	14.5	16.9	20.0	17.2	17.5						
Rwanda	1.0			0.5			13.9	4.1		15.5	4.5	
Saudi Arabia			23.6			45.8						
Senegal		11.9			20.1		13.4	19.8		50.5	58.7	
Serbia		43.2	31.0		55.5	41.3			23.4			19.1
Sierra Leone		7.3			3.5			16.0			25.6	
Singapore	4.5	6.4	9.8	5.5	11.6	16.6						
Slovak Republic	26.0	30.7	34.7	23.1	28.8	32.0		12.5	6.6		11.4	8.8
Slovenia	18.1	14.5	15.2	19.6	17.8	13.8		6.8	5.1		5.3	4.1
Somalia												
South Africa		42.7	47.2		54.7	54.6	18.0	27.4		27.0	36.8	
Spain	33.6	16.7	43.2	49.2	23.5	39.8		12.4	19.6		15.8	18.1
Sri Lanka		20.4	17.1		37.0	27.9	4.0	19.3	14.6	28.9	32.9	36.1
Sudan												
Swaziland	44.2			43.0			2.2			13.4		
Sweden	20.6	22.3	26.7	18.4	21.6	23.7		14.5	15.7		11.7	13.7
Switzerland	5.7	8.5	7.3	5.3	9.1	8.4						
Syrian Arab Republic		12.7	15.3		46.1	40.2		13.3			55.4	
Tajikistan								26.9			43.4	
Tanzania		7.4			10.1		3.2	5.3	9.5	17.5	9.1	16.9
Thailand	2.6	4.9	3.7	2.3	4.6	5.1	5.4	1.6	2.5	13.0	11.5	12.0
Timor-Leste								10.4	15.6		26.5	22.5
Togo								6.2			13.0	
Tonga	32.0	9.9		27.0	15.1		22.9			34.9		
Trinidad and Tobago	28.3	12.9	8.8	35.2	21.6	12.9						
Tunisia	33.3	31.4		29.0	29.3							
Turkey	16.9	19.5	21.0	13.1	20.6	23.1		27.3	21.9		57.9	46.9
Turkmenistan												
Uganda								3.8			13.5	
Ukraine		15.2			14.4			17.6			24.2	
United Kingdom	17.9	13.6	21.3	12.2	10.7	16.9		12.7	12.8		18.4	16.4
United States	12.5	12.4	20.8	11.6	10.1	15.8		10.7			13.8	
Uruguay	21.3	25.4	16.9	29.2	34.9	26.5	15.3	15.0	14.2	25.2	23.5	22.1
Uzbekistan												
Venezuela, RB	20.2	14.3	12.3	35.2	22.0	15.9	15.0	10.2		36.0	20.5	
Vietnam	3.4	4.4		2.9	4.9		9.3	4.6	4.3	14.3	7.4	7.9
West Bank and Gaza								21.3	19.6		37.9	30.6
Yemen, Rep.	20.2			9.8								
Zambia								21.8			22.4	
Zimbabwe	20.7	7.6		12.4	7.6							

TABLE 7 *Policies and institutions*

	Core ILO conventions ratified	Minimum wage (2005 US$ per year)		Separation cost (weeks of salary) After 1 year	After 10 years	Union membership (% of wage employment)		
	2012	2007	2010	2012	2012	1995	2005	2010
Afghanistan	5	0	0	13.0	30.3			
Albania	8	1,608	2,160	4.3	34.4			
Algeria	8	1,848	2,460	17.3	17.3			
Angola	8	1,296	1,308	8.6	80.1			
Argentina	8	2,952	4,824	8.7	52.0			
Armenia	8	540	948	13.0	13.0			
Australia	7	13,464	13,896	5.0	16.0	32	22	19
Austria	8	6,780	7,704	2.0	2.0	41	33	28
Azerbaijan	8	648	1,068	21.7	21.7			
Bangladesh	7	288	252	9.3	54.3			
Barbados	8							
Belarus	8	936	1,104	21.7	21.7			
Belgium	8	15,996	18,804	5.0	8.0	56	53	52
Belize	8	3,300	3,156	2.0	14.0			
Benin	8	600	732	5.6	18.4			
Bhutan	0	0	0	5.3	10.3			
Bolivia	8	696	960					
Bosnia and Herzegovina	8	4,092	4,356	2.0	16.4			
Botswana	8	1,308	1,164	6.7	42.0	9		
Brazil	7	2,136	3,000	5.9	20.9		30	29
Bulgaria	8	1,296	1,788	8.6	8.6	39	22	20
Burkina Faso	8	672	756	5.4	16.3			
Burundi	8	48	36	4.3	26.0			
Cambodia	8	468	444	4.3	34.4			
Cameroon	8	504	684	5.8	23.8			
Canada	5	13,104	17,952	2.0	18.0	34	30	30
Central African Republic	8	408	432	21.7	21.7			
Chad	8	552	780	4.3	20.6			
Chile	8	0	0	8.6	47.6	16	13	14
China	4	1,080	1,728	8.6	47.6	92	74	79
Colombia	8	2,076	2,628	4.3	30.0			
Congo, Dem. Rep.	8	180	696	4.2	16.8			
Congo, Rep.	8	864	1,296	4.3	17.8			
Costa Rica	8	3,600	3,852	7.1	29.5			
Côte d'Ivoire	8	0	0	5.6	22.8			
Croatia	8	4,452	5,748	4.3	25.1			
Cuba	7							
Czech Republic	8	3,996	4,608	21.7	21.7	44	20	17
Denmark	8	0	0	0.0	0.0	77	72	69
Dominican Republic	8	2,700	2,436	7.8	45.8			
Ecuador	8	1,800	2,328	14.1	54.2			
Egypt, Arab Rep.	8	276	336	13.0	67.2			
El Salvador	8	768	936	4.3	42.9			
Eritrea	7	0	0	4.0	29.3			
Estonia	8	3,264	4,236	8.6	17.2	32	9	7
Ethiopia	8	0	0	8.6	30.1			
Fiji	8	2,472	3,132	5.3	14.3			
Finland	8	18,816	22,212	4.3	17.3	80	72	70
France	8	7,284	8,484	5.2	17.3	9	8	8
Gabon	8	432	516	1.0	26.0			
Gambia, The	8	0	0	26.0	26.0			
Georgia	8	252	264	4.3	4.3			
Germany	8	9,816	12,276	6.2	39.0	29	22	19
Ghana	7	252	276	10.7	91.0			
Greece	8	10,512	12,756	24.0	24.0	31	25	24
Guatemala	8	1,776	1,992	5.1	50.6			
Guinea	8	0	0	3.2	13.0			
Guinea-Bissau	7	0	0	13.0	43.3			
Haiti	8	504	1,356	4.3	17.3			
Honduras	8	1,788	3,504	8.7	52.0			
Hungary	8	3,516	4,200	4.3	20.9	49	17	17
India	4	204	264	6.5	25.8			41
Indonesia	8	1,104	1,140	17.3	95.3	5	11	
Iran, Islamic Rep.	5	1,848	3,324	4.3	43.3			
Iraq	7	0	1,248	0.0	0.0			
Ireland	8	16,992	19,308	2.7	11.0	52	37	37
Israel	8	9,036	10,608	8.7	47.7	61	34	
Italy	8	16,236	18,768	6.5	8.7	38	34	35
Jamaica	8	2,388	2,232	2.0	26.0			
Japan	6	12,108	14,652	4.3	4.3	24	19	18
Jordan	7	1,752	2,160	4.3	4.3			
Kazakhstan	8	864	1,200	8.7	8.7			
Kenya	7	924	1,068	6.5	25.8			
Kiribati	8	0	0	4.3	4.3			
Korea, Rep.	4	6,960	6,756	8.6	47.6	13	10	10
Kosovo	0		0	13.0	26.0			
Kyrgyz Republic	8	96	132	17.3	17.3			
Lao PDR	5	300	684	11.6	84.4			

TABLE 7 *Policies and institutions,* continued

	Core ILO conventions ratified	Minimum wage (2005 US$ per year)		Separation cost (weeks of salary) After 1 year	After 10 years	Union membership (% of wage employment)		
	2012	2007	2010	2012	2012	1995	2005	2010
Latvia	8	2,424	3,816	5.3	14.0	28	19	15
Lebanon	7	2,244	3,408	4.3	13.0			
Lesotho	8			6.3	24.3			
Liberia	6	588	564	8.3	44.3			
Libya	8							
Lithuania	8	2,460	3,552	17.3	30.3	33	10	9
Macedonia, FYR	8	1,104	1,824	8.7	17.3			
Madagascar	8	288	420	3.1	21.0			
Malawi	8	192	252	6.3	34.3			
Malaysia	5	0	0	5.7	41.3	13	10	
Mali	8	156	156	9.5	18.4			
Mauritania	8	876	888	5.4	16.3			
Mauritius	8	1,188	1,692	4.7	18.6			
Mexico	6	1,368	1,332	14.6	30.0	18	18	
Moldova	8	648	1,044	18.3	27.3			
Mongolia	8	660	888	8.7	8.7			
Montenegro	8	732	1,572	28.1	28.1			
Morocco	7	2,364	2,736	6.5	36.0			
Mozambique	8	732	1,032	6.5	69.3			
Myanmar	2							
Namibia	8	0	0	5.3	14.3			
Nepal	7	360	660	8.6	47.2			
Netherlands	8	9,672	11,448	4.3	13.0	26	21	19
New Zealand	6	14,292	14,868	0.0	0.0	27	21	21
Nicaragua	8	996	1,308	4.3	21.7			
Niger	8	612	636	9.5	7.8			
Nigeria	8	0	0	6.3	26.9			
Norway	8	36,444	45,504	4.3	13.0	57	55	54
Oman	4	3,528	3,924	4.3	4.3			
Pakistan	8	372	480	8.6	47.2			
Panama	8	3,192	3,984	3.4	34.0			
Papua New Guinea	8	456	1,296	3.7	21.3			
Paraguay	8	1,464	1,824	7.1	52.9			
Peru	8	1,728	2,004	2.9	17.1			
Philippines	8	1,500	1,860	8.7	47.7	31	12	
Poland	8	2,724	4,080	8.7	26.0	31	19	15
Portugal	8	6,660	8,520	17.3	54.0	25	21	19
Romania	8	1,776	2,316	8.3	8.3	69	34	33
Russian Federation	8	2,544	3,816	17.3	17.3	76	44	43
Rwanda	8	228	0	8.6	17.3			
Saudi Arabia	5	0	0	6.5	36.8			
Senegal	8	780	828	6.4	20.6			
Serbia	8	1,296	2,196	1.4	14.4			
Sierra Leone	6	636	552	17.5	152.7			
Singapore	5	0	0	1.0	4.0	14	19	18
Slovak Republic	8	2,892	4,752	17.3	26.0	56	23	17
Slovenia	8	7,356	11,160	5.2	17.3	60	44	27
Somalia	3							
South Africa	8	5,472	5,556	5.0	14.0		32	28
Spain	8	9,432	11,400	5.0	30.7	16	15	16
Sri Lanka	8	396	384	15.2	104.3	20		
Sudan	7	780	984	4.3	47.7			
Swaziland	8	1,080	912	3.4	26.6			
Sweden	8	0	0	4.3	26.0	87	76	69
Switzerland	8	0	0	8.7	13.0	23	19	18
Syrian Arab Republic	8	1,272	1,440	8.7	8.7			
Tajikistan	8	72	156	13.0	19.5			
Tanzania	8	408	648	5.0	14.0			
Thailand	5	744	852	19.3	54.3			
Timor-Leste	4	0	0	4.3	4.3			
Togo	8	288	648	5.6	18.4			
Tonga	0	0	0	0.0	0.0			
Trinidad and Tobago	8	0	0	8.6	34.6			
Tunisia	8	1,176	1,308	6.0	17.3			
Turkey	8	4,440	5,436	8.3	51.3	13	8	6
Turkmenistan	7							
Uganda	8	36	36	4.3	13.0			
Ukraine	8	888	1,344	13.0	13.0			
United Kingdom	8	16,044	16,188	1.0	15.1	33	29	27
United States	2	13,992	13,488	0.0	0.0	15	13	12
Uruguay	8	1,560	2,532	5.2	31.2			
Uzbekistan	7	108	264	17.3	17.3			
Venezuela, RB	8	2,472	3,504					
Vietnam	5	228	408	8.7	43.3			
West Bank and Gaza	0	0	0	8.7	47.7			
Yemen, Rep.	8	1,140	1,068	8.6	47.6			
Zambia	8	840	624	13.0	91.0			
Zimbabwe	8	72	2,040	26.0	143.0			

TABLE 7 *Policies and institutions, continued*

	Labor market policies (spending in % of GDP)			Social security contributions (% of salary)			Social security coverage (% of employment)		
	1995	2005	2009	1995	2005	2010	1995	2005	2010
Afghanistan								3.7	
Albania					34.4	23.1			37.9
Algeria					34.0	34.0			
Angola									
Argentina			4.97	45.4	24.7	24.8			47.0
Armenia			1.89		3.0	3.0			32.1
Australia	1.95	0.91	0.87		9.0	9.0		90.7	
Austria	1.97	2.13	2.34		37.7	37.8		93.7	
Azerbaijan					25.0	25.0		35.4	
Bangladesh			0.09					2.5	
Barbados					17.6	17.6		83.5	
Belarus					22.0	29.5			93.5
Belgium	3.94	3.41	3.77		22.3	22.4		91.4	
Belize									61.0
Benin					14.0	12.5		5.5	
Bhutan									14.0
Bolivia					22.2	20.5			12.2
Bosnia and Herzegovina									24.5
Botswana								9.0	
Brazil				31.0	29.0	29.3			59.3
Bulgaria					30.2	21.3	81.1		78.7
Burkina Faso					14.5	18.0		1.2	
Burundi					9.5	9.5		3.5	
Cambodia									
Cameroon					12.0	10.1		16.2	
Canada	1.83	0.94	1.33		14.6	14.0	95.4		87.4
Central African Republic								1.5	
Chad					8.5	8.5		2.7	
Chile			3.13	24.7	20.3	18.0			57.7
China			0.06		32.0	32.0			33.5
Colombia			0.00		40.0	44.8			27.8
Congo, Dem. Rep.					8.5	8.5			14.2
Congo, Rep.					14.3	14.3			9.7
Costa Rica			0.60		23.3	23.8			58.6
Côte d'Ivoire				11.5	13.0	11.5		12.8	
Croatia					36.7	36.7			76.0
Cuba					14.0	14.0			
Czech Republic	0.24	0.48	0.72	34.0	34.0	31.5		95.4	
Denmark	6.02	3.92	3.33		8.0	8.0		92.9	
Dominican Republic				12.5					26.9
Ecuador					24.5	19.0		26.4	
Egypt, Arab Rep.					35.0	35.0			55.1
El Salvador									22.9
Eritrea									
Estonia		0.19	1.62		34.5	29.9		94.5	
Ethiopia					10.0	15.0			
Fiji					16.0	27.0			
Finland	5.27	2.81	2.80		32.9	28.9		89.7	
France	2.70	2.49	2.42		34.9	34.9		87.3	
Gabon									
Gambia, The								2.7	
Georgia					20.0	25.0		29.2	
Germany	3.51	2.93	2.53		41.5	38.9		86.9	
Ghana					17.5	17.5			8.7
Greece	0.78				25.2	25.2		86.0	
Guatemala					15.5	15.5			20.3
Guinea								12.1	
Guinea-Bissau								2.0	
Haiti					15.0	15.0			
Honduras					10.5	10.5			17.3
Hungary	1.29	0.69	1.15		45.5	38.5	79.9		92.0
India			6.74		22.2	22.2		10.3	
Indonesia			0.15	12.2	5.7	5.7			11.0
Iran, Islamic Rep.					30.0	30.0			
Iraq									43.1
Ireland	3.91	1.46	3.47		14.8	14.8		88.9	
Israel		1.02	0.90		6.7	8.9			
Italy		1.34	1.86		39.5	40.1		90.1	
Jamaica			0.00	5.0	5.0	5.0		17.2	
Japan	0.69	0.60	0.85		31.8	31.9		95.4	
Jordan				15.0	16.5	18.0	25.6	38.4	
Kazakhstan					10.0	10.0			62.5
Kenya			3.78		10.0	10.0	20.8	7.5	
Kiribati					15.0	15.0			
Korea, Rep.		0.32	1.02		12.4	28.8		49.5	
Kosovo									
Kyrgyz Republic				39.0	29.0	27.3	52.7		40.4
Lao PDR					9.5	9.5			

TABLE 7 *Policies and institutions,* continued

	Labor market policies (spending in % of GDP)			Social security contributions (% of salary)			Social security coverage (% of employment)		
	1995	2005	2009	1995	2005	2010	1995	2005	2010
Latvia			0.11		33.1	33.1			91.7
Lebanon					8.5	8.5		34.5	
Lesotho								4.4	
Liberia									
Libya					14.3	14.3		68.5	
Lithuania					31.2	31.3			82.9
Macedonia, FYR									52.3
Madagascar					11.8	11.8			5.3
Malawi									
Malaysia			0.57		24.3	24.3			49.0
Mali			0.22	20.0	13.0	11.5			7.9
Mauritania					6.0	6.0			
Mauritius			0.04		9.0	10.0			53.4
Mexico			0.04	26.0	7.2	7.2	32.0		27.4
Moldova					29.0	29.0			56.7
Mongolia									33.5
Montenegro									
Morocco					12.9	12.9		23.8	
Mozambique								1.9	
Myanmar									
Namibia									9.6
Nepal					20.0	20.0			3.4
Netherlands	4.14	3.31	2.92		25.5	22.4		90.7	
New Zealand	1.80	0.81	0.84						
Nicaragua					32.8	19.8			21.7
Niger								1.9	
Nigeria					15.0	15.0		8.1	
Norway	2.33	1.24			21.9	21.9		93.2	
Oman									
Pakistan			0.33		14.0	12.0			3.9
Panama					18.0	19.8			
Papua New Guinea					13.2	14.4			4.4
Paraguay					23.0	23.0		12.4	
Peru			0.06		23.2	23.2			21.7
Philippines			0.02		10.4	10.6		25.0	
Poland			0.30		26.0	26.7			81.4
Portugal	1.32	1.94	2.08		34.8	34.8		92.0	
Romania					36.8	33.7			67.9
Russian Federation					24.1	33.3		66.8	
Rwanda					8.0	8.0		4.6	
Saudi Arabia					20.0	20.0			
Senegal					16.5	16.5		5.1	
Serbia			0.13					45.0	
Sierra Leone					15.0	15.0		5.5	
Singapore					36.0	35.0	66.2		62.1
Slovak Republic	1.18	0.60	0.93		29.6	23.6	81.9	78.9	
Slovenia		0.68	0.96		37.5	37.5			87.4
Somalia									
South Africa					2.0	2.0			6.7
Spain	2.86	2.24	3.86		37.8	37.3	85.6	69.4	
Sri Lanka					20.0	20.0	21.8	24.1	
Sudan					25.0	27.0		5.2	
Swaziland									15.4
Sweden	4.62	2.44	1.84		28.7	28.7		88.8	
Switzerland	1.59	1.66			10.4	10.4		95.4	
Syrian Arab Republic					24.0	24.0			26.8
Tajikistan									
Tanzania					20.0	20.0		4.3	
Thailand			0.04		9.7	9.7		22.8	
Timor-Leste									
Togo								7.3	
Tonga									
Trinidad and Tobago			1.20		9.9	10.8			71.1
Tunisia					25.8	23.0		48.6	
Turkey			0.12		30.5	38.0	16.2		58.6
Turkmenistan					23.0	23.0			
Uganda			0.78		15.0	15.0		10.3	
Ukraine			0.00		38.8	41.8			62.1
United Kingdom	1.13	0.62	0.71		23.8	23.8		93.2	
United States	0.52	0.37	1.18		18.6	18.6		92.2	
Uruguay			0.01	40.5	35.5	32.0			78.5
Uzbekistan					36.5	29.0			
Venezuela, RB				25.5	14.2	23.9			33.9
Vietnam				20.0	20.0	23.0	9.2	19.3	
West Bank and Gaza									14.0
Yemen, Rep.				15.0			10.7	10.4	
Zambia								10.9	
Zimbabwe					6.0	8.0		20.0	

TABLE 8 *Connectedness*

	Conventions on migration ratified	Immigrants (% of population)			Emigrants (% of native population)			Remittances (% of GDP)		
	2010	1990	2000	2010	1990	2000	2010	1995	2005	2010
Afghanistan	0	0.3	0.3	0.3			6.4			
Albania	3	2.0	2.5	2.8	6.0	25.5	31.6	17.6	15.4	9.7
Algeria	2	1.1	0.8	0.7	5.9	4.2	3.3	2.7	2.0	1.3
Angola	0	0.3	0.3	0.3	2.5	2.6	2.7	0.1		0.1
Argentina	1	5.1	4.2	3.6	1.4	1.6	2.4	0.0	0.2	0.2
Armenia	2	18.6	18.7	10.5	14.0	25.1	23.9	4.5	10.2	10.6
Australia	0	21.0	21.0	21.1	2.2	2.9	2.5	0.4	0.4	0.4
Austria	0	10.3	12.4	15.6	6.8	7.0	7.8	0.4	0.9	0.9
Azerbaijan	1	5.0	4.3	2.9	13.4	16.3	14.0	0.1	5.2	2.7
Bangladesh	0	0.8	0.8	0.7	4.6	3.7	3.5	3.2	7.2	10.8
Barbados	1	8.2	9.2	10.3	27.5	26.6	30	3.3	4.5	3
Belarus	0	12.3	11.2	11.5	22.5	16.4	17.4	0.2	0.8	0.7
Belgium	1	8.9	8.6	8.9	4.3	3.5	4.4	1.7	1.9	2.2
Belize	2	16.1	14.6	13.6			14.4	2.2	4.1	5.7
Benin	1	1.6	2.1	2.6	5.4	5.2	5.8	5.0	4.0	3.8
Bhutan	0	4.3	5.6	5.5	2.7	2.1	6.1		0.2	0.3
Bolivia	1	0.9	1.1	1.5	3.3	4.2	6.5	0.1	3.6	5.5
Bosnia and Herzegovina	3	1.3	2.6	0.7	16.3	26.5	28.1		18.7	11.4
Botswana	0	2.0	3.2	5.7	5.1	2.2	3.2	1.2	1.3	0.7
Brazil	1	0.5	0.4	0.4	0.3	0.5	0.7	0.4	0.4	0.2
Bulgaria	0	0.2	1.2	1.4	7.0	8.8	13.9	0.5	5.6	2.9
Burkina Faso	3	3.7	4.7	6.3	9.8	10.6	9.3	3.3	1.0	1.1
Burundi	0	5.9	1.2	0.7	4.1	3.3	4.1		0.0	1.4
Cambodia	0	0.4	1.9	2.4	2.5	2.3	2.5	0.3	3.2	3.3
Cameroon	2	2.2	1.5	1.0	1.0	0.9	1.4	0.1	0.5	0.9
Canada	0	16.2	18.1	21.1	4.7	4.7	4.2			
Central African Republic	0	2.1	1.9	1.8	1.2	0.7	2.9	0.0		
Chad	0	1.2	1.3	3.5	2.7	1.7	2.2	0.1		
Chile	1	0.8	1.2	1.9	3.6	3.2	3.6		0.0	0.0
China	0	0.0	0.0	0.1	0.4	0.5	0.6	0.1	1.0	0.9
Colombia	1	0.3	0.3	0.2	3.0	3.7	4.4	0.9	2.3	1.4
Congo, Dem. Rep.	0	2.1	1.2	0.7	1.0	1.3	1.4			
Congo, Rep.	0	5.4	3.3	3.5	2.3	2.0	5.1	0.2	0.2	0.1
Costa Rica	0	13.6	7.9	10.5	2.7	2.8	2.9	1.1	2.1	1.5
Côte d'Ivoire	0	14.5	14.1	12.2	2.7	3.7	6.3	1.4	1.0	0.8
Croatia	0	9.9	13.9	15.8	8.2	14.1	16.9	2.5	1.6	2.2
Cuba	1	0.3	0.2	0.1	7.7	8.6	9.8			
Czech Republic	0	4.1	4.4	4.3	5.8	8.2	3.5	0.3	0.8	0.6
Denmark	0	4.6	6.9	8.7	4.1	4.1	4.9	0.3	0.3	0.2
Dominican Republic	0	4.0	4.1	4.4	6.0	9.3	9.8	5.1	8.0	6.5
Ecuador	2	0.8	0.8	2.7	2.2	4.9	7.5	1.9	6.7	4.4
Egypt, Arab Rep.	1	0.3	0.3	0.3	3.3	3.2	4.4	5.4	5.6	3.5
El Salvador	1	0.9	0.5	0.7	9.7	13.7	17.1	11.2	17.7	16.1
Eritrea	0	0.4	0.4	0.3	9.4	8.9	15.2			
Estonia	0	24.3	18.2	13.6	14.1	17.1	12.8	0.0	1.9	1.7
Ethiopia	0	2.4	1.0	0.7	0.3	0.4	0.7	0.4	1.4	0.8
Fiji	0	1.9	2	2.2	9.3	13.7	17.8	1.7	6.2	5.8
Finland	0	1.3	2.6	4.2	6.2	6.9	6.0	0.1	0.4	0.3
France	1	10.1	10.3	10.3	2.3	2.7	2.9	0.3	0.6	0.6
Gabon	0	13.7	17.0	18.9	1.7	1.4	2.0	0.1	0.1	
Gambia, The	0	12.2	14.3	16.8	2.7	3.1	4.3		9.3	11.0
Georgia	0	7.0	4.9	3.8	16.6	21.2	19.8	8.1	5.4	6.9
Germany	1	7.5	12.1	13.2	4.1	4.7	4.7	0.2	0.3	0.3
Ghana	1	4.8	7.9	7.6	2.7	2.6	3.5	0.3	0.9	0.4
Greece	0	4.1	6.7	10.0	9.8	9.3	10.6	2.5	0.5	0.5
Guatemala	2	3.0	0.4	0.4	3.4	4.8	5.7	2.4	11.3	10.2
Guinea	2	4.2	8.5	4.0	7.0	5.3	5.3	0.0	1.4	1.3
Guinea-Bissau	0	1.4	1.6	1.3	6.4	5.7	6.9	0.7	3.5	5.8
Haiti	0	0.3	0.3	0.3	6.6	8.0	9.2		23.7	22.6
Honduras	1	5.5	0.5	0.3	3.2	5.2	7.0	3.2	18.7	17.3
Hungary	0	3.3	2.9	3.7	4.0	4.2	4.6	0.3	1.8	1.8
India	0	0.9	0.6	0.4	0.9	0.9	0.9	1.7	2.7	3.2
Indonesia	0	0.3	0.1	0.1	0.6	0.9	1.0	0.3	1.9	1.0
Iran, Islamic Rep.	0	7.8	4.3	2.9	1.3	1.6	1.8	1.8	0.5	0.3
Iraq	0	0.5	0.6	0.3	3.6	4.1	4.6		2.3	0.1
Ireland	0	6.5	10.1	20.1	22.5	24.5	17.1	0.5	0.3	0.3
Israel	1	35.0	35.9	38.6	14.5	15.0	17.9	0.7	0.6	0.6
Italy	2	2.5	3.7	7.4	6.4	5.4	5.8	0.2	0.1	0.3
Jamaica	2	0.9	1.0	1.1	20.8	26.1	27.0	11.2	15.8	14.5
Japan	0	0.9	1.3	1.7	0.6	0.7	0.6	0.0	0.0	0.0
Jordan	0	36.2	40.2	49.2	32.6	27.7	19.3	21.4	19.9	13.8
Kazakhstan	0	22.1	19.3	18.9	18.7	21.8	21.9	0.6	0.3	0.2
Kenya	2	0.7	2.4	2.0	1.3	1.2	1.1	3.3	4.3	5.5
Kiribati	0	3	2.4	2	6.8	11.9	6.2	12.3		
Korea, Rep.	0	1.3	1.2	1.1	3.6	3.9	4.1	0.7	0.8	0.9
Kosovo	0								18.8	16.7
Kyrgyz Republic	2	14.2	7.6	4.1	12.7	13.2	10.6	0.1	13.1	26.6
Lao PDR	0	0.5	0.4	0.3	6.5	6.0	5.6	1.3	0.0	0.6

TABLE 8 *Connectedness,* continued

	Conventions on migration ratified	Immigrants (% of population)			Emigrants (% of native population)			Remittances (% of GDP)		
	2012	1990	2000	2010	1990	2000	2010	1995	2005	2010
Latvia	0	24.3	18.1	15.0	13.6	14.9	12.6	0.7	2.4	2.6
Lebanon	0	17.8	18.5	17.9	19.8	18.1	16.1		22.5	19.4
Lesotho	1	0.5	0.3	0.3	16.7	8.2	16.5	50.4	44.1	34.2
Liberia	0	3.8	5.6	2.4	4.3	9.0	10.0		5.9	2.7
Libya	1	10.6	10.7	10.7	1.8	2.3	1.9		0.0	0.0
Lithuania	0	9.4	6.1	3.9	15.0	14.0	12.0	0.0	2.1	4.3
Macedonia, FYR	2	5.0	6.3	6.3	11.0	15.4	18.8	1.5	3.8	4.2
Madagascar	1	0.4	0.3	0.2	0.8	0.4	0.4	0.4	0.2	
Malawi	1	12.3	2.5	1.9	3.2	2.1	1.4	0.0		
Malaysia	1	5.6	6.6	8.3	3.3	5.0	5.4	0.1	0.8	0.5
Mali	1	1.9	1.5	1.1	7.0	6.5	6.2	4.5	3.3	4.6
Mauritania	1	4.7	2.4	2.9	4.4	3.6	3.4	0.4		
Mauritius	1	0.8	3.3	3.4	8.8	6.9	10.2	3.3	3.4	2.3
Mexico	1	0.8	0.5	0.6	5.4	8.8	9.5	1.5	2.7	2.1
Moldova	1	15.7	13.0	11.5	16.4	17.0	19.6	0.1	30.8	23.6
Mongolia	0	0.3	0.3	0.4	0.1	0.2	1.2		7.1	4.5
Montenegro	2			6.7			0.0		5.3	7.3
Morocco	1	0.2	0.2	0.2	6.2	5.3	8.6	6.0	7.7	7.1
Mozambique	0	0.9	2.0	1.9	4.1	4.0	4.9	2.6	0.9	1.4
Myanmar	0	0.3	0.2	0.2	0.5	0.7	1.1			
Namibia	0	7.9	6.6	6.1	7.6	3.4	0.8	0.4	0.2	0.1
Nepal	0	2.3	2.9	3.2	3.1	3.1	3.3	1.3	14.9	21.7
Netherlands	1	8.0	10.0	10.5	5.0	5.0	6.3	0.3	0.3	0.5
New Zealand	1	15.2	17.8	22.0	10.9	13.5	15.5	2.6	0.7	0.6
Nicaragua	1	1.0	0.6	0.7	7.2	9.1	11.3	2.4	12.6	12.5
Niger	1	1.7	1.5	1.3	1.9	2.0	2.5	0.4	1.9	1.6
Nigeria	2	0.5	0.6	0.7	0.4	0.5	0.6	2.9	3.0	5.1
Norway	2	4.6	6.6	9.9	3.9	4.6	4.0	0.2	0.2	0.2
Oman	0	22.7	27.5	29.7	12.4	14.3	0.8	0.3	0.1	0.1
Pakistan	0	5.9	2.9	2.4	3.2	2.6	2.7	2.8	3.9	5.5
Panama	0	2.6	2.9	3.4	5.9	5.7	4.0	1.4	0.8	0.9
Papua New Guinea	0	0.8	0.5	0.4	0.6	0.7	0.9	0.3	0.1	0.2
Paraguay	1	4.3	3.3	2.5	7.0	7.1	7.5	3.6	3.6	3.7
Peru	1	0.3	0.2	0.1	1.3	2.6	3.6	1.1	1.8	1.6
Philippines	3	0.3	0.4	0.5	3.2	3.8	4.4	7.2	13.2	10.7
Poland	0	3.0	2.1	2.2	9.7	12.0	7.8	0.5	2.1	1.6
Portugal	2	4.4	6.2	8.6	15.7	12.2	18.7	3.4	1.6	1.6
Romania	0	0.6	0.6	0.6	7.1	5.5	11.5	0.0	4.8	2.4
Russian Federation	0	7.8	8.1	8.6	8.6	7.3	7.8	0.6	0.4	0.4
Rwanda	1	1.0	4.8	4.4	4.5	3.0	2.5	1.6	0.8	1.6
Saudi Arabia	0	29.4	25.6	26.6	1.4	1.4	0.9		0.0	0.1
Senegal	1	3.7	2.4	1.7	4.3	3.5	5.0	3.0	9.1	10.5
Serbia	2	1.3	11.4	7.2			2.8		7.9	8.7
Sierra Leone	0	3.9	2.3	1.8	1.6	3.6	4.4	2.7	0.2	3.0
Singapore	0	23.9	33.6	38.7	6.3	9.6	8.7			
Slovak Republic	0	0.8	2.2	2.4	6.6	9.3	8.9	0.1	1.5	1.8
Slovenia	2	8.9	8.8	8.0	4.3	4.8	6.5	1.3	0.7	0.7
Somalia	0	9.6	0.3	0.2	3.1	4.8	8.0			
South Africa	0	3.5	2.3	3.7	1.1	1.6	1.8	0.1	0.3	0.3
Spain	1	2.1	4.4	13.8	4.0	2.8	3.3	0.5	0.7	0.8
Sri Lanka	1	2.7	2.1	1.6	3.7	4.0	8.3	6.2	8.2	8.4
Sudan	0	6.2	3.1	2.2	2.1	2.2	2.9	2.5	3.7	2.9
Swaziland	0	8.3	3.6	3.8	8.5	4.7	13.7	4.9	3.7	2.9
Sweden	1	9.1	11.2	13.9	2.7	3.3	3.8	0.1	0.2	0.1
Switzerland	0	20.5	21.8	22.5	6.0	5.5	6.3	0.5	0.5	0.5
Syrian Arab Republic	1	5.6	5.8	10.8	3.9	3.7	4.9	3.0	2.9	2.8
Tajikistan	3	8.0	5.4	4.1	6.6	8.6	10.7		20.2	40.0
Tanzania	1	2.3	2.6	1.5	0.8	0.7	0.7	0.0	0.1	0.1
Thailand	0	0.7	1.3	1.7	0.5	1.1	1.2	1.0	0.7	0.6
Timor-Leste	1	1.2	1.1	1.2	0.5	1.9	1.5			
Togo	0	4.4	3.7	3.1	4.6	4.9	5.9	1.1	9.1	10.5
Tonga	0	3.2	1.6	0.8	22.4	31	31.5	15.1	26.5	23.7
Trinidad and Tobago	1	4.2	3.2	2.6	14.9	19.4	21.5	0.6	0.6	0.6
Tunisia	0	0.5	0.4	0.3	6.5	5.6	5.8	3.8	4.3	4.5
Turkey	1	2.1	2.0	1.9	4.5	4.6	5.6	2.0	0.2	0.1
Turkmenistan	0	8.4	5.4	4.1	9.0	7.3	5.1	0.2		
Uganda	2	3.1	2.6	1.9	1.2	2.2	2.3		3.5	5.3
Ukraine	0	13.3	11.2	11.5	14.3	11.8	13.8	0.0	0.7	4.1
United Kingdom	1	6.5	8.1	10.4	7.3	6.9	7.7	0.2	0.3	0.3
United States	0	9.3	12.3	13.8	0.7	0.8	0.9	0.0	0.0	0.0
Uruguay	2	3.2	2.7	2.4	6.9	6.8	9.7		0.4	0.3
Uzbekistan	0	8.1	5.5	4.1	5.9	6.6	6.7			
Venezuela, RB	2	5.2	4.2	3.5	1.1	1.4	1.8	0.0	0.1	0.0
Vietnam	0	0.0	0.1	0.1	1.6	2.2	2.5		6.0	7.8
West Bank and Gaza	0	46.0	46.9	49.3			60.4	18.1	17.6	
Yemen, Rep.	0	2.9	2.3	2.2	4.3	3.4	4.6	25.4	7.7	4.0
Zambia	1	3.6	3.5	1.8	2.3	1.6	1.4		0.7	0.3
Zimbabwe	0	6.0	3.3	3.0	3.0	2.9	9.3	0.6		

Technical notes

Table 1: Labor force

- **Population:** Number of people living in the territory of a country or economy; in millions; total and by gender (three indicators). Figures are from population censuses and demographic estimates. Data source: World Development Indicators (WDI), at http://data.worldbank.org/indicator/SP.POP.TOTL.

- **Working age population:** Persons aged 15 to 64 as a fraction of the population; in percent; total and by gender (three indicators). Data source: see table 9.

- **Participation rate:** Share of the working age population that is in the labor force, with the labor force defined as persons who work or are unemployed during a reference period; in percent; total, by gender and by age group (five indicators). Data source: see table 9.

- **Unemployment rate:** Share of the labor force that is unemployed, with the unemployed defined as persons who are available to work and are actively looking for a job during a reference period; in percent; total and by gender (three indicators). Data source: KILM, at http://www.ilo.org/kilm.

Table 2: Skills

- **Average schooling:** Mean of highest completed level of formal schooling among all persons aged 15 and above; in years; total and by gender (three indicators). Figures are estimated based on data from population censuses. The methodology is described by Robert J. Barro and Jong-Wha Lee, 2010, "A New Data Set of Educational Attainment in the World, 1950–2010," NBER Working Papers 15902, National Bureau of Economic Research. Data source: http://www.barrolee.com.

- **Skills as a constraint:** Share of firms identifying an inadequately skilled workforce as a "major" or "very severe" obstacle to business; in percent. Figures are from enterprise surveys covering firms with at least five employees and mainly formal. "Major" and "very severe" are the two top levels in a scale of five. Data source: International Financial Corporation/World Bank Enterprise Surveys, at http://www.enterprisesurveys.org.

- **Educational attainment:** Average score in reading, mathematics and science; units are such that the mean is 500 and standard deviation is 100. Observations from PISA are from students aged between 15 years and 3 months and 16 years and 2 months at the beginning of the assessment period. Observations from TIMSS (marked with an asterisk) are from a nationally representative sample of all students enrolled in the grade that represents 8 years of formal schooling, provided that the mean age at the time of testing is at least 13.5 years. TIMSS does not assess educational attainment in reading. Data sources: PISA at http://www.oecd.org/pisa, and TIMSS and PIRLS International Study Center, Lynch School of Education, Boston at http://timssandpirls.bc.edu/index.html.

Table 3: Employment structure

- **Employment by sector:** Share of employment in primary, secondary, and tertiary activities, based on the International Standard Industry Classification (ISIC); in percent (three indicators). The primary sector corresponds to division 1 (ISIC revision 2), tabulation categories A and B (ISIC revision 3), or tabulation category A (ISIC revision 4); it includes agriculture, hunting, forestry, and fishing. The secondary sector encompasses divisions 2–5 (ISIC revision 2), tabulation categories C–F (ISIC revision 3), or tabulation categories B–F (ISIC revision 4); it includes mining and quarrying (including oil production), manufacturing, construction, and public utilities (electricity, gas, and water). The tertiary sector corresponds to divisions 6–9 (ISIC revision 2), tabulation categories G–P (ISIC revision 3), or tabulation categories G–U (ISIC revision 4); it includes wholesale and retail trade and restaurants and hotels; transport, storage, and communications; financing, insurance, real estate, and business services; and community, social, and personal services. Data sources: see table 9.

- **Employment in civil service:** Share of total employment in the public sector; in percent. Public sector employment includes all employment of the general government as defined in System of National Accounts (SNA) 1993, plus resident and operating at central, state (or regional), and local levels of government. Persons employed directly by these institutions are included regardless of their type of employment contract; workers in state-owned enterprises are not included. Data source: LABORSTA tables on "Public Sector Employment" and "General Employment Level," at http://laborsta.ilo.org.

- **Employment by work status:** Share of employment in wage work, self employment, and farming; in percent (three indicators). The self-employed include employers and non-remunerated family workers outside farming. Data sources: see table 9.

- **Employment in urban areas:** Share of employment in cities and towns; in percent. Urban is defined by national statistical offices. Data sources: see table 9.

Table 4: Living standards

- **Wages by occupation:** Average wages of accountants, chemical engineers, bus drivers, and sewing machine operators; in annual US$ at 2005 prices (four indicators). Wages are based on data from the ILO October Inquiry database, calibrated into a normalized format referring to average monthly wage rate for an adult worker and transformed into dollars using the exchange rate of the local currency in the same year. The data are then converted to 2005 prices using the U.S. GDP deflator. The methodology is described by R.H. Oostendorp, 2012, "The Occupational Wages around the World (OWW) Database: Update for 1983–2008," background paper for the World Development Report 2013. Data source: http://www.worldbank.org/wdr2013.

- **Working poor:** Share of total employment represented by workers who are members of households living in extreme poverty; in percent. Households living in extreme poverty are identified on the basis of poverty rates computed from the international poverty line of 1.25 US$ PPP per day at 2005 prices. The use of the international poverty line means that figures are not necessarily comparable to estimates generated using national poverty lines. Data sources: see table 9, and for the poverty rate, see http://iresearch.worldbank.org/PovcalNet/.

- **Life satisfaction:** Persons aged 14 and above who answered affirmatively to a survey asking them whether they were satisfied with their life at the time of the interview; in percent of all respondents; by work status (three indicators). The question in the survey is: "All things considered, how satisfied are you with your life as a whole these days?" Possible answers range from 1("completely dissatisfied") to 10 ("completely satisfied"). Responses of 6 or higher were considered affirmative. Data source: World Values Survey, 1999–2008, at http://www.worldvaluessurvey.org.

- **Labor share of national income:** Compensation of employees as a share of GDP; in percent. Compensation of employees corresponds is measured by account D.1 in the SNA, and GDP by account B.1 in the System of National Accounts). Compensation of employees includes payments in cash and in-kind. It also includes government contributions to social insurance schemes that provide benefits to the employees. Data source: UNDATA, at http://data.un.org.

- **Gender gap in earnings:** Wage earnings for women relative to the wage earnings of men having the same characteristics; as a ratio. The estimate is based on a country-specific regression of the logarithm of monthly earnings in local currency on years of education and potential years of experience (and its square), controlling for industry, occupation, urban residence and gender. The methodology is described by Claudio E. Montenegro and Harry Anthony Patrinos, 2012, "Returns to Schooling around the World," background paper for the World Development Report 2013. Data sources: see table 9.

Table 5: Productivity

- **Value-added per worker:** Total value-added per worker; in annual US$ at 2005 prices; total and by sector of activity (four indicators). Value-added is the output of a sector net of intermediate inputs. It is calculated without making deductions for depreciation of fabricated assets or depletion and degradation of natural resources. The origin of value-added is determined by the International Standard Industrial Classification (ISIC), revision 3. Value-added data are converted to US$ using current exchange rates and then converted to 2005 prices using the U.S. GDP deflator. Data source: WDI, at http://data.worldbank.org/data-catalog/world-development-indicators.

abusive conditions and the promotion of equality of opportunity and treatment of migrant workers; and the United Nations (UN) Convention on the Protection of the Rights of All Migrant Workers and Members of Their Families. In the case of the UN Convention, accessions and successions are also treated as ratifications. Data source: ILOLEX: Database of International Labor Standards (http://www.ilo.org/ilolex/english/convdisp1 .htm; and United Nations Treaty Collection, at http://treaties.un.org/pages/View-Details.aspx?src=TREATY&mtdsg_no=IV-13&chapter=4&lang=en.

- **Immigrants:** Share of the population that is foreign born; in percent. Data source: Özden, Çaglar, Christopher Parsons, Maurice Schiff, and Terrie L. Walmsley. 2011. "Where on Earth Is Everybody? The Evolution of Global Bilateral Migration 1960–2000." *World Bank Economic Review,* 25 (1): 12–56, at http://data .worldbank.org/indicator/SM.POP.TOTL.

- **Emigrants:** Share of the native population that is residing in another country or economy; in

percent. The native population is computed as the total population minus immigrants plus emigrants. Data source: Özden, Çaglar, Christopher Parsons, Maurice Schiff, and Terrie L. Walmsley. 2011. "Where on Earth Is Everybody? The Evolution of Global Bilateral Migration 1960–2000." *World Bank Economic Review,* 25 (1): 12–56, at http://go.worldbank .org/JITC7NYTT0.

- **Remittances:** Foreign currency inflows from workers abroad; in percent of GDP. The inflows comprise current transfers by migrant workers and compensation earned by nonresident workers. Current transfers from migrant workers are considered remittances when workers have resided in the host country for more than a year, irrespective of their immigration status. Compensation earned by nonresident workers refers to the wages and salaries of migrant workers having lived in the host country for less than one year. Data source: World Development Indicators, at http://data.worldbank.org/indicator/BX.TRF .PWKR.DT.GD.ZS.

TABLE 9 Micro-data sources

	Selected databases		
	1995	2005	2010
Afghanistan		LSSN	
Albania	LSSN	LSSN	
Algeria			
Angola			
Argentina	MIX	MIX	MIX
Armenia		LSSN	
Australia	OECD/EU	OECD/EU	OECD/EU
Austria	OECD/EU	OECD/EU	OECD/EU
Azerbaijan	LSSN		
Bangladesh		LSSN	LFSN
Barbados	LFSP		
Belarus		LSSN	
Belgium	OECD/EU	OECD/EU	OECD/EU
Belize	LFSN		
Benin		LSSN	
Bhutan		LSSN	
Bolivia	LFSN	LFSN	LFSN
Bosnia and Herzegovina		LSSN	
Botswana			LSSN
Brazil	LFSP	LFSN	LFSN
Bulgaria	LSSN	OECD/EU	OECD/EU
Burkina Faso	LSSN	LSSN	
Burundi			
Cambodia	LSSN	LSSN	LSSN
Cameroon	LSSN	LSSN	
Canada	OECD/EU	OECD/EU	OECD/EU
Central African Republic	OECD/EU	LSSN	
Chad		LSSN	
Chile	LSSN	OECD/EU	OECD/EU
China	MIX	MIX	MIX
Colombia	CENSUS	LFSN	LFSN
Congo, Dem. Rep.		LSSN	
Congo, Rep.		LSSN	
Costa Rica	LFSN	LFSN	LFSN
Côte d'Ivoire			
Croatia		OECD/EU	OECD/EU
Cuba			
Czech Republic		OECD/EU	OECD/EU
Denmark	OECD/EU	OECD/EU	OECD/EU
Dominican Republic	LFSN	LFSN	LFSN
Ecuador	LFSN	LFSN	LFSN
Egypt, Arab Rep.	CENSUS	LSSN	
El Salvador	LFSN	LFSN	LFSN
Eritrea			
Estonia	OECD/EU	OECD/EU	OECD/EU
Ethiopia	LSSN	LSSN	
Fiji	CENSUS		LSSN
Finland	OECD/EU	OECD/EU	OECD/EU
France	OECD/EU	OECD/EU	OECD/EU
Gabon		LSSN	
Gambia, The			
Georgia		LSSN	LSSN
Germany	OECD/EU	OECD/EU	OECD/EU
Ghana		LSSN	
Greece	OECD/EU	OECD/EU	OECD/EU
Guatemala		LFSN	
Guinea	LSSN		
Guinea-Bissau			
Haiti			
Honduras	LFSN	LFSN	LFSN
Hungary	OECD/EU	OECD/EU	OECD/EU
India	LFSN	LFSN	LFSN
Indonesia	LSSN	LSSN	LSSN
Iran, Islamic Rep.		LSSN	
Iraq	CENSUS	LSSN	
Ireland	OECD/EU	OECD/EU	OECD/EU
Israel	OECD/EU	OECD/EU	OECD/EU
Italy	OECD/EU	OECD/EU	OECD/EU
Jamaica	LFSN		
Japan	OECD/EU	OECD/EU	OECD/EU
Jordan		CENSUS	
Kazakhstan	LFSN	LSSN	
Kenya	LSSN	LSSN	
Kiribati		LSSN	
Korea, Rep.		OECD/EU	OECD/EU
Kosovo	OECD/EU	LFSP	
Kyrgyz Republic	LSSN		
Lao PDR	LSSN		LSSN

	Selected databases		
	1995	2005	2010
Latvia	OECD/EU	OECD/EU	OECD/EU
Lebanon		LSSN	
Lesotho			
Liberia		LSSN	
Libya			
Lithuania	OECD/EU	OECD/EU	OECD/EU
Macedonia, FYR	OECD/EU	OECD/EU	MIX
Madagascar	LSSN		
Malawi	LSSN	MIX	
Malaysia			
Mali	LSSN	LSSN	
Mauritania			LSSN
Mauritius		LFSN	LFSN
Mexico	LSSN	OECD/EU	OECD/EU
Moldova		LSSN	
Mongolia			LSSN
Montenegro		LFSN	
Morocco	CENSUS	CENSUS	
Mozambique	LSSN	LSSN	LSSN
Myanmar			
Namibia	LSSN		
Nepal	LSSN	LSSN	LSSN
Netherlands	OECD/EU	OECD/EU	OECD/EU
New Zealand	OECD/EU	OECD/EU	OECD/EU
Nicaragua	LSSN	LSSN	
Niger	LSSN		
Nigeria	LSSN	LSSN	
Norway	OECD/EU	OECD/EU	OECD/EU
Oman			
Pakistan		LFSN	LFSN
Panama	LFSN	LFSN	LFSN
Papua New Guinea			LSSN
Paraguay	LFSN	LFSN	LFSN
Peru	LFSN	LFSN	LFSN
Philippines	LFSN	LFSN	LFSN
Poland	OECD/EU	OECD/EU	OECD/EU
Portugal	OECD/EU	OECD/EU	OECD/EU
Romania	LSSN	OECD/EU	OECD/EU
Russian Federation		LSSN	
Rwanda	LSSN	LSSN	
Saudi Arabia			
Senegal	LSSN	LSSN	
Serbia			LFSN
Sierra Leone		LSSN	
Singapore			
Slovak Republic	OECD/EU	OECD/EU	OECD/EU
Slovenia	OECD/EU	OECD/EU	OECD/EU
Somalia			
South Africa	LFSN	LFSN	
Spain	OECD/EU	OECD/EU	OECD/EU
Sri Lanka	LSSN	LFSN	LFSN
Sudan			
Swaziland	LSSN		
Sweden	OECD/EU	OECD/EU	OECD/EU
Switzerland	OECD/EU	OECD/EU	OECD/EU
Syrian Arab Republic		LSSN	
Tajikistan		LSSN	
Tanzania	LFSN	LFSN	LFSN
Thailand	LSSN	LSSN	LSSN
Timor-Leste		LSSN	LFSN
Togo		LSSN	
Tonga	LSSN		
Trinidad and Tobago			
Tunisia	LFSN		
Turkey	OECD/EU	OECD/EU	OECD/EU
Turkmenistan			
Uganda		LSSN	
Ukraine		LSSN	
United Kingdom	OECD/EU	OECD/EU	OECD/EU
United States	OECD/EU	OECD/EU	OECD/EU
Uruguay	LFSP	LFSP	LFSN
Uzbekistan			
Venezuela, RB	LFSN	LFSP	
Vietnam	LSSN	LSSN	LSSN
West Bank and Gaza	CENSUS	LSSN	LSSN
Yemen, Rep.		LSSN	
Zambia		LSSN	
Zimbabwe			

CENSUS	Data from population census by IPUMS
LFSN	Labor force survey with national coverage
LFSP	Labor force survey with partial coverage
LSSN	Living standards survey with national coverage
MIX	A combination of micro data from censuses with key ratios from household surveys
OECD/EU	Data from the Organisation for Economic Co-operation and Development or Eurostat

Index

Boxes, figures, maps, notes, and tables are indicated by b, f, m, n, and t following the page numbers.